PRINCIPLES OF CRIMINAL PROCEDURE: INVESTIGATION

By

Wayne R. LaFave
*David C. Baum Professor of Law Emeritus and
Center for Advanced Study Professor Emeritus,
University of Illinois*

Jerold H. Israel
*Ed Root Eminent Scholar in Trial Advocacy and Procedure,
University of Florida College of Law
and
Alene and Allan F. Smith Professor of Law Emeritus,
University of Michigan*

and

Nancy J. King
*Lee S. & Charles A. Speir Professor of Law
Vanderbilt University*

CONCISE HORNBOOK SERIES®

Mat #40234409

Concise Hornbook Series, *Westlaw*, and West Group are trademarks registered in the U.S. Patent and Trademark Office.

© 2004 West, a Thomson business
      610 Opperman Drive
      P.O. Box 64526
      St. Paul, MN 55164–0526
      1–800–328–9352

ISBN 0–314–15213–X

Preface

This book is intended to be used primarily by law students while engaged in the study of the subject of criminal procedure. This is one of two concise hornbooks that we have written on this subject; the other is *Principles of Criminal Procedure: Post–Investigation*. The present book is for use in a criminal procedure course where the focus is primarily or exclusively upon that part of the entirety of criminal procedure having to do with the detection and investigation of crime. The *Post–Investigation* book, on the other hand, can alone be used in a criminal procedure course where the focus is upon the subsequent, more formal parts of the criminal process (sometimes referred to as "bail to jail," albeit including post-conviction review). Both of these books could be used together in connection with a survey course in criminal procedure which examined both the investigation and post-investigation areas.

It has been our effort to provide as much information and analysis as is possible in a relatively short and easy to use (and carry) paperback volume. By excluding any documentation via footnotes of the various subjects considered and discussed herein (an approach requiring extraordinary self-restraint by three law professors!), we have been able to use virtually all of the space in this conveniently-sized paperback for textual elaboration of the subjects covered. Leading Supreme Court cases and, occasionally, lower court cases of special significance, are identified in the text by name and date only; full citations are available in the Table of Cases. We have provided both a very detailed Table of Contents and also an Index so that a student may easily locate topics of particular interest.

The *Investigation* and *Post–Investigation* concise hornbooks together constitute a compendious counterpart to our much more substantial undertaking, a 6–volume treatise primarily for bench and bar entitled *Criminal Procedure*. We mention that fact here only to emphasize that if on occasion a student does want to explore some topic in the present book in greater depth or to locate additional relevant cases, relevant statutes or useful secondary authorities, he or she will find it relatively easy to do so. In Westlaw, just go to the database CRIMPROC and examine the comparable material there. (Chapter 1 in the present work corresponds to parts of Chapters 1 and 2 in CRIMPROC, while Chapters 2–10 herein relate, respectively, to Chapters 3–11 in CRIMPROC. The arrangement of sections and subsections within comparable chapters is often but not inevitably the same.)

While all three of us stand responsible for the work on this book and its companion volume, *Post–Investigation*, as a whole, the initial responsibility for individual chapters in these two concise hornbooks was determined according to the allocation of responsibilities in preparation of the 6–volume treatise. Hence, as to this book Wayne LaFave had initial responsibility for chapters 2–6 and 8–9, and Jerold Israel for chapters 1, 7, and 10. Each of us would appreciate hearing from readers who have criticisms or suggestions relating to the chapters for which we had initial responsibility.

WAYNE R. LaFAVE

JEROLD H. ISRAEL

NANCY J. KING

June, 2004

Summary of Contents

*

Table of Contents

---

*

PRINCIPLES OF CRIMINAL PROCEDURE: INVESTIGATION

*

Chapter 1

THE LEGAL STRUCTURE

Table of Sections

The combined group of procedures utilized to enforce the substantive criminal law commonly is referred to as the "criminal justice process." Investigatory procedures are one component of that process. If those procedures are successful, they are followed

1

by a series of additional procedures, which include the charging of the offender, the preparation for adjudication, the adjudication by guilty plea or trial, and the sentencing of persons convicted. The principles underlying the legal regulation of these post-investigation steps are discussed in a companion volume, *Principles of Criminal Procedure: Post-Investigation.* This volume concentrates on the principles underlying the law governing criminal investigations.

Chapter One provides an introduction to this topic. Section 1.1 discusses three critical characteristics of criminal investigations in this country: (1) that we have fifty two separate legal jurisdictions providing for criminal investigations; (2) that a broad range of activities are included within criminal investigations; and (3) that a broad range of government officials are engaged in criminal investigations. The remaining sections focus on the primary task of the chapter—introducing the basic elements of the legal structure that has produced the complicated mixture of legal regulations that govern criminal investigations in the United States. An understanding of that structure is needed to place in the appropriate lawmaking context the various specific regulations discussed in the remaining chapters. Section 1.2 provides an overview of the different types of laws that provide the legal regulation of the process. Sections 1.3 to 1.5 then focus on the United States Constitution as a basic source of regulation.

§ 1.1   Different Jurisdictions, Procedures, and Actors

(a) **Accounting for Fifty-two Different Jurisdictions.** Under the American version of federalism, each of the fifty state governments retains the authority to enact its own criminal code, applicable within the territorial reach of its legislative powers. Each state also retains the power to provide for the enforcement of that criminal code through agencies and procedures that it creates. That authority has been used in each state to establish what is basically a single, general criminal justice process applicable throughout the state (although that process typically will permit some limited local variations in procedure). Congress has added to these fifty state criminal justice processes its two distinct federal criminal justice processes. First, it has created a separate criminal justice process for the District of Columbia, used to enforce a separate criminal code that applies only in the District. Second, it has created a criminal justice process for the enforcement of the general federal criminal code, which applies throughout the country. This process utilizes national law enforcement agencies and relies on prosecutions brought in the federal district courts.

In many fields in which both state and federal governments exercise regulatory authority, the enforcement of federal law by federal officials so clearly dominates the field that law school courses focus almost exclusively on the federal enforcement system. A similar focus would be most inappropriate in the field of criminal procedure. While the federal criminal justice system may be the most prominent of the nation's fifty-two criminal justice systems, the traditional statistical measures of criminal justice systems rank it simply as one of the larger, but not the largest of the fifty-two systems. Moreover, when the federal system is compared to the state systems as a group, the combined state systems clearly dominate, as they account for a much larger portion of the nation's criminal justice workload (e.g., roughly 97% of all felony prosecutions and over 99% of all misdemeanor prosecutions). Thus, the study of the law governing the criminal justice process must take account of the laws regulating the 50 state criminal justice processes as well as the two federal processes.

Taking account of fifty-two different criminal justice systems would be a less daunting task if the fifty-two jurisdictions were subject to a single law that mandated an exclusive, comprehensive regulation of each aspect of the process. There is, however, no such law. As discussed in § 1.3(d), various provisions of the Bill of Rights of the federal constitution do apply to all fifty-two jurisdictions. Those provisions do lock the fifty-two jurisdictions into the same basic procedural structure. They also prescribe a variety of requirements for specific procedures that all jurisdictions must meet. As to criminal investigations, those requirements certainly are our most significant legal regulations. However, as discussed in § 1.2(b), the regulation of the federal constitution hardly ensures uniformity among the fifty-two jurisdictions. The legal standards adopted by the individual jurisdiction also will play a significant role in regulating those aspects of the jurisdiction's process not subject to federal constitutional regulation and in adding further requirements as to many aspects subject to constitutional regulation.

With each jurisdiction regulating by its own laws, some degree of diversity is almost certain to be found among the fifty-two jurisdictions. We will not attempt in this single volume to describe all the variations that can be found in the laws of the different jurisdictions. Where major conflicts in approach exist, we will describe the basic patterns that divide one large group of jurisdictions from another. It should be kept in mind, however, that on almost any aspect of non-constitutional regulation, there will be at least a few states that depart from what we characterize as the "general rule." Similarly, when we describe state law as divided between two or three positions, there most likely will be a few states that have adopted still other positions.

(b) The Broad Range of Investigative Activities. Lawyers tend to categorize investigative activities by reference to differences in governing legal standards, and that approach largely shapes the organization of our later chapters. Criminal justice analysts, in contrast, tend to focus on the function of the procedure, and while that focus does not shape the law, it is useful in placing the different procedures in context and evaluating their practical importance. Perhaps the two most often emphasized functional distinctions look to (1) whether the procedure is utilized in a "reactive" or "proactive" investigation, and (2) whether the procedure is available to government investigators generally or only to prosecutors. Reactive investigations are responsive to information indicating a previously committed crime, with the investigation focusing on solving that past crime. Proactive investigations are aimed at unknown but anticipated ongoing or future crime. Most investigative procedures utilized in both reactive and proactive investigations are available to all government personnel authorized to act as "peace officers" (which often will include prosecutors), although those procedures usually are described as "police procedures" because used largely by the police. Commonly described as "prosecutorial investigative procedures" are those investigative procedures available only to the prosecutors.

In this subsection, we will briefly describe the major investigative practices that fall within each of the above categories. Not all of those practices will be considered in our later chapters. Some quite common investigative practices are not subject to significant legal regulation and therefore seldom are the subject of the caselaw (or statutes) discussed in those chapters. It should be kept in mind that the focus of the law (and lawyers) is on only a portion of the totality of the investigative process, and many parts of the process of great importance to enforcement agencies are barely touched upon in a course devoted to the legal regulation of the process.

Police Reactive Investigations. General purpose police agencies, such as local police departments, traditionally have devoted the vast majority of their investigative efforts to reactive investigations. These are "incident driven" or "complaint responsive" investigations, flowing from various aspects of local policing, including the neighborhood patrol and the 911 emergency telephone link. Having learned of the possible commission of a particular crime, the police then proceed to initiate an investigation of that "known" crime. The investigation will be aimed at (1) determining whether there actually was a crime committed, (2) if so, determining who committed the crime, (3) collecting evidence of that person's guilt, and (4) locating the presumed offender and taking that person into custody. A wide variety of investigative activities may be utilized to achieve these objectives. Many of these procedures will occur before a suspect is arrested (i.e., taken into custody with a purpose to charge), but often the investigation will continue after the arrest.

Pre-arrest investigative activities include: (1) the interviewing of victims; (2) the interviewing of witnesses at the crime scene; (3) canvassing the neighborhood for (and interviewing) other possible witnesses; (4) the interviewing of suspects, which may require a physical stopping of the suspect on the street and a frisking of the suspect (i.e., pat-down of the outer clothing for possible weapons); (5) the examination of the crime scene and the collection of physical evidence found there; (6) checking departmental records and computer files; (7) seeking information from informants; (8) searching for physical evidence of the crime (e.g., stolen property or weapons) in places accessible to the suspect (e.g., his home or automobile) and seizing any evidence found there; (9) surveillance of a suspect (including electronic surveillance) aimed at obtaining leads to evidence or accomplices; and (10) using undercover operatives to gain information from the suspect.

A variety of factors will determine which of the investigative practices noted above will be used in a particular investigation. One key factor is the investigative direction suggested by those "traces" of the crime that are immediately available to the police. In some instances, the limitations of available traces foreclose the use of a particular investigative practice. Any attempt to interview suspects depends upon the presence of some trace (e.g., a witness who can describe the criminal or a unique modus operandi) that allows for the designation of a manageable group of persons who might be considered possible suspects. A search for physical evidence only makes sense if the traces indicate that the criminal activity was of a type which might produce such evidence. In other instances, though the available traces will not absolutely rule out the use of particular investigative practice, they suggest that the likelihood of gaining useful information will be so remote that the time, energy, and financial costs involved simply do not make use of that practice worthwhile. There is almost always some possibility, for example, that canvassing the neighborhood will produce a witness who saw the offender, but police frequently will not canvass for witnesses unless there is a fairly substantial likelihood that such a witness might be found.

While the variation among investigations is far too great to characterize any single combination of investigative procedures as "average," even for a particular type of offense, it is clear that prearrest investigations rarely take on the characteristics of popular television depictions of the crime solving process. In general, investigations do not involve the use of scientific methods of investigation, confrontations with crafty criminals, or reliance upon informants. In many instances, almost no pre-arrest investigation will occur because a prompt response to a victim's call for assistance or an observation on patrol will allow the police officer to make an on-scene arrest or to arrest a fleeing felon within a few minutes of the commission of the crime. Thus, one study concluded that 42% of all arrests for nonviolent property (basically theft and burglary) fit that description.

Once the individual is taken into custody, additional investigative opportunities are presented through the person of the arrestee. Not all of the post-arrest procedures that produce evidence from the person are necessarily designed for that purpose. The search of the person incident to his arrest may include evidence collection as a partial objective, but it also is aimed at ensuring that the arrestee does not have access to weapons. Following that search, the arrestee commonly will be taken to the police station, where he is first "booked" (i.e., his arrest on a particular charge is recorded), and then fingerprinted and photographed. That is done without regard to whether the fingerprints and photograph will provide useful evidence as to the crime charged, as such identification data also may be valuable in the investigation of other past crimes or crimes that may be committed in the future. Assuming the arrestee does not make stationhouse bail and is not released on a summons (procedures typically available only for misdemeanors), he will then be placed in a holding facility (a jail or a police station "lock-up"), pending being presented before a magistrate within 24 hours (or 48 hours, in some jurisdictions). This placement will be accompanied by another search of the person. Although that search may produce additional evidence (missed in the search incident to the arrest), its primary purpose is to inventory the arrestee's personal belongings and to prevent the introduction of contraband into the holding facility.

Other post-arrest procedures are aimed primarily at obtaining evidence, but those are not nearly so routine. The police may seek to obtain an eyewitness identification of the arrestee by placing him in a lineup, having the witness view him individually (a "showup") or adding his picture to a group shown to a witness (a "photographic lineup"). Police also may obtain from the arrestee handwriting, hair, or bodily fluid samples that can be compared with forensic evidence obtained from the scene of the crime. The arrest also facilitates questioning the arrestee at length while he is held in custody prior to being taken before the magistrate.

Police Proactive Investigations. Proactive investigations are far less common than reactive investigations, but are used frequently in the investigation of crimes between willing participants. These investigations are aimed at uncovering ongoing criminal activity or future criminal activity that is not specifically known to the police. A proactive investigative procedure may be aimed at placing the police in a position where they can observe ongoing criminal activity that otherwise would both be hidden from public view and not reported (e.g., the possession of contraband or the transfer of drugs). It may be aimed at inducing persons who have committed crimes of a certain type, including many unknown to the police, to reveal themselves (as in a "fencing sting"). Proactive procedures also include investigative techniques designed simply to gain information that will permit the police to predict when and where a crime is likely to be committed, and techniques designed to "induce" the criminal attempt at a particular time and place by creating a setting likely to spur into action those prone to criminality. Deception is a common element of many proactive procedures. In traditional undercover operations, the police assume a false identity and present themselves as willing to participate in criminal activities (as where undercover agents "set up" fencing operations or narcotics transactions). So too, deception is the key to a "decoy tactic" of providing what appears to be an easy target for victimization (e.g., a drunk with an exposed wallet or a business of the type that is readily subject to extortion). Deception commonly also is critical to the effective use of informants. Where police utilize as informants persons whose activities expose them to a criminal milieu, they are counting on the criminals associating with those persons being deceived by a belief that those persons will not take what they have learned to the police (usually because the persons are themselves engaged in criminal activity, gain their livelihood in part from criminals, or have social ties to the criminals). Surveillance through stakeouts, covert patrols, and electronic monitoring also rests on deception by hiding the surveillance.

Other proactive techniques rely on intrusive confrontations designed to place police in a position where they can observe what otherwise would be hidden or to elicit nervous or unthinking incriminatory responses that will provide a legal grounding for taking further investigative action (e.g., an arrest or stop). Thus, police following an aggressive motorized patrol strategy will fully utilize traffic laws to maximize stops of motorists, thereby gaining greater opportunity to peer into car windows, to ask questions, and to request consent to search of the vehicle. Similarly, under a practice of heavy field interrogation, police will frequently approach pedestrians and initiate questions to determine who they are and what they are doing. Such intrusive confrontations are most often used on a selective basis, with police concentrating their efforts on those characteristics of the social environment that suggest to them possible criminality (e.g., high-crime neighborhood, suspicious class of persons, unusual behavior).

If a proactive investigation is successful, it leads to an arrest. The arrest will be followed by the various procedures discussed above as reactive post-arrest procedures. A successful proactive investigation will at some point identify a specific crime, and at that point (which may even be before arrest), the investigation commonly will turn into a reactive investigation.

Prosecutorial Investigations. The primary investigate tools available only to the prosecutor are: (1) the subpoena authority available through the grand jury; (2) the grant of immunity, which eliminates the grand jury witness' capacity to refuse to testify on the basis of the self-incrimination privilege, and (3) the capacity to offer charging and other concessions to a person charged with a crime in return for that person providing evidence against others.

The prosecutor serves as legal advisor to the grand jury, and through that position leads the grand jury in conducting investigations. As discussed in chapter seven, the grand jury has available to it the subpoena authority of the court, which enables it to call forth witness to testify under oath, and to produce documents and other physical items. The witness called before the grand jury may refuse to testify on the basis of his privilege against self-incrimination, but that privilege can be supplanted by a grant of immunity, which protects against the prosecutor using against the witness his immunized testimony or evidence derived from that testimony. See § 7.9. The combination of subpoena authority and immunity are especially valuable in investigations in which witnesses will not cooperate with the police. The broad reach of the subpoena authority is especially valuable where the primary evidence of the crime is likely to be a "paper trail," buried in voluminous records of business dealings (as the subpoena can be used to require production of such records where the police lack the probable cause predicate for obtaining those documents through a search). Such investigative authority is most likely to be needed in the investigation of crimes of public corruption (e.g., bribery), crimes involving misuse of economic power (e.g., price-fixing), and the widespread distribution of illegal services or goods (e.g., organized crime operations). The investigation of such offenses through the grand jury often has both reactive and proactive qualities. It starts with some specific information known to the prosecutor (usually through the police) that suggests a specific offense but then will extend beyond that offense to determine whether there exists similar or related criminal activity that is unknown to the prosecutor or police (a portion of the investigation often characterized as a "fishing expedition").

In various instances, the investigation can be successful only if a person charged with a crime is willing to provide information about the others engaged in that criminal activity. The prosecutor as the person setting the criminal charge, and making recommendations on sentencing, has the capacity to offer concessions to the accused in return for such cooperation. This arrangement often becomes part of a "plea bargain." A plea of guilty is entered on the basis of an agreement under which the defendant agrees to become a government witness and the prosecutor agrees to certain charging or sentencing concessions. Although used mostly in instances of multi-participant criminality, such cooperation agreements are sometimes used to obtain information from an accused about the unrelated crimes of others.

(c) **The Range of Enforcement Officials.** Over 17,000 different governmental agencies in the United States can be classified as "police agencies" in that (1) they have been given primary responsibility for the enforcement of at least a part of the criminal law, and (2) at least some of their personnel have been given special enforcement authority (e.g., special arrest powers) that distinguish the police officer from the private citizen. Within the state system, the vast majority of these police agencies are a part of local governments (e.g., municipal police departments and county sheriff's departments), although some are part of the state government (e.g., the state highway patrol). In some states, police agencies are also attached to special geographical units (e.g, parks and college campuses). In some instances, the agency responsibilities may be restricted to enforcing only certain criminal laws (as in the case of conversation officers), but most will be given enforcement responsibility as to all violations of state law within the geographic district assigned to the agency.

The vast majority of police agencies within the state system are "general agencies." Their responsibilities include not only criminal law enforcement, but also basic social services (e.g., providing emergency aid), the maintenance of public order (e.g., traffic control), and the prevention of crime (e.g., by providing a physical presence through patrol activities). In such agencies, most personnel spend most of their time on activities other than criminal investigation. Thus, in a typical local police department, patrol officers will most likely spend less than 20% of their time on activities directly related to investigating felonies. Indeed, even the detectives (who represent a small portion of the total force) spend a substantial portion of their time on other matters, such as simply closing out files in cases that obviously cannot be solved or arranging for the presentation of evidence in cases that have been solved.

Only about 10% of the police agencies enforcing state law are largely limited in their responsibilities to enforcement of the criminal law. In the general federal system, on the other hand, most agencies are so limited. The primary distinction among federal agencies relates to the range of federal criminal laws that the particular agency is assigned to enforce. While the Federal Bureau of Investigation has enforcement responsibilities as to all federal offenses, other agencies focus on a particular grouping of offenses (as in the case of the Drug Enforcement Agency and the Bureau of Alcohol, Tobacco, and Firearms). Over fifty different federal agencies have personnel with police authority and law enforcement responsibilities.

As a general matter, the legal standards governing police actions (e.g., arrests, stops, and searches) are the same for all of the different police agencies within the state. The primary legal difference will flow from any geographical limits or subject matter limits imposed on the agency. When an agency's officer acts outside of those limits (e.g., a municipal police officer acting outside the local municipality), and there is no special extension of the officer's authority (as in statutes relating to hot pursuit), the officer typically has no greater authority than a private citizen.

There are fewer varieties of prosecutors, but many states extend prosecutorial investigative authority not only to the local prosecuting attorney (known in some states as the "district attorney" or "state's attorney"), but also to the state's Attorney General. Indeed, in three states, there are no independent local prosecutors and the Attorney General's office is responsible for all prosecutions under state law.

Judges, particularly judges of courts of inferior jurisdiction, often also play a role in criminal investigations through the issuance of search warrants, arrest warrants, and other court orders. Within a single state, there may be several different types of inferior court judges who assume such traditional duties of the "magistrate." They may be lay judges who serve on a part-time basis, practicing lawyers who serve on a part-time basis as judges, and full time judges who are qualified lawyers. Very often state law will draw distinctions in the degree of authority granted to different inferior courts, based largely on the type of judges sitting in those courts.

§ 1.2   The Laws Regulating the Process

(a) **Varied Sources.** In each jurisdiction, the law governing the criminal justice process will come from several different sources. For cases in the federal system, the primary sources are: (1) the United States Constitution; (2) federal statutes; (3) the Federal Rules of Criminal Procedure; (4) rulings of federal courts based on their common law decisional authority or their supervisory authority over the administration of criminal justice (as contrasted to rulings interpreting the Constitution, statutes, or court rules); and (5) the internal regulations of the Department of Justice and other agencies involved in the administration of the federal criminal justice process. At the state level, an even larger group of sources come into play. The legal standards governing the investigative portion of the process in a state system will come primarily from eight different sources: (1) the United States Constitution; (2) federal statutes; (3) the state's constitution; (4) the state's statutes; (5) the state's general court rules; (6) rulings of the state's courts based on their common law authority or their supervisory authority; (7) the internal administrative standards of those state and local agencies involved in the administration of the process; and (8) local ordinances. The subsections that follow discuss the general character of each of the different sources, using the larger group of sources applicable to a state system.

(b) **The Federal Constitution.** The natural starting point in examining the law governing a particular procedure is the federal constitution. Under Article VI, the mandates of the federal constitution are the "Supreme Law of the Land." Thus, those mandates prevail over conflicting federal law from other sources (e.g., federal statutes), and where the constitutional mandates apply to the state system, they prevail over conflicting state law as well. As discussed in § 1.3, not all of the mandates of the federal constitution relating to the criminal justice process have been held applicable to the states. However, in its application of the selective incorporation doctrine (see § 1.3(d)), the Supreme Court has held that the Fourteenth Amendment makes applicable to the states the various Fourth, Fifth, and Sixth Amendment provisions that apply to criminal investigative practices. The Fourteenth Amendment's due process clause also has been held to have an independent regulatory content (see § 1.4) that stands apart from restraints of the Fourth, Fifth, and Sixth Amendment provisions.

As to almost all aspects of investigation, federal constitutional provisions, as interpreted by the Supreme Court, provide the primary standards of legal regulation. Accordingly, most of the discussion in the chapters that follow concentrate on the constitutional standards and the principles underlying those standards. It should be kept in mind, however, that these standards do not provide the totality of the regulation of investigative practices in either the states or the federal system. Initially, the constitutional regulation has gaps, and where the Constitution does not regulate, the individual jurisdiction will often fill the gap with its own laws. For example, the Fourth Amendment establishes the basic requirements for the issuance and execution of search warrants, but it does not impose any requirements relating to the display of the warrant or the receipt given when items are seized. These are matters commonly regulated by the individual jurisdictions. So too, the Fourth Amendment applies only to activities that constitute "searches." Most jurisdictions do not regulate police surveillance activities that fall short of a "search," but several do so under the law of the individual jurisdiction.

Where the Constitution does regulate, the individual jurisdiction always remains free to impose a more stringent regulation of police activities. Constitutional standards are only baseline standards. They prescribe prerequisites that each jurisdiction must meet at a minimum, but the jurisdiction remains free to fashion additional procedural protections if it so desires. Thus, while the Supreme Court has held that the Fourth Amendment requires the presentation of an arrestee before a magistrate within 48 hours (see § 2.5(a)), a majority of the states require that the person be presented within 24 hours. Of course, such a widespread adoption of a more stringent standard is not the norm. As to the bulk of the investigative practices discussed in the chapters that follow, most of the states have not imposed requirements more stringent than the federal constitutional mandate. However, there often will be a minority of at least a few states that have adopted more stringent regulations.

(c) Federal Statutes. In general, federal statutes regulating criminal procedure apply only to the federal system, and serve the role of local statutory regulation discussed in subsection (e) below. However, a limited body of federal legislation (e.g., the federal wiretap statute discussed in § 3.2) applies to both the state and federal criminal justice systems. Prohibitions and restrictions contained in those statutes prevail over contrary state provisions, and they therefore must be applied by state courts in state prosecutions even though the practices prohibited or restricted would pose no difficulty under state law alone.

(d) State Constitutions. Every state has a series of constitutional provisions that guarantee certain rights of the defendant and limit governmental authority in the administration of the criminal justice process. In large part, these state constitutional provisions cover the same ground as the criminal procedure guarantees in the Bill of Rights of the federal constitution. However, a state court may read its state's constitutional guarantee as imposing a more stringent limitation upon state enforcement officials than the corresponding federal guarantee. Also some state guarantees are distinct from any of the guarantees in the federal constitution (e.g., a state constitutional guarantee of a right of privacy), and therefore reach activities not subject to the federal guarantees.

(e) State Statutes. The federal system, the District of Columbia, and each of the states has an extensive group of statutory provisions regulating the criminal justice process. Initially, each jurisdiction has a series of sequentially presented provisions that typically are described as the jurisdiction's "code of criminal procedure." In only about a third of the jurisdictions, however, are these true codifications of the law of criminal procedure. Here, the "code" does set forth the basic governing standards, often accompanied by considerable procedural detail, in a conceptually integrated, comprehensive pattern of regulation. Such statutes typically have provisions on various aspects of investigative authority, including: arrest authority; issuance of summons or citations as alternatives to arrest; search authority pursuant to a warrant; electronic surveillance authority; and detention and disposition of the arrested person. Other aspects of investigation, such as police interrogation, are rarely dealt with by statute. In other states, the criminal procedure "codes" are little more than a loose conglomeration of criminal procedure statutes, providing spotty coverage on less than half of the subjects typically treated in a complete codification. These statutes are likely to deal with only a few investigative procedures, with the issuance of arrest and search warrants being the most common.

(f) **General Court Rules.** In the federal system, the Federal Rules of Criminal Procedure play a very significant role in the regulation of the criminal process. However, the Rules deal mainly with court procedures. Thus, they will provide standards only for those aspects of the investigative process that directly involve the courts, such as the issuance of warrants. They will also regulate procedures for challenging the legality of investigative practices, such as the motion to suppress (see § 9.1). The District of Columbia and roughly two-thirds of the states have their own general court rules, similar in function to the Federal Rules. In state jurisdictions, conflicts sometimes exist between statutes and court rules. In many states, as in the federal system, court rules are subject to legislative control, giving the legislature the last word on such conflicts. However, some states grant to their highest court an independent constitutional authority to prescribe rules of "practice and procedure" which prevails over contrary legislation.

(g) **Common Law Rulings.** For over a century, common law rulings were the primary source of the law governing the criminal justice process in the states. However, the introduction of comprehensive codes of criminal procedure, followed by the adoption in many states of extensive court rules, and then by the constitutionalization of the law of criminal procedure, combined to sharply reduce the role of common law rulings. Today, for all but a few states, the legal standards governing most aspects of the criminal justice process come from a combination of the federal constitution, the state's own constitution, state statutes, and state court rules (all subject, of course, to judicial interpretation). Common law rulings still dominate as to certain aspects of courtroom procedure, but only infrequently as to investigative procedures. The grand jury investigation is the one aspect of investigation in which common law rulings continue to play a significant role in many jurisdictions.

Federal courts, unlike their state counterparts, are courts of limited jurisdiction that have not been vested with "open-ended lawmaking powers," and they therefore lack authority to fashion a "general" federal common law covering the total range of substantive common law subjects. Federal courts did recognize from the outset, however, an authority to fashion common law rules of procedure where Congress had not otherwise provided. Still, over the years, they made less frequent use of that authority in shaping the criminal process than did state courts utilizing their common law authority. In part this came about because federal courts, for many years, assumed that the lack of federal legislation establishing an independent federal standard indicated a congressional intent that the federal courts conform to the procedural law of the state in which they sat as that law existed when that state was first admitted to statehood. Gradually, Congress turned to framing more federal process standards, giving federal criminal procedure a distinctive character, and the federal courts came to look to federal common law, rather than state law, where no statutory standards were specified. Two major developments, however, subsequently served to reduce sharply federal court references to the common law in their criminal process rulings. In 1946, the Federal Rules of Criminal Procedure came into effect and regulated many areas formerly governed by federal criminal law. At roughly the same time, the Supreme Court recognized a concept of supervisory authority over federal criminal justice which could provide a grounding for judicially imposed procedural requirements, fashioned apart from the interpretation of the constitution, statute, or court rule. As discussed below, federal courts have commonly cited this supervisory power in fashioning decisional rules which would be described as common law standards in other jurisdictions.

(h) Supervisory Authority Rulings. *McNabb v. United States* (1943), first announced federal court authority to establish decisional rules of criminal procedure in the exercise of "its supervisory authority over the administration of criminal justice in the federal courts." At issue in *McNabb* was the admission of confessions obtained from arrestees who allegedly had been detained and interrogated by government agents for two days before being taken before a federal magistrate (see § 5.3). The Court viewed the detention as a "flagrant disregard" of a federal statutory requirement that an arrested person promptly be brought before the nearest judicial officer. The Court acknowledged that this federal statute did not itself require exclusion of statements obtained during a detention that violated the statutory command. However, the Court had an obligation, stemming from the obligations of "judicial supervision of the administration of criminal justice in the federal courts," to maintain "civilized standards of procedure and evidence in those courts." That duty mandated exclusion of the confessions, for to allow their use as the grounding of a conviction "would stultify the policy" underlying the prompt presentment statute and make "the courts themselves accomplices in willful disobedience of law." The Court clearly did not base this ruling on the common law development of the rules of evidence. That would have required it to square its ruling with common law precedent, which had focused on the potential untrustworthiness of the individual confession and the possible invasion of some common law privilege of the accused.

The scope of the supervisory authority of the Supreme Court was not clearly defined in *McNabb*. The Court did stress that it was "not concerned with law enforcement practices except insofar as courts themselves became instruments of enforcement." Where the judicial process did become involved, however, *McNabb*'s broad description of the Court's supervisory authority suggested that the Court could shape its own standards of fairness, even apart from situations presenting a statutory violation. That came to pass in a series of later Supreme Court rulings relating to the role of trial courts in regulating the litigation process. The supervisory power was relied upon to establish general procedural standards for such matters as contempt proceedings, jury selection and disqualification, discovery and disclosure, and the permissible scope of cross-examination. However, in many of the Court's supervisory power decisions, the Court's reasoning clearly had constitutional overtones, suggesting that the procedure being required might well be constitutionally mandated. Reliance upon the supervisory power was preferred, however, as it avoided the consequences that would flow from a constitutional ruling.

United States v. Hasting (1983) reexamined the scope of the Court's supervisory power. It characterized "the purposes underlying the use of the supervisory powers * * * [as] threefold: to implement a remedy for violation of recognized rights * * *; to preserve judicial integrity by ensuring that a conviction rests on appropriate considerations validly before the jury * * *; and finally, as a remedy designed to deter illegal conduct." Lower courts subsequently sought to extend the judicial integrity grounding to dismiss indictments or exclude evidence based on an action of the prosecutor or police, taken apart from the judicial proceeding, that was viewed as "misconduct" although not prohibited by statute, court rule, or constitutional provision. In *United States v. Williams*, (1992) the Supreme Court rejected one line of such rulings and cast doubt upon the validity in general of using the supervisory authority to create misconduct standards outside of the litigation process. At issue in *Williams* was the dismissal of an indictment based upon a prosecutor's failure to present exculpatory evidence before the grand jury. The Court not only rejected use of the supervisory power to impose a prosecutorial obligation that was inconsistent with the historical traditions of the grand jury, but set forth a broad general restraint upon use of the supervisory power to dismiss indictments based on prosecutorial presentations before the grand jury. That authority, it noted, ordinarily could be used only where the prosecutorial behavior violated a legal requirement found in a statute, court rule, or constitutional command, and had a prejudicial impact upon the grand jury proceeding.

Williams reasoned that, in dealing with grand jury proceedings, which were not part of the court's own proceedings, the court's supervisory powers could be used to implement independently established legal restrictions on prosecutorial presentations, but not to create judicially additional restrictions on prosecutorial presentations. That rationale could readily be extended to bar, as a general matter, the judicial creation of prosecutorial and police misconduct standards for all portions of the criminal justice process in which the judiciary is not itself directly involved. However, the *Williams* opinion stressed the institutional independence of the grand jury, and the lower federal courts so far generally have read *Williams* as dealing only with the exercise of the supervisory power in relation to grand juries.

Two of the three uses of supervisory authority noted in *Hasting* relate to the fashioning of sanctions, both to remedy past violations of recognized rights, and to determine future violations. Supreme Court rulings, however, have imposed significant limitations on this use of supervisory authority. Two cases, *United States v. Payner* (1980) and *Hasting* itself, warned lower courts that, in fashioning supervisory authority remedies for constitutional violations, "they are not free to disregard the limitations the Supreme Court has deliberately placed on constitutional remedies." *Payner* involved the admissibility of evidence obtained through a violation of the Fourth Amendment rights of a third party, rather than the rights of the defendant. Although the Supreme Court had consistently held in its constitutional rulings that the exclusionary rule remedy was not available to the defendant unless his own Fourth Amendment rights were violated, the district court concluded that a deliberate violation taking advantage of that limitation justified exclusion in the exercise of its supervisory power. The Supreme Court, in reversing, responded that "the values assigned to the competing interests [shaping the exclusionary remedy] do not change because a court has elected to analyze the question under the supervisory power instead of the Fourth Amendment." Since the Court's Fourth Amendment rulings had concluded that the "interest in deterring illegal searches does not justify the exclusion of tainted evidence at the instance of a party who was not the victim of the challenged practice," the lower court's use of the supervisory power "amount[ed] to a substitution of individual judgment for controlling decisions of this Court."

Hasting similarly held that a lower court could not utilize its supervisory power to fashion a rule of automatic reversal of a trial conviction, based on the prosecutor's persistent disregard of a constitutional prohibition against adverse comment on the defendant's failure to testify, since the Supreme Court had earlier announced that the Constitution did not require reversal if the violation constituted harmless error. A third case, *Bank of Nova Scotia v. U.S.* (1988), held that a federal court may not invoke its supervisory role to craft a remedy inconsistent with limits imposed by a statute or a Federal Rule of Criminal Procedure (there too, a prohibition against reversal if the non-constitutional violation constituted harmless error).

(i) **Internal Administrative Standards.** All of the major participants in the administration of the criminal process are subject to regulation by what are commonly characterized as "internal administrative standards." These largely are standards of performance imposed by government agencies upon their employees or imposed by licensing bodies upon those acting in a licensed capacity. Thus, prosecutors, and police officers are subject to performance standards imposed by the governmental agencies that employ them. The focus of such standards is not on regulating the criminal justice process as such, but in setting internal standards of performance for the actors.

Prior to the Supreme Court's ruling in *United States v. Caceres* (1979), some federal lower courts, relying upon their supervisory power, had excluded evidence obtained by the government where the prosecutor or investigative agent had violated an agency policy. The *Caceres* Court ruled against exclusion in an opinion that extended well beyond the facts of the particular violation of agency regulations presented there (a violation of IRS regulations requiring the advance authorization of a Justice Department official, prior to electronic recording by an undercover agent of conversations with a suspected criminal). The Court noted that "regulations governing the conduct of criminal investigations are generally considered desirable," and the courts should not discourage use of such regulations by the rigid application of an exclusionary rule to every regulatory violation. "In the long run", the Court noted, "it is far better to have rules like those contained in the IRS Manual, and to tolerate occasional erroneous administration of the kind displayed by this record, than either to have no rules except those mandated by statute, or to have them framed in a mere precatory form." The *Caceres* opinion did not rule out the possibility that judicial relief might be available where a breach of regulations presented an exceptionally compelling case. Neither did it have before it one of those situations in which the government's failure to comply with its own regulations furnished a grounding for a constitutional violation, either because the constitutionality of the governmental action was dependent on adherence to a standard policy or "the individual * * * reasonably relied on agency regulations promulgated for his guidance or benefit and has suffered substantially because of their violation by the agency."

(j) **Local Ordinances**. Local ordinances play a comparatively minor role in the law regulating the criminal justice process. In general, municipal authority bearing upon the process is limited to the regulation of the local police. Even here, the municipality can only regulate in conformity with state law. By and large, ordinances will deal with such administrative matters as the keeping and disclosure of records, the impoundment of vehicles, and the return or other disposition of seized property. Some ordinances, however, may relate directly to investigative practices and enhance police authority. Thus, an ordinance may require that a person stopped under appropriate circumstances bear the responsibility of identifying himself. On the other side, an ordinance may direct local police to avoid utilizing certain authority (e.g., certain investigative practices) except under specified circumstances.

§ 1.3 Application of the Bill of Rights Guarantees to the States

(a) **Introduction.** As initially adopted, the Constitution said very little about criminal procedure. But once the process of obtaining state ratification produced a commitment to add amendments protecting individual rights, it became obvious that the criminal justice process would receive considerable attention in the amended Constitution. A combination of several factors—including this country's English heritage, misuse of the criminal process against colonial dissidents, and the focus of post-revolutionary political theory upon restraining the growing authority of government where it was the antagonist of the individual—had led to a heavy emphasis upon criminal process rights in the bills of rights of state constitutions. The individual rights amendments of the federal constitution, in what became the federal Bill of Rights (i.e., the first ten amendments), were requested by the ratifying states largely to perform the same function as the state bills of rights.

The guarantees of individual rights were placed in the first eight amendments (the ninth and tenth recognizing structural safeguards that also limited governmental authority). Of the twenty-seven guarantees established in those first eight amendments, sixteen dealt specifically with the criminal justice process. One additional provision, the due process clause of the Fifth Amendment, clearly applied to criminal proceedings, as it covered the criminal sanctions of loss of life, liberty, or property, although also extending to non-criminal proceedings where one of those interests (typically only property) was at stake. These seventeen provisions were certain to play a significant role in the shaping of the federal criminal justice system by Congress, and they also provided a grounding, unless narrowly construed by the federal courts, for continuous federal court regulation of that process through judicial decisions. The Bill of Rights provisions, however, applied only to the federal government. They had no bearing on the criminal justice processes of the states.

Following the civil war, the Fourteenth Amendment included a provision that clearly did apply to the states. The second sentence of section one of that amendment provided: "No state shall make or enforce any law which shall abridge the privileges or immunities of citizens of the United States; nor shall any State deprive any person of life, liberty, or property, without due process of law; nor deny to any person within its jurisdiction the equal protection of the laws." Over the many years since the adoption of the Fourteenth Amendment, a substantial portion of the Supreme Court's workload has involved the interpretation of the provisions of this second sentence. One of the more difficult recurring issues faced by the Court has been whether, and to what extent, that second sentence encompasses (and thereby makes applicable to the states) the guarantees found in the Bill of Rights. Over the years, essentially three different positions have been advanced within the Court on this issue: (1) the "total incorporation" position, advanced in numerous dissents, but never adopted by the Court majority; (2) the "fundamental fairness" position, consistently supported by a majority prior to the 1960s; and (3) the selective incorporation doctrine that has prevailed as the majority view since the mid–1960s.

Each of these positions is discussed in the subsections that follow. Since the selective incorporation doctrine has clearly won the day, one might ask why we devote two full sections to the "defeated" positions of total incorporation and fundamental fairness. Initially, an understanding of each is needed to fully appreciate the selective incorporation position. The judicial debate between the supporters of the total incorporation and fundamental fairness positions had substantial influence on the initial articulation and eventual adoption of the selective incorporation doctrine. But more significantly, strains of that debate have current vitality. As discussed in subsection (e), the concerns that were expressed by the judicial proponents of the fundamental fairness position are advanced today, in only slightly altered form, in judicial discussions of the need to provide leeway for the states in interpreting the incorporated provisions of the Bill of Rights. So too, the criticism of the totality-of-the-circumstances approach of the fundamental fairness doctrine reappears today in judicial discussions of the standards to be fashioned under the specific guarantees, as discussed in § 1.5. Finally as discussed in § 1.4, a basic strand of the fundamental fairness concept remains a viable and frequently used measure for regulating both state and federal criminal procedure under "free-standing" due process.

(b) Fundamental Fairness. The relationship between the Fourteenth Amendment and the Bill of Rights was first considered by the Supreme Court in the criminal procedure context in *Hurtado v. Cal.* (1884). The petitioner Hurtado had been tried and convicted of murder following the initiation of charges on a prosecutor's information and a determination of probable cause by a magistrate at a preliminary hearing. Hurtado claimed that Fourteen Amendment due process had been violated by the state's failure to initiate prosecution through an indictment or presentment of a grand jury. In rejecting that claim, the Court acknowledged that prosecution by indictment had a long common law history, dating back to the Magna Charta, and was required in the federal system by the Fifth Amendment's grand jury clause. However, the due process clause of the Fourteenth Amendment applied to the states only the same content as the due process clause of the Fifth Amendment applied to the federal government. That clause did not lock into the Constitution the particular practices of a particular time. It encompassed only those "fundamental principles of liberty and justice which lie at the base of all our civil and political institutions," and judicial determination of its content should look to "the very substance of individual rights" rather than "particular forms of procedure." Like the common law itself, which "dr[ew] its inspiration from every fountain of justice," due process should allow the legislature to take account of "the new and various experiences of our own situation," and looking to "the best ideas of all systems and ages," to mold basic principles of justice into "new * * * forms." Prosecution by means other than indictment had been known to the common law, and the California procedure used here, like the indictment process itself, "carefully consider[ed] and guard[ed] the substantial interests of the accused." Accordingly, it did not violate due process.

Hurtado established both prongs of what came to be known as the "fundamental fairness" or "ordered liberty" interpretation of due process. First, the due process clause protects only these rights of the individual, procedural and substantive, that are deemed to be "fundamental." Over the years, the Court variously described the standard for determining whether a right is fundamental. Due process was said to require adherence to those rights that are "implicit in the concept of ordered liberty," that are "so rooted in the traditions and conscience of our people as to be ranked fundamental," and that "lie at the base of all our civil and political institutions." As applied to criminal procedure, it was said to require "that fundamental fairness essential to the very concept of justice." The Court also repeatedly emphasized, as in *Hurtado*, that this is a flexible standard, not frozen in history. It takes account of societal change and looks to the "essence [of] just treatment," rather than the historical familiarity of form.

Second, there is no necessary correlation between the protection afforded under the specific provisions of the Bill of Rights and due process. The concept of due process has an "independent potency," which permits it to encompass rights not mentioned in the Bill of Rights (e.g., the requirement of proof beyond a reasonable doubt). At the same time, although a Fifth Amendment due process clause sat alongside the other Bill of Rights guarantees, that did not preclude the possibility that due process might overlap in its coverage with certain aspects of those guarantees. The key was the fundamental character of the particular right, whether or not mentioned in the other guarantees.

Traditional fundamental fairness analysis did not treat the recognition of a right in a Bill of Rights guarantee as a strong indicator that the right was fundamental. Some Bill of Rights guarantees, such as the grand jury clause, merely reflected the "restricted views of Eighteen Century England regarding the best method for the ascertainment of facts." Still other guarantees could encompass a fundamental right in its general conception, but not in every aspect of the guarantee as it had been interpreted by federal courts. Thus, there could be a partial overlap of the protection of a particular Bill of Rights guarantee and due process. Accordingly, as the Court indicated in *Wolf v. Colo.* (1949) (see § 2.1(a)), due process could prohibit a search that violated the Fourth Amendment, but not also mandate the evidence-exclusion remedy required by the Fourth Amendment.

(c) Total Incorporation. While total incorporation was always a minority position, it arguably had considerable influence in the Court's eventual adoption of the selective incorporation doctrine. The total incorporation position maintained that the Fourteenth Amendment incorporated and made applicable to the states all of the specific guarantees of the Bill of Rights. Most of its supporters agreed that the due process guarantee additionally protected fundamental rights not enumerated in the first eight amendments, although Justice Black maintained that due process additionally did no more than prohibit the government from departing from previously established procedures and pre-existing law. Justices advancing the total incorporation position relied in large part on their reading of the history of the Fourteenth Amendment as intended to make the Bill of Rights applicable to the states, with some arguing that purpose was reflected in the Fourteenth Amendment's privilege and immunities clause, other claiming that the Fourteenth Amendment's due process clause achieved that objective, and Justice Black looking to the Fourteenth Amendment "as a whole."

The Supreme Court first rejected a total incorporation analysis in the 1890s, but the position was pressed by dissenters again in the mid–1900s, and received four votes in *Adamson v. Cal.* (1947). The majority in each instance emphasized that the framers of the Fourteenth Amendment would have directly stated that the Bill of Rights was applicable to the states if that had been their intent. Moreover, total incorporation would have required significant changes in the then current procedures of several states, but there had been no suggestion of the need for such changes in the ratification debates, and no movement to make such changes thereafter. Indeed, the inconsistency of state procedure with total incorporation had grown, as more states did not institute criminal prosecution by grand jury indictment (as would be required by an incorporated Fifth Amendment) and did not provide jury trials in civil cases involving limited damages (although an incorporated Seventh Amendment would have required jury trials for all cases involving more than twenty dollars).

In the end, the most influential arguments of the supporters of total incorporation were not their arguments for that position, but their arguments against the "subjectivity" of the fundamental fairness doctrine. There was a need, it was argued, to have constitutional regulation rest on the "boundaries fixed by the written words of the Constitution" (i.e, the specific guarantees of the Bill of Rights), rather than the majority's "natural law" approach, which basically invited the Court "to substitute its own concepts of decency and fundamental justice for the language of the Bill of Rights." Justice Black, in particular, repeatedly criticized the Court for reaching basically idiosyncratic results under the fundamental fairness doctrine. His primary example was a pair of rulings involving police investigative practices, *Rochin v. Cal.* (1952) and *Irvin v. Cal.* (1954).

In *Rochin*, the police, having "some information" that defendant was selling narcotics, entered his home without a warrant and forced open the door to his bedroom. When the surprised defendant immediately shoved into his mouth two capsules believed to be narcotics, the police grabbed him and attempted to extract the capsules, which defendant then swallowed. The police then took the protesting defendant to a doctor, who forced an emetic solution into defendant's stomach, causing him to vomit up the capsules. Describing the total course of police action as "conduct that shocks the conscience," the Court held that due process no more permitted the use of the capsules in evidence than it would a coerced confession. "Due process," the Court added, was a principle that "precludes defining * * * more precisely than to say that convictions cannot be brought about by methods that 'offend a sense of justice.' "

In *Irvine*, the plurality described the police action as flagrant and deliberate misconduct, but held that it was not so offensive as to violate due process. The police in *Irvine* had made repeated illegal entries into defendant's home for the purpose of installing secret microphones, including one in his bedroom, from which they listened to his conversations for over a month. The plurality distinguished *Rochin* as a case involving "coercion, violence * * * [and] brutality to the person" rather than, as here, a "trespass to property, plus eavesdropping." However, Justice Frankfurter, who had written for the Court in *Rochin*, concluded that the two cases were not distinguishable. Though "there was lacking [in *Irvine*] physical violence, even to the restricted extent employed in *Rochin*," the police had engaged in "a more powerful and offensive control over Irvine's life than a single limited physical trespass."

The division of the Court in *Irvine*, Justice Black later noted, revealed that the Court's "ad hoc approach" consisted of no more than determining whether "five justices are sufficiently revolted by local police action" to "shock [the victim of that action] into the protective arms of the Constitution." Justice Frankfurter, in response, took sharp exception to Justice Black's characterization. Admittedly, the case-by-case application of the "ordered liberty" standard required the exercise of judicial judgment in an "empiric process" for which there was no "mechanical yardstick." That did not mean, however, that judges were "at large" to draw upon their "merely personal and private notions" of justice. In each case, the Court was required to undertake a "disinterested inquiry pursued in the spirit of science." It looked not to personal preferences, but to external evidence of permanent and pervasive notions of fairness, such as the positions taken in the federal constitution and early state constitutions, the standards currently applied in the various states, and viewpoints of other countries with similar jurisprudential traditions.

Also responding to Justice Black, Justice Harlan suggested that the specific provisions of the Bill of Rights that Justice Black sought to substitute for a fundamental fairness analysis often were no less amenable to a subjective interpretation than the fundamental fairness standard of due process. Under Justice Black's position, the focus of judicial inquiry would be shifted from the flexible concept of "ordered liberty" to equally flexible terms found in most of the Amendments. Terms like "probable cause," "unreasonable search," and "speedy and public trial," it was noted, are hardly self-defining. Indeed, Justice Black's own opinion in *Rochin* illustrated that ambiguity even in a provision that the Court had described as rooted in history. Justice Black had agreed that there was a constitutional violation in *Rochin*, but he had based that conclusion on the Fifth Amendment privilege against self-incrimination rather than what he described as the "evanescent" standard of fundamental fairness. To find that the privilege had been violated, however, Justice Black arguably had to make value judgments very much like those considered under a fundamental fairness analysis. To treat the stomach pumping as compulsory self-incrimination, Justice Black had to conclude that the privilege extended to the obtaining of nontestimonial evidence (as well as testimonial evidence) and prohibited physical compulsion (as well as the compulsion of a court order). The highly debatable nature of the first proposition, in particular, was evidenced by later cases in which a divided Court held that the Fifth Amendment privilege did not extend so far (see § 7.10(d)).

(d) Selective Incorporation. In 1961, Justice Brennan, in a dissenting opinion, advanced what is commonly described as the "selective incorporation" interpretation of the Fourteenth Amendment. *Cohen v. Hurley* (1961) (Brennan, J., dis.). This interpretation combines aspects of both the "fundamental rights" and "total incorporation" interpretations of the Fourteenth Amendment. Selective incorporation accepts the basic premise of the fundamental rights interpretation that the Fourteenth Amendment encompasses rights, substantive or procedural, that are so basic as to be ranked as "fundamental." It recognizes too that not all rights specified in the Bill of Rights are necessarily fundamental. It rejects the fundamental rights interpretation, however, insofar as that doctrine looks only to the character of the particular element of a specified right denied in the particular case, and evaluates that element with reference to the "totality of circumstances" of that case. Evaluating the fundamental nature of a right in terms of the "factual circumstances surrounding each individual case" is viewed as "extremely subjective and excessively discretionary." Limiting a decision to only one aspect of the specified right also is rejected as presenting the same difficulty. Accordingly, in determining whether a specified right is fundamental, the selective incorporation doctrine requires that the Court look at the total right guaranteed by the particular Bill of Rights provision, not merely at a single aspect of that right nor the application of that aspect in the circumstances of the particular case. If it is decided that a particular guarantee is fundamental, that guarantee will be incorporated into the Fourteenth Amendment "whole and intact." The specified right will then be enforced against the states in every case according to the same standards applied to the federal government. With respect to those guarantees within the Bill of Rights held to be fundamental, there is, as Justice Douglas put it, "coextensive coverage" under the Fourteenth Amendment and the Bill of Rights. *Johnson v. La.* (1972).

The selective incorporation doctrine gained majority support during the 1960s. The debate as to its adoption was presented largely in concurring and dissenting opinions, as the majority opinions typically applied the doctrine without any extensive discussion as to why the focus should be on the whole of an enumerated right. Justices opposing selective incorporation argued that it was no more than an artificial compromise between traditional fundamental fairness and the total incorporation doctrines. Supporters of the doctrine stressed that selective incorporation reduced the potential for subjectivity and "avoid[ed] the impression of personal, ad hoc adjudication" by discarding an analysis that focused on the totality of the circumstances of the individual case. Selective incorporation was also praised as promoting certainty in the law, and thereby facilitating state court enforcement of due process standards; once a specified right was held to be fundamental, the state courts were directed to the specific language of the Bill of Rights guarantee and the various decisions interpreting that guarantee in the context of federal prosecutions. This stood in contrast to the case-by-case rulings under fundamental fairness, which left the state at sea as to whether other circumstances and other aspects of a particular right would produce a different result as to what was fundamental.

The adoption of the selective incorporation position during the 1960s was accompanied by a movement towards a broader view of the nature of a "fundamental procedural right." A right was to be judged by reference to its operation within the "common law system of [criminal procedure] * * * that has been developing * * * in this country, rather than its theoretical justification as a necessary element of a 'fair and equitable procedure.'" *Duncan v. La.* (1968). The fact that another system of justice could operate without a particular right (as the civil system operated without jury trials) did not work against finding the right to be fundamental in our system. Also, an emphasis was placed upon the very presence of a right within the Bill of Rights as strong evidence of its fundamental nature.

Applying this approach, the Supreme Court in the 1960s held fundamental (and therefore applicable to the states) the three guarantees that play the largest role in the constitutional regulation of investigative practices: (1) the Fourth Amendment's regulation of searches, *Mapp v. Ohio* (1961) and *Ker v. Cal.* (1961); (2) the Fifth Amendment's prohibition against compelled self-incrimination, *Malloy v. Hogan* (1961); and (3) the Sixth Amendment's right of the accused to the assistance of counsel, *Gideon v. Wainwright* (1963). The Court also recognized as fundamental the following guarantees related to other aspects of the process: the right to a speedy trial; the right to a public trial; the right to a jury trial before an impartial jury; the right to confront opposing witnesses; the right to compulsory process for obtaining witnesses; the right to notice of the nature and cause of the accusation; and the prohibition against cruel and unusual punishment. Thus, over a brief span of the "Warren Court era," the Supreme Court made applicable to the states all but four of the 16 Bill of Rights guarantees specifically directed to criminal procedure. As for the four, the Court simply had not been presented with cases requiring incorporation rulings on three of them; the Eight Amendment prohibition of excessive bail; the Eighth Amendment prohibition against excessive fines; and the Sixth Amendment's guarantee that the jury be selected from "the state and district where the crime shall have been committed, which district shall have been ascertained by law." Indeed, it has yet to rule on these three (although lower courts have done so, unanimously assuming that the first two are fundamental and dividing on the third). As to the one remaining guarantee, the Fifth Amendment's requirement of prosecution by grand jury indictment, the Court here reaffirmed the Hurtado ruling that it is not fundamental. This is the only criminal procedure guarantee held not to apply to the states under the selective incorporation doctrine.

(e) **Selective Incorporation and Federalism.** The opinions of the Court during the era of fundamental fairness rarely failed to note the need to respect the "sovereign character of the several states" by giving the states the widest latitude consistent with ensuring fundamental fairness. Justices opposing the adoption of selective incorporation argued that the Bill of Rights provisions had long been interpreted with only the federal government in mind, and applying those provisions and their previous interpretations to the states would be inappropriate, as the state criminal justice systems operated in settings requiring far greater flexibility than the federal system. In the area of criminal investigations, for example, the much broader responsibilities of local police had to be taken in account. They enforced a "far wider spectrum of laws" than federal enforcement officers and had responsibilities that extended beyond law enforcement, such as order maintenance and traffic control, which produced a different allocation of resources and different policing techniques. A "jot for jot" application of standards developed in the context of federal proceedings could put "the states, with their differing law enforcement problem[s] * * * in a constitutional straight jacket."

Supporters of selective incorporation argued that the procedural safeguards established in the Bill of Rights simply were too important to give way to concerns relating to local control of the criminal justice process. Those safeguards had not placed the federal criminal justice system in a constitutional straight jacket, and had actually been applied with full force in the local police setting of the District of Columbia. Also, where the circumstances faced by the states were substantially different, the various guarantees were sufficiently flexible to give consideration to those differences, even if that required reexamining past precedent. Responding to this argument, Justice Harlan predicted that, to "avoid unduly fettering the states," the Court would frequently be forced to relax the constitutional standards that were now being applied to both the federal and state governments. The end result he argued, would be a "watering down [of] protections against the Federal government," thereby "discarding * * * the possibility of federal leadership by example." The supporters of selective incorporation apparently assumed, however, that the need for more flexible standards to accommodate the special problems of the states would be rare, and those standards would be carefully tied to the particular setting so as to limit their applicability.

In its subsequent application of the incorporated guarantees, the Court has in various rulings reached a result shaped by the special aspects of state criminal justice administration. It has noted in this regard a need to adopt standards sufficiently flexible to allow the states to accommodate local variations in resources. In *North v. Russell* (1976), for example, a two-tier system for the trial of misdemeanors, with non-lawyer magistrates the sole decision-maker at the first level, was sustained as an appropriate balance of the limited resources of rural communities and the procedural rights of defendants. Similarly, in *Shadwick v. City of Tampa* (1972), recognizing the "stiff and unrelenting caseloads" borne by many municipal courts, the Court held that the Fourth Amendment was not violated by the issuance of arrest warrants for municipal ordinance violations by non-lawyer clerks of municipal courts. Justice Powell's opinion for a unanimous Court initially noted that the issuance of warrants by judges or lawyers was to be preferred, but "our federal system warns of converting desirable practice into constitutional commandment. It recognizes in plural and diverse state activities one key to national innovation and vitality." In *Cady v. Dombrowski* (1973), the Court similarly recognized the special responsibilities of local police. Pointing out that previous automobile search cases had involved federal officials who did not have responsibilities relating to motor vehicles and public safety, the Court recognized a doctrinally unique warrantless search authority for obtaining a weapon located in a car that had been towed to a garage following an accident.

Rulings like *North, Shadwick, and Cady* evidence a substantial potential for accommodating constitutional interpretation to community diversity within the framework of selective incorporation. Admittedly not all claims for accommodation have been successful. Also, selective incorporation clearly provides less room for accommodation than would be available under a fundamental fairness analysis. Nevertheless, there apparently remains sufficient opportunity for recognition of local variations to convince those post–Warren–Court justices who have stressed federalism concerns in other aspects of constitutional law that there is no need to seek to overturn the selective incorporation doctrine.

§ 1.4 Free–Standing Due Process

(a) Due Process Beyond Incorporation. The selective incorporation doctrine did not challenge the traditional view that due process includes a content independent of the Bill of Rights' specific guarantees. Prior to the adoption of the selective incorporation doctrine, the fundamental fairness doctrine had given the Fourteenth Amendment's due process clause a content that not only overlapped in part with some of the specific guarantees of the Bill of Rights, but also included prohibitions that were not to be found in those guarantees. The selective incorporation doctrine challenged only the standard adopted by the earlier decisions in determining when and to what extent the Fourteenth Amendment's due process clause subjected the state criminal justice systems to restrictions identical to those imposed upon the federal system under the Bill of Rights' specific guarantees. It did not question the conception of due process as also reaching aspects of the process not regulated by those guarantees and imposing the additional restrictions as demanded by the concept of "fundamental fairness." Indeed, over the same decade during which it was selectively incorporating various Bill of Rights guarantees, the Warren Court also was relying upon the independent content of due process to impose new limitations upon the state criminal justice systems that stood apart from any of those selectively incorporated guarantees. Because they had a grounding apart from the incorporated guarantees, these ruling were often described as resting on "free-standing due process."

It was not until after the adoption of selective incorporation that the Supreme Court found it necessary to address the distinct roles of the specific guarantees and the independent content of due process in the constitutional regulation of the state criminal justice systems. The primary source of regulation, the Court noted in *Dowling v. U.S.* (1990), comes from those specific guarantees that have been selectively incorporated and thereby made applicable to the states. "Beyond the specific guarantees enumerated in the Bill of Rights, the Due Process Clause has limited operation." That is so because "[t]he Bill of Rights speaks in explicit terms to many aspects of criminal procedure, and the expansion of those constitutional guarantees under the open-ended rubric of the Due Process Clause invites undue interference with both considered legislative judgments and the careful balance that the Constitution strikes between liberty and order." In the "field of criminal law," the Court stated, "we have defined the category of infractions that violate 'fundamental fairness' very narrowly," recognizing that the due process clause does not "establish this Court as a rule-making organ for the promulgation of states rules of criminal procedure."

The Court's characterization of free-standing due process as a limited supplement to specific guarantees might suggest a sparing use of that grounding, but, in fact, a wide range of constitutional regulations of the criminal justice process are based on the independent content of due process. Free-standing due process rulings play an especially important role in regulating those stages of the process, such as sentencing, that are not regulated by any of the specific guarantees. Yet it also plays a significant role in the regulation of the criminal trial, even though the trial also is regulated by various provisions of the Fifth and Sixth Amendments. Free-standing due process rulings tend to be driven in particular by a concern for adjudication fairness (looking primarily to protection against conviction of the innocent), and that probably explains why such rulings do not play as significant a role in the regulation of criminal investigations as in the regulating of the adjudicatory stages of the process. That is not to suggest, however, that free-standing due process rulings relating to police practices are few in number or unimportant in consequence.

Due process rulings relating to criminal investigations include: the prohibition against lineups, showups, and other identification procedures that present a "substantial likelihood of irreparable misidentification" (§ 6.4); the prohibition against prosecution use of involuntary confessions(§ 5.2); the prohibition against obtaining evidence through means that "shock the conscience" (§ 1.4(c)); the mandate against police intentionally failing to preserve evidence known to be exculpatory, *Ariz. v. Youngblood* (1988); and various procedural prerequisites relating to the motion to suppress evidence as unconstitutionally obtained (§§ 9.4, 9.5).

(b) Due Process Analysis. In determining whether a procedure is consistent with free-standing due process, the Supreme Court in the post-incorporation era has looked primarily to guideposts that also were used in the Court's pre-incorporation fundamental fairness rulings. The most significant of those guideposts have been: (1) the acceptance or rejection of the challenged procedural practice under the English common law as it was adapted to the conditions of this country: (2) the current American consensus on the validity of the challenged practice, as reflected in the judicial decisions and statutes of the various states; and (3) whether the challenged practice is consistent with, or contrary to, the logical application of the over-arching structural elements of the American criminal justice process (particularly, its adherence to an adversary system of adjudication).

None of these guideposts are necessarily controlling. Thus, while the historical acceptance of a practice provides strong evidence that the practice is not contrary to those fundamental principles "rooted in the traditions and conscience of our people," the concept of due process, as *Hurtado* noted (see § 1.3(b)), is open to the lessons of new experiences and the teachings of a new age's "sense of fair play and decency." Thus, *Jackson v. Denno* (§ 9.5(a)) held invalid under due process the practice, long accepted in American common law, that allowed the trial judge to give to the jury the determination of whether a confession was obtained by methods so oppressive that it should not be admissible in evidence. Nontheless, deep common law roots are given great weight, and may well sustain a practice even though the current consensus of the states is to prohibit that practice. *Martin v. Ohio* (1987).

(c) Substantive Due Process. Where the due process claim focuses not on principles of adjudication, but on the invasion of personal liberty, it presents an issue of substantive due process. Thus, claims relating to the state's authority to exercise custodial control over a suspect, to utilize physical force against a suspect, and to subject a suspect to coercive interrogation, all have been treated as substantive due process claims. Such claims face two limitations that go beyond the prerequisites discussed in subsections (a) and (b).

The first obstacle facing substantive due process claim is the "more-specific provision" rule of *Graham v. Connor* (1989). Under the *Graham* rule, where one of the specific constitutional guarantees "provides an external textual source of constitutional protection" against a particular type of government behavior, "that Amendment, not the more generalized notion of 'substantive due process,' must be the guide for analyzing those claims." This position reflects the Court's traditional "reluctan[ce] to expand the concept of substantive due process because the guideposts for responsible decision making in this unchartered area are scarce and open-ended." The *Graham* rule requires that the due process claim identify a protected interest distinct from that protected by the specific guarantee. Thus, in *Albright v. Oliver* (1994), where the petitioner claimed that the initiation of a criminal charge on clearly unreliable evidence violated his personal liberty, the Court majority concluded that the claim was cognizable under substantive due process only if the claimed liberty interest was distinct from the pretrial deprivation of liberty produced by the criminal charge, as that interest is the focus of the Fourth Amendment's requirement of probable cause for an arrest.

A second obstacle facing a substantive due process claim is the Court's general unwillingness to applying substantive due process absent the most compelling case. Thus, in *Sacramento v. Lewis* (1998), involving a police officer's alleged reckless indifference in a high speed chase that resulted in a death, the Court majority held that acts of a government official violated substantive due process only where so egregiously abusive as to "shock the conscience." The Court concluded that the police recklessness there fell short of that standard as the police were acting on an "instant judgment" and without "harmful purpose." The conscience shocking standard requires egregiousness of the character of the forced stomach pumping which was held to violate that standard in *Rochin v. Cal.* (§ 1.3(b)). In *Chavez v. Martinez* (2003), the plurality, concurring, and dissenting opinions all recognized that "shock the conscience" was not the only substantive due process test. A substantive due process violation could also be grounded on the state having violated some "fundamental liberty interest," recognized by history and tradition as "implicit in the concept of ordered liberty." However, the Court also indicated that this requires a strong historical taboo, such as that against torture by government officials.

§ 1.5 Guideposts for Constitutional Interpretation

A variety of considerations influence the Supreme Court's interpretations of constitutional guarantees. Some of these considerations—such as the language of the guarantee and the history underlying its adoption—are staples of all constitutional interpretation. Others tend to vary with the particular guarantee, or, as in the case of the criminal process guarantees, the field of regulation. Discussed below are considerations that have been emphasized, at least since the advent of selective incorporation, in the Court's interpretation of the constitutional guarantees that apply to the criminal justice process. The weight given to the different considerations has varied with individual justices, and not all of the considerations can be said to have strong majority support today. However, each appeared to have such support at one time or another, and with the Court's rulings obviously impacted by shifts in its composition, those considerations given less weigh by today's majority can readily become the considerations given the most weight by tomorrow's majority.

(a) **The Need for Expansive Interpretations.** At any particular point in its history, the Supreme Court has viewed certain constitutional provisions as more deserving of expansive interpretations than others. Thus, the Court for the last half century has spoken of the need for "more exacting judicial scrutiny" in assessing governmental action under the First Amendment, while over the same period no such suggestion of a special need for liberal construction has been applied to the contracts clause. Although occasional earlier rulings, such as *Boyd v. U.S.* (§ 7.5(a)), spoke of a special need for expansive interpretations of the criminal process guarantees, it was not until the 1930s that the Court's rulings reflected a consistent pattern favoring such interpretations. That movement arguably lost some support in the 1940s, particularly as to the Fourth Amendment, but then regained strength in the 1950s and then reached the epitome of its strength in the 1960s. Over a stretch of several years in the 1960s, covering the latter half of Chief Justice Warren's tenure, the Court produced what commentators came to describe as the "criminal justice revolution" of the "Warren Court." That period was marked not only by the adoption of the selective incorporation doctrine, but also by expansive interpretations of the incorporated guarantees that went far beyond their previous applications to the federal criminal justice system. Supreme Court rulings in subsequent decades were far more mixed, but included a fair share of expansive interpretations, most notably producing substantial constitutional regulation of aspects of the process never given significant consideration by the Warren Court. Moreover, over that period, at times the majority, and at times individual justices, have continued to reflect in their opinions the view that the criminal procedure provisions present a special case for expansive interpretations.

The most extensive explanations of the special need for expansive interpretations of the Constitution's criminal procedure guarantees are found in academic commentary rather than Supreme Court opinions. Several of the rationales offered in that commentary, however, do find support in a series of comments, typically brief, made occasionally in opinions for the Court and more frequently in the opinions of individual justices. The rationales having such support look primarily to three factors, each discussed below: (1) the relationship of criminal procedure to the general protection of civil liberties; (2) the relationship of criminal procedure to the protection of minorities; and (3) the presence of various structural elements that enhance the Court's authority in exercising constitutional review of the criminal process.

The civil liberties concern. At least since the late 1930s, the Court has made the protection of civil liberties one of its primary concerns. It has shifted its focus from the protection of property rights to the protection of those liberties deemed more fundamental to the preservation of individual freedom. The Court has left no doubt that it considers the procedural rights of the accused to be among those more fundamental freedoms. It has accepted the premise that procedural fairness and regularity in the enforcement of the criminal law are essential to a free society. "In the end," it has explained, "life and liberty can be as much endangered from illegal methods used to convict those thought to be criminals as from actual criminals themselves." Indeed, it has added, the " 'quality of a nation's civilization can be largely measured by the methods it uses in the enforcement of its criminal law.' "

Protecting minorities. The decade of 1930s was also marked by the Court's tentative suggestion in *U.S. v. Carolene Products Co.* (1938) that one of its major functions is to protect against discrimination those "discrete and insular minorities" who cannot count on the protection of the political process. In later years that suggestion took on substantial force, particularly in the Court's application of the Fourteenth Amendment to instances of racial discrimination by government. Safeguarding the rights of the accused has been viewed as relating to the Court's role of protecting minorities in two respects. First, accused persons are themselves viewed as a highly unpopular minority. As Justice Frankfurter noted, it is precisely because appeals based on criminal process guarantees are so often made by "dubious characters" that infringement of those guarantees calls for "alert and strenuous resistance"; other constitutional protections, such as the First Amendment guarantees, "easily summon powerful support against encroachment," but criminal process guarantees are "normally invoked by those accused of crime, and criminals have few friends." In particular, the legislature is unlikely to be sympathetic to the procedural rights of the accused as "an overwhelming preponderance of political incentives favor unrestricted enforcement of the criminal law." Second, the criminal process is seen as having a special bearing upon various disadvantaged minority groups. Speaking of the Warren Court, former Solicitor General Archibald Cox noted that "[m]any purely procedural questions * * * were influenced by the realization that in another case they might affect the posture of a Negro in a hostile southern court."

"Judicial review" justifications. The special case for expansive interpretations of criminal procedure guarantees also is attributed to several factors that supposedly make the exercise of judicial review more readily supportable in the criminal justice area than in many other areas of constitutional adjudication. Initially, the structure of many of the applicable guarantees—in particular, the specificity of most of the Fourth, Fifth and Sixth Amendment guarantees—is said to permit criminal procedure rulings to be more firmly rooted in the text and history of the applicable constitutional provisions. Of course, some provisions, such as the due process clause, are open-ended, but at least they present no ambiguity as to their applicability to the criminal process.

Adding to this supposedly firmer foundation for judicial review in the criminal procedure area is the fact that the Court only infrequently is required to overturn legislative decisionmaking. Rulings on police investigative methods generally deal with practices that have been instituted by the police without formal legislative authorization. Rulings relating to trial and pretrial procedures similarly tend to deal with practices adopted by courts on their own initiative. Criminal procedure rulings, it is argued, largely bypass the concerns raised by the anti-majoritarian character of judicial overturning of legislation.

Another factor cited as contributing to the Court's willingness to act boldly in the area of criminal procedure is its presumed expertise in dealing with at least those procedural issues that relate to the process of adjudication. The Supreme Court has not described its competence in this area in quite the same way as commentators, who claim that lawyers (and judges) have unique expertise in deciding "what procedures are needed fairly to make what decisions." Yet, the Court has clearly indicated that it views itself as exercising a special responsibility in reviewing procedures of adjudication. Those procedures, it has noted, relate directly to the integrity of the judicial process. Moreover, while the Court's rulings on adjudicatory procedure undoubtedly have a bearing on the achievement of substantive policies, they do not prohibit the legislature from setting substantive standards, but merely require that proof of violation of these standards be established in a certain way. Accordingly, as Justice Jackson noted, the determination of "procedural fairness" is treated as "a specialized responsibility within the competence of the judiciary on which they do not bend before political branches of Government, as they should on matters of policy which comprise substantive law."

Finally, the Court is said to feel at home in the area of constitutional criminal procedure because its rulings here are thought to be more effective in achieving their intended reforms than its rulings in many other areas. The assumption of greater effectiveness may be grounded on either of two contrasting views of the impact of Supreme Court decisions. Under one view, procedural rulings are less likely than other rulings to be subverted and evaded. Unlike rulings in other areas, the Supreme Court's criminal procedure rulings are not seeking to institute broad social change. Even more significantly, they deal with a process that must work its way through the courts, an institution committed to adhere to the rule of law.

The second view acknowledges that effective enforcement of the Supreme Court's procedural rulings faces serious obstacles. These include: a tradition of police disregarding and evading judicial standards that they view as unrealistic; resource limitations that restrict the defense's capacity to uncover and present in court various types of constitutional violations; the prosecution's use of plea bargaining to avoid litigation on possible constitutional violations; constitutional standards that are sufficiently ambiguous to allow lower courts ample opportunity to sharply confine the impact of the Supreme Court rulings without directly disowning those rulings; and various constitutional violations arising in situations that do not result in a criminal prosecution and therefore reach the courts only if victims pursue civil actions. Taken together, these obstacles may largely offset the natural advantage (noted above) of criminal procedural rulings in gaining implementation. Commentators strongly supportive of the Warren Court argued, however, that even where that natural advantage was largely lost, Supreme Court rulings of the type issued by the Warren Court offered another strength in gaining eventual reform of the criminal justice process. The natural audience for Supreme Court rulings (lawyers and judges) coincides with the actors responsible for a good part of the administration of the process and the large part of its lawmaking. In boldly stating the basic goals of the criminal process as recognized in the Constitution, the Supreme Court's opinions had shaped the views of those actors and influenced their actions, not simply in their adherence to Supreme Court rulings, but in their general acceptance of those goals in reforming the law and practice of the criminal justice process.

(b) **Priority for Truth–Finding.** Partially supporting and partially undercutting the special case for expansive interpretations for criminal procedure guarantees is an analysis that gives primary emphasis to truth-finding guarantees. Truth-finding for this purpose goes beyond simply ensuring reliability in fact-finding and also encompasses safeguards that allocate the burden of fact-finding error so as to favor avoiding the conviction of the innocent. Fully implemented, an interpretive guideline that gives priority to truth-finding would produce substantially more expansive interpretations of truth-finding rights than truth-impairing rights (i.e., rights which withhold from the factfinder reliable relevant evidence, such as the Fourth Amendment's restrictions on searches). The priority presumably also would favor truth-finding rights over truth-neutral rights (i.e., rights which neither promote nor hinder an accurate determination of guilt or innocence, but limit the prosecution in its ability to proceed against the defendant irrespective of guilt, such as the equal protection bar against discriminatory prosecution). A truth-finding priority would further insist that the remedies allowed for violations of truth-impairing and truth-neutral guarantees be fashioned to keep to a minimum their adverse impact upon achieving a result based upon truth-finding.

Although the Supreme Court has frequently spoken of truth-finding as the "central purpose" of the trial, and has emphasized the need to interpret various trial rights in light of their objective of promoting truth-finding, it has discussed in only a handful of settings the need to differentiate among rights according to their impact upon truth-finding. Perhaps the most extensive of these discussions are found in a string of decisions interpreting the federal habeas corpus statute. That analysis of the hierarchy of claims in granting habeas relief has led the Court majority to hold that: (1) a Fourth Amendment search and seizure claim generally will not be cognizable on habeas review since the deterrence objective of the prophylactic exclusionary rule remedy for Fourth Amendment violations is adequately served without extending the exclusionary rule's truth-impairing impact to the habeas forum; (2) because the ultimate aim of the habeas safety net is to provide relief from a "fundamentally unjust incarceration," claims that would otherwise be barred by an abuse of writ in a prior habeas proceeding, or by a default in a state proceeding, will nonetheless be cognizable where based on a truth-furthering constitutional right and presented in a case in which denial of that right might have resulted in the conviction of an "actually innocent defendant"; and (3) an exception will be drawn from the usual review standard confining the habeas petitioner to the law prevailing at the time his conviction became final to permit reliance on subsequent favorable rulings that either establish that the defendant was convicted of a crime that the state constitutionally had no power to create (thereby rendering the defendant "innocent" as a matter of law), or "mandate procedures central to the accurate determination of guilt or innocence." The Court has refused, however, to limit habeas relief as a general matter to only truth-furthering guarantees.

The Court also has pointed to the need to differentiate among rights in its opinions restricting remedies that operate to deflect the truth. The truth-deflecting character of the exclusion of evidence obtained in violation of the Fourth Amendment, and in the exclusion of statements of suspects obtained in violation of the *Miranda* standards governing police interrogation, has been noted in allowing the prosecution to make use of such evidence apart from its case-in-chief (see § 8.6). However, the Court also has noted in such cases that exclusion of evidence obtained in violation of the Fourth Amendment is a "judicially created" prophylactic remedy, and the *Miranda* standards are judicially created prophylactic standards. That special prophylactic grounding (§ 1.5(e)) perhaps explains why the Court has not similarly restricted the remedy for other rights, more directly founded on constitutional guarantees, that also tend to be truth-deflecting in their operation. Thus, the prohibitions on prosecutorial use of witness statements compelled under oath via a grant of immunity (supplanting the witness' self-incrimination privilege) extend far beyond the restrictions on the use of the fruits of *Miranda* violations (see § 7.9), although the immunized statements are just as likely to be reliable as the evidence obtained through *Miranda* violations.

In many other areas, the Court has made no effort to distinguish between truth-impairing and truth-furthering constitutional rights. In some instance, the possibility of drawing such a distinction has not been noted, and in others, the distinction has been argued by concurring or dissenting opinions, but not favored by the majority. Thus, giving priority to the truth-finding function has not reached the status of a pervasive guideline for constitutional interpretation. At the same time, it appears to have had an influential role in the shaping of some rulings, and individual justices over the years would have given it a much broader influence.

(c) The Significance of Historical Acceptance. The basic strands of academic questioning of "originalism" in constitutional interpretation have failed to persuade the Supreme Court, at least in its criminal procedure jurisprudence. As evidenced by its inquiries into the historical background and legislative history of each of the Constitution's criminal process guarantees, the Court clearly has acknowledged its obligation to render decisions that are in accord with the guarantee's original design. By accepting the general direction provided by that historical background and legislative history, even when its content is not entirely consistent, the Court has rejected the contention that originalism is rarely helpful because history is almost always far too ambiguous to provide useful answers on specific interpretive issues. By treating "the intent of the Framers" and the "original understanding" as virtually synonymous interpretive guides, the Court has rendered insignificant the distinctions between determining the common understanding of the language of the guarantee at the time of its adoption and determining the subjective intent (or expectations) as to content held by the drafters (or ratifiers) of the guarantee.

The one aspect of originalism that has troubled the Supreme Court in its criminal procedure rulings is the choice of the appropriate level of generality at which the guarantee's original design should be understood. That choice has been a significant issue primarily in dealing with challenges to procedures that were known to the Framers and obviously viewed as not prohibited by the constitutional guarantee in question. Where a challenged procedure was unknown at the common law and has no close parallel in any common law practice, testing it against the original design of a guarantee necessarily requires reference to the overarching principles reflected by that design. If the Court could not look to those principles in that setting, a guarantee would operate to prohibit only "the specific abuses that give it birth," and thereby fail to fulfill the Framers' objective of enacting a fundamental legal framework for the future as well as the present. On the other hand, where a practice was widely known and considered acceptable at the time of the adoption of the Bill of Rights, or was subsequently developed and became widely known and accepted at the time of the adoption of the Fourteenth Amendment, the Court also has before it strong evidence of the apparent expectation of the Framers that the practice would not be prohibited by the guarantee they were adopting. Where that expectation appears to be inconsistent with the logical application of an overarching principle reflected in the guarantee's general design, the Court must ask whether the two can be reconciled, and if not, which conception of the Framers' design—the specific expectation or the general objective—shall prevail. The Court's response to that question has been guided by lines of analysis that are readily manipulated, leading to answers that often appear to be inconsistent.

Over the years, historical acceptance has sustained a variety of procedures that might be viewed as inconsistent with a basic function of a particular guarantee. Thus, the Court has looked to historical acceptance in holding that: the right to jury trial does not apply to prosecutions for petty offenses notwithstanding that they obviously are criminal prosecutions; the Fourth Amendment does not prohibit warrantless arrests in public places even where the arresting officer had ample time to obtain a warrant (see § 2.5(a)); the double jeopardy prohibition of successive prosecutions for the "same offence" does not apply to successive prosecutions for the same basic criminal conduct under two statutes that use different elements in defining the prohibited offense; and due process does not prohibit the forfeiture of the property of an innocent owner which had been used by others as an instrumentality of crime. In support of such rulings, the Court has noted that where a guarantee has "deep historical roots," it must be interpreted in light of its "common-law understanding." Although the general premise of the guarantee might, as a matter of logic, lead to a contrary result, there are guarantees as to which "a page of history is worth a volume of logic," and instances in which "logic * * * must defer * * * to history and experience."

On the other side, the Court has also developed a variety of countervailing rationales in holding unconstitutional various procedures with equally strong historical pedigrees which indicated that the procedures had been viewed by the Framers as constitutionally acceptable. In some instances, the Court has reasoned that changed circumstances have deprived that historical acceptance of much of its weight. Thus, in *Tenn. v. Garner* (1985) (see § 2.5(a)), the Court noted that the common law rule allowing the use of deadly force to prevent the escape of any suspected felon, without regard to the suspect's dangerousness, originally had been deemed reasonable under the Fourth Amendment, but its acceptance came at a time when "virtually all felonies were punishable by death," and when the officer's use of deadly force typically came in hand-to-hand combat that itself posed a danger. Today's setting was quite different, with almost all crimes formerly punishable by death no longer subject to that penalty, with many crimes formerly deemed misdemeanors now lifted to the felony level, and with hand guns allowing officers to use deadly force in settings where the escaping suspect poses no threat to the officer. Of course, changes of the type cited in *Garner* are not unique. With so many new developments in the criminal justice process and its administration since the adoption of the Bill of Rights (or the Fourteenth Amendment), there is almost always some change that casts upon a procedure a somewhat different light than existed at common law. Thus, the critical issue is whether the change truly alters the character of the procedure in such a way as to eliminate the characteristic that led the Framers to view the procedure as consistent with the applicable Bill of Rights guarantee. The Court has offered no clear guidelines on that issue, as evidenced by frequent disagreement over the significance of such changes.

In other instances, the Court has discounted historical acceptance of a particular procedure on the ground that the guarantee in question was designed as an "open ended provision," intended to be "molded to the views of contemporary society." Thus, the due process clause has been described as "the least frozen concept of our law—the least confined to history and the most absorptive of powerful social standards of a progressive society," and it has been applied to condemn various practices never thought to raise significant constitutional difficulties at common law. So too, the "reasonableness clause" of the Fourth Amendment has been characterized as open to interpretation "in light of contemporary norms and conditions" (leading to decisions that "ha[ve] not simply frozen into constitutional law those law enforcement practices that existed at the time of the Fourth Amendment's passage"); the prohibition against cruel and unusual punishments has been described as "draw[ing] its meaning from the evolving standards of decency that marks the progress of a maturing society"; and the equal protection clause has been held to impose a general command that requires the Court "to be open to reassessment of ancient practices." However, the extent to which a particular guarantee incorporates such an "evolving concept" is often unclear. As discussed in § 1.4(b), in recent years, in its interpretation of free-standing due process, the Court has spoken of giving great deference to historical pedigree in criminal procedure cases, notwithstanding that this guarantee supposedly is "the least confined to history." So too, the "reasonableness clause" of the Fourth Amendment has been viewed in several instances as largely controlled by historical practice, even to the point of accepting practices that appear inconsistent with general Fourth Amendment principles.

Finally, historically accepted practices have also been rejected on the ground that the practice conflicts with a more fully developed understanding of the general principles underlying a particular guarantee. Thus, the practice of not providing court appointed counsel for indigent felony defendants was held to violate the Sixth Amendment in light of experience establishing the "obvious truth that the average defendant does not have the professional legal skill" to ensure that he receives a fair trial (see § 10.1). The analysis applied in such cases is reconciled with originalism on the assumption that the Framers would not have wanted a constitutional framework designed for the future as well as the present to lock-in their specific, immediate expectations on the application of a guarantee without regard to what might be learned through subsequent experience in applying that guarantee to a variety of different settings. When such experience reveals that a practice originally thought to be consistent with the guarantee's core purpose is, in fact, in conflict with that purpose, requiring a choice between the Framers' specific expectation and their overall objective, they presumably would have expected coherence in effectuating that overall objective to prevail.

The concepts of changed circumstances, open-ended guarantees that absorb the "evolving gloss of civilized standards," and re-examination in light of the deeper, experienced-based understanding of a guarantee's core purpose, provide ample leeway for holding unconstitutional any historically sanctioned practice viewed by today's Court as inconsistent with the general thrust of its current interpretation of a particular guarantee. Whether that will occur depends in large part on that point within the spectrum of approaches to constitutional interpretation at which a Court majority can be formed. Over the years, individual justices have varied considerably in their general philosophy of constitutional interpretation, particularly as it bears on their analysis of "the original understanding," resulting in sometimes substantial and sometimes subtle shifts in the perspective commanding a Court majority.

(d) The Appropriateness of Administratively Based Per Se Rules. In many settings the Supreme Court has viewed the constitutional question at issue as naturally calling for what might be described as a "categorical" or "definitional" standard—i.e., a standard that looks to a single characteristic or event and does not adjust to the uniqueness of each case. Such a standard is imposed, for example, in determining what constitutes a criminal case for the purpose of applying the Sixth Amendment right to appointed counsel (§ 10.2(a)). In other settings, the Court has viewed the constitutional question at issue as calling for a standard requiring a fact sensitive judgment geared to a variety of circumstances that differ with each case. Such a standard is applied, for example, in determining whether police had the probable cause needed to obtain a search warrant (§ 2.3). In still other settings, the Court has concluded that, while the question at issue generally calls for a case-by-case balancing of a variety of circumstances, administrative concerns justify imposing a "per se" or "bright-line" test which finds a particular action to be constitutional or unconstitutional based on a single event or characteristic. Such a standard is similar in formulation to the usual categorical standard, but its grounding is different. The Court is not saying that the function of the applicable constitutional guarantee necessarily requires such a bright-line rule. Indeed, the Court is acknowledging that its per se standard is either over-inclusive or under-inclusive as compared to the application of that function to all relevant circumstances on a case-by-case basis. Nonetheless, practical considerations relevant to administration of the Court's ruling have convinced the Court of the need to adopt a shorthand generalization in the form of a per se rule even though the function of the guarantee might point to the ad hoc application of a totality-of-the-circumstances analysis.

Supreme Court decisions imposing categorical standards often suggest alternative lines of reasoning which leave unclear whether that standard is required logically by the function of the guarantee or has been adopted because the alternative of applying that function to the totality-of-the-circumstances would present unacceptable administrative difficulties. Nonetheless, a variety of rulings imposing categorical standards clearly indicate that the Court there carved out a bright-line rule, even though it might include more or less than the logic of the guarantee would require, because of the difficulties that would be presented in applying that logic via a standard calling for an ad hoc, multi-circumstance analysis. See e.g., *N.Y. v. Belton* (§ 2.7(a)) (allowing search of entire passenger compartment of automobile contemporaneous with driver's arrest). On the other hand, the Court also has ruled in a variety of settings that administrative concerns did not justify adopting a bright-line rule, and a fair number of those settings involved issues analogous to the issues presented in cases that did adopt administratively based bright-line standards. See e.g., *U.S. v. Dunn* (§ 2.2(d)) (refusing to adopt a "bright-line rule" that the Fourth Amendment protected area of a dwelling's "curtilage" would "extend no farther than the nearest fence surrounding a fenced house"). As might be surmised from the divergence in its rulings, the Supreme Court has not issued a bright-line rule as to when administrative concerns can appropriately lead to the choice of a categorical standard over a standard emphasizing the special circumstance of the individual case.

There is general agreement on the use of a per se standard where it provides an almost perfect fit with the result that would be reached by applying the logic of the guarantee on a case-by-case basis to the circumstances of each case. "Conclusive presumptions," the Court has noted, are "designed to avoid the costs of excessive inquiry where a per se rule will achieve the correct result in almost all cases." The key is to be able to say that, though " 'cases that do not fit the generalization may arise,' " they are " 'not sufficiently common * * * [to] justify the time and expense necessary to identify them.' " Some justices have suggested that unless the bright-line rule meets this standard by producing very little overinclusion or underinclusion (as compared to a case-by-case analysis), it bears the seeds of its own demise. Nonetheless, the Court's rulings suggest that at least three somewhat distinct administrative concerns may lead to the adoption of bright-lines that fall considerably short of an "almost perfect fit." Where these considerations apply, the Court has shown a willingness, at times, to adopt a bright-line standard which produces for the vast majority of cases the same result as the logical application of the function of the guarantee to the distinctive circumstances of the case, but

which produces as well a substantial body of applications that
result in condemning more or less than that function would otherwise require.

One setting that may lead to such an administratively based
bright-line prohibition is that in which establishing a constitutional
violation otherwise requires a difficult factual determination, such
as assessing whether an actor was motivated by bad faith or bias.
Concern that such a determination can be made accurately only by
a potentially pernicious judicial inquiry can lead the Court to prefer
a per se prohibition that avoids the necessity of making that factual
determination. A per se prohibition also may be justified on the
ground that the potential for error in such a determination poses
too great a risk that the constitutional violation will go undetected,
and as a result, an innocent person will suffer severe consequences.

Another setting is that in which the administrator lacks the
capacity, expertise, or opportunity to apply a finely tuned standard.
Thus, over the past few decades, the Supreme Court frequently has
extolled the virtues of bright-line standards in the constitutional
regulation of police activities. The Court has noted that "a single
familiar standard is essential to guide police officers, who have only
limited time and expertise to reflect on and balance the social and
individual interests in the specific circumstances they confront."
Where possible, the lawfulness of a police officer's actions should
not depend on "a highly sophisticated set of rules, qualified by all
sorts of ifs, ands, and buts and requiring the drawing of subtle
nuances and hairline distinctions," but on a "straight forward rule,
easily applied and predictably enforced." The Court has cited this
need for bright-line rules in adopting both standards over-inclusive
and under-inclusive of what a case-by-case analysis of multiple
circumstances would produce. Thus, bright-line standards governing police interrogation clearly operate to bar some confessions that
would be deemed, upon evaluation of all the circumstances, to be
obtained without violation of the Fifth Amendment's self-incrimination clause or the Sixth Amendment's right-to-counsel clause. On
the other side, bright-line standards will sustain automatically a
particular type of search notwithstanding that, on a case-by-case
analysis, there might be some situations in which that search could
be deemed unreasonable because excessive in scope or lacking a
sufficient foundation.

Although administratively based bright-line standards are commonplace in the constitutional regulation of police investigative
practices, the Court at least as frequently has rejected proposed
bright-line rules for police regulation. In some instances, the Court
has concluded that the character of the constitutional question
(e.g., what constitutes probable cause) simply does not lend itself to
a bright-line standard. In others, the proposed bright-line standard

has been viewed as not needed to provide police with sufficient guidance on the legality of their conduct. Most often, the Court has concluded that the costs of the over-inclusive or under-inclusive coverage of a bright-line simply outweigh the benefits of the administrative simplicity it would provide.

A third administrative justification for the use of bright-line rules is limited to per se prohibitions and has been discussed primarily by commentators rather than the Supreme Court. The commentators contend that the Warren Court, in particular, adopted obviously over-inclusive per se prohibitions in recognition that prohibitions in that form were needed to gain successful implementation of the Court's rulings. Having extended the Bill of Rights guarantees to the states, and having made fairness in criminal procedure a central component of the Court's responsibility in protecting civil rights, the Warren Court, it is argued, was compelled to make much heavier use of per se rules than its predecessors by virtue of the "exigencies of its efforts to provide supervision of state and federal systems of criminal justice through the use of judicial power." This was so, it was argued, because: (1) the Court's extremely limited docket restricted its opportunity to formulate comprehensive regulations through rulings tied to the facts of the individual case; and (2) the institutional units asked to administer the Court's rulings (police, prosecutors, and state courts) were highly fragmented, burdened by heavy caseloads, and "unlikely to respond automatically and with enthusiasm," leading to a need for the issuance of high visibility benchmarks that captured the attention of both those administrators and the public.

(e) The Appropriateness of Prophylactic Rules. The Supreme Court also has not formulated a bright-line standard as to when it is appropriate to utilize "prophylactic rules." Indeed, the Court has not yet settled on a standard definition of what constitutes a "prophylactic rule." The key apparently is the rationale underlying the rule rather than the form of the rule. In explaining decisions characterized as establishing prophylactic rules, the Court has emphasized two features of those rules—their function and their grounding.

Initially, as suggested by the term "prophylactic," the rules are characterized as preventive measures. Their purpose is to safeguard against a potential constitutional violation, rather than to identify what constitutes a constitutional violation. Prevention may be achieved (1) by imposing procedural safeguards that provide a protective shield for the underlying constitutional right, (2) by utilizing an evidentiary exclusionary remedy to take away the primary incentive for constitutional violations by law enforcement officers seeking to acquire evidence, or (3) by prohibiting a law enforcement practice that readily might be misused and manipulated to deprive a suspect of a constitutional right. Secondly, the prophylactic rule is grounded not on the conclusion that a violation of the rule invariably produces a violation of the core guarantee, but on the Court's exercise of its authority to craft remedies and procedures that facilitate its adjudication responsibilities.

The Court has emphasized two important consequences that follow from the special function and grounding of prophylactic rules. Because prophylactic rules may be violated without denying a constitutional right, those violations may be given remedial consequences which are narrower or which do not apply in as broad a range of proceedings as the remedies attaching to the actual violation of the constitutional right that the prophylactic rule is designed to prevent. So too, the non-constitutional grounding of prophylactic rules leaves the door open for Congress to replace those rules with other safeguards that serve the same preventive function.

Where the prophylactic rule takes the form of an evidentiary exclusionary rule, designed to deter future violations, its operation ordinarily will be tied to the presence of a constitutional violation. This is the case, for example, of the rule requiring trial exclusion of evidence obtained through Fourth Amendment violations, perhaps the most prominent prophylactic remedial measure. As illustrated in *Maine v. Moulton*, (§ 5.4(d)) however, a prophylactic remedial measure can also be used in situations in which a violation has not necessarily occurred, but the adjudicatory process would face significant obstacles in determining whether it had occurred. *Moulton* dealt with the use of an undercover agent or informant to elicit information from an indicted defendant. The Sixth Amendment prohibits the deliberate elicitation of information regarding the offense on which the defendant has been charged, but does not prohibit the elicitation of information relating to other possible criminal activities, as the defendant has not been placed in the status of an "accused" as to those uncharged offenses and the Sixth Amendment therefore does not attach. Because of concerns that law enforcement officers might mask Sixth Amendment violations, by claiming that their agents were only seeking to elicit information relating to uncharged offenses when the defendant serendipitously offered information relating to the charged offense, the Court imposed a general prohibition against prosecution use in evidence of any statements made to the undercover agent or informant relating to the charged offense. The function of the prohibition was to deter Sixth Amendment violations by removing any incentive to elicit information relating to the charged offense. To achieve this prophylactic objective, the prohibition would apply automatically, without attempting to determine whether the excluded statement was responsive to an elicitation that violated the Sixth Amendment by focusing on the charged offense or an elicitation that was acceptable under the Sixth Amendment because directed at uncharged offenses. Thus, the prophylactic remedial measure applied even though there may not have been a violation of the Sixth Amendment.

Prophylactic rules that formulate procedural prerequisites for particular police, prosecutorial, or judicial actions similarly do not declare that such actions would have produced a violation of the core guarantee without those prerequisites being followed. Rather, the prerequisites are described as necessary to combat what would otherwise be a substantial potential for constitutional violations in those actions. Such prerequisites were imposed in two Supreme Court rulings that have come to be viewed as paradigmatic of prophylactic procedural prerequisites—*Miranda v. Ariz.* (§ 5.5) and *N.C. v. Pearce* (1969). *Miranda* required the police to give various warnings to an interrogated suspect in order to ensure that custodial interrogation did not result in compulsion that would violate the suspect's privilege against self-incrimination. Absent such warnings, a statement obtained through custodial interrogation was automatically excluded from the prosecution's case-in-chief, without regard to what other circumstances might suggest as to whether the statement was compelled in violation of the Fifth Amendment. *Pearce* concluded that there is a significant likelihood that a judge who imposes a higher sentence on a defendant following that defendant's successful appeal (and subsequent retrial and conviction) is doing so vindictively, and thereby violating due process. Because it would be most difficult for the defendant to establish actual vindictiveness, the Court required, as a prophylactic safeguard, that the judge set forth the reasons for the higher sentence and rely upon "objective information concerning identifiable conduct on the part of the defendant." In the absence of such an acceptable statement of reasons, supported by factual data, the higher sentence cannot be accepted, without regard to whether it was or was not in fact a product of vindictiveness.

Edwards v. Ariz. (§ 5.9(f)) illustrates how a prophylactic ruling may shield a constitutional right by simply forbidding an activity that presents a substantial potential for invading that right. *Edwards* holds that when a suspect responds to *Miranda* warnings by requesting the assistance of counsel, police may not thereafter reinitiate interrogation (even with appropriate *Miranda* warnings) while the suspect remains in custody. This prohibition applies even when the interrogation is renewed only after the passage of a significant period of time and relates to a different crime. Any statement obtained from the suspect in response to a police initiation of interrogation that violates *Edwards* is rendered inadmissible in the prosecution's case-in-chief. Under *Mich. v. Jackson* (§ 5.4(e)), a similar prophylactic rule is applied to an accused person who requests the assistance of counsel and subsequently provides a statement in response to interrogation initiated by the police. Although it is entirely possible that a person, after requesting counsel, might change his mind and respond to subsequent police questioning with a voluntary, knowing, and intelligent waiver of the Fifth Amendment right protected by *Miranda* or the Sixth Amendment right to counsel, *Edwards* and *Jackson* impose a prophylactic prohibition against police initiated questioning after such a request because such questioning is far more likely to produce a waiver that is not voluntary, knowing, and intelligent.

Edwards and *Jackson* also illustrate the close relationship between many prophylactic rules and the administratively based, over-inclusive per se prohibition previously discussed in subsection (d). Although the Court repeatedly characterizes the *Edwards/Jackson* rules as "prophylactic" and extending beyond actual constitutional violations, it also has characterized those rules as adopting a per se approach which provides police with a bright-line standard. Consistent with the latter characterization, *Edwards/Jackson* has been described as creating a conclusive presumption that "after a defendant requests assistance of counsel, any waiver * * * given in a discussion initiated by police" is not "voluntary, knowing, and intelligent." Other prophylactic rules can similarly be cast as resting on a conclusive presumption, which is a common structure for imposing an administratively based, over-inclusive per se prohibition. *Miranda,* for example, could be cast as establishing a conclusive presumption that a statement produced by custodial interrogation is "compelled" in violation of the suspect's privilege against self-incrimination unless the suspect was given the *Miranda* warnings and voluntarily waived the rights noted in those warnings.

The Supreme Court has not explained why such rulings were established and declared to be prophylactic rules, rather than per se rules that rested on an over-inclusive interpretation of a constitutional guarantee in order to avoid the substantial administrative difficulties that would attend an ad hoc, case-by-case analysis of multiple circumstances. Presumably the latter formulation was not utilized because the generalization that would be at the heart of the per se prohibition would too often be incorrect as an empirical matter. Per se prohibitions need not always provide a close to perfect fit with the results that would be reached on a case-by-case analysis, but they should produce the same result as the case-by-case analysis in a very substantial majority of the instances that would be encompassed by the per se rule. When it becomes obvious that many (if not most) of the instances that fall within a possible conclusive presumption would not actually violate the constitutional right to be safeguarded by that presumption, the Court has presented the safeguard as a prophylactic ruling that operates apart from the violation of that constitutional right.

Although the Court's explanations of the special character of its prophylactic rulings had been less than precise prior to its ruling in *Dickerson v. U.S.* (§ 5.5(e)), that ruling managed to almost completely cloud that issue. In *Dickerson*, Justice Scalia, in a dissenting opinion joined by Justice Thomas, sharply challenged the legitimacy of the Supreme Court's prophylactic rulings. One issue presented in *Dickerson* was whether Congress could override *Miranda*. In arguing that it could, Justice Scalia rejected the defense contention that the *Miranda* was within the Court's constitutional decisionmaking authority (and therefore immune from a constitutional override) because that decisionmaking authority extended to "adopting prophylactic rules to buttress constitutional rights." Justice Scalia described that position as allowing the Court to mandate whatever procedural protections it deemed "desirable" without regard to "what the Constitutional actually requires." The *Dickerson* majority responded that *Miranda* was a decision "interpreting and applying the Constitution," and Congress therefore lacked "the constitutional authority to supersede *Miranda*." However, as Justice Scalia noted in his dissent, the majority opinion, in explaining the constitutional grounding of *Miranda*, did not refer to any special prophylactic rulemaking authority (the defense contention, which Justice Scalia rejected) or otherwise explain the special characteristics of prophylactic rulings.

The *Dickerson* majority acknowledged that *Miranda's* required warnings had been described as "prophylactic" and "not themselves rights protected by the Constitution," but disagreed with the lower court's conclusion that this description established that the "protections announced in *Miranda* are not constitutionally required." However, in explaining the constitutional grounding of the *Miranda* "guidelines," the *Dickerson* majority offered an analysis similar to that traditionally offered in sustaining per se standards. Admittedly, it noted, exclusion of all statements obtained in violation of *Miranda* was overinclusive, as that encompassed "statements which may be by no means involuntarily," but the alternative of reliance on an ad-hoc totality-of-the-circumstances analysis to identify involuntariness (the approach of the pre-*Miranda* voluntariness test) had simply presented an "unacceptably great" risk of "overlooking involuntary confessions." On the other hand, the *Dickerson* majority also acknowledged that *Miranda* contained a feature previously associated only with prophylactic rulings. The *Miranda* Court, it noted, "had concluded that something more than the totality test was necessary" to adequately protect against the self-incrimination violations that occurred through the admission of compelled confessions, but it also had acknowledged that the solution imposed in *Miranda* was not exclusive. As *Miranda* had noted, a legislative solution that differed from *Miranda* could be constitutionally acceptable, but only if it was "at least as effective" in serving the ends of the *Miranda* requirement (an issue not presented in *Dickerson*, as the Congressional legislation there merely sought to substitute the old totality test).

Dickerson put to rest any question as to the constitutional legitimacy of prophylactic rulings, and at the same time, continued to recognize a distinction between those rulings and other constitutional rulings. It provided, however, no clear answers as to how such rulings were distinguishable from other constitutional rulings (particularly per se rulings), and why their special character produced unique rules as to their implementation (including possible congressional substitution of alternative measures). Commentators speculated that the failure of the *Dickerson* opinion to more completely address these issues stemmed from a division within the Court beyond that reflected by the Scalia dissent. Three years later, the several opinions in *Chavez v. Martinez* (§ 5.5(a)) provided strong support for that speculation. There, the eight justices speaking to the issue agreed that a *Miranda* violation was quite distinct from a classic Fifth Amendment violation. They were sharply divided, however in their characterization of *Miranda's* distinctive character, and in their assessment of other Fifth Amendment rulings that might fit in that category. They did agree that *Miranda's* distinctive grounding meant that there should be no civil damage remedy for a *Miranda* violation, but they divided as to the proper rationale for that conclusion.

In *Chavez*, Justice Thomas (joined by Chief Justice Rehnquist and Justices O'Connor and Scalia) described *Miranda* as having established a "prophylactic rule." Moreover, contrary to the *Dickerson* dissent, Justice Thomas spoke of prophylactic rules as having a long history in Supreme Court jurisprudence. He described as "prophylactic," in addition to *Miranda*, several long-standing rulings dealing with self-incrimination assertions by non-defendants. These included rulings allowing witnesses to assert the privilege in civil and administrative proceeding (§ 7.8(a)), rulings prohibiting the imposition of administrative penalties on witnesses who exercise the privilege (§ 7.8(g)), and the requirement that the government, to replace the privilege, must grant immunity before compelling a witness to testify (§ 7.9). Along with the *Miranda* warnings, these rulings established "prophylactic rules designed to safeguard the core constitutional right protected by the Self–Incrimination Clause." These rulings, he added, "do not extend the scope of the constitutional right itself, just as violations of judicially crafted prophylactic rules do not violate the constitutional rights of any person." Thus, a violation of *Miranda* did not give rise to an action in damages under a statute creating a civil remedy for violations of a "constitutional right".

Another opinion in *Chavez*, by Justice Souter (joined by Justice Breyer), described somewhat differently the rulings that Justice Thomas had characterized as prophylactic. Justice Souter described these rulings (including *Miranda*) as establishing "law * * * outside the Fifth Amendment's core, with each case expressing a judgment that the core guarantee, or the judicial capacity to protect it, would be placed at some risk in the absence of some complementary protection." The special character of these "complementary-protection" rulings means that their further expansion (here creating a damage remedy) would require "a 'powerful showing,' subject to a realistic assessment of costs and risks," that the expansion was "necessary to aid the basic guarantee." No such showing had been made as to a damage remedy for a *Miranda* violation. Justice Souter's analysis arguably gives these "complementary protections" a higher status than Justice Thomas' "prophylactic rules"; yet Justice Souter also saw their violation as something less than a violation of the basic prohibition provided by the core guarantee.

In still another *Chavez* opinion, Justice Kennedy (joined by Justice Stevens and Ginsburg) offered a strikingly different characterization of the rulings protecting a witness in a non-criminal proceeding against being compelled to provide an incriminating statement. They were neither "prophylactic" nor "complimentary," but reflected the basic function of the privilege. However, Justice Kennedy (here joined only by Justice Stevens) took a different view of *Miranda*. The *Miranda* ruling, Justice Kennedy noted, is a "constitutional requirement," but one "adopted to reduce the risk of a coerced confession and to implement the self-incrimination clause." This special character produced a different analysis of needed remedies. Exclusion of a statement obtained in violation of *Miranda* was a "complete and sufficient remedy" (and, indeed, a remedy sometimes subject to exceptions); a civil damage action was not available for a *Miranda* violation standing alone, although it was available where the police employed coercive interrogation tactics (a basic Fifth Amendment violation).

All of the opinions in *Chavez* accepted the position that violations of certain constitutional rulings did not constitute violations of the core guarantee. The Court was divided as to what rulings fell in that category, although eight justices agreed that *Miranda* did so. Four were willing to describe such rulings as "judicially created prophylactic rules," but the remaining four avoided that description (as did the majority opinion in *Dickerson*, which they had joined). While the Souter and Kennedy opinions offered arguably similar alternative descriptions ("complementary protections" and requirements adopted "to reduce the risk of coerce confessions and to implement the Self–Incrimination Clause"), they adopted somewhat different perspectives in determining how that special character impacted the issue of a damage remedy (although reaching the same result on that issue). Thus, apart from their constitutional status, the Court appears to be sharply divided as to both the nature and consequences of rulings sometimes (but not always) described as "prophylactic".

How these divisions impact the creation of prophylactic rules in the future (or the interpretation of past prophylactic rulings) remains to be seen. While prophylactic rulings were viewed as a key element of the criminal law revolution of the Warren Court in the 1960s, the Court in subsequent years has not shown any strong inclination to regulate through rulings described as prophylactic. It has only sparingly adopted new prophylactic rulings or extended old prophylactic rulings. Much more frequently, it has rejected the extension of old prophylactic rulings and refused to adopt proposed new prophylactic rulings.

(f) **Weighing the Impact Upon Efficiency.** A new constitutional regulation often will impose a substantial burden upon the administration of the criminal justice process. That burden can take various forms, including increased expenses for an already underfunded system, additional hearings for already congested court dockets, and perhaps even insurmountable obstacles to the solution of some crimes. The extent to which such "practical costs" should be considered by the Court has been a matter of continuing debate among the justices. In general, the Court tends to discuss the practical impact of a ruling when it views itself as having more flexibility in fashioning its ruling. Thus, discussions of practical impact are more commonly found in decisions interpreting open-ended clauses, decisions applying the more specific clauses to new settings or settings that have been altered by changed circumstances, and decisions setting forth or applying prophylactic rules. On the other side, where the Court views the text or history of a particular provision as setting forth a "constitutional command that * * * is unequivocal," the practical costs incurred in applying that command are said to be irrelevant. The command itself strikes a balance between the rights of the accused and society's need for effective enforcement of the criminal law, and the Court is bound to accept that balance.

Where the applicability of a guarantee is acknowledged to be less than clear, the justices' views on weighing practical costs ordinarily fall within the outer boundaries marked by two distinctive positions. On the one side, there is the view that, if the burden imposed would be great, the Court should hesitate to extend the guarantee unless its extension is essential to fulfilling the function of the guarantee. On the other side, there is the view that practical costs should be a decidedly subordinate concern. They should be given weight only where the burden is substantial and clear, relates to an important state interest, and cannot be offset by other measures; and even then, they need not be controlling. This difference in perspective often extends beyond the issue of what weight (if any) should be given to the practical costs of a particular interpretation. It also appears to be reflected in the justices' evaluation of the likely extent of those costs. Thus, in *Miranda v. Ariz.* (§ 5.5), though looking at the same data, the majority concluded that its decision would "not in any way preclude police from carrying out their traditional investigatory role" and thus "should not constitute an undue interference with a proper system of law enforcement," while one dissent found that the Court was taking "a real risk with society's welfare" and another concluded that the Court's ruling would "measurably weaken" the enforcement of the criminal law and result in an inability to prosecute successfully a "good many criminal defendants."

As a result of these differences in viewpoint, the treatment of practical costs in majority opinions tends to be inconsistent. Many opinions discuss practical costs as a factor to be given serious consideration, and several refer to such costs as a primary reason for not extending a particular doctrine. Other opinions mention such costs, but promptly dismiss them, while still others fail to even acknowledge what are obviously significant administrative burdens imposed by a new ruling.

Chapter 2

ARREST, SEARCH AND SEIZURE

Table of Sections

§ 2.1   The Exclusionary Rule and Other Remedies

(a) **Origins of the Exclusionary Rule.** The Fourth Amendment remained largely unexplored until, in *Boyd v. United States* (1886), the Court held that the forced disclosure of papers amounting to evidence of crime violated the Fourth Amendment *and* that such items therefore were not admissible in the proceedings against Boyd. Though the Fourth Amendment unlike the Fifth contains no express exclusionary rule, the Court reached this result by linking the two amendments together, noting it had "been unable to perceive that the seizure of a man's private books and papers to be used in evidence against him is substantially different from compelling him to be a witness against himself." Yet in *Adams v. New York* (1904) the Court declared that "the weight of authority as well as reason" supported the common-law rule that courts will not inquire into the means by which evidence otherwise admissible was acquired.

In *Weeks v. United States* (1914), where the defendant questioned the use in a federal trial of evidence seized from his home by local police and later by federal officers, the Court held that to admit evidence illegally seized by federal officers would, in effect, put a stamp of approval on their unconstitutional conduct: "To sustain [unlawful invasion of the sanctity of his home by officers of the law] would be to affirm by judicial decision a manifest neglect, if not an open defiance, of the prohibitions of the Constitution, intended for the protection of the people against such unauthorized action." But while that evidence thus had to be excluded, the Court went on to say that the same result was not required as to the fruits of the first search, "as the 4th Amendment is not directed to individual misconduct of such officials." (In two 1927 cases, the Supreme Court concluded otherwise as to state searches with either federal participation or a federal purpose.)

Because the Bill of Rights was designed as a limitation on the federal government only, it was settled very early that the Fourth Amendment "has no application to state process." With the adoption of the Fourteenth Amendment, however, forbidding the states to "deprive any person of life, liberty, or property, without due process of law," there arose the question of the relation of that limitation upon the states to the limitations upon federal action in the first eight Amendments. Over the years, many of those guarantees were "incorporated" into the Fourteenth Amendment and applied to the states, and thus the stage was set for consideration of the issue that reached the Court in *Wolf v. Colorado* (1949): whether a state court conviction violates due process because based upon evidence that, in federal court, would have been excluded on Fourth Amendment grounds. The Court in *Wolf,* while not hesitating to say that the "security of one's privacy against arbitrary intrusion * * * which is at the core of the Fourth Amendment * * * is * * * enforceable against the States," concluded the *Weeks* exclusionary rule was another matter. Because it was "not derived from the explicit requirements of the Fourth Amendment," was not followed in "most of the English-speaking world," and had been expressly rejected in 30 states, the Court concluded it was not "a departure from basic standards" to leave the victims of illegal state searches "to the remedies of private action and such protection as the internal discipline of the police, under the eyes of an alert public opinion, may afford."

Any thought that *Wolf* meant state courts were permitted to admit all unconstitutional evidence was later dispelled in *Rochin v. California* (1952), where police engaged in a series of unlawful acts that culminated in the defendant being given an emetic by force to retrieve drugs he had swallowed. The Court held that the Fourteenth Amendment required exclusion of evidence obtained by "conduct that shocks the conscience." But it soon became apparent that *Rochin* did not require exclusion with respect to all serious Fourth Amendment violations, for it was held not to apply to illegal month-long electronic eavesdropping or to extraction of blood from an unconscious person. Another post-*Wolf* development of significance was the demise of the "silver platter" doctrine, whereby illegally obtained evidence was admitted in federal courts when obtained by state officers. In rejecting that doctrine in *Elkins v. United States* (1960), the Court emphasized that the determination in *Wolf* that Fourteenth Amendment due process prohibited illegal searches and seizures by state officers marked the "removal of the doctrinal underpinning" for the admissibility of state-seized evidence in federal prosecutions. (As for somewhat the reverse of *Elkins,* the Court had earlier held that a federal official could be enjoined from turning over such evidence and from giving testimony concerning the evidence in a state prosecution.)

In *Mapp v. Ohio* (1961), overruling *Wolf* and holding "that all evidence obtained by searches and seizures in violation of the

Constitution is, by that same authority, inadmissible in a state court," the Court reasoned:

> Since the Fourth Amendment's right of privacy has been declared enforceable against the States through the Due Process Clause of the Fourteenth, it is enforceable against them by the same sanction of exclusion as is used against the Federal Government. Were it otherwise then just as without the *Weeks* rule the assurance against unreasonable federal searches and seizures would be "a form of words," valueless and undeserving of mention in a perpetual charter of inestimable human liberties, so too, without that rule the freedom from state invasions of privacy would be so ephemeral and so neatly severed from its conceptual nexus with the freedom from all brutish means of coercing evidence as not to merit this Court's high regard as a freedom "implicit in the concept of ordered liberty."

Wolf was pushed aside as "bottomed on factual considerations" lacking "current validity," in that during the intervening years more and more states had opted for the exclusionary rule, and experience had shown that the other remedies alluded to in *Wolf* were "worthless and futile." In an oft-quoted passage the Court in *Mapp* went on to say:

> Moreover, our holding * * * is not only the logical dictate of prior cases but it also makes very good sense. There is no war between the Constitution and common sense. Presently, a federal prosecutor may make no use of evidence illegally seized, but a State's attorney across the street may, although he supposedly is operating under the enforceable prohibitions of the same Amendment. Thus the State, by admitting evidence unlawfully seized, serves to encourage disobedience to the Federal Constitution which it is bound to uphold.

(b) Purposes of the Exclusionary Rule. The deterrence of unreasonable searches and seizures is a major purpose of the exclusionary rule, as acknowledged by the Court in *Wolf, Elkins* and *Mapp*. But the rule serves other purposes as well. There is, for example, what the *Elkins* Court referred to as "the imperative of judicial integrity," namely, that the courts not become "accomplices in the willful disobedience of a Constitution they are sworn to uphold." A third purpose, as stated by some members of the Court, is that "of assuring the people—all potential victims of unlawful government conduct—that the government would not profit from its lawless behavior, thus minimizing the risk of seriously undermining popular trust in government." This is not merely another statement of the deterrence objective, for the emphasis is on the effect of exclusion upon the public rather than the police.

The purposes of the exclusionary rule are of more than academic concern, for the Court's perception of them determines the scope and, ultimately, the fate of the exclusionary rule. The Court has never deemed the latter two purposes to be so important that the rule must be unqualified, as is illustrated by the fact that the government may "profit" from wrongdoing and the court may be an "accomplice" thereto whenever the defendant lacks standing (see §§ 8.1, 8.2). Yet the reach of the exclusionary rule is affected by its perceived purposes, as is illustrated by *United States v. Calandra* (1974). The majority took into account only the deterrence function in holding that a grand jury witness may not refuse to answer questions on the ground they are based upon illegally seized evidence, reasoning that any "incremental deterrent effect which might be achieved by extending the rule to grand jury proceedings is uncertain at best." The dissenters, in reaching the contrary conclusion, stressed the other two functions and relegated deterrence to "at best only a hoped for effect of the exclusionary rule."

(c) The Exclusionary Rule Under Attack. The validity and efficacy of this exclusionary rule have been vigorously debated over the years. Much of this debate is more remarkable for its volume than its cogency. There is, for example, the oft-heard complaint that the exclusionary rule "handcuffs" the police, which is nonsense because the objection goes not to this particular remedy but to the Fourth Amendment restrictions upon police authority. That argument was rejected when the Fourth Amendment was adopted. The objection that Fourth Amendment standards are often lacking in clarity is of the same order. The concern is legitimate, but to suggest that it would vanish if the exclusionary rule were abandoned is to concede the warning in *Weeks* that without the suppression doctrine the Fourth Amendment would be no more than "a form of words." As for the complaint that the rule only comes to the aid of the guilty, it also rests upon a gross misperception. The exclusionary rule, as noted in *Elkins v. United States* (1960), "is calculated to prevent, not to repair"; suppression in a particular case is intended to influence police conduct in the future, and thus the innocent and society are the principal beneficiaries.

In *Bivens v. Six Unknown Named Agents* (1971), Chief Justice Burger asserted in dissent that the hope the Fourth Amendment could be enforced "by the exclusion of reliable evidence from criminal trials was hardly more than a wistful dream," and that "there is no empirical evidence to support the claim that the rule actually deters illegal conduct of law enforcement officials." A more accurate characterization is that the available data fall short of an empirical substantiation *or* refutation of the deterrent effect of the exclusionary rule, and thus the Chief Justice's allocation of the burden of proof is merely a way of announcing a predetermined conclusion. The exclusionary rule is like capital punishment in that it is easy to see when the deterrent effect has failed but not when it has succeeded. That the suppression doctrine has had a deterrent effect is nonetheless suggested by various post-exclusionary rule events, such as the dramatic increase in use of search warrants where nearly none were used before, stepped up efforts to educate police on Fourth Amendment law where such training had before been virtually nonexistent, and creation and development of working relationships between police and prosecutors. A majority of the Supreme Court has indicated its willingness to assume "that the immediate effect of exclusion will be to discourage law enforcement officials from violating the Fourth Amendment by removing the incentive to disregard it."

In *United States v. Leon* (1984), the Supreme Court adopted a "good faith" exception, holding that "the Fourth Amendment exclusionary rule should be modified so as not to bar the use in the prosecution's case-in-chief of evidence obtained by officers acting in reasonable reliance on a search warrant issued by a detached and neutral magistrate but ultimately found to be unsupported by probable cause." The majority reasoned: (i) that the exclusionary rule is "a judicially created remedy designed to safeguard Fourth Amendment rights generally through its deterrent effect," the applicability of which "must be resolved by weighing the costs and benefits of preventing the use" in evidence of illegally seized evidence; (ii) exclusion to deter magistrates is inappropriate, as "the exclusionary rule is designed to deter police misconduct rather than to punish the errors of judges," "there exists no evidence suggesting that judges and magistrates are inclined to ignore or subvert the Fourth Amendment," and there is no basis "for believing that exclusion of evidence seized pursuant to a warrant will have a significant deterrent effect on the issuing judge or magistrate"; (iii) in a with-warrant case, exclusion to deter the policeman is ordinarily inappropriate, for usually "there is no police illegality" because the officer justifiably relied upon the prior judgment of the magistrate; and thus (iv) "the marginal or nonexistent benefits produced by suppressing evidence obtained in objectively reasonable reliance on a subsequently invalidated search warrant cannot justify the substantial costs of exclusion."

The soundness of *Leon* is certainly open to question. The dissenters seriously questioned whether the exclusionary rule is merely a "judicially created remedy" for Fourth Amendment violations, subject to being narrowed "through guesswork about deterrence," rather than (as indicated in *Weeks*) "a right grounded in that Amendment to prevent the government from subsequently making use of any evidence so obtained." As for the majority's concern about the "costs" of the exclusionary rule, the dissenters noted that available statistics indicate "that federal and state prosecutors very rarely drop cases because of potential search and seizure problems," and that to the extent there is a cost "it is not the exclusionary rule, but the Amendment itself that has imposed this cost" by preferring freedom and privacy over more efficient law enforcement processes. As for the "benefits" of the exclusionary rule in deterrence terms, the dissenters observed that the goal of institutional deterrence is served by exclusion even when the actors in a particular case did not know they were acting illegally. Under *Leon*, by comparison, magistrates know "that they need not take much care in reviewing warrant applications, since their mistakes will from now on have virtually no consequence," and police will know "that if a warrant has simply been signed, it is reasonable, without more, to rely on it."

Whether *Leon* is a stepping-stone to adoption of a more general "good faith" exception remains to be seen. But expansion in one direction occurred in *Illinois v. Krull* (1987), holding that "a similar exception to the exclusionary rule should be recognized when officers act in objectively reasonable reliance upon a *statute* authorizing [the search in question], but where the statute is ultimately found to violate the Fourth Amendment." Despite many pre-*Leon* decisions by the Court to the contrary, the *Krull* majority concluded "[t]he approach used in *Leon* is equally applicable to the present case" because (i) application of the exclusionary rule when the police reasonably relied on a statute would "have as little deterrent effect on the officers' actions" as in the *Leon* situation, and (ii) "legislators, like judicial officers, are not the focus of the rule," as there "is nothing to indicate that applying the exclusionary rule to evidence seized pursuant to the statute prior to the declaration of its invalidity will act as a significant, additional deterrent" to the occasional enactment of a statute later determined to confer unconstitutional search authority. The dissenters, though conceding the good faith of the police who relied on the statute, stressed that statutes "authorizing unreasonable searches were the core concern of the Framers of the Fourth Amendment," and rightly so, as a "judicial officer's unreasonable authorization of a search affects one person at a time; a legislature's unreasonable authorization of searches may affect thousands or millions." Moreover, they persuasively noted, "[l]egislators by virtue of their political role are more often subjected to the political pressures that may threaten Fourth Amendment values than are judicial officers." (*Krull* has also been deemed applicable when the officer's reliance was instead upon a judicial precedent subsequently overturned.)

It is important to understand that *Leon* does not hold that the exclusionary rule is totally inapplicable whenever a warrant had been obtained. *Leon* has to do with a presumptively invalid warrant, such as one issued on less than probable cause (assumed to be so in *Leon*) or one issued with an insufficient particularity in description (assumed to be so in the companion case of *Massachusetts v. Sheppard* (1984)). Fourth Amendment violations relating to execution of the warrant are untouched by *Leon*, as is reflected by the majority's caution that its discussion "assumes, of course, that the officers properly executed the warrant and searched only those places for those objects that it was reasonable to believe were covered by the warrant." So too, *Leon* would not seem to apply where an unconstitutional warrantless search by police produced information that was then used to obtain a search warrant and the subsequent search under that warrant is challenged as the fruit of the initial warrantless search.

The *Leon* Court also emphasized that it was not suggesting "that exclusion is always inappropriate in cases where an officer has obtained a warrant and abided by its terms," and that exclusion is still required if the officer lacked "reasonable grounds for believing that the warrant was properly issued." This, the Court added, encompasses at least four situations: (1) where, under the *Franks* doctrine (see § 2.4(d)), a facially sufficient warrant is based upon knowingly or recklessly made falsehoods in the affidavit; (2) where the officer knows that the magistrate has "wholly abandoned his judicial role," as where the magistrate "allowed himself to become a member, if not the leader of the search party," and presumably also the situation earlier referred to in *Leon*, where the magistrate serves "merely as a rubber stamp for the police"; (3) where "a warrant [is] so facially deficient—i.e., in failing to particularize the place to be searched or the things to be seized—that the executing officers cannot reasonably presume it to be valid," which raises the question of how far off the mark of extant particular description requirements (see § 2.4(c), (f)) a description must be before an officer should know it is deficient (though in *Groh v. Ramirez* (2004) the Court concluded there could be no good faith where the officer failed to put the affidavit's list of things to be seized into the warrant he prepared and then failed to notice this "glaring deficiency"); and (4) where the affidavit was "so lacking in indicia of probable cause as to render official belief in its existence entirely unreasonable."

It is on this latter language that most of the post-*Leon* suppression motions in with-warrant cases have focused. Because the Court had adopted a relaxed standard of assessing probable cause just a year earlier in *Illinois v. Gates* (1983) (discussed in § 2.3(c)), whereunder it suffices if a reviewing court finds the magistrate had a "substantial basis" for concluding there was a "fair probability" evidence would be found, how if at all has *Leon*, in light of this limitation, departed from existing requirements? A partial answer may be that *Gates* and *Leon* can produce different results because of their different focus: the former is concerned with the *magistrate*'s decision, to be given deference in all "doubtful or marginal cases," while the latter involves the decision to seek and execute a warrant by the *police*, who ordinarily are entitled to assume the magistrate is acting properly. This important difference is highlighted in the assertion in *Leon* that the question to be resolved is "whether a reasonably well-trained officer would have known that the search was illegal despite the magistrate's authorization." But this seemingly hindsight perspective was thereafter rejected by the Court in another context where, purporting to follow "the same standard" as *Leon*, it was concluded that the fact that the magistrate acted favorably on the warrant request was irrelevant. This is because, the Court explained, the question "is whether a reasonably well-trained officer * * * would have known that his affidavit failed to establish probable cause and that he should not have applied for the warrant."

(d) The Significance of Underlying Motivation; More on the Deterrence Objective and Inquiry Into Subjective Matters. The question of whether a "bad" intent or motivation by the searching police officer is to be taken into account in deciding whether evidence should be suppressed was presented in *Scott v. United States* (1978), where federal agents operating a judicially authorized wiretap failed to attempt any compliance with the Fourth Amendment requirement of minimization of interception. In rejecting the petitioners' claim that this "lack of good faith efforts" required suppression even if no minimization would have been feasible in this case, the Court elected to evaluate the Fourth Amendment claim by "an objective assessment of an officer's actions in light of the facts and circumstances then known to him" and "without regard to the underlying intent or motivation of the officers involved." Generally, this is a sound rule and is fully consistent with the purposes of the Fourth Amendment and its exclusionary rule, as may be seen by examination of some of the situations in which problems of this kind arise.

One kind of case is that in which the police, though lacking the grounds required by the Fourth Amendment, decide to make an arrest or search, but before they can so act upon that decision they are confronted with additional facts supplying the requisite grounds. Most courts refuse to suppress the evidence in such circumstances, and rightly so, for the deterrence objective would not be served by exclusion in such circumstances. If the officer *does* act on his "bad" state of mind in the sense that he engages in Fourth Amendment activity despite a *mistaken* belief he lacks the grounds for such action, again suppression is not called for, as the evidence was obtained by actions—if not thoughts—entirely in accord with the Fourth Amendment. As for cases in which it might be said that the officer's "underlying intent or motivation" reflects that he was operating under the wrong legal theory, such as where an officer arrested a robbery suspect for vagrancy, but the facts at hand constituted grounds to arrest for robbery but not for vagrancy, the prevailing view is to uphold the arrest, which is correct; exclusion in the interest of deterrence is unjustified here, especially because such situations are often attributable to complicated legal distinctions between offenses or an officer's failure to record all the bases or the strongest basis upon which the arrest was made. The *Scott* rule is also correct in a case like *Abel v. United States* (1960), where immigration agents arrested Abel pursuant to an administrative warrant for deportation but with the underlying objective of acquiring evidence of espionage, but the Supreme Court declined to suppress the evidence because the record showed that the immigration agents' conduct "differed in no respect from what would have been done in the case of an individual concerning whom no such information was known to exist." Thus, the "underlying intent or motivation of the officers involved" (to use the *Scott* phrase again) does not require suppression where, even assuming that intent or motivation was the dominant one in the particular case, the Fourth Amendment activity undertaken is precisely the same as would have occurred had that intent or motivation been absent.

That highlights the remaining situation in which the Fourth Amendment activity would not have been undertaken *but for* the "underlying intent or motivation" that, standing alone, could not supply a lawful basis for the police conduct, as where the driver of an automobile suspected of unlawful drug activity is subjected to a traffic stop that leads to discovery of drugs, though the stop was not one that would have been made by an officer on routine patrol against any citizen driving in the same manner. This issue was confronted in *Whren v. United States* (1996), a case similar to the illustration set out above. (Vice squad officers patrolling a "high drug area" became suspicious of the occupants of a truck and then stopped the truck for minor traffic violations, resulting in the observation of cocaine in the vehicle.) The petitioners argued that probable cause the traffic code was being violated should not suffice for a traffic stop because "the use of automobiles is so heavily and minutely regulated that total compliance with traffic and safety rules is nearly impossible." Otherwise "a police officer will almost invariably be able to catch any given motorist in a technical violation," a situation that "creates the temptation to use traffic

stops as a means of investigating other law violations, as to which
no probable cause or even articulable suspicion exists." A *unanimous* Court rejected that proposition. Viewed as a claim that
pretextual seizures violate the Fourth Amendment, it was deemed
contrary to the Court's prior cases (especially *Scott*) treating the
officers' subjective intent as irrelevant on the constitutional issue.
Cases in which the Court had previously expressed concern about
pretextual action were distinguishable, said the Court in *Whren*,
because those decisions—unlike the instant case—involved police
searches "conducted in the absence of probable cause" and exempt
from that requirement only when made for a special purpose. The
petitioners claimed their test did not violate the *Scott* rule because
it was an objective one, "whether the officer's conduct deviated
materially from usual police practices," shown in the instant case,
they claimed, because the stop was in violation of police regulations
generally barring traffic stops by plainclothes officers in unmarked
cars. The Court answered that this was merely another attempt to
get at the pretextual stop, which is not "unreasonable" under the
Fourth Amendment because the existence of probable cause settles
the issue of reasonableness. True, some of the Court's prior cases
ascertained reasonableness by resort to a balancing analysis, but,
the *Whren* Court explained, this was done as to Fourth Amendment
activity "unusually harmful to an individual's privacy or even
physical interests." Violation of the police regulation in the instant
case was not "such an extreme practice, and so is governed by the
usual rule that probable cause to believe the law has been broken
'outbalances' private interest in avoiding police contact." Although
Whren involved a traffic stop rather than a custodial arrest, its
reasoning was deemed equally applicable to the latter form of
seizure as well in *Arkansas v. Sullivan* (2001).

(e) **Constitutional vs. Other Violations.** *Mapp* declared
that state and federal officers were obligated to respect "the same
fundamental criteria," and in *Ker v. California* (1963) the Court
held that "the standard of reasonableness is the same under the
Fourth and Fourteenth Amendments." This means that close attention must be paid to the basis of Supreme Court decisions
dealing with searches and seizures by federal officers, as a declared
standard based upon the Fourth Amendment would be equally
applicable to the states, but this would not be so as to a standard
based only upon the Court's supervisory power over federal courts.

In *Elkins v. United States* (1960), the Court abolished the so-
called "silver platter" doctrine under which federal courts could
receive the fruits of unconstitutional searches by state officers.
Thus, it is now clear that if the Fourth Amendment has been
violated the evidence must be suppressed: (i) when offered in

federal court, though the search was by state officers; (ii) when offered in state court, though the search was by federal officers; and (iii) when offered in one state, though the search was by officers of another state.

(f) Application of Exclusionary Rule in Criminal Proceedings. Questions sometimes arise as to the applicability of the exclusionary rule at stages of the criminal process other than the trial, as illustrated by *United States v. Calandra* (1974). A grand jury witness objected that he should not have to answer questions based upon information acquired by an earlier illegal search of his premises, but the Supreme Court disagreed. The Court reasoned that such "extension of the exclusionary rule would seriously impede the grand jury" by requiring suppression hearings on "issues only tangentially related to the grand jury's primary objective," damage that would not be offset by substantial benefits in terms of "incremental deterrent effect." This is because illegally seized evidence is already excludable at trial, and thus additional exclusion at the grand jury stage, the Court explained, "would deter only police investigation consciously directed toward the discovery of evidence solely for use in a grand jury investigation."

In *Costello v. United States* (1956), the Court concluded that "neither the Fifth Amendment nor any other constitutional provision prescribes the kind of evidence upon which grand juries must act," and in that case and subsequent decisions the Court rejected self-incrimination challenges to grand jury indictments. Relying upon those cases, federal courts and most state courts have refused to permit defendants to attack indictments on the ground that evidence before the grand jury was obtained in violation of the Fourth Amendment, which is a sound result. There is no feasible way to determine these issues in an adversary setting *before* the evidence is received by the grand jury, and post-indictment challenges on Fourth Amendment grounds would necessitate an elaborate assessment of all the evidence tendered to the grand jury in that case, a burden that is hardly worth whatever deterrent effect would be achieved by nullifying indictments grounded in illegally acquired evidence. That reasoning obviously does not carry over to the issue of whether the exclusionary rule should be applied to the probable cause determination at a preliminary hearing, but there as well the rule in the federal system and most but not all states is that suppression of evidence is not possible at the preliminary hearing. That result is typically explained on the ground that it thus avoids the necessity for multiple determinations of admissibility and for lesser judicial officers to pass upon complex constitutional issues.

May evidence suppressed at trial on Fourth Amendment grounds be taken into account at sentencing? Utilizing a *Calandra*-style balancing approach, it has been held that the answer is yes, as there is a need for unfettered access to information by the sentencing judge, and no appreciable increment in deterrence would result from excluding a second time at sentencing. But this is not inevitably true, and thus it is necessary to recognize two exceptions: (1) where the police are assembling a dossier to be offered to a sentencing judge should the subject ever be convicted of an offense, and (2) where police have accumulated sufficient evidence to convict and then seize additional evidence unlawfully solely to affect the sentence.

By a somewhat similar balancing process, the prevailing view in the lower courts for many years has been that the exclusionary rule generally need not be applied in proceedings to revoke a suspended sentence, probation or parole. Some courts held (and many others suggested in dictum) that the result would be different if the search was conducted by an official aware of the conditional release status of the individual. But in *Pennsylvania Board of Probation and Parole v. Scott* (1998), involving a parole officer's illegal search of the residence of a known parolee, the Court opted for *total* inapplicability of the exclusionary rule in parole board hearings. The majority declared that the cost of the exclusionary rule, altering "the traditionally flexible, administrative nature of parole revocation proceedings," was not worth the "minimal" deterrence that would result. The latter characterization was correct even in instances in which the parolee's status was known, the *Scott* majority reasoned, because even then a searching official would be deterred by the risk of evidence exclusion at a criminal trial. The four dissenters in *Scott* cogently noted that because police typically know of a parolee's status, the criminal trial exclusionary rule is less likely to deter than a parole hearing exclusionary rule, for it is generally understood that parole revocation is often preferred to a new prosecution because of the procedural ease of recommitting the individual on the basis of a lesser showing by the State.

(g) Application of Exclusionary Rule in Non-criminal Proceedings. In *One 1958 Plymouth Sedan v. Pennsylvania* (1965), the Court held that in proceedings for the forfeiture of an automobile to the state on the ground that it had been used in the illegal transportation of liquor, that use could not be proved by admission of the liquor taken from that car in an unconstitutional search. As for earlier cases holding that the government was not required to return unlawfully seized narcotics or an unregistered still, alcohol and mash, the Court noted that they "concerned objects the possession of which, without more, constitutes a crime," so that repossession would have subjected the owners to criminal penalties and "would clearly have frustrated the express public policy against the possession of such objects." By comparison, in the instant case there "is nothing even remotely criminal in possessing an automobile," and return of it "to the owner would not subject him to any possible criminal penalties for possession or frustrate any public policy concerning automobiles, as automobiles." The Court added that it would be "anomalous" to apply the exclusionary rule in a criminal proceeding for the crime in question, for which a $500 fine could be imposed, but not in proceedings intended to penalize the criminal by depriving him of a $1,000 automobile. Under the *Plymouth Sedan* analysis, the exclusionary rule does not apply in proceedings to forfeit such per se contraband as gambling devices and obscene literature. When the object is the fruits of crime, such as gambling profits, the application of *Plymouth Sedan* is unclear; it could be argued, on the one hand, that permitting the criminal to keep his ill-gotten gains frustrates public policy, and on the other that absent exclusion police will be encouraged to make lawless searches for the very purpose of depriving criminals of their profits.

In *United States v. Janis* (1976), a city police officer seized certain records and funds in a gambling raid and then turned them over to the Internal Revenue Service, where they served as the basis of an IRS assessment satisfied in part by levying upon the seized funds. Janis then sued in federal court for return of the money, and the government counterclaimed for the unpaid balance. The Supreme Court held that the exclusionary rule did not apply in those proceedings in such circumstances, reasoning that no appreciable gain in terms of deterrence would be realized by suppression in a proceeding "to enforce only the civil law of the other sovereign," as it "falls outside the offending officer's zone of primary interest." The trouble with *Janis* is that the facts of the case do not support the result, for it was shown that there was an established pattern of cooperation whereby that officer routinely notified the IRS whenever he uncovered a gambling operation involving a substantial amount of cash. Thus, as the *Janis* dissenters noted, "the deterrent purpose of the exclusionary rule is wholly frustrated" by the decision. Absent the special facts relied upon in *Janis,* the exclusionary rule is applied in civil tax proceedings, a conclusion supported by the *Plymouth Sedan* case in that here as well the penalties can far exceed those from criminal prosecution.

Courts have held or assumed that the exclusionary rule applies in a wide range of administrative proceedings, all the way from FTC hearings to uncover discriminatory pricing practices to hearings to suspend or expel a student from school. Many of these decisions are supported by the *Plymouth Sedan* reasoning that the exclusionary rule applies to proceedings that are "quasi-criminal in character," in that their object "is to penalize for the commission of an offense against the law" and could "result in even greater punishment than the criminal prosecution." Under the *Calandra* balancing approach, it may be said that the exclusion-for-deterrence point is quite strong when the search was undertaken for the specific purpose of obtaining information to offer in such administrative proceedings and relatively weak when the search was not directed at a person known to be amenable to such proceedings. As for the cost side of the *Calandra* equation, it may vary from situation to situation.

An extreme and fundamentally unsound cost-benefit analysis was utilized by the majority in *Immigration and Naturalization Service v. Lopez–Mendoza* (1984), where the Court held that the exclusionary rule is inapplicable in a civil deportation hearing. The deterrent value of the exclusionary rule in this context was deemed to be reduced because (i) "deportation will still be possible when evidence not derived directly from the arrest is sufficient to support deportation," (ii) INS agents know "that it is highly unlikely that any particular arrestee will end up challenging the lawfulness of his arrest," (iii) "the INS has its own comprehensive scheme for deterring Fourth Amendment violations" by training and discipline, and (iv) "alternative remedies" including the "possibility of declaratory relief" are available for institutional practices violating the Fourth Amendment. On the cost side, the Court continued, are these factors: (i) that application of the exclusionary rule "in proceedings that are intended not to punish past transgressions but to prevent their continuance or renewal would require courts to close their eyes to ongoing violations of the law," (ii) that invocation of the exclusionary rule at deportation hearings, where "neither the hearing officers nor the attorneys * * * are likely to be well versed in the intricacies of Fourth Amendment law," "might significantly change and complicate the character of these proceedings," and (iii) that because many INS arrests "occur in crowded and confused circumstances," application of the exclusionary rule "might well result in the suppression of large amounts of information that had been obtained entirely lawfully." The dissent correctly noted that "unlike the situation in *Janis,* the conduct challenged here falls within 'the offending officer's zone of primary interest,'" and that "the costs and benefits of applying the exclusionary rule in civil deportation proceedings do not differ in any significant way from the costs and benefits of applying the rule in ordinary criminal proceedings."

Finally, it must be asked whether the Fourth Amendment exclusionary rule applies in purely private litigation, that is, a civil action in which a governmental unit or representative is not a party. Some authority is to be found to the effect that the fruits of an illegal police search may not be used in a private lawsuit, but it is to be doubted that this conclusion is compelled under the *Calandra* approach. The *Janis* reasoning that there is no gain in deterrence when the proceeding in which the evidence is offered "falls outside the offending officer's zone of primary interest" is more persuasive here than in *Janis*.

(h) **The Exclusionary Rule and "Private" or Nonpolice Searches.** In *Burdeau v. McDowell* (1921), the Court concluded that because the Fourth Amendment's "origin and history clearly show that it was intended as a restraint upon the activities of sovereign authority and was not intended to be a limitation upon other than governmental agencies," it did not call for exclusion in the instant case, where "no official of the federal government had anything to do with the wrongful seizure * * * or any knowledge thereof until several months after the property had been taken." The *Burdeau* rule squares with the modern emphasis upon the deterrence function of the exclusionary rule, as the private searcher is often motivated by reasons independent of a desire to secure a criminal conviction and seldom engages in searches upon a sufficiently regular basis to be affected by the exclusionary sanction, and even if motivated by a desire for conviction is not under the control of the police.

It should not be assumed that a search is private whenever the physical act is done by a private person. This quite clearly is not the case when the search has been ordered or requested by a government official, when it is a joint endeavor of a private person and government official, or when the government official was standing by giving tacit approval. It is otherwise if the private person acted in direct contravention of police instructions. One recurring situation is that in which a private person examines an object and then turns it over to the police for further examination, where close attention is needed to exactly what was done on both occasions. In *Walter v. United States* (1980), for example, private persons to whom a shipment of boxes were misdelivered opened them and found packages of film with suggestive drawings and explicit descriptions of the contents on the outsides, so they turned the boxes over to FBI agents who screened the films and determined they were obscene. The Court held the screening was a governmental search because it exceeded the scope of the prior private search, and distinguished the case from one in which "the results of the private search are in plain view when materials are turned over to the Government," in which case mere observation of what remained exposed by the private search would not amount to a governmental search. (The Court later held, in *United States v. Jacobsen* (1984), that "field testing" of a white powder first uncovered by a private search did not itself constitute a search because the test would only reveal whether or not the powder was an illegal substance and thus would not "compromise any legitimate interest in privacy.") This leaves the hardest case, namely, where a private party opens a package and finds something incriminating and then repackages it and delivers it to the police, who examine the contents of the package in no greater detail than did the private party. *Walter* does not resolve this situation, but in *Jacobsen* the Court held that so long as the police conduct enabled them "to learn nothing that had not previously been learned during the private search" it "infringed no legitimate expectation of privacy and hence was not a 'search' within the meaning of the Fourth Amendment."

Courts have not hesitated to admit into evidence under the *Burdeau* rule the fruits of searches conducted by persons who, while not employed by the government, have as their responsibility the prevention and detection of criminal conduct, such as store detectives and insurance investigators. Some have argued for the contrary result, contending that the reasoning of *Marsh v. Alabama* (1946), holding that when a private company owned and operated a town it was performing a "public function" and thus was subject to constitutional restraints in the same fashion as any other town, applies here. The *Marsh* analogy is especially appealing where private police actually supplant the public police or deal regularly with the general public, particularly if it may be said they are not disinterested in criminal convictions as an aid to the private objectives of their employer, for in such instances there is both a need for and an opportunity for deterrence by application of the Fourth Amendment exclusionary rule.

Somewhat the reverse of the above situation is that in which the search was by a public employee not assigned to law enforcement responsibilities. Because *Burdeau* says the Fourth Amendment "applies to governmental actions" and is a "restraint upon the activities of sovereign authority," it follows (as the Court held in *New Jersey v. T.L.O* (1985), involving search of a student by a high school administrator) that "the Fourth Amendment [is] applicable to the activities of civil as well as criminal authorities." But in *Arizona v. Evans* (1995), the Court concluded that some government searches covered by the Fourth Amendment are nonetheless inappropriate occasions for use of the exclusionary rule, considering the kind of government official who was at fault. In *Evans*, where the defendant was arrested on the basis of an erroneous computer indication of an outstanding warrant, attributable to a court clerk's failure to advise the police that the warrant had been quashed, the Court used *Leon*-style (see § 2.1(c)) reasoning to conclude the exclusionary rule should not apply: the arresting officer acted reasonably in relying on the computer record and thus was not in need of deterrence; and exclusion would not deter such errors by court clerks, who "have no stake in the outcome of particular criminal prosecutions." *Evans* will doubtless be deemed applicable to at least some searches actually conducted by nonpolice government officials, especially those whose responsibilities would only rarely uncover evidence of criminal activity.

(i) **The Exclusionary Rule and Searches by Foreign Police.** If the police of a foreign country, acting to enforce their own law and without any instigation by American officials, conduct a search that would not meet the requirements of the Fourth Amendment if conducted in this country, and the fruits are later offered into evidence here, the evidence is not subject to suppression on constitutional grounds. The Fourth Amendment is not directed at foreign police, and no purpose would be served by applying the exclusionary rule in such a case, as it would not alter the search and seizure policies of the foreign nation. If the American authorities have actually requested or participated in the foreign search, it has been suggested that the case should be dealt with just as were state police searches in response to a federal request in the silver platter era, which means that the exclusionary rule would be applicable because of such request or participation. But this is not the law, and rightly so, as the dynamics here are quite different. The state-federal silver platter problem was one of preventing federal authorities from circumventing the Fourth Amendment by getting state officials to do what they would otherwise do themselves, while the foreign-American relationship is legitimate because investigations extending to other countries naturally depend on cooperation from the local authorities. Thus, it may generally be said that noncompliance with Fourth Amendment standards by the foreign police does not require exclusion in this situation either, as there is no reason why foreign officers need to be or could be expected to be deterred from their failure to know and follow the law of another country. There doubtless are a few special situations in which it may fairly be concluded that the exclusionary rule should apply because the circumstances indicate the American authorities are rather directly accountable for the excesses that have occurred.

Even if there has been direct U.S. involvement in the foreign search, the Fourth Amendment may be inapplicable for yet another reason. In *United States v. Verdugo–Urquidez* (1990), the Court apparently ruled that the phrase "the people" in the Fourth Amendment (and the First, Second, Ninth and Tenth Amendments) "refers to a class of persons who are part of a national community or who have otherwise developed sufficient connection with this community to be considered part of that community." The defendant in the instant case was deemed not to be such a person; he was a Mexican citizen and resident who, to be sure, just two days before the search had been turned over to U.S. authorities by Mexican police, but "this sort of presence—lawful but involuntary—is not the sort to indicate any substantial connection with our country." But, because the three dissenters agreed that the Fourth Amendment applies whenever "a foreign national is held accountable for purported violations of the U.S. criminal laws," while two concurring Justices placed great emphasis upon the inapplicability of the Fourth Amendment's warrant clause to the search in the instant case, the application of *Verdugo–Urquidez* to a foreign search of an alien's property made even without probable cause is less than clear.

(j) **Challenge of Jurisdiction.** In cases beginning with *Ker v. Illinois* (1886), the Court held that the mere fact the defendant had been arrested in violation of the Fourth Amendment does not affect the jurisdiction or power of the court to subject that individual to trial, even when the illegality amounted to total avoidance of established extradition procedures in acquiring the presence of the defendant from another country or another state. A somewhat different question is whether, when extradition processes are utilized to acquire the presence of the defendant, he is entitled to a determination in the asylum state of probable cause. In *Michigan v. Doran* (1978), where the state court had refused extradition because papers submitted by the demanding state were in conclusory form and did not set out facts showing probable cause, the Supreme Court reversed. Because the Extradition Clause of the Constitution contemplates "a summary and mandatory executive proceeding," said the Court, "once the governor had granted extradition, a court considering release on habeas corpus can do no more then decide (a) whether the extradition documents on their face are in order; (b) whether the petitioner has been charged with a crime in the demanding state; (c) whether the petitioner is the person named in the request for extradition; and (d) whether the petitioner is a fugitive." This means that "once the governor of the asylum state has acted on a requisition for extradition based on the demanding state's judicial determination that probable cause existed, no further judicial inquiry may be had on that issue in the asylum state." The Michigan court had thus taken a step not open to it under the Extradition Clause in finding the arrest warrant asserting a probable cause finding deficient merely because the factual basis of that finding was not revealed.

(k) The "Constitutional Tort." 42 U.S.C.A. § 1983 provides: "Every person who, under color of any statute, ordinance, regulation, custom, or usage, of any State or Territory, subjects, or causes to be subjected, any citizen of the United States or other person within the jurisdiction thereof to the deprivation of any rights, privileges, or immunities secured by the Constitution and laws, shall be liable to the party injured in an action at law, suit in equity, or other proper proceeding for redress." Pursuant to this statute, an action for damages may be brought in a federal court against municipal and state officers by a plaintiff alleging a violation of his Fourth Amendment rights, but it is a defense that a reasonable person in the officer's position would have a good faith belief that his conduct was lawful. In *Monell v. New York City Department of Social Services* (1978), the Court overturned its earlier ruling that governments were "wholly immune" from such suits, concluding that Congress had intended municipalities to be included "among the persons to whom § 1983 applies" whenever "execution of a government's policy or custom, whether made by its lawmakers or by those whose edicts or acts may fairly be said to represent official policy, inflicts the injury." Thus, when the question arises as to whether a Fourth Amendment violation by an officer may be said to amount to "execution of a government's policy or custom," it may be necessary for a court to resolve such questions as whether a directive in a police manual can be said to be "official policy," whether a poor hiring decision or inadequate training of police can constitute the requisite "official policy," and whether a "custom" may be established by a pattern of nondiscipline for certain Fourth Amendment violations. A municipality has no immunity from liability under § 1983 flowing from its constitutional violations and may not assert the good faith of its officers as a defense to such liability.

Though § 1983 is not applicable to federal officials, the gap was filled, at least with respect to Fourth Amendment violations, in *Bivens v. Six Unknown Named Agents* (1971), where plaintiff's complaint seeking damages for an alleged illegal arrest and search by federal officers was held to state "a cause of action under the Fourth Amendment," so that he was "entitled to recover money damages for any injuries he has suffered as a result of the agents' violation of the Amendment." If the officer invokes his qualified immunity, the "relevant question . . . is the objective (albeit fact-specific) question whether a reasonable officer could have believed" the action taken "to be lawful, in light of clearly established law and the information [the officer] possessed." Though *Bivens* was not read as also imposing liability upon the employer-government, in 1974 Congress amended the Federal Tort Claims Act to permit recovery against the government, "with regard to acts or omissions of investigative or law enforcement officers of the United States Government," for any claim arising "out of assault, battery, false imprisonment, false arrest, abuse of process, or malicious prosecution." In such an FTCA action, the government may assert the same good faith-reasonable belief defense that is available to individual officers. This FTCA amendment was not intended by Congress to provide an exclusive remedy, and thus a *Bivens* action against the offending officer is still permissible.

(*l*) **Criminal Prosecution.** 18 U.S.C.A. § 242 provides: "Whoever, under color of any law, statute, ordinance, regulation, or custom, willfully subjects any inhabitant of any State, Territory, or District to the deprivation of any rights, privileges, or immunities secured or protected by the Constitution or laws of the United States, * * * shall be fined not more than $1,000 or imprisoned not more than one year, or both; and if death results shall be subject to imprisonment for any term of years or for life." One who "acts under 'color' of law" within the meaning of that statute "may be a federal officer or a state officer," and it makes no difference that state or federal law does not affirmatively authorize the deprivation that has occurred. The "willfully" requirement has been construed by the Supreme Court to avoid vagueness objections, and as interpreted means "a purpose to deprive a person of a specific constitutional right."

(m) **Expungement of Arrest Records.** Though some legislatures have adopted statutes dealing with the use, dissemination and expungement of arrest records, the question here is whether there is a constitutional right to such expungement when the arrest violated the Fourth Amendment. Some cases have held that there is as part of the constitutional right to privacy, but the more recent cases have ruled otherwise on the strength of *Paul v. Davis* (1976), holding that this penumbral right has to do only with "matters relating to marriage, procreation, contraception, family relationships, and child rearing and education." Some authority is to be found to the effect that the expungement remedy can be grounded on the Fourth Amendment, but while dictum in some cases would suggest that an arrest without probable cause is per se a basis for expungement, the decisions do not support that proposition. Typically, expungement has occurred or been recognized as potential relief where there was a Fourth Amendment violation of an egregious nature. In any event, a balancing process is called for, which suggests that total expungement (as contrasted to limits on use) will be inappropriate when some legitimate future use could be made of the record.

(n) **Injunction.** The longstanding principle that equity will not grant relief to a petitioner who has an adequate remedy at law has proved to be no barrier to plaintiffs seeking to enjoin repeated or continuing Fourth Amendment violations, for in such circumstances neither the exclusionary rule nor an action for money damages will suffice. Another requirement is that there be a threat of imminent harm, which means injunctive relief will not be available absent a clear pattern or stated policy of continuing police action of the kind challenged. In *Rizzo v. Goode* (1976), the Court ruled that repeated unconstitutional conduct by only a few officers would justify injunctive relief only against them, not against the department at large or the officers in charge of the department.

(*o*) **Self–Help.** The common law right to resist an unlawful arrest has given way in many jurisdictions to the modern view that the use of force is not justifiable to resist an arrest that the actor knows is being made by a peace officer, although the arrest is unlawful. It has sometimes been asserted that this view cannot be squared with the Fourth Amendment, but as a general proposition this is not so. The state in removing the right to resist has merely withdrawn a remedy that not infrequently causes far graver consequences for both the officer and the suspect than does the unlawful arrest itself, and has required the arrestee to submit peacefully to the inevitable and to pursue his available remedies through the orderly judicial process. (The same reasoning applies to other forms of self-help undertaken in active resistance to a Fourth Amendment violation, such as forcible opposition to the execution of an invalid search warrant, but it does not follow that criminal punishment may be imposed for a mere failure to surrender rights under the Amendment.) But if an arrest was so flagrant an intrusion on a citizen's rights that his resistance would be virtually inevitable, it well may be that conviction for the resistance would violate due process.

§ 2.2 Protected Areas and Interests

(a) **The *Katz* Expectation of Privacy Test.** For some years the Court was of the view that for there to be a Fourth Amendment search there must have been a physical intrusion into "a constitutionally protected area." These areas were those enumerated in the Fourth Amendment itself: "persons," including the bodies and attire of individuals; "houses," including apartments, hotel rooms, garages, business offices, stores, and warehouses; "papers," such as letters; and "effects," such as automobiles. Then came *Katz v. United States* (1967), where FBI agents overheard defendant's end of telephone conversations by attaching an electronic listening and recording device to the exterior of the public telephone booth from which he was calling. The Court rejected a characterization of the issue as whether a public telephone booth is a constitutionally protected area within which a person has a right of privacy. Though the Fourth Amendment "protects individual privacy against certain kinds of governmental intrusion, * * * its protections go further, and often have nothing to do with privacy at all," while other aspects of privacy are protected by other provisions of the Constitution or left to state law. As for determining whether a particular area is "constitutionally protected," it "deflects attention" from the problem: "For the Fourth Amendment protects people, not places. What a person knowingly exposes to the public, even in his own home or office, is not a subject of Fourth Amendment protection. * * * But what he seeks to preserve as private, even in an area accessible to the public, may be constitutionally protected." It was thus deemed "clear that the reach of that Amendment cannot turn upon the presence or absence of a physical intrusion into any given enclosure," and that instead the critical point, justifying the conclusion that this activity amounted to a search, was that "a person in a telephone booth * * * who occupies it, shuts the door behind him, and pays the toll that permits him to place a call is surely entitled to assume that the words he utters into the mouthpiece will not be broadcast to the world." Justice Harlan, concurring, elaborated the point in language that has often been relied upon by lower courts in interpreting and applying *Katz*, namely, "that there is a twofold requirement, first that a person have exhibited an actual (subjective) expectation of privacy and, second, that the expectation be one that society is prepared to recognize as 'reasonable.' "

As for Harlan's first requirement, the majority in *Katz* likewise introduced a subjective element by saying that the government's conduct directed at Katz "violated the privacy upon which he justifiably relied." But while it is often rather easy to say that the police made no search because the defendant surely did not actually expect privacy, as where a person openly engaged in criminal conduct in Times Square at high noon, a subjective expectation does not add to, nor can its absence detract from, an individual's claim to Fourth Amendment protection, for otherwise the government could diminish that protection by announcing in advance an intention to do so. As for Harlan's second requirement, apparently intended to give content to the word "justifiably" in the majority statement that the eavesdropping "violated the privacy upon which he justifiably relied while using the telephone booth," the Court has since referred to this as the "reasonable 'expectation of privacy' test." While this suggests that a justified expectation is one that a reasonable man would have, based upon the statistical probability of being discovered in the circumstances, this is not really what *Katz* is all about. If two narcotics peddlers were to rely on the privacy of a desolate corner of Central Park in the middle of the night to carry out an illegal transaction, this would be a reasonable expectation of privacy; there would be virtually no risk of discovery. Yet if by extraordinary good luck a patrolman were to illuminate the desolate spot with his flashlight, the criminals would be unable to suppress the officer's testimony as a violation of their rights under the Fourth Amendment. Thus, for an expectation to be considered justified it is not sufficient that it be merely reasonable; something in addition is required; hence the suggestion that the ultimate question under *Katz* "is a value judgment," namely, "whether, if the particular form of surveillance practiced by the police is permitted to go unregulated by constitutional restraints, the amount of privacy and freedom remaining to citizens would be diminished to a compass inconsistent with the aims of a free and open society."

(b) Plain View, Smell and Hearing and Touch; Aiding the Senses. The concern here is with plain view in the sense of there being no Fourth Amendment *search* at all, as where an officer without making any intrusion sees an object on the person of an individual, in premises, or in a vehicle. While the characterization of an observation as a nonsearch plain view situation settles the lawfulness of the observation itself, it does not inevitably follow that a warrantless seizure of the observed object would be lawful. As the Supreme Court has explained, the plain view doctrine "authorizes seizure of illegal or evidentiary items visible to a police officer" only if the officer's "access to the object" itself has a "Fourth Amendment justification." If an officer standing on the public way is able to look through the window of a private residence and see contraband, he must except in extraordinary circumstances obtain a warrant before entering those premises to seize the contraband. If he had been looking into a vehicle, the warrant issue must again be resolved, though in most instances a warrant is not required in such circumstances (see § 2.7(b)). If the object had been seen on an individual, it is still necessary that the seizure of that object occur pursuant to a warrant, incident to arrest, or without warrant but under exigent circumstances. But if the object is in plain view within an accessible container then there is apparently no constitutional barrier to the seizure and opening of that container. Because in at least some other circumstances a search warrant is needed to open even an accessible container, this means that what can be properly characterized as a plain view situation in such circumstances—a matter that has caused the Court considerable difficulty—is especially important.

Just as what an officer sees where he is lawfully present is a nonsearch plain view, what he learns by reliance upon his other senses while so located is likewise no search. Thus, when surveilling officers in one motel room are able to hear with the naked ear conversations occurring in the adjoining room, this is not a search because there has been no intrusion upon a justified expectation of privacy. By like reasoning it has been held that it is no search for a lawfully positioned officer "with inquisitive nostrils" to detect incriminating odors. Even a so-called "plain touch" could amount to no search under some circumstances. However, it must be remembered that "[p]hysically invasive inspection is simply more intrusive than purely visual inspection," a point the Supreme Court emphasized in *Bond v. United States* (2000), holding that the squeezing of a bus passenger's luggage in the overhead rack, resulting in discovery of a brick-shaped object within, was an illegal search because a bus passenger justifiably expects other passengers or bus employees to "move" or "handle" his bag but does not expect that they "will, as a matter of course, feel the bag in an exploratory manner."

In *United States v. Lee* (1927), the Supreme Court held that use of a Coast Guard cutter searchlight at night to see aboard a schooner was no search, and since then courts have consistently held that use of artificial illumination by a lawfully positioned officer does not constitute a search. *Lee* likened the use of the searchlight "to the use of a marine glass or a field glass," and thus it is not surprising that the cases also agree that the use of binoculars does not, per se, constitute a search. But, while it is certainly sensible to conclude that ordinary use of such common devices for aiding the senses does not intrude upon any justified expectation of privacy (as compared to use of a magnetometer or X-ray machine or radiographic scanner to see inside an object, a gas chromatograph to identify organic compounds in an object, or use of electronic eavesdropping or wiretapping equipment to overhear conversations, all of which are Fourth Amendment searches), there may be particular situations in which the nature of the equipment or the manner of its use dictates a contrary conclusion. Illustrative would be use of a very high-powered telescope to observe from a considerable distance the contents of documents being read inside premises, or use of a flashlight to see through a minute opening what is inside a secured building.

Photo surveillance does not constitute a search even when a telescopic lens of a type generally in use is employed or when pictures taken with standard equipment are then enlarged in the development process, but the result may be otherwise when more sophisticated equipment is used. In *Dow Chemical Co. v. United States* (1986), the majority held it was no search to engage in aerial photography of the outdoor areas of a large industrial complex even though as a result it was possible to detect pipes as small as half an inch in diameter. But *Dow* was limited in several ways: (1) the Court grounded the decision in the character of the place being surveilled, and intimated the result would be different as to "an area immediately adjacent to a private home, where privacy expectations are most heightened"; (2) the Court also deemed significant what was revealed, noting that "no objects as small as ½-inch diameter such as a class ring, for example, are recognizable, nor are there any identifiable human faces or secret documents captured in such a fashion as to implicate more serious privacy concerns"; and (3) the Court indicated that, in any event, the result might be different if the surveillance involved "highly sophisticated surveillance not generally available to the public, such as satellite technology."

An infrared thermal detection device (thermal imager), without sending rays or beams into premises, can determine the amount of heat emanating therefrom by measuring differences in surface temperatures of the targeted object. When this occurs, the Supreme Court decided in *Kyllo v. United States* (2001), it constitutes a search. The majority restated the *Katz* expectation-of-privacy test in less abstract terms as to one important genre of cases, stating "that obtaining by sense-enhancing technology any information regarding the interior of the home that could not otherwise have been obtained without physical 'intrusion into a constitutionally protected area' constitutes a search where (as here) the technology in question is not in general public use." Significantly, the majority (i) refused to accept the dissenters' "off-the-wall"—"through the wall" distinction, noting that in *Katz* the device only measured vibrations on the outside surface of the phone booth; (ii) recognized a need to take a stand *now* against the increasing intrusiveness of modern technology, instead of waiting as would the dissenters until the equipment became more sophisticated and the intrusions more severe; and (iii) was unwilling to impose added burdens on those unwilling to suffer this kind of privacy intrusion, as compared to the dissenters' conclusion that such people should "make sure the surrounding area is well insulated." The most telling criticism of the dissenters concerned the majority's "not in general public use" qualification, which they condemned as "somewhat perverse because it seems likely that the threat to privacy will grow, rather than recede, as the use of intrusive equipment becomes more readily available."

In recent years police have made extensive use of specially trained dogs to detect the presence of explosives or, more commonly, narcotics. Such reliance upon the trained canine nose to detect that which the officer could not discover by his own sense of smell does not constitute a search, the Court held in *United States v. Place* (1983). The Court emphasized that "the canine sniff is *sui generis*" because unlike any other investigative procedure, it "discloses only the presence or absence of * * * a contraband item" and "does not expose noncontraband items that otherwise would remain hidden from public view." The Court's analysis apparently means that the conduct there, exposure of luggage in a public place to a trained canine, is constitutionally permissible even if done without any suspicion or in a wholesale or at random fashion. Arguably the same is not true as to use of these dogs against people, even if this can be accomplished without first detaining the person. Use of such dogs to ascertain what is inside a dwelling has been held to be a search.

(c) **Residential Premises.** If a person has abandoned the place where he formerly resided, this terminates any justified expectation of privacy that he had with respect to those premises. The question of abandonment for Fourth Amendment purposes does not turn on strict property concepts, and thus it is possible for there to be abandonment even if a tenant retained the lawful right to possession. The question in such circumstances is whether the defendant abandoned the premises in the sense of having no apparent intention to return and make further use of them. If the tenant has not left but the rental period has expired, this does not inevitably terminate the justified privacy expectation, for it may generally be said that the tenant would be justified in expecting the landlord to resort to the eviction procedures required by law rather than self-help. Because of the transitory nature of most motel and hotel rental arrangements, a guest would not be justified in assuming that the manager, at the termination of the rental period, would not immediately clear the room for occupation by another guest.

An unconsented police entry into a residential unit, be it a house, apartment, or hotel or motel room, constitutes a search under *Katz*. The mere presence of a hallway in the interior of a single family dwelling, without more, is not in itself an invitation to the public to enter, so that entry of even such a place is a search, but there is no invasion of privacy when a policeman without force enters the common hallway of a multiple-family house in the furtherance of an investigation. The result is otherwise when the apartment building hallway is accessible only by key or a buzzer system, for such safeguards give rise to a justified privacy expectation in the hallway. As for merely looking into the residence, it may generally be said that it is no search for an officer to obtain such a view from the public way, a neighbor's property, or that part of the curtilage constitutings the normal means of access to and egress from the house, while on the other hand it *is* a search for an officer to stray from that path to engage in window-peeping. But it would not be consistent with *Katz* to say there is *never* a search when the observation is from outside the building and curtilage, for there certainly is a justified expectation of privacy in not being seen or heard from vantage points not ordinarily utilized by the public or other residents. By like reasoning, the better view is that even when the officer is lawfully present in a place used by the public (e.g., the hallway of an apartment building), it is a search to engage in conduct offensive in its intrusiveness in the sense that it uncovers that which the resident may fairly be said to have sufficiently protected from scrutiny. Certainly *Katz* should not be read as permitting unrestrained peeping through keyholes and transoms.

Under the traditional pre-*Katz* view, the protections of the Fourth Amendment also extend to other structures within the curtilage, that is, all buildings in close proximity to a dwelling and used in connection therewith. On this basis, it has been held that police entry of such buildings as a garage or barn is a search, which is also the result under *Katz*. By contrast, the other aspect of the pre-*Katz* rule, which was that a garage or barn outside the curtilage was not protected by the Fourth Amendment has no current vitality; it is now necessary to inquire whether the nature of the structure and other circumstances are indicative of a justified privacy expectation. Thus, in *United States v. Dunn* (1987) the Court assumed without deciding that a barn *outside* the curtilage "enjoyed Fourth Amendment protection and could not be entered and its contents seized without a warrant," but yet held that merely peering into the barn's open front from an open fields vantage point was no search.

Lands adjoining the dwelling also fell within the pre-*Katz* curtilage concept and are clearly protected by *Katz* under some circumstances. In expectation of privacy terms, quite clearly it is not objectionable that an officer has come upon the land in the same way that any member of the public could be expected to do, as by taking the normal route of access along a walkway or driveway or onto a porch. The nature of the premises must be taken into account, for as a general matter lands adjacent to a multiple-occupancy dwelling are more likely to be viewed as public areas. Consideration must also be given to the degree of scrutiny involved; casual observation of what any visitor could have seen may be no search, while a detailed examination even in an area frequently used by the public may well constitute a search under *Katz*. Looking into protected adjoining lands from other locations is governed by considerations like those previously discussed. It is no search to observe on that land what a neighbor could readily see, but resort to extraordinary efforts to overcome the defendant's reasonable attempts to maintain the privacy of his curtilage is a search.

As for viewing by overflight, the Supreme Court took a permissive stance in *California v. Ciraolo* (1986), where police flew over defendant's fenced curtilage and saw marijuana plants growing there. Because the observations "took place within public navigable airspace" and were of "plants readily discernible to the naked eye as marijuana," the majority reasoned this was no search because "any member of the public flying in this airspace who glanced down could have seen everything that these officers observed." The four dissenters cogently reasoned that "the actual risk to privacy from commercial or pleasure aircraft is virtually nonexistent," as persons in them "normally obtain at most a fleeting, anonymous, and nondiscriminatory glimpse of the landscape and buildings over which they pass." (*Ciraolo,* involving surveillance from a fixed-wing aircraft at 1,000 feet, was relied upon in *Florida v. Riley* (1989), holding surveillance from a helicopter at 400 feet was likewise no search but denying "that an inspection of the curtilage of a house from an aircraft will always pass muster under the Fourth Amendment simply because the plane is within the navigable airspace specified by law.") *Ciraolo* does not settle what the result would be if the police in the aircraft had used some sense-enhancing equipment; in the companion case of *Dow Chemical Co. v. United States* (1986), holding use of rather sophisticated camera equipment from an airplane was no search, the decision was grounded in the nature of the premises surveilled, a large industrial plant, and the Court cautioned that the result might be different if the surveillance had been of "an area immediately adjacent to a private home, where privacy expectations are most heightened."

(d) **"Open Fields."** In *Hester v. United States* (1924), where agents retrieved evidence that had been thrown into a field, the Court held that "the special protection accorded by the Fourth Amendment * * * is not extended to the open fields." Courts applied *Hester* to virtually any land not within the curtilage, even if fenced or posted with no trespassing signs, such as wooded areas, desert, vacant lots in urban areas, open beaches, reservoirs, and open waters. Although the vitality of this *Hester* "open fields" rule was uncertain after *Katz,* it was ultimately reaffirmed in *Oliver v. United States* (1984). One reason for this result given by the *Oliver* majority, that the "persons, houses, papers, and effects" language of the Fourth Amendment means its protections cannot be extended to open fields, constitutes a literal-minded interpretation totally inconsistent with the Court's prior decisions such as *Katz.* A second reason given in *Oliver,* "that an individual may not legitimately demand privacy for activities conducted out of doors in fields, except in the area immediately surrounding the home," makes sense only if there is some good reason to proceed upon the basis of such a generalization in lieu of assessing the facts of the particular case (e.g., in *Oliver,* that the police had bypassed a locked gate and a "No Trespassing" sign in order to get to the so-called "open fields"). The *Oliver* majority concluded there was: an ad hoc approach would make it too "difficult for the policeman to discern the scope of his authority" in a particular instance. As for where the curtilage ends and "open fields" begins, in *United States v. Dunn* (1987), the Court asserted "that curtilage questions should be resolved with particular reference to four factors: the proximity of the area claimed to be curtilage to the home, whether the area is included within an enclosure surrounding the home, the nature of the uses to which the area is put, and the steps taken by the resident to protect the area from observation by people passing by."

(e) **Business and Commercial Premises.** Offices and stores and other business and commercial premises are also entitled to protection against unreasonable searches and seizures, though the nature of these premises is such that much police investigative activity directed at them will not constitute a search. Law enforcement officials may enter commercial premises at the times they are open to the public and may explore those portions of the premises to which the public has ready access, including the examination of articles available for inspection by potential customers. On the other hand, it is a search for police to enter without consent premises to which the public at large does not have access, such as the work area of a factory or a private club open only to members. Surveillance from outside business premises is governed by the same considerations discussed earlier concerning looking into dwellings. As for surveillance of the outdoor areas of businesses, such as the space between buildings within a large, fenced-in industrial complex, the Supreme Court in *Dow Chemical Co. v. United States* (1986) declared that such places "can perhaps be seen as falling somewhere between 'open fields' and curtilage, but lacking some of the critical characteristics of both." The Court intimated that with regard to physical entry of such lands the curtilage analogy would prevail, but then held that as to aerial surveillance the place was "more comparable to an open field," meaning such surveillance was no search. The four dissenters in *Dow* understandably complained about the majority's failure to "explain how its result squares with *Katz* and its progeny."

(f) **Vehicles.** There is no justified expectation of privacy in an abandoned vehicle, but abandonment in this context is not a question of whether someone had a proprietary or possessory interest in the automobile under common law property concepts, but rather whether the defendant was entitled to have a reasonable expectation that the automobile would be free from governmental intrusion. Thus, abandonment may occur not only by intending to relinquish any claim to the vehicle but by dealing with it in such a way that privacy could hardly be justifiably expected, as where a car is left behind in escaping from pursuit by the police or is left unclaimed for some time on another's property. When a car is parked by the side of the road, it is necessary to consider such factors as the condition of the vehicle, its location, and the length of time it has remained there.

Assuming lawful presence of the officer by the vehicle, generally it is no search for the officer to see or smell what is inside the car without physical intrusion into it, or for him to photograph or examine the exterior of the vehicle or perhaps even to do some "testing" of the exterior. There will occasionally be instances, however, in which the scrutiny is so intense, resulting in discovery of what had been concealed by reasonable means, that under the *Katz* rationale the police conduct must be designated a search. As for examination of vehicle identification numbers, obviously no search is involved when the number can be seen through the window of the vehicle. The cases holding that it is no search to intrude physically into the car in order to ascertain a hidden number are short on analysis and conflict with *Katz,* as the Supreme Court later concluded in *New York v. Class* (1986). More appealing is the contention that because these numbers are quasi-public information, a search of that part of the car displaying the number is but a minimal invasion of a person's privacy that may be undertaken without a warrant upon reasonable suspicion. But in *Class* the Court accepted a somewhat different proposition, namely, that inspection of the VIN "is within the scope of police authority pursuant to a traffic stop" prompted by an observed traffic violation, and that "concern for the officer's safety" justifies the officer's entry of the car to uncover the VIN on the door jamb or dashboard instead of having the driver reenter to do so.

(g) **Personal Characteristics.** In *United States v. Dionisio* (1973), the Court held that requiring the person to give voice exemplars is no search because "the physical characteristics of a person's voice, its tone and manner, as opposed to the content of a specific conversation, are constantly exposed to the public," so that "no person can have a reasonable expectation that others will not know the sound of his voice." By the same reasoning the Court ruled in the companion case of *United States v. Mara* (1973) that it is no search to require a person to give handwriting exemplars. *Dionisio* likened the sound of a person's voice to his "facial characteristics," and thus it is clear that it is not a search simply to observe those characteristics or to photograph them. The Court has also referred to fingerprinting as nothing more than obtaining "physical characteristics * * * constantly exposed to the public." At the other extreme, seizing evidence from within the body by taking a blood or urine sample quite clearly is a search. Hard situations exist in between, such as the taking of a sample of hair.

It may be said that hair is also a characteristic "constantly exposed to public view" and that consequently the taking of it is no search, but *Cupp v. Murphy* (1973) (holding it was a search to scrape visible dried blood from defendant's finger and subject it to microscopic analysis) suggests that in such cases it may make a difference whether the hair is being kept merely to preserve a readily observable characteristic or to enable much closer scrutiny than "public view" allows.

(h) Abandoned Effects. The Supreme Court has upheld the examination of certain effects on the ground that they had been abandoned, such as glass containers thrown into a field and objects put into a hotel room waste basket before checking out. Abandonment in this context may be based upon an intent to relinquish all claim to the object, as in those cases, or by simply relinquishing control of the object to such an extent and in such circumstances that examination of it by others would not be unlikely. Property is not considered abandoned when a person throws away incriminating articles due to the unlawful activities of police officers, as where the disposal was prompted by police efforts to make an illegal arrest or search. Mere denial of ownership is not proof of an intent to abandon, but at least in some circumstances courts are inclined to hold that the denial deprived the person disclaiming ownership of any justified expectation in the object.

Even inspection of one's garbage left for collection outside the curtilage of a home is no search, the Supreme Court held in *California v. Greenwood* (1988). In that case, police obtained evidence of the defendants' narcotics use by having the trash collector pick up the plastic garbage bags the defendants had left on the curb in front of their house and then give the bags to the police without first mixing the contents with refuse from other houses. The Court reasoned this was no search because the defendants had no "subjective expectation of privacy in their garbage that society accepts as objectively reasonable," as "plastic garbage bags left on or at the side of a public street are readily accessible to animals, children, scavengers, snoops, and other members of the public. * * * Moreover, respondents placed their refuse at the curb for the express purpose of conveying it to a third party, the trash collector, who might himself have sorted through respondents' trash or permitted others, such as the police, to do so." Because *Greenwood* is limited to "trash left for collection in an area accessible to the public," it should not be construed as permitting police to enter the curtilage and seize garbage kept there. It is unclear what the result should be if the police have the garbage collector make his usual pickup from within the curtilage but then turn the refuse over to them unmixed with neighbors' garbage, for that part of the *Greenwood* reasoning about defendant "conveying * * * to a third party" is seemingly applicable even there.

(i) "Mere Evidence" in General and Private Papers in Particular. In *Gouled v. United States* (1920) the Court held that a search warrant could not always be utilized "to secure evidence to be used against [a person] in a criminal or penal proceeding" because such action is permissible only "when a primary right to such search and seizure may be found in the interest which the public or the complainant may have in the property to be seized, or in the right to the possession of it." This "mere evidence" rule, whereby items were subject to lawful seizure only if they were the fruits or instrumentalities of crime, was later extended by the Court to warrantless searches as well, but was finally abandoned by the Court in *Warden v. Hayden* (1967), where the Court reasoned that "nothing in the nature of property seized as evidence renders it more private than property seized, for example, as an instrumentality." *Hayden* did not mark the end of uncertainty as to whether certain effects were immune from seizure, for the Court cautioned that "the items of clothing involved in this case are not 'testimonial' or 'communicative' in nature, and their introduction therefore did not compel respondent to become a witness against himself in violation of the Fifth Amendment."

The Court finally addressed the Fifth Amendment issue squarely in *Andresen v. Maryland* (1976), involving seizure pursuant to warrant of specified documents relating to a fraudulent sale of land. Noting that the "historic function" of the privilege against self-incrimination has been to protect a "natural individual from compulsory incrimination through his own testimony or personal records," the Court concluded there had been no Fifth Amendment violation in this case because there was no compulsion, that is, the "petitioner was not asked to say or to do anything." In particular, the Court stressed that (i) the creation of the documents by petitioner had been voluntary; (ii) he was not required to play a part in handing them over to the police; and (iii) he was not required to authenticate them at trial. This situation, then, is quite different from that in which the means of acquiring the evidence is a subpoena, where "the Fifth Amendment may protect an individual * * * because the very act of production may constitute a compulsory authentication of incriminating information." Though the Court in *Andresen* repeatedly stressed that the papers seized were "business records," it seems clear that the Court's Fifth Amendment analysis would compel the very same result were the documents much more private in nature, such as a diary.

(j) Surveillance of Relationships and Movements. One way in which law enforcement agents obtain information concerning a person's associations and activities is by examination of the detailed records kept by those agencies with which that person has had occasion to do business. Such activity is unlikely to be characterized as a search after *United States v. Miller* (1976), involving subpoenas directed at two banks for all records concerning defendant and his company in their hands. Defendant's contention that the subpoenas were defective was brushed aside because the Court concluded "that there was no intrusion into any area of which respondent had a protected Fourth Amendment interest." In support, the Court reasoned that (1) because the records in question were "the business records of the banks," respondent "can assert neither ownership nor possession"; (2) there was no "legitimate expectation of privacy concerning the information kept in bank records," as "the documents obtained, including financial statements and deposit slips, contain only information voluntarily conveyed to the banks and exposed to their employees in the ordinary course of business"; and (3) a "depositor takes the risk, in revealing his affairs to another, that the information will be conveyed by that person to the government."

Though the *Miller* result and reasoning are highly questionable, *Miller* was relied upon in *Smith v. Maryland* (1979), holding that it is no search for the police to utilize a "pen register," a device that records all telephone numbers dialed from a particular phone. The Court concluded Smith could claim no legitimate expectation of privacy because when he used his phone he "voluntarily conveyed numerical information to the telephone company and 'exposed' that information to its equipment in the ordinary course of business," and thereby "assumed the risk that the company would reveal to police the numbers he dialed." This reasoning is just as unsound as that in *Miller*. Even if it may be said that subscribers know phone companies monitors calls for internal reasons, it hardly follows that they expect this information to be made available to the general public or the government. By like reasoning, a mail cover (a form of surveillance in which law enforcement authorities have postal authorities record all external markings, including return addresses, on all mail to a particular addressee) should be considered a search, but the contrary result has been reached by resort to the all-or-nothing approach to privacy reflected in *Miller* and *Smith*. *Smith* may also support the conclusion that use of Carnivore/DCS 1000 electronic surveillance software in "pen mode" to obtain addressing information in e-mails is no search, though some argue otherwise on the grounds that it is unlike the traditional pen register in the amount and revealing nature of the information collected. But interception of the contents of communications sent by regular mail or e-mail *is* a search.

Another increasingly common surveillance technique involves the use of an electronic tracking device, as where a beacon or "beeper" is attached to a car, airplane or container and the movements of that object are then tracked by picking up the signals emitted periodically. The Supreme Court in *United States v. Karo* (1984) concluded that the mere installation of a beeper or transfer to another of a beeper-laden object is no "search," because that act alone "infringed no privacy interest" in that it "conveyed no information at all," and is no "seizure" because "it cannot be said that anyone's possessory interest was interfered with in a meaningful way." As for subsequent monitoring, the Court in *United States v. Knotts* (1983) held that such surveillance "amounted principally to the following of an automobile on public streets and highways," which if accomplished merely by visual surveillance would be no search because one "travelling in an automobile on public thoroughfares has no reasonable expectation of privacy in his movements from one place to another," and that "scientific enhancement of this sort raises no constitutional issues which visual surveillance would not also raise." In *Karo* the Court answered in the affirmative the question reserved in *Knotts,* "whether monitoring of a beeper falls within the ambit of the Fourth Amendment when it reveals information that could not have been obtained through visual surveillance." Noting first that unquestionably it would be an unreasonable search to surreptitiously enter a residence without a warrant to verify that the container was there, the Court reasoned that "the result is the same where, without a warrant, the Government surreptitiously employs an electronic device to obtain information that it could not have obtained by observation from outside the curtilage of the home. * * * Even if visual surveillance has revealed that the article to which the beeper is attached has entered the house, the later monitoring not only verifies the officers' observations but also establishes that the article remains on the premises." The Court next concluded that absent "truly exigent circumstances" such use of the beeper was governed by "the general rule that a search of a house should be conducted pursuant to a warrant." Such monitoring was characterized by the Court as "less intrusive than a full-scale search," but the Court did not have occasion to decide whether as a consequence such a warrant could issue upon reasonable suspicion rather than probable cause.

§ 2.3 Probable Cause

(a) **General Considerations.** Because the warrant clause of the Fourth Amendment provides that "no Warrants shall issue, but upon probable cause," it is apparent that a valid arrest warrant or a valid search warrant may issue only upon a showing of probable cause to the issuing authority. In the many instances in which police arrest and search without first obtaining a warrant, their conduct is governed by the other half of the Fourth Amendment, which declares the right of the people to be secure "against unreasonable searches and seizures." But it is clear that such an arrest or search is unreasonable if not based upon probable cause; as the Supreme Court explained in *Wong Sun v. United States* (1963), were the requirements less stringent than when a warrant is obtained, then "a principal incentive now existing for the procurement of * * * warrants would be destroyed."

It is generally assumed that the same quantum of evidence is required whether one is concerned with probable cause to arrest or probable cause to search. But each requires a showing of probabilities as to somewhat different facts and circumstances, and thus one can exist without the other. In search cases, two conclusions must be supported by substantial evidence: that the items sought are in fact seizable by virtue of being connected with criminal activity, and that the items will be found in the place to be searched. It is *not* also necessary that a particular person be implicated in the crime under investigation. By comparison, in arrest cases there must be probable cause that a crime has been committed and that the person to be arrested committed it, which of course can exist without any showing that evidence of the crime will be found at premises under that person's control.

The Supreme Court has long expressed a strong preference for the use of arrest warrants and search warrants. Resort to the warrant process, the Court has declared, is preferred because it "interposes an orderly procedure" involving "judicial impartiality" whereby "a neutral and detached magistrate" can make "informed and deliberate determinations" on the issue of probable cause. To leave such decisions to the police would allow "hurried actions" by those "engaged in the often competitive enterprise of ferreting out crime." This preference has resulted in a subtle difference between the probable cause required when there is no warrant and that required when there is. As the Court put it in *United States v. Ventresca* (1965), "in a doubtful or marginal case a search under a warrant may be sustainable where without one it would fail." This "deference to the decision of the magistrate to issue a warrant" means that a reviewing court is not to conduct "a de novo probable cause determination" but instead is merely to decide "whether the evidence viewed as a whole provided a 'substantial basis' for the magistrate's finding of probable cause."

When the police make an arrest or search without a warrant, they initially make the probable cause decision themselves. The "on-the-scene assessment of probable cause provides a legal justification for arresting a person suspected of crime, and for a brief period of detention to take the administrative steps incident to arrest," but an ex parte "judicial determination of probable cause [is] a prerequisite to extended restraint on liberty following arrest." This means that judicial review of probable cause for the arrest need occur only if the arrestee fails to obtain his prompt release unaccompanied "by burdensome conditions that effect a significant restraint on liberty" (see § 2.5(a)). Otherwise, a subsequent judicial determination of whether there was probable cause for the warrantless police action will ordinarily occur only if initiated by the defendant upon a motion to suppress evidence claimed to be a fruit of an illegal arrest or search.

When the police arrest or search with a warrant, the probable cause determination is made by a magistrate in the first instance. Under the traditional approach, his decision was not final; it was still open to the defendant upon a motion to suppress to argue that evidence obtained by execution of the warrant should be suppressed because the warrant was not in fact issued upon probable cause. However, in *United States v. Leon* (1984) the Supreme Court adopted a "good faith" exception to the exclusionary rule in with-warrant cases. This means that upon the motion to suppress evidence obtained pursuant to a warrant, the evidence will be admissible (without regard to whether there was in fact probable cause) if the officer could have reasonably believed that warrant was valid (see § 2.1(c)).

(b) Nature of Probable Cause. In *Brinegar v. United States* (1949), the Court characterized the probable cause requirement as "the best compromise that has been found for accommodating" the often opposing interests of privacy and effective law enforcement. This raises the question of whether this "compromise" must always be struck in precisely the same way, or whether instead probable cause may require a greater or a lesser quantum of evidence, depending upon the facts and circumstances of the individual case.

It is now clear that certain unique investigative techniques are governed by a special, less demanding probable cause test. In *Camara v. Municipal Court* (1967), for example, the Court engaged in a "balancing" of "the need to search against the invasion which the search entails" in approving such a probable cause test for housing inspection warrants; thus " 'probable cause' to issue a warrant to inspect must exist if reasonable legislative or administrative standards for conducting an area inspection are satisfied with respect to a particular building." This *Camara* balancing approach was thereafter employed in upholding other kinds of so-called administrative or regulatory searches, and was later used by the Court in *Terry v. Ohio* (1968) to support the conclusion that a brief stopping for investigation and a frisk incident thereto are permissible upon grounds falling short of probable cause to make a full-fledged arrest and a full search of the person incident thereto (see § 2.8). In both instances, the Court deemed it most significant that the practices at issue were clearly distinguishable from the typical arrest or search in that they involved a significantly lesser intrusion into freedom and privacy.

Some have argued for a more extended use of this balancing process, whereby in each case the probable cause for the investigative technique used would be determined by weighing the degree of intrusion and the law enforcement need in that particular case. But the Supreme Court has declined the invitation to adopt a proposed "multifactor balancing test" along these lines. As the Court put it in *Dunaway v. New York* (1979),

> the protections intended by the Framers could all too easily disappear in the consideration and balancing of the multifarious circumstances presented by different cases, especially when that balancing may be done in the first instance by police officers engaged in the "often competitive enterprise of ferreting out crime." * * * A single, familiar standard is essential to guide police officers, who have only limited time and expertise to reflect on and balance the social and individual interests involved in the specific circumstances they confront.

Notwithstanding this language, it might still be argued that there are a few search practices (such as eavesdropping and wiretapping, search of a private home during the nighttime, or intrusions into the human body) that, because of their unusual degree of intrusiveness, require more than the usual quantum of probable cause.

Probable cause may not be established simply by showing that the officer who made the challenged arrest or search subjectively believed he had grounds for his action. As emphasized in *Beck v. Ohio* (1964): "If subjective good faith alone were the test, the protections of the Fourth Amendment would evaporate, and the people would be 'secure in their persons, houses, papers, and effects,' only in the discretion of the police." The probable cause test, then, is an objective one; for there to be probable cause, the facts must be such as would warrant a belief by a reasonable man. (If the objective probable cause test is met, it is not also necessary to establish that the particular officer making the arrest or search subjectively believed probable cause was present.) Notwithstanding this objective test, the Supreme Court has made it clear that the expertise and experience of the officer are to be taken into account, which is as it should be. This usually means that a trained and experienced officer will have probable cause in circumstances when the layman would not, as when an officer is able to identify an illegal substance by smell, feel, or sight because of his training and experience. But sometimes an experienced officer will be held *not* to have had probable cause if a man with his special skills, though perhaps not a layman, should have recognized that no criminal conduct was involved.

Though the Supreme Court once held that a "search warrant may issue only upon evidence which would be competent in the trial of an offense before a jury," this is no longer the law. As explained in *Brinegar v. United States* (1949), in "dealing with probable cause, * * * we deal with probabilities," which "are not technical; they are the factual and practical considerations of everyday life on which reasonable and prudent men, not legal technicians, act," and thus the "standard of proof is accordingly correlative to what must be proved." Thus, information that would be inadmissible at trial on hearsay grounds may be used to show probable cause, as may a person's criminal record. But in *Spinelli v. United States* (1969), the Court characterized a general assertion of criminal reputation (i.e., that defendant was "known" as a gambler) as "a bald and unilluminating assertion of suspicion that is entitled to no weight" in determining probable cause.

The Court in *Brinegar* declared that "in dealing with probable cause, * * * as the very name implies, we deal with probabilities," but did not identify the degree of probability needed other than to say that "more than bare suspicion" and "less than evidence which would justify * * * conviction" was required. Some of the Supreme Court's decisions may be read as adopting a more-probable-than-not test, so that, for example, there would not be grounds to arrest unless the information at hand provided a basis for singling out but one person (though the Court's more recent decision in *Maryland v. Pringle* (2003), discussed in § 2.3(f), can be interpreted otherwise). But the lower court cases generally do not go this far, and instead merely require that the facts permit a fairly narrow focus, so that descriptions fitting large numbers of people or a large segment of the community will not suffice. This latter position has been defended on the ground that it strikes a fair balance between the interests of privacy and effective law enforcement, in that arrests for investigative purposes sometimes must be permitted upon somewhat general descriptions provided by crime victims and witnesses. If that is so, then it may be necessary to distinguish those cases in which the uncertainty goes not to who the perpetrator of the crime is but rather to whether any crime has occurred, as when the police observe a person engaging in suspicious activity. As to this latter situation, it is commonly said that an arrest and search based on events as consistent with innocent as with criminal activity are unlawful, so that if the observed pattern of events occurs just as frequently or even more than frequently in innocent transactions, then it is too equivocal to constitute probable cause. Utilizing the more-probable-than-not test here but not in the first situation is defensible on two grounds: (1) permitting arrests for equivocal conduct would result in more frequent interference with innocent persons than would permitting arrests upon a just-received somewhat general description from a crime victim or witness, as the latter is anchored in a time-space sense to known criminal activity; and (2) the law enforcement need is greater in the victim/witness description situation, as these cases often involve much more serious criminal activity as to which experience has shown that the likelihood of apprehending the offender is slight unless he is promptly arrested in the vicinity of the crime.

Probable cause is not defeated by an after-the-fact showing that the relevant provision in the substantive criminal law is unconstitutional. In reaching that conclusion in *Michigan v. DeFillippo* (1979), the Court reasoned: "Police are charged to enforce laws until and unless they are declared unconstitutional. The enactment of a law forecloses speculation by enforcement officers concerning its constitutionality—with the possible exception of a law so grossly and flagrantly unconstitutional that any person of reasonable prudence would be bound to see its flaws. Society would be ill served if its police officers took it upon themselves to determine which laws are and which are not constitutionally entitled to enforcement."

(c) Information From an Informant. The term "informant" is used here to describe an individual who learns of criminal conduct by being a part of the criminal milieu; it does not refer to the average citizen who by happenstance finds himself in the position of a victim of or a witness to a crime. The Supreme Court and other courts have with considerable frequency confronted the question of when probable cause may be said to exist exclusively or primarily upon the basis of information from such a person.

At issue in *Aguilar v. Texas* (1964) was a search warrant affidavit that stated: "Affiants have received reliable information from a credible person and do believe that heroin, marijuana, barbiturates, and other narcotics and narcotic paraphernalia are being kept at the above described premises for the purpose of sale and use contrary to the provisions of the law." The Court concluded this affidavit did not meet the requirements of the Fourth Amendment, because "the magistrate must be informed of some of the underlying circumstances from which the informant concluded that the narcotics were where he claimed they were, and some of the underlying circumstances from which the officer concluded that the informant, whose identity need not be disclosed, * * * was 'credible' or his information 'reliable.' " This two-pronged approach was also applied by the Court to police claims of probable cause to make an arrest or search without a warrant. Under the first or "basis of knowledge" prong, facts had to be revealed that permitted the judicial officer making the probable cause determination to reach a judgment as to whether the informant had a basis for his allegations that a certain person had been, was or would be involved in criminal conduct or that evidence of crime would be found at a certain place. By contrast, under the second or "veracity" prong of *Aguilar,* sufficient facts had to be brought before the judicial officer so that he could determine either the inherent credibility of the informant or the reliability of his information on this particular occasion.

But in *Illinois v. Gates* (1983), the Supreme Court, though casting not the slightest doubt upon the correctness of the result in *Aguilar,* decided

> to abandon the "two-pronged test" established by our decisions in *Aguilar* and *Spinelli*. In its place we reaffirm the totality of the circumstances analysis that traditionally has informed probable cause determinations. * * * The task of the issuing magistrate is simply to make a practical, common-sense decision whether, given all the circumstances set forth in the affidavit before him, including the "veracity" and "basis of knowledge" of persons supplying hearsay information, there is a fair probability that contraband or evidence of a crime will be found in a particular place. And the duty of a reviewing court is simply to ensure that the magistrate had a "substantial basis for * * * conclud[ing]" that probable cause existed. * * * We are convinced that this flexible, easily applied standard will better achieve the accommodation of public and private interests that the Fourth Amendment requires than does the approach that has developed from *Aguilar* and *Spinelli*.

The majority in *Gates* felt that the two-pronged test was too rigid and that it improperly accorded "these two elements * * * independent status," when in fact "a deficiency in one may be compensated for * * * by a strong showing as to the other." But Justice White (concurring because he found probable cause to exist by applying the *Aguilar* factors) noted that the *Gates* majority's claim that a deficiency as to one of the *Aguilar* prongs can be compensated for by a strong showing as to the other cannot be taken literally, for so interpreted, it would lead to the bizarre result (repeatedly rejected by the Court in the past) that the unsupported assertion or belief of an honest person satisfies the probable cause requirement.

Although *Gates* constitutes some "watering-down" of the probable cause standard as it had developed under *Aguilar,* this does *not* mean that lower courts are writing on a completely clean slate when they now confront the question of when an informant's information amounts to probable cause. Even the *Gates* majority agreed "that an informant's 'veracity,' 'reliability' and 'basis of knowledge' are all highly relevant in determining the value of his report." Because this is so, courts continue to rely upon the elaboration of these factors in earlier cases decided under the now-discarded *Aguilar* formula. (But it must be remembered, as the Court later emphasized, that *Gates* "did not merely refine or qualify the 'two-pronged test' " but instead abandoned it in favor of a "totality of the circumstances analysis.") Thus, while the discussion that follows relies in part upon several decisions predating *Gates,* it is nonetheless relevant on the question of what constitutes probable cause in the post-*Gates* era.

Police often attempt to establish the credibility of the informant on the basis of his past performance, as in *McCray v. Illinois* (1967), holding probable cause was established when the officer testified the informant had given him information about narcotics activities 15 or 16 times in the past, resulting in numerous arrests and convictions, and on cross-examination even named some of the persons convicted. But lower courts have consistently held that a declaration that the informant's past information led to convictions is a sufficient showing of the informer's credibility, even when information on a single past occasion produced a single conviction and even without any specific identification of the prior convictions. It will also suffice that on a prior occasion the informant said a certain object, such as narcotics, would be found at a certain place and that this information was verified by a search uncovering the object. It has frequently been held sufficient that the informant's prior information led to arrests, but the better view is that such an allegation is inadequate, as a mere statement the police decided to arrest on the prior occasion indicates nothing about the lawfulness of that arrest or whether anything learned incident to or following the arrest verified what the informant had said. And while cases may be found approving of assertions merely saying the informant's prior information proved to be "correct," "true and correct," "reliable" "reliable and accurate," or "valid," other decisions view such characterizations as conclusory and thus insufficient. Although *Gates* has occasionally been interpreted as approving such general assertions, that is incorrect. To view such allegations as alone establishing veracity would violate a cardinal principle reaffirmed by the *Gates* majority: "Sufficient information must be presented to the magistrate to allow *that official* to determine probable cause; his action cannot be a mere ratification of the bare conclusions of others." In any event, past performance relates only to the matter of veracity; as Justice White put it in *Spinelli v. United States* (1969): "The past reliability of the informant can no more furnish probable cause for believing his current report than can previous experience with the officer himself."

If no showing is made as to the informant's credibility, then it is necessary to consider whether it has been shown that the informant's information is reliable on this particular occasion. One means of showing this was recognized in *United States v. Harris* (1971), where the search warrant affidavit recited that the informant said he had purchased illicit whiskey from a named person for two years, most recently in the past two weeks, in the course of which he saw that person obtain the whiskey from a specified building. What appeared to be a majority of the Court concluded that the information given was shown to be reliable because it "was plainly a declaration against interest since it could readily warrant a prosecution and could sustain a conviction against the informant himself." The Court reasoned: "People do not lightly admit a crime and place critical evidence in the hands of the police in the form of their own admissions. Admissions of crime, like admissions against proprietary interests, carry their own indicia of credibility—sufficient at least to support finding of probable cause to search. That the informant may be paid or promised a 'break' does not eliminate the residual risk and opprobrium of having admitted criminal conduct." Certainly the admission-against-interest rationale is inappropriate when not even the police know the identity of the informant, for if the informant is not known to the police he stands no real risk of prosecution. It does not follow, as the *Harris* dissenters argued, that this is also the case if the informant's identity is known to the police but not disclosed to others. But such a case does call for particular caution, for if the informant's name is not disclosed then it is more likely (at least as a general proposition) that he is a person whose indiscretions are tolerated by the police on a continuing basis in exchange for information and who thus will perceive little risk in admitting such indiscretions. By comparison, there is much more reason to conclude that veracity is shown when the informant comes forward as an affiant or when his identity is disclosed in the affidavit or upon the motion to suppress. For a declaration against penal interest to establish reliability, the declaration must be unequivocal and have a sufficient nexus to the information critical to the probable cause determination.

Just how important it remains after *Gates* to show veracity in one of these ways is not entirely clear. The *Gates* majority says that the informant's veracity is still "highly relevant," but then asserts that a deficiency in that respect could be compensated for by a "strong showing" of basis of knowledge. Thus, "even if we entertain some doubt as to an informant's motives, his explicit and detailed description of alleged wrongdoing, along with a statement that the event was observed first-hand, entitles his tip to greater weight than might otherwise be the case." But surely the mere act of reciting a detailed account does not show veracity, nor does an informant's claim of first-hand knowledge. To conclude otherwise would be to put informants on the same footing as police and the victims of and witnesses to crime when, as Justice Brennan noted in his *Gates* dissent, "there certainly is no basis for treating anonymous informants as presumptively reliable."

The other prong of the now-abandoned *Aguilar* test concerned "basis of knowledge," which *Gates* teaches also remains a "highly relevant" consideration in determining the value of an informant's report. The most obvious and direct way of showing such a basis is by setting out for the benefit of the judicial officer who must make the probable cause decision an explanation as to exactly how the informant claims to have come by the information he gave to the officer. As Justice White explained in *Spinelli v. United States* (1969), "the informant must declare either (1) that he has himself seen or perceived the fact or facts asserted; or (2) that his information is hearsay, but there is good reason for believing it—perhaps one of the usual grounds for crediting hearsay information." But this does not mean that a basis of knowledge may be shown only in such a direct fashion. If there is not such a direct showing, said the Court in *Spinelli*, it may nonetheless be possible to assume a sufficient basis of knowledge from the wealth of detail that has been provided:

> The detail provided by the informant in *Draper v. United States* [1959] * * * provides a suitable benchmark. While Hereford, the Government's informer in that case, did not state the way in which he obtained his information, he reported that Draper had gone to Chicago the day before by train and that he would return to Denver by train with three ounces of heroin on one of two specified mornings. Moreover, Hereford went on to describe, with minute particularity, the clothes that Draper would be wearing upon his arrival at the Denver station. A magistrate, when confronted with such detail, could reasonably infer that the informant had gained his information in a reliable way. Such an inference cannot be made in the present case. Here, the only facts supplied were that Spinelli was using two specified telephones and that these phones were being used in gambling operations. This meager report could easily have been obtained from an offhand remark heard at a neighborhood bar.

If self-verifying detail can establish a basis of knowledge (clearly, it cannot show the informant's veracity), then exactly what kind of detail will suffice? What is needed, to put the proposition in the language of the *Gates* case, are details about matters sufficiently related to the criminal activity reported that it may be fairly concluded the informant "had access to reliable information of the * * * illegal activities." Such was the case in *Draper* because, as Justice White later explained in his *Gates* concurring opinion, the fact the informer could predict two days in advance what clothing Draper would be wearing suggested Draper "had planned in advance to wear these specific clothes so that an accomplice could identify him," and this gave rise to a "clear inference * * * that the informant was either involved in the criminal scheme himself or that he otherwise had access to reliable, inside information." By contrast, if in the *Aguilar* case the informant had been able to describe the furnishings inside the house (instead of, say, a particular furnishing in which it was indicated the drugs were stored), that would not give rise to such a "clear inference." It would only show that the informant or someone with whom he communicated had been in that house, and a direct assertion to that effect would not suffice to show basis of knowledge re the presence of drugs there.

Just how important it remains after *Gates* to show a basis of knowledge in one of these ways is not entirely clear. Though it is at least arguable that a basis of knowledge was established in that case, some of the majority's comments on this point are none too reassuring. As noted earlier, in abandoning the *Aguilar* two-pronged test the Court in *Gates* said that "a deficiency in one may be compensated for * * * by a strong showing as to the other." By way of example, the Court then declared that if "a particular informant is known for the unusual reliability of his predictions of certain types of criminal activities in a locality, his failure, in a particular case, to thoroughly set forth the basis of his knowledge surely should not serve as an absolute bar to a finding of probable cause based on his tip." But this assertion does not deserve to be taken too seriously, for as Justice White noted in his concurrence, the Court had "repeatedly held that the unsupported assertion or belief of an officer does not satisfy the probable cause requirement."

Although the *Spinelli* Court utilized the earlier *Draper* case to illustrate the self-verifying detail situation, *Draper* was not decided upon such a basis. Rather, *Draper* was based upon yet another device for rehabilitating what would otherwise be an insufficient or incomplete report of an informant: partial corroboration. Federal narcotics agent March had been told by an informant who had given him reliable information in the past that Draper would return from Chicago by train on one of two specified days; in addition, the informer gave a detailed physical description of Draper and of the clothing he would be wearing, and said that he would be carrying a tan zipper bag and that he habitually walked real fast. These details were not put before a magistrate. Rather, the agent maintained a surveillance at the train station and when the described person appeared as predicted he was arrested, resulting in the discovery of the heroin. In upholding the arrest and search, the majority in *Draper* emphasized that

> Marsh had personally verified every facet of the information given him by Hereford except whether petitioner had accomplished his mission and had the three ounces of heroin on his person or in his bag. And surely, with every other bit of Hereford's information being thus personally verified, Marsh had "reasonable grounds" to believe that the remaining unverified bit of Hereford's information—that Draper would have the heroin with him—was likewise true.

As for what kind or amount of corroboration is needed, *Gates* rejects the notion that corroboration of innocent activity will not suffice. "In making a determination of probable cause the relevant inquiry is not whether particular conduct is 'innocent' or 'guilty,' but the degree of suspicion that attaches to particular types of non-criminal acts." In that case, an anonymous letter said that a named couple made their living selling drugs, that the wife drives the car to Florida and flies back, after which the husband flies to Florida and drives back with a car full of drugs, and that another such trip was about to occur. A few days later the police determined that the husband had flown to Florida, and surveillance of him there established that upon arrival he took a taxi to a motel where his wife had rented a room and that the next day they left in his car and drove north on an interstate highway. On those facts a warrant to search the car and their residence was obtained. In concluding this amounted to probable cause, the *Gates* majority none too convincingly reasoned as follows: (1) the facts obtained by independent investigation were alone quite suspicious, as "Florida is well-known as a source of narcotics and other illegal drugs," and Gates' observed conduct "is as suggestive of a pre-arranged drug run, as it is of an ordinary vacation trip"; (2) the anonymous letter was then deserving of some weight, as the "corroboration of the letter's predictions that the Gates' car would be in Florida, that Lance Gates would fly to Florida in the next day or so, and that he would drive the car north toward Bloomingdale all indicated, albeit not with certainty, that the informant's other assertions also were true"; and (3) the details in the letter concerned "future actions of third parties ordinarily not easily predicted," thus suggesting the writer of the letter "also had access to reliable information of the Gates' alleged illegal activities." But, as the dissent quite properly notes, the corroboration in this case actually counts for very little. For one thing, the limited investigation established neither when the wife had gone to Florida nor whether the husband was making an immediate return trip to Illinois, and thus there was nothing inherently suspicious in what had been observed. For another, both the husband and wife had been seen together in Florida, thus disproving the assertion in the letter that they were never gone at the same time, a rather critical allegation because it squared with the further assertion that they already had "over $100,000 worth of drugs in their basement."

Upon a motion to suppress in a case where the prosecution claims information from an informant supplies probable cause, the defendant may seek the identity of the informant in an effort to learn whether the informant actually exists, whether he actually gave fruitful information in the past, and whether the informant actually gave the information alleged in this instance. Counsel will usually be thwarted in these efforts because of what is commonly referred to as the informer's privilege. In *McCray v. Illinois* (1967), the Court rejected the claim that defendants are *always* entitled upon demand to learn of the informant's name, and instead concluded "that it should rest entirely with the judge who hears the motion to suppress to decide whether he needs such disclosure as to the informant in order to decide whether the officer is a believable witness." This means that disclosure should be required on occasion, as when some aspect of the police conduct appears inexplicable if an informant actually reported what it is claimed he said. But, because it is difficult if not impossible to articulate a standard that sufficiently honors the informer's privilege and yet sufficiently guards against undetectable police perjury, a growing number of courts are utilizing the device of an *in camera* hearing, whereby the informant is produced privately for examination by the judge only.

(d) Information From a Victim or Witness. Although the Supreme Court has seldom had occasion to speak to the matter of victim-witness veracity, the Court has proceeded as if veracity may be assumed when information comes from the victim of or a witness to criminal activity, a position rather consistently taken by lower courts. But circumstances may make that presumption inoperative in a particular case; the cases holding veracity was properly presumed frequently emphasized that the police were unaware of any apparent motive to falsify. If the person who purports to have witnessed criminal activity is unwilling to identify himself to the police, then it would ordinarily be improper to presume reliability.

As for "basis of knowledge," one prong of the since-abandoned *Aguilar* test but now a "highly relevant" consideration under the *Illinois v. Gates* (1983) "totality of the circumstances" formula, it is generally not a major problem as to the so-called citizen-informer. Eyewitnesses by definition are not passing along idle rumor, for they have been the victims of the crime or have otherwise seen some portion of it. Great detail as to why the person was in a position to observe what was reported is not required, though some explanation regarding the basis of knowledge of the victim or witness is clearly called for when it appears the purported knowledge could have been obtained only by the utilization of some expertise beyond that of the typical layman.

In a victim-witness type of case there is seldom any serious problem presented concerning either veracity or basis of knowledge; rather, the major difficulty usually encountered is whether the information obtained from direct observation by a presumptively reliable person is complete and specific enough to constitute probable cause to search a particular place or (as is much more frequently in issue) to arrest a particular person. Sometimes the victim or witness can identify the perpetrator by name or by identifying his picture in police files, but more typically the police must act quickly on the basis of a description of the perpetrator. Even assuming that the Fourth Amendment probable cause test does not mean more-probable-than-not in this context (see § 2.3(b)), the description will not suffice if it was equally applicable to a great many individuals in the area. In determining what kind of description by a victim or witness together with what kind of attendant circumstances adds up to probable cause, the courts have considered these factors:

(1) Particularity of description. A victim or witness will typically describe the perpetrator in terms of some of the following characteristics: race, sex, age, height, weight, build, complexion, hair, and clothing. Generally, the more of these identifying characteristics that are available, the more likely it is there will be grounds to arrest a person found with most or all of those characteristics. But there is more to it than counting the number of points of comparison; consideration must be given to the uniqueness of the points of identification—the extent to which they aid in singling out a person from the general public.

(2) Size of the area. The time that has elapsed between the crime and the arrest is an important consideration, for it shows what distance the perpetrator of the crime could have traveled—the radius of the area within which the perpetrator might then be. If the elapsed time is short, such as five or ten minutes, then this area is fairly small, and a matching up of a person in the area with a rather general description that might not otherwise suffice will be adequate for probable cause.

(3) Number of persons in the area. The fewer persons about, the less chance there is that a description of a given particularity would fit persons other than the individual at hand. Thus, rather general descriptions have been found sufficient in the early morning hours when few persons were on the street.

(4) Direction of flight. Courts frequently take note of the fact that the police had been advised of the direction in which the

offender was fleeing on foot or by vehicle. This is appropriate, for it shows that of the total relevant area (measured by a radius the length of possible flight since the time of the crime), a particular slice is more likely than the rest to contain the individual or vehicle sought.

(5) *Actions by or condition of person arrested.* Illustrative of such additional facts are that the suspect was running in a direction away from the crime scene, that he was furtively looking back, or that upon a lawful stopping for investigation he gave an implausible explanation for his presence.

(6) *Knowledge that the person or vehicle was involved in other similar criminality on a prior occasion.* Thus the arrest of the occupants of a car for bank robbery was supported by the fact that the car was recognized as having been used to transport the fruits of an earlier robbery and one of the occupants was recognized as a person involved in that prior robbery.

(e) Information From or Held by Other Police. In *United States v. Ventresca* (1965), involving a search warrant affidavit reciting that certain events had been observed by the affiant's fellow officers, the Court in upholding the warrant stated: "Observations of fellow officers of the Government engaged in a common investigation are plainly a reliable basis for a warrant applied for by one of their number." Following the lead of *Ventresca,* lower courts have consistently held that another law enforcement officer is a reliable source and that consequently no special showing of reliability need be made as a part of the probable cause determination.

In *Ventresca,* the other officers passed on to the affiant the facts they had uncovered in their investigation, and thus that case is unlike the common situation in which a directive or request for action is circulated within or between law enforcement agencies unaccompanied by any recitation of the underlying facts and circumstances, resulting in an arrest being made by an officer who has never been told of the facts deemed to amount to probable cause. Such was the case in *Whiteley v. Warden* (1971), where a policeman arrested two men in response to a bulletin stating an arrest warrant for them had issued in another part of the state. After concluding the warrant was invalid because issued upon a conclusory complaint, the Court turned to the contention that the arrest was lawful because the policeman was entitled to assume that whoever authorized the bulletin had probable cause: "Certainly police officers called upon to aid other officers in executing arrest warrants are entitled to assume that the officers requesting aid offered the magistrate the information requisite to support an independent judicial assessment of probable cause. Where, however, the contrary turns out to be true, an otherwise illegal arrest cannot be insulated from challenge by the decision of the instigating officer to rely on fellow officers to make the arrest."

Thus, under the *Whiteley* rule police are in a limited sense "entitled to act" upon a communication through official channels. Although the Court did not elaborate upon that observation, it apparently means that the arresting officer is himself not at fault and thus should not be held personally responsible in a civil action or disciplinary proceedings if it turns out that there was no probable cause at the source. But when the question arises in the context of an effort to exclude evidence obtained as a consequence of action taken pursuant to the communication, then the question legitimately is whether the law enforcement system as a whole has complied with the requirements of the Fourth Amendment. This means that the evidence must be excluded if facts adding up to probable cause were not in the hands of the officer or agency that gave the order or made the request, for were it otherwise an officer or agency possessed of facts insufficient to establish probable cause could circumvent the Fourth Amendment by the simple device of directing or asking some other officer or agency to make the arrest and search.

Whiteley must in turn be distinguished from the case in which there has been no directive or request but the arresting or searching officer attempts to justify his action on the ground that other officers were at that time in possession of the necessary underlying facts. In such circumstances, the knowledge of other police cannot ordinarily be imputed to the arresting or searching officer, for to hold otherwise would encourage police officers to search on the hope that the total knowledge of all those officers involved in a case will later be found to constitute probable cause if the search is challenged. A contrary result has been reached when there was a close working relationship between the officer who acted and the officer who had the requisite information and in addition the circumstances indicate that had not the former officer acted the latter most certainly would have conducted the arrest or search himself.

(f) First–Hand Information. Although the kinds of suspicious events and circumstances that police on patrol confront are virtually infinite in their variety, there are a few recurring situations worth noting, such as where a person is arrested because of his association with a known offender, as in *United States v. Di Re* (1948). There, an OPA investigator was told by one Reed that he was to buy counterfeit ration coupons from one Buttitta at a certain place, so the investigator and a detective trailed Buttitta's car to the designated place. There they found Reed in the rear seat holding counterfeit coupons, and upon being asked he said he received them from Buttitta, the driver. Di Re, a passenger in the front seat, was also arrested on the theory that his presence indicated he was implicated in a conspiracy to knowingly possess counterfeit coupons, but the Supreme Court concluded that probable cause for his arrest was lacking:

> The argument that one who "accompanies a criminal to a crime rendezvous" cannot be assumed to be a bystander, forceful enough in some circumstances, is farfetched when the meeting is not secretive or in a suspicious hide-out but in broad daylight, in plain sight of passers-by, in a public street of a large city, and where the alleged substantive crime is one which does not necessarily involve any act visibly criminal. If Di Re had witnessed the passing of papers from hand to hand, it would not follow that he knew they were ration coupons, and if he saw that they were ration coupons, it would not follow that he would know them to be counterfeit. Indeed it appeared at the trial to require an expert to establish that fact. Presumptions of guilt are not lightly to be indulged from mere meetings.

Di Re intimates that when the offense does involve an "act visibly criminal," then the chances are substantially greater than a companion is more than a mere bystander, although it cannot be said that probable cause is always present upon those facts.

Di Re was distinguished in Maryland v. Pringle (2003), where an officer stopped a car at about 3 a.m. for speeding, searched the vehicle with the driver's consent, and found $763 of rolled-up money in the glove compartment and five glassine baggies of cocaine behind the upright back-seat armrest. The officer then told the three occupants (driver/owner Partlow, front-seat passenger Pringle, and back-seat passenger Smith) that if no one admitted ownership of the drugs he would arrest them all, which he did when the "men offered no information regarding the ownership of the drugs or money." Pringle was convicted on the basis of his later admission that the cocaine was his, and a unanimous Supreme Court concluded that confession was not the fruit of an unlawful arrest because Pringle had been arrested on probable cause, stating: "We think it an entirely reasonable inference from these facts that any or all three of the occupants had knowledge of, and exercised dominion and control over, the cocaine. Thus a reasonable officer could conclude that there was probable cause to believe Pringle committed the crime of possession of cocaine, either solely or jointly." The conclusion there was probable cause that Pringle alone was in possession of the drugs, never elaborated upon by the Court, is difficult to understand since Pringle seems a no more likely prospect than either of the other occupants of the vehicle, but might be explained on the notion that when the guilty party is almost certainly one of the three, then there is a sufficient probability of individual guilt as to each as to justify the arrest of all of them for post-arrest investigation. As for the notion the three men were in joint possession, the Court explained that "it was reasonable for the officer to infer a common enterprise among the three men" because the "quantity of drugs and cash in the car indicated the likelihood of drug dealing, an enterprise to which a dealer would be unlikely to admit an innocent person with the potential to furnish evidence against him." But since nothing was known about the association of the three men or when any drug dealing was to occur, and since also there is no information indicating that either the cash or the drugs were ever in the view of all occupants of the vehicle, it might be questioned whether the probable cause showing is any stronger than that found lacking in *Di Re*. The Court distinguished that case because of the statement therein that "[a]ny inference that everyone on the scene of a crime is a party to it must disappear if the Government informer singles out the guilty person," although it is not apparent that Reed's comment Buttitta had handed him the coupons would itself negate suspicion regarding Di Re, since it is doubtful Buttitta would bring a nonaccomplice with him to the scene of the intended felonious transaction.

Observation of furtive gestures is a factor that may properly be taken into account in determining whether probable cause exists. As the Supreme Court concluded in *Peters v. New York* (1968), "deliberately furtive actions * * * at the approach of strangers or law officers are strong indicia of mens rea, and when coupled with specific knowledge on the part of the officer relating the suspect to the evidence of crime, they are proper factors to be considered in the decision to make an arrest." Thus, if the police see a person in possession of a highly suspicious object and then observe that person make an apparent attempt to conceal that object from police view, probable cause is then present. But when no such object is seen and the officer merely observes a movement that could be an attempt to hide something, this does not amount to probable cause. Flight of a person from the presence of police does not alone amount to probable cause. But, as the Supreme Court recognized in *Peters,* flight is a "strong indicia of mens rea." Thus, a person's flight upon the approach of the police may be taken into account and may well elevate the pre-existing suspicion up to probable cause. But in some circumstances the flight will be so ambiguous that it cannot be considered even to that limited extent.

(g) Special Problems in Search Cases. Probable cause in arrest cases usually involves historical facts (i.e., is it probable that a certain person did at some *prior* time commit an offense), while in search cases the concern is always with facts relating to a current situation (i.e., is it probable that evidence of crime is *presently* to be found in a certain place). This is why search cases often present the unique problem of whether the information relied upon to establish probable cause has grown "stale." Illustrative is *Sgro v. United States* (1932), holding that there was not probable cause to search a hotel for illegal intoxicants where the affidavit alleged a purchase of beer there over three weeks earlier. But probable cause is not determined by merely counting the number of days between the time of the facts relied upon and the warrant's issuance, and thus, as stated in *Sgro,* the matter "must be determined by the circumstances of each case." One important factor is the character of the criminal activity under investigation; when the affidavit recites an isolated violation, probable cause ordinarily dwindles rather quickly with the passage of time, but when it recites facts indicating activity of a protracted and continuous nature the passage of time becomes less significant. Especially when the crime under investigation is not a continuing one, the nature of the property sought is an important factor, as is the opportunity those involved in the crime would have had to remove or destroy the items sought during the time that has elapsed. Because the time the facts relied upon occurred is critical in determining whether there is probable cause to search, failure to state when the alleged facts occurred is fatally defective, while statements that the events occurred "within" a specified period of time or "recently" will often but not inevitably be inadequate.

The more complicated probable cause determination that must be made in search cases may be said to include four ingredients: time; crime; objects; and place. Assuming no problem with respect to time (as discussed above), it is still necessary that there be established a sufficient nexus between (1) criminal activity, (2) the things to be seized, and (3) the place to be searched. Difficulties concerning whether the necessary relationships have been established can arise in an infinite variety of ways, but only a few illustrations will be given here. Even if the connection between things and places is clear beyond question, probable cause may still be lacking because it is not also shown to be probable that those items constitute the fruits, instrumentalities, or evidence of crime. Thus, an affidavit stating a truckload of lumber had been unloaded at defendant's residence at night makes it sufficiently probable that the lumber would be found there, but yet is defective because it fails to connect the lumber with any criminal offense. A second type of situation is that in which it is clear that certain identifiable items are connected with criminal activity, but the difficult question is whether it is probable that those items are to be found at the specified place. For example, if a warrant to search a person's apartment for drugs was based upon an affidavit disclosing that he had made an isolated street sale of drugs at a distant location, it might be doubted whether there had been a sufficient showing that he probably keeps a stash of drugs at the apartment.

§ 2.4 Search Warrants

(a) **When Warrant May Be Utilized.** Later sections of this Chapter define the various situations—such as search incident to arrest, search in response to exigent circumstances, and search by consent—in which the police may conduct a search without first obtaining a search warrant. By examination of the boundaries of those warrantless search categories, it may be determined when a search warrant *must* be obtained in order to conduct a lawful search under the Fourth Amendment. By comparison, the concern here is with whether there are some situations in which, because of what is sought, from whom it is sought, or how it would be obtained, not even the usual protections of the search warrant process will permit the search to be made. For example, whenever the seizure of large quantities of books or films or similar materials is contemplated for the purpose of bringing about their destruction as contraband, the protections afforded by the search warrant process will not suffice. Rather, under such circumstances there must be a prior judicial determination of obscenity in an *adversary* proceeding in order to avoid "danger of abridgement of the right of the public in a free society to unobstructed circulation of nonobscene books." That rule does not bar use of the usual search warrant procedures in order to obtain a limited number of copies of an allegedly obscene publication for evidentiary purposes. The usual warrant procedures will also suffice for seizure of a single copy of an allegedly obscene film, provided (i) that "a prompt judicial determination of the obscenity issue in an adversary proceeding is available at the request of any interested party," and (ii) that copying of the film is permitted "on a showing to the trial court that other copies of the film are not available" to the exhibitor pending that determination.

Some intrusions into the body are so extreme that they cannot be permitted at all, and some require more than the usual search warrant safeguards. In *Rochin v. California* (1952), the Court was confronted with a case in which the police made a forcible entry into Rochin's room and, upon observing him put two capsules in his mouth, unsuccessfully attempted to extract them by force, after which they took him to a hospital where a doctor forced an emetic solution through a tube into Rochin's stomach, resulting in vomiting by which the two capsules were retrieved. Characterizing this series of events as "conduct that shocks the conscience," the Court concluded the evidence had to be suppressed because the police actions violated Fourteenth Amendment due process. But in

Schmerber v. California (1966), where a physician took a blood sample at police direction from an injured arrestee over his objection, the majority ruled that the extraction of blood violated neither the due process clause nor the Fourth Amendment. The Court identified three factors that were critical to that holding: (i) there had been a "clear indication" that the extraction would produce evidence of crime, i.e, that defendant was intoxicated while driving; (ii) the test was "a reasonable one" in the sense that such tests are "commonplace" and involve "virtually no risk, trauma, or pain"; and (iii) the test "was performed in a reasonable manner," in that the blood was "taken by a physician in a hospital environment according to accepted medical practices." Similarly, court-ordered surgery has been allowed where (1) the evidence sought was relevant, could have been obtained in no other way, and there was probable cause to believe that the operation would produce it; (2) the operation was minor, was performed by a skilled surgeon, and every possible precaution was taken to guard against any surgical complications, so that the risk of permanent injury was minimal; (3) before the operation was performed the court held an adversary hearing at which the defendant appeared with counsel; and (4) thereafter and before the operation was performed the defendant was afforded an opportunity for appellate review. In *Winston v. Lee* (1985), the Supreme Court applied the *Schmerber* balancing test to the surgery issue by focussing "on the extent of the intrusion on respondent's privacy interests and on the State's need for the evidence," and concluded that in the case before it the lower court had properly declined to authorize surgery to remove a bullet. The Court placed particular emphasis upon two facts: (i) "the proposed surgery, which for purely medical reasons required the use of a general anesthetic, would be an 'extensive' intrusion on respondent's personal privacy and bodily integrity"; and (ii) the state's need for the bullet to establish that defendant was the robber shot by the victim was not high, as the state had "substantial additional evidence" that defendant was the robber.

Zurcher v. Stanford Daily (1978) concerned execution of a warrant at a newspaper's offices for photographs of demonstrators who had injured several policemen. The lower court had reasoned that the much less intrusive subpoena duces tecum should ordinarily be utilized against nonsuspects, and concluded "that unless the Magistrate has before him a sworn affidavit establishing proper cause to believe that the materials in question will be destroyed, or that a subpoena duces tecum is otherwise 'impractical,' a search of a third party for materials in his possession is unreasonable *per se,* and therefore violative of the Fourth Amendment." The Supreme Court disagreed, observing that there was nothing in the language or history of the Fourth Amendment to support such a distinction, and that the Amendment "has itself struck the balance between privacy and public need" by permitting issuance of warrants to search property in *all* cases upon a showing of probable cause. Dissenting Justice Stevens cogently responded that this history should not be controlling because the risk to third parties alluded to by the lower court was virtually nonexistent prior to the recent abandonment of the "mere evidence" rule. But he provided no answer to the other point made by the majority: "that search warrants are often employed early in an investigation, perhaps before the identity of any likely criminal and certainly before all the perpetrators are or could be known," so that as a practical matter it would seldom be possible for the police to show which seemingly blameless third parties were in fact involved in the criminal activity or sufficiently sympathetic to those who were involved to destroy or remove evidence implicating them.

The Court in *Zurcher* went on to reject the contention that the First Amendment ordinarily bars execution of a search warrant on the premises of a newsgathering organization, but did stress the need for courts to "apply the warrant requirements with particular exactitude when First Amendment interests would be endangered by the search." So too, courts have held that the Sixth Amendment does not preclude the issuance of warrants to search law offices, but that certain precautions may be needed, both in setting the scope of the search and in its mode of execution, because of the potential for undermining the attorney-client privilege and the work product doctrine, thereby chilling communication between lawyer and client and hampering trial preparation.

(b) The "Neutral and Detached Magistrate" Require-ment. The search warrant process is preferred because it involves a "neutral and detached magistrate" in the critical decision of wheth-er to permit the search, and thus it is necessary to ask what kinds of persons under what circumstances may be allowed to issue warrants under the Fourth Amendment. In *Coolidge v. New Hamp-shire* (1971), for example, the warrant was issued by the state attorney general, acting as a justice of the peace, although he had personally taken charge of the murder investigation to which the warrant related and was later to serve as chief prosecutor at trial. To the state's argument that the attorney general had in fact acted as a "neutral and detached magistrate," the majority responded "that there could hardly be a more appropriate setting than this for a *per se* rule of disqualification rather than a case-by-case evalua-tion of all the circumstances," as "prosecutors and policemen simply cannot be asked to maintain the requisite neutrality with regard to their own investigations." The courts are not in agree-ment as to whether this *per se* rule also applies when the person issuing the warrant had law enforcement responsibilities that did not or could not extend to the case for which the warrant was sought, but there is much to be said for the proposition that any effort to assess the neutrality of a law enforcement official in such instances on a case-by-case basis would involve the lower courts in a complicated fact-finding process better avoided by a prophylactic rule.

At issue in *Connally v. Georgia* (1977) was a warrant issued by an unsalaried justice of the peace who received five dollars for each warrant issued but nothing for reviewing and denying a warrant application. A unanimous Court held that a warrant issued under such circumstances violated the protections of the Fourth Amendment, considering that the justice's "financial welfare * * * is enhanced by positive action and is not enhanced by a negative action." The conduct of the magistrate in a particular case may also show that he was not then "neutral and detached," as is illustrated by *Lo–Ji Sales, Inc. v. New York* (1979), where a town justice issued an open-ended search warrant for obscene materials and then accompanied the police during its execution and made probable cause determinations at that time as to particular articles. In rejecting the claim that the on-the-scene determinations saved the warrant, the Court stated that there had been "an erosion of whatever neutral and detached posture existed at the outset" because the justice "allowed himself to become a member, if not the leader of the search party which was essentially a police operation."

The Court held in *Shadwick v. City of Tampa* (1972) that municipal court clerks could constitutionally issue *arrest* warrants for breach of municipal ordinances. A unanimous Court concluded that a "magistrate," in the Fourth Amendment sense, need not necessarily be a lawyer or judge, but "must meet two tests. He must be neutral and detached, and he must be capable of determining whether probable cause exists for the requested arrest or search." These tests were found to be met because the clerk worked within the judicial branch and, by virtue of his position, would be able to determine if there was probable cause as to "common offenses covered by a municipal code." *Shadwick* has been relied upon in holding that *search* warrants may be issued by nonlawyer commissioners or judges, but there is something to be said for the conclusion that search warrant cases are different because the probable cause issues are much more complex and likely to be beyond the ken of a layman.

(c) Oath or Affirmation; Record. The Fourth Amendment command that "no Warrants shall issue but upon probable cause, supported by Oath or affirmation," has prompted litigation concerning what information, transmitted in what fashion and under what circumstances, may be taken into account later in deciding whether a warrant was issued on probable cause. In *Whiteley v. Warden* (1971) the Court ruled that "an otherwise insufficient affidavit cannot be rehabilitated by testimony concerning information possessed by the affiant when he sought the warrant but not disclosed to the issuing magistrate," reasoning that a contrary rule would "render the warrant requirement of the Fourth Amendment meaningless." Where by statute or court rule a search warrant may issue only upon affidavit, a defective affidavit may not be saved by oral statements to the magistrate, even if they were given under oath. Such reliance on oral testimony does not violate the Fourth Amendment, and while it has been held that this is so even when no contemporaneous record was made, it has been persuasively argued that reliance upon oral testimony should not be allowed in such a case because there is too much leeway for after-the-fact rehabilitation of insufficient testimony. (Such utilization of oral testimony must be distinguished from the so-called oral or telephonic search warrant procedure authorized in some jurisdictions, whereby the affiant gives his sworn statement to the magistrate via telephone or other means of communication, after which if the magistrate approves issuance of the warrant he causes an original warrant to be prepared and orally authorizes the officer to prepare a duplicate warrant for use in execution; this procedure complies with the "Oath or affirmation" requirement and is not otherwise constitutionally defective.) Whether the information is transmitted orally or in writing, the "Oath or affirmation" requirement means the information must be sworn to. No particular ceremony is necessary to constitute the act of swearing; it is only necessary that something be done that is understood by both the magistrate and the affiant to constitute the act of swearing. The true test is whether the procedures followed were such that perjury could be charged therein if any material allegation contained therein is false. There is a split of authority as to whether a false-name affidavit, utilized to conceal the identity of an informer-affiant, meets that test.

(d) Probable Cause: The Facially–Sufficient Affidavit. Until *Franks v. Delaware* (1978), courts were split on whether a defendant could ever introduce additional evidence at a suppression hearing for the purpose of proving that some of the allegations in a facially-sufficient search warrant affidavit were false. The Supreme Court in *Franks,* rejecting the lower court's absolute ban upon such evidence, stressed several "pressing considerations": (i) "a flat ban on impeachment of veracity could denude the probable cause requirement of all meaning," as an officer could resort to false allegations and "remain confident that the ploy was worthwhile"; (ii) the hearing before the magistrate, because "necessarily ex parte" and "frequently * * * marked by haste," "not always will suffice to discourage lawless or reckless misconduct"; (iii) *Mapp* rejected the claim that alternative sanctions are likely "to fill the gap"; (iv) given the fact the magistrate's determination of the sufficiency of the evidence is now open to challenge at the suppression hearing, also allowing veracity challenges "would not diminish the importance and solemnity of the warrant-issuing process"; (v) probable cause is already at issue at the suppression hearing, and thus the claim this added challenge "will confuse the issue of the defendant's guilt with the issue of the State's possible misbehavior is footless"; and (vi) allowing a veracity challenge does not extend the exclusionary rule to a new area, as there is "no principled basis for distinguishing between the question of the sufficiency of an affidavit, which also is subject to a post-search re-examination, and the question of its integrity."

As for what inaccuracies jeopardize the warrant, the Court in *Franks* held it must be established "that a false statement knowingly and intentionally, or with reckless disregard for the truth, was included by the affiant in the warrant affidavit." This means, as the Court emphasized, that "allegations of negligence or innocent mistake are insufficient." *Franks* also emphasizes that the deliberate falsity or reckless disregard must be "that of the affiant, not of any nongovernmental informant." This means that if a private informer gives information to an officer who then is the affiant, reporting what he was told and why he has reason to consider the informer reliable (e.g., past experience with him), the defendant could challenge the accuracy of the officer's recitation of what he was told or why he believed the informer reliable, but may not raise the issue of whether in fact the informer was lying to the officer. *Franks* strongly intimates that the result would be otherwise if the officer-affiant received his information from another policeman, as the Court took note of its declaration on a prior occasion "that police could not insulate one officer's deliberate misstatement merely by relaying it through an officer-affiant personally ignorant of its falsity."

Franks leaves no doubt as to what consequences are to follow from the requisite inaccuracies. No hearing is needed unless "the alleged false statement is necessary to the finding of probable cause," and suppression is to occur only if the defendant proves perjury or reckless disregard *and* it then appears that "with the affidavit's false material set to one side, the affidavit's remaining content is insufficient to establish probable cause." To obtain a *Franks* hearing, the defendant must "point out specifically the portion of the warrant affidavit that is claimed to be false" and give "a statement of supporting reasons. Affidavits or sworn or otherwise reliable statements of witnesses should be furnished, or their absence satisfactorily explained." If that threshold showing is made, then a hearing is held at which the defendant has the burden to prove "by a preponderance of the evidence" that the challenged statements are false and that their inclusion in the affidavit amounted to perjury or reckless disregard for the truth. Without access to the informant it may be impossible for the defendant even to prove that the affiant (rather than the informant) lied, and thus it is to be doubted that this burden may constitutionally be imposed on defendant if at the same time the informer privilege is used to deny defendant the identity of the informant.

(e) **Particular Description of Place to Be Searched.** The Fourth Amendment provides that no warrants shall issue except those "particularly describing the place to be searched." Absolute perfection in description is not required; it is enough if the description is such that the officer with a search warrant can, with reasonable effort, ascertain and identify the place intended. As for urban premises, the common practice is to identify the place by street address. This is sufficient, but a street address is not essential when other descriptive facts identify the premises to be searched. Rural property is often described by giving the owner's name and general directions for reaching it, which will suffice. Problems arise when a facially-sufficient description is determined to be less precise than was assumed, as where the warrant refers to apartment 3 in a certain building but there are apartments with that number on each floor, or where identifying numbers and other descriptive facts do not all fit the same premises. In these circumstances, courts are inclined to permit officers to resolve the matter on the basis of other facts (e.g., owner's name) not in the warrant description but known to them from the affidavit or otherwise, or by making common-sense judgments as to which of the several descriptive facts was most likely mistaken. (While the Supreme Court in *Groh v. Ramirez* (2004), dealing instead with a lack of particularity as to the items to be seized, concluded that only information in the affidavit could be considered, and then only if the affidavit were incorporated by reference in the warrant and accompanied the warrant to the search scene, the Court emphasized it was dealing with a case where the warrant did not describe the items to be seized "at all," and distinguished other cases, such as where a warrant description contained "a mere technical mistake or typographical error.")

A search warrant for an apartment house or hotel or other multiple-occupancy building will usually be held invalid if it fails to describe the particular subunit to be searched with sufficient definiteness to preclude a search of one or more subunits indiscriminately. This is because the basic requirement of the Fourth Amendment is that the officers who are commanded to search be able from the particular description of the search warrant to identify the specific place for which there is probable cause. This means that, in the absence of a probable cause showing as to all the living units so as to justify a search of them all, a search warrant directed at a multiple-occupancy structure will ordinarily be held invalid if it describes the premises only by street number or other identification common to all the subunits located within the structure. A significant exception to that rule is: if the building in question from its outward appearance would be taken to be a single-occupancy structure and neither the affiant nor other investigating officers nor the executing officers knew or had reason to know of the structure's actual multiple-occupancy character until execution of the warrant was under way, then the warrant is not defective for failure to specify a subunit within the named building. This exception is sensible if narrowly construed so as to apply only when: (i) the multiple-occupancy character of the building was not known and could not have been discovered by reasonable investigation; (ii) the discovery of the multiple occupancy occurred only after the police had proceeded so far that withdrawal would jeopardize the search; and (iii) upon discovery of the multiple-occupancy, reasonable efforts were made to determine which subunit is most likely connected with the criminality under investigation and to confine the search accordingly.

A similar situation was involved in *Maryland v. Garrison* (1987), where police obtained and executed a search warrant for "the premises known as 2036 Park Avenue third floor apartment," only to discover thereafter that the third floor was divided into two apartments and that the contraband they had discovered was in the apartment of a person not theretofore suspected. The Court held the warrant itself was valid, though "we now know that the description of that place was broader than appropriate"; such a warrant is invalid, the Court explained, only if when obtained "the officers had known, or even if they should have known, that there were two separate dwelling units on the third floor." Similarly, the execution of the warrant was lawful as well, as "the officers' failure to realize the overbreadth of the warrant was objectively understandable and reasonable."

As for a warrant to search a vehicle, there are many descriptive facts that can be given: owner's or operator's name, make, model, year, color, license number, location, etc. A few of these, such as make-plus-license or make-plus-operator, are sufficient to meet the Fourth Amendment particularity requirement. Assuming an otherwise sufficient description, it is not necessary that the warrant indicate the location of the car or the name of the owner. When a warrant is issued for search of certain premises and "all automobiles thereon," it is likely to be vulnerable to attack because of insufficiency of description and lack of probable cause extending also to such vehicles. As for a facially-sufficient vehicle description that turns out to be partially erroneous because not all of the facts fit, the rule is the same as noted above as to premises: the warrant will still be upheld if other facts known by the executing officer or reasonable inferences by him as to where the mistake lies make it possible to identify a particular vehicle.

(f) **Particular Description of Things to Be Seized.** Another specific command of the Fourth Amendment is that no warrants shall issue except those "particularly describing the * * * things to be seized." Speaking of that limitation, the Supreme Court said in *Marron v. United States* (1927): "The requirement that warrants shall particularly describe the things to be seized makes general searches under them impossible and prevents the seizure of one thing under a warrant describing another." A particular description of the objects to be seized does aid in preventing general searches, as that description determines the permissible intensity and length of the search that may be undertaken in executing the warrant. As for the second objective of preventing the seizure of objects on the mistaken assumption that they fall within the magistrate's authorization, *Marron* goes on to say that "nothing is left to the discretion of the officer executing the warrant," but few warrants could pass such a strict test, and thus it is more accurate to say that the warrant must be sufficiently definite so that the officer executing it can identify the property sought with reasonable certainty. A third purpose underlying the particularity requirement, not mentioned in *Marron,* is to prevent the issuance of warrants on loose, vague or doubtful bases of fact. That is, the requirement of particularity is closely tied to the requirement of probable cause to search, under which it must be probable (i) that the described items are connected with criminal activity, and (ii) that they are to be found in the place searched. The less precise the description of the things to be seized, the more likely it will be that either or both of those probabilities has not been established. (By the same token, a clear statement of the objects to be seized will be defective if it is broader than can be justified by the probable cause showing.)

Consistent with these three purposes are certain general principles that may be distilled from the decided cases in this area. They are: (1) A greater degree of ambiguity will be tolerated when the police have done the best that could be expected under the circumstances, by acquiring all the descriptive facts reasonable investigation of this type of crime could be expected to uncover and by ensuring that all of those facts were included in the warrant. (2) A more general type of description will be sufficient when the nature of the objects to be seized are such that they could not be expected to have more specific characteristics. (3) A less precise description is required of property that is, because of its particular character, contraband. (4) Failure to provide all of the available descriptive facts is not a basis for questioning the adequacy of the description when the omitted facts could not have been expected to be of assistance to the executing officer. (5) An error in the statement of certain descriptive facts is not a basis for questioning the adequacy of the description if the executing officer was nonetheless able to determine, from the other facts provided, that the object seized was that intended by the description. (6) Greater care in description is ordinarily called for when the type of property sought is generally in lawful use in substantial quantities. (7) A more particular description than otherwise might be necessary is required when other objects of the same general classification are likely to be found at the particular place to be searched. (8) The greatest care in description is required when the consequences of a seizure of innocent articles by mistake is most substantial, as when the objects to be seized are books or films or the papers of a newsgathering organization. (9) The mere fact that some items were admittedly improperly seized in execution of the warrant does not mean that the warrant was not sufficiently particular. (10) The Fourth Amendment's particularity requirement does not require particularity with respect to the criminal activity suspected. (11) Some leeway will be tolerated where it appears additional time could have resulted in a more particularized description, where there was some urgency to conduct a search before the defendant had the opportunity to remove or destroy the evidence.

A defective description in the warrant sometimes may be saved by an adequate description in the affidavit. But in *Groh v. Ramirez* (2004) the Court held this is permissible only "if the warrant uses appropriate words of incorporation, and if the supporting document accompanies the warrant," apparently on the ground that even if the affiant is the executing officer and acted on the basis of the description in the affidavit, there would otherwise be lacking sufficient notice when a copy of the warrant was left with the occupant at the conclusion of the search warrant execution. While there was no such incorporation/accompaniment in *Groh*, where the warrant totally lacked the description of the things to be seized appearing in the supporting documents, it was argued that what had occurred was a reasonable warrantless search because the search "was functionally equivalent to a search authorized by a valid warrant," in that "the goals served by the particularity requirement are otherwise satisfied" because the executing officers proceeded on the basis of the description in the supporting documents. The Court rejected that premise, arguing somewhat unconvincingly that it was unclear the magistrate had intended to authorized a search of the scope requested, but then added that in any event the occupant's Fourth Amendment right to notice of the warrant's scope had not been afforded. (Whether the executing officer's claimed oral recitation of the things to be seized would suffice was not decided, as it was disputed whether a complete recitation had occurred.)

If a search warrant is issued to search a place for several items, but it is later determined that not all of those items are described with sufficient particularity or that probable cause does not exist as to all of the items described, it is often possible to sever the tainted portion of the warrant from the valid portion so that evidence found in execution of the latter will be admissible. Assume, for example, a warrant for a gun used in and money taken in a bank robbery, and assume also that there is probable cause to search for the gun and that it is particularly described but that there is either no probable cause or no adequate description of the money. If the police, while looking in a desk drawer for the gun, were to find money that by its wrappings clearly came from that robbery, the money would be admissible because found in plain view in execution of the valid part of the warrant. But if the money was found after the gun was located or by looking where the gun could not be (e.g., an envelope), the money would not be admissible.

(g) Time of Execution. Some jurisdictions provide by statute or court rule that a search warrant must be executed within a certain time after issuance, such as ten days, in which case execution after the specified time will result in exclusion of the evidence. Sometimes a delay in execution will amount to a Fourth Amendment violation, for such delay is constitutionally permissible only where the probable cause recited in the affidavit continues until the time of execution. It is possible, therefore, that an unconstitutional delay may have occurred notwithstanding execution within the time set by rule or statute, and, of course, notwithstanding the fact that the jurisdiction has set no fixed time within which warrants must be executed.

About half of the states restrict the execution of search warrants to daytime hours absent some special showing and authorization. One common restriction is that the affidavit must be "positive" the property sought is on the premises, which has not been read literally but has been construed to require a much stronger probability showing than otherwise would be necessary. A second, more sensible approach is to require a special showing of a need to execute the warrant in the nighttime. Relatively little attention has been given to the question of whether special limitations upon nighttime searches flow from the Fourth Amendment, but in *Gooding v. United States* (1974) three members of the Court took the view that a special showing of need for such a search was constitutionally required under the Fourth Amendment principle "that increasingly severe standards of probable cause are necessary to justify increasingly intrusive searches."

No special showing is needed to execute a search warrant for premises in the absence of the occupant, as such execution is not significantly different from that which would otherwise occur. An inventory is required in any event; the occupant if present could not necessarily detect or prevent a broader search; and the fact that such execution will likely require forcible entry is not a sufficient detriment to make a search unreasonable where a warrant based on probable cause has been obtained. As for when the execution of the warrant is deliberately timed to occur without being known to those living at or using the premises (e.g., entry to install wiretapping devices), which appeared to concern the Supreme Court in *Berger v. New York* (1967), the cases upholding the federal wiretapping law have stressed that normal investigative procedures were tried and failed or appeared unlikely to succeed. It has been intimated that some such showing might also be necessary for a so-called "surreptitious entry" warrant, authorizing police to enter and merely scrutinize an ongoing criminal operation (e.g., an illegal drug lab) within, permitted in some circumstances by federal legislation (18 U.S.C.A. § 1303a).

(h) Entry Without Notice. It is generally required, often by statute, that police give notice of their authority and purpose prior to making entry in the execution of a search warrant. This requirement, grounded in the Fourth Amendment, serves several worthwhile purposes: (i) it decreases the potential for violence, as an unannounced breaking and entering into a home could quite easily lead an individual to believe that his safety was in peril and cause him to take defensive measures; (ii) it protects privacy by minimizing the chance of entry of the wrong premises and even when there is no mistake, allows those within a brief time to prepare for the police entry; and (iii) it prevents the physical destruction of property by giving the occupant the opportunity to admit the officer.

Such notice is ordinarily required as a prerequisite to entry by force, by use of a pass key, or by merely opening a closed door. Whether passage through an open door is the kind of entry that ordinarily requires prior announcement is a matter that continues to divide the courts, though it would appear that the need for notice in such a case may depend upon other circumstances. Notice is not required when there is entry by ruse, as when an undercover agent gains access to premises, for in such circumstances the concerns underlying the notice requirement are not present. To comply with the notice requirement, police must identify themselves as police and indicate that they are present for the purpose of executing a search warrant, after which they may enter when admitted by an occupant or upon being refused admittance (which includes both affirmative refusal and failure to respond to the announcement).

The failure to respond situation was addressed in *United States v Banks* (2003). As for how long a wait is necessary before police may reasonably conclude they have been refused admittance, this depends upon whether, on the facts known to the police (e.g., the time of day, the size of the premises), it reasonably appears the occupant has had time to get to the door. The Court cautioned that a longer wait may be necessary when police make a forced entry, since they then should be more certain the occupant has had time to answer the door. But the foregoing limitations do not apply if, as a result of the delay, there are now exigent circumstances of the kind (discussed below) which, if existing earlier, would permit entry without notice. In such a case, the required waiting time is determined by the nature of the risk; e.g., if the risk is disposal of cocaine, the question is *not* how long it would take the occupant to get to the door, but how long it would take him to get to the bathroom or kitchen to flush the drugs down the drain. *Banks,* concerning execution of a warrant for cocaine, involved the latter situation. A unanimous Court, though conceding that the "call is a close one," concluded the 15–20 second wait by the police was sufficient, considering "the arrival of the police during the day, when anyone inside would probably have been up and around."

Police are excused from the usual notice requirement in some instances. For a time, some courts applied a so-called "blanket rule" regarding when notice was excused; for example, in some states felony drug cases were assumed to *always* carry a risk of evidence destruction and physical harm to the police sufficient to justify entry without notice. But in *Richards v. Wisconsin* (1997), the Court rejected that approach because of "two serious concerns": (i) such an exception "contains considerable overgeneralization," as "not every drug investigation will pose these risks to a substantial degree" (as illustrated by the situation in which "the only individuals present in a residence have no connection with the drug activity"); and (ii) "the reasons for creating an exception in one category can, relatively easily, be applied to others," so that a felony drug exception could lead to an armed bank robbers exception, and so on. And thus, the *Richards* Court ruled, the police are excused only when they "have a reasonable suspicion that knocking and announcing their presence, under the particular circumstances, would be dangerous or futile, or that it would inhibit the effective investigation of the crime by, for example, allowing the destruction of evidence." The Court then concluded the entry without notice in *Richards* was nonetheless lawful because, as the state trial judge had properly concluded, the facts of the particular case showed a sufficient risk of evidence destruction. Similarly, in *United States v. Ramirez* (1998), a case involving intended execution of a search warrant to enter and seize a wanted person, the Court upheld the challenged entry without notice because the police "had a 'reasonable suspicion' that knocking and announcing their presence might be dangerous to themselves or to others." While a small number of jurisdictions have adopted legislation permitting magistrates to issue so-called no-knock search warrants, it would appear that the Fourth Amendment does not require such a warrant, as the Court in another context has rejected the contention that "search warrants also must include a specification of the precise manner in which they are to be executed."

(i) **Detention and Search of Persons.** Police executing a search warrant sometimes search individuals found in the described place at the commencement of the warrant execution or who arrive there during the course of the search of that place. On occasion this occurs because the warrant describes certain premises and also a certain person. There is no inherent defect in a single warrant that authorizes search of a place and a person, and thus the search in such a case will be a valid execution of the warrant, subject of course to the possibility that upon a subsequent motion to suppress it will be found that the information supporting the warrant did not show probable cause as to the named person. A second kind of situation is that in which a person at the scene is arrested and then searched. This will constitute a valid search incident to arrest *if* the arrest was lawful, but it must be remembered that mere presence at a place for which the police have a search warrant does not alone constitute grounds to arrest.

If the person is not named in the warrant and cannot be lawfully arrested, the police may still desire to search him for the objects named in the search warrant. In *Ybarra v. Illinois* (1979), the state claimed that in such a situation the police should be entitled to search if there was only a reasonable suspicion, under the *Terry v. Ohio* (1968) standard, that this person had the named objects on his person. But the Court concluded that the interest in productive warrant execution was not so strong as to justify a departure from the usual probable cause standard, and thus the police may lawfully search the person on the premises only upon probable cause that he has the named objects on his person (not the case in *Ybarra,* where the person searched was merely a customer in a bar being searched for drugs). Another possibility is that the police will want to search persons present for their own protection, that is, to ensure they will not be attacked with weapons while they proceed with execution of the warrant; the Court in *Ybarra* concluded that the *Terry* frisk standard was applicable in this context, so that an officer may conduct such a limited search of persons present "to find weapons that he reasonably believes or suspects are then in the possession of the person he has accosted."

As for whether a person on the premises where a search warrant is being executed sometimes may be detained incident to execution of the warrant absent grounds for arrest, the Court answered in the affirmative in *Michigan v. Summers* (1981). Using the balancing test of the *Terry* case, the Court reasoned that such a detention was "substantially less intrusive" than a full-fledged arrest and served three important government interests: (i) "the legitimate law enforcement interest in preventing flight in the event that incriminating evidence is found"; (ii) "minimizing the risk of harm to the officers"; and (iii) "the orderly completion of the search," which "may be facilitated if the occupants of the premises are present." Although the *Summers* Court thus concluded that such a detention was permissible absent full probable cause, it is important to note that the Court did not merely extend *Terry* to this situation and require a case-by-case determination of whether there was reasonable suspicion sufficient to justify the detention. Rather, the Court opted to relieve police and lower courts of the necessity to engage in case-by-case balancing by announcing a general rule: detention of persons at the scene of a search warrant execution is permissible incident to that execution if (1) those persons are "occupants" (apparently meaning "residents," another term used by the Court), and (2) the warrant authorizes a "search for contraband" rather than a "search for evidence." This is a sensible rule, for it is in such circumstances that all three of the government interests mentioned above are likely to come into play.

(j) Scope and Intensity of the Search. A search made under authority of a search warrant may extend to the entire area covered by the warrant's description. For example, if the warrant authorizes a search of "premises" at a certain described geographical location, buildings standing on that land may be searched. If the place is identified by street number, the search may extend to those buildings within the curtilage and the yard within the curtilage. If the warrant specifies only a certain portion of a building, such as the first floor, only that portion may be searched, but if the warrant also refers to the curtilage the search may extend to such areas as courtyards, driveways and parking areas. Police may pass through areas adjacent to the described premises (so that what they see while doing so is a lawful "plain view") when such action is necessary to gain access to the described area.

In order to search containers in the described premises that might contain the items named in the warrant, it is not necessary that the warrant also describe those containers. But where the container is a personal item, caution is required, for the warrant will not inevitably extend to that item. In one case upholding search of a briefcase found in an office and known to belong to a co-owner of the business, the court reasoned that because he thus "had a special relation to the place, which meant that it could reasonably be expected that some of his personal belongings would be there," it was reasonable for the police to conclude that the warrant "comprehended within its scope those personal articles, such as his briefcase, which might be lying about the office." The situation would appear to be different, as to a search warrant for a residence, if the search were extended to suitcases known to belong to the tenant's overnight guest, but one court upheld a search on such facts on the ground that "it would be ineffective and unworkable to require police officers to make the distinction between which articles of clothing and personal property belong to the resident and which belong to the visitor before beginning to search." (While similar "practical realities" were an important consideration in the Supreme Court's holding in *Wyoming v. Houghton* (1999) that probable cause to search a vehicle permits search of packages belonging to passengers, *Houghton* does not itself encompass the present situation, as that holding was reached by a balancing of those realities against the "reduced expectation of privacy" that passengers have as to effects transported in vehicles.)

The permissible intensity of the search within the described premises is determined by the description of the things to be seized. As the Supreme Court has put it, "the same meticulous investigation which would be appropriate in a search for two small canceled checks could not be considered reasonable where agents are seeking a stolen automobile or an illegal still." This means the police may move objects to one side in the course of the search only if this will facilitate search into an area where the described items might be found. This means as well that in executing a warrant for certain documents, some innocuous documents will be examined, at least cursorily, in order to determine whether they are, in fact, among those papers authorized to be seized. And this also means that a search into closets, desks, boxes and other containers will exceed the authority of the warrant unless at least one of the items described in the warrant as an object of the search could be concealed therein. When the purposes of the warrant have been carried out, the authority to search is at an end. Thus, if the warrant describes only a particular package and it is found, any evidence discovered in a continuation of the search of the premises beyond that time must be suppressed. But under some circumstances, such as where the warrant authorizes search for "an unknown quantity of narcotics," the police apparently have a free hand—notwithstanding the quantity of the described item already found—to continue with the search until the entire described place has been covered. Police executing a search warrant are properly accompanied by others, even nonpolice, when the presence of the third parties directly aided in the execution of the warrant, as when the owner of sought stolen property was along to make identification, but it is a violation of the Fourth Amendment for the police to bring along persons whose presence is "not in aid of the execution of the warrant."

(k) **What May Be Seized.** At one time it was the rule that the "requirement that warrants shall particularly describe the things to be seized * * * prevents the seizure of one thing under a warrant describing another," but in *Coolidge v. New Hampshire* (1971) the Court held that unnamed objects "of incriminating character" could be seized under the "plain view" doctrine because where, "once an otherwise lawful search is in progress, the police inadvertently come upon a piece of evidence, it would often be a needless inconvenience, and sometimes dangerous—to the evidence or to the police themselves—to require them to ignore it until they have obtained a warrant particularly describing it." *Coolidge* has been properly interpreted to mean that there must exist probable cause that the object is a fruit, instrumentality or evidence of a crime.

The Court in *Coolidge* cautioned that a seizure based upon the plain view doctrine "is legitimate only where it is immediately apparent to the police that they have evidence before them; the 'plain view' doctrine may not be used to extend a general exploratory search from one object to another until something incriminating at last emerges." For many years, lower courts were inclined to permit a limited inspection of an object not named in the warrant, such as picking it up to note a brand name or serial number, *provided* there was a pre-existing reasonable suspicion the inspected item was were the fruit, evidence or instrumentality of crime. But that approach was rejected in *Arizona v. Hicks* (1987), holding full probable cause was needed to pick up an item of stereo equipment to ascertain its serial number (which revealed it was stolen property). The majority deemed it unwise "to send police and judges into a new thicket of Fourth Amendment law" by recognizing a third category of police conduct between "a plain-view inspection" requiring no suspicion and "a 'full-blown search'" requiring probable cause.

The most controversial aspect of the plain view doctrine as defined in *Coolidge* was the requirement that "the discovery of evidence in plain view must be inadvertent." Such a limitation is unsound, for it does nothing to prevent illegal entries or to limit the scope of searches under a warrant, but only protects the possessory interest of a defendant in his effects, an interest hardly worth protecting by a difficult-to-administer rule whereunder the police turn out to have greater power if it is *not* shown at the suppression hearing that they had probable cause. Such considerations doubtless influenced the Court to hold in *Horton v. California* (1990) that inadvertence "is not a necessary condition" to a plain view seizure. In *Horton,* the Court explained that adherence to the Fourth Amendment's particularity-of-description requirements "serves the interest in limiting the area and duration of the search that the inadvertence requirement inadequately protects."

(*l*) **Miscellaneous Requirements.** By statute or court rule, many jurisdictions have imposed requirements upon the execution of search warrants that go beyond those already discussed. One common provision is that an officer executing a warrant must exhibit or deliver a copy of the warrant at the place searched, so that the aggrieved party will know there is color of authority for the search. Another is that the officer must provide a receipt for the things seized in execution of the warrant. Yet another is that a prompt return of an executed warrant, accompanied by an inventory of the things seized, be made to the issuing authority. Under the traditional view, these provisions have been deemed ministerial only, so that failure to comply with them does not void an otherwise valid search, but in *Groh v. Ramirez* (2004) the Court concluded that while the Fourth Amendment does *not* require "serving the warrant on the owner before commencing the search," that Amendment was violated when the police at the conclusion of the search handed over a copy of a warrant that totally lacked specification of the things to be seized.

When a failure to leave an inventory serves to conceal from the absent occupant the fact that a search warrant execution occurred there, the problem is more serious. In striking down a state wiretapping law, the Supreme Court in *Berger v. New York* (1967) objected it "has no requirement for notice as do conventional warrants, nor does it overcome this defect by requiring some showing of special facts." (The problem is solved in the federal wiretapping law by the provision that an inventory must be served within 90 days.) The issue has recently arisen as to the so-called "surreptitious entry" warrant authorizing police to enter and look around during the occupant's absence, as to which the warrant must provide explicitly for notice within a reasonable, but short, time subsequent to the surreptitious entry.

In the context of a civil action to recover seized tangible property, the Supreme Court in *City of West Covina v. Perkins* (1999) concluded that a notice requirement exists as a matter of

Fourteenth Amendment due process. The Court declared "that when law enforcement agents seize property pursuant to warrant, due process requires them to take reasonable steps to give notice that the property has been taken so the owner can pursue available remedies for its return." In the instant case the police had left at the premises where a search warrant was executed a notice of the warrant execution and an inventory of the property seized, so the Court did not have to "decide how detailed the notice of the seizure must be or when the notice must be given." But the Court did go on to hold that there is no constitutional requirement of "individualized notice of state-law remedies which, like those at issue here, are established by published, generally available statute and case law." Because of the context of the *Perkins* case, the Court had no occasion to consider whether violation of the due process notice requirement recognized there could serve as a basis for suppression of the seized evidence in a criminal prosecution.

§ 2.5   Seizure and Search of Persons and Personal Effects

(a) **Arrest.** "To deprive a person of his liberty by legal authority" is the traditional definition of arrest, and for many years courts tended to accept such a definition, so that a mere stopping of a vehicle constituted an illegal arrest if probable cause could be established only by consideration of facts obtained subsequent to the stopping. But this is no longer true in light of *Terry v. Ohio* (1968), which established (i) that a seizure need not be called an arrest in order to subject it to the requirements of the Fourth Amendment; and (ii) that a seizure that is limited in its intrusiveness may be reasonable under the Fourth Amendment even in the absence of the probable cause traditionally required for arrest.

If a person is stopped upon less than probable cause, after which the officer sees incriminating evidence, it must be determined whether this amounts to an illegal arrest at the moment of stopping, as the defendant will claim, or a lawful arrest after observation of the evidence, as the prosecution will contend. Though the fact the officer did not make a formal announcement of arrest is not controlling, it is sometimes said that for police restraint to be an arrest it must have been performed with the intent to effect an arrest and must have been so understood by the party arrested. But, while the prosecution can hardly deny the existence of an arrest in the face of both of these elements, this is not to say that the absence of one or the other always necessitates the conclusion there was yet no arrest. Because making the issue turn upon either the subjective intent of the police officer or the subjective perception of the suspect would mean that the matter would be decided by swearing contests, courts are now inclined to use an objective test. The question is said to be what a reasonable man, innocent of any crime, would have thought had he been in the defendant's shoes. Essentially the same approach is taken when the issue is not whether there was an arrest or some lesser seizure, but instead whether there was an arrest or merely a nonseizure voluntary presence by the defendant.

The question of when an arrest occurred cannot be answered in the abstract, that is, without consideration of why the question is being asked. Courts properly take a somewhat different approach when the prosecution is contending that an arrest was made at a particular time so as to justify a search as incident to that arrest. In this context, the prosecution must be able to date the arrest as *early* as it chooses following the obtaining of probable cause, for given grounds for arrest and some degree of seizure that ripened into an arrest thereafter, the search should not be brought into question by speculation about the precise point at which the arrest occurred.

At common law, a peace officer was authorized to arrest a person for a felony without first obtaining an arrest warrant whenever he had "reasonable grounds to believe" that a felony had been committed and that the person to be arrested had committed it (i.e., what now constitutes Fourth Amendment probable cause). Under this approach, followed today by most jurisdictions, an arrest warrant is not required in a felony case even when it was feasible to obtain one. But it was not until *United States v. Watson* (1976), the first square holding that the Fourth Amendment permits a duly authorized law enforcement officer to make a warrantless arrest in a public place even though he had adequate opportunity to procure a warrant after developing probable cause for arrest, that the constitutionality of this rule was settled. The Court in *Watson* commenced with the proposition that a "strong presumption of constitutionality" was due the statute under which the arrest was made, and then concluded the presumption was not overcome in light of the fact that the statute was consistent with "the Court's prior cases," "the ancient common-law rule," and "the prevailing rule under state constitutions and statutes." The Court declined to transform its oft-stated preference for arrest warrants "into a constitutional rule" and thereby "encumber litigation with respect to the existence of exigent circumstances, whether it was practicable to get a warrant, whether the suspect was about to flee, and the like."

The common law rule with respect to misdemeanors was quite different: a warrant was required except when the offense occurred in the presence of the arresting officer, and some cases and commentators added a second requirement that the offense in question constitute a "breach of the peace." But because of the "divergent conclusions" reached on the latter point prior to adoption of the Fourth Amendment, as well as the fact that the post-Amendment history "is of two centuries of uninterrupted (and largely unchallenged) state and federal practice permitting warrantless arrests for misdemeanors not amounting to or involving breach of the peace," the Supreme Court in *Atwater v. City of Lago Vista* (2001) rejected the claim that this breach-of-the-peace limitation is a part of the Fourth Amendment's reasonableness requirement. Most jurisdictions now follow a broader rule, usually that arrest without warrant is proper for *any* misdemeanor occurring in the officer's presence, sometimes that the felony arrest rule applies also to misdemeanors, and sometimes the middle position that warrantless misdemeanor arrests are permitted on probable cause if certain exigent circumstances are believed to be present. It appears that the Fourth Amendment presents no barrier to abolition of the felony-misdemeanor distinction so as to permit warrantless arrests on probable cause in all cases. Under the "in presence" test, the prevailing view is that the officer may arrest if he has probable cause to believe the offense is being committed in his presence, provided the warrantless arrest is made at the time of the offense or as soon thereafter as circumstances permit.

Though under *Watson* an officer may arrest without first obtaining a warrant, the Court in *Gerstein v. Pugh* (1975) decided that the officer's probable cause assessment justified only the arrest and "a brief period of detention to take the administrative steps incident to arrest." At that point, "the reasons that justify dispensing with the magistrate's neutral judgment evaporate," as there is "no longer any danger that the suspect will escape or commit further crimes while the police submit their evidence to a magistrate." Consequently, the Court held in *Gerstein* "that the Fourth Amendment requires a judicial determination of probable cause as a prerequisite to extended restraint on liberty following arrest." This post-arrest probable cause showing, the Court added, may be made "without an adversary hearing" because the standard "is the same as that for arrest," which "traditionally has been decided by a magistrate in a nonadversary proceeding on hearsay and written testimony." This means the required procedure here is essentially like that utilized to obtain an arrest warrant; the magistrate must be given the underlying facts rather than more conclusions, and a complaint merely reciting the charge in the language of the statute will not suffice. *Gerstein* says the determination is to be made "promptly after arrest," but left the states with the "flexibility" to incorporate the requisite post-arrest probable cause determination into other pretrial procedures (e.g., defendant's first appearance in court). Taking both interests into account, the Court later concluded in *County of Riverside v. McLaughlin* (1991) that (1) a probable cause determination within 48 hours of arrest is presumptively reasonable, though a particular defendant may show such a delay was unreasonable because "for the purpose of gathering additional evidence to justify the arrest, a delay motivated by ill will against the arrested individual, or delay for delay's sake"; and (2) a later probable cause determination is presumptively unreasonable, meaning "the burden shifts to the government to demonstrate the existence of a bona fide emergency or other extraordinary circumstance" (i.e., something more than an intervening weekend or a desire to consolidate the probable cause determination with other pretrial proceedings). As for which defendants arrested without a warrant are entitled to a post-arrest probable cause determination, *Gerstein* clearly applies to a defendant who is unable to obtain his release on bail and consequently is held in jail pending trial, and probably applies as well when release is accompanied by substantial restraints.

The requirement of the Fourth Amendment that no warrant shall issue, but upon probable cause, supported by oath or affirmation and particularly describing the person or things to be seized, applies to arrest warrants as well as search warrants, and thus much of what has been said earlier with respect to the issuance of search warrants (see § 2.4) applies also to the obtaining of arrest warrants. For one thing, the warrant must be issued by a "neutral and detached magistrate." This is not to say that the authority to issue arrest warrants must "reside exclusively in a lawyer or judge," for a court clerk may constitutionally be given that power if he works within the judicial branch under the supervision of a judge and, though not law-trained, is capable of making the kinds of probable cause judgments needed in the category of cases that may come before him. For another, the warrant may issue only upon probable cause, and this requires a sworn complaint or testimony setting out the underlying facts and circumstances. A conclusory information sworn by the prosecutor will not suffice, but an indictment "fair on its face" returned by a "properly constituted grand jury" conclusively determines the existence of probable cause and requires issuance of an arrest warrant without further inquiry. Also, to meet the Fourth Amendment particularity requirement an arrest warrant must name the person to be arrested or give other facts that permit his identification with reasonable certainty. An arrest made pursuant to a previously issued warrant is not inevitably valid, for while an officer is entitled to assume that the warrant was issued upon the information requisite to support an independent judicial assessment of probable cause, if it turns out that this was not the case or that the arrest warrant was invalid in some other respect, the arrest cannot be upheld on the basis of the warrant. faith and had reasonable, articulable grounds to believe that the suspect was the intended arrestee.

A warrant to arrest a person as the perpetrator of a crime requires a showing of probable cause the named individual has committed that crime, but (as with warrantless arrests, as discussed below) does not in addition require any showing of a need to take custody. To be distinguished from the traditional arrest warrant in that respect is an arrest warrant for a material witness. It has been held that under the Fourth Amendment such arrest is permissible only upon a need-for-custody showing. Hence the conclusion that a material witness arrest warrant must be based upon probable cause, which must be tested by two criteria: (a) that the testimony of a person is material, and (2) that it may become impracticable to secure his presence by subpoena. The view that the first of these could be met by "a mere statement by a responsible official, such as the United States Attorney," when later subjected to a Fourth Amendment challenge, has been upheld on the ground that such an approach "strikes a proper and adequate balance between protecting the secrecy of the grand jury's investigation and subjecting an individual to an unjustified arrest." The authority to arrest and detain a person as a material grand jury witness has been increasingly relied upon especially since the 9/11/01 terrorist attack; an appellate court has rejected a district court's conclusion "that the federal material witness statute * * * does not authorize the detention of material witnesses for a grand jury investigation." The district court had concluded that the term "criminal proceeding" in the statute does not encompass grand jury proceedings because, inter alia, in such a context the judge would be unable to make a materiality determination because of grand jury secrecy.

Over the years, the prevailing assumption in most jurisdictions has been that, except for minor traffic violations, arrest is the normal way by which to invoke the criminal process. This state of affairs has rightly been criticized, and various recent law reform efforts have stressed the need for broader use of the citation alternative. As for the notion that the Fourth Amendment's reasonableness requirement is met only when probable cause is present *and* an actual need for custody exists, a bare majority of the Supreme Court has found such a claim less than persuasive. The case is *Atwater v. City of Lago Vista* (2001), a § 1983 action brought by a woman who had been subjected to a custodial arrest for misdemeanor seat belt violations punishable only by a $50 fine, pursuant to a statute allowing the officer total discretion to opt for either custodial arrest or issuance of a citation. The plaintiff's argument was that the Fourth Amendment reasonableness requirement mandated "a modern arrest rule * * * forbidding custodial arrest, even upon probable cause, when conviction could not ultimately carry any jail time and when the government shows no compelling need for immediate detention." But the *Atwater* majority, although conceding that any balancing of the interests in this particular case would certainly favor the plaintiff, concluded that the general rule required for her to prevail would lack "the values of clarity and simplicity" needed for any rule intended to govern a police decision made "on the spur (and in the heat) of the moment." In particular, police would be confounded by the necessity of making case-by-case judgments as to whether the offense in question was of the "jailable" or "fine-only" variety, and as to whether there was present some special circumstance justifying a taking of custody. Placing that burden upon the police, the majority opined, was not worth the candle, considering the substantial doubts "whether warrantless misdemeanor arrests need constitutional attention" absent a showing of "anything like an epidemic of unnecessary minor-offense arrests."

But *Watson*, the Court cautioned in *Tennessee v. Garner* (1985), should not be read as meaning that if the probable cause "requirement is satisfied the Fourth Amendment has nothing to say about *how* that seizure is made." Thus, the Court in *Garner* held that "use of deadly force to prevent the escape of all felony suspects, whatever the circumstances, is constitutionally unreasonable," but "if the suspect threatens the officer with a weapon or there is probable cause to believe that he has committed a crime involving the infliction or threatened infliction of serious physical harm, deadly force may be used if necessary to prevent escape, and if, where feasible, some warning has been given." As the Court elaborated on a subsequent occasion, the Fourth Amendment reasonableness standard (1) applies to "*all* claims that law enforcement officers have used excessive force—deadly or not—in the course of an arrest, investigatory stop, or other 'seizure' of a free citizen"; (2) "requires careful attention to the facts and circumstances of each particular case, including the severity of the crime at issue, whether the suspect poses an immediate threat to the safety of the officers or others, and whether he is actively resisting arrest or attempting to evade arrest by flight"; (3) "must embody allowance for the fact that police officers are often forced to make split-second judgments—in circumstances that are tense, uncertain, and rapidly evolving—about the amount of force that is necessary in a particular situation"; and (4) asks "whether the officers' actions are 'objectively reasonable' in light of the facts and circumstances confronting them, without regard to their underlying intent or motivation."

(b) Search of the Person at Scene of Prior Arrest. In *Chimel v. California* (1969), the Court declared that when an arrest is made "it is reasonable for the arresting officer to search the person arrested in order to remove any weapons that the latter might seek to use in order to resist arrest or effect his escape" and also "to search for and seize any evidence on the arrestee's person in order to prevent its concealment or destruction." This language highlighted a very significant issue that the Court did not have to resolve on that occasion: whether, on the one hand, the right to make such searches of the person flows automatically from the fact a lawful arrest was made, or whether, on the other, such searches may be undertaken only when the facts of the individual case indicate some likelihood that either evidence or weapons will be found. Lower courts were divided on the issue until the Supreme Court, in *United States v. Robinson* (1973) and the companion case of *Gustafson v. Florida* (1973), held that the broader view was consistent with the protections of the Fourth Amendment. In *Robinson,* where heroin had been found in a cigarette package in defendant's pocket following his arrest for driving after revocation of his license, the court of appeals held the search to be unreasonable because there was no evidence to search for, given the nature of the offense, and because the officer's interest in self-protection could have been met by only a frisk of the arrestee. But the Supreme Court, noting its "fundamental disagreement" with the court of appeals' "suggestion that there must be litigated in each case the issue of whether or not there was present one of the reasons supporting the authority for a search of the person incident to a lawful arrest," concluded:

> A police officer's determination as to how and where to search the person of a suspect whom he has arrested is necessarily a quick ad hoc judgment which the Fourth Amendment does not require to be broken down in each instance into an analysis of each step in the search. The authority to search the person incident to a lawful custodial arrest, while based upon the need to disarm and to discover evidence, does not depend on what a court may later decide was the probability in a particular arrest situation that weapons or evidence would in fact be found upon the person of the suspect. A custodial arrest of a suspect based on probable cause is a reasonable intrusion under the Fourth Amendment; that intrusion being lawful, a search incident to the arrest requires no additional justification. It is the fact of the lawful arrest which establishes the authority to search, and we hold that in the case of a lawful custodial arrest a full search of the person is not only an exception to the warrant requirement of the Fourth Amendment, but is also a "reasonable" search under that Amendment.

The majority in *Robinson* justified this result by claiming that the prior decisions of the Court and also the "original understanding" of the Fourth Amendment established that the "general authority" to search a person incident to arrest is "unqualified."

There is reason for concern about the application of this "general authority" to search in cases involving traffic violations. "There is," as the *Robinson* dissenters put it, "always the possibility that a police officer, lacking probable cause to obtain a search warrant, will use a traffic arrest as a pretext to conduct a search." What avenues are open to deal with the pretext arrest problem, which the *Robinson* majority preferred to "leave for another day"? The most obvious is to meet it head on by excluding evidence obtained in a search incident to a traffic arrest upon a showing that the arrest was nothing more than a pretext to search for evidence. But this result has been virtually foreclosed as a result of the Supreme Court's decision in *Whren v. United States* (1996) (discussed in § 2.1(d)) that when a purportedly pretextual traffic stop has been made on sufficient evidence of the traffic violation, no Fourth Amendment challenge may be undertaken on the grounds that "the actual motivations of individual officers" was to stop in order to investigate some other offense or that "the officer's conduct deviated materially from usual police practices." Another way of dealing with the problem might be to remove the temptation to engage in pretext arrests by broadening the exclusionary rule so as to exclude from evidence anything but a weapon found in a search incident to an arrest for a crime, such as a traffic violation, for which there existed no justification to search for anything but a weapon. However, the Supreme Court has not indicated it is receptive to such an extension of the exclusionary rule. Yet another possibility, inasmuch as *Robinson* declares what may be done incident to a "custodial arrest," (i.e., a seizure of the person with the intention of thereafter having him transported to the police station or other place to be dealt with according to law), would be to require that there be established by legislation or police regulation some rational scheme for determining when a noncustodial alternative (i.e., a citation) should be utilized as the means for invoking the criminal process. But when the Supreme Court nearly thirty years later finally confronted that issue head on in *Atwater*, a bare majority of the Court rejected the proposition that such a requirement could be derived from the Fourth Amendment's reasonableness requirement.

The other issue considered by the court of appeals in *Robinson*, what the officer could do in the absence of a "custodial arrest," was not reached by the Supreme Court in that case but was later resolved in part in *Knowles v. Iowa* (1998). An officer stopped Knowles for speeding and then, pursuant to a statute authorizing but not requiring him to issue a citation in lieu of arrest for most bailable offenses, issued a citation. The officer then made a full search of Knowles' car and found a bag of marijuana. That search was upheld by the state courts on the ground that because a state statute declared that issuance of a citation in lieu of arrest "does not affect the officer's authority to conduct an otherwise lawful search," it sufficed that the officer had probable cause to make a custodial arrest. A unanimous Supreme Court reversed on the ground that the two search-incident-arrest rationales discussed in *Robinson* did not justify the search in the instant case. The "threat to officers safety from issuing a traffic citation * * * is a good deal less than in the case of a custodial arrest," where (as it was put in *Robinson*) there is "the extended exposure which follows the taking of a suspect into custody and transporting him to the police station." And thus the "concern for officer safety" incident to a traffic stop is sufficiently met by the officer's authority under existing decisions of the Court: he could order the driver and passengers out of the car, "perform a 'patdown' of a driver and any passengers upon a reasonable suspicion they may be armed and dangerous," and conduct a patdown "of the passenger compartment of a vehicle upon reasonable suspicion that an occupant is dangerous and may gain immediate control of a weapon." As for the "need to discover and preserve evidence," the Court continued, there was no such need in the instant case, as "no further evidence of excessive speed was going to be found on the person of the offender or in the passenger compartment of the car." Thus left unresolved in *Knowles* was the question of whether, incident to citation for an offense for which there *could be* evidence on the person or in the vehicle, the officer would have the search authority he would have if he instead had opted for custodial arrest, or whether instead any search would have to be justified on the ground that there existed probable cause to *search* (a question distinct from whether there is probable cause to arrest).

Police sometimes find it necessary to employ force in conducting a search of a person at the arrest scene. Such force cannot be used as a matter of course as a part of the previously discussed "standardized procedures," and thus it is necessary at the outset that the officer act on probable cause to believe that specific evidence is being disposed of. If that is the case, then the police may use reasonable force to prevent loss of the evidence. The problem usually arises when the arrestee attempts to swallow evidence, as to which the police may properly respond by forcing open his mouth or choking him to the extent necessary to prevent swallowing of the evidence.

(c) Search of the Person During Post–Arrest Detention.
When an arrested person has been delivered to the place of his forthcoming detention, he may be subjected to a rather complete search of his person. One ground upon which such searches are commonly upheld is as a search incident to arrest; in *United States v. Edwards* (1974) the Court held "that searches and seizures that could be made on the spot at the time of arrest may legally be conducted later when the accused arrives at the place of detention." As already noted, no advance probable cause is needed to justify such a search except that which establishes grounds for the preceding arrest.

A second theoretical justification for search of an arrestee's person upon his arrival at the station is that of inventory incident to his booking into jail. This inventory, which is a search for Fourth Amendment purposes, has been rather consistently upheld by the courts as meeting these legitimate objectives: (1) protecting the arrestee's property while he is in jail; (2) protecting the police from groundless claims that they have not adequately safeguarded the defendant's property; (3) safeguarding the detention facility by preventing introduction therein of weapons or contraband; and (4) ascertaining or verifying the identity of the person arrested. That view has been taken by the Supreme Court where "standardized inventory procedures" have been followed, even if the contents of containers such as a purse are examined in the process. In those few jurisdictions that have adopted a search-incident-to-arrest rule narrower than *Robinson,* the extent of legitimate inventory activity is likely to be litigated and on occasion results in a decision imposing limits grounded in state law upon that conduct, such as that the inventory may not extend to closed containers.

Assuming a lawful search upon defendant's arrival at the station, there remains the question of what may be seized. There is authority that here as with search at the arrest scene, objects may be seized only upon probable cause that they constitute evidence, instrumentalities or fruits of crime, while another view is that after a person has been deprived of the possession of his property upon being incarcerated, he may not thereafter complain if police have his property examined. The latter position makes sense only if an arrestee has no privacy interest in the effects being held for him, an issue that is raised more directly by consideration of whether the arrestee and his effects remain legitimate targets of search during the entire period of custody.

An issue of that kind reached the Supreme Court in *United States v. Edwards* (1974), where defendant was arrested and jailed for attempting to break into a post office and then, a day later, his clothing was taken from him to determine whether it contained paint chips from the window the burglar had tried to pry open. The

Court upheld this warrantless search, reasoning "that Edwards was no more imposed upon than he could have been at the time and place of the arrest or immediately upon arrival at the place of detention," and that "it is difficult to perceive what is unreasonable about the police examining and holding as evidence those personal effects of the accused that they already have in their lawful custody as the result of a lawful arrest." In trying to identify the scope of the *Edwards* holding, it is useful to note at the outset that the broad issue of whether an arrestee's person and effects remain "fair game" for search during his incarceration can be broken down into two inquiries: whether a warrant is required; and whether probable cause the search will produce evidence is required. In *Edwards* the Court focused on the warrant issue and concluded no warrant was needed, hardly a surprising result because, though there were no exigent circumstances, the clothing was clearly evidence of the crime and was in plain view at the time of seizure. But the Court says that the result would be the same had the police seized evidence then "held under the defendant's name in the 'property room' of the jail," and thus it may fairly be concluded that *Edwards* means at least that no warrant is needed when (i) an object lawfully came into police view at the time of a search upon the arrestee's arrival at the place of detention, (ii) later investigation established that this item is of evidentiary value, and (iii) the item remains in police custody as a part of the arrestee's inventoried property. In contrast to that situation, which might be characterized as a second look-probable cause type of case, is that in which what is involved is a search into the arrestee's effects to discover that which was not found in the booking inventory. Even here the prevailing view is that no warrant is required in such a case because the warrant process is intended to determine whether probable cause exists, and thus is unnecessary because these searches may be made without probable cause; in the language of the *Edwards* majority, the police may do during the entire period of incarceration what "they were entitled to do incident to the usual custodial arrest and incarceration." But *Edwards* has not settled this point, for the Court there cautioned that such warrantless searches must still be reasonable and that in the instant case "probable cause existed for the search and seizure of respondent's clothing."

(d) Other Search of the Person. Sometimes the police will conduct a warrantless search of a person and find evidence of crime and then place that individual under arrest. Although a search may not both precede an arrest and serve as part of its justification, sometimes a broader rule is asserted, namely, that a search of the person without a search warrant is unlawful when it is made prior to an arrest. But that is not the case; as the Supreme Court concluded in *Rawlings v. Kentucky* (1980), "where the formal arrest followed quickly on the heels of the challenged search of petitioner's person, we do not believe it particularly important that the search preceded the arrest rather than vice versa," so long as the fruits of the search were "not necessary to support probable cause to arrest."

As for searching a person for evidence without any arrest at all, the Court confronted this issue in *Cupp v. Murphy* (1973), where defendant voluntarily appeared at the station in connection with the strangulation murder of his wife, police asked him to submit scrapings from under his fingernails when they saw what appeared to be dried blood on his finger, and when he refused the police proceeded to take the scrapings without a warrant. The Court, though stressing it was not holding "that a full *Chimel* search would have been justified in this case," concluded that in light of the circumstances (including that Murphy began rubbing his fingers together when he ascertained the police believed there was evidence on them), the police were justified "in subjecting him to the very limited search necessary to preserve the highly evanescent evidence they found under his fingernails." At a minimum, therefore, *Cupp* establishes that (i) if there is probable cause for arrest but no arrest, and (ii) if the suspect is reasonably believed to be in the actual process of destroying "highly evanescent evidence," then (iii) that evidence may be preserved if this can be accomplished by a search "very limited" as compared to a full search of the person. Many lower court cases, however, support a broader but sound rule: a warrantless search is proper if the officer had probable cause to believe that a crime had been committed and probable cause to believe that evidence of the crime in question would be found and that an immediate, warrantless search was necessary in order to prevent the destruction or loss of evidence. This means, for example, that when a person reasonably believed to have been driving under the influence is taken to a hospital for treatment instead of arrested, a warrantless taking of a blood sample to determine alcohol content would be proper in the same way as if that person had been arrested.

(e) Seizure and Search of Containers and Other Personal Effects. If the police lawfully arrest a person, may they then search containers and other personal effects belonging to that individual on the ground that this is a legitimate search incident to arrest? The teaching of *Chimel v. California* (1969) is that, at a minimum, the arrestee's effects may be examined on a search-incident-to-arrest theory only if they can be said to be " 'within his immediate control'—construing that phrase to mean the area from within which he might gain possession of a weapon or destructible evidence." At one time, courts were inclined to uphold searches of effects as searches incident to arrest without close attention to whether in the particular case the police restraints upon the arrestee or the nature of the fastening devices on the container were such that there was no realistic opportunity for the arrestee to gain access to the *interior* of that container, which would seem to be the issue posed by *Chimel*. It was as if the carried container was an extension of the person and thus subject to search under *United States v. Robinson* (1973) without any showing of justification based upon the facts of the individual case, and likewise subject to search under *United States v. Edwards* (1974) even after it had been taken from the arrestee.

But the Court's later decision in *United States v. Chadwick* (1977) indicated the search-incident-to-arrest theory was much more limited than customarily assumed. There, the defendants were arrested while standing next to an open auto trunk into which they had just placed a double-locked footlocker the agents believed contained marijuana; the defendants, the car and the footlocker were all taken to the federal building, where the agents unlocked and searched the locker without a warrant. The Court held this was not a lawful search incident to arrest, as "once law enforcement officers have reduced luggage or other personal property not immediately associated with the person of the arrestee to their exclusive control, and there is no longer any danger that the arrestee might gain access to the property to seize a weapon or destroy evidence, a search of that property is no longer an incident of the arrest." Though the reach of *Chadwick* was somewhat unclear because the Court did not say whether the result would be different had the police *immediately* searched the footlocker, the case appeared to have this effect: (i) the right to routinely search incident to arrest without showing any need in the particular case, recognized as to search of the person in *United States v. Robinson* (1973), also extends to containers on the person such as a wallet and containers such as a purse that are "immediately associated" with the person; (ii) in all other instances probable cause and (absent true exigent circumstances) a search warrant is needed whenever the police have—or, could have—taken exclusive control of the container, even if the container was in the arrestee's control at the moment of arrest.

But the vitality of the second half of that equation is to be doubted in light of the Court's more recent analysis in *New York v. Belton* (1981). The Court there adopted the general rule that incident to the arrest of an occupant of a car the passenger compartment of the vehicle (including containers found therein) may be searched as a matter of routine. Because the Court had earlier held that the Fourth Amendment protection of a container is the same whether it is within or without a vehicle, and because the assertion in *Belton* of a need for a "bright line" on what constitutes "immediate control" seems equally applicable to containers not found in cars, the likely consequence of *Belton* is a comparably broad search-of-container-incident-to-arrest rule. This would mean that a container in the arrestee's possession may be searched incident to arrest if the search is contemporaneous with the arrest, without regard to any of the following: (i) whether on the facts of the particular case there was a likelihood the arrestee could get into the container; (ii) whether the police had already subjected the container to their exclusive control; or (iii) whether there was a likelihood that a weapon or evidence of the crime for which the arrest was made would be found.

A second possible basis upon which to justify a search into containers possessed by an arrestee is the need to inventory them incident to the arrestee's booking and post-arrest detention. There is authority that whenever the defendant's suitcase or some similar container was properly impounded by the police at the time of his arrest (or otherwise lawfully came into the custody of the police), an item-by-item inventory of its contents at the station is permissible both to preserve the property of the accused and to forestall the possibility that the accused may later claim that some item has not been returned to him. That view was adopted by the Supreme Court in *Illinois v. Lafayette* (1983), permitting "a stationhouse search of every item carried on or by a person who has lawfully been taken into custody by the police," if done pursuant to "standardized inventory procedures," because it "will amply serve the important and legitimate governmental interests involved." As for the position theretofore taken by a minority of courts that it would suffice if the container was merely sealed and secured without examination of the contents, the Court rejected this as a Fourth Amendment limitation on the grounds that it could not "second-guess police departments as to what practical administrative method will best deter theft by and false claims against its employees and preserve the security of the stationhouse," and that "it would be unreasonable to expect police officers in the everyday course of business to make fine and subtle distinctions in deciding which containers or items may be searched and which must be sealed as a unit."

Another potential basis for upholding a warrantless search of personal effects is that the search in question was made (i) upon probable cause to believe that the effects contained evidence of crime and (ii) when it would not have been practicable to obtain a search warrant first because of certain exigent circumstances. The significant issue here is precisely what constitutes exigent circumstances in this context. At one time, courts were inclined to permit

warrantless searches of containers by analogy to the rules governing vehicle searches (see § 2.7(b)), especially the ruling in *Chambers v. Maroney* (1970) that "for constitutional purposes" there was
no difference between seizing the item to be searched and holding it
while a warrant is obtained, and simply proceeding to make an
immediate warrantless search. This meant that if the circumstances were sufficiently exigent as to justify a warrantless seizure
of a container, it somehow followed that an immediate warrantless
search was also permissible. But that conclusion was rejected by the
Supreme Court in the previously described *Chadwick* case, where it
was reasoned that because "a person's expectations of privacy in
personal luggage are substantially greater than in an automobile,"
the rule for automobiles could not be extended to such containers;
rather, when the circumstances are sufficiently exigent to allow the
police to make a warrantless seizure of the luggage, this does not
permit the "far greater intrusion" of examining the contents thereof but only the continued possession of the container while a
warrant is sought. Any thought that these "substantially greater"
expectations derived from the special steps taken by the defendant
in *Chadwick,* who was transporting a double-locked footlocker, was
dissipated by *Arkansas v. Sanders* (1979), holding that *Chadwick*
also applied to a "small, unlocked suitcase" because "respondent's
failure to lock his suitcase [did not] alter its fundamental character
as a repository for personal, private effects."

This means a search warrant is needed to search containers
absent true exigent circumstances, such as that the object contained evidence which would lose its value unless the container
were opened at once or that immediate search would facilitate the
apprehension of confederates or the termination of continuing
criminal activity, unless (as stated in a caveat in *Sanders*) the
container is one of those that "by their very nature cannot support
any reasonable expectation of privacy because their contents can be
inferred from their outward appearance." The holding in *Sanders*,
that a search warrant is needed even when the container is located
within a vehicle, was later overruled in *California v. Acevedo* (1991)
(discussed in § 2.7(c)). But because *Acevedo* is grounded primarily
in a perceived need for "one clear-cut rule to govern automobile
searches," whether the requisite probable cause extends to the
automobile generally or only to a specific container therein, that
decision does not appear to eliminate the warrant requirement for
search of containers *not* found in vehicles. However, it will doubtless be argued by some that *Acevedo* should be extended to the
latter situation as well, for (as the concurring opinion in that case
put it) "it is anomalous for a briefcase to be protected by the
'general requirement' of a prior warrant when it is being carried

along the street, but for that same briefcase to become unprotected as soon as it is carried into an automobile.''

A variation of sorts on the plain view situation referred to in *Sanders* is the so-called "controlled delivery." When police lawfully see the contents of a container in transit (most likely because it was lawfully opened by a customs official upon its entry into the country or by the suspicious agents of a private domestic courier), they often arrange for it to be delivered under surveillance, after which the recipient is arrested and the container seized and opened. No warrant is needed to justify the opening of the container, the Supreme Court explained in *Illinois v. Andreas* (1983), because this does not amount to a Fourth Amendment search. "No protected privacy interest remains in contraband in a container once government officers lawfully have opened that container and identified its contents as illegal. The simple act of resealing the container to enable the police to make a controlled delivery does not operate to revive or restore the lawfully invaded privacy rights." In *Andreas* (1983), the container (a metal container with a wooden table inside, within which a customs inspector found marijuana) had been out of police view inside defendant's apartment 30 to 45 minutes before he reemerged with it, but the Court concluded that did not require a different result absent "a substantial likelihood that the contents of the container had been changed during the gap in surveillance." Because of the "unusual size of the container, its specialized purpose, and the relatively short break in surveillance," the Court deemed it "substantially unlikely that the respondent removed the table or placed new items inside the container while it was in his apartment."

§ 2.6 Entry and Search of Premises

(a) Basis for Entry to Arrest. *Payton v. New York* (1980) holds "that the Fourth Amendment * * * prohibits the police from making a warrantless and nonconsensual entry into a suspect's home in order to make a routine felony arrest." The Court first noted it was "a 'basic principle of Fourth Amendment law' that searches and seizures inside a home without a warrant are presumptively unreasonable," while "objects * * * found in a public place may be seized by the police without a warrant." The *Payton* majority then concluded that "this distinction has equal force when the seizure of a person is involved" because "an entry to arrest and an entry to search for and to seize property implicate the same interest in preserving the privacy and the sanctity of the home, and justify the same level of constitutional protection." The Court reasoned that any differences in the intrusiveness of entries to search and entries to arrest are merely ones of degree rather than kind. The two intrusions share this fundamental characteristic: the breach of the entrance to an individual's home. The Fourth Amendment protects the individual's privacy in a variety of settings. In none is the zone of privacy more clearly defined than when bounded by the unambiguous physical dimensions of an individual's home—a zone that finds its roots in clear and specific constitutional terms: "The right of the people to be secure in their * * * houses * * * shall not be violated." * * * In terms that apply equally to seizures of property and to seizures of persons, the Fourth Amendment has drawn a firm line at the entrance to the house. Absent exigent circumstances, that threshold may not reasonably be crossed without a warrant.

In response to the contention that "only a search warrant based on probable cause to believe the suspect is at home at a given time can adequately protect the privacy interests at stake," the Court in *Payton* declared that while it "is true that an arrest warrant requirement may afford less protection than a search warrant requirement," "it will suffice to interpose the magistrate's determination of probable cause between the zealous officer and the citizen," for if "there is sufficient evidence of a citizen's participation in a felony to persuade a judicial officer that his arrest is justified, it is constitutionally responsible to require him to open his doors to the officers of the law." This makes sense if there is some reason why it is unnecessary to have a judicial determination of "probable cause to believe the suspect is at home," which would seem to be the case. Though it appears that such probable cause is needed, this requirement would often be an insurmountable barrier if it could be met only by specific facts in the individual case instead of by inference. Because rudimentary police procedure dictates that a suspect's residence be eliminated as a possible hiding place before a search is conducted elsewhere, it is permissible for the police to infer that the defendant is home except when they have "special knowledge" indicating otherwise. That being so, the Court in *Payton* was quite correct in concluding there was no need to involve the magistrate in simply applying that inference.

When the police wish to enter the premises of a third party to make an arrest, it is clear that they must have probable cause to believe that the named suspect is present within at the time. Quite obviously this probable cause can be established only by facts of the particular case rather than by inference, and quite obviously as well this probable cause determination is central to protection of the privacy rights of the third party. This explains why the Supreme Court in *Steagald v. United States* (1981) held that a search warrant, based upon a magistrate's determination that it is probable the person to be arrested is now in those premises, is the kind of warrant needed in those circumstances.

In *Payton,* the Court noted it had "no occasion to consider the sort of emergency or dangerous situation, described in our cases as 'exigent circumstances,' that would justify a warrantless entry into a home" to make an arrest. The Court's prior cases have only declared that any possible warrant requirement was obviated when the police were in "hot pursuit" of the offender. Many lower courts utilize this list of considerations: (1) whether a grave offense is involved; (2) whether the suspect is reasonably believed to be armed; (3) whether there is a clear showing of probable cause of the person's guilt; (4) whether there is strong reason to believe that the suspect is in the premises; (5) whether there is a likelihood that the suspect will escape if not swiftly apprehended; (6) whether the entry is made peaceably; and (7) whether the entry is made at night, which on the one hand is more intrusive and on the other may show the impracticality of getting a warrant. Though declining to express approval of all of these factors, the Court in *Welsh v. Wisconsin* (1984) placed great emphasis (too much, it would seem) on the first of these factors in concluding that "it is difficult to conceive of a warrantless home arrest that would not be unreasonable under the Fourth Amendment when the underlying offense is extremely minor." In *Welsh* police had entered defendant's home without a warrant to arrest him for the offense of driving while intoxicated, in which he had been engaged in the immediate vicinity just minutes before. The state claimed exigent circumstances, namely, a need to obtain evidence of the defendant's blood alcohol level, which the Supreme Court had previously found compelling in other circumstances. But the Court concluded "the best indication of the state's interest in precipitating an arrest" was the fact that the state had "chosen to classify the first offense for driving while intoxicated as a noncriminal, civil forfeiture offense for which no imprisonment is possible," and thus held that in such circumstances "a warrantless home arrest cannot be upheld simply because evidence of the petitioner's blood-alcohol level might have dissipated while the police obtained a warrant." As the two dissenters correctly observed, the statutory scheme was doubtless adopted "to increase the ease of conviction and the overall deterrent effect of the enforcement effort" and thus hardly manifested an expression that the defendant's conduct was so insignificant as to be undeserving of effective enforcement.

The *Payton–Steagald* warrant requirement is inapplicable when the police are otherwise lawfully present within the premises, such as to execute a search warrant or by virtue of consent. There is likewise no need for a warrant, the Court concluded in *United*

States v. Santana (1976), if the arrested defendant was standing directly in the doorway, but *Payton* teaches it is not enough that the door is open and the person to be arrested is clearly visible within. The lower courts are not in agreement as to whether *Santana* may be extended to cases in which the defendant was "at" but not "in" the door, but the better view is that such de minimis physical intrusions as reaching in to seize the person do not invoke the warrant requirement. Such a warrantless arrest is not rendered illegal by the fact that the police summoned the defendant to the door without revealing their intention to arrest him or by resort to noncoercive subterfuge, but the result is otherwise when the police utilize coercion or a false claim of authority to gain the defendant's presence at (or even outside) the door.

Assuming now a situation in which the *Payton–Steagald* warrant requirement *is* applicable and in which the police are armed with the requisite warrant, the Fourth Amendment requires "that police actions in execution of a warrant be related to the objectives of the authorized intrusion." This means, for one thing, that police entering the premises to execute the warrant may not be accompanied by others whose presence therein "was not related to the objectives of the authorized intrusion." Such was the holding in *Wilson v. Layne* (1999), concluding that the Fourth Amendment was thus violated when police entering a private dwelling to execute an arrest warrant allowed members of the news media to accompany them. Violation of the rule in *Wilson* (which was a § 1983 action) would appear to have significance in an exclusionary rule context, if at all, only if the persons improperly present discovered evidence now to be introduced at defendant's trial.

(b) Entry Without Notice to Arrest. The proposition that police must ordinarily give notice of their authority and purpose prior to making an entry of premises to arrest a person therein, which has common law credentials and is often found expressed by statute, seems to have been viewed by the Supreme Court in *Ker v. California* (1963) as a Fourth Amendment requirement, just as the Court later held regarding entry to execute a search warrant. It reduces the potential for violence to both the police officers and the occupants of the house into which entry is sought, guards against the needless destruction of private property, and symbolizes the respect for individual privacy summarized in the adage that a man's house is his castle. The requirement applies to entry by force, by use of a pass key, by merely opening an unlocked door, and at least in some circumstances to passage through an already open door, but it does not extend to entry by ruse because such activity does not intrude upon the aforementioned interests.

What is required is that a police officer, upon identifying himself as such an officer, demand that he be admitted to such premises for the purpose of making the arrest. He may then enter upon submission by the occupant or if his demand is not promptly complied with, which means he must give the occupant a reasonable opportunity to come to the door. The Supreme Court's discussion in *United States v. Banks* (2003) of such failure to respond in the case of search warrant execution (see § 2.4(h)) would seem equally applicable here. Entry without such notice is permissible in an emergency, that is, when the officer acts on a reasonable and good faith belief that compliance would increase his peril, frustrate an arrest, or permit the destruction of evidence. Some jurisdictions followed the so-called "blanket rule" under which an emergency can be grounded upon the general category of the case involved, but the Supreme Court's recent rejection of that approach re search warrant execution (see § 2.4(h)) would seem equally applicable here. Thus, it is not enough that the person to be arrested is known to own a weapon or is involved in criminal activity typically necessitating use of easily disposable evidence. What is necessary is that the police "had a 'reasonable suspicion' that knocking and announcing their presence might be dangerous to themselves or to others." (A few jurisdictions authorize the issuance of so-called no-knock warrants, whereunder the magistrate would authorize entry without prior notice because of a sufficient showing to him of a need to do so.) Announcement is also unnecessary when it would be a "useless gesture," that is, when the authority and purpose of the police is already known to those inside.

(c) Search Before and Incident to Arrest. In *Warden v. Hayden* (1967), the Supreme Court made clear the unquestioned authority of police lawfully within premises for the purpose of making an arrest to search those premises to the extent necessary to find the individual to be arrested. Such a search is ordinarily limited to examining places where a fugitive could conceal himself, but *Hayden* also establishes that sometimes the police may do more. There one officer found weapons in a bathroom flush tank and another found clothing of the type described by the victim in the washing machine, and the Court upheld the search into those places because it was necessary for the police to ensure that they "had control of all weapons which could be used against them or to effect an escape." Because the Court stressed that these searches occurred "as part of an effort to find a suspected felon, armed, within the house into which he had run only minutes before," it is to be doubted that a weapons search is permissible as a matter of course in every case in which the police enter to arrest.

The longstanding rule that if the defendant was arrested in his own premises this automatically justified a warrantless search of the entire premises incident to that arrest was rejected in *Chimel v. California* (1969). After noting that it is reasonable to search the *person* of the arrestee to prevent him from concealing or destroying evidence and to prevent resistance or escape, the Court continued:

> And the area into which an arrestee might reach in order to grab a weapon or evidentiary items must, of course, be governed by a like rule. A gun on a table or in a drawer in front of one who is arrested can be as dangerous to the arresting officer as one concealed in the clothing of the person arrested. There is ample justification, therefore, for a search of the arrestee's person and the area "within his immediate control"—construing that phrase to mean the area from within which he might gain possession of a weapon or destructible evidence.
>
> There is no comparable justification, however, for routinely searching any room other than that in which an arrest occurs—or, for that matter, for searching through all the desk drawers or other closed or concealed areas in that room itself. Such searches, in the absence of well-recognized exceptions, may be made only under the authority of a search warrant. The "adherence to judicial processes" mandated by the Fourth Amendment requires no less.

The Court thus wisely limited the authority to search without warrant incident to arrest by circumscribing that authority in terms of the rationale for making such a search.

Especially in the years that immediately followed *Chimel,* courts applied the rule loosely by finding unhesitantly that the arrestee had a substantial area "within his immediate control" notwithstanding his arrest. The correct approach is to inquire what places it would be *possible* for the arrestee presently to reach, which necessitates consideration of such factors as (1) whether the arrestee was placed in some form of restraints, such as handcuffs; (2) the position of the officer vis-a-vis the defendant in relation to the place searched; (3) the ease or difficulty of gaining access within the container or enclosure searched; and (4) the number of officers present in relation to the number of arrestees or other persons. (More recently, in *New York v. Belton* (1981), the Court adopted a more generous search-incident-arrest rule for search of vehicles after arrest of passengers (see § 2.7(a)), but gave no indication that *Chimel* itself was being expanded.) Courts generally have not considered whether *Chimel* obligates the police to take measures to narrow the range of the arrestee's control, but when the police rely upon their purported knowledge of the arrestee's dangerous propensities in support of a search somewhat broader than might otherwise be permissible, their claim may be rejected because of their failure to take appropriate steps to restrain the arrestee.

(d) Search and Exploration After Arrest. If the defendant is arrested at a particular place in the premises, even at the front door, the circumstances may be such that he will be allowed to move about the premises prior to departure, as where it is necessary for him to change his clothes or put on additional clothing. In such a situation, it is proper for the police in the interest of self-protection to accompany the defendant to the other part of the residence where the clothes are to be obtained and inspect the interior of a closet or drawer where the defendant says he wants to obtain clothing.

After a defendant is arrested within premises, the police sometimes make a cursory inspection of other parts of those premises for the purpose of determining whether there are possible accomplices present. Such a search has been upheld when the police had *some* reason to anticipate finding accomplices, but is not justified if police enter to arrest defendant for a past offense it is known he committed alone or for which all confederates are known to have been apprehended. But at least when the criminal activity is rather serious, exploration for potential accomplices is reasonable even absent concrete information indicating the accomplices are now present.

Yet another reason why police sometimes make a cursory inspection of the balance of the premises is to ensure their own safety while departing with the arrestee. The question of when such a "protective sweep" is permissible reached the Supreme Court in *Maryland v. Buie* (1990), where the Court adopted a two-part sweep rule: (1) "that as an incident to the arrest the officers could, as a precautionary matter and without probable cause or reasonable suspicion, look in closets and other spaces immediately adjoining the place of arrest from which an attack could be immediately launched"; and (2) that for a more extensive sweep "there must be articulable facts which, taken together with the rational inferences from those facts, would warrant a reasonably prudent officer in believing that the area to be swept harbors an individual posing a danger to those on the arrest scene." No effort was made to define either the "immediately adjoining" category or the factors bearing on this variety of reasonable suspicion. As to the latter, lower court decisions have said this is a matter that requires consideration of the seriousness of the offense, the likelihood that the crime for which the arrest was made involved confederates, the likelihood that other persons are now present in the premises, and the extent to which the circumstances and surroundings make difficult a safe withdrawal from the premises with the arrestee.

As for whether the police may accompany the defendant into the home following his arrest outside so that the defendant may obtain identification, get his effects, or change clothes, the Supreme Court answered in the affirmative in *Washington v. Chrisman* (1982). Such action was deemed permissible without regard to the likelihood that the arrestee would attempt to escape; as the Court put it in *Chrisman,* "it is not 'unreasonable' under the Fourth Amendment for a police officer, as a matter of routine, to monitor the movements of an arrested person, as his judgment dictates, following the arrest."

(e) Warrantless Entry and Search for Evidence. In earlier days, the Supreme Court sometimes intimated that a warrantless search of premises for evidence could *never* be justified under the Fourth Amendment, and sometimes alluded to the possibility that such a search would be upheld upon a showing of genuine exigent circumstances. No case concerning this issue reached the Court in the pre-*Chimel* era, for then the police could usually avoid the issue by the simple expedient of arresting the defendant there and then searching the entire premises incident to that arrest. But after *Chimel* a case seemingly raising this issue, *Vale v. Louisiana* (1970), reached the Court. Police set up a surveillance of a house in which Vale was thought to be residing, as they had a warrant to arrest him because of a bond increase on his previous narcotics charge. They saw him come out of the house and apparently make a drug sale to a person who drove up and sounded his horn, so the police moved in and arrested Vale just as he was about to reenter the house. The police then took him inside and made a cursory inspection of the house, during which time Vale's brother and mother entered the premises, and the officers then proceeded to search the house and discovered Vale's stash of narcotics. Though the state claimed that the search was lawful because made on probable cause narcotics would be found and in response to a risk the narcotics would be disposed of if the police were to delay for a search warrant, the Court in *Vale* disagreed.

One response by the Court was that the state's rationale "could not apply to the present case, since by their own account the arresting officers satisfied themselves that no one else was in the house when they first entered the premises." This observation does not square with the facts, which again were that when the detailed search uncovering the drugs was undertaken two close relatives of the defendant were on the premises. Equally baffling is the assertion that because the officers "were able to procure two warrants for the appellant's arrest" and "had information that he was residing at the address where they found him," there was "no reason * * * to suppose that it was impracticable for them to obtain a search warrant as well." The facts support precisely the opposite conclusion; a search warrant for drugs could hardly have issued merely because Vale's bond was being raised, as the probable cause for the warrant came into being only minutes before the search was conducted. But putting those two points aside, *Vale* is significant because it appears to recognize that a warrantless search of a dwelling for evidence may be undertaken in "an exceptional situation," and also because it seemingly asserts that the risk-of-evidence-loss "emergency" is to be very narrowly circumscribed. In concluding no such emergency existed in the instant case, the Court emphasized that the "goods ultimately seized were not in the process of destruction" nor "about to be removed from the jurisdiction." Although some courts have resisted a broader formulation on the ground that the police can too easily conjure up reasons why evidence within premises might be subject to future destruction or disposal, most lower courts have not accepted the *Vale* formulation as controlling. They have been inclined to state the exception in broader terms, covering instances in which the police reasonably conclude that the evidence would be destroyed or removed before they could secure a search warrant.

What one thinks of this formulation is likely to depend upon one's assumptions as to whether the police could resolve their dilemma by some less intrusive alternative, which naturally leads to the so-called impoundment alternative. It has sometimes been suggested that it would be preferable for officers to impound the dwelling until they can obtain a search warrant, during which time those occupants who could not lawfully be arrested would be forced to leave the building or else remain under police surveillance. In recent years more and more courts have expressed their approval of the impoundment alternative. For impoundment to be reasonable, these decisions indicate, the persons present when the police enter should be permitted to leave if they choose that option, and in any event the period of impoundment should be relatively short.

The Supreme Court addressed this important practice, albeit in a somewhat obscure manner, in *Segura v. United States* (1984). There police made a warrantless entry of an apartment, arrested all the occupants (who were promptly removed from the scene), and then remained within 19 hours until a search warrant was obtained and executed. The Court held "that where officers, having probable cause, enter premises, and with probable cause, arrest the occupants who have legitimate possessory interests in its contents and take them into custody and, for no more than the period here involved, secure the premises from within to preserve the status quo while others, in good faith, are in the process of obtaining a warrant, they do not violate the Fourth Amendment's proscription against unreasonable seizures." The Court went on to hold that in any event any illegality in the initial entry would not require suppression of the evidence first discovered in the later execution of the search warrant. Curiously, the first holding in *Segura* was elaborated and explained in a part of the opinion joined in by only two members of the Court, who concluded that the entry could be disregarded; absent exigent circumstances, the entry might constitute an illegal *search* (as the lower court had held), but it had nothing to do with the *seizure* because the interference with possessory interests was no greater than had the officers guarded the premises without entry. This would make the 19 hours of occupation irrelevant, but presumably only because those persons with a possessory interest in the premises were in custody during that time.

A somewhat different tactic was at issue in *Illinois v. McArthur* (2001), where two police officers stood by outside to keep the peace while defendant's wife removed her effects from the family residence, a trailer. Upon exiting, she told the officers her husband had hidden marijuana under the couch, so the officers sought his permission to search the premises. When he refused, one officer left to obtain a search warrant, while another officer remained on the porch with defendant, who was told he could not reenter unless he was accompanied by the officer. A warrant was obtained and executed two hours later, but in the interim defendant entered the trailer two or three times, and on each occasion the officer stood just inside the door and observe his actions. The Court held "that the restriction at issue was reasonable, and hence lawful, in light of" four enumerated circumstances: (i) "the police had probable cause to believe that McArthur's trailer home contained evidence of a crime and contraband, namely, unlawful drugs"; (ii) "the police had good reason to fear that, unless restrained, McArthur would destroy the drugs before they could return with a warrant," as they reasonably concluded that even before the requested consent to search he realized his angry wife had informed the police about the drugs; (iii) "the police made reasonable efforts to reconcile their law enforcement needs with the demands of personal privacy" by imposing "a significantly less strict restraint" than a warrantless search of the premises; and (iv) "the police imposed the restraint for a limited period of time, namely, two hours."

Of a quite different order from the situations previously discussed are those in which an immediate search of premises is necessary because of a risk of bodily harm or even death. Such a warrantless search may be undertaken upon reasonable cause to believe that those premises contain (1) individuals in imminent danger of death or serious bodily harm; or (2) things imminently likely to burn, explode, or otherwise cause death, serious bodily harm, or substantial destruction of property; or (3) things subject to seizure that will cause or be used to cause death or serious bodily harm if their seizure is delayed. Some courts for years recognized yet another exception to the general rule, namely, that police could enter without a warrant to conduct an investigation at the scene of a possible homicide. But in *Mincey v. Arizona* (1978), after noting that no "emergency threatening life or limb" had been established, the Court "decline[d] to hold that the seriousness of the offense under investigation itself creates exigent circumstances of the kind that under the Fourth Amendment justify a warrantless search," and thus concluded "that the 'murder scene exception' created by the Arizona Supreme Court is inconsistent with the Fourth and Fourteenth Amendments." *Mincey* lacks *all* of the characteristics that lower courts traditionally relied upon in recognizing such an exception: this was not an investigation into a then unknown cause of death, as the police knew it was murder and knew who the perpetrator was; this was not a case in which an occupant of the premises had summoned police and tacitly approved of the investigation; and this was not an investigation kept within narrow temporal and spatial dimensions. This makes it more understandable why the Court failed to permit some degree of warrantless investigation as it had done just a few weeks before in the analogous case of *Michigan v. Tyler* (1978), concerning investigation within premises of the cause of a fire (see § 2.9(e)). But in the more recent case of *Thompson v. Louisiana* (1984), lacking the various extreme circumstances present in *Mincey*, the Court again declined to recognize a murder scene exception to the warrant requirement. Absent a warrant, the Court declared, evidence would be admissible only if discovered in plain view while police were assisting the injured party or were checking the premises for other victims or the killer.

(f) Warrantless Entry and Search for Other Purposes. Police may enter a dwelling without a warrant to render emergency aid and assistance to a person they reasonably believe to be in distress and in need of that assistance. If they entered because of a purported emergency and find evidence of crime, that evidence will be admissible only if the state shows that the warrantless entry fell within the exception, using and an objective standard as to the reasonableness of the officer's belief. But that standard is to be applied by reference to the circumstances then confronting the officer, including the need for a prompt assessment of sometimes ambiguous information concerning potentially serious consequences. The question is whether the officers would have been derelict in their duty had they acted otherwise. Police may also enter private property for the purpose of protecting the property of the owner or occupant or some other person. The most common case is that in which the police have reason to believe that the premises in question have been burglarized or vandalized. If the police are lawfully on the premises for this purpose, they may look to see if the burglar or vandal is still present, and may also take necessary steps to identify the occupant so that he may be notified.

The other reasons for which police or other public officials might enter private premises are so varied that generalization is virtually impossible, though it is useful to ask in all such cases whether there was a "compelling urgency" for the action taken. Thus in *G.M. Leasing Corp. v. United States* (1997), where IRS agents made a warrantless entry of corporate offices to levy on property subject to seizure, the Court rejected the government's contention "that the warrant protections of the Fourth Amendment do not apply to invasion of privacy in furtherance of tax collection," and thus held the agents' entry unreasonable because there had been no showing of exigent circumstances.

(g) **What May Be Seized.** Assuming now a lawful warrantless entry or search of private premises on one of the bases heretofore discussed, there remains the separate question of what may be seized. The Court in *Coolidge v. New Hampshire* (1971) indicated "plain view" seizures would often be proper in such circumstances, and then referred to *Warden v. Hayden* (1967), which teaches that to justify such a seizure there must be "a nexus—automatically provided in the case of fruits, instrumentalities or contraband—between the item to be seized and criminal behavior," that is, probable cause "to believe that the evidence sought will aid in a particular apprehension or conviction." Except when there is some established justification for more closely examining an object (e.g., where it is within the "immediate control" of the arrestee for *Chimel* purposes), this probable cause, the Court also said in *Coolidge,* must be "immediately apparent," as "the 'plain view' doctrine may not be used to extend a general exploratory search from one object to another until something incriminating at last emerges." For a time, many lower courts held it was nonetheless proper for police to pick up an item and take closer note of its character and identifying characteristics, *provided* there was a pre-existing reasonable suspicion the object was subject to seizure, but that approach was rejected in *Arizona v. Hicks* (1987), holding full probable cause was needed to pick up an item of stereo equipment to ascertain its serial number (which revealed it was stolen property). The majority deemed it unwise "to send police and judges into a new thicket of Fourth Amendment law" by recognizing a third category of police conduct between "a plain-view inspection" requiring no suspicion and "a 'full-blown search' " requiring probable cause.

Yet another requirement set out in *Coolidge* was "that the discovery of evidence in plain view must be inadvertent," but it was ultimately rejected by the Court in *Horton v. California* (1990). The Court indicated its disapproval of Fourth Amendment "standards that depend upon the subjective state of mind of the officer," and added that adherence to the Fourth Amendment's particularity-of-description requirements "serves the interest in limiting the area and duration of the search that the inadvertence requirement inadequately protects." Somewhat different than the "inadvertent discovery" doctrine is the notion that evidence found within premises will be suppressed if the entry was a subterfuge, as where the police passed up a prior opportunity to arrest defendant on the street and followed him home and then entered the premises to arrest, though there was absolutely no reason for foregoing the earlier arrest opportunity. But the cases adopting this position appear to have been deprived of their vitality by the subsequent Supreme Court decisions in *Scott v. United States* (1978)and *Whren v. United States* (1996), which foreclose pretext-type claims grounded in either the officer's subjective motivation or material deviation from usual practice.

§ 2.7   Search and Seizure of Vehicles

(a) Search Incident to Arrest. Back when courts generally permitted a full warrantless search of the defendant's premises merely because of his arrest there, a comparable unrestrained search was permitted of vehicles in the possession or general control of the arrestee at the time of his arrest. But then came *Chimel v. California* (1969), in which the Court held that because the rationale underlying search incident to arrest is the need to prevent the arrestee from obtaining a weapon or destroying evidence, such a search could extend only to "the arrestee's person and the area 'within his immediate control'—construing that phrase to mean the area from within which he might gain possession of a weapon or destructible evidence." Though it was sometimes held that the *Chimel* rule did not carry over to vehicles, the prevailing view was otherwise, although any need for such a case-by-case assessment was largely obviated by *New York v. Belton* (1981). In that decision, the majority reasoned: (1) Fourth Amendment protections "can only be realized if the police are acting under a set of rules which, in most instances, make it possible to reach a correct determination beforehand as to whether an invasion of privacy is justified in the interest of law enforcement"; (2) "no straight-forward rule has emerged from the litigated cases respecting the question involved here"; (3) this has caused the courts "difficulty" and has put the appellate cases into "disarray"; (4) the cases suggest "the generalization that articles inside the relatively narrow compass of the passenger compartment of an automobile are in fact generally, even if not inevitably, within 'the area into which an arrestee might reach in order to grab a weapon or evidentiary item' "; and thus (5) "the workable rule this category of cases requires" is best achieved by holding "that when a policeman has made a lawful custodial arrest of the occupant of an automobile, he may, as a contemporaneous incident of that arrest, search the passenger compartment of that automobile," inclusive of "the contents of any containers found within the passenger compartment." The wisdom of the *Belton* rule is open to question. The Court is unconvincing in its claim that a case-by-case application of the *Chimel* principle in vehicle cases has proved unworkable. Moreover, the results produced under the *Belton* "bright line" well exceed those that usually would be reached by a case-by-case application of *Chimel*. This is particularly troubling when it is considered that *Belton* permits broad searches of vehicles without any probable cause that evidence will be found therein, provided only that there is probable cause to arrest an occupant. This is no less than an invitation to subterfuge, for police wishing to search a car but lacking grounds to do so need only await the commission of some minor offense by the driver or other occupant and then arrest before the search.

   Belton applies only when there has been a "custodial arrest," and therefore such search of an automobile incident to arrest is not permissible when the person merely receives a citation at the scene, even though he will be allowed to reenter his car and go his way. *Belton* requires that the arrest and search be "contemporaneous," and thus it appears that the search of the vehicle must occur at the place of arrest and not later at the station. There is disagreement as to whether *Belton* also means the search must be made before the arrestee is taken from the scene, but clearly it is unnecessary that he have continuing access to the car. Thus, a search of a vehicle under *Belton* is permissible even after the defendant has been removed from the car, handcuffed and placed in a squad car, and even if he is in the custody of several officers. The term "passenger compartment" in *Belton* has been construed to mean all areas reachable without exiting the vehicle, without regard to the likelihood that such reaching actually occurred in the particular case. It would seem, notwithstanding the fears of the *Belton* dissenters of a contrary interpretation, that the *Belton* "bright line" rule does not permit the dismantling of the vehicle to get inside door panels, the opening of sealed containers, or other searches into particular places to which the arrestee unquestionably had no access immediately preceding his apprehension.

   Purportedly to maintain its bright-line character, *the Belton* rule was broadly construed in *Thornton v. United States* (2004), a step actually revealing further doubts about the soundness of *Belton*'s theoretical underpinnings. In *Thornton*, defendant stopped and alighted from his vehicle of his own accord before the police accosted him concerning the tags on his vehicle belonging to another car, after which drugs were lawfully found on defendant's person, resulting in his arrest and a *Belton*-grounded search of his car uncovering a weapon. In rejecting defendant's claim that *Belton* should be limited to instances, unlike the present case, where contact was initiated while the person was still in the vehicle, a bare majority responded (i) that such a limitation "would obfuscate" *Belton*'s limits because the officer would have to determine whether he had successfully made contact prior to the person exiting the car; and (ii) that such a limitation would not square with the need underlying *Belton*, as "the arrest of a suspect who is next to a vehicle presents identical concerns regarding officer safety and the destruction of evidence as the arrest of one who is inside the vehicle." *Belton* was thus deemed applicable to "both 'occupants' and 'recent occupants,'" though it was cautioned that the latter status "may turn on [the person's] temporal or spatial relationship to the car at the time of the arrest and search," an matter deemed not before the Court in the instant case because "beyond the question on which we granted certiorari."

Emphasizing that the vehicle search in *Thornton* occurred *after* the defendant "was handcuffed and secured in the back of the officer's squad car," Justice Scalia's concurring opinion considered and then rejected three possible defenses to a vehicle search in such circumstances: (1) The notion that the search might be "justified to protect officer safety or prevent concealment or destruction of evidence" involves nothing but a "speculative fear," for the "risk that a suspect handcuffed in the back of a squad car might escape and recover a weapon from his vehicle is surely no greater than the risk that a suspect handcuffed in his residence might escape and recover a weapon from the next room–a danger we held insufficient to justify a search in *Chimel*." (2) The notion that the officer should not be penalized for his safety precautions, and thus must have the same search authority he would have if the arrestee were still unshackled and by the car was also deemed wanting, for a *Chimel* search "is not the Government's right" but rather "an exception" only "justified by necessity," absent in the instant case (and, perhaps, only unjustifiably present if the officer failed to take such safety precautions). (3) The notion that the "benefits of a bright-line rule justify upholding that small minority of searches that, on their particular facts, are not reasonable" depends upon the accuracy of the claim in *Belton* that the passenger compartment is "in fact generally, even if not inevitably," within the suspect's immediate control, belied by the government's admission that the "practice of restraining an arrestee on the scene before searching a car that he just occupied is so prevalent that holding that *Belton* does not apply in that setting would ... 'largely render *Belton* a dead letter.' " Scalia thus concluded that *if* the *Belton* case were to survive (as to which he was equivocal), it should not be explained as "a mere application of *Chimel*" but instead as a search of a place with "a reduced expectation of privacy" permissible when (and only when, as in the instant case) "it is reasonable to believe evidence relevant to the crime of arrest might be found in the vehicle." But if Scalia's alternative theory involves something more than the well-established right to conduct warrantless searches of vehicles for evidence on probable cause (see § 2.7(b)), as appears to be the case, it would extend significantly beyond existing Fourth Amendment doctrine.

(b) Search and Seizure to Search for Evidence. The Supreme Court considered the question of whether a warrantless automobile search for evidence was lawful in the prohibition-era case of *Carroll v. United States* (1925). Federal agents stopped a car they had probable cause to believe contained illegal liquor and immediately subjected it to a warrantless search. In upholding that action, the Court recognized "a necessary difference between a search of a store, dwelling house, or other structure in respect of which a proper official warrant readily may be obtained and a search of a ship, motor boat, wagon, or automobile for contraband goods, where it is not practicable to secure a warrant, because the vehicle can be quickly moved out of the locality or jurisdiction in which the warrant must be sought." On the facts of *Carroll*, the point was well taken, for the officers lacked a basis for "in presence" misdemeanor arrests of the occupants and thus could not have prevented them from moving the vehicle while a warrant was being sought.

Some courts concluded *Carroll* could not be extended to cases in which the vehicle occupants were arrested for the simple reason that exigencies do not exist when the vehicle and the suspect are both in police custody. But the Supreme Court, in *Chambers v. Maroney* (1970), did not agree. In upholding the warrantless search at the police station of a station wagon seized upon arrest of the occupants for a just-committed armed robbery, the Court stated:

> Neither *Carroll,* nor other cases in this Court require or suggest that in every conceivable circumstance the search of an auto even with probable cause may be made without the extra protection for privacy that a warrant affords. But the circumstances that furnish probable cause to search a particular auto for particular articles are most often unforeseeable; moreover, the opportunity to search is fleeting since a car is readily movable. Where this is true, as in *Carroll* and the case before

us now, if an effective search is to be made at any time, either
the search must be made immediately without a warrant or the
car itself must be seized and held without a warrant for
whatever period is necessary to obtain a warrant for the
search. * * *

Arguably, because of the preference for a magistrate's
judgment, only the immobilization of the car should be permitted until a search warrant is obtained; arguably, only the
"lesser" intrusion is permissible until the magistrate authorizes the "greater." But which is the "greater" and which the
"lesser" intrusion is itself a debatable question and the answer
may depend on a variety of circumstances. For constitutional
purposes, we see no difference between on the one hand seizing
and holding a car before presenting the probable cause issue to
a magistrate and on the other hand carrying out an immediate
search without a warrant. Given probable cause to search,
either course is reasonable under the Fourth Amendment.

On the facts before us, the blue station wagon could have
been searched on the spot when it was stopped since there was
probable cause to search and it was a fleeting target for a
search. The probable-cause factor still obtained at the station
house and so did the mobility of the car unless the Fourth
Amendment permits a warrantless seizure of the car and the
denial of its use to anyone until a warrant is secured. In that
event there is little to choose in terms of practical consequences between an immediate search without a warrant and
the car's immobilization until a warrant is obtained.

This passage from *Chambers* is truly remarkable. There is no
explanation as to why it is a "debatable question" whether the
seizure of a car is a lesser intrusion than a search of its interior,
when the Court just months before had found not at all debatable a
similar issue. Secondly, the choices are characterized as "immediate
search" and "holding a car before presenting the probable cause
issue to a magistrate," thus ignoring the fact that the case involved
neither of these but instead a holding of the car followed by a
warrantless search. Thirdly, the Court jumped to the conclusion
that "the mobility of the car" "still obtained at the station house,"
though the owner of the car was among those arrested for a serious
crime; he clearly would be in no position to claim the car in the
interval needed to get a warrant, and there is no indication that the
owner asked that the car be turned over to some third party. That
is, resort to the warrant process in order to protect the owner's
privacy interest would not have involved any greater intrusion
upon the owner's possessory interest in the car. Because *Chambers*
cannot be rationalized in terms of the oft-stated principle that a
search warrant is required except in exigent circumstances, it was

perhaps inevitable that members of the Court would later disagree frequently as to its application.

In *Coolidge v. New Hampshire* (1971), the police, after months of investigation, arrested defendant for murder and contemporaneously seized his car from his driveway and later searched it because it was believed to have been used in commission of the crime. Though the car was seized pursuant to a warrant, the warrant was invalid, and thus an effort was made to justify it as a lawful warrantless seizure and search. Four members of the Court noted that "the police had known for some time of the probable role of the Pontiac car in the crime" and that the defendant "had already ample opportunity to destroy any evidence he thought incriminating," which might well distinguish *Coolidge* from *Chambers* and *Carroll* if the notion were that a warrant is necessary when there is neither a need for an immediate search nor a need for an immediate seizure. But in concluding the warrantless seizure and search were unlawful, they emphasized other purported distinguishing characteristics: that the objects sought "were neither stolen or contraband nor dangerous"; that this was not a car "stopped on the open highway" but "an unoccupied vehicle, on private property"; and that the police had taken steps so that neither Coolidge nor his wife could gain access to the car. But, as other members of the Court correctly noted, none of those three facts distinguishes the case from *Chambers*. *Coolidge* was limited to its facts in a series of subsequent decisions all upholding warrantless search of vehicles. Though in some of these cases the Court pretended that exigent circumstances were necessary, it became apparent (as the Court finally acknowledged in *United States v. Chadwick (1977)*) that warrantless vehicle searches were being permitted "in cases in which the possibilities of the vehicle's being removed or evidence in it destroyed were remote, if not non-existent." On what basis? Because, as the majority said in *Chadwick*: "One has a lesser expectation of privacy in a motor vehicle because its function is transportation and it seldom serves as one's residence or as the repository of personal effects * * *. It travels public thoroughfares where both its occupants and its contents are in plain view." Putting aside the fact that this characterization is certainly not beyond dispute, it would appear to provide the only possible basis for explaining *Chambers* and the post-*Coolidge* cases. Then came *California v. Carney* (1985), where the *Chambers* vehicle exception was held applicable to a motor home that "is being used on the highways, or if it is readily capable of such use and is found stationary in a place not regularly used for residential purposes." The majority emphasized both justifications for the vehicle exception, noting that a motor home in such circumstances is "readily mobile" and has "a reduced expectation of privacy stemming from its use as a licensed motor vehicle subject to a range of police regulation inapplicable to a fixed dwelling." As the Supreme Court in recent years has come to emphasize more and more not merely the mobility factor but also the lesser expectation of privacy notion, one point has emerged clearly regarding vehicle searches: a warrantless search of a vehicle may be upheld with virtually no inquiry into the facts of the particular case, as whether or not any kind of exigent circumstances claim could plausibly be put forward is totally irrelevant.

(c) **Search of Containers and Persons Within.** In *United States v. Chadwick* (1977), three persons were arrested for transportation of marijuana, following which the police seized and later searched without a warrant a double-locked footlocker that had just been put into the open trunk of a car belonging to one of the defendants. The Court declined to uphold the search by analogy to the previously-discussed vehicle cases, reasoning that vehicles have a "diminished expectation of privacy" but that the footlocker did not because it was "not open to public view" or "subject to regular inspections and official scrutiny on a continuing basis" and because it "is intended as a repository of personal effects." But because "the Government does not contend that the footlocker's brief contact with Chadwick's car makes this an automobile search," *Chadwick* did not settle the questions of whether containers in a vehicle may be searched without a warrant in an otherwise lawful warrantless search of the vehicle.

That issue was first considered by the Court in the subsequently-overruled case of *Arkansas v. Sanders* (1979), involving a warrantless search of an unlocked suitcase found in the trunk of a cab in which the arrestee had been riding at the time of his arrest. Thus confronted with "the task of determining whether the warrantless search of respondent's suitcase falls on the *Chadwick* or the *Chambers/Carroll* side of the Fourth Amendment line," the Court ruled "that the warrant requirement of the Fourth Amendment applies to personal luggage taken from an automobile to the same degree it applies to such luggage in other locations." This is because the container's location within a vehicle affected neither the defendant's expectation of privacy as to the container's contents nor the true exigencies of the situation; the use of a suitcase "as a repository for personal items" is especially evident in such circumstances, and once the police have taken the case from the car its mobility is no longer affected by its prior location. Thus, said the Court in *Sanders,* the police should have seized the suitcase and then held it while a search warrant was sought, as there were no truly exigent circumstances mandating an immediate search. But *Sanders* was later limited to the special situation present in that case, where there was probable cause to search a particular container but not probable cause to search the vehicle generally. When the latter, broader form of probable cause exists, the Court held in *United States v. Ross* (1982), "the scope of the warrantless search authorized by [the automobile] exception is no broader and no narrower than a magistrate could legitimately authorize by warrant," so that if "probable cause justifies the search of a lawfully stopped vehicle, it justifies the search of every part of the vehicle and its contents that may conceal the object of the search." Thus in *Ross,* where (unlike *Chadwick* and *Sanders*) there was probable cause to search the entire vehicle for drugs, the police lawfully searched a brown paper bag and a zippered pouch found in the trunk. The *Ross* Court explained that it was justified by the practical consideration that "prohibiting police from opening immediately a container in which the object of the search is most likely to be found and instead forcing them first to comb the entire vehicle would actually exacerbate the intrusion on privacy interests."

The distinction drawn in *Ross* is now irrelevant, however, for in *California v. Acevedo* (1991), involving search of a paper bag in a car on probable cause limited to the bag, the Court concluded "that it is better to adopt one clear-cut rule to govern automobile searches and eliminate the warrant requirement for closed containers set forth in *Sanders*." The Court could see "no principled distinction in terms of either the privacy expectation or the exigent circumstances between the paper bag found by the police in *Ross* and the paper bag found by the police here," for in each case the container was "equally easy for the police to store and for the suspect to hide or destroy." Also, the Court reasoned, the distinction drawn in *Ross* (i) "provided only minimal protection for privacy," given the search-incident-to-arrest rule of *Belton* and the inducement that *Ross* offers for police stretching probable cause to include the entire vehicle, and (ii) "impeded effective law enforcement" because police had experienced difficulty in determining whether *Ross* or *Sanders* was applicable in particular cases.

Assuming a lawful warrantless search of a vehicle, may it automatically extend to the person of an occupant? No, the Supreme Court held in *United States v. Di Re* (1948), for the need to do so is no greater than the necessity "for searching guests of a house for which a search warrant had issued," which the government conceded would not be lawful. However, it has been argued that if the objects sought are not found in the car and they are of a size that they could be concealed on the person, then the occupants of the vehicle should be subject to search if the officer has reason to suspect one of them has the objects concealed on his person. In support, it is said that the *Di Re* analogy is unsound and that it is absurd to say that the occupants can take the narcotics out of the glove compartment and stuff them in their pockets, and drive happily away after the vehicle has been fruitlessly searched.

However, *Di Re* was not overturned but only distinguished when the Court later confronted the related question of when a passenger's effects may be searched. In *Wyoming v. Houghton* (1999), the state court had held that while an officer with probable cause to search a vehicle may search all containers that might conceal the object of the search, if the officer knows or should know that a container belongs to a passenger who is not suspected of criminal activity, then that container is outside the scope of the search unless someone had the opportunity to conceal contraband within it to avoid detection. But the Supreme Court instead decided that "when there is probable cause to search for contraband in a car, it is reasonable for police officers * * * to examine packages and containers without a showing of individualized probable cause for each one," meaning that the search may extend to "a passenger's personal belongings, just like the driver's belongings or containers attached to the car like a glove compartment." And this is so, the Court added, even without any information suggesting either involvement by that passenger in the criminality under investigation or placement of contraband into the passenger's effects by the driver. Such a rule, the Court explained, was justified by "the balancing of the relative interests" involved: (i) "passengers, no less than drivers, possess a reduced expectation of privacy with regard to the property that they transport in cars," as distinguished from the "heightened protection" re search of the person recognized in *Di Re*; and (ii) the "practical realities" are that "a car passenger * * * will often be engaged in a common enterprise with the driver" or else the criminal "might be able to hide contraband in a passenger's belongings as readily as other containers in the car * * * without the passenger's knowledge or permission," thus justifying a bright-line rule here because of the difficulty that would be involved in sorting out, on a case-by-case basis, such questions as whether the passenger's claim of ownership is valid, whether the passenger was a confederate, or whether the driver might have introduced the contraband into the package even without the passenger's knowledge.

(d) Seizure for Other Purposes. If a vehicle is itself evidence of crime, may it be seized without a warrant as evidence in plain view? Not necessarily, concluded at least four members of the Court in *Coolidge v. New Hampshire* (1971), as a warrantless seizure on a plain view theory is permissible only upon "inadvertent discovery" of the item seized, because the "requirement of a warrant to seize imposes no inconvenience whatever" when "the police know in advance the location of the evidence and intend to seize it." But in *Cardwell v. Lewis* (1974), involving the warrantless seizure of defendant's car from a public parking lot some time following his arrest elsewhere, four members of the Court deemed this lawful; no mention was made of the "inadvertent discovery" limitation, though it was claimed the instant case differed from *Coolidge* "in the circumstances of the seizure," apparently a reference to the possibility that the defendant's wife might have gained access to the car had it not been immediately seized. In *Horton v. California* (1990), the Court rejected the *Coolidge* "inadvertent discovery" requirement but then seemingly endorsed the *result* in *Coolidge* as grounded in noncompliance with two other conditions of a plain view warrantless seizure: (i) the seized objects' incriminating character "must also be 'immediately apparent,' " which was not the case in *Coolidge* because "the cars were obviously in plain view, but their probative value remained uncertain until after the interiors were swept and examined microscopically"; and (ii) "not only must the officer be lawfully located in a place from which the object can be plainly seen, but he or she must also have a lawful right of access to the object itself," which was not the case in *Coolidge* because "the seizure of the cars was accomplished by means of a warrantless trespass on the defendant's property."

Coolidge and *Cardwell* predate the broad rule in *California v. Carney* (1985) allowing warrantless search of vehicles for evidence absent any genuine exigent circumstances, and thus it might be argued that the *Carney* rule also applies in this context to permit a warrantless seizure of a car seized *as* evidence. But, *Carney* focuses upon the low privacy interest in the vehicle, while seizure of a vehicle as evidence is also likely to amount to a major intrusion upon a possessory interest, for the vehicle itself will probably be held a substantial period of time, much longer than necessary to facilitate the typical *Carney* search. This being the case, it might be concluded that the initial seizure of a vehicle as evidence is permissible without a warrant (by analogy to *Carney*), but that a substantial continuation of that dispossession would require a warrant.

It is common at both the federal and state level to find statutes authorizing the seizure and subsequent forfeiture of a vehicle because it was used in certain criminal activity. The courts were once in disagreement as to whether such seizures could be made without a warrant, but over time more and more lower courts upheld the warrantless seizure of automobiles for forfeiture, usually by analogy to the *Chambers–Carney* line of cases. The matter was finally settled when the Supreme Court, in *Florida v. White* (1999), upheld the warrantless seizure of a vehicle from a public place on probable cause that it constituted forfeitable contraband under a state forfeiture statute. Taking note of "the special considerations recognized in the context of movable items" in the above-mentioned line of cases, the Court concluded the need was "equally weighty when the *automobile,* as opposed to its contents, is the contraband that the police seek to secure." Next noting that "our Fourth Amendment jurisprudence has consistently accorded law enforcement officials greater latitude in exercising their duties in public places," the Court in *White* deemed the instant case "nearly indistinguishable" from *G.M. Leasing Corp. v. United States* (1977), involving a warrantless seizure of automobiles from public streets and lots as part of a levy on a corporation's assets for tax deficiencies. A unanimous Court in *G.M. Leasing* upheld the seizures with the brief comment that the seizures "did not involve any invasion of privacy," but went on to hold that the rule was otherwise as to warrantless searches, and thus unanimously held the agents had violated the Fourth Amendment when they entered the premises of the corporation and seized its books. The Court explained this was because under the *Camara* principle (see § 2.9(a)) the where-to-search issue could not be left to the discretion of an agent in the field, which highlights the fact that the Court never satisfactorily explained why the what-to-seize issue (i.e., was the corporation the alter ego of the taxpayer, subjecting its cars to levy) should be left to the agents in the field.

Police impound vehicles for a variety of reasons. This occurs when a vehicle is found abandoned, illegally parked or in unsafe mechanical condition, and, most frequently, when the owner or operator of the vehicle has been arrested in or near the car. Generally, courts are of the view that when a person is arrested away from home, the police may impound the personal effects that are with him at the time to ensure the safety of those effects. But the better view, consistent with *Dyke v. Taylor Implement Manufacturing Co.* (1968), is that immediate impoundment of a car after the driver has been arrested for a minor traffic violation is improper because the police are obligated to give the defendant a reasonable opportunity to post his bail and obtain his prompt release. Moreover, if the driver is not afforded the usual opportunity to post bond, as provided by statute, rule of court or perhaps even police custom, then his improper continued detention contaminates the impoundment of the vehicle resulting therefrom, so that whatever is found in the course of an inventory during impoundment must be suppressed.

A broader question, relevant whatever the cause of the vehicle operator's arrest, is whether impoundment should be considered the only feasible disposition of the car or whether, instead, the police should consider other possible alternatives or even consult the arrestee concerning them. Some courts took the latter positions, but in *Colorado v. Bertine* (1987), the Court rejected, as a

Fourth Amendment matter, the argument that the impoundment of the car was improper because the arrested driver was not "offered the opportunity to make other arrangements." Rejecting an "alternative 'less intrusive' means" approach, the Court concluded impoundment was lawful "even though courts might as a matter of hindsight be able to devise equally reasonable rules requiring a different procedure." But the Court cautioned that the individual officer's impound-or-lock-and-leave decision must be made "according to standard criteria," which was deemed to be met in the instant case because a police "directive establishes several conditions that must be met before an officer may pursue the park and lock alternative." This latter conclusion seems erroneous, for the applicable police regulation placed *no* restrictions upon resort to the impoundment alternative.

(e) Search for Other Purposes. It is common practice for the police to conduct an inventory of the contents of vehicles they have taken into their custody in order to protect the vehicle and the property in it, and to safeguard the police or other officers from claims of lost possessions. This practice received little attention from the Supreme Court until *South Dakota v. Opperman* (1976), in which defendant's illegally parked car was towed to the city impound lot where an officer, observing articles of personal property in the car, proceeded to inventory it, finding a bag of marijuana in the unlocked glove compartment. The Court concluded:

> The Vermillion police were indisputably engaged in a caretaking search of a lawfully impounded automobile. * * * The inventory was conducted only after the car had been impounded for multiple parking violations. The owner, having left his car illegally parked for an extended period, and thus subject to impoundment, was not present to make other arrangements for the safekeeping of his belongings. The inventory itself was prompted by the presence in plain view of a number of valuables inside the car. * * * [T]here is no suggestion whatever that this standard procedure, essentially like that followed throughout the country, was a pretext concealing an investigatory police motive.

> On this record, we conclude that in following standard police procedures, prevailing throughout the country and approved by the overwhelming majority of courts, the conduct of the police was not "unreasonable" under the Fourth Amendment.

Although some jurisdictions have as a matter of local law taken a narrower view, such as that noninvestigative police inventory searches of automobiles without a warrant must be restricted to safeguarding those articles that are within plain view of the officer's vision, most courts are likely to follow what they perceive to be the implications of the *Opperman* holding.

The Court in *Opperman* was unwilling to impose upon the police, in the case where they have impounded a car without contemporaneous contact with the owner or possessor, the burden of complying with the procedure proposed by the four dissenters: "reasonable efforts under the circumstances to identify and reach the owner of the property in order to facilitate alternative means of security or to obtain his consent to the search." What then of the more common situation in which the car was impounded incident to arrest of the operator? The four *Opperman* dissenters concluded that in such a case "his consent to the inventory is prerequisite to an inventory search." But in *Colorado v. Bertine* (1987), the Court rejected the notion that resort to such "alternative 'less intrusive' means" is ever necessary. (However, the Court indicated that if such alternatives are sometimes utilized, then this must occur pursuant to "standardized criteria" set out in police regulations.)

In *Opperman* the vehicle was kept at "the old county highway yard," only partially fenced and a situs of past vandalism. The Court was unwilling to impose the burden of providing secure impoundment facilities as an alternative to inventory. There remained the claim, however, that if a particular jurisdiction does have secure facilities, then it has no need for inventory. But in *Bertine* the Court rejected such a claim, reasoning that "the security of the storage facility does not completely eliminate the need for inventorying; the police may still wish to protect themselves or the owners of the lot against false claims of theft or dangerous instrumentalities." Yet another issue is whether some special need vis-a-vis the particular car is necessary to trigger the authority to inventory. Because the Court's opinion in *Opperman* notes that the "inventory was prompted by the presence in plain view of a number of valuables inside the car," the case may be read as permitting inventory only upon such an observation. But that would be an unsound limitation; whatever right of inventory otherwise exists need not be "triggered" by the observation of such articles, for their absence does not reduce the likelihood of personal effects being present elsewhere in the car. To put the matter another way, the right to inventory is not limited by a probable cause requirement in the sense that there must be a case-by-case determination of the likelihood of valuables being in the vehicle. Rather, it is sufficient that a particular inventory is not arbitrary, that is (as it was put in *Opperman*), that it "was carried out in accordance with *standard procedures* in the local police department."

Finally, assuming that a particular inventory is otherwise lawful, *Opperman* does not foreclose challenge regarding the permissible scope of a vehicle inventory. The Court approved of examination within the unlocked glove compartment, "since it is a customary place for documents of ownership and registration, * * * as well as a place for the temporary storage of valuables." This would indicate that inventories may routinely extend to unlocked glove compartments, and also supports the conclusion that there is *no* right to "inventory" those parts of a vehicle in which one would not expect to find valuables stored. The inventory in *Opperman* did not extend to the locked trunk, and thus the case did not settle whether the police might search a locked trunk or other compartment. But *Bertine*, although not involving inventory into a trunk, rather clearly indicates such an inventory would be approved by the Court, as the Court upheld inventory within a vehicle kept in a secure storage facility on the ground the police are entitled "to protect themselves * * * against false claims of theft or dangerous instrumentalities."

The *Opperman* inventory did not involve an opening of containers in the vehicle, and the dissenters were thus prompted to stress that "the Court's opinion does not authorize the inspection of suitcases, boxes, or other containers which might themselves be sealed, removed and secured without further intrusion." However, the Supreme Court thereafter held "that it is not 'unreasonable' for police, as part of the routine procedure incident to incarcerating an arrested person, to search any container or article in his possession, in accordance with established inventory procedures." Relying on that case, the Court in *Bertine* upheld an inventory extended to a backpack within the vehicle, and held that extending a vehicle inventory to containers therein did not depend upon the likelihood "that the containers might serve as a repository for dangerous or valuable items." While *Bertine* indicated a majority of the Court would deem it "permissible for police officers to open closed containers in an inventory search only if they are following standard police procedures that mandate the opening of such containers in every impounded vehicle," the Court's later decision in *Florida v. Wells* (1990) suggests that something short of this will likely suffice. The holding in *Wells*, agreed to by the entire Court, is only that the inventory there was unlawful because the police agency "had no policy whatever with respect to the opening of closed containers encountered during an inventory search." But dictum in *Wells* goes on to say that "a police officer may be allowed sufficient latitude to determine whether a particular container should or should not be opened in light of the nature of the search and characteristics of the container itself."

Courts have also upheld warrantless searches into vehicles for a variety of other purposes. If an arrestee's car is not impounded but is to be left at the scene of the arrest, some limited police activity to secure the car and its contents is reasonable. If a person's car, because of an accident or other circumstances, is to remain in a location where it is vulnerable to intrusion by vandals, then the police, if they have probable cause that the vehicle contains a weapon or similar device that would constitute a danger if it fell into the wrong hands, may conduct a warrantless search for that item. A limited search of an automobile in an effort to ascertain ownership is permissible in some circumstances, such as where the car has apparently been abandoned or where the arrested driver is possibly not the owner and does not otherwise establish the matter of ownership. Also, if "an officer has probable cause to believe that a vehicle has been the subject of burglary, tampering, or theft, he may make a limited entry and investigation, without a search warrant, of those areas he reasonably believes might contain evidence of ownership." And if the police find a person unconscious or disoriented and incoherent in a vehicle, it is reasonable for them to enter the vehicle for the purpose of giving aid to the person in distress and of finding information bearing upon the cause of his condition.

(f) **Plain View, Subterfuge and Related Matters.** Police may ordinarily seize evidence in plain view without a warrant, provided the initial intrusion that brings the police within plain view of such an article is itself lawful, and thus when police seize evidence from a vehicle pursuant to any of the activities heretofore discussed, it is necessary at the outset to ascertain the lawfulness of the activity by which the police obtained the car and entered it. An object may not be seized from a car merely because the police plain view of it was lawfully acquired; there must be probable cause that the object is a fruit, instrumentality or evidence of crime. And under the "immediately apparent" requirement of *Coolidge v. New Hampshire* (1971), this probable cause must be determined without examination of the object other than is justified by the purpose underlying police entry of the vehicle.

Somewhat related is the question of under what circumstances the police may conduct an examination of some object (a car or personalty found therein) subsequent to the time they have taken custody of it. If the basis of the initial seizure of the item is that it constitutes evidence, it is plainly within the realm of police investigation to subject such an object to scientific testing and examination for the purpose of determining its evidentiary value. If a vehicle is seized because it is reasonably believed to contain evidence, we have seen in *Chambers v. Maroney* (1970) that the search may be undertaken later at the station instead of at the scene, and this is so even though it was feasible to conduct the search at the scene. It would seem, however, that *Chambers* "contemplated some expedition in completing the searches so that automobiles could be released and returned to their owners." In *United States v. Johns* (1985), where packages in a truck were opened three days after the vehicle was seized on probable cause the packages contained marijuana, the Court in upholding the search cautioned that possession of the vehicle "indefinitely" was not being approved and noted that in the instant case the defendants "never sought return of the property." A third situation is that in which a vehicle is in police custody for some other reason (e.g., an impoundment), and there then develops for the first time probable cause to search the car. Warrantless searches have been upheld in such circumstances, a result which might be defended on the ground that the vehicle was no less mobile than the vehicle in *Chambers* at the time of the search. Finally, it must be asked whether a lawfully impounded vehicle or items removed therefrom for safekeeping may later be searched or examined without probable cause that evidence will be discovered. *United States v. Edwards* (1974), discussed earlier (see § 2.5(c)), seems to permit doing later what could have been done earlier, and thus may support the argument that when items have been exposed to police view under unobjectionable circumstances, then no reasonable expectation of privacy is breached by an officer taking a second look at such items.

Though it has occasionally been held that evidence found in a vehicle inventory must be suppressed if the police had suspected they might find such an item, this makes no sense whatsoever. What makes an inventory search reasonable under the requirements of the Fourth Amendment is not that the subjective motives of the police were simplistically pure, but rather that the facts of the situation indicate that an inventory search was reasonable under the circumstances, i.e., that per *Opperman* and *Bertine* it was conducted pursuant to "standard police procedures." In light of *Whren v. United States* (1996), a pretext objection to a vehicle search will only rarely be possible. *Whren* involved a pretextual traffic stop, and as to it the Court applied this rule: when certain police conduct is permitted upon probable cause, the existence of that probable cause establishes the reasonableness of the police conduct, and thus neither the officer's ulterior motives nor his departure from ordinary practice or governing police regulations makes that conduct unreasonable under the Fourth Amendment. The Court in *Whren* then distinguished the expression of concern about "pretext" in *Bertine* by explaining that in an inventory context, where a search is being allowed without probable cause because of the special purpose being served, the exemption from the usual probable cause requirement would not obtain if the search was not made for that purpose.

§ 2.8   Stop and Frisk and Similar Lesser Intrusions

(a) Stop and Frisk: Fourth Amendment Theory. The issue of whether the police have the right to stop and question a suspect, without his consent, in the absence of grounds for an arrest was confronted by the Supreme Court in *Terry v. Ohio* (1968). A Cleveland police officer, after seeing three men repeatedly look into a store as if they were "casing" it for a stickup, approached the men and asked them to identify themselves and, when they only mumbled something, patted them down and found weapons on two of them. After stating the issue in the narrowest possible terms, "whether it is always unreasonable for a policeman to seize a person and subject him to a limited search for weapons unless there is probable cause for an arrest," the Court concluded:

> Each case of this sort will, of course, have to be decided on its own facts. We merely hold today that where a police officer observes unusual conduct which leads him reasonably to conclude in light of his experience that criminal activity may be afoot and that the persons with whom he is dealing may be armed and dangerous, where in the course of investigating this behavior he identifies himself as a policeman and makes reasonable inquiries, and nothing in the initial stages of the encounter serves to dispel his reasonable fear for his own or others' safety, he is entitled for the protection of himself and others in the area to conduct a carefully limited search of the outer clothing of such persons in an attempt to discover weapons which might be used to assault him.
>
> Such a search is a reasonable search under the Fourth Amendment, and any weapons seized may properly be introduced in evidence against the person from whom they were taken.

It soon became clear that *Terry* was not limited to cases based upon direct observations by the investigating officer, as in *Adams v. Williams* (1972) the Court concluded that "reasonable cause for a stop and frisk" had been provided when an informant who had given reliable information in the past said a man seated in a nearby car was carrying narcotics and had a gun at his waist.

One important contribution of the *Terry* case to Fourth Amendment theory was the Court's conclusion that restraining a person on the street is a "seizure" and an exploration of the outer surfaces of his clothing is a "search," without regard to the labels that police or others choose to put on those activities. Another was the Court's further development of its recently-adopted balancing test as a means for judging the constitutionality of unique practices. Just the year before, in *Camara v. Municipal Court* (1967) (discussed in § 2.9(a)), the Court, by "balancing the need to search against the invasion which the search entails," held that warrants for housing inspections could be issued without the traditional quantum of case-by-case probable cause if appropriate legislative or administrative standards for area or periodic inspections were met. The *Camara* balancing test was quoted and relied upon in *Terry,* but it was now applied in a slightly different way: the police conduct had to be justified upon the facts of the individual case, but a lesser quantum of evidence was required. A third contribution to Fourth Amendment theory in *Terry* lies in the Court's response to the argument that a police power to stop and frisk should not receive express recognition because police have often utilized such street encounters for improper purposes, such as the wholesale harassment of minority groups. To this, the Court noted that the exclusionary rule "is powerless to deter invasions of constitutionally guaranteed rights where the police either have no interest in prosecuting or are willing to forego successful prosecution in the interest of serving some other goal." Read with another comment by the Court, namely, that the "exclusionary rule * * * cannot properly be invoked to exclude the products of legitimate police investigative techniques on the ground that much conduct which is closely similar involves unwarranted intrusions upon constitutional protections," it appears the Court's point is really this: If exclusion of the fruits of *all* street encounters by declaring them all to be in violation of the Fourth Amendment would somehow put a stop to those engaged in for harassment and other improper purposes, it could at least be argued that the benefits derived would be worth the cost, but no such argument can be made here because the illegal encounters are usually motivated by objectives other than conviction and thus cannot be influenced by the exclusionary rule.

(b) Dimensions of a Permissible "Stop." If, as *Terry* teaches, there is a certain kind of police conduct, typically called a "stop," which may be undertaken upon less evidence than is needed for arrest because it is a lesser intrusion than an arrest, then it is obviously important to know just what kind of a seizure, undertaken for what purpose and made in what manner, can qualify as that lesser intrusion. For example, because in *Terry* the officer acted in the interest of crime *prevention,* which was stressed by the Court, and because all members of the Court agreed some added power was necessary for that purpose, it might be asked if *Terry* stops may also be made for the purpose of crime *detection.* The proper answer is yes. When immediately after the perpetration of a crime the police may have no more than a vague description of the possible perpetrator, it would be irrational to deprive the officer of the opportunity to "freeze" the situation for a short time, so that he may make inquiry and arrive at a considered judgment about further action to be taken. This conclusion is supported by *United States v. Hensley* (1985), where the Court concluded that a *Terry* stop on less than full probable cause would sometimes be permissible for the purpose of investigating criminal activity that had occurred on some prior occasion. But the Court cautioned that the "factors in the balance may be somewhat different" in such a case, so that the reasons for permitting a seizure merely upon reasonable suspicion might not always be compelling. Thus, the Court cautiously limited its holding, expressly authorizing the stopping of "a person suspected of involvement in a past crime" only as to "felonies or crimes involving a threat to public safety," where "it is in the public interest that the crime be solved and the suspect detained as promptly as possible." Similar reasoning supports the conclusion that a *Terry* stop may be made of a nonsuspect who might be able to supply information, though it may well be that the Fourth Amendment does not permit the stopping of potential witnesses to the same extent as those suspected of crime.

As for whether a *Terry* stop may be made for investigation of all types of crimes or only those of a relatively serious nature, the *Adams* decision is sufficiently ambiguous that this may fairly be said to be an open question outside the *Henley* type of situation. Though admittedly articulation of offense-category limits as a matter of Fourth Amendment interpretation (as opposed to a policy reflected in a statute) would be most difficult, in support of such limits it may be said (i) that the need factor of the *Camara* balancing test cannot be sufficiently assessed without consideration of the seriousness of the crime under investigation, (ii) that meaningful review of police action is most difficult as to minor offenses such as loitering or disorderly conduct because these crimes are so diverse and diffuse, and (iii) that permitting stops for such minor crimes as marijuana possession presents the most obvious temptation to abuse the frisk as an occasion for searching for contraband.

Another important issue is whether the police conduct may still qualify as a lesser intrusion and thus a *Terry* stop if it includes force or a threat of force. Though it has occasionally been held that such action as surrounding the suspect or drawing weapons converts the police conduct into an arrest because the restriction of liberty of movement was complete, this is in error, for a stopping differs from an arrest not in the incompleteness of the seizure but in the brevity of it. The better view, therefore, is that surrounding the suspect will sometimes be an appropriate way of making the stop and maintaining the status quo, just as the drawing of weapons will sometimes be a reasonable precaution for the protection of officers and bystanders. Handcuffing ordinarily is improper, but may be resorted to when necessary to thwart the suspect's attempt to frustrate further inquiry. Although as a general matter it is not proper to place the detainee in a police car, such a step is permissible when dictated by special circumstances (e.g., inclement weather). There may occasionally be instances in which the use of physical force to make the stop will be justified, and also instances in which entry of private premises will be necessary to seize a fleeing suspect.

The police conduct should be judged in terms of what was done rather than what the officer involved may have called it at the time. If an officer tells the suspect he is under arrest but then conducts only a frisk and finds a weapon, a later determination that grounds for arrest were lacking should not render inadmissible the discovered weapon if there were in fact grounds for a stop and the frisk. Obviously the result would be otherwise if the search exceeded that permissible under *Terry*. In *Peters v. New York* (1968) the Court approved the reverse of the above proposition, so that if an officer perceives his conduct as a stop only but he makes a full search of the person rather than a mere frisk, the evidence found is admissible if in fact the officer had grounds to arrest.

Though the Court in *Terry* had little to say about the stopping part of the stop-and-frisk phenomenon, it did stress that an arrest "is a wholly different kind of intrusion upon individual freedom * * * inevitably accompanied by future interference with the individual's freedom of movement," thus intimating that there were time and place limits upon a lawful stop. (*Terry* also says that the officer's actions must be "reasonably related in scope to the circumstances which justified the interference in the first place," a requirement later emphasized in *Hiibel v. Sixth Judicial District Court* (2004), holding that refusal to state one's name during a lawful *Terry* stop may be criminalized only if the request for identification was so "reasonably related.") The permissible length depends upon the circumstances of the particular case. The results of the initial stop may arouse further suspicion or may dispel the questions in the officer's mind. If the latter is the case, the stop may go no further and the detained individual must be free to go. If, on the contrary, the officer's suspicions are confirmed or are further aroused, the stop may be prolonged and the scope enlarged as required by the circumstances. This is not to say that the detention may continue as long as the reasonable suspicion persists; rather, it must be asked whether the police are diligently pursuing a means of investigation likely to resolve the matter one way or another very soon and whether there is a reason for continuing the suspect's presence during that interval. In *Florida v. Royer* (1983), a plurality asserted that a *Terry* stop should "last no longer than is necessary to effectuate the purpose of the stop" and that "the investigative methods employed should be the least intrusive means reasonably available to verify or dispel the officer's suspicion in a short period of time." But more recently, the Court has cautioned against "unrealistic second-guessing," and has declared that the "question is not simply whether some other alternative was available, but whether the police acted unreasonably in failing to recognize or to pursue it."

In pre-*Terry* days courts were inclined to hold that any movement of the suspect, even to a police call box a block away, converted the detention into an arrest for which full probable cause was required, but today courts are inclined to permit some movement of the suspect in the immediate area of the stop. It has been held that it is improper to transport the suspect to the crime scene, even if it is relatively close, for possible identification by the victim or witnesses when there exist less intrusive and more reasonable alternatives, such as bringing the victim and witnesses to the detention scene or arranging for such a confrontation on some future occasion. The prevailing view is to the contrary, and rightly so; usually the matter can be resolved most expeditiously by transporting the suspect, and if the identification is delayed the risks of error are substantially increased. However, a taking of the suspect to the police station in lieu of conducting the investigation at the scene will ordinarily take the police conduct outside the *Terry* rule.

As noted in *United States v. Hensley* (1985), whether a *Terry* stop has been kept within lawful bounds depends upon whether the circumstances "justified the length and intrusiveness of the stop and detention that actually occurred." The temporal limitation means, e.g., that any consent to search be obtained before the time has run out, while the intrusiveness limitation means, e.g., that any interrogation even before expiration of the time must concern an offense for which there was then reasonable suspicion. But when it comes to those stops made for a traffic infraction (what courts call "routine traffic stops," although in fact such stops are frequently made on a hunch that the vehicle contains drugs), the *Terry* limitations are honored more often in the breach than in the observance. For one thing, the temporal limits are loosely observed, and courts even go so far as to state that such limits may be even extended briefly in the interest permitting procedures only relevant to drug law enforcement. For another, the intensity limitation is treated as if it did not exist at all, so that nonsearch investigative procedures undertaken to uncover drugs are deemed permissible so long as they actually or approximately occurred within whatever temporal limits are being observed.

In support of watered-down temporal limits upon traffic stops, it is argued that while a person stopped for a traffic violation typically is given a citation and released, *Atwater v. City of Lago Vista* (2001) holds that when there is probable cause (usually the case as to a traffic stop) the Constitution allows the police to place the person in custody and take him to be booked, meaning that although traffic stops usually proceed like *Terry* stops, the Constitution does not require this equation. This is nothing more than a determination of the lawfulness of a seizure because of what the police might have done, rather than what they actually did, and hence cannot be squared with *Knowles v. Iowa* (1998), holding that where an officer engages in a traffic stop/citation for speeding, a full search of the car cannot be undertaken incident to that stop even though the officer could have made such a search had he opted to make a full custodial arrest. The correct view, therefore, is that the *Terry* temporal limits do apply to traffic stops, meaning that the appropriate time limits are those necessary to serve the traffic enforcement purposes justifying the stop in the first place.

As for the intensity limitation of *Terry*, it is contended that a traffic stop is not limited to investigation of the traffic offense because, e.g., since the Supreme Court has held in *Florida v. Bostick* (1991) that "mere police questioning does not constitute a seizure," it follows that because questions are neither searches nor seizures, police may question about drugs incident to a traffic stop. But the fatal flaw in this analysis is the assumption that unless certain conduct is itself a search or seizure, it cannot be taken into account in judging the intrusiveness of a stop under the *Terry* limitations. This view conveniently ignores the fact that detention involves official coercion and therefore concerns quite a different relationship of the police officer to the person questioned than when there is no custody at all. And thus the correct view is that incident to a traffic stop when there does not also exist reasonable suspicion of drug possession, the officer may not question the vehicle occupants about drugs, may not quiz them about the details of their past and pending travels, may not seek a consent to search the vehicle for drugs, and may not lead a drug-sniffing dog around the stopped vehicle.

(c) Action Short of a Stop. Not all police-citizen contacts constitute Fourth Amendment "seizures" that must be justified by showing grounds for the detention. "Only when the officer, by means of physical force or show of authority, has in some way restrained the liberty of a citizen," said the Court in *Terry*, "may we conclude that a 'seizure' has occurred." The Court then proceeded to "assume" that no seizure had occurred in that case until the frisk because it was unnecessary to pinpoint the precise earlier time at which the seizure commenced. The issue of what constitutes an encounter short of a *Terry* stop was presented more directly in *United States v. Mendenhall* (1980), where federal drug agents approached the defendant as she was walking through an airport concourse, identified themselves and asked to see her identification and airline ticket, which she produced for their inspection. Justice Stewart, in a part of his opinion joined by only one other member of the Court, concluded there had been no seizure, explaining:

> We conclude that a person has been "seized" within the meaning of the Fourth Amendment only if, in view of all of the circumstances surrounding the incident, a reasonable person would have believed that he was not free to leave. Examples of circumstances that might indicate a seizure, even where the person did not attempt to leave, would be the threatening presence of several officers, the display of a weapon by an officer, some physical touching of the person of the citizen, or the use of language or tone of voice indicating that compliance with the officer's request might be compelled. * * * In the absence of some such evidence, other inoffensive contact between a member of the public and the police cannot, as a matter of law, amount to a seizure of that person.

By way of footnote, it was added that "the subjective intentions of the DEA agent in this case to detain the respondent, had she attempted to leave, is irrelevant except insofar as they may have been conveyed to the respondent." More recently, a majority of the Supreme Court has endorsed the Stewart "reasonable person" standard, which probably takes into account obvious and common characteristics (e.g., youth) of the particular suspect (cf. *Yarborough v. Alvarado* (2004), discussed in § 5.6(c)).

However, in *Florida v. Bostick* (1991), the Court recognized that literal application of the "free to leave" test would be inappropriate in some circumstances (e.g., the present case, where defendant was questioned on a bus he did not want to leave in any event), and thus said that in such circumstances "the appropriate inquiry is whether a reasonable person would feel free to decline the officers" requests or otherwise terminate the encounter. The Court applied the *Bostick* standard in *United States v. Drayton* (2002), where during a scheduled stop the bus driver left the bus in the hands of three police officers; one stood guard at the front of the bus and another at the rear while the third questioned the passengers individually without informing them of their right not to cooperate. In holding there had been no seizure, the *Drayton* majority emphasized that the questioning officer did not brandish a weapon or make any intimidating movements, left the aisle free, spoke in a polite and quiet voice, and said nothing to indicate the person was barred from leaving the bus or otherwise terminating the encounter. Noting that "had this encounter occurred on the street, it would be constitutional," the majority concluded that the "fact that an encounter takes place on a bus does not on its own transform standard police questioning of citizens into an illegal seizure" and that, indeed, "because many fellow passengers are present to witness officers' conduct, a reasonable person may feel even more secure in his or her decision not to cooperate with police on a bus than in other circumstances."

The lower court cases tend to find that it is not a seizure to approach a stationary pedestrian and ask him a question, or even to overtake a walking pedestrian and ask him to halt or to summon him to where the officer is, but that more dramatic steps, such as stopping a vehicle, do bring the Fourth Amendment into play. Though the proposition is seldom articulated in precisely this form, the lower court decisions for the most part can be reconciled by this proposition: there is no Fourth Amendment seizure when the policeman, although perhaps making inquiries that a private citizen would not be expected to make, has otherwise conducted himself in a manner consistent with what would be viewed as a nonoffensive contact if it occurred between two ordinary citizens.

In *California v. Hodari D.* (1991), after a group of youths fled upon approach of a police car, one officer pursued Hodari on foot, prompting Hodari to throw to the ground what upon inspection proved to be cocaine. The state court concluded that Hodari had been "seized" when he saw the officer pursuing him, and that consequently the cocaine was the fruit of that illegal (because without reasonable suspicion) seizure, but the Supreme Court disagreed. The word "seizure" in the Fourth Amendment, the Court declared, means "a laying on of hands or application of physical force to restrain movement, even when it is ultimately unsuccessful," and also a "*submission* to the assertion of authority," but it did not encompass a "show of authority" as to which "the subject does not yield." As for Hodari's reliance on the *Mendenhall* test, the Court responded that the requirement "a reasonable person would have believed that he was not free to leave" "states a necessary, but not a *sufficient* condition for seizure * * * effected through a 'show of authority.' "

(d) **Grounds for a Permissible "Stop."** Although the Court in *Terry* claimed it was "decid[ing] nothing today concerning the constitutional propriety of an investigative 'seizure' upon less than probable cause," a lesser standard was suggested when the Court related the holding to a situation "where a police officer observes unusual conduct which leads him reasonably to conclude in light of his experience that criminal activity may be afoot." The Court later indicated in *Adams v. Williams* (1972) that a stopping for investigation could be made even when "there is no probable cause to make an arrest," but made no effort to articulate exactly what the standard was. More recently, in *United States v. Cortez* (1981), the Court noted that the various phrases used by the lower courts, such as "founded suspicion," were "not self-defining" but that the essence of the standard was that "the detaining officers must have a particularized and objective basis for suspecting the particular person stopped of criminal activity." Because a " 'totality of the circumstances' principle * * * governs the existence *vel non* of 'reasonable suspicion,' " the various factors relied upon to establish such suspicion are not to be independently assessed one-by-one and rejected if susceptible to an innocent explanation. Assuming a sufficient degree of suspicion, it is *not* also necessary that there be unavailable a less intrusive investigative technique.

The most common type of investigative stop situation occurs when, as in *Terry,* a patrolman observes suspicious conduct. The protean variety of observed circumstances that might lead to a stop makes generalization about this situation virtually impossible, but a few comments are in order: (1) Most such stops are for investigation of property crimes, and thus often are based upon the fact that the suspect is carrying some object in suspicious circumstances or is in a suspicious relationship to a car or building. (2) Because deliberate furtive actions and flight at the approach of strangers or law officers are strong indicia of *mens rea,* efforts to avoid the police or avoid being seen by them can contribute to grounds for a stop. Although it has occasionally been held that if the means of avoidance are sufficiently extreme they alone may justify the stop, that conclusion may be in some doubt as a result of *Illinois v. Wardlow* (2000). In that decision, the majority held there were grounds for a *Terry* stop where the defendant engaged in "[h]eadlong flight," "unprovoked flight upon noticing the police," where there was the additional factor of defendant's "presence in an area of heavy narcotics trafficking." The other four Justices, concurring in part and dissenting in part, (i) made much of the majority's failure to endorse the state's proposed *per se* rule regarding the sufficiency of "unprovoked flight upon seeing a clearly identifiable police officer"; (ii) appeared to admit that flight under the proper circumstances would justify a police inference of wrongdoing; but (iii) then cogently found the majority's ultimate conclusion unsound "because many factors providing innocent motivations for unprovoked flight are concentrated in high crime areas." (3) It is proper to consider the surrounding circumstances and the suspect's relationship to them, such as whether he "fits" the area in which he is found, whether it is a high crime area, whether he is about at a time of day when the suspected criminality is most likely to occur, and whether he is in the company of one who can be arrested for a present or recent crime. (4) It is proper to take account of the suspect's past criminal record, though such a record standing alone is never a basis for a stop. (5) The officer, based upon his training and experience, is allowed to make inferences and deductions that might well elude an untrained person, but if his actions are later challenged he must be able to explain those inferences and deductions so as to show that there was a particularized and objective basis for the stop. (6) If during an earlier nonseizure contact the person made contradictory or otherwise suspicious remarks, those comments may be taken into account.

Another common situation is that in which a stop is made because a person is found near the scene of a recent crime and the police wish to determine if that person was the perpetrator. Though a "dragnet approach" is impermissible, detentions greater in number than the number of known perpetrators are proper if selective investigative procedures are utilized that provide a reasonable possibility that any person stopped is a perpetrator. In making that judgment, officers may properly consider: (1) the particularity of the description of the offender or the vehicle in which he fled; (2) the size of the area in which the offender might be found, as indicated by such facts as the elapsed time since the crime occurred; (3) the number of persons about in that area; (4) the known or probable direction of the offender's flight; (5) observed activity by the particular person stopped; and (6) knowledge or suspicion that the person or vehicle stopped has been involved in other criminality of the type presently under investigation.

A third kind of situation, that in which the stopping is made on the basis of information received from an informant, occurs with much less frequency, but reached the Supreme Court in *Adams v. Williams* (1972), where an informant told the officer a man in a nearby car was carrying narcotics and had a gun at his waist. The Court concluded this "information carried enough indicia of reliability to justify the officer's forcible stop of Williams," as the "informant was known to him personally and had provided him with information in the past," the "informant here came forward personally to give information that was immediately verifiable at the scene," and under state law the informant was "subject to immediate arrest for making a false complaint had Sgt. Connolly's investigation proven the tip incorrect." The question raised by *Adams* is to what extent there is a lesser standard here than when a full arrest or search is made on an informant's tale, in which case probable cause is usually lacking unless (i) the underlying circumstances show reason to believe that the informant is a credible person, and (ii) the underlying circumstances show the basis of the conclusions reached by the informant. As to the first or credibility aspect, the points relied upon in *Adams* are extremely weak; merely saying the informant had given information in the past without even indicating whether it proved to be accurate does not show credibility, and in the absence of any suggestion that the informer was aware of the seldom-used false complaint statute it cannot be said that credibility has been shown by the fact the informer was in the area and could have been arrested if his story proved to be

false. As for the second or basis-of-knowledge prong, the Court in
Adams offers nothing; the informer never said how she knew what
she claimed to know, and certainly she did not give so many details
as to permit an inference that she had a reliable source. Because of
this failure of the Court in *Adams* to explain what departure from
the then extant *Aguilar v. Texas* (1964) formula, if any, was
permissible, the post-*Adams* lower court cases were in disarray and
not infrequently permitted stops based upon an informant's story
though there was *absolutely no indication* of that informant's
credibility or basis of knowledge.

There is much to be said for the proposition that just as strong
a showing of both credibility and basis of knowledge should be
required here as for arrest, though here the facts would not need to
show as high a probability of criminal conduct. But when the Court
revisited this area in *Alabama v. White* (1990), it decided otherwise:
"Reasonable suspicion is a less demanding standard than probable
cause not only in the sense that reasonable suspicion can be
established with information that is different in quantity or content
than that required to establish probable cause, but also in the sense
that reasonable suspicion can arise from information that is less
reliable than that required to show probable cause." In *White,*
police received an anonymous call that the defendant, Ms. White,
would leave a certain apartment in a certain vehicle, would be
going to a certain motel, and would be in possession of an ounce of
cocaine inside a brown attache case. A woman was then seen to
leave the building where that apartment was, get in the described
vehicle and drive in the direction of the motel, at which point she
was stopped. The Court declared: (i) that it was not prepared to say
that an anonymous call by itself "could never provide the reasonable suspicion necessary for a *Terry* stop"; (ii) that nonetheless the
call in this case was standing alone insufficient, for like the letter in
Illinois v. Gates (1983) it gave absolutely no indication of reliability
or basis of knowledge; (iii) that some corroboration of the anonymous informant's story is clearly insufficient, such as the discovery
of the described vehicle outside the specified apartment, for "anyone could have 'predicted' that fact because it was a condition
presumably existing at the time of the call"; and (iv) that the total
corroboration in the instant "close case" was sufficient, as "the
caller's ability to predict respondent's *future behavior,* because it
demonstrated inside information—a special familiarity with respondent's affairs," meant it was "reasonable for police to believe that a
person with access to such information is likely to also have access
to reliable information about that individual's illegal activities."
But that is a questionable conclusion; as the three dissenters in
White noted, "anybody with enough knowledge about a given
person to make her the target of a prank, or to harbor a grudge

against her, will certainly be able to formulate a tip about her like the one predicting Vanessa White's excursion."

In *Florida v. J. L.* (2000), where police, acting solely on an anonymous telephone tip that a described person at a certain bus stop had a gun, frisked that person and found a gun, the Court held the tip "lacked the moderate indicia of reliability present in *White*," for mere confirmation of the suspect's present location and appearance "does not show that the tipster has knowledge of concealed criminal activity." As for the so-called "firearms exception" to *White* theretofore adopted by several lower courts, the Court responded it "would rove too far," as it "would enable any person seeking to harass another to set in motion an intrusive, embarrassing police search of the targeted person simply by placing an anonymous call falsely reporting the target's unlawful carriage of a gun." The Court in *J. L.* declined "to speculate about the circumstances under which the danger alleged in an anonymous tip might be so great as to justify a search even without a showing of reliability," as with "a report of a person carrying a bomb," and also left open what result would obtain regarding places such as schools where "the reasonable expectation of Fourth Amendment privacy is diminished."

As for stops made on the basis of information received via police channels, a useful illustration is provided by a lower court case, where an officer stopped a van on the basis of a radio message that it contained several illegal aliens, and *after* the stop observed circumstances providing grounds for an arrest that when made resulted in the discovery of certain evidence. The defendant relied upon *Whiteley v. Warden* (1971), holding that an arrest made in response to a police bulletin may be upheld only upon a subsequent showing of probable cause at the source (which had not been done here), but the court responded that no such showing was needed to support an investigatory stop instead of an arrest. Such a conclusion is in error and has been properly rejected by other courts, for to accept all police bulletins at face value is to abandon any requirement of an "indicia of reliability" (to use the *Adams* language). By the same token, there is no reason to be more demanding than *Whiteley* in this context, and thus (as the Supreme Court held in *United States v. Hensley* (1985)) a stopping in reliance upon a conclusory flyer issued by another department indicating the person is wanted for investigation of a felony is lawful, *provided* the flyer "has been issued on the basis of articulable facts supporting a reasonable suspicion." In other words, with a *Terry* stop as with a full-fledged arrest, it suffices that the facts justifying the seizure were then in the hands of the directing or requesting agency.

In *Brown v. Texas* (1979), in the course of holding that police did not have grounds to stop a man who was seen walking away

from another man in an alley in an area with a high incidence of
drug traffic, a unanimous Court emphasized that under the Fourth
Amendment a seizure must either "be based on specific, objective
facts" or "be carried out pursuant to a plan embodying explicit,
neutral limitations on the conduct of individual officers." In support of the latter part of this statement, the Court cited *Delaware v.
Prouse* (1979) and *United States v. Martinez–Fuerte* (1976), which
state that stopping of all cars at a checkpoint to examine drivers'
licenses or to question occupants about their alienage would be
lawful because the intrusion is not "subject to the discretion of the
official in the field." This raises the question of whether this
standardized procedures approach, which originated in *Camara v.
Municipal Court* (1967) (see § 2.9) and has been utilized generally
in assessing so-called inspections or administrative searches, has
any application to stop-and-frisk cases. That is, if in *Brown* it had
been established that the officers stopped the defendant pursuant
to a police department "plan" to question all pedestrians found in
the "high drug problem area," would the outcome have been
different? Though certainly there is a good reason to favor such law
enforcement planning by police agencies, it is rather doubtful that
resort to that kind of plan, in lieu of continued reliance upon an
individualized suspicion approach, would be permitted. This is
because, as the Supreme Court has intimated, the neutral plan
approach is for use in those situations "in which the balance of
interests precludes insistence upon 'some quantum of individualized suspicion.' " If a plan dealing generally with a certain constant
law enforcement concern, such as drug trafficking, could somehow
be more carefully and tightly formulated than suggested above, it is
of course possible that it would be deemed to pass muster under
Camara. More likely, however, is the possibility that a plan addressing a "special" problem existing at a certain time and place
would be upheld.

(e) **"Frisk" for Weapons.** In determining the lawfulness of a
frisk, two matters are to be considered: (i) whether the officer was
rightly in the presence of the party frisked so as to be endangered if
that person was armed; and (ii) whether the officer had a sufficient
degree of suspicion that the party frisked was armed and dangerous. As to the first, Justice Harlan helpfully commented in his
separate *Terry* opinion that if "a policeman has a right * * * to
disarm a person for his own protection, he must first have a right
not to avoid him but to be in his presence." Thus a mere bulge in a
pedestrian's pocket, insufficient to justify a stopping for investigation, would not be a basis for a frisk by a passing officer, though
quite clearly the same bulge would entitle the officer to frisk a
person he had already lawfully stopped for investigation. And while
some language in *Terry* could be read as saying a frisk would be in

order incident to a lawful stop only if a preliminary inquiry were made and did not clear up the matter, such a limitation would be unsound and has not been followed by the Supreme Court or the lower courts.

As for the second factor, *Terry* says that what is required is that the officer's observations lead him "reasonably to conclude * * * that the persons with whom he is dealing may be armed and presently dangerous." The use of the phrase "may be" makes it apparent that it will suffice that there is a substantial possibility the person is armed, and that there need not be the quantum of evidence that would justify an arrest for the crime of carrying a concealed weapon. Sometimes this possibility may be said to exist merely because of the nature of the crime under investigation, while on other occasions something in addition will be required, such as a bulge in the suspect's clothing, a sudden movement by the suspect toward a pocket or other place where a weapon could be hidden, or awareness that the suspect was armed on a previous occasion. The test is an objective one, and thus the officer need not later demonstrate that he was in actual fear. If the *Terry* test for a frisk cannot be met, this does not mean that the officer is powerless to do anything in the interest of self-protection. The teaching of *Pennsylvania v. Mimms* (1977) is that without any showing the particular suspect may be armed, an officer may require a person lawfully stopped to alight from his car in order to diminish "the possibility, otherwise substantial, that the driver can make unobserved movements." The *Mimms* rule is equally applicable to passengers; though there has been no reason to detain the passenger, as a practical matter the passenger is detained whenever the vehicle is stopped, and so again a minimal added intrusion is justified in the interest of the officer's safety.

The Court in *Terry* emphasized that what is here referred to as a "frisk" must "be confined in scope to an intrusion reasonably designed to discover guns, knives, clubs, or other hidden instruments for the assault of the police officer," and found the officer had so limited his actions by patting down the clothing first and reaching inside only upon feeling a weapon. In the companion case of *Sibron v. New York* (1968), the officer was deemed to have exceeded the permissible scope of such a search in that he made "no attempt at an initial limited exploration for arms" but instead "thrust his hand into Sibron's pocket." Though this means that usually a frisk must commence with a pat-down, *Adams v. Williams* (1972) indicates there are exceptions, for there the officer's conduct was upheld though he immediately reached into the suspect's clothing. Because the informant in that case had indicated the exact location of the weapon, some courts have taken that to be the basis of the *Adams* exception, but a more reasonable interpretation is that the immediate search was upheld because the suspect's failure to comply with the officer's request that he get out of the car made the possible weapon, as the Court put it, "an even greater threat." As for the permissible extent of the pat-down, the Court in *Terry* unfortunately quoted a rather distressing description, in fact intended to describe what may be done after arrest and before transportation to the station. The need is only to find implements that could be reached by the suspect during the brief face-to-face encounter, not to uncover items cleverly concealed and to which access could be gained only with considerable delay and difficulty, and thus the pat-down should be limited accordingly. In any event, once the officer is satisfied that an object in the suspect's pocket is *not* a weapon, then the officer may not continue the tactile examination of it in an effort to ascertain whether it is otherwise incriminating.

In *Terry,* the Court stressed that the officer "did not place his hands in [the suspects'] pockets or under the outer surface of their garments until he had felt weapons." But the officer need not be absolutely certain that the individual is armed, and thus the question is whether there was anything in the officer's perception to indicate it was not a weapon either because of its size or density. This would, for example, bar a search when only a soft object was felt in the pat-down. Assuming grounds for a search because of the pat-down, that search must be limited to retrieving and inspecting the suspect object; as the Court stressed in *Terry,* the officer there, once he felt what appeared to be weapons, "merely reached for and removed the guns."

As for whether such a protective search may ever extend beyond the person of the suspect, one way in which this question arises is when an officer searches within a vehicle in which the stopped suspect was riding. In *Michigan v. Long* (1983), the Supreme Court held "that the search of the passenger compartment of an automobile, limited to those areas in which a weapon may be placed or hidden, is permissible if the police officer possesses a reasonable belief based on 'specific and articulable facts that, taken together with the rational inferences from those facts, reasonably warrant' the officers in believing that the suspect is dangerous and the suspect may gain immediate control of weapons." In *Long,* an officer actually saw a knife in the car before the search and the person under investigation for erratic driving was being allowed to reenter the car to get the vehicle registration. But the Court unfortunately took an expansive view of what constitutes danger in the context of a *Terry* stop of a person in an automobile, understandably prompting the dissenters to declare that "the implications of the Court's decision are frightening." For one thing, the Court in *Long* asserted that if the investigation did not result in an arrest, then the suspect "will be permitted to reenter his automobile, and he will then have access to any weapons inside." Just why the suspect would want to attack the officer who had told him he was free to go was not explained. For another, the Court stressed the risk that a *Terry* suspect might "break away from police control and retrieve a weapon from his automobile." One might think that in any case where such a danger was perceived by the officer, who is entitled to order the suspect out of the car, he would move him a sufficient distance away or take other steps to overcome the danger. But the Court in *Long* declared that officers are not required to "adopt alternate means to insure their safety in order to avoid the intrusion involved in a *Terry* encounter."

Another circumstance in which the question arises whether a protective search may extend beyond the person of the suspect is when the officer examines the contents of items carried by the suspect, such as a purse, shopping bag, or briefcase. Though case authority upholding such conduct is to be found, there is much to be said for the notion that the officer should simply put the object out of the suspect's reach for the duration of the encounter. But given the Supreme Court's approach in *Long,* it may be argued that even this alternative means can be disregarded.

(f) Roadblocks. The use of checkpoints to uncover violations of a certain type by persons passing by is one kind of regulatory search discussed later (see § 2.9(f), (g)). By contrast, the concern here is with utilization of a roadblock for much the same purpose as in many stop-and-frisk situations: discovery and apprehension of a person who recently has committed a particular crime in the area. Illustrative would be a case in which, following a bank robbery and information the robber had left town in a vehicle via a certain road, all cars travelling that road were stopped at a checkpoint so that each of them could be checked for the robber. It has been suggested that if an officer has reasonable cause to believe that a felony has been committed and stopping all or most vehicles moving in a particular direction or directions is reasonably necessary to permit a search for the perpetrator or victim of such felony in view of the seriousness and special circumstances of such felony, then he may order the drivers of such vehicles to stop, and may search such vehicles to the extent necessary to accomplish such purpose. While the Supreme Court has never dealt with the issue, and the lower court cases are not particularly helpful, it would seem that the Fourth Amendment limits on use of roadblocks should be somewhat different than those upon an ordinary *Terry* stop: (1) a roadblock should be permitted only upon a reliable report of a crime, and not upon suspicion of criminal conduct; (2) a roadblock should be permitted only for a rather serious crime carrying with it a strong public interest in prompt apprehension of the perpetrator; (3) a roadblock should be permitted only if reasonably located, that is, there must be some reasonable relation between the commission of the crime and the establishment and location of the roadblock, which necessitates consideration of police knowledge concerning the number of alternative paths of escape or the particular direction in which the perpetrator is reasonably believed to be headed.

Sometimes roadblocks are set up at or near a recent crime scene in order to seek information from passersby who might have also passed the scene at the time of the crime. In *Illinois v. Lidster* (2004), the Court held the reasonableness of a particular information checkpoint depends upon "[1] the gravity of the public concerns served by the seizure, [2] the degree to which the seizure advances the public interest, and [3] the severity of the interference with individual liberty." Applying this test, the Court upheld the roadblock at issue because (i) "the stop's objective was to help find the perpetrator of a specific and known crime," one which "had resulted in a human death"; (ii) the police had "appropriately tailored their checkpoint stops to fit important criminal investigatory needs" by establishing the checkpoint at a place and time which held promise of obtaining some information from driver's who had been there at the time of the accident after completing night shifts at nearby industrial complexes; and (iii) "the stops interfered only minimally with liberty of the sort the Fourth Amendment seeks to protect," as each stop required a wait of "a very few minutes at most," involved contact with police "only a few seconds," consisted "simply of a request for information," and did not involve unnecessary police discretion because the police "stopped all vehicles systematically."

(g) Detention at the Police Station for Investigation. In *Davis v. Mississippi* (1969), petitioner and 24 other black youths were detained for questioning and fingerprinting in connection with a rape for which the only leads were a general description and a set of fingerprints. The Court held that petitioner's prints should have been excluded as the fruits of a seizure in violation of the Fourth Amendment, but intimated that a detention at the station might sometimes be permissible on evidence insufficient for arrest:

> Detentions for the sole purpose of obtaining fingerprints are no less subject to the constraints of the Fourth Amendment. It is arguable, however, that because of the unique nature of the fingerprinting process, such detentions might, under narrowly defined circumstances, be found to comply with the Fourth Amendment even though there is no probable cause in the traditional sense. * * * Detention for fingerprinting may constitute a much less serious intrusion upon personal security

than other types of police searches and detentions. Fingerprinting involves none of the probing into an individual's private life and thoughts that marks an interrogation or search. Nor can fingerprint detention be employed repeatedly to harass any individual, since the police need only one set of each person's prints. Furthermore, fingerprinting is an inherently more reliable and effective crime-solving tool than eyewitness identifications or confessions and is not subject to such abuses as the improper lineup and the "third degree." Finally, because there is no danger of destruction of fingerprints, the limited detention need not come unexpectedly or at an inconvenient time. For this same reason, the general requirement that the authorization of a judicial officer be obtained in advance of detention would seem not to admit of any exception in the fingerprinting context.

The *Davis* dictum has had considerable impact. Statutes or court rules authorizing brief detention at the station by court order on less than the grounds needed for arrest, where the purpose of the detention is to conduct various identification procedures, were adopted in several jurisdictions. These provisions have been upheld by the courts, and other cases have upheld such procedures even in the absence of a specific statute or rule.

(h) Brief Seizure of Objects. A detention for investigation of a somewhat different kind, involving objects rather than a person, was involved in *United States v. Van Leeuwen* (1970). A postal clerk advised a policeman that he was suspicious of two packages of coins just mailed, and the packages were then held at that post office while an investigation was conducted that culminated in the issuance of a warrant and search of the packages there 29 hours after they were mailed. Citing *Terry,* a unanimous Court declared that the suspicious circumstances "certainly justified detention, without a warrant, while an investigation was made." But the Court then disposed of the case with a broader pronouncement: "No interest protected by the Fourth Amendment was invaded by forwarding the packages the following day rather than the day when they were deposited. The significant Fourth Amendment interest was in the privacy of this first class mail; and that privacy was not disturbed or invaded until the approval of the magistrate was obtained."

Van Leeuwen was an easy case because the defendant was unable to show that the invasion intruded upon either a privacy interest in the contents of the packages or a possessory interest in the packages themselves. It thus did not resolve the constitutionality of the practice of detaining the luggage possessed by suspected drug couriers at airports while further investigation (typically, exposure of the suitcases to a drug-detection dog) was conducted, later confronted by the Court in *United States v. Place* (1983). Using the *Terry* balancing of interests approach, the Court there concluded that "the governmental interest in seizing the luggage briefly to pursue further investigation is substantial," and that because "seizures of property can vary in intrusiveness, some brief detentions of personal effects may be so minimally intrusive of Fourth Amendment interests that strong countervailing governmental interests will justify a seizure based only on specific articulable facts that the property contains contraband or evidence of a crime." But the Court then cautioned that "in the case of detention of luggage within the traveler's immediate possession, the police conduct intrudes on both the suspect's possessory interest in his luggage as well as his liberty interest in proceeding with his itinerary," in that "such a seizure can effectively restrain the person since he is subjected to the possible disruption of his travel plans in order to remain with his luggage or to arrange for its return." For this reason, said the Court in *Place*, "the limitations applicable to investigative detentions of the person * * * define the permissible scope of an investigative detention of the person's luggage on less than probable cause." This would appear to mean that in such circumstances the container may be detained without full probable cause only so long as could the suspect from whose possession it was taken, so that the suspect at his option may also remain at the place of the seizure for that length of time and then reclaim the container unless in the interim the suspicion has grown into probable cause.

§ 2.9   Inspections and Regulatory Searches

(a) **General Considerations.** In the discussion that follows, the concern is with a variety of rather special search practices commonly described either as "inspections" or as "regulatory searches." These practices are directed toward certain unique problems unlike those ordinarily confronted by police officers in their day-to-day investigative and enforcement activities. Some of the practices, such as the examination of the effects of persons entering the country from abroad, have been followed for many years and have rather strong historical credentials, while others, such as the airport hijacker detection screening process, are rather recent innovations undertaken in an effort to respond to new problems. However, they all have this in common: it is generally assumed that the problems to which they are addressed could not be adequately dealt with under the usual Fourth Amendment restraints and that consequently the practices must be judged by somewhat different standards.

A theoretical basis for doing precisely this did not clearly emerge until the Supreme Court's decision in *Camara v. Municipal Court* (1967). In the course of holding that unconsented safety inspections of housing could be conducted pursuant to a warrant issued upon less than the usual quantum of probable cause, the Court declared that "there can be no ready test for determining reasonableness other than by balancing the need to search against the invasion which the search entails." Under this balancing theory, the Court continued, it is necessary to consider (i) whether the practice at issue has "a long history of judicial and public acceptance," (ii) whether the practice is essential to achieve "acceptable results," and (iii) whether the practice involves "a relatively limited invasion of * * * privacy." Assessing those factors, the Court in *Camara* held that inspection warrants could issue pursuant to "reasonable legislative or administrative standards" even without case-by-case probable cause. That is, searches of the kind at issue could occur so long as procedures were followed to ensure against the arbitrary selection of those to be subjected to them. The *Camara* balancing test was later used in *Terry v. Ohio* (1968) to permit brief seizures for investigation on the street upon evidence less than that required for a full-fledged arrest. There a case-by-case determination was required, but the special circumstances justified the practice on what one might call a "watered-down" version of probable cause. Use of the *Camara–Terry* balancing test in assessing the various practices discussed herein has frequently resulted in the conclusion that these practices may constitutionally be undertaken on one or both of the bases just described, that is, upon a showing in the individual case of reasonable suspicion short of traditional probable cause, or upon a showing that the individual case arose by application of standardized procedures involving neutral criteria.

It must be emphasized, however, that (in contrast to *Terry*) the situations discussed in this section are typically justified in terms of what it is that necessitates deviation from the usual Fourth Amendment requirements, usually described in terms of some "special need" distinct from ordinary law enforcement. That being the case, the special need must itself be something other than an ordinary law enforcement goal, and, indeed, must in any event be sufficiently divorced from ordinary law enforcement. But, as is illustrated by *United States v. Knights* (2001), when the Court is able to justify one of the special search rules discussed herein on the basis of general Fourth Amendment theory instead of by reliance upon the "special needs" doctrine, then the aforementioned limitation apparently disappears.

(b) Inspection of Housing. In *Camara v. Municipal Court* (1967), concerning the constitutionality of the San Francisco housing inspection scheme whereunder "routine" inspections for violations of the city housing code could be made without a warrant, the Court had occasion to resolve two important issues: (i) whether such inspections must be conducted pursuant to a warrant; and (ii) what grounds are needed to undertake such inspections. On the warrant issue, the majority reasoned that because no showing had been made "that fire, health, and housing code inspection programs could not achieve their goals within the confines of a reasonable search warrant requirement," and because also the searches at issue "are significant intrusions" that "when authorized and conducted without a warrant procedure lack the traditional safeguards which the Fourth Amendment guarantees," unconsented housing inspections could ordinarily be conducted only pursuant to a search warrant. But then, utilizing the balancing test described above, the Court rejected appellant's claim that such a warrant requires "probable cause to believe that a particular dwelling contains violations of the minimum standards prescribed by the code being enforced," and instead held that reasonable standards based upon such factors as the passage of time, the nature of the building, or the condition of the entire area would suffice.

As for the extent of the *Camara* warrant requirement, the Court stressed its holding was not "intended to foreclose prompt inspections, even without a warrant, that the law has traditionally upheld in emergency situations." Such an emergency is unlikely to arise in this context. Most housing code violations cannot readily be concealed without being corrected; to the extent that householders take advantage of notice to correct deficiencies, the purposes of the housing code are advanced rather than thwarted. Warrantless entry is permissible in the face of an imminent and substantial threat to life, health, or property, but such a danger is unlikely as to an inspection that is merely part of an area or periodic inspection plan. *Camara* also indicates that "warrants should normally be sought only after entry is refused," and thus the consent alternative has been given preferred status.

(c) Inspection of Businesses. In *See v. City of Seattle* (1967), concerning defendant's conviction for not permitting a warrantless fire inspection of his locked commercial warehouse, the Court concluded that a "businessman, like the occupant of a residence, has a constitutional right to go about his business free from unreasonable official entries upon his private commercial property" and that consequently the *Camara* holding extended to the instant case. But the Court cautioned it was not implying "that business premises may not reasonably be inspected in many more situations than private homes, nor do we question such accepted regulatory techniques as licensing programs which require inspections prior to operating a business or marketing a product." A few years later, in *Colonnade Catering Corp. v. United States* (1970), the Court ruled the *See* warrant requirement was inapplicable to inspection of the business premises of a liquor licensee. This conclusion was based upon "the long history of the regulation of the liquor industry during pre-Fourth Amendment days" rather than any close analysis of the benefits or burdens of requiring a warrant in this context. Then came *United States v. Biswell* (1972), upholding a warrantless inspection pursuant to a statute authorizing such inspections during business hours of the premises of any firearms or ammunition dealer for the purpose of examining required records and the firearms or ammunition stored there. The Court reasoned that (1) such inspections are a "crucial part of the regulatory scheme" for controlling the firearms traffic; (2) that the negligible protections of a warrant were offset by the fact that a warrant requirement "could easily frustrate inspection" here, as under this inspection scheme (unlike that in *Camara*) "unannounced, even frequent, inspections are essential," and the "necessary flexibility as to time, scope and frequency is to be preserved"; and (3) that these inspections "pose only limited threats to the dealer's justifiable expectations of privacy," as when he "chooses to engage in this pervasively regulated business and to accept a federal license, he does so with the knowledge that his business records, firearms and ammunition will be subject to effective inspection."

Colonnade and *Biswell* were distinguished in *Marshall v. Barlow's, Inc.* (1978), because each concerned a "closely regulated industry," while the statutory provision held unconstitutional in the instant case permitted warrantless OSHA inspections of "any factory, plant, establishment, construction site, or other area, workplace or environment where work is performed by an employee." Though it was acknowledged that the act in question "regulates a myriad of safety details that may be amenable to speedy alteration or disguise," the Court in *Barlow's* deemed this an insufficient reason to permit warrantless inspections, for "the great majority of businessmen can be expected in normal course to consent to inspection without a warrant." *Barlow's* was in turn distinguished in *Donovan v. Dewey* (1981), upholding a statute authorizing warrantless inspections of underground and surface mines. While in *Barlow's* the statutory scheme was so loose as to leave matters in the "unbridled discretion" of administrative officers, that was not true in the instant case because "the statute's inspection program * * * provides a constitutionally adequate substitute for a warrant." The *Dewey* Court stressed that (1) "the Act requires inspection of *all* mines and specifically defines the frequency of inspection;" (2) a mine operator could know the inspector's purpose and the limits of the inspection because "the standards with which a mine operator is required to comply are all specifically set forth" in the statute and published administrative regulations; and (3) "the Act provides a specific mechanism for accommodating any special privacy concerns that a specific mine operator might have," as if entry is refused the government may only seek to enjoin future refusals, a proceeding which "provides an adequate forum for the mine owner to show that a specific search is outside the federal regulatory authority, or to seek from the District Court an order accommodating any unusual privacy interests that the mine owner might have." Similarly, in *New York v. Burger* (1987), upholding a warrantless inspection of an auto junkyard, the Court stressed the presence of these factors: (1) the business was "closely regulated," considering the duration and extensive nature of the regulatory scheme; (2) "a 'substantial' government interest," combatting auto theft, supported the regulatory scheme; (3) warrantless inspections are "necessary to further [the] regulatory scheme," as frequent and unannounced inspections are necessary to detect stolen cars and parts; (4) the statutory inspection scheme "provides a 'constitutionally adequate substitute for a warrant' " by informing the businessman that inspections will occur regularly, of their permissible scope, and who may conduct them; and (5) the permitted inspection is "carefully limited in time, place, and scope" (business hours only, auto dismantling business only, and of records, cars and parts only).

As for the grounds needed to conduct a business inspection, the Court in *Barlow's* followed the *Camara* standard, stating: "A warrant showing that a specific business has been chosen for an OSHA search on the basis of a general administrative plan for the enforcement of the Act derived from neutral sources such as, for example, dispersion of employees in various types of industries across a given area, and the desired frequency of searches in any of the lesser divisions of the area, would protect an employer's Fourth Amendment rights." Thus, the magistrate is to determine that there are reasonable legislative or administrative standards in existence and that the proposed inspection would conform to those standards, especially in terms of selection of the place to be inspected. As for the grounds needed when no warrant is required, the lower court cases are silent on the question, and the Supreme Court has not been very helpful regarding whether the authorities ever need show why they selected a particular business in a no-warrant situation.

(d) Welfare Inspections. The question in *Wyman v. James* (1971) was whether a recipient of welfare benefits may be required to submit to a warrantless home visit by a caseworker as a condition to the continued receipt of those benefits. The Court answered in the affirmative, but relied primarily upon two erroneous notions (that a home visit is not a "search * * * in the Fourth Amendment meaning of that term"; and that the Fourth Amendment limits of *Camara* have no application when criminal prosecution is not threatened), making it unnecessary to confront directly the basic questions of whether either the warrant requirement or the usual probable cause requirement should apply in such circumstances. Under a *Camara*-type analysis, it would suffice that a particular home visit was in accordance with an established schedule to make such visits at designated intervals or was undertaken upon a "watered-down" probable cause showing that the child's welfare was in danger, and a warrant would be required except upon a suspicion the child is in some immediate jeopardy.

(e) Inspections at Fire Scenes. As the Supreme Court put it in *Michigan v. Tyler* (1978), a "burning building clearly presents an exigency of sufficient proportions to render a warrantless entry 'reasonable'," as "it would defy reason to suppose that firemen must secure a warrant or consent before entering a burning structure to put out the blaze." But the question here is whether, when the occupant's justified expectation of privacy remains notwithstanding the fire, it is permissible for the authorities to conduct an inspection of those premises for the purpose of determining the cause of the fire. *Camara* suggests an affirmative answer; applying the balancing test to this situation, it may be reasoned that the "need to search" is in part a need to ascertain if the cause is one that could result in a renewal of the fire, hardly a matter that can be determined by external observation of the premises, and that there is here as in *Camara* a "limited invasion" because once again the inspection does not require rummaging through personal effects but instead is directed toward such facilities as the heating, ventilation, gas and electrical systems and the possible accumulation of combustibles. The Court in *Tyler* did not engage in such an assessment, but reached a result consistent with it, namely, that the mere fact a fire has occurred on the premises justifies officials "to remain in a building for a reasonable time to investigate the cause of a blaze after it has been extinguished," and that if later entries "detached from the initial exigency and warrantless entry" are made, then a warrant is required.

It is to be doubted that requiring a warrant here after the "initial exigency" has passed makes sense, provided that the authorities give "fair notice of an inspection." So the argument goes, a warrant is unnecessary to prevent arbitrariness in this context, for the places subject to such an inspection are limited and determined by a prior event that is beyond dispute—that the fire

department recently extinguished a fire there. The majority in
Tyler felt a warrant was nonetheless useful as a means of reassuring the property owner of the legality of the entry and "preventing
harassment by keeping that invasion to a minimum," but more
recently a majority of the Court declined to require a warrant for a
with-notice post-fire inspection into the cause of the fire. Unaffected by this development is the other *Tyler* holding, namely, that "if
the investigating officials find probable cause to believe that arson
has occurred and require further access to gather evidence for a
possible prosecution, they may obtain a warrant only upon a
traditional showing of probable cause applicable to searches for
evidence of crime." Such a warrant can confer greater search
authority than an administrative warrant obtained to ascertain the
cause of the fire.

(f) **Border Searches and Related Activities.** In *United
States v. Ramsey* (1977), the Court declared that "searches made at
the border, pursuant to the long-standing right of the sovereign to
protect itself by stopping and examining persons and property
crossing into this country, are reasonable simply by virtue of the
fact that they occur at the border." Thus, routine searches of
persons and things may be made upon their entry into the country
without first obtaining a search warrant and without establishing
probable cause or any suspicion at all in the individual case.
Ramsey held that the same was true of incoming international mail,
at least if that mail is of a nature to contain more than correspondence and the inspection does not include the reading of correspondence. These routine border searches may be made at the border
when entry is by land from Canada or Mexico, at a place where a
ship finally docks after coming from foreign waters, or a place
where aircraft land at the end of an international flight, and there
is also authority that they may be conducted inland at a functional
equivalent of the border or if there has been virtual constant
surveillance since the time of the border crossing, thus ensuring
that whatever is found in the search can be said to be an object that
crossed the border. In the main, these routine searches can be
justified by resort to the *Camara* balancing analysis, as there is a
vital national interest in preventing illegal entry and smuggling and
the searches are a limited invasion in the sense that they are
directed at a morally neutral class of persons who have it within
their power to determine the time and place of the search.

Certain kinds of border searches are deemed to be more than
routine and to require some kind of case-by-case justification. Thus
a strip search, where the person is forced to disrobe to a state that
would be offensive to the average person, may be undertaken only
upon a "real suspicion" supported by objective, articulable facts

that would reasonably lead an experienced, prudent customs official to suspect that the individual is concealing something on his person contrary to law. This standard lies somewhere in the nebulous region between mere suspicion and probable cause. As for a border search involving examination of the rectum, examination of the vagina, or the use of laxatives or emetics to determine what is in the stomach, it may be conducted only upon a "clear indication" of smuggling, which is also a standard that falls below the usual probable cause requirement. No search warrant is required even as to these non-routine and highly intrusive searches, a state of affairs that has frequently been questioned. But intrusions into the body are unreasonable if not done by medical personnel in medical surroundings utilizing customary medical techniques. "But the reasons that might support a requirement of some level of suspicion in the case of highly intrusive searches of the person—dignity and privacy interests of the person being searched—simply do not carry over to vehicles," the Court concluded in *United States v. Flores–Montano* (2004), and thus removal and disassembling of a vehicle's gas tank does not require reasonable suspicion, though "it may be true that some searches of property are so destructive as to require a different result." Because of the increasing utilization of alimentary canal smuggling, customs agents sometimes detain suspects at the border to await the "call of nature." The Court addressed this practice in *United States v. Montoya de Hernandez* (1985), holding: (i) "that the detention of a traveler at the border, beyond the scope of a routine customs search and inspection, is justified at its inception if customs agents, considering all the facts surrounding the traveler and her trip, reasonably suspect that the traveler is smuggling contraband in her alimentary canal"; and (ii) that such a detention is "reasonably related in scope to the circumstances which justified it initially" if the suspect is held so long as is "necessary to either verify or dispel the suspicion." This means that if, as in *de Hernandez*, the suspect declines to submit to an x-ray, then the detention on reasonable suspicion may continue until a bowel movement occurs.

To be distinguished from these border searches are a variety of activities conducted in the interior in an effort to identify and apprehend illegal aliens. One, the use of roving patrols to stop and search vehicles on the highways for illegal aliens without a warrant and without probable cause, was held in *Almeida–Sanchez v. United States* (1985) to violate the Fourth Amendment; it could not be upheld under the *Carroll–Chambers* rule (see § 2.7(b)) because that rule applies only when there is probable cause, and it could not be upheld as a *Camara* administrative search because that case condemned searches "at the discretion of the official in the field." But in *United States v. Brignoni–Ponce* (1975), the Court held that roving patrols may stop vehicles for the purpose of questioning the occupants upon facts "that reasonably warrant suspicion that the vehicles contain aliens who may be illegally in the country." Factors that may be taken into account, the Court helpfully added in *Brignoni,* include: (i) the "characteristics of the area," including its "proximity to the border, the usual patterns of traffic on the particular road, and previous experience with alien traffic"; (ii) "information about recent illegal border crossings in the area"; (iii) the "driver's behavior," such as "erratic driving or obvious attempts to evade officers"; (iv) the type of vehicle, such as a station wagon with large compartments, which "are frequently used for transporting concealed aliens"; (v) that the vehicle seems "heavily loaded" or has "an extraordinary number of passengers"; (vi) that persons are observed "trying to hide"; (vii) "the characteristic appearance of persons who live in Mexico, relying on such factors as the mode of dress and haircut"; and (viii) such other facts as are meaningful to the officer "in light of his experience detecting illegal entry and smuggling."

Two other decisions of the Court are concerned with the use of fixed checkpoints to discover illegal aliens. In *United States v. Ortiz* (1975), involving use of a checkpoint at which all cars travelling on a certain road were required to stop for investigation and were sometimes searched as a part of that investigation, the Court held "that at traffic checkpoints removed from the border and its functional equivalents, officers may not search private vehicles without consent or probable cause." As for utilizing a fixed checkpoint merely to stop vehicles and question the occupants, the Court in *United States v. Martinez–Fuerte* (1976) held this to be permissible under the *Camara* balancing test, as "the potential interference with legitimate traffic is minimal," and the "checkpoint operations both appear to and actually involve less discretionary enforcement activity."

(g) Vehicle Use Regulation. Although the practice of stopping vehicles at random to check drivers' licenses and vehicle registrations and determine that the vehicles are in proper mechanical condition had been upheld by the lower courts, the Supreme Court decided otherwise in *Delaware v. Prouse* (1979) "by balancing its intrusion on the individual's Fourth Amendment interests against its promotion of legitimate governmental interests." The Court thus held

> that except in those situations in which there is at least articulable and reasonable suspicion that a motorist is unlicensed or that an automobile is not registered, or that either the vehicle or an occupant is otherwise subject to seizure for violation of law, stopping an automobile and detaining the

driver in order to check his driver's license and the registration
of the automobile are unreasonable under the Fourth Amendment. This holding does not preclude the State of Delaware or
other States from developing methods for spot checks that
involve less intrusion or that do not involve the unconstrained
exercise of discretion. Questioning of all oncoming traffic at
roadblock-type stops is one possible alternative.

It thus appears that the Court would uphold the use of a checkpoint, as have the lower courts, when used to check drivers' licenses
and vehicle registrations or to conduct safety inspections of vehicles. And while the *Prouse* majority describes the practice in terms
of dealing with "all oncoming traffic," it is not necessary for a
checkpoint to stop every car in order to be systematic but only for
officers to be following some pattern that will minimize their
discretion in choosing whether to stop a particular auto. Also, the
Court in *Prouse* explained its ruling was not intended to "cast
doubt on the permissibility of roadblock truck weigh stations and
inspection checkpoints, at which some vehicles may be subject to
further detention for safety and regulatory inspection than are
others," another procedure that has been upheld by the lower
courts.

The sobriety checkpoint, at which traffic is stopped at a temporary location so that each driver may be observed to see if he is
under the influence and, if signs of intoxication are detected, may
be directed out of the traffic flow for further scrutiny and perhaps
sobriety tests, was upheld in *Michigan Dept. of State Police v. Sitz*
(1990). Utilizing a balancing test similar to that employed in
Prouse, the majority in *Sitz* stressed these factors: (1) the states'
strong interest in eradicating the serious drunken driving problem;
(2) the slight "intrusion on motorists subjected to a brief stop at a
highway checkpoint," where (as in the instant case) "checkpoints
are selected pursuant to [established] guidelines, and uniformed
police officers stop every approaching vehicle"; and (3) that it is for
"politically accountable officials" to decide "as to which among
reasonable alternative law enforcement techniques should be employed."

The Coast Guard is authorized by statute to stop vessels upon
the high seas and waters of the United States to conduct inspections. These special inspection powers do not extend to search into
private books, papers or personal belongings, but it is permissible
to examine safety equipment, inspect documentation papers, check
the identification number on the beam or frame to ensure it
matches the number in those papers, and otherwise identify the
ship when no documentation is supplied. The *Prouse* decision does
not bar or limit exercise of that statutory authority, the Court
concluded in *United States v. Villamonte–Marquez* (1983), for the

"nature of waterborne commerce in waters providing ready access to the open sea is sufficiently different from the nature of vehicular traffic on highways as to make possible alternatives to the sort of 'stop' made in this case less likely to accomplish the obviously essential governmental purposes involved."

Whenever departure from the usual warrant and/or probable cause requirements is claimed to be justified on the basis of some "special need," as is ordinarily the case with respect to a vehicle checkpoint, it is necessary that this need be something other than the state's general law enforcement interest, as is illustrated by *City of Indianapolis v. Edmond* (2000). The Court there held that city-operated vehicle checkpoints, complete with drug dogs, undertaken to interdict unlawful drugs, contravened the Fourth Amendment. As for the city's reliance on *Martinez–Fuerte, Prouse* and *Sitz*, the *Edmond* majority distinguished those cases because in none of them "did we indicate approval of a checkpoint program whose primary purpose was to detect evidence of ordinary criminal wrongdoing." As for the city's response that securing the border and apprehending drunk drivers "are * * * law enforcement activities, and law enforcement officers employ arrests and criminal prosecutions in pursuit of these goals," the Court responded that analysis at that "high level of generality" would mean there "would be little check on the ability of the authorities to construct roadblocks for almost any conceivable law enforcement purpose." *Edmond* was later deemed not to bar an informational roadblock seeking witnesses to a recent homicide because, as explained in *Illinois v. Lidster* (2004), the "stop's primary law enforcement purpose was *not* to determine whether a vehicle's occupants were committing a crime, but to ask vehicle occupants, as members of the public, for their help in providing information about a crime in all likelihood committed by others."

(h) **Airport Searches.** When airplane hijacking became a major problem in the late 1960's, the government first attempted to deal with it by establishing procedures for identifying a relatively select group of air passengers who should be subjected to close preboarding screening. When a passenger checked in for a flight, the agent would apply a behavioral profile, based upon a detailed study of all then known hijackers, to determine if he was a potential hijacker. In the boarding area, a person so identified would have to pass through a magnetometer set to detect the amount of metal in a small handgun. A person who both fit the profile and triggered the magnetometer would be interviewed, and if he failed to supply adequate identification he would be frisked and his carry-on luggage searched. Consequently, these more intrusive actions were undertaken against a very small percentage of passengers. Utilizing the balancing test, courts upheld these searches on the ground that they were based upon the reasonable suspicion required by *Terry v. Ohio* (1968). On the need side of the equation there was the fact that air piracy presented extreme dangers to the traveling public and could be effectively dealt with only if the potential hijacker was intercepted on the ground. On the intrusion side, it was relevant that the searches were of a morally neutral class who must voluntarily come to and enter the search area and were under the supervision of airlines who have a substantial interest in assuring that their passengers are not unnecessarily harassed. Those considerations made it reasonable to conduct the searches upon the degree of suspicion provided by the profile-plus-magnetometer-plus-questioning selection process, which experience had shown produced a person carrying a weapon six per cent of the time.

In 1973, efforts to utilize this selective process were abandoned in favor of a program whereunder *all* passengers were checked before boarding. Every passenger was required to pass through the magnetometer, and his carry-on luggage was inspected either by hand or by passing it through an X-ray device. If the magnetometer sounded, the passenger had to remove items from his person until he was able to pass through the device without triggering it, and if the X-ray detected a suspicious object the passenger was not allowed to proceed unless he permitted an examination of the contents of the luggage. Especially because use of the magnetometer and X-ray both qualify as searches, the question arose as to whether subjecting all passengers to these searches was constitutionally permissible. Employing the balancing test once again, the courts decided this procedure also passed Fourth Amendment muster, not because there was a reasonable suspicion of those searched, but rather because (as in *Camara*) it involved a general regulatory scheme without the potential for arbitrariness. Even under this system, *Terry* reasonable suspicion sometimes comes into play, as where a person has "passed" the inspection in the literal sense but it has produced facts of a highly suspicious nature.

As a consequence of the tragic events of 9/11/01, Congress enacted the Aviation and Transportation Security Act of 2001, which placed all airport screening in the hands of a new agency, the Transportation Security Administration. The screening procedures required under the Act are considerably more intrusive and intensive than those earlier mandated by the FAA, and now include examination of checked luggage for explosives by "a variety of methods—bomb-scan machines, dog sniffs, and manual searches." But, while the screening of passengers and their luggage has generally become more intense than in the past, it has often proved impossible to give the "full treatment" to each and every traveler, and hence some degree of selectivity has proved necessary. Whether a selective process tending to focus upon Arab Muslim men is justified has been a matter of vigorous debate. A new computerized screening system, claimed "not to use race or ethnicity as criteria," is being made operational, but because it would involve gathering much background information about travelers it is a matter of concern on that basis.

Analysis similar to that used in the airport screening cases has been used to uphold other inspection schemes contemplating examination of all persons who wish to enter a particular place where there are special security needs. Illustrative are checkpoint inspections of visitors to a penal institution, to a military installation, or to government buildings which have been the targets of violence or threats of violence.

(i) Searches Directed at Prisoners. In keeping with the Supreme Court's earlier declaration that "a prisoner is not wholly stripped of constitutional protections when he is imprisoned for crime," many courts held that prisoners have a Fourth Amendment expectation of privacy of a diminished scope; under that approach, a "shakedown" search of the cell and personal effects of prisoners could be undertaken only pursuant to standardized procedures or upon reasonable suspicion. But that approach was rejected by the Supreme Court in *Hudson v. Palmer* (1984), concluding that a "right of privacy in traditional Fourth Amendment terms is fundamentally incompatible with the close and continual surveillance of inmates and their cells required to ensure institutional security and internal order. We are satisfied that society would insist that the prisoner's expectation of privacy always yield to what must be considered the paramount interest in institutional security." It is unclear whether *Hudson* also applies to searches and seizures of the person of a prisoner.

The Supreme Court in *Procunier v. Martinez* (1974), concerning censorship of prison mail, declared that an "obvious example of justifiable censorship of prisoner mail would be refusal to send or deliver letters concerning escape plans or containing other information concerning proposed criminal activity, whether within or without the prison," and lower courts have reasoned that by implication this permits the inspection of all mail for such contents. The same reasoning has been used to justify eavesdropping upon conversations of prisoners and visitors. It has been questioned, however, whether the risk of escape or further criminal conduct is sufficiently great as to *all* types of detainees to justify those practices across the board. In one post-*Hudson* decision, the Supreme Court concluded that when prison regulations affect outgoing mail, as opposed to incoming mail, there must be a "closer fit between the regulation and the purpose it serves," but yet concluded that in neither case must the regulation satisfy a "least restrictive means" test. It is thus not surprising that more recent lower court decisions have upheld the review of prison inmates' outgoing general correspondence.

(j) **Searches Directed at Probationers and Parolees.** A variety of theories have been articulated by the courts in purported justification for holding that probationers and parolees may be lawfully subjected to searches which, absent their status, would be deemed unlawful because of the absence of probable cause or a search warrant or both. Three of them—that such persons are in the "constructive custody" of the government; that parole or probation is an "act of grace" that may be attended by whatever restrictions upon privacy the government may deem appropriate; and that searches of such persons are proper because voluntarily consented to as part of the "contract" of release—are less than convincing. There is yet another theory that *does* make sense, which is that some "special" Fourth Amendment rules apply in this area by application of the *Camara* balancing test. On the need side of the equation, the basic point is that the very existence of these forms of conditional release for convicted criminals reflects a legislative judgment that these men can achieve effective rehabilitation only with the aid of supervision and guidance from governmental officials, and that in certain types of cases, at least, close surveillance tends to reduce the rate of recidivism. Such was the approach taken in *Griffin v. Wisconsin* (1987), upholding search of a probationer's home without a warrant or full probable cause because of the "special needs" of the probation system. The warrant requirement was deemed inappropriate for probation officers, who "have in mind the welfare of the probationer" and must "respond quickly to evidence of misconduct." The usual probable cause standard was deemed inapplicable because it "would reduce the deterrent effect of the supervisory arrangement" and because "the probation agency must be able to act based upon a lesser degree of certainty than the Fourth Amendment would otherwise require in order to intervene before a probationer does damage to himself or society."

Considering that part of the *Camara* balancing test requiring that the special search authority be limited to the unique problem giving rise to the need for it, it would seem that the rehabilitation objective is best served by giving the special authority only to parole and probation officers and not to the police, and by deeming the search unlawful if a probation or parole officer used his special power as nothing more than the agent of the police. Those conclusions, consistent with the reasoning in *Griffin*, seemed even more solid as a result of the Court's later decisions holding that "special needs" analysis could be used only when the interests served were other than ordinary law enforcement. But the Supreme Court then found it possible to avoid any such limitations in the probationer search area by developing a different supporting theory in *United States v. Knights* (2001). After Knights' state conviction for a drug offense, he was placed on probation subject to the condition that he "[s]ubmit his ... person, property, place of residence, vehicle, personal effects, to search at any time, with or without a search warrant, warrant of arrest or reasonable cause by any probation officer or law enforcement officer." Three days later, a sheriff's detective, without the knowledge or participation of probation officials, made a warrantless search of Knights' residence on reasonable suspicion he was involved in vandalism, resulting in federal charges. The district court granted his motion to suppress the evidence found in his home on the ground that the search had been "investigatory" rather than "probationary," and the court of appeals affirmed. But the Supreme Court, after noting that *Griffin* expressly declared that its "special needs" holding made it "unnecessary to consider whether" warrantless searches of probationers were otherwise reasonable within the meaning of the Fourth Amendment, proceeded to answer the reserved question in the affirmative. The Court declared that the search in the instant case passed muster "under our general Fourth Amendment approach of 'examining the totality of the circumstances'" and then determining reasonableness "by assessing, on the one hand, the degree to which it intrudes upon an individual's privacy and, on the other, the degree to which it is needed for the promotion of legitimate government interests." Proceeding with the balancing of interests, the Court concluded (a) that the "probation order clearly expressed the search condition and Knights was unambiguously informed of it," meaning the "probation condition thus significantly diminished Knights's reasonable expectation of privacy"; (b) that because a probationer "will be more likely to engage in criminal conduct than an ordinary member of the community," the State's "interest in apprehending violators of the criminal law * * * may therefore justifiably focus on probationers in a way that it does not on the ordinary citizen"; and (c) that "the balance of these considerations requires no more than reasonable suspicion to conduct a search of this probationer's house" and "render[s] a warrant requirement unnecessary." The Court then concluded: "Because our holding rests on ordinary Fourth Amendment analysis that considers all the circumstances of a search, there is no basis for examining official purpose."

(k) Searches Directed at Students. Searches directed at the persons or effects of students while on the premises of an educational institution have on occasion been upheld even when they could not pass the Fourth Amendment requirements applicable in the typical criminal investigation. The Supreme Court dealt with this general problem in *New Jersey v. T.L.O.* (1985), involving search of a high school student's purse. The Court held that "the Fourth Amendment applies to searches conducted by school authorities," but that under the *Camara* balancing test such a search could be conducted without a warrant and without full probable cause. What is required is that the search of the student be justified at its inception (i.e., that there be "reasonable grounds for suspecting that the search will turn up evidence that the student has violated or is violating either the law or the rules of the school") and that it be reasonable in scope (i.e., that "the measures adopted are reasonably related to the objectives of the search and not excessively intrusive in light of the age and sex of the student and the nature of the infraction"). The Court also cautioned that there were several issues regarding searches directed at students it had not resolved, such as "whether individualized suspicion is an essential element of the reasonableness standard," "whether a schoolchild has a legitimate expectation of privacy in lockers, desks, or other school property provided for storage of school supplies," and whether a higher standard would be needed in "assessing the legality of searches conducted by school officials in conjunction with or at the behest of law enforcement agencies."

Later, in *Vernonia School District 47J v. Acton* (1995), the Court held that on the facts presented there was one type of search that did *not* require individualized suspicion: drug testing of student athletes. The Court deemed the privacy expectations intruded upon to be somewhat limited, as per *T.L.O.* all school children are subject to considerable supervision and control, and student athletes' expectations "are even less" because they voluntarily chose to subject themselves to greater regulation, "somewhat like adults who choose to participate in a 'closely regulated industry.'" Also, the intrusion upon privacy complained of was limited, as the tests were taken under conditions "nearly identical to those typically encountered in public restrooms," and the test results "are disclosed only to a limited class of school personnel who have a need to know." That intrusion, the Court concluded, was outweighed by the legitimate government interests advanced: deterring drug use by school children and, in the case, of student athletes, preventing physical harm to drug users and other players. The less intrusive alternative of testing only upon individualized suspicion was dismissed by the *Acton* majority as "probably impracticable." *Acton* was applied so as to uphold drug testing of students in much less compelling circumstances in *Board of Education of Independent School District No. 92 of Pottawatomie County v. Earls* (2002), where the random testing policy was applicable to middle and high school students participating in *any* extracurricular activity. This was accomplished by holding that the *Acton* emphasis upon the especially low privacy expectations of student-athletes "was not essential to our decision" in the earlier case and that, "in any event," all students who "voluntarily subject themselves" to additional regulations by opting for extracurricular activities have as a consequence "a limited expectation of privacy," and that the fact that in *Acton* the athletes were at the heart of the drug problem there "was not essential to the holding" in that case, which "did not require the school to test the group of students most likely to use drugs."

At the college level, the cases in the main have concerned searches of rooms in dormitories maintained by the educational institution and rented to students matriculating there. One view is that here as well the reasonable suspicion test applies, and the emphasis once again is upon the special need to maintain a proper educational atmosphere. The contrary view is that traditional Fourth Amendment standards apply to such searches, a conclusion that is supported by the fact that application of the *Camara* balancing test here does not produce a convincing showing that broader authority is needed. For one thing, the searches at issue cannot be characterized as a limited intrusion; a student's dormitory room is his house and home for all practical purposes, and he has the same interest in the privacy of his room as any adult has in the privacy of his home, dwelling, or lodging. Nor is the need as strong as at the high school level. College students are more mature and less in need of general supervision, their presence is not compelled by attendance laws, they are not in day-long close contact with one another in a single location, and their dorm rooms are not concerned with the academic affairs of the university community.

(*l*) Searches Directed at Public Employees. *O'Connor v. Ortega* (1987), a § 1983 action challenging search by a doctor's supervisors of his desk and filing cabinets at the state hospital where he was employed, focused attention upon the somewhat limited Fourth Amendment rights of public employees. Though the Court was firmly of the view that "[s]earches and seizures by government employers or supervisors of the private property of their employees * * * are subject to the restraints of the Fourth Amendment," the protections of the Amendment were deemed to be somewhat different in this context. Even assuming that the facts of the particular case show that the employee had a justified expectation of privacy in the particular area searched, it is necessary in this context to "balance the invasion of the employee's legitimate expectations of privacy against the government's need for supervision, control and the efficient operation of the workplace." One consequence of this balancing is that no search warrant is needed for intrusions "for legitimate work-related reasons wholly unrelated to illegal conduct." Moreover, intrusions "for noninvestigatory, work-related purposes, as well as for investigation of work-related misconduct, should be judged by the standard of reasonableness under all the circumstances" rather than the traditional quantum of probable cause.

Drug testing of government employees (or, of private employees pursuant to government regulation) has been addressed by several courts recently. Upon a weighing of the competing public and private interests, most lower courts have concluded that such testing is constitutional at least in those instances in which there was reasonable individualized suspicion. These cases reflect the judgment that the individualized suspicion test fairly accommodates the legitimate interest in employee privacy without unduly restricting the employer's opportunity to monitor and control drug use by employees. Whether random or more generalized testing is also permissible upon some special showing is a more difficult question, though the Supreme Court has upheld two such inspection schemes where testing was triggered by a specific event and where, in addition, it was concluded a special need existed for testing in such circumstances. In *Skinner v. Railway Labor Executives Ass'n* (1989), concerning blood and urine tests required of railroad employees following major train accidents or incidents and breath and urine samples authorized to be taken from railroad employees who violate certain safety rules, the Court stressed the need "to prevent or deter that hazardous conduct" by "those engaged in safety-sensitive tasks" and also the "limited discretion exercised" by the testing employers. In *National Treasury Employees Union v. Von Raab* (1989), concerning urinalysis tests required of Customs Service employees upon their transfer or promotion to positions having a direct involvement in drug interdiction or requiring the carrying of firearms, the Court emphasized the "Government's compelling interests in preventing the promotion of drug users to positions where they might endanger the integrity of our Nation's borders or the life of the citizenry."

The two drug testing cases just mentioned, as well as the testing-of-students cases (*Acton; Earls*), must be distinguished from *Ferguson v. City of Charleston* (2001), where a task force made up of representatives of the Charleston public hospital, police and other public officials developed a policy for identifying and testing pregnant patients suspected of drug use and then turning the results over to law enforcement agents without the knowledge or consent of the patients. This policy, which also contained procedures for arresting patients and for prosecuting them for drug offenses and/or child neglect, was challenged by a group of obstetrical patients at that hospital who had been arrested after testing positive for cocaine. The Court answered in the negative the question of "whether the interest in using the threat of criminal sanctions to deter pregnant women from using cocaine can justify a departure from the general rule that an official nonconsensual search is unconstitutional if not authorized by a valid warrant." The instant case, the majority reasoned, was different from the Court's prior drug testing cases in two material respects: (1) in the previous cases "there was no misunderstanding about the purpose of the test or the potential use of the test results, and there were protections against the dissemination of the results to third parties"; and (2) the "critical difference" between the earlier cases and the instant one "lies in the nature of the 'special need' asserted as justification for the warrantless searches," for in all the earlier cases the "special need" advanced was "one divorced from the State's general interest in law enforcement," while here "the central and indispensable feature of the policy from its inception was the use of law enforcement to coerce the patients into substance abuse treatment."

§ 2.10 Consent Searches

(a) **Nature of Consent.** Consent searches are sometimes relied upon by police when probable cause is present but they feel either that they do not have time to get a warrant or that they would simply like to avoid that time-consuming process, but more often an effort is made to obtain consent where probable cause is lacking and no warrant could be obtained. The practice of making searches based on consent is by no means a disfavored one. The issue of whether a consent search is simply a matter of the consenting party having acted voluntarily or whether instead the waiver of a constitutional right is involved, so as to bring into play the need to show "an intentional relinquishment or abandonment of a known right" was finally resolved in *Schneckloth v. Busta-monte* (1973). The Court there upheld a consent to search a car given during a street encounter in which no Fourth Amendment warnings were given. Noting that the voluntariness standard was the traditional means for balancing the interests in the police interrogation area, the Court observed that in the consent search area there are also "two competing concerns [which] must be accommodated * * *—the legitimate need for such searches and the equally important requirement of assuring the absence of coercion." A "fair accommodation" of those competing interests, the majority concluded in *Schneckloth,* lies in "the traditional definition of 'voluntariness,'" as a need to show the consenting party was aware of his rights would "create serious doubt whether consent searches could continue to be conducted" in light of the prosecution's difficulty in proving such awareness.

As for the suggestion that this would not be so if the police advised a person of his rights before eliciting his consent, the Court responded:

> [I]t would be thoroughly impractical to impose on the normal consent search the detailed requirements of an effective warning. Consent searches are part of the standard investigatory techniques of law enforcement agencies. They normally occur on the highway, or in a person's home or office, and under informal and unstructured conditions. The circumstances that prompt the initial request to search may develop quickly or be a logical extension of investigative police questioning. The police may seek to investigate further suspicious circumstances or to follow up leads developed in questioning persons at the scene of a crime. These situations are a far cry from the structured atmosphere of a trial where, assisted by counsel if he chooses, a defendant is informed of his trial rights. * * * And, while surely a closer question, these situations are still immeasurably, far removed from "custodial interrogation" where, in *Miranda v. Arizona,* we found that the Constitution required certain now familiar warnings as a prerequisite to police interrogation.

Thus, while a "strict standard of waiver" applies "to those rights guaranteed to a criminal defendant to insure * * * a fair criminal trial," it need not extend to the "protections of the Fourth Amendment," which "are of a wholly different order, and have nothing whatever to do with promoting the fair ascertainment of truth at a criminal trial."

A somewhat different issue concerning the meaning of consent in this context is illustrated by *United States v. Elrod* (1971), where Wright consented to a search of a room occupied by him and Elrod, revealing the fruits of a bank robbery, but that evidence was suppressed because of later-acquired information showing that Wright was mentally incompetent at the time that he signed the consent form. The court explained: "No matter how genuine the belief of the officers is that the consenter is apparently of sound mind and deliberately acting, the search depending on his consent fails if it is judicially determined that he lacked mental capacity." Some courts, however, have articulated the consent search standard in a way that would produce a different result on the *Elrod* facts; the issue is said to be whether the officers, as reasonable men, could conclude that defendant's consent was given. When *Schneckloth* was decided, the Court's "voluntariness" test from the confession cases would have supported the *Elrod* result, for it was then accepted that a confession could be "coerced" by innocent conduct of the police when a condition of the suspect was unknown to them. But the rule is now otherwise as to confessions (see § 5.2(b), (c)), and presumably this means that the *Schneckloth* rule will not produce the result reached in *Elrod*. Other aspects of *Schneckloth* also lend support to that conclusion. The Court emphasized both the value of searches made by consent and the fact that the Fourth Amendment is unique because it does not protect against police action undertaken upon "reasonably though mistakenly believed" facts. Both of these considerations underlie the appealing notion that because the Fourth Amendment is only concerned with discouraging unreasonable activity on the part of law enforcement officers, it is not violated when a search is conducted upon a reasonable (albeit mistaken) belief that voluntary consent has been granted.

(b) Factors Bearing on Validity of Consent. The Court held in *Schneckloth* that "the question whether a consent to a search was in fact 'voluntary' or was the product of duress or coercion, express or implied, is a question of fact to be determined from the totality of the circumstances." One factor likely to produce a finding of no consent under this test is a claim by the police that they can make the search in any event. Thus, if the police claim that they have a search warrant and the person then submits to a search because of that claim, but it later turns out that the police actually had no warrant or the prosecution later declines to rely upon the warrant as the basis for the search, the evidence must be suppressed because it was obtained by a submission to a claim of lawful authority. The same is true when the police have incorrectly asserted that they have a right to make a warrantless search under the then existing circumstances or have intimated as much by merely declaring that they have come to search or are going to search. A threat by the police to *obtain* a search warrant is not materially different from a claim that a warrant has already issued, and thus such a threat is likely to invalidate a subsequent consent if there were not then grounds upon which a warrant could issue. But if there were grounds for issuance of a search warrant, then the advice of a law enforcement agent that, absent a consent to search, a warrant can be obtained does not constitute coercion, as in such a case the person has been correctly advised of his legal situation. In the eyes of some courts, a police threat to *seek* a search warrant is not coercive because the officer was merely telling the defendant what he had a legal right to do. But it is to be doubted whether the ordinary person, when confronted with a request by an officer to consent to a search, would discriminate between the statement that otherwise the officer would *get* a search warrant, as compared with a statement that otherwise he would *apply for* a warrant. Absent such claims, consideration must be given to whether the circumstances were coercive, which necessitates attention to whether the person was confronted with many officers or a display of weapons, whether he was in custody and if so whether the circumstances of the custody were coercive, and whether the alleged consent was obtained in the course of stationhouse interrogation. Of course, if the prior police restraint was itself illegal, the consent may also be challenged as the fruit of the poisonous tree (see § 8.4(b)).

In *Schneckloth,* the majority, in responding to the argument that the failure to require the prosecution to establish knowledge as prerequisite to a valid consent would relegate the Fourth Amendment to the special province of "the sophisticated, the knowledgeable, and the privileged," observed that the "traditional definition of voluntariness we accept today has always taken into account evidence of minimal schooling [and] low intelligence." Consistent with this position, courts determining the voluntariness of a consent must assess whether the individual was immature and impressionable or experienced and well-educated, and whether that person was in an excited emotional state, mentally incompetent, or under the influence of drugs or alcohol at the time the purported consent was given. (But, by virtue of the significant change in the "voluntariness" test that has occurred in the law on confessions as a result of *Colorado v. Connelly* (1986), involuntariness cannot be grounded solely in the defendant's mental condition, for "the crucial element of police overreaching"—that is, "coercive" police conduct, such as exploiting defendant's deficient mental condition—must be present.) A consent is suspect if given by one who earlier refused to consent, unless some reason appears to explain the change in position. By like reasoning, if the consent is preceded by a valid confession or by cooperation in the investigation generally, this enhances the chances that the consent was voluntary, and the same may be said of cooperation in the search itself. What then if the consent was by a person suspected of the crime under investigation but who denied his guilt? One view, taken in *Higgins v. United States* (1954), is that if such a denial preceded an alleged consent that led to the discovery of incriminating evidence, then the consent must be held invalid, as "no sane man who denies his guilt would actually be willing that policemen search his room for contraband which is certain to be discovered." But *Higgins* has not received general acceptance. Sometimes it is simply distinguished away, which is certainly correct in cases where it appears the defendant thought the incriminating evidence had been removed or was cleverly concealed and thus not likely to be discovered, or where the objects found were not obviously incriminating in character. On other occasions the *Higgins* test has been rejected as an unworkable test based upon hindsight which, in any event, is based upon the erroneous assumption that the pressure exerted on a criminal by the realization that the "jig is up" amounts to coercion. The Supreme Court has summarily rejected a *Higgins*-type argument by asserting the question is what a reasonable innocent person would have done.

The Supreme Court in *Schneckloth,* as a consequence of adopting the voluntariness test for consent searches, concluded that "while the subject's knowledge of a right to refuse is a factor to be taken into account, the prosecution is not required to demonstrate such knowledge as a prerequisite to establishing a voluntary consent." That is, consent may be established without a showing that the police warned the consenting party of his Fourth Amendment rights or that he was otherwise aware of those rights. Indeed, as the Court emphasized in a later case, it is *not* the case that "a presumption of invalidity attaches if a citizen consented without explicit notification that he or she was free to refuse to cooperate." (Relying on *Schneckloth,* the Court later held that if a person has been lawfully seized, for example, because of commission of a traffic violation, and following the point at which the detainee would be free to go he consents to a search, that consent is not made involuntary by virtue of the officer's failure to specifically advise the detainee that he was free to go.) Though the Court in *Schneckloth* emphasized that the decision was "a narrow one," extending only to the situation in which "the subject of the search is not in custody," a few years later the Court extended the *Schneckloth* rule to a case in which the consent was obtained from a person in police custody. In that case, *United States v. Watson* (1976), it was stressed that the "consent was given while on a public street, not in the confines of the police station," but lower courts have in the main utilized the "totality of the circumstances" approach without regard to the nature of the custody. Such an extension of *Schneckloth,* it may be argued, ignores the teaching of *Miranda v. Arizona* (1966) that there is "compulsion inherent in custodial surroundings" and overlooks the fact that the concern in *Schneckloth* about warnings being "impractical" under the "informal and unstructured conditions" of a roadside search does not extend to situations in which the person has been taken into custody. In any event, proof by the prosecution that the consenting party was warned of his rights or that he was aware of his rights is often a significant factor leading to a finding of voluntary consent, and sometimes will be essential if prior coercion is to be overcome.

Some courts have held that a consent to search given during custodial interrogation must be preceded by *Miranda* warnings because the request to search is a request that defendant be a witness against himself he is privileged to refuse under the Fifth

Amendment. But the prevailing and better view is to the contrary, for a consent to search, as such, is neither testimonial nor communicative in the Fifth Amendment sense. Although the giving of *Miranda* warnings may contribute to a finding of voluntariness, these warnings are not equivalent to Fourth Amendment warnings in terms of overcoming prior coercion, for a defendant might well not understand that the "silence" referred to covers not allowing a search. There may be circumstances in which a consent to search will be invalidated because made without counsel or waiver of the right to counsel. The Supreme Court has held that "a person's Sixth and Fourteenth Amendment right to counsel attaches only at or after the time that adversary judicial proceedings have been initiated against him," and then only as to a "critical stage," which means when "the accused required aid in coping with legal problems or assistance in meeting his adversary." A post-charge solicitation of the defendant to consent to a search would appear to be such a situation. And in any event, a pre-consent refusal of a person's request to consult counsel would weigh heavily against finding that consent to be voluntary.

(c) **Consent by Deception.** A rather special type of consent case, involving considerations different from those discussed above, is that in which the police have obtained consent to intrude into a certain private area by resort to deceit. One situation, which the Supreme Court has confronted with some frequency, is that in which the person conceals the fact that he is a policeman or that he has already agreed to act on behalf of the police. In *On Lee v. United States* (1952), where an informant wired for sound entered defendant's laundry and engaged him in incriminating conversations, the Court rather summarily concluded that "Chin Poy entered a place of business with the consent, if not by the implied invitation, of the petitioner," and that "the claim that Chin Poy's entrance was a trespass because consent to his entry was obtained by fraud must be rejected." Similarly, in *Hoffa v. United States* (1966), where an old friend of the defendant gave incriminating testimony based upon his visits to defendant's hotel room as an agent of the government, the Court characterized the situation as one of "misplaced confidence" and concluded that it was *not* true that "the Fourth Amendment protects a wrongdoer's misplaced belief that a person to whom he voluntarily confides his wrongdoing will not reveal it." *Lewis v. United States* (1966), decided the same day, involved a situation in which a federal drug agent gained access to defendant's home by misrepresenting his identity and expressing a willingness to purchase narcotics. Stressing that "the petitioner invited the undercover agent to his home for the specific purpose of executing a felonious sale of narcotics," the Court concluded that "when, as here, the home is converted into a commercial center to which outsiders are invited for purposes of transacting unlawful business, that business is entitled to no greater sanctity than if it were carried on in a store, a garage, a car, or on the street. A government agent, in the same manner as a private person, may accept an invitation to do business and may enter upon the premises for the very purposes contemplated by the occupant." These decisions, then, appear to support the following proposition: when an individual gives consent to another to intrude into an area or activity otherwise protected by the Fourth Amendment, aware that he will thereby reveal to this other person either criminal conduct or evidence of such conduct, the consent is not vitiated merely because it would not have been given but for the nondisclosure or affirmative misrepresentation that made the consenting party unaware of the other person's identity as a police officer or police agent.

Though some consider even *Lewis* as objectionable on the ground that deliberate deception about an obviously material fact should be regarded as inconsistent with voluntariness, a more appropriate concern is that of keeping the above-stated principle within reasonable bounds. One attractive proposal is that permissible deception by a stranger *must* include a stated intention on his part to join the consenting party in criminal activity, for in that way innocent persons will be spared from intrusions upon their privacy by deception. But lower courts in the main have not recognized such a limitation, and have instead relied upon the broader proposition that the Fourth Amendment affords no protection to the person who voluntarily reveals incriminating evidence to another in the mistaken belief that the latter will not disclose it. Even that formulation should often bar some of the more extreme forms of deception, such as police entry of a private home in the guise of an employee of the gas company.

A somewhat different kind of case is that in which the consenting party knows he is dealing with a law enforcement officer or agent, but there is some deception as to the latter's objective or purpose. Certainly it is not objectionable that the agent has manifested a willingness to be bribed. But what of a misrepresentation as to the reason a consent to search was being sought, as in *Alexander v. United States* (1968), where officers seeking stolen marked money obtained consent to search by claiming they were looking for stolen jewelry? Though the court there concluded the "fraudulent warning" deprived the consent of its validity, it is by no means clear that this is so. The fact remains that the police did not "see * * * anything that was not contemplated," an important factor in *Lewis;* that such deception has been tolerated in the voluntariness-of-confession cases; and that this kind of deception does not pose a risk to innocent persons because it will likely produce a consent that would otherwise have been withheld only from a person guilty of the undisclosed crime. By comparison, when the police misrepresentation of purpose is so extreme that it deprives the individual of the ability to make a fair assessment of the need to surrender his privacy, as where police gained entry to defendant's apartment on the false claim they were investigating a gas leak, the consent should not be considered valid.

(d) Third Party Consent: General Considerations. Although in *Schneckloth* it was noted that under some circumstances a person's privacy may be lawfully invaded by virtue of consent obtained by police from a third party, the Court has experienced some difficulty in identifying just what it takes to give a certain third party this power. In *Stoner v. California* (1964), holding a hotel clerk could not consent to search of a guest's room, the Court reasoned that the guest could surrender his rights only "directly or through an agent" and found no evidence that the "clerk had been authorized by the petitioner" to permit the police to enter his room. In *Bumper v. North Carolina* (1968), holding the consent by defendant's grandmother had been coerced, the Court left little doubt that but for the coercion the evidence would have been admitted because she "owned both the house and the rifle," that is, the place searched and the thing seized. Then, in *Frazier v. Cupp* (1969), holding defendant's cousin could consent to a search of a duffel bag that he held and in which both he and his cousin kept some of their personal effects, the Court appeared to abandon the agency and property theories in favor of an "assumption of risk" formulation: "Petitioner, in allowing [his cousin] Rawls to use the bag and in leaving it in his house, must be taken to have assumed the risk that Rawls would allow someone else to look inside."

Then came *United States v. Matlock* (1974), where, following defendant's arrest in the yard of the house in which he lived, a woman consented to search of the bedroom she shared with defendant. The Court deemed it clear that the prosecution "may show that permission to search was obtained from a third party who possessed common authority over or other sufficient relationship to the premises or effects sought to be inspected." The Court then dropped this explanatory footnote:

> Common authority is, of course, not to be implied from the mere property interest a third party has in the property. The authority which justifies the third-party consent does not rest upon the law of property, with its attendant historical and legal refinements, * * * but rests rather on mutual use of the property by persons generally having joint access or control for most purposes, so that it is reasonable to recognize that any of the co-inhabitants has the right to permit the inspection in his

own right and that the others have assumed the risk that one of their number might permit the common area to be searched.

The Court thus identified two bases for its "common authority" rule: (i) that the consenting party could permit the search "in his own right"; and (ii) that the defendant had "assumed the risk" a co-occupant might permit a search. It is important to keep both of them in mind in assessing the issues that commonly arise about the circumstances which will validate or invalidate a search by third party consent:

(1) Does the validity of third party consent depend upon the existence of amicable relations between that party and the defendant? In one case, where defendant's wife summoned police to their home to have him arrested on a charge of beating her and then showed them where he kept his supply of illegal liquor, the court answered in the affirmative, suppressing the evidence because "her actions were hostile to her husband and obviously to his interests." But the prevailing and better view is to the contrary, for the antagonism does not bear upon the two considerations stressed in *Matlock*. By remaining in the marital household the wife has maintained her "equal authority" over those premises, and the defendant's expectations of privacy are, if anything, diminished as a consequence of his assault upon another occupant of those premises.

(2) Can a third party give effective consent after being instructed by defendant not to do so? In one case, police obtained the consent of defendant's wife to search the family home, but the evidence obtained thereby was suppressed because the police "knew her husband had instructed her not to consent and, under these circumstances, were not entitled to rely upon her consent as justification for their conduct." If the *Stoner* agency theory were the sole basis upon which a third party consent could be upheld, there would be little reason to question that result. But it cannot be squared with the two *Matlock* bases. In light of the third party's ability to permit the search "in his own right," it may be said that defendant's instructions cannot invalidate consent that did not depend on his authority in the first place. As for the "assumption of risk" aspect, certainly there is a risk, stronger in some cases than in others, that the other occupant will not comply with such a request.

(3) Is a third party's consent invalidated by the defendant's prior or contemporaneous refusal to consent to such a search? Yes, it has sometimes been held, because constitutional rights may not be defeated by the expedient of soliciting several persons successively until the sought-after consent is obtained. But the cases holding to the contrary may be more readily squared with *Matlock,* for here

again the other occupant retains his "own right" to allow a search and the defendant has participated in a living situation in which there inheres the risk that in defendant's absence another occupant might admit the police. What then if defendant was *present* and objecting at the time? *Matlock* cautiously puts this situation to one side, for the Court there said that "the consent of one who possesses common authority over premises or effects is valid as against the *absent,* nonconsenting person with whom that authority is shared." One view is that even here *Matlock* permits the third party to act in his own or the public interest, while the contrary position is that the consent of both is required when both are present because persons with equal rights in a place would ordinarily accommodate each other by not admitting persons over another's objection while he was present. So the argument would proceed, using *Matlock* terminology, a person's authority to consent in his "own right" does not go so far as to outweigh an equal privacy claim by another occupant who is actually present asserting his right, and the defendant by his joint occupancy or use has only "assumed the risk" as to what will happen when he is not present to protect his own interests. Even if this is so, there will be cases in which some other circumstance justifies giving one of these "equal" rights greater recognition than the other, and of course there are also cases in which the rights of the two occupants are not equal and the matter can thus be resolved by giving recognition to the superior interest.

(4) Is a third party's consent ineffective when the police bypassed an opportunity to seek consent from the defendant? The cases answer no, and they appear to be supported by both the facts and the rationale of *Matlock*. This is generally a sound result, perhaps even when the bypassed opportunity was at the time of the defendant's arrest while present at the place later searched. But when the positions of the two persons are not equal, so that it may be said the police passed up an obvious opportunity to seek consent from a defendant with a clearly superior interest in the place, this has been held to invalidate the consent obtained from the third party with a lesser interest.

(5) Is a third party's consent affected by the fact that the defendant maintained exclusive control as to certain areas or effects? *Matlock* is rather ambiguous on this point, for the Court said the question was whether Ms. Graff had "common authority" over the premises, which was deemed to rest on "mutual use of the property" by one "having joint access or control for most purposes." Perhaps it is of no significance that the Court failed to allude specifically to the principle, recognized in prior lower court decisions, that persons sharing premises may nonetheless retain areas of exclusive control. But it is well to remember that the Court

has taken a firm stand against extreme or strained applications of the exclusive control concept. In *Frazier v. Cupp* (1969), in response to defendant's argument that his cousin (who possessed and consented to search of defendant's duffel bag) only had permission to use one compartment in the bag, the Supreme Court declined to "engage in such metaphysical subtleties in judging the efficacy of Rawls' consent" and concluded defendant had assumed the risk by allowing Rawls to use the bag and in leaving it in his house. Thus, while it has sometimes been suggested that under *Matlock* police are obligated to ascertain the possibly unique pattern of living arrangements between defendant and the third party so as to determine the extent of the "common authority," courts generally are not inclined to be that demanding.

(6) May a third party consent be upheld when the police had a reasonable but mistaken belief that the third party had authority over the place searched? In *Stoner v. California* (1964), in response to the argument that the police "had a reasonable basis for the belief that the [hotel] clerk had authority to consent to the search" of a guest's room, the Court properly asserted that "the rights protected by the Fourth Amendment are not to be eroded * * * by unrealistic doctrines of 'apparent authority.' " The police in *Stoner* were fully aware of the relevant facts (i.e., that the person consenting was a clerk and that defendant was currently renting the room in question), and thus the mistake was as to the clerk's *legal* authority, which if it were to prevail would in effect allow the police to expand the law of third party consent by their misperceptions of what the Fourth Amendment allows. But what if the error was as to a *factual* matter and the reasonably assumed fact, if true, would put the consenting party in a position to give a valid consent; that is, what if in *Stoner* the police had acted upon the clerk's consent in the reasonable but mistaken belief that no one was renting the room in question? In such a case, the Supreme Court concluded in *Illinois v. Rodriguez* (1990), the search is lawful, for what the defendant "is assured by the Fourth Amendment itself * * * is not that no government search * * * will occur unless he consents; but that no such search will occur that is 'unreasonable.' " In this and many other Fourth Amendment contexts, a police officer's actions can be reasonable even when grounded in factual assumptions which turn out to be incorrect. But the Court in *Rodriguez* cautioned it was *not* suggesting "that law enforcement officers may always accept a person's invitation to enter premises. Even when the invitation is accompanied by an explicit assertion that the person lives there, the surrounding circumstances could conceivably be such that a reasonable person would doubt its truth and not act upon it without further inquiry," in which case "warrantless entry

without further inquiry is unlawful unless authority actually exists."

(7) May a third party consent be upheld when the defendant had a reasonable but mistaken belief as to the extent of the risk involved? This interesting question is prompted by a case in which defendant *A* stored containers of marijuana in a barn with the consent of *B,* who *A* was led to believe had exclusive possession and control of that barn, but in fact the barn belonged to and was under the control of *C,* who consented to a police search of the barn. In upholding the consent, the court concluded that *C*'s "independent right * * * to authorize the search of her property" could not be affected by *B*'s conduct in misleading *A.* In other words, when the two bases of the *Matlock* "common authority" rule come into conflict, the consenting person's authority to permit the search "in his own right" is to prevail over a showing that the defendant had not "assumed the risk" of consent by the person who gave it. This is a sound result, as (a) it is still important in such circumstances to recognize the owner's "legitimate interest in exculpating himself or herself from possible criminal involvement with the suspected contraband," as the court put it; (b) *A* was ignorant as to the true identity of the person in possession, but in a more general sense "assumed the risk" that whoever was in possession might for some reason admit others; and (c) permitting the police to proceed on the situation as it appears to the person who summoned them and consented to the search is to be preferred over a rule that nullifies the search by an after-the-fact assessment of defendant's reasonably mistaken impressions of the situation.

(e) Common Relationships in Third Party Consent. It may generally be said that one spouse may give consent to a search of the family residence that will be effective against the other spouse. At one time there was a tendency to view consent by the wife with greater suspicion on the ground that the husband is the head of the household, but the modern view is that the wife has no less authority than the husband because she normally exercises as much control over the property in the home as the husband. It is possible in a particular case that the consent will be held ineffective because the area searched was within the "exclusive control" of the defendant, but this is much less likely in husband-wife cases than in other shared occupancy situations. There is somewhat greater reluctance to uphold a wife's consent to search of her husband's car, but it is not inconsistent with *Matlock* to suggest that the wife's consent should suffice if the vehicle is the family car, without regard to whether the wife is a registered co-owner or uses it as a driver instead of only as a passenger.

If a son or daughter, whether or not still a minor, is residing in the home of the parents, generally it is within the authority of the father or mother to consent to a police search of that home that will be effective against the offspring. This is unquestionably so as to areas of common usage, and is also true of the bedroom of the son or daughter when a parent has ready access for purposes of cleaning it or when because of the minority of the offspring the parent is still exercising parental authority. Because in the latter circumstances the parent's rights are superior to the rights of children who live in the house, a parent's consent would prevail even if the child were present and objecting and even if the child had taken special measures in an effort to ensure he had exclusive use of the area searched. When the tables are turned and it is the offspring who has consented and a parent is the defendant, the effectiveness of the consent depends upon: (1) the age of the child, because as children grow older they gradually acquire discretion to admit whom they will on their own authority; and (2) the scope of the consent given, in that a teenager could admit police to look about generally but a child of eight could merely admit police to that part of the house that any caller would be allowed to enter.

Turning to property relationships, it may generally be said that a lessor who has granted the lessee exclusive possession over a certain area may not, during the period of the tenancy, give an effective consent to a police search of that area. This is so whether the arrangement involves the rental of a house, an apartment, a room in a rooming house, hotel or motel, or even a locker. The rule is not otherwise merely because the lessor has by express agreement or by implication reserved the right to enter for some special and limited purpose. The landlord may consent to search of common areas, such as a hallway in an apartment building. It logically follows that the tenant may consent to a search of the area he has leased, but not a portion of the premises the landlord has retained as his own. Where two or more persons occupy a dwelling place jointly, the general rule is that a joint tenant can consent to police entry and search of the entire house or apartment, even though they occupy separate bedrooms. This is certainly true of common areas such as a kitchen or bathroom, but not as to places under the "exclusive control" of another tenant, a matter the police are obligated to make some inquiry about in ambiguous situations. Similarly, while a host can consent to a search of his premises occupied by a guest, this does not inevitably extend to a suitcase or like object in which a person has a high expectation of privacy even when a guest in another's home. Generally, a guest cannot give consent to a search of the premises which will be effective against his host. In bailment cases, the bailee may give effective consent if the nature of the bailment is such, as it was in *Frazier v. Cupp*

(1969), where defendant left his duffel bag with his cousin, that defendant has "assumed the risk" the bailee would do so. The bailor does not have authority to consent to an intrusion into the bailee's possessory interest, but in some circumstances may have the power to terminate the bailment for violation of its terms by the bailee and to then allow the search.

In employment relationships, where the question arises whether an employee's consent was effective, courts are inclined to assess the responsibilities of the particular employee, which makes sense from both an agency and an assumption of risk point of view. Thus, a caretaker left in charge of a farm for a few weeks has greater authority to consent to a search there than a farm hand working at a particular location on the farm while his employer is occupied elsewhere on the property. Courts are understandably influenced by the "status" of the employee (e.g., officer manager vs. clerk) and the character of the place searched (e.g., warehouse vs. private office). When the consent is by the employer and the objecting defendant is an employee, courts consider (1) the extent to which the particular area searched had been set aside for the personal use of the employee, and (2) the extent to which the search was prompted by a unique or special need of the employer to maintain close scrutiny of employees. Finally, there are the third party consent cases involving what might be called the educational relationship, in which a student objects to a search allowed by a school official. Generally, it may be said that the courts have upheld such searches when made of lockers in a high school, but not when made of a college dorm room. These cases reflect both that such consent is more likely to be upheld in order to maintain discipline over young students and that it is less likely to be upheld when the place in question is a residential area having only a tangential relationship to the educational enterprise.

(f) Scope of Consent. Even if it is determined that the consent of the defendant or another authorized person was "voluntary" within the meaning of *Schneckloth,* it does not inevitably follow that evidence found in the ensuing search will be admissible. This is because it is also necessary to take account of any express or implied limitations on the consent that mark the permissible scope of the search in terms of its time, duration, area or intensity. The matter of scope, the Supreme Court has decided, is to be determined by neither the subjective intentions of the consenting party nor the subjective interpretation of the searching officer; rather, the standard is "that of 'objective' reasonableness—what would the typical reasonable person have understood by the exchange between the officer and the suspect?" Police customarily ask for consent not in the abstract but in terms of a particular place, such as a certain residence or vehicle, and if the person responds with a consent that is general and unqualified, then ordinarily the police may conduct a general search of that place. This means that when the object the police indicated they are looking for could be concealed therein, they may even search unlocked containers found in that place, but not that they may break into locked containers or otherwise do physical damage in carrying out the search. The scope of the search must be more narrowly confined when expressly stated to cover only a portion of a certain place, when the thing the police say they are looking for quite obviously necessitates looking only in a particular place, or when the person giving the consent makes it apparent that he does not expect that the police can gain access to a certain part of the designated place. The most common limitation on the scope of a search by consent is that upon the intensity of the police activity permitted. This limitation is not ordinarily expressly stated by the consenting party, but arises from the fact that the police have indicated that the consent is being sought for a particular purpose. But if the police search only where the items they purport to be looking for could be concealed, under the "plain view" doctrine they may seize other items if they have probable cause they are the fruits, instrumentalities or evidence of some crime.

As a general rule, it would seem that a consent to search may be said to have been given on the understanding that the search will be conducted forthwith and that only a single search will be made. Though there is some authority that consent once given may not be withdrawn, the better view is that though a consent to search is not terminated merely by a worsening of the consenting party's position, a consent may be withdrawn or limited at any time prior to the completion of the search. A revocation of consent does not operate retroactively to render unreasonable a search conducted prior to the time of revocation, any more than the giving of consent may be said to retroactively validate a search conducted prior to the time the consent was given.

Chapter 3

WIRETAPPING AND ELECTRONIC SURVEILLANCE

Table of Sections

§ 3.1 Historical Background

(a) The *Olmstead* Case. The first wiretapping case to reach the United States Supreme Court was *Olmstead v. United States* (1928), involving the interception by federal agents of messages passing over telephone wires. In a 5–4 decision, the Court held that such activity did not amount to a Fourth Amendment search or seizure because (1) the agents obtained access to the telephone wires without any "entry of the houses or offices of the defendants," meaning that no "place" had been searched within the meaning of the Amendment; and (2) the agents obtained the content of the conversations that passed over the wires but did not acquire any physical objects, and thus no "things" had been seized within the meaning of the Amendment. It made no difference that the conduct was in violation of a state law making it a misdemeanor to "intercept" telegraphic or telephonic messages, as that statute did not declare evidence so obtained was inadmissible and, in any event, a state statute "can not affect the rules of evidence applicable in courts of the United States."

As discussed later, both reasons given in *Olmstead* for holding the Fourth Amendment inapplicable have since been rejected by the Supreme Court. It is not surprising, therefore, that in recent years the forceful dissents in *Olmstead* have received the greatest attention. In an exhaustive dissenting opinion, Justice Brandeis argued that "every unjustifiable intrusion by the Government upon the privacy of the individual, whatever the means employed, must be deemed a violation of the Fourth Amendment." In addition, he contended that the government, as "the omnipresent teacher," should not be upheld in its admitted violation of a state wiretapping law. Justice Holmes, in a brief separate dissent on the latter ground only, characterized wiretapping in violation of state law as "dirty business" that a judge should not "allow * * * to succeed." In an oft-quoted passage, Holmes reasoned that it is "a less evil that some criminals should escape than that the Government should play an ignoble part."

(b) Section 605. The majority in *Olmstead* noted that "Congress may of course protect the secrecy of telephone messages by making them, when intercepted, inadmissible in evidence in federal criminal trials." The Federal Communications Act of 1934 was later enacted, and it provided in part in § 605 that "no person not being authorized by the sender shall intercept any communication and divulge or publish the existence, contents, substance, purport, effect, or meaning of such intercepted communication to any person." Though this legislation did not contain an express declaration of an exclusionary rule as apparently contemplated by *Olmstead,* it was interpreted to have this effect in *Nardone v. United States*

(1937). But in *Schwartz v. Texas* (1952), involving the use of state-gathered wiretap evidence in a prosecution in a state court, the Court held the evidence obtained in violation of § 605 admissible, reasoning that "in the absence of an expression by Congress, this is simply an additional factor for a state to consider in formulating a rule of evidence for use in its own courts." But in *Benanti v. United States* (1957), the Court excluded state-gathered wiretap evidence proffered in a federal prosecution on the ground that the statute "contains an express, absolute prohibition against the divulgence of intercepted communications." *Schwartz* was then overruled in *Lee v. Florida* (1968) because "nothing short of mandatory exclusion of the illegal evidence will compel respect for the federal law 'in the only effectively available way—by removing the incentive to disregard it.' " *Lee* was held to be nonretroactive, and thus had a limited impact because just two days later the electronic surveillance provisions of the Crime Control Act of 1968 were signed into law.

(c) Non-telephonic Electronic Eavesdropping. After *Olmstead,* highly sophisticated means of electronic eavesdropping were developed and put into use, but were largely uncontrolled by the law. They were not within the prohibitions of § 605, for it applied only when telephone, telegraph or radiotelegraph conversations were overheard. Moreover, the protections of the Fourth Amendment applied only if there was a physical invasion or "trespass" into a constitutionally protected area. No such trespass was deemed to exist in *Olmstead,* where the taps from house lines were made in the streets near the house; in *Goldman v. United States* (1942), where federal officers merely placed a detectaphone against the wall of an adjoining office where they were lawfully present; or in *On Lee v. United States* (1952), where incriminating statements were picked up via a "wired for sound" former acquaintance of petitioner who entered his premises with consent. The trespass requirement began to give way in later electronic eavesdropping cases, and then any lingering doubts were dispelled by *Katz v. United States* (1967). The issue in *Katz* was whether recordings of defendant's end of telephone conversations, obtained by attaching an electronic listening and recording device to the outside of a public telephone booth, had been obtained in violation of the Fourth Amendment. Expressly rejecting the "trespass" doctrine of *Olmstead* and *Goldman,* the Court held that the government action constituted a search and seizure within the meaning of the Fourth Amendment. This was because that conduct "violated the privacy upon which [the defendant] justifiably relied while using the telephone booth." *Katz* thus made it clear that, with the possible exception of the case in which a conversation is overheard or recorded with the consent of a party to the conversation, wiretapping and electronic eavesdropping are subject to the limitations of the Fourth Amendment.

§ 3.2   Title III and the Fourth Amendment

(a) **Summary of Title III.** About a year after the Supreme Court in *Berger v. New York* (1967) held that a certain state eavesdropping statute violated the Fourth Amendment, the Congress adopted comprehensive legislation on the subject of wiretapping and electronic surveillance. This legislation is commonly referred to simply as Title III (as it will be hereinafter), as it makes up that part of the Omnibus Crime Control and Safe Streets Act of 1968 (18 U.S.C.A. §§ 2510–2520, to which there was added in 1986 §§ 2701–2710, having to do with stored wire and electronic communications and transactional records access, for which there is no statutory exclusionary rule and which are not discussed extensively herein). Title III was adopted because there was common agreement that its predecessor, § 605, was the worst of all possible solutions. Private citizens and public officials could ignore the prohibition against wiretapping without fear of prosecution, while law enforcement officers could not use electronic surveillance to investigate and prosecute even the most serious crimes.

Under Title III, the Attorney General or certain specified subordinates may authorize application to a federal judge for an order permitting interception of wire or oral communications (i.e., wiretapping or electronic eavesdropping) by a federal agency having responsibility for investigation of the offense as to which application is made, when such interception may provide evidence of certain enumerated federal crimes. A comparable provision permits, when authorized by state law, application by a state or county prosecutor to a state judge when the interception may provide evidence of "murder, kidnapping, gambling, robbery, bribery, extortion, or dealing in narcotic drugs, marijuana or other dangerous drugs, or other crime dangerous to life, limb, or property, and punishable by imprisonment for more than one year." The judge may only grant an interception order as provided under the Act, and evidence obtained in the lawful execution of such order is admissible in court.

An interception order may be issued only if the judge determines on the basis of facts submitted that there is probable cause for belief that an individual is committing, has committed, or is about to commit one of the enumerated offenses; probable cause for belief that particular communications concerning that offense will be obtained through such interception; that normal investigative procedures have been tried and have failed or reasonably appear to be unlikely to succeed if tried or to be too dangerous; and probable cause for belief that the facilities from which, or the place where, the communications are to be intercepted are being used, or are about to be used, in connection with the commission of such offense, or are leased to, listed in the name of, or commonly used by such person. Each interception order must specify the identity of the person, if known, whose communications are to be intercepted; the nature and location of the communications facilities as to which, or the place where, authority to intercept is granted; a particular description of the type of communication sought to be intercepted, and a statement of the particular offense to which it relates; the identity of the agency authorized to intercept the communications and of the person authorizing the application; and the period of time during which such interception is authorized, including a statement as to whether or not the interception shall automatically terminate when the described communication has been first obtained. No order may permit interception "for any period longer than is necessary to achieve the objective of the authorization, nor in any event longer than thirty days." Extensions of an order may be granted for like periods, but only by resort to the procedures required in obtaining the initial order.

Interception without prior judicial authorization is permitted whenever a specifically designated enforcement officer reasonably determines that "(a) an emergency situation exists that involves (i) immediate danger of death or serious physical injury to any person, (ii) conspiratorial activities threatening the national security interest, or (iii) conspiratorial activities characteristic of organized crime, that requires a wire, oral or electronic communication [defined in § 3.3(a)] to be intercepted before an order authorizing such interception can with due diligence be obtained, and (b) there are grounds upon which an order could be entered." In such a case, application for an order must be made within 48 hours after the interception commences, and, in the absence of an order, the interception must terminate when the communication sought is obtained or when the application for the order is denied, whichever is earlier. Title III does not limit the constitutional power of the President to act for various purposes, such as to obtain foreign intelligence information deemed essential to the security of the United States.

Within a reasonable time but not later than 90 days after the filing of an application that is denied or the termination of an authorized period of interception, the judge must cause to be served on the persons named in the order or application and other parties to the intercepted communications, an inventory that shall include notice of (1) the fact of the entry of the order or application; (2) the date of the entry and the period of authorized interception, or the denial of the application; and (3) the fact that during the period communications were or were not intercepted. A similar inventory is required as to interceptions terminated without an order having been issued.

Where the disclosure would be in violation of Title III, "no part of the contents of [an intercepted wire or oral] communication and no evidence derived therefrom may be received in evidence in any trial, hearing, or other proceeding in or before any court, grand jury, department, officer, agency, regulatory body, legislative committee, or other authority of the United States, a State, or a political subdivision thereof." Any intentional interception or disclosure of any wire, oral or electronic communication without the prior consent of a party thereto, except as authorized under Title III, is a criminal offense punishable by a fine, imprisonment for not more than five years, or both. Any person whose wire, oral or electronic communications are intercepted, disclosed or used may bring a civil action against the offending party and may recover the actual damages suffered or statutory damages (the greater of $10,000 or $100 a day for each day of violation); plus punitive damages and a reasonable attorney's fee and other reasonable litigation costs. A good faith reliance on a court order or legislative authorization constitutes a complete defense to any civil or criminal action brought. Willful violations are also a basis for a civil action against the United States and administrative discipline of the offending officer or employee.

(b) Continued Surveillance. The most obvious difference between a search for tangible items and the search for wire, oral or electronic communications allowed under Title III is the time dimension of the latter kind of search. A search warrant for some physical object permits a single entry and prompt search of the described premises (see § 2.4(j)), while Title III permits continuing surveillance up to 30 days, with extensions possible, during which time all conversations over the tapped line or within the bugged room may be overheard and recorded without regard to their relevance. As reflected in *Berger*, this striking difference accounts for the major constitutional obstacle to legalized electronic surveillance. In holding a New York law unconstitutional, the Court emphasized that it (1) permitted installation and operation of surveillance equipment for 60 days, "the equivalent of a series of intrusions, searches, and seizures pursuant to a single showing of probable cause"; (2) permitted renewal of the order "without a showing of present probable cause for the continuance of the eavesdrop"; and (3) placed "no termination date on the eavesdrop once the conversation sought is seized." While Title III permits extensions only upon a new showing of probable cause and requires that interception cease once "the objective of the authorization" is achieved, it does permit continued surveillance for up to 30 days upon a single showing of probable cause, and thus goes well beyond the kind of with-warrant electronic surveillance the Supreme Court has approved or indicated would be permitted.

As was emphasized in *Berger*, the bugging of a secret agent earlier upheld by the Court in *Osborn v. United States* (1966) was pursuant to an order which "authorized one limited intrusion rather than a series or a continuous surveillance. And, we note that a new order was issued when the officer sought to resume the search and probable cause was shown for the succeeding one. Moreover, the order was executed by the officer with dispatch, not over a prolonged and extended period." Similarly, in *Katz v. United States* (1967), the Court noted that the "surveillance was so narrowly circumscribed that a duly authorized magistrate * * * clearly apprised of the precise intrusion * * * could constitutionally have authorized * * * the very limited search and seizure that the Government asserts in fact took place." The surveillance in *Katz* was limited in that the agents had probable cause to believe defendant was using certain public telephones for gambling purposes about the same time almost every day and thus activated the surveillance equipment attached to the outside of the phone booth only when defendant entered the booth.

Decisions holding that continued surveillance may also be squared with the Fourth Amendment rely upon the analysis of Justices Harlan and White, who dissented in *Berger*. Their contention was that an electronic surveillance that is continued over a span of time is no more a general search than the typical execution of a search warrant over a described area. As Justice White argued:

> Petitioner suggests that the search is inherently overbroad because the eavesdropper will overhear conversations which do not relate to criminal activity. But the same is true of almost all searches of private property which the Fourth Amendment permits. In searching for seizable matters, the police must necessarily see or hear, and comprehend, items which do not relate to the purpose of the search. That this occurs, however, does not render the search invalid, so long as it is authorized by a suitable search warrant and so long as the police, in executing that warrant, limit themselves to searching for items which may constitutionally be seized. Thus, while I would agree with petitioner that individual searches of private property through surreptitious eavesdropping with a warrant must be carefully circumscribed to avoid excessive invasion of privacy and security, I cannot agree that all such intrusions are constitutionally impermissible general searches.

This analogy is less than perfect unless it may be concluded that the overhearing or recording of a series of conversations is merely a search, from which certain particularly described conversations will thereafter be seized, a matter on which a majority of the Supreme Court has never spoken clearly. But this has not deterred the lower courts from consistently holding that Title III is not rendered unconstitutional solely because it authorizes wiretaps which may last several days and encompass multiple conversations. So too, lower courts have held that the Fourth Amendment permits issuance of a search warrant that authorizes a silent ongoing video surveillance through the installation of a hidden video camera in places believed to be used in criminal activities, although the non-technical requirements of Title III (e.g., the inappropriateness of alternative, "normal investigative procedures") have been viewed as prerequisites for compliance with the Fourth Amendment in issuing such warrants.

(c) **Lack of Notice.** The Supreme Court in *Berger* also found the New York eavesdropping law "offensive" because it "has no requirement for notice, as do conventional warrants, nor does it overcome this defect by requiring some showing of special facts. On the contrary, it permits uncontested entry without any showing of exigent circumstances. Such a showing of exigency, in order to avoid notice would appear more important in eavesdropping, with its inherent dangers, than that required when conventional procedures of search and seizure are utilized." This criticism goes to the very heart of all eavesdropping practices because, as the Court observed, success inevitably depends upon secrecy.

The *Berger* Court did not explore this matter in greater detail, and thus it is not entirely clear whether Title III is somewhat vulnerable on this basis. However, the lower courts have consistently rejected constitutional challenges to the legislation on such grounds with the following arguments: (1) One reason for advance notice is to guard the entering officer from attack on the mistaken belief he is making a criminal entry, and this danger is generally not present in eavesdropping cases. Either the eavesdropping is accomplished without any trespass or else a covert entry to plant an eavesdropping device is made at a time when it is known no one is present within. (2) Another reason for notice is so that the individual will be aware that a search was conducted, but in the more typical search case this notice may come only after the event by discovery of the warrant and a receipt at the place searched. That notice is comparable to the Title III requirement of service of an inventory within 90 days. (3) In executing search warrants for physical evidence, prior notice is not required when there is reason to believe such notice would result in the destruction or removal of the evidence sought (see § 2.4(h)). Though the Court in *Berger* was unwilling to uphold all eavesdropping without notice on this ground, this "exigency" does exist in some circumstances. One of these circumstances, so the argument goes, is that which must exist under Title III by virtue of the requirement of a showing that "normal investigative procedures have been tried and have failed or reasonably appear to be unlikely to succeed if tried or to be too dangerous." The Supreme Court in *Katz v. United States* (1967) intimated that it finds these arguments compelling.

(d) **Probable Cause.** One aspect of the more general Fourth Amendment issue of whether the "probable cause" requirement is a fixed or a variable test (see § 2.3(b)), is the question of whether the probable cause needed to conduct a Title III surveillance is in some respects greater than the probable cause ordinarily required to obtain a search warrant. Justice Stewart spoke to this question in his concurring opinion in *Berger,* where he concluded that though the evidence in the instant case "might be enough to satisfy the standards of the Fourth Amendment for a conventional search or arrest," it "was constitutionally insufficient to constitute probable cause to justify an intrusion of the scope and duration that was permitted in this case." However, defendants who have made this type of argument to the lower courts have not prevailed

(e) **Particular Description.** The eavesdropping statute struck down in *Berger* required very little by way of particularizing the conversations to be seized; it merely required the naming of "the person or persons whose communications * * * are to be overheard or recorded." The Court held this did not meet the Fourth Amendment requirement that the things to be seized be particularly described, and declared that the "need for particularity * * * is especially great in the case of eavesdropping [because it] involves an intrusion on privacy that is broad in scope." Title III requires a particular description of the "type of communication sought to be intercepted, and a statement of the particular offense to which it relates," and it is now generally accepted that this particularization requirement can be fulfilled by indicating the offense under investigation, without further details about the anticipated conversations. Despite that development, the lower courts have rather consistently held that the statutory formula in Title III is sufficient to meet the Fourth Amendment particularity requirement as explicated in *Berger.* The reasoning is that it would be virtually impossible to predict in advance the exact language of a conversation which has not yet occurred, and that to demand more would render Title III totally ineffective.

(f) **Covert Entry.** In *Dalia v. United States* (1979), FBI agents entered an office to install a bug and reentered to remove it, all pursuant to a court order that allowed the interception of all oral communications at that office concerning a certain conspiracy but that did not explicitly authorize entry of those premises. In upholding the surveillance, the Court concluded (1) that the "Fourth Amendment does not prohibit *per se* a covert entry performed for the purpose of installing otherwise legal electronic bugging equipment"; (2) that Congress had intended to authorize such an entry pursuant to the Title III procedures; and (3) that the entry violated petitioner's Fourth Amendment privacy rights because the authorizing court did not explicitly set forth its approval of the covert entries. Regarding the last point, the Court found nothing in the Fourth Amendment or prior decisions under it suggesting that "search warrants also must include a specification of the precise manner in which they are to be executed. On the contrary, it is generally left to the discretion of the executing officers to determine the details of how best to proceed with the performance of a search authorized by warrant—subject of course to the general Fourth Amendment protection 'against unreasonable searches and seizures.' " The Court in *Dalia* added that it "would promote empty formalism * * * to require magistrates to make explicit what unquestionably is implicit in bugging authorizations: that a covert entry, with its attendant interference with Fourth Amendment interests, may be necessary for the installation of the surveillance equipment."

(g) Emergency Interception Without a Warrant. There has been virtually no use of the provision in Title III that permits interception without prior judicial approval when there are grounds for an interception order but an emergency exists involving "(i) immediate danger of death or serious physical injury to any person, (ii) conspiratorial activities threatening the national security interest, or (iii) conspiratorial activities characteristic of organized crime, that requires a wire, oral, or electronic communication to be intercepted before an order authorizing such interception can with due diligence be obtained." As a consequence the courts have not been called upon to assess its constitutionality.

In *Katz v. United States* (1967), the Supreme Court condemned the warrantless eavesdropping challenged in that case, but the facts made it perfectly clear that there was ample time to secure a warrant. *Katz* therefore cannot be read as prohibiting all warrantless electronic surveillance. The Fourth Amendment doubtless would permit such surveillance under at least some circumstances, but it is unclear whether that may be said of all of the situations that might be fit within the statutory language just quoted. This is attributable in part to the fact that the relevant statutory terms are ambiguous and are not clarified by legislative history, and in part to the uncertainty that generally exists as to when a warrantless search is permissible to prevent the destruction or loss of evidence. It does seem, however, that the case in which the strongest showing of need could be made falls within the more recently enacted item (i) of the statutory exception.

(h) Use of Secret Agents. Because Title III declares interception to be lawful where "one of the parties to the communication has given prior consent to such interception," it does not forbid the use of eavesdropping equipment to record or transmit what a suspect says to a secret agent. Whether this practice can be squared with the Fourth Amendment is an issue the Supreme Court has had before it on several occasions, culminating in *United States v. White* (1971), where a government informer engaged defendant in conversations in a restaurant, defendant's home, and the informer's car while the informer was carrying a concealed radio transmitter. The court of appeals held that this electronic eavesdropping constituted a search, but the Supreme Court did not agree. Asserting that *Katz* "left undisturbed" the notion "that however strongly a defendant may trust an apparent colleague, his expectations in this respect are not protected by the Fourth Amendment when it turns out that the colleague is a government agent regularly communicating with the authorities," the Court concluded:

> If the law gives no protection to the wrongdoer whose trusted accomplice is or becomes a police agent, neither should it protect him when that same agent has recorded or transmitted the conversations which are later offered in evidence to prove the State's case.

> Inescapably, one contemplating illegal activities must realize and risk that his companions may be reporting to the police. If he sufficiently doubts their trustworthiness, the association will very probably end or never materialize. But if he has no doubts, or allays them, or risks what doubt he has, the risk is his. In terms of what his course will be, what he will or will not do or say, we are unpersuaded that he would distinguish between probable informers on the one hand and probable informers with transmitters on the other. Given the possibility or probability that one of his colleagues is cooperating with the police, it is only speculation to assert that the defendant's utterances would be substantially different or his sense of security any less if he also thought it possible that the suspected colleague is wired for sound. At least there is no persuasive evidence that the difference in this respect between the electronically equipped and the unequipped agent is substantial enough to require discrete constitutional recognition,

particularly under the Fourth Amendment which is ruled by fluid concepts of "reasonableness."

The Court added that this result was bolstered by the fact that a recording will often produce a "more reliable rendition of what a defendant has said than will the unaided memory of a police agent," and that "with the recording in existence it is less likely that the informant will change his mind," and there is "less chance that threat or injury will suppress unfavorable evidence and less chance that cross-examination will confound the testimony." In a forceful dissent, Justice Harlan argued that recording should be treated differently because of "the expectation of the ordinary citizen, who has never engaged in illegal conduct in his life, that he may carry on his private discourse freely, openly, and spontaneously without measuring his every word against the connotations it might carry when instantaneously heard by others unknown to him and unfamiliar with his situation or analyzed in a cold, formal record played days, months, or years after the conversation."

§ 3.3   Title III: What Surveillance Covered

(a) Meaning of "Interception." Title III prohibits, except as provided therein, any "interception" of communications, defined as "the aural or other acquisition of the contents of any wire, electronic or oral communication through the use of any electronic, mechanical, or other device." To determine the precise scope of this definition, three questions must be answered: (1) what communications are protected—that is, what is included within the categories of "wire communication," "electronic communication," and "oral communication"? (2) What means of interception are covered—that is, what is "any electronic, mechanical, or other device"? (3) What kind of activity is covered—that is, what are the "contents" of a communication and what constitutes their "aural or other acquisition"?

Wire communication: The extensive statutory definition establishes several prerequisites that combine to classify an intercepted communication as a "wire communication" (1) Because wire communications are limited to "aural transfer[s]," defined as "transfer[s] containing the human voice," communications through wire that transfer only printed or electronic data are not protected under this provision (although they are likely to fall within the definition of "electronic communications," discussed later). The transfer only need contain the human voice at some point between and including the point of origin and the point of reception, and thus a communication remains a wire communication even though a voice signal is converted to digital form in the course of transmission. (2) An aural transfer is a wire communication only if it is transmitted, at least in part, through the "aid of wire, cable, or other like connection between the points of origin and reception (including the use of such connection in a switching station)." This language carries the definition of "wire communication" beyond the standard "land line" telephone communication to also cover telephone transmissions carried by fiber optic cable and the cellular telephone. The reference to a "switching station" connection makes it clear that cellular transmissions are included even when made between telephones that are both cellular. (3) Since the aural transfer need be made only "in part" by "wire, cable, or other like connection," a transfer of the human voice does not lose its characterization as a wire communication simply because other means are also used in carrying the voice between the points of origin and reception. That is the situation as to cellular technology utilizing radio signals in the initial stage of its transmission, voice communication made by telephone and then transmitted by radio to a person carrying a pager, and telephone calls carried in part by wire (or by fiber optic cable) and in part by microwave (commonplace in long distance telephone calls).

A 1986 amendment specifically included in the definition the "electronic storage" of an aural transfer made in whole or in part through wire, cable, or other like connection so as to encompass the voice mail communication. However, the core Title III protection extends only to the "interception" of the aural transfer, which occurs as the voice mail transfer is made and placed in storage, and thus to gain access to completed voice mail messages already held in storage, law enforcement officers only need comply with less demanding statutory provisions not enforced by an exclusionary remedy. (By a 2001 amendment, the term "electronic storage" was removed from the definition of an aural transfer, which with other changes made it clear that it is lawful—rather than unlawful but not a basis for exclusion—to obtain unopened voice mail messages (just as with e-mail messages) by a regular search warrant instead of a Title III warrant.) The 1986 amendment also provides that conversations transmitted entirely by radio are not "wire communications," but radio transmissions may be protected under the new category of electronic communications.

Electronic communication. The category of "electronic communication," added to the statute in the 1986 amendment, was not placed on same plane as the "wire communication" and "oral communication" categories. Although unauthorized interception of protected electronic communications is prohibited, authorization requirements are not as stringent, and violation of the prohibition is not grounds for suppression of the evidence obtained. The critical distinction between wire and electronic communications is that the former is limited to aural transfers and only the aural transfers by specific electronic means (in whole or in part by wire, cable or other like connection). When a communication is transferred by those specified means, it will constitute a wire communication insofar as it contains the human voice, but it will be an electronic communication if it is a non-aural transfer. Thus, electronic mail, which typically consists of typewritten messages transferred over telephone lines, falls within the electronic communications category. Where the technology of transmission does not meet the requirements for wire communications (e.g., it is a radio transmission), the transmitted communication will be an electronic communication even if it does contain the human voice (as in a microwave transmission of a closed circuit video teleconference). If the technology is being used not to transfer a voice communication from one device to another, but simply to pick up the sound waves transmitted as a person speaks in the presence of another, then the communication is an oral communication, and it will not constitute an electronic communication even though it arguably involves a transfer transmitted "in part" through the electronic device used to pick up those sound waves. The definition of electronic communications also specifies exceptions that exclude (i) the tone-only paging device communication, (ii) the tracking device communication, and (iii) electronic funds transfer information stored by a financial institution in a communications system used for electronic storage and transfer of funds. An additional exception removes from the protection of the electronic communications category those radio communications that lack the attributes of privacy characteristic of the non-radio electronic communications that fall within that category.

Oral communication. The category of oral communications is defined as "any oral communication uttered by a person exhibiting an expectation that such communication is not subject to interception under circumstances justifying such expectation, but such term does not include any electronic communication." The mode of communication here is sound waves as opposed to an electronic medium, which ordinarily means that the speaker is communicating to a listener who is within normal hearing distance. The critical element of the definition is its limitation to persons having a justifiable expectation that their conversations would not be intercepted, intended to reflect existing law on the Fourth Amendment "reasonable expectation of privacy standard" as set forth in *Katz v. United States* (1967) (see § 2.2(a)). This being so, it would seem that the Supreme Court's decisions interpreting that Fourth Amendment standard (see § 2.2) should be the touchstone for applying the "justifiable expectation" component of the oral communication definition. If there is any doubt about this, it is because some of the legislative history goes into more detail and thus arguably deprives the statute of some of the opportunity for the "growth" that *Katz* has experienced on the Fourth Amendment level.

"Electronic, mechanical, or other device." Title III applies only to interception through the use of any "electronic, mechanical, or other device." Section 2510(5) defines such a device as "any device or apparatus which can be used to intercept a wire, oral, or electronic communication" other than two exempted groups of devices. The first exempted group is "any telephone or telegraph instrument, equipment or facility or any component thereof (i) furnished to the subscriber or user by a provider of wire or electronic communication service in the ordinary course of its business and being used by the subscriber or user in the ordinary course of its business or furnished by such subscriber or user for connection to the facilities of such service and used in the ordinary course of its business; or (ii) being used by a communications common carrier in the ordinary course of its business or by an investigative or law enforcement officer in the ordinary course of his duties." The second exempted group consists of "a hearing aid or similar device being used to correct subnormal hearing to not better than normal."

The major form of interception occurring without the use of a "device or apparatus" is the overhearing with the naked ear. Of course, a conversation that can be overheard by the naked ear ordinarily would not constitute a protected "oral communication" because there would be no justifiable expectation that the communication would not be intercepted. It is partly for that reason that conversations overheard with the naked ear can also be tape recorded surreptitiously without violating Title III. However, even if a person were hidden in such a way that there would be a reasonable expectation that the conversation could not be overheard, thus presenting a protected oral communication, there would be no Title III interception if the communication was overheard without an artificial aid.

The first of the two exceptions has been the subject of considerable litigation. Courts have held that this exception exempts nonconsensual listening to conversation over an extension phone by other members of the same household, employer use of extension phones and other elements of the employer's phone system to monitor calls by employees under some circumstances, and the police officer who answers a telephone while lawfully on the premises (including that in which the caller is misled as to the identity of the answerer). The exemption's provisions on use in the ordinary course of business by a communications service provider has been held to apply to the listening in by a telephone operator who sought to verify that the call was connected and by a telephone lineman who broke into a line to check out a complaint of excessive noise.

The ordinary course of duties exemption for police use has been held applicable primarily to police monitoring of calls from and to prisoners at jail and the routine monitoring and recording of all calls at police stations.

"Aural or other acquisitions." The Act does not define the phrase "aural acquisition," but that lack of definition has not created difficulties in the application of Title III. Courts are in agreement that replaying a recording of an intercepted conversation does not constitute a new "aural acquisition," which would make necessary an additional authorization. So too, where an individual hears a conversation without an auditory device, his surreptitiously recording of that conversation uniformly has been held not to violate Title III. At one time, there was some disagreement as to whether a recording constituted an aural acquisition when nobody was listening to the recording at the time, but unmonitored recording is presently viewed as covered by the statute. To treat an unattended recording as not constituting a aural transfer and then to allow disclosure of the recording on the ground that there had never been an interception would clearly be contrary to the purpose of the statute. The 1986 amendment giving protection to electronic communications (which includes non-voice communications such as electronic mail) also expanded the reference to "aural acquisition" in the definition of "intercept" to read "aural or other acquisition," which has been held to apply only to acquiring the contents of the communication as it takes place, not to gaining subsequent access to stored non-voice communications.

"Contents." Interception applies only to the "contents" of the wire, oral, or electronic communication, defined as "including any information concerning the substance, purport, or meaning of the communication." In *United States v. New York Telephone Co.* (1977), the Supreme Court held that "the language of the statute and its legislative history establish beyond any doubt that pen registers," devices that do not record phone conversations but merely make a record of the numbers dialed from a given phone and the time of dialing "are not governed by Title III." The Court reasoned:

> Pen registers do not "intercept" because they do not acquire the "contents" of communications, as that term is defined by 18 U.S.C. § 2510(8). Indeed, a law enforcement official could not even determine from the use of a pen register whether a communication existed. These devices do not hear sound [and thus] do not accomplish the "aural acquisition" of anything. They decode outgoing numbers by responding to changes in electrical voltage caused by the turning of the telephone dial (or the pressing of buttons on push button telephones) and

present the information in a form to be interpreted by sight rather than by hearing.

At the time that *New York Telephone* was decided, the statutory definition of contents referred to information concerning "the identity of the parties" to the communication or the "existence" of the communication. To both codify *New York Telephone* and to ensure that devices similar to the pen register would be given similar treatment, the 1986 amendment deleted that language. Thus, it is now clear that "transactional information"—i.e., information that only reveals that a communication occurred (and between what parties or devices), without revealing what was said or communicated—are not within the protection of Title III. This is what is described by statute as a "trap and trace device"—"a device which captures the incoming electronic or other impulses which identify the originating number of an instrument or device from which a wire or electronic communication was transmitted." So too, Title III does not regulate silent video surveillance. (1986 legislation prohibits use of pen registers and trap and trace devices without proper authorization, but law enforcement use is allowed upon judicial order, in emergency situations without court order, and pursuant to the Foreign Intelligence Surveillance Act.)

(b) Phone Company Activities. By virtue of the limitations upon the meaning of "interception" in the context of Title III, discussed above, it is clear that certain activities engaged in by telephone companies are not at all proscribed by the Act. This includes the making and keeping of toll records, the use of pen registers or other call-tracing devices to see if a particular person is making harassing phone calls or is otherwise misusing the telephone service, and the use of a diode trap whereby annoying phone calls can be traced by preventing disconnection when a call is made to a phone to which the device is attached. But sometimes investigations conducted by telephone companies go beyond this. Especially when the company is investigating the fraudulent use of company lines by the use of a "blue box" or other equipment permitting the bypassing of long distance automatic billing mechanisms, investigators will actually monitor and record calls to determine the speakers' identities and the extent of illegal use.

Because such activity *does* fall within the statutory definition of what constitutes an interception, it must be assessed under a special provision declaring that it is not unlawful "for an operator of a switchboard, or an officer, employee, or agent of a provider of wire or electronic communication services, whose facilities are used in the transmission of a wire or electronic communication, to intercept, disclose, or use that communication in the normal course of his employment while engaged in any activity which is a necessary incident to the rendition of his service or to the protection of the rights or property of the provider of that service." (This statute goes on to say that these providers may "not utilize service observing or random monitoring except for mechanical or service quality control checks.") Monitoring by the company to obtain evidence for a wire fraud prosecution falls within the "protection of the rights of property" part of the statute. Such monitoring has been upheld where it continued for several weeks, where it continued after the identity of one perpetrator was learned but it was known unidentified others were involved, and even where entire conversations were recorded. As for the "rendition of his service" part of the statute, it has been held to permit, for example, a long distance operator to remain on the line to verify that the call has been connected, and a telephone lineman to intercept a conversation while checking the noise level on a line.

(c) Consent. An important exception to the usual Title III requirement that an interception occur only pursuant to a court order is that which has to do with interceptions made by prior consent. The Act specifically provides that it "shall not be unlawful under this chapter for a person acting under color of law to intercept a wire, oral or electronic communication, where such person is a party to the communication or one of the parties to the communication has given prior consent to such interception." A similar provision covers persons not acting under color of law. It is thus clear that law enforcement authorities are free to make consensual interceptions in a variety of ways: (1) by having the consenting party wear or carry a tape recorder with which he records his face-to-face conversations with another; (2) by having the consenting party wear a transmitter which broadcasts his conversations to agents equipped with a receiver; or (3) by having the consenting party to a telephone conversation record it or permit another to listen in on an extension. Another consent provision allows the victim of a "hacker" under some circumstances to consent to interception of the hacker's messages transmitted to, through or from the victim's computer.

(d) National Security Surveillance. When Title III was enacted, there was included in it an express declaration that nothing therein "shall limit the constitutional power of the President to take such measures as he deems necessary to protect the Nation against actual or potential attack or other hostile acts of a foreign power, to obtain foreign intelligence information deemed essential to the security of the United States, or to protect national security information against foreign intelligence activities," or "to protect the United States against the overthrow of the Government by force or other unlawful means, or against any other clear and present danger to the structure or existence of the Government." Since at least 1940, there had been presidential sanction for warrantless electronic surveillance in furtherance of national security, and the apparent purpose of the above language was not to disturb whatever powers in this regard the President actually has under the Constitution.

The matter is now dealt with by another statute, the Foreign Intelligence Surveillance Act of 1978 (50 U.S.C.A. §§ 1801–1811). This Act provides that the Chief Justice of the United States is to publicly designate 11 district judges from seven of the federal judicial circuits "who shall constitute a court which shall have jurisdiction to hear applications for and grant orders approving electronic surveillance anywhere within the United States under the procedures set forth in this Act," and that he is also to publicly designate three judges from the federal district courts or courts of appeals who shall "comprise a court of review which shall have jurisdiction to review the denial of any application made under this Act." Upon a proper application, a judge of the former court is to enter an ex parte order approving electronic surveillance for 90 days or until its purpose is achieved, whichever is less, if he finds, inter alia, that "there is probable cause to believe" that "the target of the electronic surveillance is a foreign power or an agent of a foreign power" and that "each of the facilities or places at which the electronic surveillance is directed is being used, or is about to be used, by a foreign power or an agent of a foreign power." But, it is further provided that "no United States person may be considered a foreign power or an agent of a foreign power solely upon the basis of activities protected by the first amendment to the Constitution of the United States."

The FISA also deals with warrantless surveillance. It provides that "the President, through the Attorney General, may authorize electronic surveillance without a court order under this title to acquire foreign intelligence information for periods of up to one year" if, inter alia, the Attorney General certifies in writing under oath (with a copy of that certification transmitted under seal to the special court) that the surveillance is "solely directed at" the acquisition of the contents of communications "transmitted by means of communications used exclusively between or among foreign powers" and that "there is no substantial likelihood that the surveillance will acquire the contents of any communication to which a United States person is a party."

Evidence acquired in noncompliance with FISA is subject to suppression by "an aggrieved person" in "any trial, hearing, or other proceeding in or before any court, department, officer, agency, regulatory body, or other authority of the United States, a State or a political subdivision thereof." However, "if the Attorney General files an affidavit under oath that disclosure or an adversary hearing would harm the national security of the United States," then the appropriate federal district court must "review in camera and ex parte the application, order and such other materials relating to the surveillance as may be necessary to determine whether the surveillance of the aggrieved person was lawfully authorized and conducted. In making the determination, the court may disclose to the aggrieved person, under appropriate security procedures and protective orders, portions of the application, order, or other materials relating to the surveillance only where such disclosure is necessary to make an accurate determination of the legality of the surveillance."

§ 3.4   Title III: Application for and Issuance of Court Order

(a) **Application Procedure.** In contrast to the situation that generally obtains as to conventional search warrants, which may be sought by any law enforcement officer, application for a Title III order must be authorized by a high-level official. In the federal system, only the "Attorney General, Deputy Attorney General, Associate Attorney General, or any Assistant Attorney General, any acting Assistant Attorney General, or any Deputy Assistant Attorney General or Acting Assistant Attorney General in the Criminal Division specially designated by the Attorney General, may authorize an application." This provision is intended to centralize in a publicly responsible official subject to the political process the formulation of law enforcement policy on the use of electronic surveillance techniques. In *United States v. Giordano* (1974), where the Court was confronted with a violation of this authorization requirement (the Attorney General's executive assistant, not an official designated by the statute, had in fact been the person who placed the Attorney General's initials on an authorizing memo that the Attorney General had not seen), it was held "that the provision for pre-application control was intended to play a central role in the statutory scheme and that suppression must follow when it is shown that this statutory requirement has been ignored."

In adding protection for electronic communications in 1986, Congress departed from the requirements of high level authorization within the Justice Department by providing that "any attorney for the Government" (which includes a United States Attorney and "an authorized assistant of a United States attorney") may apply for court authorization of an interception of an electronic communication. This statute also allows for broader use of interception of electronic communications by allowing application to be made in connection with the investigation of "any federal felony," rather than the limited group of felonies specified as to the interception of wire or oral communications, but in other respects the application process is the same.

(b) Contents of Application. Each Title III application must "be made in writing upon oath or affirmation" and must include a considerable amount of information specified in the statute. It must "state the applicant's authority to make such application," which presumably can be met merely by identifying that person as holding the office specified in the statute, and it must also disclose "the identity of the investigative or law enforcement officer making the application, and the officer authorizing the application." In *United States v. Chavez* (1974), the Supreme Court concluded this identification requirement was not so central to the protections of Title III as to require suppression of the evidence obtained as a consequence of that application.

Next, the statute requires that the application set out "a full and complete statement of the facts and circumstances relied upon by the applicant to justify his belief that an order should be issued." Certain particulars are then specified in the statute, beginning with "details as to the particular offense that has been, is being, or is about to be committed," which has been interpreted to require only an indication of the general nature of the criminal conduct under investigation rather than a specification of a particular statute. Another requisite particular is "a particular description of the nature and location of the facilities from which or the place where the communication is to be intercepted," which in the case of a wiretap can be met by giving the particular phone number or (if the probable cause showing permits) by referring to all phones at a certain address. Under the so-called "roving tap" provision added in 1986, specification of the facilities or place may be excused upon a particularized showing of need. Still another particular is "a particular description of the type of communications sought to be intercepted," which courts have generally read as requiring no more than an indication of the offense under investigation. In justification, it is said that the actual content need not and cannot be stated since the conversations have not yet taken place at the time the application is made and it is virtually impossible for an applicant to predict exactly what will be said.

The fourth particular, "the identity of the person, if known, committing the offense and whose communications are to be intercepted," has proved a source of difficulty and has twice been considered by the Supreme Court. One question, dealt with in *United States v. Kahn* (1974), concerns just what the obligation of the government is to discover and name the persons to be heard, which arose because the wiretap at issue to intercept bookmaking-related conversations "of Irving Kahn and others as yet unknown." On the question of what persons must be identified in the application, the Court held "that Title III requires the naming of a person in the application or interception order only when the law enforcement authorities have probable cause to believe that that individual is 'committing the offense' for which the wiretap is sought," and that nothing in the statute supports "an additional requirement that the Government investigate all persons who may be using the subject telephone in order to determine their possible complicity." The question in *United States v. Donovan* (1977) was what the consequences of noncompliance with this part of the statute, as construed in *Kahn,* must be. There, government agents lawfully executing a wiretap learned the named individuals were discussing gambling with several other persons, but in obtaining an extension they failed to name these other persons, though there was probable cause as to them. The Court held that suppression was not required; the "naming" requirement was deemed not to play a "substantive role" in the regulatory scheme, in that even with the omissions "the application provided sufficient information to enable the issuing judge to determine that the statutory preconditions were satisfied."

The statute also requires that the application contain "a full and complete statement as to whether or not other investigative procedures have been tried and failed or why they reasonably appear to be unlikely to succeed if tried or to be too dangerous." This is an important part of the legislative scheme. As the Supreme Court has explained, it is designed to assure that that electronic eavesdropping is not "routinely employed as the initial step in criminal investigation" or "resorted to in situations where traditional investigative techniques would suffice to expose the crime." Yet, the requisite showing is not great and is to be tested in a practical and commonsense fashion, and in practice the standard has been watered down to one of investigatory utility, rather than necessity. The showing can be made in any one of three ways: (1) by showing the failure of other methods, which need not go so far as to indicate that every conceivable investigatory alternative has been unsuccessfully attempted; (2) by showing other methods are unlikely to succeed, which can be accomplished, for example, by indicating the difficulty in penetrating a particular conspiracy or by asserting that a conventional search warrant would not likely produce incriminating evidence; or (3) by showing other methods would be too dangerous, either in terms of disclosing the investigation or placing an officer or informant in physical danger.

Title III also requires that the application contain "a statement of the period of time for which the interception is required to be maintained." Moreover, if "the nature of the investigation is such that the authorization for interception should not automatically terminate when the described type of communication has been first obtained," then "a particular description of facts establishing probable cause to believe that additional communications of the same type will occur thereafter" is also required. When the objective is to intercept a particular conversation, it is usually not difficult to state the time period, but most cases are not of that kind. The statute contemplates that where "a course of conduct embracing multiple parties and extending over a period of time is involved, the order may properly authorize proportionally longer surveillance." In such circumstances, making the requisite showing has not proved difficult; where there is probable cause of a continuing offense, almost inevitably there is probable cause to believe that there will be more than one relevant conversation.

The application must also include "a full and complete statement of the facts concerning all previous applications known to the individual authorizing and making the application, made to any judge for authorization to intercept, or for approval of interceptions of, wire, oral, or electronic communications involving any of the same persons, facilities or places specified in the application, and the action taken by the judge on each such application." This provision serves to prevent "judge shopping" and also provides the judge with a basis upon which to assess the statements of probable cause and investigative necessity in the application. If the earlier request was granted, the judge is alerted to inquire why there is a need for further surveillance; if it was denied, the judge is alerted to determine whether its deficiencies carry over to the present application. The "previous applications" provision is central to the statutory scheme, so that a deliberate omission of that information requires suppression of evidence obtained by a warrant issued pursuant to the defective application. It must be emphasized, however, that the provision only requires disclosure of what is "known" by the person authorizing and making the application, and also that it does not cover prior interceptions of the same person pursuant to an application in which that person was not named or required to be named.

The final requirement, applicable only "where the application is for the extension of an order," is that the application contain "a statement setting forth the results thus far obtained from the interception, or a reasonable explanation of the failure to obtain such results." It is designed to provide the issuing judge with an opportunity to evaluate the actual investigative need for continued electronic surveillance at the time the extension application is presented.

(c) Review of Application. In reviewing a Title III application, the judge "may require the applicant to furnish additional testimony or documentary evidence in support of the application." Though such inquiry is discretionary, resort to it may sometimes be critical, for it provides an informal and expeditious means of curing minor, technical defects, or supplying even a major element omitted by oversight, such as an informant's "track record." Use of the word "testimony" highlights the fact that information in support of any search warrant must be given under oath. A suitable record should be made of it, and the best practice in this regard is to use a court reporter.

Before an eavesdropping order may be entered by the judge, Title III requires that he determine on the basis of the facts submitted that

(a) there is probable cause for belief that an individual is committing, has committed, or is about to commit a particular offense enumerated in section 2516 of this chapter;

(b) there is probable cause for belief that particular communications concerning that offense will be obtained through such interception;

(c) normal investigative procedures have been tried and have failed or reasonably appear to be unlikely to succeed if tried or to be too dangerous;

(d) except as provided in [the] subsection [on "roving taps"], there is probable cause for belief that the facilities from which, or the place where, the wire or oral communications are to be intercepted are being used, or are about to be used, in connection with the commission of such offense, or are leased to, listed in the name of, or commonly used by such person.

Absent a finding of each of the four matters listed in the statute, the judge may not issue the order. But by the statute's use of the word "may," it would appear that the judge has discretion not to issue the order even if such findings can be made, although there is not complete agreement as to whether this is so. In any event, denial of an application is appealable but should only be overturned on appeal if it is clearly erroneous.

(d) Contents of Order. A Title III interception order must specify certain matters that go to satisfying the particularity of description requirement of the Fourth Amendment. These are: "(a) the identity of the person, if known, whose communications are to be intercepted; (b) the nature and location of the communications facilities as to which, or the place where, authority to intercept is granted; (c) a particular description of the type of communications sought to be intercepted, and a statement of the particular offense to which it relates." These requirements are comparable to those that exist as to the application, and what was said about them in that context earlier (see § 3.4(b)) is equally applicable here. The order must also identify the person authorizing the application, as to which the same may be said, and in addition must identify the agency authorized to intercept the communications.

The order must also contain several directives concerning its execution, most of which go to the time of the permitted surveillance. There must be "a provision that the authorization to intercept shall be executed as soon as practicable," which reflects not only the need for prompt execution before the probable cause information becomes stale (see § 2.3(g)) but also the fact that eavesdropping devices often cannot be installed as promptly as a conventional warrant may be executed. The order must also specify "the period of time during which such interception is authorized," which may not be "for any period longer than is necessary to achieve the objective of the authorization, nor in any event longer than thirty days." That specification must include "a statement as to whether or not the interception shall automatically terminate when the described communication has been first obtained." In addition, the order must contain a provision that it "must terminate upon attainment of the authorized objective, or in any event in thirty days." Apart from these time limits, the order must also contain a directive that the interception "be conducted in such a way as to minimize the interception of communications not otherwise subject to interception," and, at the discretion of the court, "may require reports to be made to the judge who issued the order showing what progress has been made toward achievement of the authorized objective and the need for continued interception." These reports constitute an extremely important safeguard when the authorized surveillance is lengthy. Finally, in a case in which the applicant has so requested, the order is to "direct that a provider of wire or electronic communication service, landlord, custodian, or other person shall furnish the applicant forthwith all information, facilities, and technical assistance necessary to accomplish the interception unobtrusively and with a minimum of interference with the services that such service provider, landlord, custodian, or person is according to the person whose communications are to be intercepted."

§ 3.5   Title III: Executing the Order

(a) **Recording.** Execution of a Title III order has no functional or theoretical equivalent in traditional search warrant law. The traditional warrant typically is served very promptly, is executed in a brief period of time, results in the seizure of a few objects, and by its observed execution or receipt of an inventory assures that the subject of the search is promptly made aware of the search and what was seized. By contrast, a Title III order often cannot be executed very promptly, is likely to be executed over a considerable span of time, usually results in the interception of many communications, and is executed secretly and thus without the subject of the search being aware of it or of what had been seized. For this reason, certain special requirements have understandably been imposed by statute with respect to execution of Title III orders.

One such requirement is that the contents of any intercepted communication "shall, if possible, be recorded on tape or wire or other comparable device * * * in such way as will protect the recording from editing or other alterations." The purpose of this requirement is to ensure that an accurate record of the conversation is made in the first instance and not altered in the interim before its use. This means that monitoring agents should record everything that is overheard by them, whether or not it is deemed pertinent.

(b) Minimization. One very important provision in Title III requires that an interception order be executed "in such a way as to minimize the interception of communications not otherwise subject to interception under this chapter." This minimization duty implements a constitutional prerequisite to the validity of all court-ordered electronic surveillance, for the Supreme Court, in striking down the New York eavesdropping statute in *Berger v. New York,* (1967), deemed that statute to permit unconstitutional general searches because it allowed seizure of "the conversations of any and all persons coming into the area covered by the device * * * indiscriminately and without regard to their connection to the crime under investigation."

What is to be minimized is the interpretation of "communications not otherwise subject to interception" under Title III, which appears to mean communications other than those "concerning" the offense that was the basis of the order. This suggests that a communication is pertinent and thus not subject to the minimization limitation if it in some respect provides information helpful to the investigation, without regard to whether it includes an incriminating remark directly implicating the speaker in criminal activity. As for the other, nonpertinent communications, it must be emphasized that the statute does not forbid their interception, but merely requires that measures be adopted to reduce the extent of such interception to a practical minimum. In determining whether the surveying agents sufficiently complied with the minimization requirement, it is necessary to assess the facts of the particular case.

The Supreme Court has had one occasion to make such an assessment, in *Scott v. United States* (1978), where government agents intercepted for a one-month period virtually all conversations over a particular telephone suspected of being used in furtherance of a conspiracy to import and distribute narcotics, though only forty percent of those conversations were shown to be narcotics related. In the course of concluding that the minimization requirement had not been violated, the Court enumerated a number of factors that are to be taken into account in deciding the minimization issue, such as (1) that in the case of "very short," "one-time only" or "ambiguous" calls, or those apparently involving "guarded or coded language," "agents can hardly be expected to know that the calls are not pertinent prior to their termination"; (2) that "it is also important to consider the circumstances of the wiretap," e.g., whether "the investigation is focusing on what is thought to be a widespread conspiracy [requiring] more extensive surveillance," and the "type of use to which the telephone is normally put"; and (3) that "it may be important to determine at exactly what point during the authorized period the interception was made," for during "the early stages of surveillance the agents may be forced to intercept all calls to establish categories of nonpertinent calls which will not be intercepted thereafter." In the instant case, the Court reasoned, most of the 60% of the calls that turned out not to be material to the narcotics investigation were either "very short," "ambiguous in nature," or "one-time conversations" that fit into no previously established category, and thus there had been no minimization violation.

A more controversial aspect of the *Scott* case concerns the fact that the district court had found the surveilling agents "made no attempt to comply" with a minimization requirement and had concluded that this standing alone was a basis for suppression. The Supreme Court rejected that position in favor of the notion that "[s]ubjective intent alone * * * does not make otherwise lawful conduct illegal or unconstitutional," meaning that the officers' presumed failure to make even a good-faith effort to comply with the minimization requirement was not itself a reason for excluding the evidence obtained. The Court asserted this was sound Fourth Amendment doctrine and also good Title III law.

(c) Amendment and Extension. It is necessary to distinguish the Title III procedures for extension of an eavesdropping order from those dealing with what amounts to a retrospective amendment of a prior order. As for extension, this is possible only upon an application that meets the usual requirements and only after the court makes the findings usually required before an interception order may issue. "The period of extension shall be no longer than the authorizing judge deems necessary to achieve the purposes for which it was granted and in no event for longer than thirty days," but there is no prohibition on obtaining successive extensions of the same original order. The statute does not require by its own terms a fresh showing of probable cause in the extension application, but it has been suggested that such a showing is essential in light of the *Berger v. New York* (1967) prohibition upon protracted electronic searches upon a single showing of probable cause.

When officers are conducting a court-ordered surveillance under Title III with respect to one particular crime, they will sometimes intercept conversations that refer to or are evidence of some other type of crime. The contents of such communications are for some purposes treated just like the contents of communications of the type named in the order; that is, an officer with authorized knowledge of them may use them "to the extent such use is appropriate to the proper performance of his official duties" and also "may disclose such contents to another investigative or law enforcement officer to the extent that such disclosure is appropriate to the proper performance of the official duties of the officer making or receiving the disclosure." But, the contents of these communications concerning other crimes may be testified to in a federal or state proceeding only if a judge finds upon subsequent application, "made as soon as practicable," that "the contents were otherwise intercepted in accordance with the provisions of this chapter." This latter situation does not include instances in which these contents are merely set out and sworn to in an application for another Title III order or in a complaint for an arrest warrant.

Though the statute does not state what is to appear in the amendment application, the legislative history indicates it should include a showing that the original order was lawfully obtained, that it was sought in good faith and not as subterfuge search, and that the communication was in fact incidentally intercepted during the course of a lawfully executed order. The courts have not been very demanding with respect to the "as soon as practicable" timing limitation on an amendment application, but these cases have been criticized on the ground they disregard the principle of ongoing judicial supervision embodied in that part of the Act.

(d) Post–Surveillance Notice. Title III also provides that certain persons are to receive post-surveillance notice that the surveillance occurred. The judge is required to serve this notice "[w]ithin a reasonable time but not later than ninety days after the filing of an application for an order of approval * * * which is denied or the termination of the period of an order or extensions thereof," except that upon "an ex parte showing of good cause to a judge of competent jurisdiction the serving of the inventory required by this subsection may be postponed." The "reasonable time" requirement has been broadly construed. As for the "good cause" for postponement, it has been held to include such reasons as protecting the integrity of an ongoing investigation or ensuring that persons would not flee to avoid arrest. By statute, this notice is to include "(1) the fact of the entry of the order or the application; (2) the date of the entry and the period of authorized, approved or disapproved interception, or the denial of the application; and (3) the fact that during the period wire, oral, or electronic communications were or were not intercepted."

The notice is to be served "on the persons named in the order or the application, and such other parties to intercepted communications as the judge may determine in his discretion that is in the interest of justice." This in no event covers a person who is merely identified in the communications of another, and as to parties to communications not named in the order or application appellate courts have been disinclined to question the discretion exercised by the judge in deciding which of them should receive notice. Because "a judge is likely to require information and assistance beyond that contained in the application papers and the recordings of intercepted conversations made available by law enforcement authorities" in order to exercise his discretion intelligently, the Supreme Court concluded in *United States v. Donovan* (1973) that those authorities have a "routine duty to supply the judge with relevant information," "at a minimum, knowledge of the particular categories into which fall all the individuals whose conversations have been intercepted." In *Donovan,* where two names had been omitted from the list and those individuals thus did not receive notice until they were indicted eight months later, the Court held this did not require suppression because Congress did not mean for "post intercept notice * * * to serve as an independent restraint on resort to the wiretap procedure." The *Donovan* Court emphasized that the omission was inadvertent and had not prejudiced the defendants, which has been taken to mean that suppression is required if names are deliberately withheld or if prejudice resulted from lack of timely notice. Courts are generally disinclined to find that a defendant has established prejudice, but it would seem prejudice exists when the conversation is not inherently incriminating but is subject to explanation and interpretation and the delay in notice has diminished the speaker's opportunity to marshal his explanations.

(e) Sealing. Title III also requires that "the contents of any wire, oral, or electronic communication intercepted by any means authorized by this chapter shall, if possible, be recorded on tape or wire or other comparable device" and that such recording "be done in such way as will protect the recording from editing or other alterations." It further provides that "immediately upon the expiration of the period of the order, or extension thereof, such recordings shall be made available to the judge issuing such order and sealed under his direction." The Title III sealing requirement, intended to ensure the reliability and integrity of evidence obtained by means of electronic surveillance, has an explicit exclusionary remedy for noncompliance: "the presence of the seal provided for by this subsection, or a satisfactory explanation for the absence thereof, shall be a prerequisite for the use or disclosure of the contents of any wire, oral, or electronic communication or evidence derived therefrom." *United States v. Ojeda Rios* (1990) held that (1) the requirement is not that of "just any seal but a seal that has been obtained *immediately* upon expiration of the underlying surveillance order"; (2) consequently the "absence" the Government must explain "encompasses not only the total absence of a seal but also the absence of a timely applied seal"; (3) the required "satisfactory explanation" requires "that the Government explain not only why such a delay occurred but also why it is excusable"; and (4) the Government may establish a reasonable excuse for delay by showing reliance upon an erroneous interpretation of Title III which "was objectively reasonable at the time."

§ 3.6 Title III: Remedies

(a) **Violations Requiring Exclusion.** If a particular instance of electronic eavesdropping does not meet the requirements of the Fourth Amendment, then of course the judicially-created exclusionary rule for that Amendment comes into play, in which case what is said elsewhere herein about the dimensions of that rule is applicable. Of concern here, by contrast, is the statutory exclusionary rule of Title III. The statute at one point declares that no information derived from eavesdropping "may be received in evidence in any trial, hearing, or other proceeding * * * if the disclosure of that information would be in violation of this chapter." This language is somewhat misleading, and it has been properly suggested that it should be read as requiring the exclusion of evidence the *seizure* of which was in violation of the chapter. In any event, more attention has been focused upon the wording of another provision to the effect that a suppression motion may be made "on the grounds that (i) the communication was unlawfully intercepted; (ii) the order of authorization or approval under which it was intercepted is insufficient on its face; or (iii) the interception was not made in conformity with the order of authorization or approval." While the Fourth Amendment exclusionary rule was intended only as a restraint upon the activities of sovereign authority, and thus has no application to purely private searches (see § 2.1(h)), the Title III exclusionary rule expresses no such limitation, and thus several courts have held it is also applicable to private searches otherwise covered by that legislation.

In 1986, Title III was substantially amended so as to also cover the interception of any "electronic communication," defined as "any transfer of signs, signals, writing, images, sounds, data, or intelligence of any nature transmitted in whole or in part by a wire, radio, electromagnetic, photoelectronic or photooptical system that affects interstate or foreign commerce." However, neither of the two exclusionary rule provisions quoted above was amended, so that both continue to be limited only to violations having to do with wire or oral communications (defined in § 3.3(a)). The legislative history expressly declares that the Title III statutory exclusionary rule has no application to the interception of electronic communications, but no rationale for this curious distinction is given.

In *United States v. Giordano* (1974), the government argued that the phrase "unlawfully intercepted" in that provision meant only an interception obtained in violation of the Constitution. The Supreme Court rejected that contention and concluded from the legislative history that "Congress intended to require suppression where there is failure to satisfy any of those statutory requirements that directly and substantially implement the congressional intention to limit the use of intercept procedures to those situations clearly calling for the employment of this extraordinary investigative device." As the Court put it later in *Giordano,* suppression under this statutory exclusionary rule is required whenever the particular statutory provision violated "was intended to play a central role in the statutory scheme." At issue in *Giordano* was a failure to comply with the statutory requirement that the "Attorney General, or any Assistant Attorney General specifically designated by the Attorney General" must authorize application for a federal surveillance order. That requirement, the Court concluded, did play a "central role" because the statute reflected a Congressional intent to limit eavesdropping not merely by a probable cause requirement and a nature-of-offense limitation but also by having "a senior official in the Department of Justice" decide that the situation was one warranting resort to such surveillance.

By comparison, in *United States v. Chavez* (1974) the Court concluded that the misidentification of the authorizing official in the application and order "did not affect the fulfillment of any of the reviewing or approval functions required by Congress" because the statutory provisions thereby violated do "not establish a substantive role to be played in the regulatory system." And in *United States v. Donovan* (1977), where the violation was the failure to include in the application the names of all persons as to whom there was probable cause and who were likely to be overheard, the Court concluded *Chavez* rather than *Giordano* was controlling because the missing information would not "have precluded judicial authorization of the intercept," and even without that information "the application provided sufficient information to enable the issuing judge to determine that the statutory preconditions were satisfied." The "insufficient on its face" part of the statutory exclusionary rule was also addressed in *Chavez*; the Court concluded that it applies only when the order can be determined to be insufficient without resort to other facts. Thus, because in that case the order did identify a person as having authorized the application who had the authority to give such authorization, the fact it was subsequently shown he actually did not give the requisite approval "does not detract from the facial sufficiency of the order." As for the "not made in conformity" statutory language, the Court in *Giordano* observed it concerns only "the manner of conducting the court-approved interceptions" and thus was not in issue there.

One final problem, addressed in another branch of the *Donovan* case, needs to be specially noted. The government in that case also failed to inform the judge of all identifiable persons whose conversations were intercepted, thus making it impossible for the judge to exercise fully his discretionary authority to decide what parties should receive notice. In concluding that violation did not require suppression, the Court reasoned:

> Nothing in the structure of the Act or this legislative history suggests that incriminating conversations are "unlawfully intercepted" whenever parties to those conversations do not receive discretionary inventory notice as a result of the Government's failure to inform the District Court of their identities. At the time inventory notice was served on the other identifiable persons, the intercept had been completed and the conversations had been "seized" under a valid intercept order. The fact that discretionary notice reached 39 rather than 41 identifiable persons does not in itself mean that the conversations were unlawfully intercepted.

One way to read that paragraph is as just another illustration of the "central role" test being used to admit evidence notwithstanding the statutory violation, but another plausible reading is that any noncompliance subsequent to a lawful interception, no matter how serious, cannot operate to retroactively invalidate the prior interception. Though this latter view is arguably supported by a literal reading of the statute, it may be that courts are empowered to exclude evidence, even beyond what is provided for in the Title III exclusionary rule, when they do so for the purpose of overcoming prejudice or deterring deliberate statutory violations. The Court in *Donovan* appears to have left these issues open by carefully noting that the defendants made no claim of prejudice and also that the violation was unintentional.

(b) Who May Exclude When. Fourth Amendment standing, including the ruling in *Alderman v. United States* (1969) that in an eavesdropping case the parties to the conversation and the persons with a possessory interest in the place where the conversation occurs all have standing, is discussed elsewhere herein (see § 8.1(b)). Regarding Title III standing, the statute says that any "aggrieved person" may move for suppression, and that term is defined as meaning "a person who was a party to any intercepted wire, oral, or electronic communication or a person against whom the interception was directed." Read literally, this definition would seem to be narrower in some respects and broader in some respects than Fourth Amendment standing; it seems to leave out the person with the possessory interest in the place surveilled and to include the target of the surveillance who was neither that person nor one of the speakers. But, as the Court noted in *Alderman*, the legislative history shows this definition was intended "to reflect existing law," and thus the Court there concluded Congress had not extended the exclusionary rule. Thus, courts are inclined to define Title III standing as being exactly the same as Fourth Amendment standing, and even take into account developments in the Fourth Amendment area that have occurred after enactment of Title III.

There is another way, however, in which the Fourth Amendment exclusionary rule and the Title III exclusionary rule are unquestionably different. The former, as a creature of the Supreme Court, need be applied only in circumstances the Court believes will further its objectives (see § 2.2(f), (g)); illustrative is *United States v. Calandra* (1974), refusing to allow a grand jury witness to invoke the exclusionary rule because a contrary result "would achieve a speculative and undoubtedly minimal advance in the deterrence of police misconduct at the expense of substantially impeding the role of the grand jury." But the Title III exclusionary rule, by virtue of the statute, applies "in any trial, hearing, or proceeding in or before any court, department, officer, agency, regulatory body, or other authority of the United States, a State, or a political subdivision thereof," meaning it may be invoked, for example, by a party in a bail hearing, a parole revocation proceeding, or a police department disciplinary proceeding.

The legislative history of the language quoted above unequivocally states that "[b]ecause no person is a party as such to a grand jury proceeding, the provision does not envision the making of a motion to suppress in the context of such a proceeding itself," but only that if a motion to suppress is granted in another context "its scope may include use in a future grand jury proceeding." This means, for example, that a prospective defendant cannot merely by virtue of that status invoke the Title III exclusionary rule before the grand jury considering his case. But in *Gelbard v. United States*

(1972), the Court held that a grand jury witness may refuse to testify where his testimony is sought on the basis of illegal electronic surveillance. This is because, the Court explained, that testimony would constitute "evidence derived" from violation of Title III, and another part of the Act expressly provides that such evidence may not "be received in evidence in any trial, hearing, or other proceeding in or before any court, *grand jury,* department, officer, agency, regulatory body, legislative committee, or other authority of the United States, a State, or a political subdivision thereof." The Court reasoned that if that prohibition was "not available as a defense to the contempt charge, disclosure through compelled testimony makes the witness the victim, once again, of a federal crime." *Gelbard* was a 5–4 decision in which a majority was achieved only with the concurring opinion of Justice White, who suggested a different result would obtain "where the Government produces a court order for the interception" but "the witness nevertheless demands a full-blown suppression hearing to determine the legality of the order," as "hearings in these circumstances would result in protracted interruption of grand jury proceedings" but "the deterrent value of excluding the evidence will be marginal at best."

(c) Disclosure of Illegal Electronic Surveillance. After enacting Title III, Congress recognized that victims of illegal wiretapping might have grounds to suspect, but yet have difficulty proving, that wiretapping had occurred. It thus enacted a provision that in "any trial, hearing, or other proceeding in or before any court, grand jury, department, officer, agency, regulatory body, or other authority of the United States," upon a claim by "a party aggrieved" that the evidence is inadmissible as the fruit of an "unlawful act," "the opponent of the claim shall affirm or deny the occurrence of the alleged unlawful act." To put the government to the task of responding, the aggrieved party must articulate a colorable basis for his claim of surveillance. Once that burden has been met, the government must make a factual, unambiguous, and unequivocal response, normally in the form of sworn testimony or an affidavit indicating the results of inquiry of all appropriate investigative agencies to determine if any of them have conducted surveillance of the complaining party.

(d) Disclosure of Electronic Surveillance Records. Under Title III, suppression is provided for not only as to the contents of an illegally intercepted wire or oral communication, but also as to "evidence derived therefrom," which raises the question of what procedures are required to facilitate a determination whether other evidence is the fruit of such a surveillance. This issue reached the Supreme Court in a series of cases not involving Title III: *Alderman v. United States, Ivanov v. United States,* and *Butenko v. United*

States (1969), where the defendants sought disclosure of all surveillance records so that they might show that some of the evidence admitted against them grew out of illegally overheard conversations. The government urged that in order to protect innocent third parties participating or referred to in irrelevant conversations overheard by the government, surveillance records should first be subjected to in camera inspection by the trial judge, who would then turn over to defendants and their counsel only those materials "arguably relevant" to defendants' convictions. The Court held that a defendant should receive *all* surveillance records as to which he has standing; the government's proposal was rejected on the ground that the trial judge often would not be in a position to determine what conversations were relevant, as an "apparently innocent phrase, a chance remark, a reference to what appears to be a neutral person or event, the identity of a caller or the individual on the other end of a telephone, or even the manner of speaking or using words may have special significance to one who knows the more intimate facts of an accused's life." To protect innocent third parties, the Court added, the trial court could place defendants and counsel under enforceable orders against unwarranted disclosure of the materials they would be entitled to inspect.

Giordano v. United States (1969) emphasized that disclosure under *Alderman* was available only to one who "has standing to assert the illegality of the surveillance" and that "a finding by the District Court that the surveillance was lawful would make disclosure and further proceedings unnecessary." And in *Taglanetti v. United States* (1969), the Court rejected defendant's contention that he was entitled to examine additional surveillance records to establish that he might be a party to some other conversations. Distinguishing *Alderman,* the Court concluded that the trial judge could be expected to identify defendant's voice without the defendant's assistance.

By statute, Congress has attempted to limit the impact of *Alderman* in the federal courts. For one thing, records of an unlawful surveillance which occurred prior to the enactment of Title III need not be disclosed "unless such information may be relevant to a pending claim of * * * inadmissibility," which presumably is to be determined by the judge in camera. For another, on the legislative finding that "there is virtually no likelihood" that evidence offered to prove an event would have been obtained by exploitation of an unlawful surveillance occurring more than five years prior to that event, no such claim is to be considered. The constitutionality of these provisions is open to some doubt, as the *Alderman* decision was cast in terms of "the scrutiny which the Fourth Amendment exclusionary rule demands."

(e) Civil Remedies. Title III expressly provides that "any person whose wire, oral, or electronic communication is intercepted, disclosed, or intentionally used in violation of this chapter may in a civil action recover from the person or entity which engaged in that violation" appropriate relief, including: appropriate equitable or declaratory relief; damages and punitive damages in appropriate cases; and a reasonable attorney's fee and other reasonable litigation costs. The damages may be the greater of the sum of the plaintiff's actual damages and the violator's resulting profits, or statutory damages of the greater of $100 a day or $10,000. Good faith reliance on a court warrant or order, grand jury subpoena, legislative authorization, or request of a law enforcement officer is a defense. Any willful violation of the provisions on interception and disclosure of wire, oral or electronic communications or on access to stored communications provides the basis for a civil action against the United States to collect money damages of $10,000 or actual damages, whichever is greater, plus reasonable litigation costs. Where there are "serious questions" about whether an officer or employee of the U.S. acted willfully or intentionally in that regard, an investigation must promptly be initiated to determine whether disciplinary action is warranted.

(f) Criminal Penalties. Title III makes it a crime for a person, except as permitted by the statute, to "intentionally" intercept, endeavor to intercept, or procure another to intercept or endeavor to intercept a communication; to "intentionally" disclose or endeavor to disclose to another the contents of a communication "knowing or having reason to know" that it was obtained by an illegal interception; or to "intentionally" use or endeavor to use the contents of a communication "knowing or having reason to know" that it was obtained by an illegal interception. The "intentionally" mental state was substituted for "willfully" in 1986 to emphasize that inadvertent interception is not criminal. Under this provision, a person acts intentionally if his conduct or the result thereof was his conscious objective. The "good faith reliance" defense is also available in a criminal prosecution. With limited exceptions, a person convicted of this offense may be fined, imprisoned not more than five years, or both. Another provision with like penalties makes it a crime to possess, manufacture, distribute, advertise or mail "any electronic, mechanical, or other device, knowing or having reason to know that the design of such device renders it primarily useful for the purpose of the surreptitious interception of wire, oral, or electronic communication." Exceptions are provided for law enforcement agents and their suppliers and for providers of wire or electronic communication service and their agents.

Chapter 4

POLICE "ENCOURAGEMENT" AND THE ENTRAPMENT DEFENSE

Table of Sections

---

§ 4.1 Encouragement of Crime and the Defense of Entrapment

(a) Encouragement of Criminal Activity. Certain criminal offenses present the police with unique and difficult detection problems because they are committed privately between individuals who are willing participants. Consequently, in addition to employing search and seizure techniques, routine and electronic surveillance, and informants to expose such consensual crime, law enforcement officers actually encourage commission of these offenses. An environment is created in which the suspect is presented with an opportunity to commit a crime. The simulation of reality must be accurate enough to induce the criminal activity at the point in time when the agents are in a position to gather evidence of the crime. The tactics used vary from case to case. Some solicitations are

255

innocuous, but since persons engaged in criminal activity are generally suspicious of strangers, government agents typically do more than simply approach a target and request the commission of a crime. Multiple requests or the formation of personal relationships with a subject may be necessary to overcome that suspicion. In addition, appeals to personal considerations, representations of benefits to be derived from the offense, and actual assistance in obtaining contraband or planning the details of the crime are frequently employed.

(b) Entrapment Defense as a Limit. The more extreme forms of encouragement activity are a matter of legitimate concern for a variety of reasons. Of central concern is the possibility that the encouragement might induce a person who otherwise would be law-abiding to engage in criminal conduct. Yet, as a historical matter, the traditional response of the law was that there were no limits upon the degree of temptation to which law enforcement officers and their agents could subject those under investigation. Even today, neither courts nor legislatures have affirmatively developed detailed guidelines for police and their agents to follow when engaging in encouragement activity. However, there did ultimately develop, originally in the state courts, a defense called "entrapment" that may be interposed in a criminal prosecution. Beginning with the decision in *Sorrells v. United States* (1932), the development of the law of entrapment became largely an activity of the federal courts, with the states then adopting the doctrine thereby created. The classic definition of entrapment is that articulated in *Sorrells:* "Entrapment is the conception and planning of an offense by an officer, and his procurement of its commission by one who would not have perpetrated it except for the trickery, persuasion, or fraud of the officer."

(c) Scope of the Defense. The defense of entrapment has been asserted in the context of a wide variety of criminal activity, although the great majority of the cases involve a charge of some drug offense. There is a dearth of case authority on the question of whether the entrapment defense is available no matter what the nature of the charge brought against the defendant. But in *Sorrells* there appears a caution that the defense might be unavailable where the defendant is charged with a "heinous" or "revolting" crime, and the Model Penal Code formulation of the defense expressly makes it "unavailable when causing or threatening bodily injury is an element of the offense charged and the prosecution is based on conduct causing or threatening such injury to a person other than the person perpetrating the entrapment." This latter limitation has been explained on the ground that one "who can be persuaded to cause such injury presents a danger that the public cannot safely disregard, and that the impropriety of the inducement will likely be dealt with by punishment of the conniving or cooperating officers."

The defense of entrapment does not extend to *all* inducements, and thus another important issue concerning the scope of the defense is that of whose inducements may result in entrapment. Entrapment can occur through an undercover agent, a confidential informant or a private citizen knowingly acting under the direction of government agents. This is not to suggest, however, that any sort of relationship between the police and a private citizen will suffice; for example, it is not enough that the police had earlier made an informal request for potential future information to the person who made the inducements. On the other hand, a sufficient agency relationship can exist even when the police did not expressly request the particular inducement techniques later challenged via an entrapment defense, as the government cannot make such use of an informer and then claim disassociation through ignorance.

As for the troublesome question of whether entrapment can occur through a third party who is not knowingly furthering a government scheme, it is necessary to distinguish between three different situations, beginning with what might be called "private entrapment" in the purest sense, an instance in which a private individual, of his own will and without any official involvement, induces another person to commit a crime. The entrapment defense does not extend to such inducements. If the entrapment defense was conceived of as being based upon the notion that a person is not culpable whenever he engages in what would otherwise be criminal conduct because of the strong inducement of another person, this limitation would be open to serious question. What this limitation reflects, then, is that the purpose of the defense is to deter misconduct in enforcing the law.

The two other situations are "vicarious entrapment" and "derivative entrapment." In the case of vicarious entrapment, a private individual, who himself has been induced by an undercover law enforcement officer or agent, now in turn induces someone else to join in the scheme. The views of some courts is that even when the government has no reason to expect that a target of an investigation will induce a nonessential collaborator to join in criminal activity, the third party should still be able to plead entrapment if it is found that the initial target was himself entrapped, as in such a case the third party is another victim of the same misconduct. But other courts deem it inappropriate to confer an entrapment defense upon individuals never targeted by the government in the first place. Consistent with the latter view but going further are those decisions that assert, in effect, that the entrapment defense is *never* available to a defendant who was not directly induced by a law enforcement officer or an agent knowingly acting on the officer's behalf. Such a broad rule would, of course, extend even to the third situation, "derivative entrapment," by which is meant the case in which the undercover government officer or agent uses the unsuspecting middleman as a means of passing on an inducement to a distant target. Some other federal and state courts, however, have taken the view that the entrapment defense should be available to the distant target under these circumstances. The notion is that it should make no difference that the intermediary is unwitting, for the purpose behind allowing such a defense is to prevent the government from circumventing rules against entrapment merely by deploying intermediaries, only one degree removed from the officials themselves, who carry out the government's instructions to persuade a particular individual to commit a particular crime using a particular type of inducement.

Though the defense of entrapment is ordinarily interposed in the context of a criminal prosecution, a number of states have recognized entrapment as a defense to an administrative proceeding involving revocation or suspension of a license to practice a profession, trade, or business. Few courts have considered the issue, and the cases in which the matter is alluded to at all usually reflect nothing but the tacit assumption that the defense is available in administrative proceedings but inapplicable to the case at bar. Nevertheless, extension of the entrapment defense to administrative disciplinary proceedings seems to be warranted by the policies underlying its application in criminal cases.

§ 4.2 Subjective Versus Objective Test for Entrapment

(a) The Subjective Approach. There are currently two major approaches to the defense of entrapment, each involving a distinct test and rationale and each with somewhat different procedural consequences. The majority view is usually referred to as the "subjective approach," although it is also called the federal approach or the *Sherman–Sorrells* doctrine, a reference to the fact that this test was adopted by a majority of the Supreme Court in the cases of *Sherman v. United States* (1958) and *Sorrells v. United States* (1932). This subjective approach is still followed in the federal courts, and has also been adopted in about two-thirds of the states as well. A two-step test is used under the subjective approach: the first inquiry is whether or not the offense was induced by a government agent; and the second is whether or not the defendant was predisposed to commit the type of offense charged. A defendant is considered to have been predisposed if he was ready and willing to commit the crimes charged whenever an opportunity was afforded. If the accused is found to be predisposed, the defense of entrapment may not prevail. The emphasis under the subjective approach is clearly upon the defendant's propensity to commit the offense rather than on the officer's misconduct.

In *Jacobson v. United States* (1992), where the defendant ordered sexually explicit photos of children through the mail after the government, over 2–1/2 years, made repeated efforts through five fictitious organizations and a bogus pen pal to explore his willingness to do so, the Court held the government had failed to establish defendant's predisposition. In so concluding, the Court emphasized that it was not enough the defendant was "ready and willing" by the time he was specifically asked to engage in the proscribed conduct; the government needed and failed to prove "that this predisposition was independent and not the product of the attention" the government had directed at him over that previous time span. The defendant's purchase of a similar publication before any government contact *and* before the conduct was made illegal did not establish predisposition, "for, there is a common understanding that most people obey the law even when they disapprove of it." Moreover, the defendant's later communication with the government's fictitious organizations, while "indicative of * * * a predisposition to view photographs of preteen sex," could "hardly support an inference that he would commit the crime of receiving child pornography through the mails."

The underlying rationale of the subjective approach is grounded in the substantive criminal law. The defense is explained in terms of the defendant's conduct not being criminal because the legislature intended acts instigated by the government to be excepted from the purview of the general statutory prohibition. As stated by the majority in *Sorrells:* "We are unable to conclude that it was the intention of the Congress in enacting this statute that its processes of detection and enforcement be abused by the instigation by government officials of an act on the part of persons otherwise innocent in order to lure them to its commission and to punish them."

(b) The Objective Approach. There is growing support for the objective approach, variously described as the "hypothetical person" approach or the Roberts–Frankfurter approach (after the writers of the concurring opinions in *Sorrells* and *Sherman*). The objective approach is favored by a majority of the commentators, is reflected in the formulation of the entrapment defense appearing in the American Law Institute's Model Penal Code, and has been adopted by about one-third of the states.

This approach focuses upon the inducements used by the government agents, as entrapment has been established if the offense was induced or encouraged by employing methods of persuasion or inducement which create a substantial risk that such an offense will be committed by persons other than those who are ready to commit it. In applying this test, it is necessary to consider the surrounding circumstances, such as evidence of the manner in which the particular criminal business is usually carried on. Though such practices as appeals to sympathy or friendship, offers of inordinate gain, or persistent offers to overcome hesitancy are suspect, courts in jurisdictions using the objective test have been reluctant to lay down absolutes. Though such temptations may be impermissible in some instances, each case must be judged on its own facts. Thus, it would seem that this "objective" focus upon the propriety of the police conduct leaves as much room for value judgments to be made as does the "subjective" focus upon the defendant's state of mind.

The rationale behind the objective approach is grounded in public policy considerations. Proponents of this approach reject the legislative intent argument. They believe that courts must refuse to convict an entrapped defendant not because his conduct falls outside the proscription of the statute, but rather because, even if his guilt has been established, the methods employed on behalf of the government to bring about the crime cannot be countenanced. To some extent, this reflects the notion that the courts should not become tainted by condoning law enforcement improprieties. If government agents have instigated the commission of a crime, then the courts should not in effect approve that abhorrent transaction by permitting the induced individual to be convicted. But the primary consideration is that an affirmative duty resides in the courts to control police excesses in inducing criminal behavior, and that this duty should not be limited to instances in which the defendant is otherwise "innocent." So viewed, the entrapment defense appears to be a procedural device (somewhat like the Fourth Amendment and *Miranda* exclusionary rules) for deterring undesirable governmental intrusions into the lives of citizens.

As currently applied, the two approaches differ more than merely at the theoretical level, although neither of the two approaches is uniformly more favorable to defendants. Under the subjective approach, if *A*, an informer, makes overreaching appeals to compassion and friendship and thus moves *D* to sell narcotics, *D* has no defense if he is predisposed to narcotics peddling, while under the objective approach a defense would be established because the police conduct, not *D*'s predisposition, determines the issue. Under the subjective approach, *A*'s mere offer to purchase narcotics from *D* may give rise to the defense provided *D* is not predisposed to sell, but a contrary result would be reached under the objective approach because a mere offer to buy hardly creates a serious risk of offending by the innocent.

(c) Objections to the Subjective Approach. Proponents of the objective approach raise three main arguments against the subjective approach. First of all, the "legislative intent" theory is attacked as sheer fiction; it is argued that the Congress or state legislature intended to proscribe precisely the conduct in which the defendant engaged, as is reflected by the fact that the conduct is unquestionably criminal if the temptor was a private person rather than a government agent. Because the prior innocence of the defendant will not sustain the defense of entrapment, then, so the argument proceeds, the public policies of deterring unlawful police conduct and preserving the purity of the courts must be controlling. Those policies, it is concluded, are not effectuated by looking to the defendant's predisposition.

A second criticism of the subjective approach is that it creates, in effect, an "anything goes" rule for use against persons who can be shown by their prior convictions or otherwise to have been predisposed to engage in criminal behavior. This is because if the trier of fact determines that a defendant was predisposed to commit the type of crime charged, then no level of police deceit, badgering or other unsavory practices will be deemed impermissible. Such a result is unsound, it is argued, because it ignores the possibility that no matter what his past crimes and general disposition the defendant might not have committed the particular crime unless confronted with inordinate inducements. Moreover, so this reasoning proceeds, this notion that the permissible police conduct may vary according to the particular defendant is inconsistent with the objective of equality under the law.

Yet a third objection to the subjective approach is that delving into the defendant's character and predisposition not only has often obscured the important task of judging the quality of police behavior, but also has prejudiced the defendant more generally. This is because once the entrapment defense is raised, certain usual evidentiary rules are discarded, and the defendant will be subjected to a searching inquiry into his own conduct and predisposition as bearing upon that issue. This means a prosecutor may admit evidence of a prior criminal record, reputation evidence, acts of prior misconduct, and other information generally barred as hearsay or as being more prejudicial than probative.

(d) Objections to the Objective Approach. Proponents of the subjective approach have likewise raised various criticisms concerning the objective approach. One of them is that defendant's predisposition, at least if known by the police when the investigation in question was conducted, has an important bearing upon the question of whether the conduct of the police and their agents was proper. For example, if it is known that a particular suspect has sold drugs in the past, then it is proper to subject that person to more persuasive inducements than would be permissible as to an individual about whose predisposition the authorities knew nothing. By like token, knowledge that a target has a weakness for a vice crime but is currently abstaining is also a fact that merits consideration when assessing an agent's conduct. Thus, the objective approach is said to be inherently defective because it eliminates entirely the need for considering a particular defendant's criminal predisposition.

A second major criticism of the objective approach is that the "wrong" people end up in jail if a dangerous, chronic offender may only be offered those inducements that might have tempted a hypothetical, law-abiding person. This is because, for example, the fact that the defendant in a particular case has been a shrewd, active member of a narcotics ring prior to and continuing through the incident in question is irrelevant under the objective test to a determination of the propriety of the inducements used. So the argument continues, to avoid this acquittal of wary criminals, courts are likely to allow agents substantial leeway in determining the limits of permissible inducement, with the result that this same freedom will allow the police to lead astray the "unwary innocent."

Still another criticism directed at the objective approach to entrapment is that it will foster inaccuracy in the factfinding process. It is argued that the nature of the inducement offered in secret is a factual issue less susceptible to reliable proof than the issue of predisposition. This is because if a defendant claims that an inducement was improper, the agent can take the stand and rebut the allegations, resulting in a swearing match. Especially because the defense of entrapment ordinarily assumes an admission of guilt (unless inconsistent defenses are permitted), this means the factfinder will often have to make the "imponderable choice" between the testimony of an informer, often with a criminal record, and that of a defendant who has admittedly committed the criminal act.

A fourth objection relates to the public policy justifications of the objective approach. It is questioned whether the "purity" of the courts is itself a sufficient justification, and whether the objective approach can be expected to serve the deterrence objective in a meaningful way. Because courts are disinclined to adopt per se rules regarding what are impermissible police inducements, it is doubted whether there will actually result significant restrictions upon the types of inducements that police are entitled to utilize. Moreover, so the argument continues, even if such limitations are developed the police will still be left with the discretion to decide upon the context or target of encouragement activity. To this are added the familiar arguments against other attempts to deter the police, such as that they can be thwarted by police perjury or that they will be totally ineffective when the police are acting for objectives other than conviction. For all these reasons, this line of argument concludes, the deterrence objective should be dismissed in favor of an effort to do justice to the individual defendant in the particular case.

§ 4.3   Procedural Considerations

(a) **Admissibility of Evidence of Defendant's Past Conduct.** Entrapment has sometimes been characterized as a dangerous defense that should only be used in a few cases with ideal fact situations or in desperate circumstances where no other defense is possible. This perceived danger is largely attributable to various procedural consequences that attend interposition of an entrapment defense where the majority, subjective approach is followed. And of the procedures that are relevant in this respect, certainly of primary importance is the readiness with which evidence of defendant's past conduct is received as bearing upon defendant's predisposition. In most jurisdictions, once entrapment has been raised as a defense the usual evidentiary rules are no longer followed. For the purported purpose of allowing the factfinder access to all information bearing upon the "predisposition" issue, courts have allowed the receipt into evidence of defendant's prior convictions, prior arrests, and information about his "reputation" and even concerning "suspicious conduct" on his part. The result is that otherwise inadmissible hearsay, suspicion and rumor are brought into the case and the defendant, in effect, is put on trial for his past offenses and character.

This indiscriminate attitude toward predisposition evidence is by no means a necessary feature of the subjective test. This is because less prejudicial means of determining the readiness and willingness of a defendant to engage in the criminal conduct will often be available. The most promising alternative is testimony about the defendant's actions during the negotiations leading to the charged offense, such as his ready acquiescence, his expert knowledge about such criminal activity, his admissions of past deeds or future plans, and his ready access to the contraband. Another possibility is evidence obtained in a subsequent search or otherwise showing the defendant was involved in a course of ongoing criminal activity.

(b) **Triable by Court or Jury.** Traditionally, the entrapment defense has been regarded as a matter for the jury rather than for determination by the judge. (Even where this is unquestionably the case, the judge may rule on the sufficiency of the proof to raise the issue in the first place, and where uncontradicted evidence supports the conclusion that the defendant was entrapped the issue may of course be decided as a matter of law by the court.) Under the majority, subjective approach to entrapment, grounded upon the implied exception theory, the issue of whether a defendant has been entrapped is for the jury as part of its function of determining the guilt or innocence of the accused. In support of this state of affairs, it has been argued that determining matters of credibility and assessing the subjective response to the stimulus of police encouragement are peculiarly within the ken of the jury. Also, it has been observed that if the matter is placed in the hands of the jury there is an opportunity for jury nullification, meaning that the jury, if it wishes, can acquit because of the moral revulsion that the police conduct evokes in them, notwithstanding any amount of convincing evidence of the defendant's predisposition.

Under the objective approach to entrapment, in favor of having the matter decided by the judge is the notion that it is the function of the court to preserve the purity of the court. Similarly, it may be said that to the extent the objective approach rests upon a deterrence-of-police rationale this function also is the proper responsibility of the court, just as it is when the court rules on suppression motions. And there is the added point that only the court, through the gradual evolution of explicit standards in accumulated precedents, can give significant guidance for official conduct for the future. However, not all of the states that have adopted the objective approach submit the issue to the judge instead of the jury. Perhaps this is because the issue is deemed an appropriate one for the jury because the jury has particular competence on the question of what temptations would be too great for an ordinary law-abiding citizen.

(c) Inconsistent Defenses. The traditional view has been that the defense of entrapment is not available to one who denies commission of the criminal act with which he is charged, for the reason that the denial is inconsistent with the assertion of such a defense. However, a trend in the opposite direction appears to be developing, and there is much to be said in favor of this latter position. For one thing, it avoids serious constitutional questions concerning whether a defendant may be required, in effect, to surrender his presumption of innocence and his privilege against self-incrimination in order to plead entrapment. Also, it would seem that the adversary process is itself a sufficient restraint upon resort to positions that are truly inconsistent, for in a case where two positions are unquestionably logically inconsistent, a defendant who pursued both positions would certainly be found to be lacking credibility. The matter was settled in the federal courts by *Mathews v. United States* (1988), where the Supreme Court held that even if a defendant denies one or more elements of the crime, he is entitled to an entrapment instruction whenever there is sufficient evidence from which a reasonable jury could find entrapment.

Even in jurisdictions where the traditional view persists, the defendant must be allowed to raise the defense of entrapment without admitting the crime whenever the circumstances are such that there is no inherent inconsistency between claiming entrapment and yet not admitting commission of the criminal acts. Thus, the inconsistency rule does not apply when the government in its own case in chief has interjected the issue of entrapment into the case. And if a defendant testifies that a government agent encouraged him to commit a crime that he had never contemplated before that time and that he resisted the temptation nonetheless, there is nothing internally inconsistent in thereby claiming entrapment and that the crime did not occur. Asserting the entrapment defense is not necessarily inconsistent with denial of the crime even when it is admitted that the requisite acts occurred, for the defendant might nonetheless claim that he lacked the requisite bad state of mind.

(d) Burden of Proof. In those jurisdictions following the majority, subjective approach to entrapment, it is generally accepted that the defendant has the burden of establishing the fact of inducement by a government agent. Some courts require a defendant to sustain a burden of persuasion by proving government inducement by a preponderance of the evidence, but many give the defendant only the burden of production, which can be met by coming forward with "some evidence" of government conduct creating a risk of persuading a nondisposed person to commit a crime. In any event, once the defendant's threshold responsibility is satisfied, the burden is then on the government to negate the defense by showing beyond a reasonable doubt defendant's predisposition or an absence of inducement.

Where the objective approach is followed, the entire burden of production and persuasion is on the defendant, who must establish the impropriety of the police conduct by a preponderance of the evidence. This is a consequence of the entrapment defense under this approach being an "affirmative defense" rather than something that negatives the existence of an element of the crime charged. Such an allocation of the burden of proof might be questioned on the ground that as a general matter the government is in a much better position than the defendant to obtain and preserve evidence on the question of what kinds of government inducements were utilized in the particular case. This has led to the suggestion that perhaps the real basis for placing the burden of persuasion on the defendant is that entrapment is a disfavored defense, so that factual doubts should be resolved against it.

§ 4.4 Other Challenges to Encouragement Practices

(a) **Contingent Fee Arrangements.** From time to time the courts have given consideration to whether additional restraints upon encouragement practices by police and their agents are needed. The restraints considered in some respects resemble the entrapment defense, for they are also concerned with situations in which a government agent has induced a crime. But they are clearly different than the majority, subjective approach to entrapment, for these other restraints (if imposed) would protect even those defendants predisposed to commit the crime charged. They are also different in some respects from the objective approach to entrapment, though they share with it the purpose of deterring the police from improper practices.

One practice occasionally a cause of concern is that of entering into a contingent fee arrangement with a person acting on behalf of the police to bring about commission of a crime by some other person. The compensation may be monetary, but frequently it takes the form of offers of leniency regarding charges pending against the informant. Depending upon the particular arrangement, contingent fee arrangements may provide the informant with an incentive to engage in unfair tactics and then misrepresent the nature of those tactics subsequently. If the contingency only involves providing a controlled opportunity to another person to engage in criminal conduct, then the incentive to employ unfair tactics may not be great. But if the compensation is contingent upon the subject's commission of a controlled offense, the informer's testimony about that commission in court, or the conviction of the subject for commission of that offense, then the risks of misrepresentation and unfair tactics substantially increase.

Occasionally an appellate court, concerned about the risk of a "frame-up" where contingent fees of one of the latter types was involved, has reversed defendant's conviction. But the current view is that such a contingency is merely a matter for the jury to consider in weighing the credibility of the witness-informant. That position finds support in the Supreme Court's expressed unwillingness in *United States v. Russell* (1973) to establish "fixed rules" of due process in the entrapment area or to give the federal judiciary "a 'chancellor's foot' veto" over law enforcement practices of which it disapproves.

(b) **Inducements to Those Not Reasonably Suspected.** It has sometimes been suggested that a government agent should not be permitted to solicit an offense absent at least "reasonable suspicion" that his target is engaged in such criminal activity. Such a requirement would to some degree lend support to the entrapment doctrine's objective of ensuring that the police detect but not create crime, though its main thrust would be to protect the interests of privacy and freedom from unreasonable intrusions. Some authority is to be found that reasonable suspicion is an encouragement prerequisite, but most of the decisions on this issue have rejected this theory. *Russell* seems to have sapped it of any remaining vitality by indicating that the entrapment defense is intended to protect nondisposed defendants rather than to control police conduct.

(c) Government "Overinvolvement" in a Criminal Enterprise. In *Sorrells* and *Sherman*, the entrapment doctrine was explained in terms of the presumed intention of Congress rather than as a matter of constitutional law. This means, of course, that Congress may depart from the *Sorrells–Sherman* test if it wishes, and that state courts and legislatures may do likewise. In short, the law of entrapment is not itself of constitutional dimension. But there remains for consideration the question of whether certain kinds of government involvement in a criminal enterprise would warrant the conclusion that the due process rights of the person induced had been violated.

In *United States v. Russell* (1973), an undercover agent supplied the defendant and his associates with 100 grams of propanone, an essential but difficult to obtain ingredient in the manufacture of methamphetamine ("speed"); they used it to produce two batches of "speed," which pursuant to agreement the agent received half of in return. The defendant, convicted of unlawfully manufacturing and selling the substance, conceded on appeal that the jury could have found him predisposed, but claimed that the agent's involvement in the enterprise was so substantial that the prosecution violated due process. In particular, he contended that prosecution should be precluded when it is shown that the criminal conduct would not have been possible had not the agent "supplied an indispensable means to the commission of the crime that could not have been obtained otherwise, through legal or illegal channels." The Court in *Russell* found it unnecessary to pass on that contention because the record showed that propanone "was by no means impossible" to obtain by other sources. Though acknowledging that "we may some day be presented with a situation in which the conduct of law enforcement agents is so outrageous that due process principles would absolutely bar the government from invoking judicial processes to obtain a conviction," the majority concluded "the instant case is distinctly not of that breed" because the agent had simply supplied a legal and harmless substance to a person who had theretofore been "an active participant in an an illegal drug manufacturing enterprise." (Three dissenters urged adoption of the objective approach to entrapment and asserted that if pronanone "had been wholly unobtainable from other sources" the agent's actions would be "conduct that constitutes entrapment under any definition.")

Then came *Hampton v. United States* (1976), where petitioner, convicted of distributing heroin, objected to the denial of his requested jury instruction that he must be acquitted if the narcotics he sold to government agents had earlier been supplied to him by a government informant. Three members of the Court concluded that the difference between the instant case and *Russell* was "one of degree, not of kind," for here the government supplied an illegal substance that was the corpus delicti of petitioner's crime and thus "played a more significant role" in enabling the crime to occur. But such conduct as to a predisposed defendant was deemed not to violate due process. Significantly, two concurring Justices, while agreeing that "this case is controlled completely by *Russell*," expressed their unwillingness "to join the plurality in concluding that, no matter what the circumstances, neither due process principles nor our supervisory power could support a bar to conviction in any case where the Government is able to prove disposition." The three dissenters in *Hampton* urged that conviction be "barred as a matter of law where the subject of the criminal charge is the sale of contraband provided to the defendant by a Government agent." The instant case, they contended, was different from *Russell* because (i) here the supplied substance was contraband, and (ii) here the "beginning and end of this crime" coincided with the government's involvement. "The Government," they protested, "is doing nothing less than buying contraband from itself through an intermediary and jailing the intermediary."

Russell and *Hampton,* then, indicate that a majority of the Court accepts the notion that there may well be *some* circumstances in which a due process defense would be available even to a defendant found to be predisposed. However, those two cases do not provide clear guidance as to how the police conduct is to be assessed in making this judgment, though they do justify the conclusion that instances of government conduct outrageous enough to violate due process will be exceedingly rare. Among the possibilities are (1) an instance in which government agents induce others to engage in violence or threat of violence against innocent parties; (2) where concern for overreaching government inducement overlaps with concern for first amendment freedoms, as where the government sends provocateurs into political organizations to suggest the commission of crimes; (3) where the government initiated or exploited a sexual relationship to bring about the crime; (4) where the government offered such extraordinarily large financial inducements as to bring about a coercive situation; and (5) the situation put by the *Russell* dissenters, supplying contraband "wholly unobtainable from other sources" so as to "make possible the commission of an otherwise totally impossible crime."

Chapter 5

INTERROGATION AND CONFESSIONS

Table of Sections

---

§ 5.1   Introduction and Overview

(a) The Need for Confessions. No area of constitutional criminal procedure has provoked more debate over the years than that dealing with police interrogation. In large measure, the debate has centered upon two fundamental questions: (1) how important are confessions in the process of solving crimes and convicting the perpetrators? and (2) what is the extent and nature of police abuse in seeking to obtain confessions from those suspected of crimes? Conclusive evidence on these two points is lacking, and thus it is not surprising that this debate continues.

As to the first question, some respond that many criminal cases, even when investigated by the best qualified police departments, are capable of solution only by means of an admission or confession from the guilty But it is difficult to quantify that proposition, as available statistics are inconclusive. Those tending to show that confessions are offered into evidence in only a small fraction of criminal prosecutions for serious crimes fail to show how many of the considerable number of cases disposed of by guilty plea were not contested precisely because the defendant had given a confession. As for statistics offered to show that confessions are frequently relied upon in criminal prosecutions, they do not, standing alone, establish there existed a need in those cases to resort to interrogation instead of some other form of investigation. And even if we could fairly assess the availability of alternatives, there remains the question of whether interrogation is necessarily the most undesirable of the lot, or whether it is to be preferred over sole reliance upon eyewitness identification, perhaps attended by a higher risk of unreliability.

(b) The Extent of Police Abuse. As the Supreme Court noted in *Miranda v. Arizona* (1966), police interrogation "still takes place in privacy," which "results in secrecy and this in turn results in a gap in our knowledge as to what in fact goes on in the interrogation rooms." Because of this secrecy (for some a sufficient indication in itself of abuse), there is lacking sufficient empirical evidence to assert with confidence what always, usually, or often occurs in the course of police interrogation. This being so, attention has often turned to celebrated cases of confessions later proved false or to judicial opinions (including many Supreme Court decisions) revealing outrageous police tactics, but some claim such incidents have no relation to ordinary day-to-day police operations. Moreover, to say, as conceded in *Miranda,* that "the modern practice of in-custody interrogation is psychologically rather than physically oriented," is not to conclude that police abuse is nonexistent, but rather that it has become somewhat more difficult to determine exactly what ought to be encompassed within the term "abuse."

(c) The Supreme Court's Response. From 1936 to nearly thirty years later, the Supreme Court dealt with confessions admitted in state criminal proceedings in terms of the fundamental fairness required by the Fourteenth Amendment due process clause. A so-called "voluntariness" test, which depended upon the "totality of the circumstances," was used to determine whether the Constitution required exclusion of a confession. The dimensions of this test changed over the years as the Supreme Court's concerns about the interrogation process broadened. At first, the question was simply one of whether the methods used had produced a confession that was unreliable; then the Court undertook to deter unfair police interrogation practices even if they produced reliable statements; and still later the Court's decisions reflected concern with whether the interrogated defendant had been substantially deprived of the choice whether or not to talk to the police. As the years passed, it became increasingly apparent that this test was most difficult to administer because it required a finding and appraisal of all relevant facts surrounding each challenged confession.

Essentially the same approach was used by the Supreme Court during this period on the infrequent occasions when confessions admitted in federal prosecutions were reviewed. In such instances, it might logically be thought that the Court was then relying upon the due process clause of the Fifth Amendment. However, the tendency was to refer to earlier holdings in which the basis of exclusion was the Fifth Amendment privilege against self-incrimination or a common law rule of evidence. The anticipated move away from sole reliance upon the voluntariness test occurred in *Escobedo v. Illinois* (1964), suppressing the defendant's confession because it was obtained in violation of his right to counsel at the time of interrogation. *Escobedo* was a cautious step carefully limited to the unique facts of the case, but it was generally assumed that this newly established right to counsel in the police station would thereafter be expanded on a case-by-case basis. That did not occur, for in the now famous case of *Miranda v. Arizona* (1966) the Court moved off in a different direction by relying instead upon the Fifth Amendment privilege against self-incrimination. But thereafter the Court returned to the right-to-counsel theory as a means of deciding certain cases not amenable to easy resolution under *Miranda*.

In *Miranda*, the Court held that a person "deprived of his freedom of action in any significant way" could not be questioned unless he waived his rights after being properly advised by the police. Today *Miranda* is most often invoked in confession suppression hearings, and thus the emphasis herein is upon the basis and meaning of that decision, although this is not to suggest that today the admissibility of an incriminating statement is determined only by application of the *Miranda* rules. For one thing, there will be times when *Miranda* is not applicable, either because the defendant was not in custody or otherwise "deprived of his freedom of action in any significant way" or because the police did not engage in interrogation or its "functional equivalent." As for the right to counsel, it will be applicable only to those cases in which the statement was obtained after that right has attached, but in such cases it may be extremely important because, for example, police conduct can violate that right even if it does not constitute interrogation under *Miranda*. As for the "voluntariness" due process test, it is always worthy of consideration; it is possible that there has been an effective waiver of *Miranda* rights followed by police conduct that made the subsequent confession involuntary.

§ 5.2 The "Voluntariness" Test

(a) **The Common Law Rule.** Under the early common law, confessions were admissible at trial without any restrictions whatsoever; even an incriminating statement obtained by torture was not excluded. But some time prior to the middle of the eighteenth century, English trial judges began placing restrictions on the admissibility of confessions. Sometimes the question was put in terms of whether the defendant's confession had been induced by a promise of benefit or threat of harm, while on other occasions the inquiry was more directly put in terms of whether the circumstances under which the defendant had spoken impaired the reliability of the confession. But it became more common for the courts simply to ask whether the confession had been made "voluntarily," that is, without certain improper inducements. These included actual or threatened physical harm, a promise not to prosecute, a promise to provide lenient treatment upon conviction, and deceptive practices so extreme that they might have produced a false confession (not merely using a fellow prisoner as an undercover agent or misleading the defendant as to the strength of the case against him). There was no attempt to assess the effect of an inducement on a particular suspect.

The Supreme Court's early decisions on the admissibility of confessions in federal courts relied upon the common law rule. The rule was stated by the Court in terms of whether there had been such an inducement that "the presumption upon which weight is given to such evidence, namely, that one who is innocent will not imperil his safety or prejudice his interests by an untrue statement, ceases." In *Bram v. United States* (1897), the Court appeared to base exclusion upon violation of the Fifth Amendment privilege against self-incrimination, but the Court later pulled back from that position. Nonetheless, *Bram* influenced the Court to state the rule of exclusion more broadly, so that it was not merely a matter of whether the confession was reliable or whether a forbidden inducement had been used, but rather whether the confession "was, in fact, voluntarily made." So expanded, the common law standard seems merged into the definition of due process voluntariness developed in the state court cases subsequently decided by the Court.

(b) Due Process and the "Complex of Values". It was not until *Brown v. Mississippi* (1936) that the Court barred the use of a confession in the state courts. It could not, of course, dispose of the state confession on the same grounds as were resorted to in the earlier cases. Under our federal system, the Supreme Court may not proscribe mere rules of evidence for the states, and the Fifth Amendment privilege was then not deemed applicable to the states. Thus the confessions in *Brown,* obtained by brutally beating the suspects, were struck down on the notion that interrogation is part of the process by which a state procures a conviction and thus is subject to the requirements of the Fourteenth Amendment due process clause. Though *Brown* declared that due process was violated when a conviction was rested "solely" upon a confession so obtained, later cases made it clear that the mere use at trial of such a confession was unconstitutional.

This due process test is customarily referred to as the "voluntariness" requirement, the term used by the Court in enunciating the due process requisites for admissibility. But that term is not at all helpful in determining the policies underlying this particular constitutional limitation. As the Court candidly put it in *Blackburn v. Alabama* (1960), "a complex of values underlies the stricture against use by the state of confessions which, by way of convenient shorthand, this Court terms involuntary." A closer examination of the Court's decisions in this area over the years reflects three important values deserving specific mention here.

In *Brown*, the confessions clearly were of doubtful reliability, and thus that case might be read as announcing a due process test for excluding confessions obtained under circumstances presenting a fair risk that the statements are false. Concern with this risk was emphasized in several subsequent cases, and this led many state courts to the conclusion that unfairness in violation of due process exists when a confession is obtained under circumstances affecting its testimonial trustworthiness. But while ensuring the reliability of confessions is *a* goal under the due process voluntariness standard, it is incorrect to define the standard in terms of that one objective. In *Rogers v. Richmond* (1961), defendant's confession was obtained after the police pretended to order his ailing wife arrested for questioning, and the state court had ruled that the statement need not be excluded "if the artifice or deception was not calculated to procure an untrue statement." The Supreme Court disagreed, emphasizing that convictions based upon coerced confessions must be overturned "not because such confessions are unlikely to be true but because the methods used to extract them offend an underlying principle in the enforcement of our criminal law: that ours is an accusatorial and not an inquisitorial system." *Rogers* thus made certain what had been strongly intimated in several earlier cases, namely, that the due process exclusionary rule for confessions (in much the same way as the Fourth Amendment exclusionary rule for physical evidence) is also intended to deter improper police conduct.

In *Townsend v. Sain* (1963), the ailing defendant had been given a drug with the properties of a truth serum, after which he gave a confession in response to questioning by police who were unaware of the drug's effect. Although the confession was not obtained by conscious police wrongdoing and apparently was reliable, the Court nonetheless held its use impermissible: "Any questioning by police officers which *in fact* produces a confession which is not the product of free intellect renders that confession inadmissible." *Townsend* thus highlights another theme running through many of the earlier cases: the confession must be a product of the defendant's "free and rational choice." This phrase, however, was not used in an absolute sense, but rather in conjunction with a recognized need to exert some pressure to obtain confessions. As the Court seems to have acknowledged in *Miranda v. Arizona* (1966), the question of whether a confession was "voluntary" had theretofore been determined by a lesser standard than, say, the question of whether a testator's will was his voluntary act.

Viewing the voluntariness test in terms of its underlying values, then, it might be said that the objective of the test is to bar admission of those confessions (i) of doubtful reliability because of the practices used to obtain them; (ii) obtained by offensive police practices even if reliability is not in question (for example, where there is strong corroborating evidence); or (iii) obtained under circumstances in which the defendant's free choice was significantly impaired, even if the police did not resort to offensive practices. But in *Colorado v. Connelly* (1986), the Court in effect denied the existence of the third category listed above, holding that the state court had erred in excluding a confession volunteered to police by a defendant who suffered from a psychosis that interfered with his ability to make free and rational choices. Absent "the crucial element of police overreaching," the Court reasoned, "there is simply no basis for concluding that any state actor has deprived a criminal defendant of due process." *Townsend* was distinguished as a case involving "police wrongdoing" in questioning a person who had been given a truth serum, though in fact the Supreme Court in that earlier case proceeded on the assumption that neither the police doctor who administered the drug nor the police who did the questioning were aware of the drug's truth serum character. *Connelly* is grounded in the notion that "state action" beyond merely receiving defendant's confession into evidence is necessary, that at a minimum there must be "police conduct causally related to the confession," and that this conduct must be "coercive" (such as exploiting defendant's deficient mental condition). *Connelly* also emphasized the narrow reading that must be given to the first category listed above. The Court conceded that a "statement rendered by one in the condition of respondent might be proved to be quite unreliable," but then declared that "this is a matter to be governed by the evidentiary laws of the forum * * * and not by the Due Process Clause of the Fourteenth Amendment." This is so, the Court explained, because the aim of the due process requirement "is not to exclude presumptively false evidence, but to prevent fundamental fairness in the use of evidence, whether true or false." Moreover, because the Fourteenth Amendment only covers state action, the "most outrageous behavior by a private party," even if it produces an unreliable confession, "does not make that evidence inadmissible under the Due Process Clause" (see § 5.10(b)).

In *Chavez v. Martinez* (2003), where a majority agreed that a § 1983 plaintiff had no Fifth Amendment claim regarding persistent police interrogation of him over his objection and while he was suffering from serious injuries because the confession obtained was never admitted against him in a criminal case (see § 5.5(a)), another majority held: "Whether Martinez may pursue a claim of liability for a substantive due process violation is * * * an issue that should be addressed on remand, along with the scope and merits of any such action that may be found open to him." Some members of the Court, however, had no doubt what the outcome should be, and in the process expressed quite different views on what constituted due process in that context. Three Justices declared that the "shocks the conscience" test would apply but would not be met on these facts, and that the due process protection of any "fundamental liberty interest" test would not either because there is nothing in the Court's jurisprudence supporting the position "that freedom from unwanted police questioning is a right so fundamental that it cannot be abridged absent a compelling state interest." Three others, however, citing *Brown*, asserted that the due process requirement of a voluntary confession makes it "a simple enough matter to say that use of torture or its equivalent in an attempt to induce a statement violates an individual's fundamental right to liberty of the person."

(c) Relevant Factors in the "Totality of Circumstances." The Fourteenth Amendment due process voluntariness test requires examination of the "totality of circumstances" surrounding each confession. As a general matter, this means that it is necessary to assess carefully the conduct of the police in obtaining the confession. Indeed, it has long been the case that if the conduct of the police was "inherently coercive," then suppression in the interest of deterring such conduct in future cases is appropriate without first making any judgment about the impact of that conduct upon the particular defendant. In the pre-*Connelly* era, when the question came down to whether *this* defendant's free choice was substantially impaired, any facts that tended to show that he was more or less susceptible to pressures than the average person were particularly relevant. Since *Connelly*, as will be discussed further herein, it is less clear just what relevance the characteristics and status of the person who gave the confession has in determining whether the requisite element of "police overreaching" is present.

A significant number of the confession cases that have reached the Supreme Court have involved actual or threatened physical brutality or deprivation, such as whipping or slapping the suspect, depriving him of food or water or sleep, keeping him in a naked state or in a small cell, holding a gun to his head or threatening him with mob violence. As the Court noted in *Stein v. New York* (1953), when such outrageous conduct is present "there is no need to weigh or measure its effects on the will of the individual victim." However, this *per se* approach is subject to limitations even as to the use or threatened use of violence.

The *Stein* approach was not applied by either the majority or the dissent in a much more recent coerced confession case involving a threat of force, *Arizona v. Fulminante* (1991). That case involved a defendant who confessed to a fellow prison inmate (who was actually a government agent) after that inmate stated that he had heard that Fulminante was "starting to get some tough treatment" from the other inmates and suggested that he might be able to protect Fulminante, but only if he was told the truth. The Court majority found *both* that the circumstances presented "a credible threat of physical violence unless Fulminante confessed" *and* that, as a result, "Fulminante's will was overborne in such a way as to render his confession the product of coercion." The four dissenters found no grounding in the record for the majority's conclusion that the defendant (described by the dissent as "an experienced habitué of prisons and able to fend for himself") had "his capacity for self-determination critically impaired" by a perceived need for protection against possible physical recriminations by his fellow inmates. Neither the *Fulminante* majority nor the dissenters sought to distinguish the per se approach of *Stein*. However, the Court did cite as analogous *Payne v. Arkansas* (1958), a case where the police interrogator offered protection from mob violence, and it noted that *Payne* also was a case in which it had found that there was a credible threat of violence that had in fact operated on the particular defendant to overbear his will. The assumption seems to be that where the threat of physical violence stems not from the interrogator who holds the defendant in custody, but from third persons, the cogency of the threat is less apparent, making inappropriate a conclusive presumption that it operated to overbear the free will of the defendant. Even where force was actually applied by the police, lower courts have held that *Stein's per se* approach is limited to those confessions made substantially concurrently with physical violence, so that those sufficiently attenuated from such misconduct are subject to the more lenient totality of the circumstances test.

Another very important "totality of the circumstances" factor is whether the defendant was subjected to extended periods of incommunicado interrogation. Of particular significance in this regard is whether the suspect was subjected to lengthy and uninterrupted interrogation, whether he was kept in confinement an extended period of time even though subjected only to intermittent questioning, whether he was moved from place to place and questioned by different persons so as to be disoriented, whether he was questioned in solitary confinement or at some isolated place away from the jail, and whether he was held incommunicado up until the time of the confession (especially if family, friends or counsel were turned away). Under the more extreme of these circumstances, such as where there have been a couple of weeks of uninterrupted detention or virtual nonstop interrogation for 36 hours, the situation is "inherently coercive" and suppression of the confession is mandated. But in less extreme circumstances the confession has typically been excluded only upon a showing that the defendant was especially susceptible to coercion.

In *Bram v. United States* (1897), the Court declared that a confession "obtained by any direct or implied promises, however slight," is not voluntary. Read literally, this passage suggests a standard holding automatically involuntary any confession that was a "but for" product of a promise that might benefit the defendant. But *Fulminante* noted that such a reading of the *Bram* passage "under current precedent does not state the standard for determining the voluntariness of a confession." The role of the promise must be evaluated in light of the totality of the circumstances, and the promise must have been sufficiently compelling to overbear the suspect's will in light of those circumstances. Supreme Court opinions suggest, however, that certain promises, by their very nature, can be presumed to have that impact absent special circumstances pointing in the opposite direction. Illustrative are *Rogers v. Richmond* (1961), holding defendant's confession was coerced where it was obtained in response to a police threat to take defendant's wife into custody, and *Lynumn v. Illinois* (1963), deciding that the confession was coerced where defendant was told she could lose her welfare payments and the custody of her children but that if she cooperated the police would help her and recommend leniency.

Similarly, lower courts have often held that a confession is involuntary if made in response to a promise that the result will be nonprosecution, the dropping of some charges, medical treatment, or a certain reduction in the punishment defendant may receive (although in recent years there has been a movement away from treating such promises of leniency as *per se* producing involuntariness, especially in light of *Fulminante's* reading of *Bram*). Merely promising to bring defendant's cooperation to the attention of the prosecutor is not objectionable, nor is a promise that if defendant confesses the prosecutor would *discuss* leniency. Also, more generalized assurances that assistance will be sought or that certain facilities are available are not inherently coercive. But the cases go both ways on the question of what the result should be when a confession has been obtained in response to a police assertion that cooperation would facilitate prompt release on bail or would mean that the defendant would fare better in subsequent proceedings. In the latter situation, the difficulty is in attempting to reconcile the voluntariness requirement with the plea bargaining process and especially the role of the police in that practice.

The Court in *Bram* also stated that a confession was involuntary if obtained by any other "improper influence," but the courts have not had an easy time in trying to resolve what other police conduct deserves to be so characterized. This is particularly true with respect to police trickery and deception. Although dictum in *Miranda v. Arizona* (1966) was highly critical of such activity, as a general matter it may be said that the courts have not deemed such conduct sufficient by itself to make a confession involuntary. One type of trickery involves misrepresenting to the suspect the strength of the existing case against him, as in *Frazier v. Cupp* (1969). During the interrogation of Frazier concerning a homicide, the police told him that his cousin Rawls, with whom he had been on the evening in question, had been brought in and had already confessed. The Court concluded that the "fact that the police misrepresented the statements that Rawls made is, while relevant, insufficient in our view to make this otherwise voluntary confession inadmissible." Similarly, lower courts have held confessions admissible when they were prompted by such misrepresentations as that the murder victim was still alive, that the police only sought defendant's statement as a witness, that nonexistent witnesses have been found, that the murder weapon had been uncovered, that defendant's prints were found at the crime scene, that an accomplice had confessed and implicated the defendant, or that the results of defendant's polygraph exam showed that he had lied. Courts are much less likely to tolerate misrepresentations of law, such as that defendant's confession could not be used against him at trial or that the previously obtained confession of an accomplice could be so used.

Another type of deceit is the so-called "false friend" technique, whereby the interrogator represents that he is a friend acting in the suspect's best interest. Extreme versions of this technique have been condemned by the Supreme Court. In *Leyra v. Denno* (1954) a confession was held involuntary where obtained by a police psychiatrist who was represented as a general practitioner brought in to relieve his acutely painful sinus attack, and in *Spano v. New York* (1959) a confession was ruled involuntary where obtained by a policeman who was a close friend of the defendant and who told defendant he would be in trouble unless defendant confessed. Dictum in the *Miranda* case was critical of the "Mutt and Jeff" routine, whereby the defendant is questioned by a hostile interrogator and then a supposedly sympathetic one. But the courts have not generally disapproved of the police giving "friendly" advice to the defendant or expressing sympathy for him. A quite different kind of "false friend" situation, that in which by deception the defendant is made unaware that the person with whom he is conversing is a police officer or police agent, clearly does not make the defendant's statement involuntary even though he acted in the mistaken impression that this person could be trusted not to reveal it. Police appeals to the defendant's sympathies, such as by the now-famous "Christian burial speech" ploy, do not automatically render a confession involuntary, and the same is true of exhortations to tell the truth or assertions that the suspect had been lying.

Under *Miranda*, certain warnings must precede custodial interrogation, and this means a failure to give those warnings will result in exclusion of the confession under that decision. Nonetheless, on occasion the question may arise as to the relevance of the absence of such warnings to the voluntariness issue. This can occur when the confession at issue (i) was obtained prior to the *Miranda* decision, (ii) was obtained from a suspect not in custody and thus not covered by *Miranda,* or (iii) is admissible for a special purpose if voluntary notwithstanding the *Miranda* violation. As the Court put it in *Procunier v. Atchley* (1971), failure to give the warnings is not inherently coercive, but is "relevant only in establishing a setting in which actual coercion might have been exerted." On the other hand, the fact the warnings were given is an important factor tending in the direction of a voluntariness finding. This fact is important in two respects. It bears on the coerciveness of the circumstances, for it reveals that the police were aware of the suspect's rights and presumably prepared to honor them. And, as with the factors discussed below, it bears upon the defendant's susceptibility, for it shows that the defendant was aware he had a right not to talk to the police. Where, however, the police give the warnings but then suggest that the exercise of the right to consult with a lawyer would be prejudicial, denying the defendant all opportunities for leniency, that action not only will render involuntary the waiver of *Miranda* rights but also add a coercive element to the interrogation that could render the statement itself involuntary. (This additional consequence may become important because limitations upon the prosecution's use of involuntary statements extend beyond the limitation upon the use of statements that are voluntary but obtained in violation of *Miranda* (see §§ 8.5(a), 8.6(b)).)

Especially in an otherwise close case, it is appropriate also to take account of the particular characteristics of the person who was subjected to interrogation, in order to judge the extent of his ability to resist the external pressures brought to bear upon him. The Supreme Court has taken into consideration the suspect's age, sex, and race whenever those factors have tended to indicate less than average ability to resist. Likewise relevant is the fact that the defendant might have been more willing to confess because he was suffering from a physical injury, physical illness, physical fatigue, mental illness, mental deficiency, emotional distress, or an abnormality caused by drugs or alcohol. Courts have also taken into account the suspect's education level, and his prior experience with the police. But *Connelly,* discussed above, makes it clear that such characteristics of the defendant, in isolation, cannot alone "ever dispose of the inquiry into constitutional 'voluntariness' "; there must also exist "the crucial element of police overreaching," which was not present in that case because the police merely received the confession of a person who approached them and volunteered it. *Connelly* thus leaves uncertain how the "overreaching" judgment is to be made in the more typical interrogation situation. There is a split of authority as to whether the very act of interrogating one known to be under a substantial mental disability supplies the requisite coercion. It would seem, however, that the propriety of the investigative and interrogation techniques used must be judged in light of what the police knew or should have known about defendant's ability to comprehend the events and circumstances.

Connelly also highlights the fact that coercive tactics utilized by private persons cannot alone produce a confession that is involuntary in the constitutional sense. (Under the law of some states, however, such private coercion may be a basis for suppression on some other grounds.) However, the "police overreaching" language of *Connelly* should not be taken literally, for a government employee need not be a law enforcement official for his questioning to implicate the strictures of the Fifth Amendment.

(d) Critique of the "Voluntariness" Test. One major defect in the due process "voluntariness" test is that it is so imprecise as to leave the police without needed guidance. Secondly, the ambiguous due process standard impaired the effectiveness and the legitimacy of judicial review. Even conscientious trial judges were left without guidance for resolving confession claims. Moreover, the "totality of circumstances" approach both facilitated pro-police rulings at suppression hearings and diminished the chances that the defendant would obtain relief at the appellate level. Perhaps the strongest evidence of the ineffectiveness and the unworkability of the voluntariness test is the case of *Davis v. North Carolina* (1966). No one other than the police had spoken to the defendant during the sixteen days of detention and interrogation that preceded his confessions, and in holding the confessions involuntary the Court noted it had "never sustained the use of a confession obtained after such a lengthy period of detention and interrogation as was involved in this case." Yet two state courts and two federal courts had previously held that these confessions were lawfully admitted into evidence against Davis. While in *Davis* the relevant facts clearly appeared on the record and were uncontested, the more typical case is one in which there is a "swearing contest" over what happened behind closed doors, and thus a third major defect in the due process voluntariness test is that its application is fatally dependent upon resolution of that swearing contest.

§ 5.3   The Prompt Appearance Requirement

(a) The *McNabb–Mallory* Rule. Beginning in 1943 the Supreme Court developed another line of authority, not expressly grounded in the Constitution, that was frequently utilized in federal criminal prosecutions. Under what became known as the *McNabb–Mallory* rule, the Court required the suppression of any confession obtained during custody that was illegal by virtue of a failure to honor a defendant's right to be brought promptly before a judicial officer following his arrest. The rule had an uncertain beginning in *McNabb v. United States* (1943), where the Court exercised "its supervisory authority over the administration of criminal justice in the federal courts" to exclude such confessions. Later, in *Mallory v. United States* (1957), a unanimous Court held that a confession was inadmissible because procured in violation of a provision in the federal rules (not extant when *McNabb* was decided) to the effect that an arrested person must be taken before a committing magistrate "without unnecessary delay." As for the meaning of that term, the Court explained: "Circumstances may justify a brief delay between arrest and arraignment, as for instance, where the story volunteered by the accused is susceptible of quick verification through third parties. But the delay must not be of a nature to give opportunity for the extraction of a confession."

Early Supreme Court decisions marked other important limits upon this particular exclusionary rule, namely: a confession obtained during a period of lawful detention is not subject to suppression merely because of a subsequent failure promptly to take the confessing defendant before a magistrate; at least absent a showing that a subterfuge was involved, a confession for one crime is not subject to suppression where it was obtained upon remand of defendant to the police following his prompt appearance before a magistrate on a different (even lesser) charge; and a confession obtained by federal agents from a defendant in state custody is not subject to suppression even where exclusion would have been required if the custody had been federal, unless it appears there was a "working arrangement" between state and federal officials. And in the post-*Mallory* case of *Cleary v. Bolger* (1963) the Court, stressing the traditional reluctance of federal courts to interfere with state proceedings, held it was improper for a federal court to enjoin a state official from testifying at a state criminal trial about his witnessing of a confession that would have been inadmissible in federal court under *McNabb–Mallory*.

(b) Reactions to the Rule. Reactions to the *McNabb–Mallory* rule over the years were mixed. Some saw the prompt appearance requirement coupled with an exclusionary sanction as preventing wholesale or dragnet arrests on suspicion and giving force to the notion that an arrest (even on probable cause) is not properly a vehicle for the investigation of crime. Others objected to the rule on the ground that it unwisely tended to "collapse" the arrest and charging decisions and to prevent even fair questioning intended to determine whether a person lawfully arrested should be charged. Such views prompted repeated efforts to have Congress either repeal or revise the *McNabb–Mallory* rule, finally accomplished as a part of the Omnibus Crime Control and Safe Streets Act of 1968. One provision states that a voluntary confession "shall not be inadmissible solely because of delay" in bringing the person before a magistrate "if such confession was made or given by such person within six hours immediately following his arrest or other detention," to which there is added the proviso that this time limitation "shall not apply in any case in which the delay in bringing such person before such magistrate or other officer beyond such six-hour period is found by the trial judge to be reasonable considering the means of transportation and the distance to be traveled to the nearest available such magistrate or other officer." Though that language would seem to restrict the *McNabb–Mallory* rule to confessions obtained after the six-hour period and reasonable extensions thereof, other provisions declare that any confession shall be admissible in a federal prosecution "if it is voluntarily given" and that delay in appearance before a magistrate is but one of several factors "to be taken into consideration by the judge" but which "need not be conclusive on the issue of voluntariness."

This confusing combination of provisions has produced disagreement among lower courts as to what is left of the *McNabb–Mallory* rule. One view is that exclusion based solely on impermissible delay is no longer allowed, and that impermissible delay is merely a factor to be considered in judging voluntariness. A contrary position holds that *McNabb–Mallory* survives, but is now applicable only to a delay occurring prior to the confession that extended beyond the six hour period and that was unreasonable as measured by the logistical concerns noted in the statute. A middle position holds that the per se exclusion formerly mandated by *McNabb–Mallory* is no longer appropriate, but that a federal court retains discretion to employ an exclusionary remedy as a response to unreasonable delay beyond the six hour period. In *United States v. Alvarez–Sanchez* (1994), which unanimously held that the statute "does not apply to statements made by a person who is being held solely on state charges," the Supreme Court took note of the aforementioned division among the lower courts but found no need to resolve it.

(c) Prompt Appearance in the States. Early on in the development of the *McNabb–Mallory* rule, the Supreme Court held that it was not constitutionally mandated and that consequently it was not applicable to trials in the state courts. But prompt appearance is a common if not universal requirement under state law, and thus there remains the possibility that a state might adopt an exclusionary rule as a means of enforcing such a law. The vast majority of state courts passing on the question have rejected the *McNabb–Mallory* approach outright, but several states follow the *McNabb–Mallory* approach in some respect, some utilizing a per se rule of exclusion and others requiring a showing of a causal connection between the illegal delay and the challenged confession.

§ 5.4 The Right to Counsel

(a) The *Massiah* Case. Although by the late 1950's a minority of the Court was asserting that a suspect had a constitutional right to have counsel present during police interrogation, the argument that the right to counsel attaches when the defendant is indicted and his status thereby changes from "suspect" to "accused" was finally accepted by the Court in a case that did not even involve custodial interrogation. In *Massiah v. United States* (1964), Massiah, indicted for federal narcotics violations, retained counsel, pled not guilty and was released on bail. Codefendant Colson, who unknown to Massiah was cooperating with the authorities and had a radio transmitter in his car, invited Massiah to discuss the pending case, and during their conversations in that car Massiah's damaging admissions were overheard by a federal agent, who testified as to them at Massiah's trial. Perhaps to avoid a difficult eavesdropping issue, the Supreme Court decided *Massiah* on Sixth Amendment grounds, holding "that the petitioner was denied the basic protections of that guarantee when there was used against him at his trial evidence of his own incriminating words, which federal agents had deliberately elicited from him after he had been indicted and in the absence of his counsel." Although *Massiah* was also applied in state proceedings, it had a rather limited impact until revitalized and expanded in *Brewer v. Williams* (1977). In the confessions area, it was overshadowed by *Escobedo v. Illinois* (1964), decided just a few weeks later, and by *Miranda v. Arizona*

(1966), which came two years later. Lower courts were inclined to give *Massiah* as narrow an interpretation as possible.

(b) The *Escobedo* Case. Just five weeks after *Massiah,* the Court decided the case of *Escobedo v. Illinois* (1964). Escobedo was taken into custody and questioned concerning the fatal shooting of his brother-in-law, but his retained counsel obtained his release. About ten days later one DiGerlando told police that Escobedo had fired the fatal shots, so Escobedo was again arrested and then told of that allegation. He repeatedly asked to see his retained attorney, who came to the police station but was barred from seeing his client. After the police arranged a confrontation between DiGerlando and Escobedo, Escobedo incriminated himself in the killing, and this enabled an assistant prosecutor to obtain a more elaborate written confession, which was admitted at Escobedo's trial. He was convicted of murder, but the Supreme Court reversed the conviction. The majority opinion was highly critical of reliance upon confessions in general and interrogation of those without counsel in particular, but the *Escobedo* holding was cautiously limited to the facts of the case:

> We hold, therefore, that where, as here, [1] the investigation is no longer a general inquiry into an unsolved crime but has begun to focus on a particular suspect, [2] the suspect has been taken into police custody, [3] the police carry out a process of interrogations that lends itself to eliciting incriminating statements, [4] the suspect has requested and been denied an opportunity to consult with his lawyer, and [5] the police have not effectively warned him of his absolute constitutional right to remain silent, the accused has been denied "the Assistance of Counsel" in violation of the Sixth Amendment to the Constitution as "made obligatory upon the States by the Fourteenth Amendment," * * * and that no statement elicited by the police during the interrogation may be used against him at a criminal trial.

The combination of sweeping language at some points and the above limited holding engendered conflicting views about the implications of the case. But *Escobedo* appeared to be a landmark decision that could only expand as the Court further considered the Sixth Amendment's application at the police station. This did not happen because just two years later the Court instead, in *Miranda v. Arizona* (1966), adopted a much broader rule based upon the Fifth Amendment privilege against self-incrimination, and the Supreme Court itself ultimately came to treat *Escobedo* as nothing more than a "false start" toward the new approach to the confessions problem undertaken later in *Miranda.*

(c) The *Williams* Case. After the Supreme Court decided *Miranda v. Arizona* (1966), grounded in the Fifth Amendment privilege against self-incrimination, it remained unclear at best whether the "pure" Sixth Amendment right to counsel approach continued to have any vitality or significance in the confession area until the Supreme Court decided *Brewer v. Williams* (1977). Williams was arraigned in Davenport, Iowa on an outstanding arrest warrant prior to his transportation to Des Moines on a murder charge. Though the police had assured Williams' lawyer that he would not be interrogated during the trip, a detective made a "Christian burial speech," to the effect that because of the worsening weather it would be necessary to find the body now to ensure the victim a Christian burial. Williams then directed the police to the body. On Williams' motion to suppress all evidence relating to or resulting from the statements he made to the police, the trial judge found that "an agreement was made between defense counsel and the police officials to the effect that the Defendant was not to be questioned on the return trip to Des Moines" and that the evidence had been elicited from Williams during "a critical stage in the proceedings requiring the presence of counsel on his request," but ruled that Williams had "waived his right to have an attorney present during the giving of such information." The state supreme court affirmed.

On federal habeas corpus, the district court concluded that Williams had not waived any of his constitutional protections, and ruled for him on three alternative and independent grounds: (1) that he had been denied his constitutional right to the assistance of counsel; (2) that he had been denied his rights under *Escobedo* and *Miranda;* and (3) that in any event his self-incriminatory statement had been involuntarily made. The federal court of appeals affirmed on the first two grounds, and then the Supreme Court affirmed the judgment of the court of appeals. The majority concluded there was "no need" to assay the voluntariness or *Miranda* issues because "it is clear that the judgment before us must in any event be affirmed upon the ground that Williams was deprived of a different constitutional right—the right to the assistance of counsel" because "[t]he circumstances of this case are * * * constitutionally indistinguishable from those presented in *Massiah*." Though *Massiah* was a post-indictment case, it was now clear under *Kirby v. Illinois* (1972) that the right to counsel arises "at or after the time that judicial proceedings have been initiated," which was the case here because Williams had been arraigned on the warrant in Davenport. It was also clear that the detective had "designedly set out to elicit information from Williams." Moreover, the fact that "the incriminating statements were elicited surreptitiously in [*Massiah*], and otherwise here," was deemed "constitutionally irrelevant." The

Williams majority then rejected the state court's conclusion that waiver had occurred here merely because during the trip Williams did not assert that right or a desire not to talk in the absence of counsel.

(d) When the Right to Counsel Begins. Although the *Massiah* right to counsel had generally been interpreted as arising only upon indictment, in *Brewer v. Williams* (1977) the Court declared that "the right to counsel granted by the Sixth and Fourteenth Amendments means at least that a person is entitled to the help of a lawyer at or after the time that judicial proceedings have been initiated against him—'whether by way of formal charge, preliminary hearing, indictment, information, or arraignment.' " Noting that a warrant had been issued for Williams' arrest and that he had been arraigned on that warrant before a judge and that he had been committed by the court to confinement in jail, the Court concluded there "can be no doubt in the present case that judicial proceedings had been initiated."

Clearly this test is not met merely because the defendant had been arrested without a warrant, nor is it met, the Court later held in *Hoffa v. United States* (1966), merely because the investigation has focused upon the defendant. There is a split of authority on the question of whether the filing of a complaint is alone sufficient, though the difference probably is explainable by the fact that this document is used for multiple purposes. Cases holding that filing the complaint suffices under *Williams* typically stress express recognition in that jurisdiction of the complaint as one type of charging document, while decisions holding that filing the complaint (or, indeed, filing the complaint and issuance of an arrest warrant thereon) does not have this effect emphasize use of the complaint simply as a means of obtaining a warrant. The Court in *Williams* did not discuss the circumstances behind the issuance of the complaint and warrant in that case; perhaps the assumption was that whatever the reasons underlying the complaint-warrant process, at least from the time defendant is brought into court and arraigned on the warrant (at which point it or the complaint underlying it becomes a tentative charging document) the Sixth Amendment right to counsel applies. The Court later declared in *Michigan v. Jackson* (1986) that "arraignment," in the sense of defendant's initial appearance, "signals the initiation of adversary proceedings."

Assuming that "judicial proceedings have been initiated," is it in addition essential to recognition of the Sixth Amendment right that counsel actually have been retained by or appointed for the defendant? While in both *Massiah* and *Williams* the defendant was already represented by an attorney at the time in question, the

Court later held this was not necessary. What then if such judicial proceedings have not been initiated but the defendant in fact has counsel appointed for or (more likely) retained by him? In *Moran v. Burbine* (1986), the Court concluded that "it makes little sense to say that the Sixth Amendment right to counsel attaches at different times depending on the fortuity of whether the suspect or his family happens to have retained counsel," especially since the Sixth Amendment, "by its very terms, * * * becomes applicable only when the government's role shifts from investigation to accusation."

If judicial proceedings have been initiated and the *Massiah–Williams* right to counsel has thus attached, does it attach for all purposes or only with respect to matters related to those proceedings? This issue reached the Supreme Court in *Maine v. Moulton* (1985), where, after Colton and Moulton were indicted for theft, Colton told police of Moulton's suggestion a state witness be killed and agreed to record later conversations with Moulton, and the recorded statements thereafter obtained in which Moulton discussed the thefts were admitted in his trial on those and other charges. The Court in *Moulton* agreed that the fact a defendant had been charged with one offense was no reason to give him special protection in the investigation of other, uncharged crimes, and thus concluded that "to exclude evidence pertaining to charges as to which the Sixth Amendment right to counsel had not attached at the time the evidence was obtained, simply because other charges were pending at that time, would unnecessarily frustrate the public's interest in the investigation of criminal activities." From this, the four dissenters reasoned there was no basis for exclusion in the instant case, as the simple fact was that the *Massiah–Brewer* Sixth Amendment right did not apply where, as here, "the police undertook an investigation of separate crimes." Though there is some logic to that position, the *Moulton* majority rejected it on essentially pragmatic grounds in favor of the conclusion that any statements obtained in such circumstances are admissible at trial of the uncharged crime but not at trial of crimes theretofore charged. The majority saw this as "a sensible solution to a difficult problem" because the dissenters' approach "invites abuse by law enforcement personnel in the form of fabricated investigations."

Although the Court thereafter characterized the Sixth Amendment right as "offense-specific," some lower courts concluded that it carried over to closely related but uncharged crimes. One such case, where the right to counsel that attached upon defendant being charged with burglary was held to apply as well to the murders of the occupants of the premises burglarized, reached the Supreme Court in *Texas v. Cobb* (2001). The majority, in reversing the state court, rejected the claim that a truly offense-specific limitation would permit the police almost total license to conduct unwanted and uncounseled interrogations, responding (1) that defendants still have the protections of *Miranda*; and (2) that the Constitution does not negate society's interest in the ability of the police to talk to those witnesses and suspects charged with other offenses. But, the *Cobb* majority added, the definition of "offense" under the Sixth Amendment is not limited to the four corners of the charging document; it has the same meaning as in the double jeopardy clause, and thus "the test to be applied to determine whether there are two offenses or only one, is whether each provision requires proof of a fact which the other does not."

(e) Waiver of Counsel. The Court in *Brewer v. Williams* (1977) acknowledged that the right to counsel there recognized could be waived, and that such waiver would not inevitably necessitate the participation of the defendant's lawyer. The majority declared it was *not* holding "that under the circumstances of this case," namely, where an attorney had actually advised defendant not to talk to the police and had extracted an agreement from the police not to question defendant, "Williams *could not,* without notice to counsel, have waived his rights under the Sixth and Fourteenth Amendments." *Williams* is thus consistent with prior authority that the Sixth Amendment right to counsel is the right of the client rather than the attorney, so that it may be waived by the client without counsel's participation.

Seemingly inconsistent with this conclusion is the Court's statement in *Miranda* that in *Escobedo* the conduct of the police in turning away the lawyer was by itself "a violation of the Sixth Amendment." If, as noted above, the right is that of the defendant, then it might be asked why there is any violation here if the defendant on his own waives the right. As to such tactics, perhaps the point is that they bear upon the effectiveness of any waiver of the right to counsel by the defendant. If, as in *Escobedo,* the defendant was aware that his lawyer was being prevented from seeing him, this certainly should cast doubt upon any waiver of counsel subsequently obtained from the defendant, for defendant's realization may well have underscored the police dominance of the situation. Even absent such awareness, it has sometimes been held that if police failed to admit counsel to a person in custody or to inform the person of the attorney's efforts to reach him, then they cannot thereafter rely on defendant's "waiver" of counsel because, having been denied facts critical to his decision, he cannot be said to have made a knowing choice. The Supreme Court rejected this latter conclusion in a *Miranda* context, but has thereafter asserted that "in the Sixth Amendment context, this waiver would not be valid."

The Court in *Williams* emphasized in various ways that courts should be reluctant to find a waiver of the right to counsel. It was noted that the burden of showing waiver is on the prosecution, that what must be shown is "an intentional relinquishment or abandonment of a known right," that the right is not lost merely by a lack of request by the defendant, that "every reasonable presumption" must be indulged against waiver, and that a "strict standard" equal to that concerning waiver of counsel at trial applies. Whether this means that waiver of the "pure" right to counsel under *Williams* calls for something more than the waiver of counsel under *Miranda* is a matter on which lower courts were divided until the issue was resolved in *Patterson v. Illinois* (1988). Taking the "pragmatic approach" that the warnings and waiver procedure required depend largely upon "the scope of the Sixth Amendment right to counsel" at the particular stage of the criminal process at issue, the *Patterson* majority concluded the requirements of *Miranda* would suffice because the "State's decision to take an additional step and commence formal adversarial proceedings against the accused does not substantially increase the value of counsel to the accused at questioning, or expand the limited purpose that an attorney serves when the accused is questioned by authorities." However, the Court in *Patterson* noted that the defendant had not yet retained or accepted appointment of counsel to represent him, and stated that "once an accused has a lawyer, a distinct set of constitutional safeguards aimed at preserving the sanctity of the attorney-client relationship take effect." Based on that language, it has been held that when defendant *is* represented by counsel a response to police questioning after *Miranda* warnings is not a sufficient waiver of the Sixth Amendment right.

In *Williams* the Supreme Court stressed that "waiver requires not merely comprehension but relinquishment." Thus, while it there appeared that defendant "had been informed of and appeared to understand his right to counsel," any claim of relinquishment was refuted by his "consistent reliance upon the advice of counsel in dealing with the authorities," his statements "that he desired the presence of an attorney before any interrogation took place," his awareness of the agreement between the police and his counsel "that no interrogation was to occur during the journey," and that the police "made no effort at all to ascertain whether Williams wished to relinquish that right." Lower courts take into account such factors as whether there was a police agreement with counsel not to interrogate, whether defendant asserted his right to counsel, whether the police tried to talk defendant out of consulting with counsel, and whether defendant's statement was volunteered.

Waiver is a possibility only when the defendant makes a statement to one known to be in a position adverse to him, such as a police officer, police agent, or examining psychiatrist. As the Supreme Court ruled in *United States v. Henry* (1980), "the concept of a knowing and voluntary waiver of Sixth Amendment rights does not apply in the context of communications with an undisclosed undercover informant acting for the government." This is because in such an instance the defendant, being unaware the other person "was a government agent expressly commissioned to secure evidence, cannot be held to have waived his right to the assistance of counsel" by freely communicating with him.

The special waiver-after-assertion-of-rights rules that govern in the *Miranda* area as to a case in which the defendant, upon receiving the *Miranda* warnings from police, invoked his right to counsel (see § 5.9(f)), also apply to the Sixth Amendment right. Thus the Court held in *Michigan v. Jackson* (1986) that when the Sixth Amendment right has attached, "if police initiate interrogation after a defendant's assertion, at an arraignment or similar proceeding, of his right to counsel, any waiver of the defendant's right to counsel for that police-initiated interrogation is invalid." "Preserving the integrity of an accused's choice to communicate with police only through counsel is the essence" of *Jackson*, and thus the bar on any police-initiated interrogation does not arise automatically with the filing of the charging instrument but requires as well the accused's invocation of this right to the assistance of counsel. And in any event, because the Sixth Amendment right is "offense-specific" and "cannot be invoked once for all future prosecutions," it follows that "its *Michigan v. Jackson* effect of invalidating subsequent waivers in police-initiated interviews is offense-specific." This means, for example, that if a defendant exercises his Sixth Amendment right when brought into court on an armed robbery charge, that is no bar to subsequent police-initiated questioning about an unrelated murder.

(f) Infringement of the Right. Assuming now a situation in which the Sixth Amendment right to counsel has attached, and assuming also that this right has not been waived by the defendant, there remains the question of what activity constitutes an infringement of that right so as to require suppression of any statement obtained thereby. In *Massiah v. United States* (1964), the police arranged for a codefendant to discuss their pending trial with the defendant while they were in the codefendant's car, which had a radio transmitter concealed in it. The Court declared that defendant's right to counsel was violated "when there was used against him at his trial evidence of his own incriminating words, which federal agents had deliberately elicited from him." And in *Brewer v. Williams* (1977), where the activity objected to was the "Christian burial speech" on the ride from Davenport to Des Moines, the

Court deemed *Massiah* applicable because the detective "deliberately and designedly set out to elicit information from Williams just as surely as—and perhaps more effectively than—if he had formally interrogated him." Both *Massiah* and *Williams* at some point refer to the police conduct as "interrogation," but the facts of those cases make it clear that this does not mean interrogation in the narrow sense of the word, and the Court has since made it perfectly clear in *Fellers v. United States* (2004) that deliberately eliciting information is enough whether or not the police conduct constituted "interrogation."

The claim that the "decisive fact in *Massiah* * * * was that the police set up the confrontation between the accused and a police agent" was rejected in *Maine v. Moulton* (1985), finding an infringement of the right to counsel even when it was the defendant who initiated the meeting with his codefendant, who by the time of the meeting was a police agent. As the Court explained, while "the Sixth Amendment is not violated whenever—by luck or happenstance—the State obtains incriminating statements from the accused," a "knowing exploitation by the State of an opportunity to confront the accused without counsel being present is as much a breach of the State's obligation not to circumvent the right to assistance of counsel as is the intentional creation of such an opportunity."

Though the language used in the *Massiah* and *Brewer* cases would seem to require action undertaken with the specific intent to evoke an inculpatory disclosure, some doubt was created by *United States v. Henry* (1980). *Henry* is a "jail plant" case; government agents contacted a federal informant serving a term in a city jail and "told him to be alert to any statements made by the federal prisoners, but not to initiate any conversation with or question Henry regarding the bank robbery." The informant later reported "that he and Henry had engaged in conversation and that Henry had told him about the robbery of the Janaf bank," and he so testified at Henry's trial. Though the government argued before the Supreme Court that the incriminating statements were "not the result of any affirmative conduct on the part of government agents to elicit evidence," the majority in *Henry* held that the incriminating statements had been "deliberately elicited" by the government "intentionally creating a situation likely to induce Henry to make incriminating statements." That language was understandably criticized by the dissenters, who noted that it removed the word "deliberately" from the *Massiah–Williams* test and "would cover even a 'negligent' triggering of events resulting in reception of disclosures." But despite the unfortunate "likely to induce" phrase, *Henry* appears to be viewed by the majority as a genuine "deliberately elicited" type of case.

The majority in *Henry* cautioned it was not "called upon to pass on the situation where an informant is placed in close proximity but makes no effort to stimulate conversations about the crime charged." Later, in *Kuhlmann v. Wilson* (1986), the Court ruled that because "the primary concern of the *Massiah* line of decisions is secret interrogation by investigatory techniques that are the equivalent of direct police interrogation," "a defendant does not make out a violation of that right simply by showing that an informant, either through prior arrangement or voluntarily, reported his incriminating statements to the police." *Kuhlmann* illustrates, however, the difficulty in drawing the line between "active" and "passive" efforts. Defendant first gave his cellmate the same story of noninvolvement he had earlier given the police, to which the cellmate, placed there by police with instructions not to question defendant but to listen for information, responded that the explanation "didn't sound too good." The defendant did not alter his story until a few days later, after his brother visited him and expressed the family's concern with his apparent involvement in a murder. The majority concluded this meant defendant's confession had not been "deliberately elicited" by his cellmate, but three dissenting Justices thought otherwise because, though "the *coup de grace* was delivered by respondent's brother," the "informant, while avoiding direct questions, nonetheless developed a relationship of cellmate camaraderie with respondent and encouraged him to talk about his crime." After *Kuhlmann*, it seems clear that the mere use of an inanimate electronic device as a "listening post" does not infringe upon the right to counsel, for it cannot be said that the bugging in any sense increases the defendant's predisposition toward making an incriminating response.

(g) Critique of the Right to Counsel Approach. Whether the *Massiah* rule, as elaborated and extended in such cases as *Williams* and *Henry,* is a sensible and desirable doctrine is a matter on which opinions differ. In criticism, it is asserted that the *Massiah* rule is unnecessary because *Miranda* protects against the coercive pressures of custodial interrogations while the due process voluntariness test affords sufficient protection in noncustodial situations. On the other hand, some do find offensive certain police practices likely to be reached only by the *Massiah* rule, such as use of an undercover agent to elicit incriminating remarks, and for them the problem with the rule is that it is too narrow because not extended to similar conduct that occurs after formal arrest. In answer to the latter criticisms, it might be observed that *Massiah,* after all, is grounded in the Sixth Amendment right to counsel and thus should be assessed in terms of its protection of that right instead of as some sort of alternative to or extension of either *Miranda* or the voluntariness test. But even when *Massiah* is so viewed, there is disagreement about whether the Sixth Amendment should function as a shield, enabling the defendant to frustrate the state's efforts to obtain evidence directly from him. And even if it should, so that there properly comes a point after which the Sixth Amendment right to counsel protects against all self-incrimination, compelled or not, there is room for dispute as to whether that point has been correctly defined in the *Massiah* line of cases. One question is whether the right to counsel rule turns on distinctions that are unresponsive to the government's need for evidence. It thus might be asked whether *Massiah,* which erected a Sixth Amendment shield around a defendant who had been arrested and indicted many months earlier, is more understandable than *Williams,* where such a shield was erected around a defendant shortly after his arrest and apparently before even the magnitude of the crime had been ascertained by the proper prosecuting authority. A second question is whether these distinctions are objectionable because often, albeit not in *Williams,* they are conducive to manipulation by the police.

(h) The "Repeal" of the *Massiah* Rule. In the Crime Control Act of 1968, Congress purported to "repeal" the *Massiah* rule for federal prosecutions. This was done by providing that in the federal courts a confession "shall be admissible in evidence if it is voluntarily given," and that various, enumerated factors to be taken into account on the voluntariness issue, including "whether or not such defendant was without the assistance of counsel when questioned and when giving such confession," "need not be conclusive on the issue of voluntariness." This legislation has been largely ignored, and properly so, for to the extent it purports to nullify the Sixth Amendment right to counsel as recognized in *Massiah* and subsequent Supreme Court decisions it is most certainly unconstitutional.

§ 5.5 The Privilege Against Self–Incrimination; *Miranda*

(a) The Privilege in the Police Station. The Fifth Amendment of the United States Constitution provides that no person "shall be compelled in any criminal case to be a witness against himself." A literal reading of that language certainly suggests that the privilege against self-incrimination has no application to unsworn statements obtained by station-house interrogation, but the Supreme Court in *Bram v. United States* (1897) seemed quite clearly to conclude otherwise, for it was there asserted that "[i]n criminal trials, in the courts of the United States, wherever a question arises whether a confession is incompetent because not voluntary, the issue is controlled by that portion of the fifth amendment * * * commanding that no person 'shall be compelled in any criminal case to be a witness against himself.' " This assertion was not relied upon by the Court in subsequent confession cases, and the Court later expressed doubt that the privilege was relevant in confession cases. Then came *Malloy v. Hogan* (1964), which did not involve a confession but nonetheless was important in two significant respects to the ultimate acceptance of the privilege against self-incrimination as a constitutional restraint upon police interrogation practices. *Malloy* held that the privilege was applicable to the states, and then supported that conclusion by declaring that "today the admissibility of a confession in a state criminal prosecution is tested by the same standard applied in federal prosecution since 1897" in the *Bram* decision. Any lingering doubts were dispelled two years later by *Miranda v. Arizona* (1966), holding that the privilege "is fully applicable during a period of custodial interrogation."

The applicability of the privilege at the police station, in a quite different sense, was much later the central issue in *Chavez v. Martinez* (2003), which, although a civil case, is worthy of consideration here. Martinez was interrogated by police officer Chavez under circumstances that would have made his resulting confession inadmissible under *Miranda* in a criminal case, but Martinez was not thereafter even charged with a crime. In a § 1983 action for damages, Martinez relied in part upon the Fifth Amendment, and was upheld in that respect by the district court and court of appeals, but a splintered Supreme Court reversed. Four members of the Court, relying upon the literal language of the Fifth Amendment, concluded: "Martinez was never made to be a 'witness' against himself in violation of the Fifth Amendment's Self–Incrimination Clause because his statements were never admitted as testimony against him in a criminal case." Two other Justices, while also rejecting the self-incrimination claim, did so in less absolute terms, noting that on occasion the Court had previously applied the privilege in other circumstances, always "expressing a judgment that the core guarantee, or the judicial capacity to protect it, would be placed at some risk in the absence of such complementary protection." But, they added, Martinez had not made the requisite "powerful showing" needed to come within that line of cases, especially since he "offers no limiting principle or reason to foresee a stopping place short of liability in all * * * cases" where *Miranda* was violated. The remaining members of the Court, dissenting on this point, asserted that the self-incrimination clause "provides both assurance that a person will not be compelled to testify against himself in a criminal proceeding and a continuing right against government conduct intended to bring about self-incrimination. * * * The principle extends to forbid policies which exert official compulsion that might induce a person into forfeiting his rights under the Clause." "The conclusion that the Self–Incrimination Clause is not violated until the government seeks to use a statement in some later criminal proceeding," they lamented, "strips the Clause of an essential part of its force and meaning."

(b) The *Miranda* Rules. In *Miranda,* the majority began by examining "various police manuals and texts," a "valuable source of information about present police practices." From the several psychological ploys and stratagems outlined therein, the Court concluded that even without resort to brutality "the very fact of custodial interrogation exacts a heavy toll on individual liberty and trades on the weaknesses of individuals." Next examining the facts of the four cases under collective consideration, the Court concluded that even though it "might not find the defendants' statements to have been involuntary in traditional terms," those statements were obtained under circumstances in which the "potentiality for compulsion is forcefully apparent." In each case the defendant was interrogated by police who had custody of him and who did not advise him that he could remain silent or otherwise "insure that the statements were truly the product of free choice." The Court thus concluded that "[u]nless adequate protective devices are employed to dispel the compulsion inherent in custodial surroundings, no statement obtained from the defendant can truly be the product of his free choice."

The necessary "protective devices" were then described in some detail in what the *Miranda* dissenters disparagingly called a "constitutional code of rules for confessions." *Miranda* thus represents a striking contrast to both *Escobedo v. Illinois* (1964) and the Court's usual "totality of circumstances" approach to the due process voluntariness issue, for it contains a set of rules to be followed by police in all future custodial interrogations. These rules, discussed further in the remaining sections of this Chapter, may be summarized as follows:

(1) These rules are required to safeguard the privilege against self-incrimination, and thus must be followed in the absence of "other procedures which are at least as effective in apprising accused persons of their right of silence and in assuring a continuous opportunity to exercise it."

(2) These rules apply "when the individual is first subjected to police interrogation while in custody at the station or otherwise deprived of his freedom of action in any significant way," and not to "[g]eneral on-the-scene questioning as to facts surrounding a crime or other general questioning of citizens in the fact-finding process" or to "[v]olunteered statements of any kind."

(3) Without regard to his prior awareness of his rights, if a person in custody is to be subjected to questioning, "he must first be informed in clear and unequivocal terms that he has the right to remain silent," so that the ignorant may learn of this right and so that the pressures of the interrogation atmosphere will be overcome for those previously aware of the right.

(4) The above warning "must be accompanied by the explanation that anything said can and will be used against the individual in court," so as to ensure that the suspect fully understands the consequences of foregoing the privilege.

(5) Because this is indispensable to protection of the privilege, the individual also "must be clearly informed that he has the right to consult with a lawyer and to have the lawyer with him during interrogation," without regard to whether it appears that he is already aware of this right.

(6) The individual must also be warned "that if he is indigent a lawyer will be appointed to represent him," for otherwise the above warning would be understood as meaning only that an individual may consult a lawyer if he has the funds to obtain one.

(7) The individual is always free to exercise the privilege, and thus if he "indicates in any manner, at anytime prior to or during questioning, that he wishes to remain silent, the interrogation must cease"; and likewise, if he "states that he wants an attorney, the interrogation must cease until an attorney is present."

(8) If a statement is obtained without the presence of an attorney, "a heavy burden rests on the Government to demonstrate that the defendant knowingly and intelligently waived his privilege against self-incrimination and his right to retained or appointed counsel," and such waiver may not be presumed from the individual's silence after warnings or from the fact that a confession was eventually obtained.

(9) Any statement obtained in violation of these rules may not be admitted into evidence, without regard to whether it is a confession or only an admission of part of an offense or whether it is inculpatory or allegedly exculpatory.

(10) Likewise, exercise of the privilege may not be penalized, and thus the prosecution may not "use at trial the fact that [the defendant] stood mute or claimed his privilege in the face of accusation."

Although these rules sound inflexible and unbending, neither the Supreme Court nor the lower courts have generally taken a rigid approach in the application of *Miranda*.

(c) The Experience Under *Miranda*. Various surveys and empirical studies have been undertaken in an effort to gauge the impact of the *Miranda* decision upon police interrogation practices. Although the early verdict on *Miranda* was that it had little impact, the extent to which this is still true today, now that *Miranda* has become a part of our culture and presumably the rights declared therein are more widely perceived by the public at large, is not entirely clear. The conflicting assessments are doubtless attributable to the fact that we lack sufficient reliable empirical data on *Miranda*'s impact and that, consequently, existing evidence is amenable to differing interpretations. This is so both as to the the ultimate question of the "cost" of *Miranda* in terms of lost convictions, and with respect to the basic question of how the post-*Miranda* confession rate compares with that which existed prior to the *Miranda* decision.

(d) Critique of the *Miranda* Approach. There exists a considerable difference of opinion concerning the extent to which *Miranda* has "solved" pre-existing problems concerning police interrogation practices in this country. Nonetheless, it is possible to identify some of the strengths and weaknesses of *Miranda*. On the plus side, it may be said that *Miranda* (1) serves important symbolic functions, such as correcting the appearance that the poor and the unsophisticated were particularly vulnerable to police exploitation; (2) serves the educational purpose of ensuring that police are frequently reminded of the rights of the people with whom they deal; (3) provides much needed guidance for the police by prescribing a series of set procedures to be followed in every instance of custodial interrogation; and (4) simplifies to some extent judicial review of police interrogation practices. Yet there appears to be a very fundamental inconsistency in the *Miranda* majority's analysis. The Court places heavy emphasis on the notion that the decision of one in custody whether or not to incriminate himself cannot be truly voluntary but yet concludes that the choice to dispense with counsel can be voluntary in the same circumstances. Moreover, a cogent criticism of the old "voluntariness" test namely, that because the critical events occur in secrecy the admissibility of the confession will be determined by the outcome of a "swearing contest" in court, applies to *Miranda* as well, for the heralded warnings need not be given by a disinterested person, and the defendant's decision to waive his rights need not be made before a disinterested party or recorded in any fashion.

(e) The "Repeal" of *Miranda*. In the Crime Control Act of 1968, Congress purported to "repeal" the *Miranda* decision in federal prosecutions. This was done by providing that in the federal courts a confession "shall be admissible in evidence if it is voluntarily given," and that various enumerated factors taken into account on the voluntariness issue, such as "whether or not such defendant was advised or knew that he was not required to make any statement and that any such statement could be used against him," "whether or not such defendant had been advised prior to questioning of his right to the assistance of counsel," and "whether or not such defendant was without the assistance of counsel when questioned and when giving such confession," "need not be conclusive on the issue of voluntariness."

In *Dickerson v. United States* (2000), the Court determined that "Congress intended by its enactment to overrule *Miranda*," and thus found it necessary to address the critical question of "whether Congress has constitutional authority" to do so. Because Congress "retains the ultimate authority to modify or set aside any judicially created rules of evidence and procedure that are not required by the Constitution" but "may not legislatively supersede our decisions interpreting and applying the Constitution," the case consequently turned "on whether the *Miranda* Court announced a constitutional rule or merely exercised its supervisory authority to regulate evidence in the absence of congressional direction." In deciding it was the former, the majority in *Dickerson* emphasized: (i) "that both *Miranda* and two of its companion cases," as well as many cases in which the Court later interpreted and applied *Miranda*, involved "prosecutions arising in state courts," as to which the Supreme Court's authority "is limited to enforcing the commands of the United States Constitution"; (ii) that the *Miranda* majority opinion "is replete with statements indicating that the majority thought it was announcing a constitutional rule"; and (iii) that the contrary is not shown by the Court's later decision's narrowing *Miranda*, for those decisions (as well as others broadening the application of *Miranda*) "illustrate the principle—not that *Miranda* is not a constitutional rule—but that no constitutional rule is immutable." The Court in *Dickerson* then turned to a critical passage in *Miranda* reading as follows:

> It is impossible for us to foresee the potential alternatives for protecting the privilege which might be devised by Congress or the States in the exercise of their creative rule-making capacities. Therefore we cannot say that the Constitution necessarily requires adherence to any particular solution for the inherent compulsions of the interrogation process as it is presently conducted. Our decision in no way creates a constitutional straitjacket which will handicap sound efforts at reform nor is it intended to have this effect. We encourage Congress and the States to continue their laudable search for increasingly effective ways of protecting the rights of the individual while promoting efficient enforcement of our criminal laws. However, unless we are shown other procedures which are at least as

effective in apprising accused persons of their right of silence and in assuring a continuous opportunity to exercise it, the following safeguards must be observed.

Despite this "invitation for legislative action" in *Miranda*, the *Dickerson* Court concluded that above-described statute could not be upheld in light of that invitation's clearly-expressed "requirement that a legislative alternative to *Miranda* be equally as effective in preventing coerced confessions." This is because the statute merely "reinstates the totality test as sufficient," while the *Miranda* Court "concluded that something more than the totality test was necessary." And even taking into account the fact "that there are more remedies available for abusive police conduct than there were at the time *Miranda* was decided," those remedies and this statute are not together "an adequate substitute for the warnings required by *Miranda*." Having thus concluded that the statutory provision "cannot be sustained if *Miranda* is to remain the law," the Court in *Dickerson* next declared it would *not* strike down *Miranda*. Longstanding "principles of *stare decisis* weigh heavily against overruling it now," the Court explained, for its " 'doctrinal underpinnings' " have not been undermined, and it "has become embedded in routine police practice to the point where the warnings have become part of our national culture." And while under *Miranda* it may sometimes be the case that "a guilty defendant go[es] free," the Court deemed that a lesser disadvantage than trying to operate exclusively under a totality-of-the-circumstances test, which "is more difficult than *Miranda* for law enforcement officers to conform to, and for courts to apply in a consistent manner."

§ 5.6 *Miranda*: When Interrogation Is "Custodial"

(a) "Custody" vs. "Focus." Because these *Miranda* safeguards were deemed necessary to counteract the combined effects of interrogation and custody, the meaning of the Court's "custodial interrogation" phrase is a matter of considerable importance. By way of explanation, the Court said this meant "questioning initiated by law enforcement officers after a person has been taken into custody or otherwise deprived of his freedom of action in any significant way," but then confused matters by appending thereto a footnote stating: "This is what we meant in *Escobedo* when we spoke of an investigation which had focused on an accused." This is incorrect, for *Escobedo* held that the Sixth Amendment right to counsel attached when a series of events coincided, including *both* "focus" and "custody," thus making it quite plain that the Court had *not* then viewed the two terms as synonymous. The "focus" approach was expressly rejected in *Beckwith v. United States* (1976), where petitioner claimed he was entitled to the full *Mi-*

randa warnings when he was interviewed at home by IRS agents because he was at that time the focus of a criminal investigation. Similarly, a plurality of the Court in *United States v. Mandujano* (1976) rejected the argument that a "putative" or "virtual" defendant called before a grand jury is entitled to the *Miranda* warnings, which "were aimed at the evils seen by the Court as endemic to police interrogation of a person in custody."

(b) Purpose of Custody. *Mathis v. United States* (1968) posed the question of whether *Miranda* applies when the purpose of the custody is unrelated to the purpose of the interrogation. There an IRS agent failed to give petitioner the *Miranda* warnings when questioning him about his prior income tax returns while petitioner was incarcerated in a state jail serving a state sentence. The government argued that *Miranda* was inapplicable because the petitioner had not been jailed by the interrogating federal officers but was there for an entirely different offense, but the Court rejected that distinction as "too minor and shadowy to justify a departure from the well-considered conclusion of *Miranda* with reference to warnings to be given to a person held in custody." Thus, it is now clear that *Miranda* applies to interrogation of one in custody for another purpose or with respect to another offense, although jail and prison inmates are not necessarily in custody for purposes of *Miranda* (see § 5.6(e)).

(c) Subjective vs. Objective Approach. A most fundamental question concerning the *Miranda* "custody" element is whether it is to be determined by some subjective factor, either that the suspect in fact believed he was in custody or that the police officer intended to take custody, or whether instead an objective test of the "reasonable man" type governs. The first subjective approach relates directly to the "potentiality for compulsion" the Court was concerned in *Miranda*, but would place upon the police the burden of anticipating the frailties or idiosyncracies of every person they question. The second subjective approach, at one time utilized by the Supreme Court, would on the other hand be easy for the officer to understand, but would make no sense in terms of the "potentiality for compulsion." Moreover, both of these subjective approaches have a common defect: the governing test would involve matters exceedingly difficult for courts to determine after the fact. Doubtless this is why a majority of the lower courts came to adopt an objective standard.

The Supreme Court expressly adopted this position in *Berkemer v. McCarty* (1984), involving roadside interrogation of a motorist stopped for a traffic violation. The Court, after holding *Miranda* is inapplicable in that context (see § 5.6(e)), confronted the fact that apparently the trooper who made the stop "decided as soon as respondent stepped out of his car that respondent would be taken into custody and charged with a traffic offense," though he "never communicated his intention to respondent." This did not require a different result, the Court concluded, for a "policeman's unarticulated plan has no bearing on the question whether a suspect was 'in custody' at a particular time; the only relevant inquiry is how a reasonable man in the suspect's position would have understood his situation." Under *Berkemer,* the question is *not* whether a reasonable person would believe he was not free to leave, but rather whether such a person would believe he was in police custody of the degree associated with formal arrest.

This objective approach often requires a careful examination of all the circumstances of the particular case. Account must be taken of those facts intrinsic to the interrogation: when and where it occurred, how long it lasted, how many police were present, what the officers and the defendant said and did, the presence of physical restraint or the equivalent (e.g., drawn weapons, guard stationed at the door), and whether the defendant was being questioned as a suspect or as a witness. Events before the interrogation are also relevant, especially how the defendant got to the place of questioning—whether he came completely on his own, in response to a police request, or escorted by police officers. The Supreme Court and the lower courts have also looked to what happened after the interrogation, relying upon the fact that the suspect was allowed to leave following the interrogation as strong evidence that the interrogation was not custodial. But as a matter of logic it is unsound to say that what happens later has some bearing on how a reasonable person would have perceived the situation at some earlier time. The same objection may be made as to the reliance by some courts on whether there was "focus." As a matter of logic, neither "focus" nor its absence (when not communicated to the suspect) has any direct bearing upon how a reasonable man would perceive the situation. Perhaps these cases reflect only the fact that courts are more willing to accept police representations of a noncustodial environment when it appears they lacked a basis for arrest and even after the questioning elected not to arrest.

The *Berkemer* "reasonable person" test probably requires consideration of certain unique characteristics of the suspect (e.g., his youth), notwithstanding *Yarborough v. Alvarado* (2004). Though the majority concluded the court of appeals, in emphasizing defendant's "age [17] and inexperience with law enforcement," had "ignored the argument that the custody inquiry states an objective rule designed to give clear guidance to the police, while consideration of a suspect's individual characteristics—including his age— could be viewed as creating a subjective inquiry," this hardly settles the matter, for: (i) *Yarborough* was a deferential-review habeas corpus case in which the issue was *only* whether the state court, in not taking those characteristics into account, had made an unreasonable application of clearly established law; (ii) when the majority hypothesized about what the outcome would be on de novo review, it only said that reliance on the suspect's prior history with law enforcement would be "improper" because in "most cases, police officers will not know a suspect's interrogation history"; (iii) the four dissenters concluded that Alvarado's age should have been considered on the custody issue, as it was "known to the police" and is "a widely shared characteristic that generates commonsense conclusions about behavior and perception" that consequently would "not complicate the 'in custody' inquiry"; and (iv) one member of the majority allowed that Alvarado's age might have been relevant had he not been "almost 18 years old at the time of his interview."

(d) **Presence at Station.** One situation given specific mention in *Miranda* as being custodial is where the individual is "in custody at the station." This is obviously so when, as in the four cases involved in *Miranda,* the defendant is being held at the police station following his arrest. It does not follow, however, that all presence at the station is custodial in nature. To take the most obvious case, there is no custody if the person came to the station on his own initiative. It has also been held that there is no custody when the person is present at the station in response to an "invitation" from the police, although in such cases a close look at all the surrounding circumstances is necessary. In *Oregon v. Mathiason* (1977), a police officer left a note at the apartment of defendant, a parolee, stating he wanted "to discuss something with you," so defendant called the officer and arranged to meet him at the state patrol office a few blocks from the apartment. When defendant appeared, he was told he was not under arrest and that the officer wanted to talk to him about a burglary. Later the officer falsely told defendant that his fingerprints had been found at the burglary scene, and defendant then confessed, after which he left the station. The Supreme Court's conclusion that defendant "came voluntarily to the police station" and thus was not initially in custody is unobjectionable. However, the Court's added conclusion that the circumstances never became custodial is open to serious question. It is true, as the Court put it in *Mathiason,* that the requirement of warnings is not imposed "simply because the questioning takes place in the station house, or because the questioned person is one whom the police suspect." But it is rather difficult to accept the conclusion that a parolee who is told his fingerprints had been found at a burglary scene would believe he was still free to leave.

If the so-called "invitation" involves the person going to the station in the company of the police, then a finding of custody is much more likely. *Dunaway v. New York* (1979), though not involving a *Miranda* issue, is illustrative. Acting on instructions to "pick up" petitioner and "bring him in," officers found him at a friend's house and drove him to the station. He was not told he was under arrest, no weapons were displayed, no handcuffs or any touching of petitioner was resorted to, and he was not booked, but he was then subjected to interrogation and was not told that he was free to go. The Court concluded there was "little doubt that petitioner was 'seized' in the Fourth Amendment sense when he was taken involuntarily to the police station," as "the detention of petitioner was in important respects indistinguishable from a traditional arrest." On the facts of *Dunaway,* it would seem that it also could be concluded that the situation was "custodial" for *Miranda* purposes. The result would be different if the suspect had been clearly and unequivocally advised that he was not under arrest and was free to leave at any time, or if it was made to appear that the person's presence was sought only as a witness.

(e) Presence Elsewhere. The *Miranda* Court stated that interrogation is custodial if it occurs while the individual is "in custody at the station or otherwise deprived of his freedom of action in any significant way." One reason for the latter part of this disjunctive definition is obvious: if *Miranda* governed only station-house interrogations, the police could easily circumvent the warning requirements by conducting interrogations in such places as hotel rooms or squad cars. Thus, it has been held that *Miranda* applies where, for example, a person has been apprehended and is in a police car at the time of his interrogation.

On the other hand, courts are much less likely to find the circumstances custodial when the interrogation occurs in familiar or at least neutral surroundings. Thus the Supreme Court in *Beckwith v. United States* (1976) held, as have many lower court decisions, that interrogation in the suspect's home was noncustodial. Generally, the notion is that the suspect was in familiar surroundings and thus did not face the same pressures as in the police-dominated atmosphere of the station house. But the circumstances of each case must be carefully examined. The view that at-home questioning is noncustodial is strengthened when the suspect's friends or family members were present at the time. By contrast, in *Orozco v. Texas* (1969) the Supreme Court concluded *Miranda* applied where four police officers entered defendant's bedroom at 4 a.m. to question him about a shooting, a proper result in that the circumstances produced a "potentiality for compulsion" equivalent to station house interrogation. Questioning has also been held to be noncustodial where it occurred at the home of a friend or relative, a place of employment, a place of public accommodation, or a hospital, although once again it must be emphasized that the circumstances of the particular case need to be carefully assessed. Thus, the situation might well be different as to an employee who was marched off to a security office of his employer, or as to a hospital patient who was taken to the hospital by the police or who was put into a police-dominated situation. But a person is not in custody for *Miranda* purposes merely because of his compelled appearance at a judicial proceeding to give testimony.

In *Minnesota v. Murphy* (1984), a probationer met with his probation officer at her office pursuant to her order and admitted in response to her questioning that he had committed a rape and murder some years ago. The Court held *Miranda* was inapplicable because there was not custody:

> Custodial arrest is said to convey to the suspect a message that he has no choice but to submit to the officers' will and to confess. * * * It is unlikely that a probation interview, arranged by appointment at a mutually convenient time, would give rise to a similar impression. * * * Many of the psychological ploys discussed in *Miranda* capitalize on the suspect's unfamiliarity with the officers and the environment. Murphy's regular meetings with his probation officer should have served to familiarize him with her and her office and to insulate him from psychological intimidation that might overbear his desire to claim the privilege. Finally, the coercion inherent in custodial interrogation derives in large measure from an interrogator's insinuations that the interrogation will continue until a confession is obtained. * * * Since Murphy was not physically restrained and could have left the office, any compulsion he might have felt from the possibility that terminating the meeting would have led to revocation of probation was not comparable to the pressure on a suspect who is painfully aware that he literally cannot escape a persistent custodial interrogator.

Though the language of *Murphy* might suggest otherwise, and though the Supreme Court on an earlier occasion assumed that a person serving a prison sentence is "in custody" for *Miranda* purposes, lower courts have often found questioning of those serving prison sentences to be not custodial. The notion is that the coercive effects that *Miranda* found to be associated with custodial interrogation arise in the prison context only if an inmate's liberty is limited beyond the usual conditions of his confinement.

In *Miranda,* the Court declared: "General on-the-scene questioning as to facts surrounding a crime or other general questioning of citizens in the factfinding process is not affected by our holding.

* * * In such situations the compelling atmosphere inherent in the process of in-custody interrogation is not necessarily present." This is not to suggest, however, that all "on-the-scene" questioning falls outside *Miranda,* even if the person questioned is under arrest. As stated in *New York v. Quarles* (1984), "the ultimate inquiry is simply whether there is a 'formal arrest or restraint on freedom of movement' of the degree associated with a formal arrest." Such was the case in *Quarles,* where the questioning occurred in a supermarket minutes after defendant's arrest by four police officers with guns drawn and after defendant had been handcuffed. By contrast, the Court in *Berkemer v. McCarty* (1984) concluded that *Miranda* warnings are not required in the circumstances present there, where defendant was subjected to roadside questioning during a routine traffic stop. The Court acknowledged that the defendant had been "seized" for Fourth Amendment purposes, but noted the seizure was a limited one, much like a *Terry* stop for investigation, and then concluded as to both that the "comparatively nonthreatening character" of the detentions justified the holding "that persons temporarily detained pursuant to such stops are not 'in custody' for the purposes of *Miranda.*" Specifically, the Court deemed it significant that such detentions are "presumptively temporary and brief" and are so perceived by the detainees, and that the circumstances of the stops are not such that a detainee "feels completely at the mercy of the police," as the stops occur in public and involve only one or two officers. Applying *Berkemer,* lower courts have held that *Miranda* does not apply in various settings judged to involve no more than a *Terry* stop, but the circumstances of some *Terry* stops have been deemed coercive so as to constitute "custody" for *Miranda* purposes even if they are not full-fledged arrests in a Fourth Amendment sense.

(f) **Other Considerations.** In ascertaining, as called for by *Miranda,* whether the deprivation of freedom of action was "significant," it is particularly important whether some indicia of arrest are present. A court is not likely to find custody for *Miranda* purposes if the police were not even in a position to physically seize the suspect, but is likely to find custody if there was physical restraint such as handcuffing, drawing a gun, holding by the arm, or placing into a police car. Merely having the suspect move a short distance to facilitate conversion does not itself constitute custody. Also relevant are whether or not the suspect was told that he was free to leave and, if the events occur at the station, whether or not booking procedures were employed. Because the Court in *Miranda* expressed concern with the coerciveness of situations in which the suspect was "cut off from the outside world" and "surrounded by antagonistic forces" in a "police dominated atmosphere" and interrogated "without relent," circumstances relating to those kinds of concerns are also relevant on the custody issue. Thus, custody is less likely to be deemed present when the questioning occurred in the presence of the suspect's friends or other third parties, and more likely to be found when the police have removed the suspect from such individuals. A court is more likely to find the situation custodial when the suspect was confronted by several officers instead of just one, when the demeanor of the officer was antagonistic rather than friendly, and when the questioning was lengthy rather than brief and routine. And surely a reasonable person would conclude he was in custody if the interrogation is close and persistent, involving leading questions and the discounting of the suspect's denials of involvement.

§ 5.7　*Miranda*: "Interrogation"

(a) The "Functional Equivalent" Test. Just what is encompassed within the "interrogation" part of *Miranda's* "custodial interrogation" term has caused the courts considerable difficulty. One view often taken, which finds support in the *Miranda* Court's explanation that "we mean questioning initiated by law enforcement officers," was that nothing but the asking of questions will bring a case within the constraints of *Miranda*. Another view, consistent with the observation in *Miranda* that it is the placing of an individual "into police custody" and then subjecting him "to techniques of persuasion" which together produce the "compulsion to speak," was that the word "interrogation" should not be given a narrow or literal interpretation. So matters stood until the Supreme Court finally resolved this fundamental dispute in *Rhode Island v. Innis* (1980).

In *Innis,* defendant was arrested for robbery with a sawed-off shotgun and promptly given his *Miranda* warnings, at which he said he wished to speak with a lawyer. The arresting officers then began their journey to the station with the prisoner, and during this time the officers conversed among themselves about the desirability of finding the shotgun because there was a school for handicapped children in the vicinity. At this, defendant said he would show the officers where the gun was located, which he did. His murder conviction was overturned by the state supreme court, as the gun and testimony about its discovery was held to have been improperly admitted because defendant had been subjected to "subtle coercion" equivalent to *Miranda* "interrogation," A majority of the Supreme Court, though ultimately concluding that "respondent was not 'interrogated' within the meaning of *Miranda*," nonetheless opted for a rather broad definition of what constitutes "interrogation" by concluding that the *Miranda* safeguards come into play whenever a person in custody is subjected to either express questioning or its functional equivalent. That is to say, the term "interrogation" under *Miranda* refers not only to express questioning, but also to any words or actions on the part of the police (other than those normally attendant to arrest and custody) that the police should know are reasonably likely to elicit an incriminating response from the suspect. The latter portion of this definition focuses primarily upon the perceptions of the suspect, rather than the intent of the police. This focus reflects the fact that the *Miranda* safeguards were designed to vest a suspect in custody with an added measure of protection against coercive police practices, without regard to objective proof of the underlying intent of the police. A practice that the police should know is reasonably likely to evoke an incriminating response from a suspect thus amounts to interrogation. But, since the police surely cannot be held accountable for the unforeseeable results of their words or actions, the definition of interrogation can extend only to words or actions on the part of police officers that they *should have known* were reasonably likely to elicit an incriminating response.

The *Innis* definition of "interrogation" was expressly noted to be "not necessarily interchangeable" with the *Brewer v. Williams* (1977)and *Massiah v. United States* (1964) definition of what constitutes a violation of the Sixth Amendment right to counsel once that right has attached. For one thing, the *Williams–Massiah* "deliberately elicited" test focuses upon the intent of the police, while the *Innis* test does not. Only Justice Stevens, dissenting in *Innis,* felt that " 'interrogation' must include any police statement or conduct that has the same purpose or effect as a direct question," that is, both those "that appear to call for a response from the suspect" and "those that are designed to do so." But one of the ambiguities of *Innis* is just how far apart these two positions actually are. In an apparent attempt to bridge the gap, the majority dropped a footnote saying that the intent of the police is not irrelevant, "for it may well have a bearing on whether the police should have known that their words or actions were reasonably likely to evoke an incriminating response." This footnote goes on to say that "where a police practice is designed to elicit an incriminating response from the accused, it is unlikely that the practice will not also be one which the police should have known was reasonably likely to have that effect," which drew the following footnote rejoinder by Justice Stevens: "This factual assumption is extremely dubious. I would assume that police often interrogate suspects without any reason to believe that their efforts are likely to be successful in the hope that a statement will nevertheless be forthcoming."

This exchange is indicative of more fundamental problems with both the majority opinion and the Stevens dissent. To take the latter first of all, it surely does not make sense to conclude that under *Miranda* the existence of "interrogation" (any more than the existence of "custody," see § 5.6(c)) depends upon the undisclosed intentions of the officer. *Miranda* is grounded in the notion that custody plus interrogation produces a coercive atmosphere, which makes sense only when the suspect is aware of both the custody and the interrogation. The court noted in *Innis* that it would not constitute "interrogation" for the police merely to drive past the site of the concealed weapon while taking the most direct route to the police station, and surely the result should not be different even if the police admitted their "purpose" in driving by was to elicit an incriminating response. To take a phrase from *Miranda,* the "potentiality for compulsion" would be no different in the latter situation than in the former. Justice Stevens was apparently attracted to his intention-of-the-officer alternative because it would largely overcome what he saw as a glaring weakness in the majority's approach in *Innis*. His reading of the majority's (perhaps unfortunate) "reasonably likely to elicit" language is that it necessitates a determination of the apparent probability that police speech or conduct will elicit an incriminating response. This interpretation cannot be dismissed out of hand; for one thing, it would explain the otherwise questionable *Innis* result. But so interpreted the *Innis* test would not provide adequate guidance to police and lower courts. However, that does not appear to be what the *Innis* majority really meant, for such a view of the case is inconsistent with the majority's professed aim of defining "interrogation" in a manner consistent with *Miranda*'s underlying policy of prohibiting all speech or conduct that is the "functional equivalent" of direct questioning.

Just what *Innis* does mean is a matter of some uncertainty, although it would seem to turn upon the *objective* purpose *manifested* by the police. Thus, an officer "should know" that his speech or conduct will be "reasonably likely to elicit an incriminating response" when he should realize that the speech or conduct will probably be viewed by the suspect as designed to achieve this purpose. To ensure that the inquiry is entirely *objective,* the proposed test could be framed as follows: If an objective observer (with the same knowledge of the suspect as the police officer) would, on the sole basis of hearing the officer's remarks, infer that the remarks were designed to elicit an incriminating response, then the remarks should constitute "interrogation." This interpretation is consistent with the result reached in *Innis,* would not be difficult to apply because it is an objective test not requiring a determination of the actual perception of the suspect, but yet is fully responsive to the concerns in *Miranda* because it identifies the situation in which the suspect will experience the "functional equivalent" of direct questioning by concluding that the police are trying to get him to make an incriminating response. Moreover, it has the added advantage that it would put to rest a concern expressed by one member of the Court in *Innis:* that the police were expected to "evaluate the suggestibility and susceptibility of an accused."

Consistent in some respects with the preceding interpretation is *Arizona v. Mauro* (1987), where, after defendant invoked his right to counsel, the police acceded to a request of his wife, also a suspect in the investigation of their son's death, to speak with defendant, but had a police officer and tape recorder conspicuously present at the meeting. The Court held this did not constitute "interrogation" under the *Innis* formulation. *Mauro* apparently reflects an unwillingness of a majority of the Court to ground the "interrogation" determination in the subjective intentions of the police. The state supreme court had concluded that the proper focus was upon the intent of the police and that this intent was "so clear" that it was unnecessary to "address appellant's perceptions," and this approach was accepted by the four dissenters in *Mauro.* The *Mauro* majority, on the other hand, asserted that there was no such intent shown and added, even more unconvincingly, that the police were not even aware of "a sufficient likelihood of incrimination" under the legal standard articulated in *Innis.* But what seems to lie at the heart of the majority position in *Mauro* is that neither the subjective intentions of the police nor their perception of a significant likelihood that a certain scenario will prompt incriminating statements by the defendant is determinative. This is reflected in the majority's statement that "the weakness of Mauro's claim that he was interrogated is underscored by examining the situation from his perspective. * * * We doubt that a suspect, told by officers that his wife will be allowed to speak to him, would feel that he was being coerced to incriminate himself in any way." That is, the bottom line in *Mauro,* as the majority sees it, is that "Mauro was not subjected to compelling influences, psychological ploys, or direct questioning."

There is much to be said for the proposition, which *seems* to underlie the majority's position in *Mauro* notwithstanding all the disclaimers, that neither the officers' intentions nor their strong expectations should be decisive. Rather, as suggested earlier, it makes more sense to consider the objective purpose manifested by the police—that is, what an objective observer with the same knowledge as the suspect would conclude the police were up to. *If* that is the proper approach, then it is by no means clear that the majority in *Mauro* reached the correct result. When the defendant was suddenly confronted with what must have appeared to him as a police-arranged meeting with his wife at which the police maintained a presence with a tape recorder operating, it would seem that he was subjected to the "functional equivalent" of interrogation. This is because Mauro had learned that those having custody of him had produced a scenario that (in the language of Justice Stevens in *Innis*) "appear[ed] to call for a response."

(b) Questioning. The Court in *Innis* set out to determine what "words or actions on the part of the police" other than "express questioning" constitute "interrogation" within the meaning of *Miranda*. Putting the matter this way would certainly suggest that *any* time a person in custody is asked a question, surely the *Miranda* requirements apply. But no such absolute rule had been recognized by the lower courts prior to *Innis,* and it does not seem that all of those decisions are cast in doubt by the *Innis* decision. If other "words or actions" fall within *Miranda* only if "the police should know [they] are likely to elicit an incriminating response," then it is not fanciful to suggest that certain types of questioning also do not come within *Miranda* because they are unlikely to produce that kind of response. Or if, as suggested above, the unfortunate "likely to elicit" language is ignored in favor of an inquiry whether an objective observer would infer that the remarks were designed to elicit an incriminating response, it still does not follow that *all* questioning of those in custody is governed by *Miranda*.

Miranda requirements are inapplicable to questioning that produces an incriminating response not "testimonial" in nature. Illustrative is *Pennsylvania v. Muniz* (1990), where the defendant, under arrest for driving under the influence, was asked a series of questions about his name, address, birthday, age, etc. The Court concluded that though defendant's videotaped responses incriminated him because his slurred speech manifested his drunkenness, the lack of *Miranda* warnings did not require suppression. Relying upon the established distinction between "testimonial" and "real or physical evidence" for purposes of the privilege against self-incrimination (see § 6.2(a)), the Court concluded "that any slurring of speech and other evidence of lack of muscular coordination revealed by Muniz's responses to [the officer's] direct questions constitute nontestimonial components of those responses. Requiring a suspect to reveal the physical manner in which he articulates words, like requiring him to reveal the physical properties of the sound produced by his voice, * * * does not, without more, compel him to provide a 'testimonial' response for purposes of the privilege."

The *content* of one of the defendant's answers in *Muniz*, that he did not know the date of his sixth birthday, was incriminating because it would allow the inference that his mental state was confused. Four members of the Court believed this also fell into the "real or physical evidence" category, but the majority disagreed. They explained that even if the matter inferred had to do with physical condition, the critical issue "is whether the inference is drawn from a testimonial act or from physical evidence. * * * Whenever a suspect is asked for a response requiring him to communicate an express or implied assertion of fact or belief, the suspect confronts the 'trilemma' of truth, falsity, or silence and hence the response (whether based on truth or falsity) contains a testimonial component." Under this test, the sixth birthday question "required a testimonial response": the coercive environment precluded the option of remaining silent, and the truth (that he did not know the date) was incriminating, as would have been a false statement (an incorrect guess).

Both prior to and following *Muniz*, lower courts—usually relying upon the *Innis* assertion that "interrogation" does not include those words and actions "normally attendant to arrest and custody"—have held that routine inquiries during the booking process are lawful even absent *Miranda* warnings. *Muniz*, in holding admissible the answers given to a series of booking questions, supports this conclusion; four members of the Court concluded the answers were admissible "because the questions fall within a 'routine booking question' exception which exempts from *Miranda's* coverage questions to secure the 'biographical data necessary to complete booking or pretrial services,' " while four others deemed it "unnecessary to determine whether the questions fall within the 'routine booking question' exception to *Miranda*" because they believed the defendant's responses "were not testimonial."

A related but more difficult issue concerns questions asked for purposes of identification (e.g., "what is your name?", "where do you live?") other than as part of the booking process. For example, in the unlikely event that an on-the-street interrogation were deemed custodial, may the police make inquiries limited to the purpose of identifying a person found under suspicious circumstances or near the scene of a recent crime? An affirmative answer is suggested by *California v. Byers* (1971), holding that a statute requiring the driver of a car involved in an accident to stop and give the driver of the other car his name and address does not violate the privilege against self-incrimination, even without a restriction on the use of the required disclosures, because the required conduct was not "testimonial" in the Fifth Amendment sense and did not entail a "substantial risk of self-incrimination." As the Court explained, a name "identifies but does not by itself implicate anyone in criminal conduct," and although identity, "when made known, may lead to inquiry that in turn leads to arrest and charge, those developments depend on different factors and independent evidence." Application of *Byers* to the situation here under discussion (which finds support in the many holdings that the privilege presents no bar to various other identification techniques, see § 6.2(b)) would not seem inconsistent with the *Innis* definition of "interrogation." This is especially so if the identification request is merely for the suspect's name, for in *Hiibel v. Sixth Judicial District Court* (2004), upholding defendant's conviction for failing to comply with a statutory command to provide his name during a lawful *Terry* stop, the Court in rejecting defendant's self-incrimination challenge indicated such would be the result in most cases because "[a]nswering a request to disclose a name is likely to be so insignificant in the scheme of things as to be incriminating only in unusual circumstances."

There can be circumstances in which purported identification questions that would otherwise be innocuous will constitute interrogation under *Innis* because the circumstances of the particular case gave the officer reason to know that the suspect's answer would likely incriminate him. But the mere fact that an innocuous question results in an incriminating response is not enough; as the Court put it in *Innis*, "the police surely cannot be held accountable for the unforeseeable results of their words or actions." As for questions not quite so innocuous but not accusatory either (e.g., "what happened?", "what's going on here?") the issue has been infrequently litigated because those situations usually arise in the context of a brief noncustodial encounter between an officer and citizen. However, there is authority that such situations fall within the *Miranda* Court's statement that "[g]eneral on-the-scene questioning as to facts surrounding a crime or other general questioning of citizens in the fact-finding process is not affected by our holding." In any event, it would seem that at least some such inquiries are not interrogation under the suggested interpretation of *Innis*: whether an objective observer would infer the remarks were designed to elicit an incriminating response. Such an inference might well not be drawn when the question is very general in nature, not directed at one particular person, obviously asked before it is known that any criminal conduct has occurred or before there has been any sorting of suspects from witnesses, apparently asked about a seemingly innocuous matter not directly related to the police intervention, obviously spontaneous in nature, or seemingly a natural question anyone would ask given defendant's condition or other unusual circumstances.

Still another type of case is that in which the authorities claim that they were questioning for the purpose of protecting themselves or others from weapons by asking the defendant whether he had a gun or where a gun was located. Illustrative is *New York v. Quarles* (1984), where police chased a rape suspect, who was reportedly armed, inside a supermarket and then arrested him there; a frisk uncovered an empty shoulder holster, so one officer asked him "Where is the gun?"; the suspect gestured toward a stack of soap cartons and said, "The gun is over there," and police then found a revolver behind the cartons. A majority of the Supreme Court concluded that "on these facts there is a 'public safety' exception to the requirement that *Miranda* warnings be given." The Court characterized *Miranda* as representing a willingness by the Court to impose procedural safeguards "when the primary social cost of those added protections is the possibility of fewer convictions," to be distinguished from the instant situation in which the cost would be an inability "to insure that further danger to the public did not result from the concealment of the gun." It was thus concluded that the need for answers to questions in a situation posing a threat to the public safety outweighs the need for the prophylactic rule protecting the Fifth Amendment's privilege against self-incrimination. Otherwise, the *Quarles* majority recognized, police would be "in the untenable position of having to consider, often in a matter of seconds, whether it best serves society for them to ask the necessary questions without the *Miranda* warnings and render whatever probative evidence they uncover inadmissible, or for them to give the warnings in order to preserve the admissibility of evidence they might uncover but possibly damage or destroy their ability to obtain that evidence and neutralize the volatile situation confronting them." (Somewhat similar is the so-called "rescue doctrine," under which it has been held that *Miranda* warnings are unnecessary before custodial questioning undertaken to save life (e.g., in an effort to locate a kidnap victim).)

The most troublesome aspect of *Quarles* is the apparent breadth of the exception that has been created. Though the record below did not indicate that the police questioning was prompted by an actual concern for public safety, the majority disposed of that problem by declaring that the public safety exception "does not depend upon the motivation of the individual officers involved." That is, the notion put forward by the majority is that the facts of the case, objectively viewed, show that the police, "in the very act of apprehending a suspect, were confronted with the immediate necessity of ascertaining the whereabouts of a gun which they had every reason to believe the suspect had just removed from his empty holster and discarded in the supermarket. So long as the gun was concealed somewhere in the supermarket, with its actual whereabouts unknown, it obviously posed more than one danger to the public safety; an accomplice might make use of it, a customer or employee might later come upon it." But the facts in *Quarles* shows no such thing. At the time of the questioning, Quarles was himself handcuffed and in the custody of four armed officers, there was not the slightest suggestion of an accomplice, and the possibility that some other person might come onto the gun before the police could locate it, this seems equally fanciful in light of the facts that the events occurred after midnight when the store was apparently deserted and that the police knew the gun had been discarded in the immediate vicinity. But at least we know the *Quarles* exception is not broad enough to encompass any questioning about the location of a weapon, for the majority distinguished *Orozco v. Texas* (1969), where police entered the sleeping defendant's room and then questioned him about a gun used in a murder at a restaurant several hours earlier, as there "the questions about the gun were clearly investigatory" because "they did not in any way relate to an objectively reasonable need to protect the police or the public from any immediate danger associated with the weapon."

One other special purpose type of questioning deserves mention, especially because it has been specifically considered by the Supreme Court. In *Estelle v. Smith* (1981), defendant was indicted for murder and the state announced its intention to seek the death penalty. Though defense counsel had not interposed an insanity defense or questioned his client's competency to stand trial, defendant was subjected to a psychiatric examination and the psychiatrist testified at the penalty phase of the trial concerning defendant's "future dangerousness," after which defendant was sentenced to death. The state claimed that a psychiatric examination did not infringe upon Fifth Amendment interests because an inquiry into defendant's state of mind was like obtaining a blood sample or voice and handwriting exemplars, but the Court rejected this contention. Because the doctor's testimony "was not based simply on his observation of respondent" but came "largely from respondent's account of the crime during their interview," the "Fifth Amendment privilege * * * is directly involved here because the State used as evidence against respondent the substance of his disclosures during the pretrial psychiatric examination." The Court added that the result would have been otherwise had the doctor testified at a hearing on defendant's competency to stand trial, for "no Fifth Amendment issue would have arisen" in that context. The Court also emphasized that the instant case was not analogous

> to a sanity examination occasioned by a defendant's plea of not guilty by reason of insanity at the time of his offense. When a defendant asserts the insanity defense and introduces supporting psychiatric testimony, his silence may deprive the State of the only effective means it has of controverting his proof on an

issue that he interjected into the case. Accordingly, several courts of appeals have held that, under such circumstances, a defendant can be required to submit to a sanity examination conducted by the prosecution's psychiatrist.

The Court did not have occasion to rule on such a situation in *Smith,* and in the later case of *Buchanan v. Kentucky* (1987) found it necessary only to hold that "if a defendant requests [a psychiatric] evaluation or presents psychiatric evidence, then, at the very least, the prosecution may rebut this presentation with evidence from the reports of the examination that the defendant requested."

(c) Other "Words or Actions." The major impact of *Innis* is with respect to conduct other than express questioning. Prior to that decision there was a split of authority as to what the outcome should be when the police engaged in such tactics as confronting the defendant with physical evidence, with an accusing accomplice, or with the confession of an accomplice. One explanation given for admitting incriminating statements obtained in these ways was that questioning does not exist absent verbal conduct by the police, a notion *Innis* clearly repudiates. Indeed, under *Innis* such tactics will usually be characterized as "interrogation." This may seem less likely after *Mauro,* discussed earlier (see § 5.7(a)), rejecting the conclusion of the four dissenters "that a police decision to place two suspects in the same room and then to listen to or record their conversation may constitute a form of interrogation even if no questions are asked by any police officers." Perhaps that is so, though the majority distinguished the situation before it from those in which the police resorted to " 'psychological ploys, such as to "posi[t]" "the guilt of the subject" * * *.' "

Another line of reasoning in the pre-*Innis* cases is that it is not unfair to communicate to the defendant information about the strength of the case against him, for such information is relevant to an intelligent decision by him as to whether he should cooperate or remain silent. To the extent that this view persists, there will doubtless be pressure not to apply *Innis* to every instance in which such information has been made available to a defendant. And in any event, *Innis* is not so broad; as noted earlier, it is best interpreted as covering those instances in which the officer's words or actions would be viewed by an objective observer as designed to elicit an incriminating response, which is preferable to asking (to take some of the language in *Innis*) whether the police should have known the activity was "reasonably likely to elicit an incriminating response." This point is best illustrated by two situations that have been viewed as not within *Miranda's* constraints and as to which *Innis* is not likely to produce a different result: where the defendant made a confession after being identified in a lineup or after witnessing police discovery of physical evidence, In terms of the probability of a defendant making an incriminating remark, these two situations probably are not significantly different from many of the others described above. But the important fact about these two situations is that the police were engaged in activity calculated to produce evidence against the defendant by other means, and thus objectively viewed they would not appear to be designed to get an incriminating response from the defendant.

Another kind of case that requires closer analysis after *Innis* is where the police within the hearing of defendant engage in comments or conversation short of questions put to the defendant. *Innis* itself was this kind of case, as it involved a conversation among the officers about the desirability of finding the shotgun so that it would not fall into the hands of a handicapped child. The majority concluded this was not *Miranda* interrogation because the comments were just "a few off-hand remarks" rather than a "lengthy harangue," were not made to one the police knew "was peculiarly 'evocative,' " and were not made to one the police knew "was peculiarly susceptible to an appeal to his conscience concerning the safety of handicapped children." Though *Innis* is a close case, surely there are other instances in which the comments or conversations of the police will be deemed interrogation. Illustrative is the "Christian burial" speech in *Brewer v. Williams* (1977). Though the Court decided that case on other grounds, prompting concern that it was not prepared to extend the concept of interrogation as it later did in *Innis,* certainly the conduct of the police in *Williams,* where the remarks were directed at the defendant by police who knew of and were taking advantage of the fact he was deeply religious, amounts to interrogation.

But there are other instances in which the police activity will not amount to "interrogation" or a functional equivalent, though it is clear beyond dispute that an officer directed words to the suspect. Illustrative is *Pennsylvania v. Muniz* (1990), where the defendant, arrested for driving under the influence, made incriminating remarks when asked by officers to perform physical sobriety tests and to submit to a breathalyzer examination. The Court concluded there was no "interrogation within the meaning of *Miranda*" because the "limited and focused inquiries were necessarily 'attendant to' the legitimate police procedure * * * and were not likely to be perceived as calling for any incriminating response." The Court earlier reached the same conclusion as to a police request that a suspect take a blood alcohol test, while lower courts have so ruled as to police statements to the suspect by way of warning him of his rights or explaining why he was arrested.

Finally, it must be asked what the significance of *Innis* is in the so-called "jail plant" case, where an undercover agent is placed with the defendant while he is in custody and listens to defendant's remarks or even encourages the defendant to make remarks about the crime. In *Hoffa v. United States* (1966), involving a "plant" of a government agent with an unincarcerated defendant, the Court summarily dismissed the claim that Hoffa's incriminating statement had been obtained in violation of the Fifth Amendment. The Court there noted that "a necessary element of compulsory self-incrimination is some kind of compulsion," and that Hoffa's choice to make incriminating remarks in the agent's presence was "wholly voluntary" and not "the product of any sort of coercion, legal or factual." It has sometimes been questioned, however, whether the same result should obtain when the defendant is in jail. So the argument goes, the confinement increases a suspect's anxiety and makes him more likely to seek discourse with others to relieve this anxiety, meaning he will be more susceptible to an undercover investigator seeking information. Moreover, though *Hoffa* was fooled he at least had the choice of his companions, but when the suspect's ability to select people with whom he can confide is completely within police control, they have a unique opportunity to exploit the suspect's vulnerability.

While the Supreme Court has applied the *Massiah* rule (available only after the right to counsel has attached) to the "jail plant" situation, at least when the plant has taken some affirmative steps to bring about the defendant's statements (see § 5.4(g)), the Court more recently held in *Illinois v. Perkins* (1990) "that an undercover law enforcement officer posing as a fellow inmate need not give *Miranda* warnings to an incarcerated suspect before asking questions that may elicit an incriminating response." The Court in *Perkins* concluded that conversations "between suspects and undercover agents do not implicate the concerns underlying *Miranda*," as the "essential ingredients of a 'police-dominated atmosphere' and compulsion are not present when an incarcerated person speaks freely to someone that he believes to be a fellow inmate." Because coercion "is determined from the perspective of the suspect," the Court added, it follows that when "a suspect considers himself in the company of cellmates and not officers, the coercive atmosphere is lacking."

(d) "Volunteered" Statements and Follow–Up Questioning. The *Miranda* Court emphasized that "there is no requirement that police stop a person who enters a police station and states that he wishes to confess to a crime, or a person who calls the police to offer a confession or any other statement he desires to make. Volunteered statements of any kind are not barred by the Fifth Amendment and their admissibility is not affected by our holding today." It is thus clear that a statement not preceded by the *Miranda* warnings will be admissible when, for example, the defendant walks into a police station and confesses or blurts out an admission when approached by an officer near a crime scene. More important, because *Miranda* found only custody-plus-interrogation coercive, a statement may qualify as "volunteered" even though made by one in custody, one who had previously asserted his right to silence, or one who had previously requested counsel. Indeed, a statement following a police officer's question may qualify as at least the equivalent of being volunteered when it is unresponsive, as when an officer's question is met by a bribery attempt.

Assuming a truly volunteered statement, may the police follow up that statement with some questions? *Miranda* is not entirely clear on this issue; at one point custodial interrogation is defined as "questioning initiated by law enforcement officers," suggesting that police questioning designed to clarify or amplify a volunteered statement is permissible, but elsewhere it is said that the suspect must be warned "prior to any questioning." Except in extreme circumstances, courts have generally been quite willing to admit the answers to follow-up questions on the ground that these answers are a continuation of the volunteered statement. The better view, however, is that the part of defendant's statement given after the follow-up questions is volunteered only if the questions are neutral efforts to clarify what has already been said rather than apparent attempts to expand the scope of the statement previously made. This means a question that would clarify a prior ambiguous statement (e.g., "did what?" in response to "I did it") would not constitute *Miranda* interrogation but a question that would enhance the defendant's guilt or raise the offense to a higher degree would. *Innis* should not be read as a prohibition upon all follow-up questions, though the *Innis* Court's unfortunate "likely to elicit an incriminating response" language, if applied literally, it would seem to foreclose even a clarifying question.

§ 5.8 *Miranda*: Required Warnings

(a) Content. The Supreme Court in *Miranda* held that before a person in custody may be subjected to interrogation he "must be adequately and effectively apprised of his rights." In particular, "he must first be informed in clear and unequivocal terms" (1) "that he has the right to remain silent," (2) "that anything said can and will be used against the individual in court," (3) "that he has the right to consult with a lawyer and to have the lawyer with him during interrogation," and (4) "that if he is indigent a lawyer will be appointed to represent him." Whether the warnings must be given in precisely that language reached the Court in *California v. Prysock* (1981), on review of a lower court decision grounded in the proposition that the "rigidity of the *Miranda* rules and the way in which they are to be applied was conceived of and continues to be recognized as the decision's greatest strength." The Supreme Court noted that it "has never indicated that the 'rigidity' of *Miranda* extends to the precise formulation of the warnings given" and that, "[q]uite the contrary, *Miranda* itself indicates that no talismanic incantation was required to satisfy its strictures." The Court in *Prysock* thus concluded that what is required is not "a verbatim recital of the words of the *Miranda* opinion" but rather words that in substance will have "fully conveyed to [defendant] his rights as required by *Miranda.*" Just when that has been accomplished, of course, is sometimes a difficult question.

As for the warning "that he has the right to remain silent" one variation that has surfaced, telling the suspect he "need not make any statement," has usually been held acceptable. As for the second warning, concerning possible use of anything said by the suspect, in the excerpt quoted above the Court employed the overstatement "can and will be used," but at an earlier point the Court described the warning as being that what is said "may be used," and this alternative has been consistently approved by the lower courts. The courts have also upheld other formulations, including use of "can" alone, of "might," and of "could." The part of the second warning cautionings about use of the statement "against" the suspect has sometimes been changed so that he is told what he says may be used "for or against you." Some courts have disapproved of this variation because it is not only misleading but is likely to undercut the effect of the warning by offering an inducement to speak, while others have criticized it but yet held it not an impermissible deviation from the *Miranda* formula.

Under *Miranda,* it is necessary that these warnings cover the right to appointed counsel and the immediacy of the right in the sense that it exists both before and during interrogation. This has given rise to the question of whether the statement about appointment of counsel must particularize that appointment will precede questioning. No such language appears in the warnings quoted above, but at another point the *Miranda* Court said the defendant must be warned "that if he cannot afford an attorney one will be appointed for him prior to any questioning if he so desires." However, in *Prysock* the Court held that where defendant "was told of his right to have a lawyer present prior to and during interrogation" and also of "his right to have a lawyer appointed at no cost if he could not afford one," these warnings collectively "conveyed to respondent his right to have a lawyer appointed if he could not afford one prior to and during interrogation." Somewhat different from *Prysock* is the case in which the police warnings convey the message that appointed counsel cannot be made available until some future time. Such a case reached the Court in *Duckworth v. Eagan* (1989), where the defendant was given the full *Miranda* warnings (including: "You have a right to talk to a lawyer for advice before we ask you any questions, and to have him with you during questioning"), but was also told: "We have no way of giving you a lawyer, but one will be appointed for you, if you wish, if and when you go to court." In holding these warnings sufficient, the

Court stressed that the "if and when" statement "accurately described the procedure for the appointment of counsel in Indiana" and squared with *Miranda,* which "does not require that attorneys be producible on call. * * * If the police cannot provide appointed counsel, *Miranda* requires only that the police not question a suspect unless he waives his right to counsel."

Assuming incomplete or inadequate *Miranda* warnings are given, may the prosecution overcome this by showing the suspect was in fact knowledgeable concerning the rights the warnings did not cover? The *Miranda* Court answered no, explaining that

> we will not pause to inquire in individual cases whether the defendant was aware of his rights without a warning being given. Assessments of the knowledge the defendant possessed, based on information as to his age, education, intelligence, or prior contact with authorities, can never be more than speculation; a warning is a clearcut fact. More important, whatever the background of the person interrogated, a warning at the time of the interrogation is indispensable to overcome its pressures and to insure that the individual knows he is free to exercise the privilege at that point in time.

As the Court put it at another point, giving warnings to the knowledgeable suspect "will show the individual that his interrogators are prepared to recognize his privilege should he choose to exercise it." Most courts have thus properly concluded that the warnings must be given even to lawyers and other suspects knowledgeable as to their *Miranda* rights.

A somewhat similar issue is whether omission of that part of the *Miranda* warnings concerning appointment of counsel can later be excused by a showing that the defendant was not indigent and thus would not have qualified for appointed counsel. The *Miranda* Court recognized some leeway was permissible here, stating that while "a warning that the indigent may have counsel appointed need not be given to the person who is known to have an attorney or is known to have ample funds to secure one, the expedient of giving a warning is too simple and the rights involved too important to engage in ex post facto inquiries into financial ability when there is any doubt at all on that score." Some courts have read this as meaning that it must be shown the police were actually aware of defendant's ability to retain counsel, while others have deemed it sufficient if the prosecution later established that the defendant did have that ability at the time of the interrogation. The latter view is unobjectionable, but the same cannot be said of those decisions holding that a defendant has the burden of showing he was indigent and thus entitled to warnings about appointment of counsel.

The characteristics of the particular suspect are relevant when the issue is whether the police did enough in giving the warnings in the language set out in *Miranda.* To take the most obvious case, if the suspect does not comprehend English then the warnings must be given in a language he understands. If the suspect is illiterate or of low intelligence, then great care must be taken to ensure that he understands his rights. If the police commenced giving the *Miranda* warnings only to be interrupted by the suspect, the courts are somewhat more sympathetic to the prosecution's position. When the interruption in effect stated what the police omitted (e.g., "I know I don't have to make a statement"), courts are inclined to conclude that *Miranda* has been complied with. Some courts reach the same result when the interruption is a more general declaration, such as "I know my rights," though the better view is that such an ambiguous assertion does not foreclose the need for specification of those rights by the police. But even when there is the latter type of interruption or one that includes no reference to *Miranda* rights, the subsequent statement will be admissible in any event if it was volunteered.

(b) **Time and Frequency.** With respect to the timing of the *Miranda* warnings, one question which arises is whether the warnings were given soon enough. The Supreme Court reached this issue in *Missouri v. Seibert* (2004), which involved an increasingly popular "police protocol for custodial interrogation that calls for no warnings of the rights to silence and counsel until interrogation has produced a confession," intended "to get a confession the suspect would not make if he understood his rights at the outset," a likely consequence because giving the warnings *after* the defendant has already confessed "could lead to an entirely reasonable inference that what he had just said will be used, with subsequent silence being of no avail." The Court held Seibert's second confession must be suppressed because the circumstances in which *Miranda* warnings were given meant they could not "function 'effectively' as *Miranda* requires." The "relevant facts that bear on whether *Miranda* warnings delivered midstream could be effective enough to accomplish their object" are "the completeness and detail of the questions and answers in the first round of interrogation, the overlapping content of the two statements, the timing and setting of the first and second, the continuity of police personnel, and the degree to which the interrogator's questions treated the second round as continuous with the first."

Assuming the warnings were given in a timely fashion, the question then may be whether they became "stale" after the passage of time. It is generally accepted that fresh warnings are not required after the passage of just a few hours. Authority is also to be found to the effect that this is also true even after the passage of several days where the custody has been continuous, but the contrary view has much to commend it. Clearly the passage of weeks or months is too long. Even when the passage of time has been fairly brief, consideration must be given to changes in the circumstances in the interim. However, the courts have generally taken the position that new warnings are not required just because there has been a change in the locale of the interrogation, in the officers doing the questioning, or in the subject matter of the investigation. Even a combination of these circumstances is not deemed to call for new warnings. In any event, repetition of the *Miranda* warnings will be necessary if the authorities are to "undo" the effects of coercive conduct following the initial warnings.

(c) **Manner; Proof.** In *Miranda,* the Court declared that "[s]ince the State is responsible for establishing the isolated circumstances under which the interrogation takes place and has the only means of making available corroborated evidence of warnings given during incommunicado interrogation, the burden is rightly on its shoulders." Though this would suggest that it is desirable to tape record the warnings or have them stenographically reported, most courts have not imposed such a requirement. Indeed, the uncorroborated testimony of a police officer that the warnings were given (if sufficiently detailed) will suffice even in the face of contradictory testimony by the defendant.

The warnings may be given either orally or in writing, though it has been noted that the better practice is to do both. Though giving the warnings in writing alone will suffice, it must be shown that the defendant could and did read the warnings and that he acknowledged an understanding of them. More commonly the warnings are given orally by the officer reciting the provisions from a *"Miranda* card." This alone is sufficient, provided of course that the reading is not done in a hurried or mechanical fashion. If both oral and written warnings were given but one version was defective or incomplete, courts have held it suffices that the one set of warnings was complete and correct. This may be a sensible result when the difference between the two sets of warnings is merely that something was omitted from one of them, but a contrary result is necessary if the conflict between the two is such that the suspect would be confused by the discrepancy. Two sets of warnings, *each* of which is deficient, may not be read together to create one valid set of warnings.

(d) **Additional Admonitions.** Defendants have sometimes contended that warnings other than those set out earlier are generally or in particular circumstances required by *Miranda.* For example, because the Court in *Miranda* noted that many suspects will assume that "silence in the face of accusation is itself damning and will bode ill when presented to a jury," it might well be argued that suspects are entitled to be explicitly warned of another important part of the *Miranda* holding—that the "prosecution may not * * * use at trial the fact that he stood mute or claimed his privilege in the face of accusation." But, neither the Supreme Court nor the lower courts have mandated the giving of such a warning. Similarly, while the *Miranda* Court recognized that a defendant has a right to stop answering questions at any time, this right was not included within the mandated warnings and thus lower courts have concluded that such a warning is not necessary.

The Supreme Court concluded in *Colorado v. Spring* (1987) that there is no affirmative obligation on the police to advise the defendant about the crime concerning which they wish to interrogate—even when the circumstances rather strongly suggest the desired questioning will be about a matter quite different from that later encompassed by the interrogation. Although in *Spring* the arrest had been by federal ATF agents but the post-arrest questioning after a *Miranda* waiver was about an unreported homicide in another state, defendant's statements were held to be admissible even absent any pre-waiver warning that questions about the homicide would be asked. The Court reasoned that since the defendant had been told he had a right to remain silent and that *anything* he said could be used against him, he had all the information necessary for a knowing and intelligent waiver of his Fifth Amendment rights; "the additional information could affect only the wisdom of a *Miranda* waiver, not its essentially voluntary and knowing nature." As for the statement in *Miranda* that "any evidence that the accused was threatened, tricked, or cajoled into a waiver will * * * show that the defendant did not voluntarily waive his privilege," the Court responded that mere "official silence" about the desire to question concerning the murder did not constitute trickery, and cautiously left unresolved whether a waiver of *Miranda* rights would be valid had there been "an affirmative misrepresentation by law enforcement officials as to the scope of the interrogation."

When a foreign national has sought suppression of his confession because police failed to advise him of his right under a treaty to contact a consular official, the courts have responded that violation of rights created by treaty is not a constitutional error and thus does not require use of the exclusionary rule.

§ 5.9 *Miranda:* Waiver of Rights

(a) **Express or Implied.** Although the Court in *Miranda* ruled that interrogation when accompanied by custody is so likely to be coercive that the defendant must be warned of his right not to talk to the police and to have the assistance of counsel before and during any questioning, this does not mean the police are free to interrogate whenever they have given the requisite warnings. The Court in *Miranda* went on to hold that if thereafter the defendant is interrogated and a statement is obtained, it will be admissible only if the government meets its "heavy burden" of demonstrating "that the defendant knowingly and intelligently waived his privilege against self-incrimination and his right to retained or appointed counsel." Moreover, if "the individual indicates in any manner, at any time prior to or during questioning, that he wishes to remain silent, the interrogation must cease," for he has thus "shown that he intends to exercise his Fifth Amendment privilege."

While the tone and language of the majority opinion in *Miranda* seemed to indicate that the Court would be receptive to nothing short of an express waiver of the rights involved, most lower courts nonetheless took the position that the *Miranda* waiver of rights did not have to be express, and this view was ultimately adopted by the Supreme Court in *North Carolina v. Butler* (1979). There defendant was given his *Miranda* rights orally at the time of arrest and later at the FBI office he read an "Advice of Rights" form which he said he understood, after which he said he would talk to the agents but would not sign the waiver on the form. The state supreme court excluded defendant's incriminating statement on the ground that a waiver of *Miranda* rights "will not be recognized unless such waiver is 'specifically made' after the *Miranda* warnings have been given," but the Supreme Court disagreed:

> An express written or oral statement of waiver of the right to remain silent or of the right to counsel is usually strong proof of the validity of that waiver, but is not inevitably either necessary or sufficient to establish waiver. The question is not one of form, but rather whether the defendant in fact knowingly and voluntarily waived the rights delineated in the *Miranda* case. As was unequivocally said in *Miranda,* mere silence is not enough. That does not mean that the defendant's silence, coupled with an understanding of his rights and a course of conduct indicating waiver, may never support a conclusion that a defendant has waived his rights. The courts must presume that a defendant did not waive his rights; the prosecution's burden is great; but in at least some cases waiver can be clearly inferred from the actions and words of the person interrogated.

(b) Competence of the Defendant. The Court in *Butler* indicated that the question of whether there has been a waiver of *Miranda* rights must be ascertained on "the particular facts and circumstances surrounding that case, including the background, experience, and conduct of the accused." This highlights the fact that whether the defendant has (as the *Miranda* Court put it) "knowingly and intelligently waived" his rights depends in part upon the competency of the defendant—that is, upon his ability to understand and act upon the warnings *Miranda* requires the defendant have received. *Tague v. Louisiana* (1980) stresses that this showing of competency was part of the "heavy burden" to be carried by the government. The arresting officer there "could not recall whether he asked petitioner whether he understood the rights as read to him, and * * * 'couldn't say yes or no' whether he rendered any tests to determine whether petitioner was literate or otherwise capable of understanding his rights," but the state court held that "it can be presumed that a person has capacity to understand, and the burden is on the one claiming a lack of capacity to show that lack." The Supreme Court summarily reversed, noting that the lower's court's position was clearly contrary to the previously quoted language from *Miranda* and *Butler*.

In assessing the personal characteristics of the defendant, one factor that obviously must be considered is his youthfulness. Especially when a youth has had no prior experience with the police or has a low IQ, his waiver may be found ineffective. This is not to suggest, however, that a valid waiver cannot be given by an underage defendant, for courts have frequently found waivers by juveniles to be valid. In *Fare v. Michael C.* (1979) the Supreme Court held that the "totality of the circumstances approach is adequate to determine whether there has been a waiver even where interrogation of juveniles is involved." Thus, the Court continued, what is mandated is an "evaluation of the juvenile's age, experience, education, background, and intelligence, and into whether he has the capacity to understand the warnings given him, the nature of his Fifth Amendment rights, and the consequences of waiving those rights." Most states follow this "totality of the circumstances" approach, while the others have opted for the so-called "interested adult" rule, under which a juvenile's waiver is not effective unless he was allowed to consult and have with him an adult interested in his welfare.

If the defendant is seriously mentally retarded, this reduces the chances that his waiver will be found valid. Either limited schooling or a low IQ can contribute to a finding of an ineffective waiver, but waivers have not infrequently been upheld notwithstanding such circumstances. A waiver can be effective even though the defendant was emotionally upset at having been apprehended or by other circumstances, though again this condition can contribute to a contrary determination. Obviously, the fact a defendant is well-educated and mature enhances the likelihood of a finding that his waiver was effective. If at the time of the alleged waiver the defendant was in considerable pain from a serious injury, this can contribute to a finding that the waiver was not effective. But defendants have generally been unsuccessful in claiming that their *Miranda* waivers should be held invalid because they were either intoxicated or under the influence of drugs or medication at that time.

It must be emphasized, however, that such personal characteristics of the defendant existing at the time of the purported waiver are often relevant only as they relate to police overreaching. Such is the teaching of *Colorado v. Connelly* (1986), rejecting a state court ruling that a defendant's *Miranda* waiver was not voluntary because he suffered from a psychosis that interfered with his ability to make free and rational choices. Noting that the "voluntariness of a waiver * * * has always depended on the absence of police overreaching, not on 'free choice' in any broader sense of the word," the Court in *Connelly* concluded that "*Miranda* protects defendants against government coercion" but "goes no further than that." The Court's later teaching in *Colorado v. Spring* (1987)—that a *Miranda* waiver must be *both* (i) "voluntary in the sense that it was the product of a free and deliberate choice" and (ii) "made with full awareness both of the nature of the right being abandoned and the consequences of the decision to abandon it"— serves to mark *Connelly*'s limits: it has to do only with the first of these two requirements.

A great many defendants who give *Miranda* waivers are not "competent" to do so in a certain sense, for the tactical error of that decision was not perceived by them. But this is no bar to an effective waiver for *Miranda* purposes, for a waiver need not be wise to be "intelligent" within the meaning of that case. This result is consistent with *Miranda's* emphasis upon the need to overcome the coerciveness of in-custody interrogation, and also may be explained in part by the impracticability of inquiring into defendant's awareness of all possible tactical considerations.

(c) Conduct of the Police. *Miranda* also says it must be shown that the defendant did "voluntarily waive his privilege," and as to this the conduct of the police will be particularly relevant. In *Fare v. Michael C.* (1979), the Court declared that the "totality of the circumstances approach is adequate to determine whether there has been a waiver," which indicates that the two categories of inducement that were considered sufficiently compelling to render a resulting confession inadmissible under longstanding and traditional confessions law—promises and threats—have a like adverse effect upon *Miranda* waivers. Lower courts have held waivers involuntary where obtained by a promise of some benefit or a threat of some adverse consequence. The Court in *Miranda* indicated that even absent such threats or promises a waiver would not be upheld if obtained under coercive circumstances, and that "the fact of lengthy interrogation or incommunicado incarceration before a statement is made is strong evidence that the accused did not validly waive his rights." Lower courts have held waivers invalid where the defendant had been held in custody an extended period of time before being given the warnings, or where the defendant had first been subjected to persistent questioning.

The *Miranda* Court also asserted that "any evidence that the accused was threatened, tricked, or cajoled into a waiver will, of course, show that the defendant did not voluntarily waive his privilege." This condemnation of the use of trickery suggests that using interrogation techniques creating either false confidence or resignation in a defendant will per se make the defendant's subsequent waiver ineffective. As we have seen, trickery has no such per se effect under the voluntariness approach to confessions, and thus the language from *Miranda* just quoted would suggest that a waiver-of-rights analysis is, at least in this respect, more demanding than the old voluntariness inquiry. But the lower courts have not reached this conclusion; rather, they have taken an approach that, if anything, is strengthened by the Supreme Court's more recent use of "totality of the circumstances" language in this context, namely, that trickery bears on the waiver issue in essentially the same way that it does on the due process voluntariness-of-confession issue. Under this approach, *Miranda* waivers have been upheld even when obtained after the police had misrepresented the strength of the case against the defendant or the seriousness of the matter under investigation. Even assuming that these cases can be squared with *Miranda* because the trickery concerned only the wisdom of exercising the rights of which the defendant had been warned, it still follows that there is an absolute prohibition upon any trickery that misleads the suspect as to the existence or dimensions of any of the applicable rights or as to whether the waiver really is a waiver of those rights.

Though some lower courts had held that a defendant's waiver of counsel is not sufficiently "knowing and intelligent" if police withheld from him information that an attorney had sought to consult him, the Supreme Court ruled otherwise in *Moran v. Burbine* (1986). The Court reasoned that "events occurring outside of the presence of the suspect and entirely unknown to him," as compared to defendant's knowledge an attorney had been barred access, "can have no bearing on the capacity to comprehend and knowingly relinquish a constitutional right." This is so even if the withheld information "might have affected his decision to confess," as a valid waiver only requires that the defendant "understand the nature of his rights and the consequences of abandoning them." As for the defendant's other argument, that such deception should be constitutionally proscribed because it was "inimical to the Fifth Amendment values *Miranda* seeks to protect," the Court declined to disturb *Miranda's* clarity by introducing new questions about just what events would require the police to give a defendant additional information. As to the dissenters' fears that the doors had been opened to all sorts of deception by the police, the majority responded that on unspecified "facts more egregious that those presented here police deception might rise to a level of a due process violation." *Burbine* stresses that the privilege against self-incrimination is personal to the defendant, from which it also follows that a defendant's *Miranda* rights cannot be invoked by a third party.

(d) **Implied Waiver.** While inquiry into the defendant's competency may indicate whether he *could* knowingly and intelligently waive his rights, and assessment of the police conduct may show whether such a waiver *would* be voluntary, it is still necessary to scrutinize the defendant's words and actions to see if he did *in fact* waive his *Miranda* rights. Assuming the other two inquiries present no bar to finding a waiver, the relatively easy cases are those in which the defendant makes an "express written or oral statement of waiver" constituting "strong proof of the validity of that waiver," or in which at the other extreme the defendant explicitly asserts his right to remain silent or his right to counsel. But courts are frequently confronted with fact situations lying at neither of these extremes.

As noted earlier, the Supreme Court in *North Carolina v. Butler* (1979) held that "an explicit statement of waiver is not invariably necessary to support a finding that the defendant waived the right to remain silent or the right to counsel guaranteed by the *Miranda* case." But if this is so, then even in cases not complicated by conduct of the defendant arguably constituting a feeble attempt to assert his rights, there remains the difficult question of what facts will justify a finding of waiver by implication. On this issue, *Butler* instructs that "mere silence is not enough" but that this "does not mean that the defendant's silence, coupled with an understanding of his rights and a course of conduct indicating waiver, may never support a conclusion that a defendant has waived his rights." This certainly means, as the lower courts and the Supreme Court itself have held, that a waiver is not established merely by showing that a defendant was given the complete *Miranda* warnings and thereafter gave an incriminating statement.

But what if the defendant expresses an understanding of the *Miranda* warnings he has received and thereafter an incriminating statement is obtained from him? In the language of *Butler,* does this amount to a showing of "an understanding of his rights and a course of conduct indicating waiver"? Several courts have answered this question in the affirmative. There is, however, authority to the contrary, and it has been argued with some force that his acknowledgement of understanding adds nothing more to the circumstances beyond mere silence. The point, quite simply, is that an understanding of rights and an intention to waive them are two different things, and the latter should not be inferred merely because the former is now clearly established. That is true, yet when it is clear the defendant does understand his rights it is somewhat easier to make some judgments about the significance of his subsequent conduct in terms of whether or not those rights are being invoked. Thus, while an acknowledgment of understanding should not inevitably carry the day, it is especially significant when defendant's incriminating statement follows immediately thereafter. On the matter of waiver by implication, courts have also taken into account the fact the defendant initiated the conversation that occurred after the warnings were given and that the defendant's contact with the police was attributable to his cooperation. Moreover, a finding of waiver is likely when the defendant has engaged in certain conduct falling a bit short of an express waiver, such as a declaration of a cooperative attitude or even a nod or a shrug.

(e) "Qualified" or Limited Waiver. A second group of cases in which the focus is primarily upon the conduct of the defendant presents an added complication, as where there is conduct that in isolation seems to amount to a waiver, but it is accompanied by other conduct that can be interpreted as a refusal to waive or even as an assertion of rights. Illustrative are the facts of *North Carolina v. Butler* (1979), where the defendant read a written "Advice of Rights" form, stated he understood his rights, and then refused to sign the form but nonetheless indicated he would talk. (The Court in *Butler* did not hold that this constituted a waiver, but only rejected the state court's view that nothing short of an express waiver would suffice under *Miranda*.) Another illustration would be where the suspect indicates he is willing to talk but is unwilling to have his remarks reduced to writing, as in *United States v. Frazier* (1979).

The court in *Frazier* held that the waiver was effective notwithstanding the defendant's unwillingness to permit note taking, and some other courts have similarly ruled that a waiver is effective notwithstanding the defendant's refusal to permit taping of his oral confession or to sign a copy of his confession, and that an oral waiver is effective in the face of defendant's refusal to sign a written waiver. As the court put it in *Frazier*, since the suspect there had the capacity to comprehend the warnings, the police officer questioning him was not required to "place a legal interpretation on the language of *Miranda* warnings he was directed to give." But this approach conflicts with *Miranda's* policy of trying to place the accused on a more equal footing with the police at the interrogation stage and gives the accused minimal protection against a misunderstanding of the warnings. It overlooks the fundamental point noted by the *Frazier* dissenters: "capacity to understand the warnings does not by any means guarantee that they will actually be understood."

An objective view of the facts of the *Frazier* case strongly suggests that the defendant acted as he did because of a mistaken impression that an oral confession not contemporaneously recorded could not be used against him. Similarly, the *Butler* facts certainly suggest the defendant misperceived the effect of a waiver that was oral rather than written. Under such circumstances, there is much to be said for the view that the police are under an obligation to clear up misunderstandings of this nature which are apparent to any reasonable observer. Short of this, it certainly makes sense in such cases to conclude that the defendant's conduct should significantly increase the prosecution's burden to overcome the presumption against waiver of *Miranda* rights.

Somewhat similar to *Frazier* is *Connecticut v. Barrett* (1987), where after receiving his *Miranda* warnings the defendant repeatedly asserted his willingness to talk about the incident and his unwillingness to give a written statement unless his attorney was present. Though the state court had ruled this amounted to an invocation of the right to counsel for all purposes, the Supreme Court concluded otherwise: "Barrett's limited requests for counsel * * * were accompanied by affirmative announcements of his willingness to speak with the authorities. The fact that officials took the opportunity provided by Barrett to obtain an oral confession is quite consistent with the Fifth Amendment. *Miranda* gives the defendant a right to choose between speech and silence, and Barrett chose to speak." Significantly, the Court in *Barrett* emphasized that the defendant's distinction between oral and written statements might have been "illogical," but that this alone would not make the waiver ineffective. But the Court also emphasized the defendant had testified to a full understanding of his *Miranda* warnings, and thus *Barrett* was not a case in which the partial or limited character of the waiver demonstrated an insufficient understanding by the defendant of the warnings he had received.

In other instances the question is the scope of the waiver, as is illustrated by *Wyrick v. Fields* (1982). Fields, charged with rape, after release on bail and consultation with privately retained counsel, agreed to a polygraph examination. Prior to the examination, he executed a waiver of *Miranda* rights, both in writing and orally. At the conclusion of the examination, an agent told him there had been some deceit and asked him if he would explain why his answers were bothering him. Fields then admitted the intercourse but claimed it was with consent, and that statement was admitted against him at trial. A federal court held this waiver covered only the polygraph examination and that a new set of warnings was required once the polygraph examination had been discontinued and Fields was asked if he could explain the test's unfavorable results. The Supreme Court disagreed, stressing that discontinuing the polygraph "effectuated no significant change in the character of the interrogation" and that neither Fields nor his attorney could have reasonably assumed "that Fields would not be informed of the polygraph readings and asked to explain any unfavorable result."

(f) Waiver After Assertion of Rights. The discussion up to this point has been concerned with the question of what the prosecution must do in order to carry its "heavy burden" of showing a waiver of *Miranda* rights. A somewhat special problem, reserved to this point, is whether the situation is different once the defendant has actually asserted his rights. Are the police then foreclosed from thereafter seeking a waiver from that defendant? If not, is the burden in such circumstances even heavier?

The significance of the defendant's invocation of the right to remain silent reached the Supreme Court in *Michigan v. Mosley* (1975). There, defendant was arrested for several robberies and at the station was given his *Miranda* warnings; he declined to discuss the robberies and no effort was made to have him reconsider his position. Two hours later another detective in another part of the building sought to question defendant about an unrelated murder; he was given the *Miranda* warnings again and thereafter gave an incriminating statement. The *Mosley* Court concluded that the propriety of this action depended upon the interpretation to be given language in *Miranda* that if "the individual indicates in any manner, at any time prior to or during questioning, that he wishes to remain silent, the interrogation must cease," and that "any statement taken after the person invokes his privilege cannot be other than the product of compulsion, subtle or otherwise," as without "the right to cut off questioning, the setting of in-custody interrogation operates on the individual to overcome free choice in producing a statement after the privilege has been once invoked." After rejecting two "possible literal interpretations" of this language—that it permits "the continuation of custodial interrogation after a momentary cessation," or at the other extreme, that it constitutes "a blanket prohibition against the taking of voluntary statements or a permanent immunity from further interrogation, regardless of the circumstances"—the *Mosley* Court continued:

> The critical safeguard identified in the passage at issue is a person's "right to cut off questioning." Through the exercise of his option to terminate questioning he can control the time at which questioning occurs, the subjects discussed, and the duration of the interrogation. The requirement that law enforcement authorities must respect a person's exercise of that option counteracts the coercive pressures of the custodial setting. We therefore conclude that the admissibility of statements obtained after the person in custody has decided to remain silent depends under *Miranda* on whether his "right to cut off questioning" was "scrupulously honored."

As for application of the *Mosley* "scrupulously honored" test, the majority concluded it was met on the facts of that case because "the police here immediately ceased the interrogation, resumed questioning only after the passage of a significant period of time and the provision of a fresh set of warnings, and restricted the second interrogation to a crime that had not been a subject of the earlier interrogation." Some courts have viewed the latter fact an essential one to a finding that defendant's rights were "scrupulously honored," and there is much to be said for this position. Other courts have not deemed a change in the subject matter of the inquiry to be essential. Perhaps that is unobjectionable when it is the defendant who initiated the subsequent conversation, but in other circumstances it is a highly questionable position. In any event, the "scrupulously honored" test is not met where the police did not honor the original in-custody assertion of the right to remain silent, ignored that assertion and expressed sympathy for defendant's plight, resumed questioning after a short interval, or made repeated attempts to obtain a waiver.

The defendant in *Mosley* had not invoked his *Miranda* right to counsel, and concurring Justice White suggested that had he done so the result might well be different. He later made the point for a majority of the Court in *Edwards v. Arizona* (1981), which held "that an accused, * * * having expressed his desire to deal with the police only through counsel, is not subject to further interrogation by the authorities until counsel has been made available to him, unless the accused himself initiates further communication, exchanges or conversations with the police." This result, the Court noted, is consistent with the language in *Miranda* that "[i]f the individual states that he wants an attorney, the interrogation must cease until an attorney is present." (Consequently, the Court clarified in a later case, the "available to him" language in *Edwards* means "that when counsel is requested, interrogation must cease, and officials may not reinitiate interrogation without counsel present, whether or not the accused has consulted with his attorney.") Thus the defendant's confession in *Edwards* was inadmissible, for the police had visited the defendant in his cell and obtaining a waiver of *Miranda* rights the morning after defendant had declared he wanted an attorney.

Edwards, best viewed as a *per se* rule proscribing any interrogation of a person held in custody who has invoked his right counsel absent the individual's subsequent initiation of conversation, thus limits the application of *Mosely's* "scrupulously honored" test to those cases where only the right to silence was invoked. This is evidenced by *Arizona v. Roberson* (1988), holding that *Edwards* rather than *Mosely* governs even when the later interrogation concerns a wholly unrelated crime. The *Roberson* majority emphasized the desirability of maintaining *Edwards* as a "bright line rule," without qualifications or exceptions, where there has been an unlimited invocation of the *"Miranda"* right to counsel, and noted that a defendant's manifestation "that he did not feel sufficiently comfortable with the pressures of custodial interrogation to answer questions without an attorney" should no more be limited to a particular offense than is a waiver of *Miranda* rights.

In *Oregon v. Bradshaw* (1983), eight members of the Court agreed that the admissibility of a confession given by a defendant who earlier invoked his *Miranda* right to counsel is to be determined by a two-step analysis. It first must be asked whether defendant "initiated" further conversation. This means that the impetus must come from the accused, not from the officers. However, if there has been some kind of police conduct preceding and allegedly contributing to the defendant's supposed "initiation," the question then becomes how that conduct is to be judged in determining where the "impetus" lies. One view, certainly subject to dispute, is that the prior police conduct is not relevant unless it actually amounted to interrogation or its functional equivalent under *Innis*. Another finds police initiation also in certain conduct not falling within the *Innis* formulation, though even under this approach certain police contacts which are insignificant, regarding unrelated matters, or made for other legitimate purposes concerning the case do not constitute such initiation. *Bradshaw* goes on to say that if it is found the defendant "initiated" further conversation, it must then be inquired whether defendant waived his right to counsel and to silence, "that is, whether the purported waiver was knowing and intelligent * * * under the totality of the circumstances, including the necessary fact that the accused, not the police, reopened the dialogue with the authorities."

As for what constitutes "initiation," by the defendant, those eight Justices in *Bradshaw* could not agree. The four-Justice plurality concluded that "inquiries or statements * * * relating to routine incidents of the custodial relationship" would not suffice but that questions "evinc[ing] a willingness and a desire for a generalized discussion about the investigation" would. The four dissenters defined "initiation" more narrowly as "communication or dialogue *about the subject matter of the criminal investigation.*" As for the defendant's statement in *Bradshaw*, "Well, what is going to happen to me now?", the plurality concluded this was initiation under their test, while the dissenters asserted it was not under theirs. But an objective assessment of the circumstances in that case would seem to justify only one conclusion—as the dissenters put it, the defendant was merely trying "to find out where the police were going to take him." That would not amount to "initiation" under either of the tests, and is quite different from the conduct lower courts have quite properly found sufficient to establish that the defendant had reopened the dialogue about the criminal investigation. Uncertainty about the applicable test persists after *Bradshaw,* as the other member of the Court, Justice Powell, rejected the two-step approach and deemed the confession admissible merely because there had later occurred a knowing and intelligent waiver by defendant of his rights.

In *Smith v. Illinois* (1984), the Supreme Court characterized the *Edwards* holding as a "bright-line rule" prohibiting all police overreaching, be it "deliberate or unintentional." This suggests, as the lower courts have rather consistently held, that police conduct can violate the *Edwards* prohibition even when the particular officer who makes contact was unaware of the defendant's prior invocation of his right to counsel. Sometimes this interpretation of *Edwards* is stated in terms of others within the same investigatory authority, and sometimes it is stated more broadly as extending to all law enforcement officers who subsequently deal with the suspect. On the other hand, some lower courts have recognized another type of limitation on *Edwards*: a break in custody concludes the special hands-off status a defendant has by virtue of having invoked his right to counsel. This is because the release of the defendant, after the defendant has invoked his right to counsel while in police custody, ends the need for the *Edwards* rule because the defendant is no longer under the inherently compelling pressures of continuous custody. But absent such a break, the mere passage of time between the time defendant invoked his right to counsel and the next interrogation does *not* make *Edwards* inapplicable.

(g) Ambiguous, Equivocal, Limited and Untimely Assertions of Rights. The Court in *Miranda* emphatically declared that if "the individual indicates in any manner at any time prior to or during questioning, that he wishes to remain silent, the interrogation must cease" and that if he "states that he wants an attorney, the interrogation must cease until an attorney is present." Whether there has been such an assertion of rights is of considerable importance; as we have seen, under the *Mosley* and *Edwards* doctrines the assertion puts the defendant into a somewhat "special" situation in terms of the subsequent dealings of the police with him.

As for assertion of the right to remain silent, any declaration of a desire to terminate the contact or inquiry (e.g., "Don't bother me") should suffice. The same is true of silence in the face of repeated questioning, or an effort to end the contact with the interrogator. On the other hand, a statement that is much more limited expressing an unwillingness to respond to a particular interrogator (e.g., "I don't want to talk to you guys"), an unwillingness to discuss the matter at a particular time (e.g., not "right now"), or an unwillingness or inability to respond to a particular inquiry (e.g., "You've done asked me a question I can't answer") is not a general claim of the privilege. Depending upon the surrounding circumstances, even a statement that itself appears to amount to an assertion of the right to remain silent (e.g., "I ain't saying nothing") may be held not to have that effect. As for assertion of the right to counsel, an indication by the defendant that he will only want counsel at some future time or for some other purpose is not an assertion of the right to counsel for *Miranda* purposes, just as a current reference by defendant to the fact that he had actually spoken to an attorney on a prior occasion is not a present invocation of the right to counsel.

Whether a request for someone other than an attorney constitutes an invocation of *Miranda* rights confronted the Supreme Court In *Fare v. Michael C.* (1979). There, a juvenile in custody on suspicion of murder was given his warnings and he then asked to have his probation officer present; this request was denied, a waiver of rights was obtained, and the juvenile then made incriminating statements. The Court held that the request to see the probation officer was not a per se invocation of *Miranda* rights (that is, not the equivalent of asking for a lawyer), but rather was merely a factor to be considered in the "totality of circumstances" determination of the voluntariness of the subsequent waiver. The majority explained that the per se aspect of *Miranda* was

> based on the unique role the lawyer plays in the adversary system of criminal justice in this country. Whether it is a minor or an adult who stands accused, the lawyer is the one person to whom society as a whole looks as the protector of the legal rights of that person in his dealing with the police and the courts. For this reason the Court fashioned in *Miranda* the rigid rule that an accused's request for an attorney is *per se* an invocation of his Fifth Amendment rights, requiring that all interrogation cease.

A probation officer, on the other hand, the Court continued, "is not trained in the law, and so is not in a position to advise the accused as to his legal rights," and is actually an adversary of the juvenile because "the probation officer is duty bound to report wrongdoing by the juvenile when it comes to his attention, even if by communication from the juvenile himself." This latter language suggests the situation would be different if a juvenile were to request the presence of a parent, but the *Fare* rule has sometimes been applied even to such facts. But certainly a different result is called for if the juvenile manifests a desire to see his parent in order to obtain an attorney.

If the defendant's conduct suffices to constitute an invocation of one of his *Miranda* rights, then there is no need for the police to seek clarification, and thus the Court held in *Smith v. Illinois* (1984) that a defendant's "*post-request* responses to further interrogation may not be used to cast retrospective doubt on the clarity of the initial request itself." This is as it should be, for otherwise police could disregard a defendant's invocation of his rights in the hope that subsequent interrogation would cast retrospective doubt upon it. The other side of the coin, it would seem, is that if the defendant's assertion *was* equivocal or ambiguous and thus not alone sufficient to constitute invocation of the defendant's *Miranda* rights, then it is *permissible* for the police to seek clarification. A significant body of lower court authority to this effect is to be found with respect to both the right to silence and the right to counsel.

But in *Davis v. United States* (1994), the Court held that in a post-waiver setting the *Edwards* rule of would not be extended so as to *require* "law enforcement officers to cease questioning immediately upon the making of an ambiguous or equivocal reference to an attorney." The Court recognized that its holding "might disadvantage some suspects who—because of fear, intimidation, lack of linguistic skills, or a variety of other reasons—will not clearly articulate their right to counsel although they actually want to have a lawyer present," but deemed that consideration to be outweighed by the fact that the "clarity and ease of application" of the bright-line *Edwards* rule (see § 5.9(f)) "would be lost" if "we were to require questioning to cease if a suspect makes a statement that might be a request for an attorney." But the *Davis* majority then went on to assert without further explanation that the cautious approach of the officers in the instant case, who obtained clarification of the ambiguous statement from the suspect and proceeded with the interrogation only when he said he did not want an attorney, was "good police practice" yet not a requirement under the *Miranda–Edwards* line of cases. (The *Davis* rule has been deemed equally applicable to post-waiver ambiguous references to the right to remain silent.)

It is possible that the defendant's invocation of his right to counsel will be limited in some way, in which case application of the *Edwards* rule is limited to the same extent, as the Supreme Court concluded in *Connecticut v. Barrett* (1987). The record there reflected a clear understanding by defendant of his *Miranda* warnings, and thus his assertion of a desire to have counsel present before making a written statement meant only that "[h]ad the police obtained such a statement without meeting the waiver standards of *Edwards*, it would clearly be inadmissible"; defendant's oral statements were not likewise barred by *Edwards*.

In *Michigan v. Jackson* (1986), the Court held that when the Sixth Amendment right to counsel has attached, "if the police initiate interrogation after a defendant's assertion, at an arraignment or similar proceeding, of the right to counsel, any waiver of the defendant's right to counsel for that police-initiated interrogation is invalid." Does it follow that such an assertion is an invocation of the *Miranda* right to counsel as to any uncharged offense? No, the Court later held in *McNeil v. Wisconsin* (1991), reasoning that invocation of the Sixth Amendment interest does not also constitute invocation of *Miranda* as to other, uncharged offenses, for a defendant "might be quite willing to speak to the police without counsel present concerning many matters, but not the matter under prosecution." Moreover, the Court noted, a contrary rule would not be wise policy, for it would mean that "most persons in pretrial custody for serious offenses would be *unapproachable* by police officers suspecting them of involvement in other crimes, *even though they have never expressed any unwillingness to be questioned.*" But *McNeil* would appear to have even broader significance given several of the Supreme Court's observations therein: that the Court had "never held that a person can invoke his *Miranda* rights anticipatorily, in a context other than 'custodial interrogation' "; that "[m]ost rights must be asserted when the government seeks to take the action they protect against"; and that the Court's conclusion a *Miranda* assertion of a right to counsel remains in effect "does not necessarily mean that we will allow it to be asserted initially outside the context of custodial interrogation, with similar future effect." Several cases have taken this to mean that for there to be a valid assertion of *Miranda* rights, the authorities must be conducting custodial interrogation, or such interrogation must be imminent.

§ 5.10 *Miranda:* Nature of Offense, Interrogator, and Proceedings

(a) Questioning About Minor Offense. Although the Supreme Court in *Miranda* gave no indication that its holding regarding warning and waiver of rights prior to custodial interrogation was somehow limited to serious cases, a number of lower courts concluded that such a limitation existed, so that *Miranda* was deemed inapplicable to misdemeanors or at least to traffic offenses. But in *Berkemer v. McCarty* (1984), where a unanimous Court rejected any such exception to *Miranda,* the Court first noted that the exception for misdemeanor traffic offenses proposed there "would substantially undermine" a "crucial advantage" of the *Miranda* doctrine—its clarity. Police would often be uncertain in a particular instance what the magnitude of the crime was and consequently whether warnings were required, and courts would become involved in "doctrinal complexities" concerning, for example, when a misdemeanor investigation escalates into or is a pretext for a felony investigation. The Court then concluded that the purposes of *Miranda*—relieving the inherent compelling pressure of custodial interrogation, and freeing courts from the necessity of making frequent case-by-case voluntariness determinations—are also served in the context of police interrogation related to minor traffic offenses.

(b) Questioning by Private Citizen. In the *Miranda* case the Court defined interrogation as "questioning initiated by law enforcement officers." Because of this and also because of the general doctrine that state action is a prerequisite to application of constitutional protections, it is clear that *Miranda* does not govern interrogation by private citizens acting on their own. This covers such instances as where the defendant was questioned by the victim, an arresting private citizen, a friend, a relative, or a newspaper reporter. Even if the private citizen falsely held himself out to the defendant as a police officer, so that it may be said the defendant was under just as much pressure as if his interrogator had been an actual officer, *Miranda* still does not apply because of the absence of state action.

That situation must be distinguished from one in which the defendant is questioned by a person who is not a government employee but who has employment responsibilities of a law enforcement nature, such as a department store security guard. In such circumstances, it might be argued that the protections of *Miranda* would be appropriate, for such security personnel also utilize detention, privacy, the appearance of authority, and psychologically coercive methods to facilitate fruitful interrogation. Moreover, it could well be contended that in such cases the "state action" hurdle may be overcome by a public function analysis, i.e., that persons performing functions essentially like those ordinarily left to governmental agencies are also subject to constitutional restraints. However, the courts have rather consistently held that such persons as security officers, store detectives, railroad detectives, insurance investigators, and private investigators are not required to comply with the *Miranda* procedures. A contrary result has sometimes been reached if the interrogator, though then serving private security functions, has been given police powers by a governmental unit.

Some courts have concluded that the private person exception does not apply when the person is at the time acting as an agent of the police. Thus, *Miranda* has been held to govern where such persons as the victim, a private security officer, the defendant's parents, the defendant's friend, or the victim's attorney questioned the defendant at the behest of the police. But, more compelling is the view that unless a person realizes he is dealing with a police agent, their efforts to elicit incriminating statements from him do not constitute "police interrogation" within the meaning of *Miranda*. It is the impact on the suspect's mind of the interplay between police interrogation and police that creates "custodial interrogation" within the meaning of *Miranda*. This, of course, is precisely the theory that was adopted by the Supreme Court in *Illinois v. Perkins* (1990) regarding the very similar "jail plant" situation (see § 5.7(c)).

(c) **Questioning by Non-police Official.** In cases where the interrogator is a public employee and thus not outside the "state action" requirement, but yet is someone other than a police officer, the *Miranda* definition of interrogation as "questioning initiated by law enforcement officers" takes on added significance. Though the extent to which the decisions rest upon this particular point is often clouded by uncertainty as to whether the defendant was even in a "custodial" situation, the courts have generally held that government agents not primarily charged with enforcement of the criminal law are under no obligation to comply with *Miranda*. Thus, at least where the official has not been given police powers, *Miranda* has been held inapplicable to questioning by school officials, welfare investigators, medical personnel, prison counselors, and parole or probation officers.

The notion that *Miranda* does not inevitably apply whenever questions are asked in a custodial setting by a government employee is an appealing one, for not all such interrogations would seem to have a coercive impact comparable to the police questioning that concerned the Court in *Miranda*. This is not to say, however, that the decisions referred to above are beyond dispute, for the Supreme Court in *Mathis v. United States* (1968) seems to have rejected the notion that *Miranda* applies only to criminal law enforcers. In *Mathis* the questioning was by an IRS agent and—more importantly for present purposes—one who was a "civil investigator * * * required, whenever and as soon as he finds 'definite indications of fraud or criminal potential,' to refer a case to the Intelligence Division for investigation by a different agent who works regularly on criminal matters." Such a referral occurred eight days *after* the questioning in issue, and there was no suggestion that it was improperly delayed, but yet the Court held that *Miranda* applied. The *Mathis* majority acknowledged that "tax investigations differ from investigations of murder, robbery, and other crimes" because they "may be initiated for the purpose of a civil action rather than criminal prosecution," but then concluded this was not a controlling difference because, "as the investigating revenue agent was compelled to admit, there was always the possibility during his investigation that his work would end up in a criminal prosecution." Additional proof that the Court does not view *Miranda* as limited to interrogation by police officers is provided by *Estelle v. Smith* (1981), holding *Miranda* applicable to a psychiatric examination. The Court declared: "That respondent was questioned by a psychiatrist designated by the trial court to conduct a neutral competency examination, rather than by a police officer, government informant, or prosecuting attorney is immaterial."

Viewed in terms of the theory underlying *Miranda,* neither *Mathis* nor *Smith* is particularly objectionable. Mathis was doubtless under just as much pressure to talk to the "civil investigator" who visited him in jail as the criminal investigator who called on him later, and certainly Smith would feel compelled to converse with a psychiatrist appointed by the court to examine him. Because that is so and because the Court in these two cases did not explore the issue in greater depth, those decisions cannot be read as settling that *all* public-official interrogation of those in custody is governed by *Miranda.* They do, however, lend support to the conclusion some courts have reached that custodial interrogation (other than routine interviews) by a probation or parole officer is governed by *Miranda* because the probationer or parolee is under heavy psychological pressure to cooperate with one who can recommend his imprisonment. They also support the conclusion that questioning by any government employee comes within *Miranda* whenever prosecution of the defendant being questioned is among the purposes, definite or contingent, for which the information is elicited, as will often be manifested by the fact the questioner's duties include the investigation or reporting of crimes.

(d) Questioning by Foreign Police. Foreign police, even when investigating an American citizen, can hardly be expected to know and follow all of the procedures that would be required if that individual were under investigation in his own country. Thus, even if (as commonly assumed) a defendant may be entitled to keep out of a prosecution in this country a confession by him that was involuntarily given to a foreign policeman, he may not obtain the suppression of a confession obtained by such an official merely because the *Miranda* warnings were not given. This result is ordinarily explained on the same grounds customarily given for not suppressing evidence obtained in a foreign search: the exclusion would have little if any deterrent effect upon foreign officials.

This is not to say that *Miranda* has no extraterritorial effect. Law enforcement officers of this country are bound by *Miranda* even when interrogating on foreign soil. Moreover, it has been recognized that foreign police are governed by *Miranda* when they are acting as the agents of United States law enforcement authorities. But in this context it will take a bit more to establish the requisite agency than when police obtain the assistance of private citizens in this country. This is because cooperative efforts among police agencies of different countries is a natural and desirable arrangement, and thus should not be inherently suspect as a likely effort to accomplish indirectly that which could not be done directly. At least where the foreign police were also serving law enforcement interests of their own country, it is not enough that American officers have played a substantial role in events leading up to the arrest or that the cooperation has the character of a joint venture.

(e) Proceedings at Which Confession Offered. Finally, there is the question of the kinds of proceedings at which a person may object to receipt of his incriminating statements because they were obtained in violation of the *Miranda* procedures. Because *Miranda* is grounded in the Fifth Amendment privilege against self-incrimination, this presents a question of exactly what constitutes incrimination within the meaning of the Amendment. As a general matter, this constitutional provision itself supplies the answer, for it declares that no person "shall be compelled in any criminal case to be a witness against himself." This most certainly means, as occurred in *Miranda,* that an improperly obtained confession is subject to suppression when offered in a criminal trial as evidence of defendant's guilt of the crime charged. Some of the cases discussed earlier holding *Miranda* inapplicable to certain minor offenses, though ordinarily explained in terms of the subject matter of the interrogation, might be read as meaning *Miranda* rights cannot be invoked in a criminal trial of a minor offense. If so viewed, they are even more clearly in error.

What if the confession is tendered only at the sentencing stage of the trial? This issue confronted the Court in *Estelle v. Smith* (1981), for there defendant's statements to an examining psychiatrist were received at the penalty phase of a capital case on the crucial issue of his future dangerousness. The state argued that this raised no Fifth Amendment issue because "incrimination is complete once guilt has been adjudicated," but the Court could "discern no basis to distinguish between the guilt and penalty phases of respondent's capital murder trial so far as the protection of the Fifth Amendment privilege is concerned," given that an "effort by the State to compel respondent to testify against his will at the sentencing hearing clearly would contravene the Fifth Amendment." This point, fully consistent with the Court's analysis in *Miranda,* indicates that *Smith* is not limited to capital case penalty phase hearings, for it is more generally true that the privilege protects against use of compelled testimony in setting the sentence.

Smith also teaches that *Miranda* cannot be invoked at every proceeding somehow connected to a criminal case. The state attempted to exempt the case from the reach of *Miranda* by pointing out that the psychiatrist's examination of defendant had been undertaken in the first instance for the beneficial purpose of determining if defendant was competent to stand trial. The Court quite properly responded that this made no difference given the use actually made of defendant's statements. But the Court then added that "if the application of Dr. Grigson's findings had been confined to serving" the function of "ensuring that respondent understood the charges against him and was capable of assisting in his defense," then "no Fifth Amendment issue would have arisen." In other words, *Miranda* could not be invoked at a competency-to-stand-trial hearing. Similarly, it appears that *Miranda* has no application at a parole or probation revocation proceeding, though by virtue of *Smith* the result would be otherwise at a probation revocation proceeding involving deferred sentencing. And in *Baxter v. Palmigiano* (1976), holding that "prison disciplinary hearings are not criminal proceedings" for Fifth Amendment purposes, the Court asserted in passing that *Miranda* had no relevance in that context.

On the other hand, the *Smith* approach would appear to make it certain that *Miranda* applies in juvenile delinquency proceedings, for the Supreme Court earlier held in *In re Gault* (1967) that the Fifth Amendment privilege is otherwise applicable in juvenile court proceedings. In explaining this result in *Gault,* the Court asserted at one point that the "Constitution guarantees that no person shall be 'compelled' to be a witness against himself when he is threatened with a deprivation of his liberty," a statement that might be read as saying the Fifth Amendment privilege (and thus *Miranda*) is applicable in any proceeding that could result in a deprivation of liberty. But *Gault* does not go this far. In *Allen v. Illinois* (1986), the Court characterized *"Gault's* sweeping statement" as "plainly not good law," and went on to hold that admissions obtained in violation of *Miranda* requirements were thus properly received in a sexually dangerous persons proceeding against the petitioner. This conclusion was grounded in the fact that the applicable statute had a "civil label" and in addition was not "punitive either in purpose or effect" because "the State has disavowed any interest in punishment, provided for the treatment of those it commits, and established a system under which committed persons may be released after the briefest time in confinement. The Act thus does not appear to promote either of 'the traditional aims of punishment—retribution and deterrence.' Neither the fact that the statute applied only to those charged with crime nor the fact that it required many of the safeguards applicable to criminal trials made such proceedings 'criminal' within the meaning of the Fifth Amendment."

Chapter 6

IDENTIFICATION PROCEDURES

Table of Sections

---

§ 6.1 Introduction

(a) The Problem of Misidentification. Eyewitness identification can be a powerful piece of evidence in a criminal prosecution. It is frequently an essential piece of evidence as well, as more scientific forms of identification evidence, such as fingerprint and handwriting analyses, are not always available. Yet it is well known that eyewitness evidence is inherently suspect and that suggestive procedures may prejudicially affect the ultimate identification. A pretrial identification proceeding may increase the risk of mistaken identification, as it occurs outside the courtroom and therefore is beyond the immediate supervision of the court. There is considerable evidence that th problem of misidentification is a serious one; especially telling is the fact that mistaken eyewitness identifications were a major cause in sixty of the first eighty-two DNA exonerations handled by the Innocence Project in New York.

(b) The Causes of Misidentification. Identification testimony has at least three components. First, witnessing a crime, whether as a victim or a bystander, involves perception of an event actually occurring. Second, the witness must memorize details of the event. Third, the witness must be able to recall and communicate accurately. Dangers of unreliability in eyewitness testimony arise at each of these three stages of the identification process, for whenever people attempt to acquire, retain and retrieve information accurately they are limited by normal human fallibilities and suggestive influences. *Perception* is a highly selective process in which details later shown to be important can be missed, and perceptual inaccuracies are often caused by the brain's inherent limitations, the circumstances of the observation, plus anxiety and fear. *Memory* is constantly undergoing change; some details are forgotten while others are added or altered to resolve the cognitive dissonance that arises when new information differs from the original memory representation. *Recall* is another source of errors, for a narrative description unprompted by questions results in incomplete information retrieval, while structured questioning undertaken to achieve completeness causes responses to become more inaccurate.

(c) The Supreme Court's Response. Traditionally, eyewitness identification testimony has been readily accepted in American criminal trials. The witness will be asked if he sees in the courtroom the person who committed the crime, and will almost invariably answer in the affirmative and identify the defendant. Moreover, it is now generally accepted that the hearsay doctrine does not bar receipt as substantive evidence of the fact that this witness on a prior occasion, such as at a police lineup, identified the defendant as the perpetrator of the crime charged. Indeed, this earlier identification is likely to be the most important of the two.

Except in the unusual case in which the identification testimony would be the fruit of an illegal arrest of the person identified (see § 8.4(d)), there was for many years no solid constitutional basis upon which an objection to the receipt of eyewitness identification testimony could be grounded. In contrast to the situation that obtains as to the defendant's confession, the Fifth Amendment privilege against self-incrimination does not afford a criminal suspect a right of nonparticipation in identification procedures. But in 1967 the Supreme Court recognized two constitutional grounds upon which such testimony could sometimes be successfully challenged. In *United States v. Wade* (1967), the absence of counsel at a post-indictment lineup was held to make inadmissible at trial testimony about the lineup identification and also identification testimony at trial that was the fruit of the earlier identification. But the Court has since given *Wade* a narrow reading, and consequently it has had a limited impact. In *Stovall v. Denno* (1967), the Court held that identification testimony must be suppressed if the confrontation "was so unnecessarily suggestive and conducive to irreparable mistaken identification" as to constitute a denial of due process of law. *Stovall* has likewise been given a limited application, and consequently some commentators believe that a need exists for additional safeguards regarding potentially unreliable eyewitness testimony.

§ 6.2 The Privilege Against Self–Incrimination

(a) **The *Schmerber* Rule.** In the case of *Schmerber v. California* (1966), the Supreme Court upheld the taking of a blood sample by a physician at police direction from the defendant over his objection after his arrest for drunken driving. Among the grounds upon which the defendant challenged the admission of the blood sample into evidence against him was that it violated his Fifth Amendment privilege not to be "compelled in any criminal case to be a witness against himself." The Court rejected this contention, holding that "the privilege protects an accused only from being compelled to testify against himself, or otherwise provide the State with evidence of a testimonial or communicative nature, and that the withdrawal of blood and use of the analysis in question in this case did not involve compulsion to these ends." As the Court elaborated, "the privilege has never been given the full scope which the values it helps to protect suggest," but instead is limited to those situations in which the state seeks to submerge those values by obtaining evidence from the defendant "by the cruel, simple expedient of compelling it from his own mouth." This explained, the Court added, why "both federal and state courts have usually held that it offers no protection against compulsion to submit to fingerprinting, photographing, or measurements, to write or speak for identification, to appear in court, to stand, to assume a stance, to walk, or to make a particular gesture."

(b) Application to Identification Procedures. The Supreme Court held in *United States v. Wade* (1967) that requiring a defendant to appear in a lineup and to say "put the money in the bag" did not violate his privilege against self-incrimination. The *Wade* majority reasoned: "We have no doubt that compelling the accused merely to exhibit his person for observation by a prosecution witness prior to trial involves no compulsion of the accused to give evidence having testimonial significance. * * * Similarly, compelling Wade to speak within hearing distance of the witnesses, even to utter words purportedly uttered by the robber, was not compulsion to utter statements of a 'testimonial' nature; he was required to use his voice as an identifying physical characteristic, not to speak his guilt." On like reasoning the Court held in the companion case of *Gilbert v. California* (1967) that the taking of handwriting exemplars did not violate the defendant's rights.

The dissenters in *Wade* and *Gilbert* argued that *Schmerber* was wrongly decided, in that the privilege was designed to bar the government from forcing a person to supply proof of his own crime. Alternatively, assuming *Schmerber* was controlling, the dissenters claimed the instant cases were distinguishable in that in each of them the defendant had been compelled "actively to cooperate—to accuse himself by a volitional act." But the majority's conclusion that the privilege does not necessarily apply even when the defendant is put into an active rather than a passive posture still prevails, as is indicated by the fact that the Supreme Court has since reaffirmed that there is no Fifth Amendment privilege not to give handwriting exemplars or voice exemplars. The lower courts have followed the *Schmerber–Wade–Gilbert* view and have thus held the Fifth Amendment privilege inapplicable to a great variety of identification procedures. Included are fingerprinting, physical examination, examination of the defendant by X-rays or ultraviolet light, taking casts of defendant's teeth or requiring him to show his teeth, requiring the defendant to remove his glasses or to put on a hat, shoe, jacket, mask or wig and beard, or requiring him to display a limp or a tattoo.

(c) Refusal to Cooperate. What happens if a defendant refuses to cooperate in an identification procedure requiring his active participation? One possibility is that the prosecutor may be permitted to comment on the refusal to cooperate. If the identification procedure in which the defendant has refused to participate or cooperate, such as a lineup or taking of exemplars, is not protected by the Fifth Amendment, then of course there is no right to refuse and thus the act of refusal is not itself a compelled communication. Rather, that refusal is considered circumstantial evidence of consciousness of guilt just as is escape from custody, a false alibi, or flight. But if the refusal to speak follows the giving of the *Miranda* right-to-silence warning to the defendant, and that warning did not clearly distinguish between speech in terms of communications and speech for voice identification, then the silence is insolubly ambiguous and thus cannot be treated as some evidence of defendant's guilt.

Yet another possibility is that the police will proceed to conduct the identification procedure over the defendant's objection. It has been suggested, however, that the use of force to compel the accused to mount the stage and remain there would make the proceeding unduly suggestive and thus a violation of due process under *Stovall v. Denno* (1967). But since the *Stovall* rule extends only to identifications that are "unnecessarily suggestive," it may be argued in response that the suggestiveness has been made necessary by the defendant's resistance. Indeed, it has been reasoned that a refusal to participate in a lineup would justify the use by the police of a showup procedure in which defendant is alone viewed by the witness and, if *United States v. Wade* (1967) applies, in which substitute counsel is provided. Although it has also been suggested that the use of force by the police in carrying out the identification procedure may be sufficiently shocking to the conscience of the Court to require exclusion of the real evidence so obtained under the due process rule of *Rochin v. California* (1952), it is not objectionable that the authorities have used only so much force as is necessary to overcome the defendant's resistance.

(d) Change in Appearance. A related question is what may be done in response to a suspect's drastic alteration of his appearance between the time of arrest (or the occurrence of the crime) and his appearance in a lineup. One possibility is that this alteration will be brought to the attention of the jury for consideration as some evidence of defendant's guilt. Courts have concluded that evidence of defendant's alteration in appearance may be received, and even that it is appropriate to give an instruction to the jury that the evidence may be considered an indication of consciousness of guilt.

A second possibility is that the identification procedure will be conducted in such a way as to simulate the defendant's prior appearance. Illustrative is *People v. Cwikla* (1979), where defendant appeared at a pretrial identification hearing with his head and face newly shaved, allegedly for medical reasons. On application of the prosecutor, the defendant was required to don a wig and false beard for purposes of the identification hearing. Though the defendant claimed this violated his privilege against self-incrimination, the court ruled "it was not error to compel defendant to conform his appearance at the lineup to his appearance at the time of the crime." On like reasoning, other courts have held it lawful to require the defendant to dye his hair, to wear a wig, to wear an artificial goatee, and even to submit to extensive work by makeup experts who changed his appearance to conform to an earlier photograph of him. In the case of more severe measures (e.g., requiring defendant to shave his beard because he had been clean-shaven at the time of the crime) the prosecution bears the burden of establishing substantive justification for action that would deprive the defendant of his constitutionally protected right to determine his personal appearance.

§ 6.3   The Right to Counsel and to Confrontation

(a) **Procedures Required.** In *United States v. Wade* (1967), the Supreme Court confronted the question of "whether courtroom identifications of an accused at trial are to be excluded from evidence because the accused was exhibited to the witnesses before trial at a post-indictment lineup conducted for identification purposes without notice to and in the absence of the accused's appointed counsel." The defendant had been placed in a lineup made up of himself and five or six other prisoners, and each person had been required to wear strips of tape on each side of his face and to say "put the money in the bag," the words used by the perpetrator of a recent bank robbery. This lineup was conducted over a month after defendant had been indicted for the robbery and fifteen days after defense counsel had been appointed, but counsel was not notified of and was not present at the identification proceeding. At defendant's trial, two bank employees identified defendant as the robber and testified that they had earlier identified him in the lineup. The Court ruled that those procedures had been constitutionally inadequate, and thus concluded "that for Wade the post-indictment lineup was a critical stage of the prosecution at which he was 'as much entitled to such aid [of counsel] * * * as at the trial itself.' * * * Thus both Wade and his counsel should have been notified of the impending lineup, and counsel's presence should have been a requisite to conduct of the lineup, absent an 'intelligent waiver.' "

The lineup was a "critical stage," the Court elaborated, because "the confrontation compelled by the State between the accused and the victim or witnesses to a crime to elicit identification evidence is peculiarly riddled with innumerable dangers and variable factors which might seriously, even crucially, derogate from a fair trial." As the Court explained, under past lineup practices, the defense was often unable "meaningfully to attack the credibility of the witness' courtroom identification" because of several factors that militate against developing fully the circumstances of a prior lineup identification by that witness. In particular: (1) other participants in the lineup are often police officers, or, if not, their names are rarely recorded or divulged at trial; (2) neither witnesses nor lineup participants are apt to be alert for or schooled in the detection of prejudicial conditions; (3) the suspect (often staring into bright lights) may not be in a position to observe prejudicial conditions, and, in any event, might not detect them because of his emotional tension; (4) even if the suspect observes abuse, he may nonetheless be reluctant to take the stand and open up the admission of prior convictions; and (5) even if he takes the stand, his version of what transpired at the lineup is unlikely to be accepted if it conflicts with police testimony. Moreover, the Court pointed out, the need to learn what occurred at the lineup is great; the risk of improper suggestion is substantial, and once the witness has picked out the accused in a lineup, he is unlikely to go back on his word in court.

The intended constitutional foundation of the *Wade* decision was not entirely clear from the Court's decision. The Court talked about the lineup being "a critical stage" at which defendant was as much entitled to counsel as at trial, which would seem to indicate that *Wade* was grounded in the Sixth Amendment right to counsel. But in explaining why this was so, the *Wade* majority referred to the fact that "presence of counsel itself can often * * * assure a meaningful confrontation at trial." Indeed, the Court repeatedly referred to the Sixth Amendment right to confrontation and cross-examination in *Wade*, suggesting that the decision was grounded in the Sixth Amendment right of confrontation and cross-examination, with counsel being required simply to give sufficient protection to that other right. But when the choice between these two theories later became important in determining the scope of *Wade*, the Supreme Court opted for the narrower right to counsel theory (see § 6.3(b)).

The *Wade* majority emphasized that lineups as they were customarily conducted constituted a "critical stage" for right to counsel purposes, but that it might be otherwise if appropriate reforms were adopted: "Legislative or other regulations, such as those of local police departments, which eliminate the risks of abuse and unintentional suggestion at lineup proceedings and the impediments to meaningful confrontation at trial may also remove the basis for regarding the stage as 'critical.' " Just what substitute procedures would suffice, so that the lineup could be constitutionally conducted without counsel, is not entirely clear. The answer may depend to some extent upon precisely what the function of counsel at the lineup is thought to be, about which there is less than complete agreement (see § 6.3(e)). But in any event it seems clear that an adequate substitute must at least provide for a means whereby the defendant can have an opportunity at trial effectively to reconstruct the procedure by which he was identified in a pretrial lineup.

(b) Time of Identification. Because both *Wade* and the companion case of *Gilbert v. California* (1967) involved lineups held after indictment and appointment of counsel, lower courts were in disagreement as to whether counsel was required at any pre-indictment identifications. The issue was finally resolved by the Supreme Court in the case of *Kirby v. Illinois* (1972), which involved a police station identification of the defendant shortly after his warrantless arrest and before he had been formally charged in any way. The Court held that the *Wade–Gilbert* rule applies only to identifications occurring "at or after the initiation of adversary judicial criminal proceedings—whether by way of formal charge, preliminary hearing, indictment, information, or arraignment." The rationale was that the constitutional right to counsel has traditionally been so limited, and with good reason, in that only after such initiation is a defendant "faced with the prosecutorial forces of organized society, and immersed in the intricacies of substantive and procedural criminal law." Thus, some have objected, the Court in *Kirby* managed to limit *Wade* by treating it as a "pure" right to counsel case, necessitating a determination of when that right begins, instead of, as it seemed to be, a case grounded in the Sixth Amendment right to confrontation at trial, which is threatened no matter when the pretrial identification occurs. As a result, so the argument goes, the right to counsel is afforded the defendant where he least needs it, namely, for post-arraignment lineups typically conducted to refresh uncertain identifications previously made.

On the other hand, if one accepts the *Kirby* right to counsel characterization, then the ruling there is certainly an understandable one. Even accepting the premise that the need for counsel is often equivalent in the post-indictment and pre-indictment lineup, it does not necessarily follow that appointment of counsel is constitutionally required in both situations, for the Sixth Amendment does not provide for counsel at every stage in which counsel's assistance is helpful. Moreover, that characterization of *Wade* perhaps can best be explained on the ground that the Court deemed it impractical to impose a counsel requirement on *all* police-conducted identification proceedings, especially on-the-scene confrontations occurring just after the commission of the crime. By treating the issue solely in right to counsel terms, it was possible to exclude the earlier stages of the criminal process from the strictures of the *Wade* procedures, a limitation that would be much more difficult to rationalize under the right of confrontation theory. To some, this limitation is advantageous because police are encouraged and enabled to conduct identification proceedings more expeditiously, at a time when the recall of witnesses will be fresher and thus the identifications will generally be more reliable.

Except for the language quoted earlier, the Court in *Kirby* did not explore exactly what it takes to "initiate" adversary judicial criminal proceedings and thus bring the *Wade–Gilbert* rule into play. But that language was later relied upon by the Court in *Moore v. Illinois* (1977), where it was held that an identification at a preliminary hearing was governed by *Wade*. The Court in *Moore* emphasized that it was "plain that 'the government ha[d] committed itself to prosecute'" by that time and that defendant "faced counsel for the State" at that time. By this reasoning, it seems clear that the *Wade* right to counsel comes into existence even before the preliminary hearing. On the other hand, it seems clear under the *Kirby–Moore* test that the *Wade* right to counsel does not ripen merely because the defendant has first been subjected to a warrantless custodial arrest. This means that a person so arrested may be viewed in a lineup without the presence of counsel if that occurs prior to the time of his appearance before a magistrate, except in those jurisdictions providing as a matter of state law for a broader right to counsel at identification proceedings. And if a person is summoned to appear before a grand jury for purposes of being identified, there is again no *Wade–Gilbert* right to counsel, as the government was still in the process of investigation. There is a split of authority on the question of whether the issuance of an arrest warrant marks the initiation of adversary judicial proceedings within the meaning of *Kirby*. This may be attributable in part to the fact that a document called a "complaint" is sometimes used as a basis for issuance of an arrest warrant and on other occasions is utilized to manifest the prosecutor's preindictment charging decision. But where the complaint simply serves to provide the probable cause to issue an arrest warrant, which may be needed for reasons having nothing to do with charging (see § 2.6(a)), it makes no sense under the *Kirby–Moore* formula to view either the issuance of the warrant or the arrest of the defendant pursuant to the warrant as marking the commencement of the *Wade* right to counsel. Moreover, if the right to counsel has not otherwise attached, it does not attach merely because the defendant is represented by counsel.

(c) Nature of Identification Procedure. Regardless of when they occur, certain types of identification procedures will not trigger the right to counsel. For example, as held in *United States v. Ash* (1973), there is no right to have counsel present when the police show photographs of the defendant and others to witnesses, and this is so even if the defendant has already been indicted.

Throughout the expansion of the constitutional right to counsel to certain pretrial proceedings, said the majority in *Ash,* "the function of the lawyer has remained essentially the same as his function at trial," which is to give the accused "aid in coping with legal problems or assistance in meeting his adversary." This being so, the Court reasoned that there is no such right at photo-identification, as unlike a lineup there is no "trial-like confrontation" involving the "presence of the accused." Although the defendant in *Wade* had not been confronted with legal questions, the lineup offered opportunities for the authorities to take advantage of the accused, a problem that the Court in *Ash* concluded did not exist with respect to identification by use of a photo display. Moreover, the *Ash* majority emphasized that absence of counsel from the photo-identification would not impair effective cross-examination at trial as would absence from a lineup, for photographic identifications are relatively easy to reconstruct.

Justice Stewart, concurring in *Ash,* objected to the majority's distinction of *Wade* as a situation in which the lawyer is giving advice or assistance to the defendant at the lineup. He construed the lawyer's role to be that of "an observer," but then concluded that such a role need not be performed with respect to photo-identification, as in that context "there are few possibilities for unfair suggestiveness." Certainly the notion in *Ash* that the function of counsel in a pretrial setting is "the same as his function at trial" is a dubious one, for in post-indictment lineups, it is not readily apparent what immediate assistance an attorney can provide. He cannot stop the lineup or see that it be conducted in a certain manner, nor can he give legal advice, proffer defenses, or advance arguments. Rather, his only function is as a trained observer. The critical question in *Ash,* therefore, was really whether such a "trained observer" was needed at identifications made by examination of photographs. Justice Stewart did perceive this as the issue but, as noted, answered in the negative; the three dissenters, however, presented a most forceful argument to the contrary. They noted that the risk of impermissible suggestiveness is equally present in photo-identifications as it is in lineups, and that in the former situation there is even less likelihood any irregularities will ever come to light because even the accused is not present to observe them. Moreover, photographic identifications lack scientific precision and are difficult to fully reconstruct at trial.

One unfortunate consequence of the *Ash* case is that police are encouraged to resort to photo-identification in lieu of lineups in order to obviate the necessity to have defense counsel present at the identification. This is unfortunate, as a photographic identification, even when properly obtained, is clearly inferior to a properly obtained corporeal identification. Some state courts have appreciated this problem and thus, as a matter of local law, have gone beyond *Ash* in some way. One view is that photo-identification is an improper identification procedure when the suspect is in custody and could be placed in a lineup, while another is that in such circumstances a photo-identification must be conducted in the presence of defense counsel.

Whether the lawyer is viewed as an advisor and advocate or as merely a trained observer, it is clear that the right to counsel does not attach to more scientific identification procedures, such as the taking of a blood sample. As the Court explained in *United States v. Wade* (1967): "Knowledge of the techniques of science and technology is sufficiently available, and the variables in techniques few enough, that the accused has the opportunity for a meaningful confrontation of the Government's case at trial through the ordinary processes of cross-examination of the Government's expert witnesses and the presentation of the evidence of his own experts." The procedures for taking and analyzing blood samples, fingerprints, clothing, hair and the like are distinguishable from lineups and photographic arrays in that they do not depend for their reliability on the recollection of a witness. Rather, their reliability depends on the scientific validity of the techniques and the skill and precision with which they are administered. The risk of suggestiveness present in eyewitness identification simply does not extend to such procedures. On similar reasoning, the Supreme Court held in *Gilbert v. California* (1967) that the taking of handwriting exemplars is not a critical stage entitling the defendant to the assistance of counsel, for "there is minimal risk that the absence of counsel might derogate from his right to a fair trial." While the suspect might benefit from counsel's advice as to whether to give the exemplars or refuse and suffer the consequences, this does not involve a constitutional right to which the right to counsel might be linked.

Although the *Wade* holding is stated in terms of a right to counsel at a "lineup," unquestionably it extends beyond that. In *Moore v. Illinois* (1977), the holding in *Wade* was more expansively stated as being "that a corporeal identification is a critical stage of a criminal prosecution for Sixth Amendment purposes," and thus the Court concluded that there was a right to counsel at a one-on-one showup. Indeed, as the Court observed, such a procedure is so highly suggestive that the need for counsel is especially great. The identification in *Moore* occurred at a preliminary hearing when the prosecutor asked a rape victim to point out her assailant in the courtroom, but the Court rejected the contention that there is no right to counsel at an identification procedure conducted in the course of a judicial proceeding. Though the more formal proceeding involved in *Moore* may have reduced substantially the chances of undetectable suggestiveness as compared with the typical police lineup, this was offset in the eyes of the Court by the fact that in the judicial setting the lawyer could more readily have caused something to be done to avoid the suggestiveness.

Finally, in the case of corporeal identification there is the question of whether the *Wade* right to counsel applies only to the time of the viewing of the defendant by the witness or whether it extends as well to the time at which the witness communicates to the police the fact of identification. There is much to be said for the broader view, which some courts have adopted, as otherwise the defendant has no way of knowing whether the witness was improperly led, or whether the witness was hesitant or unsure in his identification. There is, however, authority to the contrary, and it seems more consistent with the approach taken by the Supreme Court in *Ash*.

(d) Waiver or Substitution of Counsel. In *United States v. Wade* (1967), the Supreme Court indicated that there could be an "intelligent waiver" of counsel, in which case presence of an attorney at the identification procedures would not be required. Although this may seem consistent with the waiver permitted in *Miranda v. Arizona* (1966), it might be questioned whether the right to counsel at an identification should be subject to waiver. The argument is that while waiver of counsel under *Miranda* serves the legitimate objective of permitting the suspect to bear witness to the truth, no comparable value is served by waiver under *Wade*. However, the lower courts have consistently held that the right to counsel at identification procedures can be waived, provided of course the waiver is both intelligent and voluntary. Waiver of counsel for another purpose will not suffice, and thus a waiver following receipt of the *Miranda* warnings does not carry over to the lineup.

The *Wade* opinion does not dwell upon the question of what is required to show an effective waiver, although it seems likely that an approach similar to that dictated by *Miranda* is to be followed here. This means that a "heavy burden" rests upon the government to show an express waiver following the requisite warnings, which at least must include notice to the defendant that he has a right to counsel for this particular purpose and that counsel will be provided for him if he is indigent. The better practice is also to advise the defendant that the lineup will be delayed for a reasonable time after the lawyer is notified, in order to allow the lawyer to appear. Because the privilege against self-incrimination does not extend to identification procedures, surely there is no need to tell the defendant that he has a right not to participate or that any identification will be used against him at trial.

While there is language in *Wade* which, if read literally, would seem to support the view that waiver of counsel must occur in the presence of counsel, it is fully consistent with waiver of counsel in the confessions area to conclude that the right is that of the defendant rather than the lawyer and that consequently it may be waived by the defendant alone. Indeed, there is a sense in which a broader variety of waiver must be recognized here than in the confession context. The police have no right to require a suspect to converse with them, but surely there is a police-prosecution-public interest in a prompt lineup of a person who has been lawfully arrested. This being so, a defendant who is not indigent and thus could hire a lawyer but unreasonably delays in doing so may be deemed to have waived his right to counsel at the identification proceeding.

The Court in *Wade,* in response to the argument that a counsel requirement would "forestall prompt identifications," deliberately opted to "leave open the question whether the presence of substitute counsel might not suffice where notification and presence of the suspect's own counsel would result in prejudicial delay." Given the state's interest in a prompt lineup, it would seem that substitute counsel would suffice where he was sufficiently apprised of the circumstances so as to be able effectively to represent the defendant. On the other hand, it is not sufficient that there was a lawyer present at the lineup for some other purpose, such as to represent another individual, for that attorney could not be expected to be alert to any problems that existed as to the defendant. Moreover, police claims that they had somehow provided substitute counsel are not likely to be favorably received by the courts where it appears the police had taken their good time in arranging the lineup, so that no prejudicial delay could have resulted from permitting defendant to engage his own attorney.

(e) Role of Counsel. *Wade* stresses the need to protect the defendant's "right meaningfully to cross-examine the witnesses against him and to have effective assistance of counsel at the trial itself," while in *Ash* the *Wade* rule was explained on the basis that "[c]ounsel was seen by the Court as being more sensitive to, and aware of, suggestive influences than the accused himself, and better able to reconstruct the events at trial." This indicates that the lawyer is to be only an observer at the lineup so that, at the trial, he would then be in a position to decide on the basis of his earlier observations whether it is tactically wise to bring out the lineup identification in order to cast doubt upon an in-court identification. And, if he decides to do so, he will better know what questions to ask the witness about the circumstances of the lineup. If the lawyer is to serve as an observer because, as the Court indicated in *Wade* and *Ash,* he is better able than the defendant and others present to recognize suggestive influences, then this would suggest that it may well be necessary for him to take the stand himself to testify as to what went on at the lineup. This places the defense attorney in a dilemma. Under the Model Rules of Professional Conduct, if a lawyer learns he will be required to be a witness at trial for his client, except as to an uncontested issue, he should withdraw from the case unless doing so "would work substantial hardship on the client."

A second position with respect to defense counsel's function is that the identification procedure is to be a fully adversary proceeding in which the counsel for the suspect may make objections and proposals, which if they are proper or even reasonable must be respected. Support for this position can be found in the Supreme Court cases. *Wade* says that "presence of counsel itself can often avert prejudice" and assist law enforcement "by preventing the infiltration of taint in the prosecution's identification evidence," and this prompted the dissenters to find in *Wade* "an implicit invitation to counsel to suggest rules for the lineup and to manage and produce it as best he can." Similarly, in *Ash* the Court asserts that "[c]ounsel present at lineup would be able to remove disabilities of the accused." If the defense lawyer is to have an active role then, as a matter of tactics, he will have to decide in each case whether to try to prevent and remedy the suggestive aspects of the identification process or whether instead simply to allow them to occur so that he can bring them out at trial to the possible advantage of his client. But, it is by no means clear that he would or ought to have these choices, for if defense counsel is allowed to take an active role in setting up the lineup, then it might well be that no challenges to the physical staging of the lineup could successfully be raised beyond objections raised at the time of the lineup. Such a waiver rule seems undesirable, and this suggests that the notion of defense counsel playing an active role at the identification proceeding is unsound if this is to be the consequence. If the possibility of such waiver exists, then defense counsel would be obligated to raise every conceivable objection unless there was a sound tactical reason for not doing so, a hard choice for an attorney at a very early stage of his contact with the case. Moreover, it would result in courts frequently being confronted with incompetency of counsel claims because of the defense attorney's inaction at the identification proceeding.

The situation is quite different when the identification procedure in question occurs in court rather than at the police station. With respect to an in-court identification, made on the record and in the presence of a judicial officer and other observers, it is difficult to make a convincing argument that presence of a lawyer is essential to reveal otherwise undiscoverable suggestiveness. Yet the Court in *Moore v. Illinois* (1977) unhesitantly extended the *Wade* rule to in-court identifications, and in doing so emphasized that the identification in that case had been done in a "suggestive manner" and that "[h]ad petitioner been represented by counsel, some or all of this suggestiveness could have been avoided." In this context, then, in contrast to the police station identification, the defense attorney *is* properly considered to have an active role to play. The reasons militating against that role at the police station do not obtain here; defense counsel's proposals as to how the identification should be conducted can be countered by the prosecutor and ruled on by the judge, and the case is now sufficiently far along that it is not unfair to expect defense counsel to make binding tactical choices.

(f) Consequences of Violation. If the procedures mandated by the *Wade* case are not followed and consequently a pretrial identification occurs without counsel, what are the consequences of this violation of defendant's Sixth Amendment rights? One is that testimony as to the fact of that pretrial identification is inadmissible at trial, for, as the Court explained in *Gilbert v. California* (1967), such testimony "is the direct result of the illegal lineup 'come at by exploitation of [the primary] illegality' " and the state is thus "not entitled to an opportunity to show that that testimony had an independent source." Under this *per se* exclusionary rule, the Court explained in *Gilbert,* if evidence of the pretrial identification was received at trial, then any resulting conviction must be reversed unless the appellate court is "able to declare a belief that it was harmless beyond a reasonable doubt."

What then of a subsequent in-court identification by a witness who earlier identified the defendant at an improperly conducted pretrial identification proceeding? This, the Court declared in *Wade,* presents a "fruit of the poisonous tree" problem that, consistent with the approach generally taken as to that kind of issue (see § 8.3), necessitates a determination of "[w]hether, granting establishment of the primary illegality, the evidence to which instant objection is made has been come at by exploitation of that illegality or instead by means sufficiently distinguishable to be purged of the primary taint." And this means, the Court added, that the prosecution must "establish by clear and convincing evidence that the in-court identifications were based upon observations of the suspect other than the lineup identification." The relevant factors, the Court explained in *Wade,* include

the prior opportunity to observe the alleged criminal act, the existence of any discrepancy between any pre-lineup description and the defendant's actual description, any identification prior to lineup of another person, the identification by picture of the defendant prior to the lineup, failure to identify the defendant on a prior occasion, and the lapse of time between the alleged act and the lineup identification. It is also relevant to consider those facts which, despite the absence of counsel, are disclosed concerning the conduct of the lineup.

While the taint approach of the Court in *Wade* does not accord with psychological theory concerning identification, when confronted with illegal pretrial identifications the lower courts have easily found an "independent source" for an in-court identification and have readily avoided reversing convictions by stretching, often beyond reason and logic, the doctrines of independent source and harmless error. As a practical matter, the burden is on the defense to show the presence of taint. This being so, it may well be asked whether it would be preferable, as Justice Black contended in *Wade*, that all in-court identifications be admissible so long as not supplemented or corroborated by admission of the earlier illegal identification, or whether instead the per se exclusionary rule should be extended to in-court identifications by witnesses who participated in earlier illegal identifications.

(g) The "Repeal" of the Right. In the Omnibus Crime Control and Safe Streets Act of 1968, the Congress purported to "repeal" the *Wade–Gilbert* rule in federal prosecutions. The Act provides: "The testimony of a witness that he saw the accused commit or participate in the commission of the crime for which the accused is being tried shall be admissible in evidence in a criminal prosecution in any trial court ordained and established under article III of the Constitution of the United States." Though the Court in *Wade* said that the need for counsel could be removed by "[l]egislative * * * regulations * * * which eliminate the risks of abuse and unintentional suggestion at lineup proceedings and the impediments to meaningful confrontation at trial," this statute hardly does that and thus cannot be treated as having nullified the *Wade* decision.

§ 6.4 Due Process: "The Totality of the Circumstances"

(a) Generally. A companion case to *Wade* and *Gilbert*, both recognizing a right to counsel at postindictment lineups, was *Stovall v. Denno* (1967). There, a victim of a stabbing was hospitalized for major surgery, and defendant, arrested for the offense, was brought to the victim's hospital room for a confrontation. The defendant was handcuffed to one of the seven law enforcement officials who brought him to the hospital room, and he was the only black person in the room. After being asked by an officer whether the defendant "was the man," the victim identified him. At his trial, both the victim and the police who were present in the hospital room testified to that identification.

Although the defendant in *Stovall* had not been accompanied by counsel, the Court declined to decide the case under the *Wade–Gilbert* rule, holding instead that the principles in those cases would not be applied retroactively but would affect only those identification procedures conducted after the date those decisions were handed down. But the Court then went on to recognize another basis upon which identification testimony could be challenged on constitutional grounds. It must be determined, said the Court in *Stovall,* by a consideration of "the totality of the circumstances," whether the confrontation "was so unnecessarily suggestive and conducive to irreparable mistaken identification" that the defendant was denied due process of law. As the Court later explained, when the issue is whether a witness at the earlier identification may now identify the defendant at trial, then it must be determined whether the identification procedure "was so impermissibly suggestive as to give rise to a very substantial likelihood of irreparable misidentification." "While the phrase was coined as a standard for determining whether an in-court identification would be admissible in the wake of a suggestive out-of-court identification, with the deletion of 'irreparable' it serves equally well as a standard for the admissibility of testimony concerning the out-of-court identification itself."

(b) The "Unnecessarily Suggestive" Element. Under the two-pronged *Stovall* due process test, the first question to be asked is whether the initial identification procedure was "unnecessarily" or "impermissibly" suggestive. (The burden is on the defendant to prove by a preponderance of the evidence that the identification was unnecessarily suggestive.) This first inquiry can in turn be broken down into two constituent parts: that concerning the suggestiveness of the identification, and that concerning whether there was some good reason for the failure to resort to less suggestive procedures. As for what is sufficiently suggestive to prompt a *Stovall* inquiry, the Court in that case found itself confronted with one such situation, noting that the "practice of showing suspects singly to persons for the purpose of identification, and not as part of a lineup has been widely condemned." This should not be taken to mean that resort to a lineup procedure inevitably means there is an absence of suggestiveness. As the Court later concluded in *Foster v. California* (1969), the manner in which a particular lineup is conducted may make it suggestive in the *Stovall* sense. Similarly, as the Court concluded in *Simmons v. United States* (1968), in some circumstances a photographic array may be suggestive.

Assuming suggestive circumstances, the question then is whether they were impermissible or unnecessary. The Court gave a negative answer in *Stovall,* quoting the following language from the lower court's decision in support of the conclusion that "an immediate hospital confrontation was imperative":

Here was the only person in the world who could possibly exonerate Stovall. Her words, and only her words, "He is not the man" could have resulted in freedom for Stovall. The hospital was not far distant from the courthouse and jail. No one knew how long Mrs. Behrendt might live. Faced with the responsibility of identifying the attacker, with the need for immediate action and with the knowledge that Mrs. Behrendt could not visit the jail, the police followed the only feasible procedure and took Stovall to the hospital room. Under these circumstances, the usual police station line-up, which Stovall now argues he should have had, was out of the question.

Although the *Stovall* Court's conclusion that the law enforcement authorities in that case were confronted with an emergency is open to question, as is the Court's assumption that less suggestive identification procedures could not have been resorted to at the hospital, the lower courts have usually applied the *Stovall* necessity analysis broadly. Many cases have upheld hospital room showups where there has been a serious injury to the victim or witness or to the defendant; even when it appears that the hospitalized person will recover, such a procedure has been justified merely because a period of extended hospitalization lies ahead. Some courts, however, have been more demanding and thus find hospital showups unnecessary if no immediate danger of death to the suspect or witness exists.

A somewhat different kind of emergency was recognized in *Simmons*, where the Court noted that

it is not suggested that it was unnecessary for the FBI to resort to photographic identification in this instance. A serious felony had been committed. The perpetrators were still at large. The inconclusive clues which law enforcement officials possessed led to Andrews and Simmons. It was essential for the FBI agents swiftly to determine whether they were on the right track, so that they could properly deploy their forces in Chicago and, if necessary, alert officials in other cities. The justification for this method of procedure was hardly less compelling than that which we found to justify the "one-man lineup" in *Stovall v. Denno.*

The *Simmons* notion that suggestive procedures may be necessary when there is a need for law enforcement officials "to determine whether they were on the right track" has most often been applied by lower courts to justify identification procedures conducted within several hours of the crime. Perhaps because the Supreme Court in *Simmons* went on to discuss the fact that in the circumstances there present the chances of misidentification were slight, these lower court cases typically emphasize the reliability of the identification as well. These cases often give the impression, though the point is not articulated, that the finding of a need for immediate identification is balanced against the unreliability factor, in the sense that a higher risk of error will be tolerated when there was a strong need to conduct the identification procedure at that time.

Another type of case involves the so-called "accidental" showup, not planned by the police, as where a witness just happens to see the defendant in custody in the corridors of the courthouse or at the police station. Some courts seem to take the view that no due process issue exists in such circumstances, apparently because the confrontation was not due to the fault of the police or prosecutor. But this appears to be an unwarranted broadening of the *Stovall–Simmons* exception, for the mere fact that the confrontation was not deliberate does not mean that it was necessary. Perhaps because of doubts about the legitimacy of this extension, the courts frequently proceed to the next step of assessing these "accidental" showups in terms of their unreliability.

In *Neil v. Biggers* (1972), the Court found it unnecessary to decide "whether, as intimated by the District Court, unnecessary suggestiveness alone requires the exclusion of evidence." But the Court recognized that such a result might be explained on grounds similar to the Fourth Amendment and *Miranda* exclusionary rules, namely, to induce the police to follow proper procedures in the future. But such a per se rule was later rejected in *Manson v. Brathwaite* (1977) in favor of a "more lenient" test based on the "totality of the circumstances":

> The *per se* rule * * * goes too far [in furnishing protection against the use of unreliable eyewitness testimony] since its application automatically and peremptorily, and without consideration of alleviating factors, keeps evidence from the jury that is reliable and relevant.
>
> * * * Although the *per se* approach has the more significant deterrent effect, the totality approach also has an influence on police behavior. The police will guard against unnecessarily suggestive procedures under the totality rule, as well as the *per se* one, for fear that their actions will lead to the exclusion of identifications as unreliable.
>
> The third factor is the effect on the administration of justice. Here the *per se* approach suffers serious drawbacks. [I]n those cases in which the admission of identification evi-

dence is error under the *per se* approach but not under the totality approach—cases in which the identification is reliable despite an unnecessarily suggestive identification procedure— reversal is a Draconian sanction. Certainly, inflexible rules of exclusion, that may frustrate rather than promote justice, have not been viewed recently by this Court with unlimited enthusiasm.

The two dissenters in *Manson* objected that there were "two significant distinctions" between the per se rule being advocated and other exclusionary rules: (1) the evidence suppressed is not "forever lost," as "when a prosecuting attorney learns that there has been a suggestive confrontation, he can easily arrange another lineup conducted under scrupulously fair conditions"; and (2) the exclusion is not of "relevant and usually reliable evidence," as exclusion "both protects the integrity of the truth-seeking function of the trial and discourages police use of needlessly inaccurate and ineffective investigatory methods." This reasoning takes on added appeal when it is considered, as noted below, that lower courts have applied the risk of misidentification element of the *Stovall* rule in such a way that due process violations are seldom found to exist.

(c) The Risk of Misidentification Element. If, as the Court has made clear, unnecessary suggestiveness without more does not violate due process, then it might be thought that the unreliability of the pretrial identification or the trial identification, whichever is being challenged, must be established by the defendant as part of his burden to show that his constitutional rights have been violated. However, the courts, though seldom speaking to the issue, have been inclined to allocate the burden of showing reliability to the prosecution. As one court explained: "Having utilized an unfair means to establish the defendant's guilt, the State must show that the defendant was not harmed by its own transgression."

When the question is the reliability of the in-court identification, the issue is phrased in terms of whether the earlier suggestive procedure created "a very substantial likelihood of irreparable misidentification." When, on the other hand, the question is the reliability of the earlier identification occurring in the context of the unnecessarily suggestive procedure, the standard is quite similar; the same language, "with the deletion of 'irreparable,'" is utilized. It is unlikely but theoretically possible that there could be a risk of misidentification which was substantial but not irreparable, meaning that in a particular case applying the *Stovall* rule the pretrial identification would be suppressed but not the at-trial identification by the same person. Both issues necessitate evaluation of "the totality of the circumstances," and the factors to be considered, the Court explained in *Manson,* "include the opportunity of the witness to view the criminal at the time of the crime, the witness' degree of attention, the accuracy of his prior description of the criminal, the level of certainty demonstrated at the confrontation, and the time between the crime and the confrontation. Against these factors is to be weighed the corrupting effects of the suggestive evidence itself."

These and similar factors have been utilized by the lower courts. Generally, however, these lower court cases show that a *Stovall* due process violation will not be found except in outrageous situations and that a variety of very suggestive lineup procedures are being upheld. This is particularly worrisome when it is considered that the *Manson* reliability test is not very demanding in the first place and is not in all respects in accord with established psychological knowledge of the phenomenon of eyewitness identification. The "level of certainty demonstrated at the confrontation" by the witness, for example, is not a valid indicator of the accuracy of the recollection. Unrelated evidence corroborating defendant's guilt has no bearing on an identification's reliability (but can be considered in determining whether identification resulting from unnecessarily suggestive procedures was harmless error).

(d) Lineups. It may generally be said that lineups are the most useful and least questionable witness identification procedure. They are obviously less suggestive than one-man showups, and are also more reliable than photographic identifications. Yet not every lineup is free from the danger of suggestive procedures. An apt illustration of a due process violation in a lineup identification is provided by *Foster v. California* (1969). In that case, the defendant was convicted of robbing a Western Union office. The manager viewed a police station lineup in which the defendant was placed with two other men who were half a foot shorter and was the only one wearing a leather jacket similar to that worn by the robber. When this did not lead to positive identification, the police permitted a one-on-one confrontation, but the witness' identification was still tentative. Ten days later another lineup was arranged at which defendant was the only person who had also appeared in the first lineup, and at last the manager was "convinced" that defendant was the man. The Supreme Court quite properly concluded that "the suggestive elements in this identification procedure made it all but inevitable" that the suspect would be identified "whether or not he was in fact 'the man.' In effect, the police repeatedly said to the witness, '*This* is the man.' "

Unfortunately, most courts have not applied the due process test this vigorously and thus have often held suggestive lineups not violative of due process under the ambiguous "totality of the circumstances" approach. For example, while commentators agree that lineups should contain about six similar participants, lower courts have upheld lineups of as few as three people. And while it seems obvious that similarity of race, physical features, size, age and dress of lineup participants is a prerequisite to avoidance of suggestion, courts have been reluctant to find due process violations even where there were significant dissimilarities of appearance or dress. Suggestive police statements, photographic displays or confrontations with the suspect occurring before the actual lineup can cast serious doubt upon the reliability of the witness' subsequent identification. When a lineup has failed to result in a successful identification, a flagrant form of police suggestion, as in *Foster,* has been the viewing of another lineup in which the suspect reappears. Courts have held, however, that multiple confrontations do not necessarily violate due process. When a suspect has an unusual physical characteristic or defect that was included in the witness' earlier description, it is desirable that the noticeable abnormality be either concealed or duplicated by other members of the lineup, but identification procedures in which the abnormality was apparent have often been upheld.

(e) **Use of Pictures.** Several factors bear upon the suggestiveness of photographic identification procedures. Certainly a photographic array should so far as practicable include a reasonable number of persons similar to any person then suspected whose likeness is included in the array. As the number of photographs displayed decreases the suggestivity increases, and obviously displaying a single photograph to a witness is very suggestive. Still, courts have been reluctant to hold that display of a single photograph violates due process, frequently relying on the witness' prior opportunity to view the defendant. Though certainly the array should not be arranged so that a particular individual stands out, courts have generally not found violations of due process simply because the contents of an array point to a particular suspect. Even if the size, color, or repetitious nature of photographs of suspects are not suggestive by themselves, the manner of presentation by the police may indicate to the witness exactly which person is suspected by the police. Yet an improper remark by a police officer will not necessarily be viewed as a due process violation, nor will the use of successive photo arrays in which only the defendant's picture reappears. In short, while photographic identifications are generally less reliable than lineup identifications and thus deserving of greater precautions to ensure maximum reliability, the courts have generally been unsympathetic to defendants attacking the suggestiveness of photographic identification procedures.

(f) One–Man Showups. As the Supreme Court acknowledged in *Stovall,* "[t]he practice of showing suspects singly to persons for the purpose of identification, and not as part of a lineup, has been widely condemned." This would suggest that showups should be deemed to violate due process absent the most imperative circumstances, but courts generally are not this demanding. Showups are commonly permitted when they occur within several hours of the crime; the two justifications given are the need for quick solution of the crime and the desirability of fresh, accurate identification by eyewitnesses. This may be convincing in the case of an on-the-scene identification, but courts have been inclined also to uphold the showup procedure when it does not take place at the scene of the crime and when it occurs many hours after the occurrence of the crime. Similarly, courts have been reluctant to hold that a showup violates due process when the confrontation is accidental, when some sort of emergency exists, when the suspect is unknown or at large, or when external factors "prove" the accuracy of the identification. Here as well, therefore, courts have relied upon the vagueness of the "totality of the circumstances" test to brush over substantial due process claims.

(g) In–Court Identifications. If a one-on-one confrontation at the police station is highly suggestive, then surely such a confrontation in court is the most suggestive situation of all, for the witness is given an even stronger impression that the authorities are already satisfied that they have the right man. As the Supreme Court declared in *Moore v. Illinois* (1977), where after defendant was led to the bench for his preliminary hearing the rape victim was called upon to make her first corporeal identification of him, it "is difficult to imagine a more suggestive manner in which to present a suspect to a witness for their critical first confrontation than was employed in this case." The due process issue was not before the Court in *Moore,* and thus the Court declined to state exactly what must be done to avoid such a situation.

The Court did, however, mention some ways in which the suggestiveness might have been prevented had defendant been represented by counsel. "For example, counsel could have requested that the hearing be postponed until a lineup could be arranged at which the victim would view petitioner in a less suggestive setting." A leading case on this point, *Evans v. Superior Court* (1974), held that due process requires the prosecution to honor a defense request for a lineup where "eyewitness identification is shown to be a material issue and there exists a reasonable likelihood of a mistaken identification which a lineup would tend to resolve." Other decisions are also to be found holding that a defense request for a lineup should have been granted, although generally courts are inclined to say merely that whether such relief is called for is left to the trial court's discretion. The Court in *Moore* also noted that "counsel could have asked that the victim be excused from the courtroom while the charges were read and the evidence against petitioner was recited, and that petitioner be seated with other people in the audience when the victim attempted an identification." Here as well, the prevailing view is to leave the matter largely within the trial judge's discretion. This is surprising, as an identification more unreliable than the witness's familiar selection of the conspicuous defendant is difficult to imagine.

Perhaps because of the fact that it is within the judge's discretion whether to grant such requests, defense counsel have on occasion resorted to self-help, sometimes with unfortunate consequences. In a case in which the defense attorney used a decoy without the trial judge's knowledge or approval, the decoy was convicted and temporarily jailed. Defense counsel's act of substituting another person for the defendant at counsel table without the court's permission or knowledge has been viewed as a violation of ethical standards and an obstruction of justice punishable by contempt.

(h) The "Repeal" of the Right. As a part of the Omnibus Crime Control and Safe Streets Act of 1968, Congress in its wisdom adopted this provision: "The testimony of a witness that he saw the accused commit or participate in the commission of the crime for which the accused is being tried shall be admissible in evidence in a criminal prosecution in any trial court ordained and established under article III of the Constitution of the United States." Just as Congress cannot by such an act destroy the constitutional right to counsel under the *Wade–Gilbert* rule, it surely cannot do away with a defendant's right under *Stovall* not to be convicted on the basis of an identification so unreliable as to violate due process.

§ 6.5   Additional Possible Safeguards

(a) Jury Instructions. Because the *Wade* and *Stovall* rules have not resulted in the substantial elimination of the danger of unrealistic eyewitness identification, it is appropriate to consider other possible safeguards such as jury instructions. Instructions cannot make the identifications any more reliable, but hopefully they can alert the jury to the necessity for a most careful assessment of identification evidence. In *United States v. Telfaire* (1972), the court set out an instruction for use in future identification cases. It states in part:

> Identification testimony is an expression of belief or impression by the witness. Its value depends on the opportunity

the witness had to observe the offender at the time of the offense and to make a reliable identification later.

In appraising the identification testimony of a witness, you should consider the following:

(1) Are you convinced that the witness had the capacity and an adequate opportunity to observe the offender?

Whether the witness had an adequate opportunity to observe the offender at the time of the offense will be affected by such matters as how long or short a time was available, how far or close the witness was, how good were lighting conditions, whether the witness had had occasion to see or know the person in the past. * * *

(2) Are you satisfied that the identification made by the witness subsequent to the offense was the product of his own recollection? You may take into account both the strength of the identification, and the circumstances under which the identification was made.

If the identification by the witness may have been influenced by the circumstances under which the defendant was presented to him for identification, you should scrutinize the identification with great care. You may also consider the length of time that lapsed between the occurrence of the crime and the next opportunity of the witness to see defendant, as a factor bearing on the reliability of the identification. * * *

(3) You may take into account any occasions in which the witness failed to make an identification of defendant, or made an identification that was inconsistent with his identification at trial.

(4) Finally, you must consider the credibility of each identification witness in the same way as any other witness, consider whether he is truthful, and consider whether he had the capacity and opportunity to make a reliable observation on the matter covered in his testimony.

I again emphasize that the burden of proof on the prosecutor extends to every element of the crime charged, and this specifically includes the burden of proving beyond a reasonable doubt the identity of the defendant as the perpetrator of the crime with which he stands charged. If after examining the testimony, you have a reasonable doubt as to the accuracy of the identification, you must find the defendant not guilty.

A few other federal circuits have likewise strongly recommended that such an instruction be given when identification is a key issue in the case, while others have recommended such a special instruction in those circumstances but leave the trial judge with considerable discretion in deciding whether to use the instruction. Some state courts also utilize an instruction like that in *Telfaire,* while some others take the view that such an instruction is inappropriate because the matter is best left to final argument by the parties. Also, there is some authority that an instruction regarding the risks of cross-racial identification should be given.

(b) **Expert Testimony.** Some have argued that in a case in which eyewitness testimony is of central importance, the defendant should be entitled to have a psychologist testify in his behalf on such circumstances as may be present in the particular case (e.g., presence of stress or passage of time, cross-racial or cross-ethnic identification) that psychological research has shown may cast doubt upon an eyewitness identification. But the appellate cases typically say that whether to receive such expert testimony lies within the sound discretion of the trial court. In holding that the trial judge acted within the scope of his discretion in not permitting such testimony, these cases make such assertions as that work in the field is not sufficiently developed, that the testimony would invade the province of the jury or have undue influence upon the jury, that the undue consumption of time would substantially outweigh its probative value, and that what the expert has to offer can be effectively communicated to the jury by probing questioning of the identification witnesses. In recent years, however, there has been somewhat greater willingness by trial courts to receive such evidence.

(c) **Improved Police Procedures.** *Wade* and *Stovall* mark only the constitutional minimum of what must be done rather than the maximum of what should be done to enhance the reliability of eyewitness identifications. As some police agencies have discovered, this is an area in which the existence of clear regulations, in the formulation of which law enforcement agencies have themselves participated, are especially beneficial. Setting clear and reasonable standards for each type of identification procedure can be of great benefit to those suspected of crime and also those charged with the responsibility of enforcing the law. There are, thus, real benefits to be realized by the prosecution, and the public it represents, in presenting evidence of a pretrial identification made under conditions which vouch for its fairness, and hence, its probable accuracy. Beyond this, improvements in police investigative activities directed toward uncovering evidence corroborating eyewitness identifications are especially desirable.

As the body of scientific knowledge in this area has grown over recent decades, the gap between the procedures used by most police forces and procedures demonstrated by the eyewitness research to produce superior eyewitness evidence became increasingly obvious.

Consequently, psychologists have intensified their efforts to influence police identification procedures, culminating in the publication of various proposed "guidelines" for law enforcement. The recommendations most often made are: (1) The witness should be instructed that the actual perpetrator may or may not be in the lineup or photo array, and that consequently they should not feel that they have to make an identification. (2) The lineup or photo array should be composed in such a way that the suspect does not unduly stand out. (3) A clear statement should be taken from the witness at the time of identification, and prior to any feedback, indicating the degree of confidence by the witness that the person identified is the perpetrator. (4) The person conducting the lineup or photo array should not know the identity of the suspect. (5) Mock witnesses should be used to test the neutrality of the lineup or photo array. (6) Sequential rather than simultaneous identification procedures should be used.

Chapter 7

GRAND JURY INVESTIGATIONS

Table of Sections

-----

§ 7.1 The Investigative Role of the Grand Jury

(a) **Dual Functions.** The common law grand jury was said to operate as both "the shield and the sword" of the American criminal justice process. It was likened to a shield in its performance as a screening agency interposed between the government and the individual. In deciding whether to issue an indictment, the grand jury reviewed the government's evidence and, in effect, screened the prosecutor's decision to charge. By refusing to indict when the evidence was insufficient or the prosecution otherwise appeared unjust, the grand jury was said to "function as a shield, standing between the accuser and the accused, protecting the individual citizen against oppressive and unfounded government prosecution." The grand jury was likened to a sword in its perform-ance as an investigative body. Here the grand jury was not review-ing cases that the prosecutor believed to be ready for prosecution, but rather examining situations that were still at the inquiry stage. Utilizing its investigative authority, the grand jury uncovered evi-dence not previously available to the prosecution, and thereby provided the sword that enabled the government to secure convic-tions that might otherwise not be obtained.

It was the screening function that led to inclusion of a grand jury clause in the Fifth Amendment and in the constitutions of most of the original states, but that clause also indirectly recog-nized the grand jury's investigative function. The grand jury clause requires that prosecutions for all felonies be brought by a grand jury's "indictment" or "presentment." The more common indict-ment was the charging instrument presented before the grand jury by the prosecuting official and approved by it, as a "true bill," upon a finding that the government's evidence was sufficient to proceed. The presentment was a charging instrument issued by the grand jury on its own initiative, and was commonly based on its own knowledge and investigation.

At the time of the adoption of the Constitution, the grand jury was an institution revered not only for its independence in screen-ing, but also for its service as a "public watchdog," uncovering and proceeding against public corruption and other criminal activity that the local officials chose to ignore or were unable to investigate. Over the nineteenth century, local police forces were created and their investigative capacity expanded. At the same time, local prosecutors came to have a virtual monopoly over the decision to prosecute, and private parties no longer were able to take their cases directly to the grand jury. The end result was a diminished use of the grand jury as a investigative body. The need for grand jury screening was also challenged, as many states moved to allow-ing prosecutions to be brought on a prosecutor's information fol-lowing a magistrate's finding of probable cause at a preliminary hearing.

Today, of the fifty-two American jurisdictions, only twenty (the federal system, the District of Columbia, and eighteen states) still require prosecution by indictment in all felony cases. All of these states continue to use grand juries for investigations as well as screening. The vast majority of matters coming before the grand jury, however, are fully developed cases presented only for screen-ing. The next largest group will be matters requiring only limited use of the grand jury's investigative authority. A case will be almost fully investigated, and the grand jury will be utilized to compel production of certain evidence to complete the investigation. Final-ly, the smallest group will be cases in which the grand jury will play a major role in the investigation. These are primarily cases of the type described in § 7.2. Because the federal system deals with a much larger percentage of such cases than the typical state, a much larger (though still minority) percentage of the workload of its grand juries involves investigations. Of course, when the grand jury's investigation is completed, the jury turns into a screening grand jury, as it then must decide whether to indict.

Twenty eight states do not require prosecution by indictment for any felonies. All but two of these states still allow for grand jury indictments, and all recognize grand juries exercising investigative powers. In some of these states, grand juries are regularly available because they are used to screen and indict in certain limited types of cases. The same is true in the four states that require grand jury indictments for either capital or formerly capital (now life-imprisonment) offenses. Where, as in these jurisdictions, grand juries are regularly impaneled, though only for a limited group of cases, their availability is likely to lead to their use as well for both partial investigations and full investigations. In other information states, if a grand jury should be needed for an investigation, it must be impaneled specially, as grand juries are never used simply for screening. Here, grand juries are not utilized for partial investigations, and less frequently utilized for full investigations. A not unusual pattern is to find that grand jury investigations are a regular practice only in the state's larger counties. In still other information states, the grand jury is a forgotten institution, as no grand jury has been impaneled for decades. Prosecutors here largely rely on the federal system to deal with the types of crimes that ordinarily can be investigated only through a grand jury.

(b) The Investigative Structure. At one point, investigative grand juries in particular, tended to have a "blue ribbon" composition. The jurors were selected from a limited slice of the citizenry, consisting primarily of persons who occupied positions of responsibility and leadership in the community. Starting in the 1960s, as petit jury selection procedures were altered to provide more representative trial juries, that objective was carried over to grand juries as well. Legislative reforms imposed cross-section requirements upon grand juries, and various judicial decisions suggested that was a constitutional requirement as well. The end result was the elimination of the blue ribbon grand jury. Today, the grand jury array is drawn from the same constituency, and selected in the same manner, as the array for the petit jury.

The change in composition of the grand jury arguably worked alongside other developments to strengthen the position of the prosecutor in leading the grand jury. The prosecutor traditionally has been the legal advisor to the grand jury, but that position carried with it only limited authority. The prosecutor's ability to shape the grand jury investigation therefore depended largely upon the grand jury's willingness to follow the prosecutor's suggestions. While that remains true in some jurisdictions today, many others have given the prosecutor the right to make presentations before the grand jury. These jurisdictions give the prosecutor the authority to obtain the issuance of subpoenas duces tecum and ad testificandum, directing appearance before the grand jury, without prior consultation with the grand jury. Even in such jurisdictions, however, the grand jury retains ultimate control over the scope of the investigation through its authority to go beyond the evidence produced by the prosecutor. Initially, the jurors have a right to ask their own questions, although the prosecutor may request that he be allowed to screen the questions to ensure that they are proper as to form and content. The grand jury also has the authority to require the production of additional witnesses or other evidence relevant to the proposed charges being presented by the prosecutor. Indeed, it even has the power to initiate an investigation into an entirely different subject matter, and if the prosecutor fails to follow its direction, to seek from the supervisory court the appointment of an independent prosecutor to assist the grand jury.

Critics of continued judicial reliance on early precedents granting grand juries sweeping investigative powers claim that the courts have been blinded by the historic examples of truly independent grand juries. Today, they argue, such independence is simply theoretical, resting on independent powers of the grand jury that are almost never exercised. In reality, they argue, the sweeping powers of the grand jury are exercised by the prosecutor alone. Working with the police, the prosecutor determines what witnesses will be called and when they will appear. The prosecutor examines the witnesses and advises the grand jury on the validity of any legal objections the witnesses might present. If a witness refuses to comply with a subpoena, it is the prosecutor who seeks a contempt citation. If a witness refuses to testify on grounds of self-incrimination, it is the prosecutor who determines whether an immunity grant will be obtained. The grand jury, it is argued, must almost invariably look to the prosecutor's leadership, as the prosecutor has the expertise, and the supplementary resources, needed for success in their venture. What the courts must do, the critics argue, is set aside the precedent that was developed during an era when grand juries were largely independent, and subject grand jury investigative power to the same kinds of limitations as are imposed upon other investigative weapons in the government's arsenal (typically exercised by police).

Responding supporters of continued judicial deference acknowledge that instances of "runaway" grand juries (i.e., grand juries which pursue investigations over the objection of the prosecutor) are rare. They note, however, grand jury secrecy precludes a fully informed judgment on the extent to which grand juries help to shape investigations without coming into direct conflict with the prosecutor. Moreover they argue, assuming that the prosecutor does control the investigation, this development dates back over one hundred years, preceding many of the decisions that speak most eloquently of the necessary breadth of the grand jury's investigative authority. The key to the historical grant of that authority, they argue, was a legal structure that rendered the government's use of the grand jury's investigative powers subject to the veto of the jurors, who sat as community representatives. That structure has not been substantially altered, and its very presence, the argument continues, serves to hold the prosecutor in check and to distinguish grand jury investigations from investigatory tools granted directly to the prosecutor or the police. The fact that the grand jury only occasionally exercises its power to override the prosecutor does not detract from the significance of that power. The prosecutor must respect the existence of that power and act in a way that he knows, from past experience, will be acceptable to the jurors.

While there have been some exceptions, most courts have refused to reexamine the historical precedents granting the grand jury broad investigative authority. The Supreme Court, over some dissents, has been a leader in this regard. The Court has continued to adhere to the philosophy expressed in *Blair v. U.S.* (1919). The *Blair* Court noted that the grand jury's authority to resort to compulsory process had been recognized in England as early as 1612, and the inquisitorial function of the grand jury was well established at the time of the Constitution's adoption. Both the Fifth Amendment and the earliest federal statutes recognized an investigative authority of the grand jury that included the "same powers that pertained to its British prototype." The Supreme Court would not view that authority with suspicion and subject it to new limitations. The latest Supreme Court discussion of federal court supervisory power over federal grand juries, *U.S. v. Williams* (1992), expressed a similar philosophy. As discussed below, *Williams* indicated that any major alteration of the grand jury's broad authority to shape its own procedures, as reflected in the "history of the grand jury institution," must come from the legislature, not the judiciary.

(c) **Judicial Supervision.** As the Supreme Court noted in *Brown v. U.S.* (1959), "A grand jury is clothed with great independence in many areas, but it remains an appendage of the court, powerless to perform its investigative function without the court's aid, because powerless itself to compel the testimony of witnesses."

At one time, the grand jury's reliance upon the authority of the court was thought to give the court supervisory power over all aspects of grand jury's basic structure. Over the years, however, judicial control over various structural elements of the grand jury has been limited by statute or court rule. For example, while the decision to impanel an investigatory grand jury traditionally rested within the discretion of the court, many jurisdictions now require automatic impanelment upon request of the prosecutor. Similarly, while it was formerly said that a court could discharge a grand jury "at any time, for any reason or no reason," many jurisdictions now permit an early discharge only where justified by "cause."

The scope of the court's supervisory authority over the operations of the grand jury is most often discussed in connection with challenges to indictments, where the primary focus is upon judicial prescription of standards designed to ensure "fairness" in grand jury screening. However, courts are also called upon to exercise their supervisory authority over grand jury investigations, usually upon a motion of a witness challenging a grand jury subpoena or a proposed contempt sanction, but sometimes upon a motion of the target of the investigation. State and lower federal court decisions supporting extensive use of the court's supervisory authority in that context include: a ruling insisting that the prosecutor either present certain information to the grand jury on a particular manner or allow the private complainant to present the matter; a ruling suspending the continued investigation of a state official, which had been marked by extensive leaks, until after the forthcoming election; rulings requiring that the grand jury itself participate in demands for evidence or applications for judicial imposition of contempt sanctions; rulings requiring a preliminary government showing of legitimacy as a prerequisite for enforcement of a subpoena; rulings requiring a preliminary government showing of need as a prerequisite for enforcement of a subpoena that might chill the target's relationship with counsel; and rulings imposing transcription or disclosure requirements beyond what is required by grand jury statutes.

The above rulings reflect a perspective that places the court's supervisory authority over grand jury proceedings on much the same plane as the court's supervisory authority over courtroom and related pretrial proceedings. Grand jury proceedings are seen as an out-of-court appendage of the judicial process, no less subject to judicial supervision and regulation than, for example, pretrial discovery. Other courts reject this view, stressing both the independence of the grand jurors and the prerogatives of the prosecutor that come with the responsibility of the executive branch for investigation and prosecution. They adhere to a standard of limited intervention, as suggested in the following, widely-quoted formulation: "[T]here should be no curtailment of the inquisitorial power of the grand jury except in the clearest case of abuse, and mere inconvenience not amounting to harassment does not justify judicial interference with the functions of the grand jury." For the federal courts, the Supreme Court's majority opinion in *U.S. v. Williams* (1992) clearly favors the latter position, if not an even more tightly confined supervisory power.

Williams presented the question of whether a district court could dismiss an indictment based upon the prosecutor's failure to comply with a court-created standard requiring the presentation of known exculpatory evidence before the grand jury. In holding that a court could not impose such a standard (and therefore could not dismiss an indictment based upon a failure to comply with the standard), the *Williams* Court distinguished between a federal court's use of supervisory power "as a means of enforcing or vindicating legally compelled standards of prosecutorial conduct before the grand jury" that are set forth in a Federal Rule of Criminal Procedure or in a federal statute, and a federal court's use of supervisory power "as a means of prescribing those standards of prosecutorial conduct in the first instance." The former use is appropriate, as the federal courts here are merely assuring adherence to "those few clear rules which were carefully drafted and approved by this Court and by Congress to ensure the integrity of the grand jury's functions." The prescription of standards, on the other hand, assumes a federal court authority to create a "common law" of grand jury practice, which is inconsistent with the "grand jury's functional independence from the judicial branch." The *Williams* Court concluded as to such efforts to exercise superintending control: "Because the grand jury is an institution separate from the courts, over whose functioning the courts do not preside, we think it clear that, as a general matter at least, no such 'supervisory' authority exists."

Though the *Williams* Court dealt with the prescription of standards relating to the grand jury's decision to indict, its analysis of the federal court's limited supervisory power clearly extends as well to the regulation of the investigatory process. The *Williams* majority opinion stressed the federal courts' traditional recognition of the "grand jury's functional independence from the judicial branch," particularly with respect to the grand jury's "power to investigate criminal wrongdoing." It reasoned that "the Fifth Amendment's constitutional guarantee presupposes an investigative body 'acting independently of either prosecuting attorney or judge.'" This "tradition of independence," *Williams* added, has led the Court to "insist * * * that the grand jury remain 'free to pursue its investigations unhindered by external influence or supervision so long as it does not breach upon the legitimate rights of any witnesses called before it.' " Not surprisingly, federal lower courts have concluded that *Williams* requires a reexamination of their earlier, expansive supervisory rulings of the type noted above. Unless those rulings can be explained as enforcing standards prescribed by statute, court rule, or the Constitution, the limits they placed on grand jury investigations must be discarded.

(d) **Alternative Investigative Procedures.** The primary investigative tool of the grand jury investigation is the subpoena. Many jurisdictions make that tool available as well to other investigative authorities. A few grant directly to prosecutors an investigative deposition authority. Several states authorize judicial inquests, giving the court the authority under limited circumstances to subpoena witnesses and documents in order to determine whether a crime has committed. Most federal administrative agencies, and many state agencies, may utilize administrative subpoenas to investigate possible violations of regulatory statutes within their enforcement domain, and very often these violations may constitute crimes as well as civil wrongs.

The investigatory processes of such institutions lack many of the key characteristics of the grand jury proceeding: they are not secret, but open; the lawyer may accompany the witness; there is no lay participation, and the enforcement of the subpoena commonly is through a standard civil action. Accordingly, many of governing legal standards differ from those applied to grand jury investigations. However, their use of the subpoena presents similar issues as Fourth Amendment limitations (§ 7.5) and the application of the privilege against self-incrimination (§§ 7.8–7.11).

§ 7.2 Investigative Advantages

Compared to police investigations, grand jury investigations are expensive, time consuming, and logistically cumbersome. However, the grand jury also offers certain investigative advantages over the police. Those advantages stem mainly from five elements in the grand jury process—(1) subpoena authority backed up by potential contempt sanctions, (2) closed proceedings, (3) immunity grants, (4) grand jury secrecy requirements, and (5) lay participation. For the investigation of most crimes, these aspects of the grand jury process are superfluous. Police investigations work as well and do so at far less cost. There are certain types of cases, however, in which prosecutors are likely to view the grand jury's investigatory assistance as either essential or highly desirable, and therefore worth the extra costs of the grand jury process. These are primarily cases in which investigators face one or more of the following tasks: unraveling a complex criminal structure, dealing with victims or other witnesses reluctant to cooperate, obtaining information contained in extensive business records, keeping a continuing investigative effort from the public gaze, or counteracting public suspicion of political manipulation of the investigation. Criminal activities likely to present such investigative problems include governmental corruption (e.g., bribery), misuse of economic power (e.g., price-fixing), and widespread distribution of illegal services (e.g., gambling, money laundering, and loan-sharking).

(a) Subpoena Authority. The basic investigative advantage of the grand jury stems from its ability to use the subpoena authority of the court that impaneled it. The grand jury may utilize the subpoena duces tecum to obtain tangible evidence and the subpoena ad testificandum to obtain testimony. Both subpoenas are supported by the court's authority to hold in contempt any person who willfully refuses, without legal justification, to comply with a subpoena's directive. That authority encompasses both civil and criminal contempt, although use of the former is far more common than use of the latter. Under civil contempt, the witness is sentenced to imprisonment or to a fine (which may increase daily), but he may purge himself by complying with the subpoena. It is said that he "carries the keys of the prison in his own pockets." The civil contemnor who refuses to purge himself will remain under sentence until the grand jury completes its term and is discharged. Moreover, if the information that the contemnor possesses is still needed, he may be subpoenaed by a successor grand jury and again held in contempt if he continues to refuse to supply that information. Where the information is no longer needed, or the recalcitrance is not likely to be overcome, the witness may be charged with the crime of criminal contempt.

Subpoena ad testificandum. The subpoena ad testificandum is especially useful in obtaining statements from persons who will not voluntarily furnish information to the police. Faced with the threat of contempt, a recalcitrant witness often will have a change of heart and will give the grand jury information that he has refused to give to the police. Of course, the recalcitrant witnesses called before the grand jury may rely upon the standard privileges that would also be available at trial. Thus, if the information sought could be incriminating, the recalcitrant witness (unless granted immunity) may still refuse to cooperate by relying on his privilege against self-incrimination. Many persons, however, are unwilling to furnish information to the police, yet will provide that information before the grand jury, without regard to the availability of the privilege, because they feel more comfortable providing information in that setting. Thus, an employee may wish to avoid the appearance of voluntarily assisting police investigating his employer, yet testify freely under the compulsion of a subpoena.

The grand jury subpoena ad testificandum also has the advantage of requiring witnesses to give information under oath. If a witness fails to tell the truth, he may be prosecuted for perjury. Apart from the federal system, a person who gives false information to an investigating officer ordinarily will not have committed a crime. Accordingly, where a witness might be willing to talk to the police, but also is likely to "shade his story," requiring him to testify before a grand jury may produce a more complete and truthful statement. Even where a witness is willing to give an entirely truthful statement to the police, there may be value in requiring him to testify before the grand jury. Once a person has testified under oath, he is likely to think twice about changing his testimony at trial and thereby providing the grounds for a perjury prosecution based on inconsistent sworn statements.

Subpoena duces tecum. The grand jury subpoena duces tecum offers several advantages over the primary device available to the police for obtaining records and physical evidence—the search pursuant to a warrant. Unlike the search warrant, the subpoena duces tecum can issue without a showing of probable cause. Moreover, even where probable cause could be established, there are times when the subpoena will have administrative advantages. For example, there may be a need to seize so many records from various locations that a search would be impractical. With a subpoena duces tecum, the party served may be required to undertake the extensive task of bringing together records from several different locations and sorting through them to collect those covered by the subpoena. At other times, there may be a need to obtain records from uninvolved third parties (e.g., a bank), and a subpoena will be preferred because it will be far less disruptive to the third party's business operations. So too, the prosecution may desire to keep from the target and the public the grounding for the selection of particular records and evidence, readily achieved with a subpoena duces tecum since it requires no statement of grounding. A search warrant, in contrast, requires an affidavit setting forth that grounding, and preventing its disclosure requires a not-readily-available affidavit sealing order. Finally, the remedy for a search that turns out to be unconstitutional often is suppression of the evidence seized. Where a subpoena duces tecum is impermissible in scope or issuance, the challenge must be raised prior to the response and the consequence is the quashing of the subpoena. This allows the government to refashion the subpoena to meet the sustained objections, so there is no loss of evidence that could have been obtained through a curable illegality.

(b) Closed Proceedings and Psychological Pressure. The psychological pressure exerted by the grand jury setting also is cited as a factor that frequently enables the grand jury to obtain information from witnesses unwilling to cooperate with the police. Proponents of grand jury investigations claim that this pressure stems from the moral force exerted by the lay group of jurors. Critics, however, claim the psychological pressure stems from what they describe as the "star chamber setting" of grand jury interrogation. "In all of the United States legal system," they note, "no person stands more alone than a witness before a grand jury; in a secret hearing he faces an often hostile prosecutor and 23 strangers with no judge present to guard his rights, no lawyer present to counsel him, and sometimes no indication of why he is being questioned."

As noted in § 7.12(b), a substantial number of states have altered this setting by allowing the witness to be accompanied by a lawyer before the grand jury. Also, in other jurisdictions, such as the federal, the witness may have retained counsel located immediately outside the grand jury room, and the witness will be allowed to leave that room for consultation with counsel, at least as to the possible exercise of a testimonial privilege. See § 7.12(c). Even with counsel available, however, the witness still faces the pressure of knowing that he is testifying under oath, and that the prosecutor may ask questions, potentially embarrassing, almost without limitation as to subject matter.

(c) Immunity Grants. An immunity grant is a court order granting a witness sufficient immunity from future prosecution to supplant the witness' self-incrimination privilege. Once the witness has been granted immunity, he may no longer rely upon the privilege. Since immunity grants are tied initially to the exercise of the privilege by a person under a legal obligation to testify, they are not available to persons who simply refuse to give a statement to the police. At the investigatory stage, almost the only way the prosecution can make use of an immunity grant is in conjunction with a subpoena directing the uncooperative witness to testify before the grand jury. The immunity grant may be used to gain information from various types of recalcitrant witnesses. For example, immunity quite frequently is given to a lower-level participant in order to obtain testimony against higher-level participants. It also often is used to force testimony from witnesses who are not themselves involved in criminal activities, but desire not to give testimony that may hurt others. Although the privilege is not available simply to protect others, witnesses who do not actually fear personal incrimination have been known to claim that they do in order to avoid testifying against their friends. Since such claims are difficult to dispute, the prosecutor may simply prefer to grant the witness immunity.

(d) Secrecy. Grand jury secrecy requirements are commonly cited as another investigative advantage of the grand jury. Initially, those requirements are said to facilitate keeping the target of the investigation "in the dark" as to the nature of the inquiry. A person may be investigated without even knowing that he is the subject of an investigation or, if he is aware of his "target" status, without knowing which of his activities are being examined or who is providing information on those activities. Keeping these matters from the target may be essential where there is a likelihood that he might flee to avoid possible indictment or might attempt to destroy evidence or tamper with possible grand jury witnesses.

Secondly, grand jury secrecy requirements are said to have the independent value of keeping the investigation from coming to the attention of the public. When the target of a possible investigation occupies a position of prominence, public disclosure of the investigation may cause irreparable harm to his reputation even though the investigation eventually reveals no basis for prosecution. Accordingly, where investigations are likely to become public, the prosecutor might hesitate to initiate an investigation unless fairly well convinced that it will lead to a prosecution. On the other hand, with the grand jury process keeping the investigation secret, the prosecutor might be willing to undertake an investigation on the basis of suspicions that have far less grounding. If the suspicions prove erroneous, the suspect's reputation will not have been harmed; but if the suspicions prove well founded, the prosecution will have the basis for a prosecution that otherwise might never have been brought.

Third, secrecy requirements are said to encourage "free and untrammeled disclosure" by witnesses. Initially, the secrecy of the grand jury proceeding may keep the target of the investigation from learning that the witness (often an associate or employee of the target) is providing testimony. Even if the target becomes aware that the witness has testified or will testify, the cloak of secrecy permits the witness to describe his testimony to the target as the witness pleases.

As discussed in § 7.3, grand jury secrecy today recognizes a series of exceptions that may largely undermine these supposed advantages. The exemption for witnesses (§ 7.3(c)) means that a witness friendly to the target may discuss his appearance with the target, and a witness not so friendly may disclose the nature of the investigation to those who will give the investigation wide circulation within the community. Even if the witnesses all desire to keep secret their role in the investigation, the secrecy requirements imposed on investigators may not preclude official statements that give the public a glimpse of the investigation (see § 7.3(b)), and illegal leaks, difficult to trace, may reveal much more. Also, under governing discovery standards, witnesses know that their testimony before the grand jury will eventually be made available to the target if the target is prosecuted (§ 7.3(e)).

(e) Lay Participation and Public Confidence. Assuming that the investigation will become known to the public sooner or later, grand jury participation often helps in maintaining community confidence in the integrity of the investigatory process, a particularly valuable asset when the person under investigation is a public official. The community tends to be suspicious of partisan influences in such investigations, especially where the investigation results in a decision not to prosecute. As one court noted: "Where corruption is charged, it is desirable to have someone outside the administration [i.e., the grand jury] act, so that the image, as well as the fact of impartiality in the investigation can be preserved and allegations of cover-up or white-wash can be avoided." The prosecutor may also look to the grand jury to help allay other public concerns, as in cases in which investigated parties are almost certain to claim police and prosecutor harassment.

§ 7.3 Grand Jury Secrecy

(a) Statutory Requirements. Grand jury secrecy was recognized at common law, but today, in almost every jurisdiction, the precise scope of that secrecy is set by statute or court rule. Undoubtedly the most complex secrecy provision is Rule 6(e) of the Federal Rules of Criminal Procedure. Rule 6(e) includes: (1) a general rule of secrecy, stating that specified persons present during a grand jury proceeding (basically prosecutors, clerks, stenographers, and grand jurors) are bound not to disclose any matter occurring before the grand jury except as authorized by the Rule; (2) a list of several specified exceptions, some requiring court authorization and others allowing disclosure without prior judicial approval; (3) procedural provisions governing applications for court approved disclosure; (4) a provision authorizing the sealing of indictments until the defendant has been taken into custody; (5) a requirement of a closed judicial hearing where necessary to avoid disclosure of grand jury matter, subject to "any right to an open hearing in a contempt proceeding"; (6) a provision for keeping various records under seal as a security measure; and (7) a provision making a "knowing violation of Rule 6 * * * punish[able] as contempt of court".

While various states have provisions modeled after Rule 6(e), most have provisions that are less complete. They will set forth a general requirement of secrecy, but then leave to trial courts, exercising their supervisory powers, the formulation of appropriate procedures to preserve that secrecy. Where courts have such discretion, they tend to take diverse approaches, in particular, on the closing of hearings. A variety of motions made by witnesses, targets, criminal defendants, and other interested parties will require consideration of grand jury transcripts and involve discussions of what occurred before the grand jury. If those hearings are not held in camera, they may become a prime vehicle for public disclosure of grand jury proceedings. Although court hearings traditionally are open, Rule 6(e) requires that all hearings that reveal grand jury matter be closed, making an exception only for any constitutional right of a defendant in a contempt proceeding to an open proceeding. Where state courts have discretion, some follow a practice similar to that commanded by Rule 6(e), but others will often keep open hearings that bear upon grand jury matter, especially where the hearing does not involve a direct challenge to grand jury procedures.

(b) Protected Information. The information protected by grand jury secrecy provisions varies with the jurisdiction. Federal Rule 6(e)'s secrecy provision applies to any "matter occurring before the grand jury." Many state provisions contain similar language. Also, since the federal courts have applied a functional analysis in determining what information is within the protection of the federal secrecy provision, federal precedent has a significant influence even in states with somewhat different statutory language.

The first lesson of the federal precedent is that the phrase "matter occurring before the grand jury" is a term of art, not to be construed literally as encompassing only events that have taken place before the grand jury. Thus, the caselaw has established the following basic principles as guides to determining what constitutes grand jury matter: (1) the protection of grand jury secrecy extends to what will come before the grand jury as well as what already has come before it; (2) that protection extends beyond testimony to encompass all substantive aspects of the proceedings; and (3) events that occurred outside the grand jury room (in particular, events within the prosecutor's office) may fall within that protection where the events have a sufficiently close connection to the grand jury process and the disclosure of information relating to those events is likely to reveal what has occurred or will occur in the grand jury room.

The application of the third principle cited above undoubtedly has caused the courts the greatest difficulty. Certain events occurring outside the grand jury are readily viewed as creating "grand jury matter." Thus, courts uniformly hold that grand jury secrecy covers the fact that a grand jury subpoena has been served on a particular person. Memorandums and records that describe or analyze information presented to the grand jury will constitute grand jury matter even though prepared by the prosecution and not part of the official record of the grand jury. Courts have divided, however, as to whether Rule 6(e) governs prosecutorial disclosure of the contents of statements made to the police by persons who will later testify before the grand jury. Although the subsequent grand jury testimony might differ from the interview record, disclosure of the interview is likely to reveal the substance of that witness' testimony, and for some courts, that is enough to constitute disclosure of "grand jury matter." Other courts suggest that as long as the interview statement was not itself presented to the grand jury, the fact that it might suggest the content of a witness' subsequent testimony is irrelevant, as it was not part of "what transpired in the grand jury room." Relying on a similar analysis, one court held that where the prosecutor's office revealed publicly that it was considering the possibility of bringing certain charges, that statement did not reveal grand jury matter as it did not state that "an indictment has been sought or will be sought," or that the prosecution's consideration of the charges related to any evidence presented to a grand jury (as opposed to evidence simply collected by investigators).

(c) **Disclosure by a Witness.** Roughly a dozen states impose an obligation of secrecy on the grand jury witness, subject to the exemption of the witness' discussion of his testimony with counsel. In *Butterworth v. Smith* (1990), the Supreme Court sustained a First Amendment challenge to a state statute that imposed a secrecy obligation upon a grand jury witness—so broad as to prohibit disclosure of the "content, gist, or import" of the witness' testimony—insofar as that secrecy obligation extended beyond the point of discharge of the grand jury. The Court reasoned that several of the traditional functions of grand jury secrecy were no longer served by a witness-secrecy requirement once the grand jury's investigation ended, and those functions that remained were "not sufficient to overcome [the witness'] First Amendment right to make a truthful statement of information he acquired on his own." *Butterworth* does not necessarily preclude a permanent disclosure prohibition (at least with an exemption possible upon a showing of compelling justification) where that prohibition is limited to a discussion of the specific content of the grand jury testimony itself, as opposed to the broader prohibition presented in *Butterworth*, which was interpreted as preventing the witness from describing his personal knowledge of the events that were the subject of his testimony. Such a limited prohibition could be viewed as analogous to the secrecy obligation imposed upon the grand jurors and prosecutors.

In the federal system and the vast majority of states, the witness is not bound by secrecy. In Federal Rule 6(e) and many similar state provisions, the secrecy provision initially sets forth a list of persons subject to the secrecy obligation (e.g., jurors, and prosecutors), which does not include witnesses. The provision then adds that "no obligation of secrecy may be imposed on any person" except in accordance with that provision. What the absence of a secrecy obligation means is that witnesses, if they so choose, can freely disclose publicly or privately both their own testimony and whatever information was revealed to them by the grand jurors or prosecutor in the course of giving that testimony. Although this exception has been criticized as creating a gigantic loophole in grand jury secrecy, it has been justified on grounds of practical necessity and the need to prevent grand jury abuses. Imposition of a witness secrecy requirement has been characterized as "impractical and unreal—a partner, an employee, a relative, a friend called on to testify will come back and tell the person concerning whom he testified, and it should be so." The key to encouraging "free and untrammeled disclosures" by witnesses, it is argued, is to assure the witness who desires secrecy that others will not disclose his testimony, not to require secrecy from those witnesses who feel duty bound to disclose. Some commentators add that the ability of a witness to "go public" stands as a deterrent against grand jury harassment of witnesses.

(d) Disclosure to Further Criminal Law Enforcement. Since only one or two prosecutors will ordinarily appear before the grand jury, provision must be made, as a matter of practical necessity, for disclosure by those attorneys to other members of the prosecutor's staff (including nonattorney support personnel) and police officers assisting in the investigation. Almost all jurisdictions will allow disclosure to such persons without court order. In the federal system, the investigative staff may include agents borrowed from administrative agencies that may later have an interest in pursuing a civil or administrative action against the target. Rule 6(e) therefore includes a provision restricting such personnel to use of the disclosed material in assisting the prosecuting attorney in the performance of "a duty to enforce criminal law." If the administrative agency desires access to grand jury matter, even that disclosed to its borrowed personnel, it must seek a court order as discussed in subsection (f). The same principle limits prosecutors in their use of grand jury matter. If an Assistant United States Attorney first participates in a grand jury investigation and then joins a government legal team pursuing a civil action relating to the same matter, that attorney cannot reveal the grand jury matter to those other attorneys or otherwise disclose the matter in the civil action, unless first obtaining a court order.

In the course of a grand jury investigation and a subsequent prosecution, the prosecutor or assisting personnel may have need to reveal grand jury matter to third parties in a variety of settings relating to the resolution of the investigation and prosecution. These include asking a possible witness about grand jury matter in determining whether that person should be subpoenaed, asking a possible recipient of an immunity grant about grand jury matter, asking a grand jury witness or a trial witness about grand jury matter not provided by that witness, revealing grand jury matter to the defendant or defense counsel in the course of plea negotiations or providing informal discovery, and revealing grand jury matter to a court in connection with a judicial hearing on such matters as sentencing or the issuance of a search warrant. While such disclosures are made in the performance of the prosecutor's "duty to enforce criminal law," here, unlike disclosures made under that principle to investigative personnel, the disclosure is to persons who would not constitute agents of the prosecutor and therefore would not be subject to the prosecutor's obligation of secrecy.

Although such disclosures must be quite common, the caselaw is quite sparse, with the courts reaching mixed results. Moreover, much of that caselaw comes from the federal system, where the presence of a special provision on disclosures to government personnel arguably suggests a special concern that even disclosures for law enforcement purposes be made only to persons who are under an obligation of continued secrecy. Where feasible, prosecutors will attempt to bypass the issue by shaping the disclosure so as to avoid identifying the information as coming from the grand jury. Several cases have suggested that secrecy provisions are not violated when prosecutors or investigators refer to grand jury matter in interviewing a prospective witness without identifying the matter as coming from the grand jury. Also, in some settings (e.g., disclosures to a court in a sentencing hearing), the prosecutor will have ample opportunity to obtain in advance a court order authorizing the disclosure.

(e) Disclosure to Defendant Pursuant to Discovery Rules. Approximately a dozen states grant defendant a complete transcript of the grand jury proceedings that produced his indictment. Apart from those states, pretrial discovery of grand jury matter tends to be treated no differently than discovery of other material of the same character. Thus, documents and physical evidence subpoenaed by the grand jury are treated the same as documents and physical evidence otherwise obtained by the prosecution. They are discoverable insofar as they meet the traditional standards for discovery of such material—that it was obtained from the defendant, will be introduced by the prosecutor, or will be material to the defendant's preparation of a defense.

Similarly, recorded grand jury testimony tends to be treated no differently than other prior recorded statements (e.g., recorded statements made to by the police). Thus, in the substantial number of states which provide pretrial discovery of the prior recorded statements of prosecution witnesses, the defendant can obtain pretrial the grand jury testimony of those witnesses. A witness testifying before a grand jury in such states must recognize that his testimony will eventually be disclosed if the grand jury issues an indictment and the government then lists him as a possible trial witness. In the federal system and the many states that do not permit pretrial discovery of a witness' prior recorded statement, but grant a right to such statements at trial for use in impeachment, the same standards apply to the trial witness' grand jury testimony. Here, the grand jury witness stands a better chance of not having his testimony disclosed, because even if an indictment is issued and the grand jury witness is likely to be needed as a trial witness, the defendant will only be able to demand disclosure if the trial occurs, and most cases are resolved by a guilty plea.

Several states appear to still recognize a secrecy interest in grand jury material that restricts defense discovery of a witness' recorded grand jury testimony as compared to his other prior recorded statements. In large part, however, grand jury secrecy no longer plays a significant role in itself in limiting pretrial and trial discovery of grand jury material by defendants. Two changes in perspective have contributed to this development. First, courts have come to view the "traditional reasons for grand jury secrecy" as "largely inapplicable" to post-indictment disclosure of a trial witness' grand jury testimony, particularly where disclosure is delayed until the witness testifies at trial. Second, the interest of the defendant and the judicial system in ensuring that "a criminal conviction not be based on the testimony of untruthful or inaccurate witnesses" is generally recognized as having substantially higher priority than the interests supporting grand jury secrecy.

(f) Disclosure to Third Parties. All jurisdictions recognize the authority of the court, under certain circumstances, to order disclosure of grand jury matter to third parties (i.e., persons other than prosecution personnel or defendants) for use in other proceedings. The most common third party recipients are litigants in a civil suit, administrative agencies, and government personnel outside of the law enforcement field. In jurisdictions with provisions similar to Federal Rule 6(e), disclosures to such persons are governed by a provision authorizing court ordered disclosure "preliminary to or in connection with a judicial proceeding." In jurisdictions with less detailed provisions, third party disclosures may be authorized under a general exception for disclosure "upon written order of the court."

The traditional standard applicable to court ordered disclosures to third parties is the "particularized need" standard set forth by the Supreme Court in *Douglas Oil Co. of California v. Petrol Stops Northwest* (1979). It requires third parties seeking disclosure to "show that the material they seek is needed to avoid a possible injustice in another judicial proceeding, that the need for disclosure is greater than the need for continued secrecy, and that their request is structured to cover only material so needed." Although a showing of need that is particularized is a part of this standard, it is only one component of what *Douglas Oil* described as a "balancing process" attuned to the "relevant circumstances of a particular case." Supreme Court and lower federal court decisions point to a variety of factors that should be weighed in this balancing process.

Initially, the court will look to the status of the investigation that produced the requested grand jury material. The need for secrecy clearly is greatest while the jury is still gathering evidence and considering whether to indict. As a result, third party disclosure during the pendency of an investigation rarely will be granted. On the other hand, once the grand jury is finished with the matter, the need for secrecy declines, and the petitioner's burden in establishing a particularized need outweighing secrecy is reduced. However, as the *Douglas Oil* noted, the value of grand jury secrecy is only "reduced," not "eliminated," by the termination of the investigation. Consideration must be given to the long term impact of the disclosure extending beyond the individual case. In particular, witnesses in future investigations "will be consider[ing] the likelihood that their testimony may one day be disclosed to outside parties," and each instance of a court-ordered disclosure may magnify that risk in their minds.

Another factor to be weighed is whether the third party seeks disclosure that might subject grand jury witnesses to "retribution or social stigma." One of the considerations that the Supreme Court found to weigh against disclosure to a participant in a civil antitrust suit was that witnesses in an antitrust investigation often are employees of the target companies, or their customers or suppliers, and might face discharge or other forms of retaliation if their testimony were disclosed to their employers. *U.S. v. Procter & Gamble* (1958). On the other hand, if there already has been substantial disclosure of the grand jury materials to the investigated companies (as where the companies were indicted and gained the witness' statements in the course of criminal discovery), disclosure to the other parties in the parallel civil suit is less likely to cause concern.

An additional consideration is the narrowness of the disclosure requested. Under a standard of "particularized" need, a request for broad disclosure will almost certainly work against the petitioner, as it did in *Procter & Gamble*, where the Court characterized the rejected request as seeking "wholesale discovery." As the Supreme Court noted in *Douglas Oil*, the "typical showing of particularized need arises when a civil litigant seeks to use the grand jury transcript at the trial to impeach a witness, to refresh his recollection, to test his credibility and the like." The disclosure there "can be limited to those portions of a particular witness' testimony that bear upon his * * * direct testimony at trial." In addition, such requests are less likely to be based on a speculative judgment as to need, while the use involved serves the important interest of ensuring that the factfinder is not misled. In assessing need even as to fairly limited disclosure, however, the court also must take into consideration the availability of alternative means (such as civil discovery) that might produce the same information. The fact that disclosure will avoid the significant expense and delay of the alternative means is not in itself sufficient to establish the requisite need.

Where the request for disclosure comes from a governmental agency pursuing an administrative or civil claim, many courts have required a somewhat lesser showing of particularized need. The Supreme Court has rejected the contention that a government agency can justify disclosure simply by showing the relevancy of the requested material, but it has also said that the balancing process may be somewhat different for disclosure to government bodies as opposed to private parties. The Court has noted in particular that "the district court may weigh the public interest, if any, served by disclosure to a government body—along with the requisite particularized need—in determining whether the need for disclosure is greater than the need for continued secrecy." *Ill. v. Abbot & Associates* (1983). Thus, where the contemplated disclosure was to civil attorneys within the government for the purpose of deciding whether to file a civil action, the district court could properly take into account the likelihood that the disclosure would "sav[e] the Government, the potential defendants, and witnesses, the pains of costly and time consuming depositions and interrogatories which might later have turned out to be wasted if the Government decided not to file a civil action after all." *U.S. v. John Doe, Inc. I* (1987). Accordingly too, while the governmental agency's capacity to obtain the same information through its own investigative authority is a consideration weighing against the need for disclosure, that factor cannot be treated as a per se bar against authorizing disclosure. Indeed, that authority may strengthen the case for disclosure as it responds to another concern noted by the *John Doe*

Court—that the use of grand jury materials by other government agencies not "threaten to subvert the limitations applied outside the grand jury context on the Government's powers of discovery and investigation."

Under Federal Rule 6(e) and similar state provisions, a showing of particularized need is combined with the additional requirement that the disclosure be "preliminary to or in connection with a judicial proceeding." As the Supreme Court noted in *U.S. v. Baggot* (1983), this requirement "reflects a judgment that not every beneficial purpose or even every valid government purpose, is an appropriate reason for breaching grand jury secrecy." The Rule "contemplates only uses related fairly directly to some identifiable litigation, pending or anticipated," as measured by the "primary purpose of the disclosure." *Baggot* held that disclosure for use in an IRS audit of civil tax liability did not meet this prerequisite since the agency's determination of tax liability and its collection of any amount determined to be due did not require judicial intervention. The mere possibility that the taxpayer might bring a court action to challenge the agency's non-judicial means of enforcing its determination would not make the agency proceeding "preliminary to a judicial proceeding."

§ 7.4 The Right to Every Man's Evidence

(a) The Public's Right and the Individual's Duty. The grand jury's investigative authority is commonly said to rest largely on "the long standing principle that 'the public has a right to every man's evidence.'" Indeed, no aspect of grand jury power is more frequently extolled by the courts, particularly in cases rejecting challenges to subpoenas, than its right to compel the testimony of any person, subject only to "constitutional, common law or statutory privilege." The Supreme Court has described the grand jury's authority to compel testimony as "[a]mong the necessary and most important of the powers * * * [that] assure the effective functioning of government in an ordered society." While the Court has never stated precisely why it views this authority as so essential to the "welfare of society," its opinions appear to support the conventional explanation that effective law enforcement requires the cooperation of the public, and that there are many instances in which such cooperation would not be forthcoming if it could not be compelled.

The modern tradition has been to relieve citizens of any legal responsibility to assist the police or prosecutor in the investigation of crime. Misprision is no longer a crime in most jurisdictions, and the individual has no obligation (even when there is absolutely no possibility of personal incrimination) to respond to police inquiries.

At the same time, increased urbanization may have produced a setting in which fewer people feel a responsibility to the community and hence a responsibility to assist law enforcement officials. The grand jury's authority to compel testimony therefore takes on added importance. That authority is accepted, the Court has noted, not simply because it is "historically grounded," but because the "obligation of every person to appear and give testimony" is "indispensable to the administration of justice." Without that authority, criminal activity could be hidden behind a "wall of silence" which finds no justification in legal privilege, but is based simply on the individual's desire not to get "involved," fear of retaliation, dislike for the substantive law, or private code against "snitching."

Assuming that the authority to compel cooperation must of necessity be lodged somewhere, the courts find wisdom in the traditional delegation of that authority to the grand jury—an independent body, composed of laymen and having a membership that shifts from one term to the next. The structure of the grand jury provides assurance that investigations will be carried out free from political pressures. The capacity of a grand jury to take an investigation wherever it may lead serves to counteract suspicions of corruption and partisanship in criminal law enforcement. The grand jury therefore has the capacity not only to ferret out hidden crimes, but to relieve public concern generated by false rumors. The courts stress, however, that to serve its purpose, the grand jury must be free to carry forward wide ranging investigations.

Two points in particular have been stressed with respect to the necessary breadth of grand jury investigations. First, the grand jury must be "free from any restraint comparable to * * * [a] specific charge and showing of probable cause." It must be able to investigate "merely on suspicion that the law is being violated, or even just because it wants assurance that it is not." The jurors must be able to "act on tips, rumors, evidence offered by the prosecutor, or their own personal knowledge." They must have the capacity to "run down every available clue" and to examine "all witnesses * * * in every proper way." It is recognized, in this connection, that "if the investigation is to be meaningful, some exploration or fishing necessarily is inherent and entitled to exist."

Second, courts frequently note that the grand jury must be free of technical rules that would cause grand jury proceedings to be punctuated by litigation and delay. Judicial rulings must not provide the recalcitrant witness with a long list of challenges that can be used "to tie the grand jury into knots—to drag out the proceedings with technicalities instead of matters of substance." In determining whether a particular objection should be recognized, a court must consider whether that holding "would saddle a grand jury with minitrials and preliminary showings [that] would assuredly impede its investigation and frustrate the public's interest in the fair and expeditious administration of the criminal laws." The grand jury must be left "free to pursue its investigations unhindered by external influence or supervision so long as it does not trench upon the legitimate rights of a witness called before it."

The Supreme Court has acknowledged that the obligation of the citizen to appear and testify before the grand jury is not without its burdens. Appearance may be "onerous at times" and required answers "may prove embarrassing or result in an unwelcome disclosure of * * * personal affairs"; but such personal sacrifices, the Supreme Court has noted, are "part of the necessary contribution of the individual to the welfare of the public." In this regard, the duty to testify before the grand jury is sometimes compared to the duty to testify at trial, which is imposed simply upon a determination of one of the parties that a particular person should be subpoenaed. There are, of course, certain distinctions in the two situations. The witness summoned to testify at trial knows the subject to be considered, and is not himself the target of the inquiry. In the grand jury setting, the subject under inquiry may not be revealed, and the person summoned may well be a prospective defendant. The witness at trial testifies in public while the witness before the grand jury testifies in a closed proceeding. Justice Thurgood Marshall suggested that a grand jury appearance may carry with it a substantial stigma, not attached to a trial appearance, since "the public often treats an appearance before a grand jury as tantamount to a visit to the stationhouse." Courts recognize that such distinctions may require a somewhat different treatment of the grand jury witness in a few situations, but they also have concluded that the protection afforded the grand jury witness is sufficient to impose a general duty to appear similar to that imposed upon the trial witness. That protection is said to stem from four sources. First, the grand jury witness retains the same constitutional, statutory and common law privileges as the trial witness. Second, the secrecy of the grand jury proceeding affords the witness protection against damage to his reputation and mitigates any element of embarrassment in his testimony. Third, the witness has the protection afforded by the presence of the grand jurors, who, as Justice Black once noted, "have no axes to grind and are not charged personally with the administration of the law." Finally, grand juries remain subject to judicial supervision.

(b) Privileges and Other Protections. In every jurisdiction, a subpoenaed person may challenge the subpoena itself, or a question put by the grand jury, if compliance would violate a testimonial privilege recognized in that jurisdiction. With one exception, the privilege against self-incrimination, we leave the discussion of the testimonial privileges to the evidence treatises. The self-incrimination privilege is considered at length (§ 7.8–7.11) because of its central role in grand jury investigations.

§ 7.5 Fourth Amendment Challenges to Subpoenas

(a) Applicability of the Fourth Amendment to Subpoenas for Documents. The application of the Fourth Amendment to court orders requiring production of documentary evidence began with *Boyd v. U.S.* (1886), a widely celebrated case that in most respects has little current vitality. *Boyd* involved a customs forfeiture proceeding in which the government sought to utilize an 1847 statutory provision allowing it to gain documentary evidence from the importer of the property to be forfeited. The provision authorized the trial judge, on motion of the government describing a particular document and indicating what it might prove, to issue a notice directing the importer to produce that document. The petitioners in *Boyd* challenged a notice that directed them to produce the invoice for thirty-five cases of plate glass allegedly imported without payment of customs duties. The Supreme Court sustained their challenge, holding that the notice and the statute authorizing it violated both the Fourth Amendment and the self-incrimination clause of the Fifth Amendment.

Speaking to the Fourth Amendment, the *Boyd* Court acknowledged that the notice procedure "lacked certain aggravating incidents of actual search and seizure, such as forcible entry into a man's house and searching among his papers," but stressed that it nonetheless "accomplish[ed] the substantial object of those acts in forcing from a party evidence against himself." Accordingly, a "compulsory production of a man's private papers" would be treated as "within the scope of the Fourth Amendment to the Constitution, in all cases in which a search and seizure would be." Having found the Fourth Amendment applicable, the *Boyd* opinion turned to the question as to whether this particular "search and seizure, or what is equivalent thereto," was unreasonable within the meaning of that Amendment. It concluded that the compelled production of a private document was per se unreasonable.

Boyd cited several factors in concluding that the Fourth Amendment simply did not allow a search, or its equivalent, as to private papers. It relied, in part, on the landmark English ruling in *Entick v. Carrington & Three Other King's Messengers* (1765), which had found a trespass in government officials entering the plaintiff's home and breaking open his boxes and examining his papers. This decision, which undoubtedly influenced "those who framed the Fourth Amendment," had spoken of the individual's papers as his "dearest property," and it was the invasion of the individual's indefeasible right in that property, rather than the "breaking of his doors and the rummaging of his drawers" that was the "essence" of the violation of individual liberty in that case. The Court also noted that the "compulsory extortion" of private papers to be used as evidence to convict the individual was parallel to compelling testimony for the same purpose, and here, "the Fourth and Fifth Amendments run into each other." What "is condemned in the Fifth Amendment throws light on * * * what is an 'unreasonable search and seizure' " and renders per se unreasonable a search which is not "substantially different from compelling [a person] * * * to be a witness against himself."

The *Boyd* position on per se unreasonableness was short-lived. In *Hale v. Henkel* (1906), decided twenty years later, the Supreme Court rejected that position, but reaffirmed the applicability of the Fourth Amendment to a "compulsory production of a man's private papers." The *Hale* majority initially noted that *Boyd* had erred in reading together the Fourth and Fifth Amendment protections. Any absolute prohibition against compelled production of documentary items lay in the self-incrimination clause alone, and that clause had no application in the case before it; the challenged grand jury subpoena was directed to corporate documents and corporations did not have the benefit of the self-incrimination privilege. However, the Court continued, the corporation was entitled to the protection of the Fourth Amendment, and "an order for the production of books and papers" could still constitute "an unreasonable search and seizure." While it was true that "a search ordinarily implies a quest of an officer of the law, and a seizure contemplates a forcible dispossession of property, still, as was held in *Boyd,* the substance of the offense is * * * [unreasonable] compulsory production, whether under a search warrant or a subpoena duces tecum."

The *Hale* Court announced, with little explanation, that the Fourth Amendment's protection was violated by a subpoena duces tecum that is "far too sweeping in its terms to be regarded as reasonable." That overbreadth was present in the subpoena before the Court. It required production of corporate papers relating to transactions with various different companies, and such a broad request was capable of preventing the corporation from carrying on its business. While the government might have need for many of these documents, it would have to make some showing of "materiality" before it could "justify an order for the production of such a mass of papers."

Justice McKenna, concurring separately in *Hale*, argued that the Fourth Amendment should not apply in any respect to a subpoena to compel the production of documents. The service of the subpoena involved "no element of trespass or force," nor was it "secret and intrusive." The subpoena could not be "finally enforced except after challenge, and a judgment of the court upon the challenge." These safeguards and limitations, from Justice McKenna's perspective, clearly distinguished the subpoena from the search. Justice McKenna also considered the possibility that the majority was saying that a subpoena did not involve a search except where it was "too sweeping," but he could not understand how that quality alone, improper though it may be, could transform the subpoena into a search.

The *Hale* majority failed to respond to Justice McKenna's criticism, apart from its reference to *Boyd*'s analysis. It failed also to explain why the subpoena, though governed by the Fourth Amendment, was not subject to the usual Fourth Amendment requirement of probable cause, but simply an overbreadth prohibition. Commentators and lower courts have sought to provide answers where *Hale* failed to do so. Explaining *Hale* as a Fourth Amendment case, they have offered two somewhat different explanations for the positions taken there.

One explanation rests in large part on Fourth Amendment concepts that had not been articulated at the time of the *Hale* ruling. Those concepts are: (1) the Fourth Amendment's reach must be determined by reference to its primary function of protecting expectations of privacy; and (2) the Fourth Amendment imposes different standards of reasonableness depending upon the character of the search involved. In light of the obvious expectation of privacy in private papers, the state is said to engage in activity within the reach of the Fourth Amendment when it examines papers not voluntarily exposed. The examination invades privacy without regard to whether there is an additional invasion of privacy in placing the state agent in the location where that examination is possible. However, the search conducted through the use of the subpoena is less invasive because the agent looks only at the papers subpoenaed (not the premises in which they were kept) and the subpoena provides an opportunity for a prior judicial challenge. Taking these factors into consideration, along with the long history of grand jury subpoenas issued without probable cause, *Hale* is seen as the forerunner of a series of later Supreme Court cases that sustained under the Fourth Amendment regulatory searches made without probable cause (see § 2.9(a)). Here, the special context of a search by subpoena limits Fourth Amendment reasonableness to requiring no more than a showing that the subpoena is restricted to documents material to the investigation.

This first explanation, however, does not fully explain *Hale*. It does not suggest that the Fourth Amendment protection be conditioned on the subpoena compelling production of a substantial body of documents (as *Hale's* overbreadth analysis seemed to suggest) or that overbreadth be tested by reference to the economic burden imposed upon the individual or entity by being forced to relinquish those documents (as *Hale* clearly did).

A second explanation of *Hale* builds upon Justice McKenna's suggestion that the *Hale* majority found the Fourth Amendment applicable only when the subpoena was overlybroad. The theory here is that the subpoena which is too sweeping, which calls for a mass of documents without regard to what is relevant, necessarily requires a sifting through of the documents to obtain those that are needed. Whether that sifting takes place on the premises of the owner or in the offices of the prosecutor assisting the grand jury, it constitutes a search. Thus, *Hale* and other courts have compared the overbroad subpoena to a "general warrant." While this explanation arguably fits the fact situation in *Hale*, it fails to explain the various lower court rulings that have applied *Hale*'s condemnation of subpoena overbreadth to subpoenas that did not require a large volume of documents.

Forty years after *Hale*, in *Oklahoma Press Publishing Co. v. Walling* (1946) the Supreme Court suggested still a third explanation—that the Fourth Amendment had no direct application to subpoenas, but was looked to only by analogy to protect against a different form of "officious intermeddling by government officials." In that case, which involved an administrative agency subpoena duces tecum, the Court acknowledged that certain misconceptions had arisen due to the failure of lower courts to distinguish between "so-called 'figurative' or 'constructive'" searches by subpoena and "cases of actual search and seizure." The Court noted that "only in * * * [an] analogical sense can any question related to search and seizure be thought to arise" in subpoena cases. It stressed that the Fourth Amendment, "if applicable," did no more than "guard against abuse only by way of too much indefiniteness or breadth" in the subpoena. The interests to be protected were "not identical with those protected against invasion by actual search and seizure" but arose out of the right of persons to be free from "officious examination [that] can be expensive, so much so that it eats up men's substance," and thereby "become[s] persecution when carried beyond reason."

In its post-*Oklahoma Press* rulings the Supreme Court has returned to referring to the prohibition against "overbreadth" in the subpoena of documents as a Fourth Amendment requirement. It has not, however, retreated from *Oklahoma Press's* explanation of the function of the overbreadth limitation. Thus, lower courts applying that limitation to grand jury subpoenas have looked in large part to the avoidance of undue burdens upon the subpoenaed party. In some instances, however, those rulings have appeared to take into consideration as well the especially private nature of the papers involved. A survey of those lower court rulings is set forth in subsection (b) below. Because a very similar limitation is found in provisions like Federal Rule 17(c), which provides protection against subpoenas duces tecum that are "unreasonable or oppressive," the decisions applying those provisions, described in § 7.6(b) and (c), must also be considered in assessing the potential for successful objections based upon the "too sweeping" reach of a subpoena.

(b) Applying the Overbreadth Prohibition. Courts applying the constitutional prohibition against overlybroad subpoenas duces tecum frequently start out by noting that the stated standard, proscribing breadth "far too sweeping * * * to be regarded as reasonable," necessarily requires a fact-specific judgment, with each ruling tied to the circumstances of the individual case. At the same time, the courts have sought, with limited success, to develop some general criteria to guide that judgment. Initially, the question arises as to whether the party challenging the subpoena must establish sufficient breadth to suggest that compliance will be burdensome. While there is language in Supreme Court opinions suggesting that is a prerequisite and most successful challenges have involved such subpoenas, a small group of rulings have struck down subpoenas that would have presented no significant burdens in collecting and relinquishing the records. Those cases involved subpoenas that either suggested on their face that no effort had been made to limit the subpoena to what was needed or that dealt with sensitive information.

Assuming some potential for overbreadth, courts then will turn to the three "components" of reasonableness initially developed by the lower federal courts: (1) the subpoena may command only the production of things relevant to the investigation being pursued; (2) specification of things to be produced must be made with reasonable particularity; and (3) production of records covering only a reasonable period of time may be required.

The second element of this formulation is commonly described as having "two prongs": first, "particularity of description" so that the subpoenaed party "know[s] what he is being asked to produce"; and second, "particularity of breadth" so that the subpoenaed party "is not harassed or oppressed to the point that he experiences an unreasonable business detriment." The requirement of adequate notice rarely poses significant difficulty, although ambiguities may arise where documents are described by their relationship to a particular event. Accordingly, courts looking to the second component tend to focus on the second factor, the degree of burden imposed by production.

While many courts have treated the elements of relevancy, sufficient particularity to avoid an undue burden of production, and reasonableness of time period as separate requirements of reasonableness, so that deficiency as to any one element can invalidate the subpoena, it is clear that the three elements are interrelated. Greater particularity, by narrowing the range of documents to be produced, will extend the time period into which the subpoena may reach. On the other hand, as a subpoena reaches farther into the past, a court is more likely to require a stronger showing of relevancy. So too, the significance of the burden of production will be weighed against the strength of the showing as to relevancy and the reasonableness of the time period. Thus, courts have noted that a subpoena that clearly meets the relevancy and time-period requirements will be rejected on the basis of a substantial burden of production only in the most extreme cases.

While the subpoenaed party bears the ultimate burden of establishing that a challenged subpoena is unreasonable, many courts insist that the government make an initial showing of relevancy since it alone knows the precise nature of the grand jury inquiry. Ordinarily, this showing requires no more than a general description of the relationship of the material sought to the subject matter of the investigation. A critical factor here will be the character of that subject matter. Some activities (e.g., crimes involving the illicit use of funds) will render relevant all financial records, as total income and receipts must be traced. The possibility of unknown conspirators similarly opens up the range of documents relating to other parties. Similarly, antitrust investigations demand a broad range of documents since the violation may be reflected in many different aspects of a company's business.

Courts generally give grand juries considerable leeway in judging relevancy. They recognize that "some exploration or fishing necessarily is inherent" since the grand jury will not ordinarily have a "catalog of what books and papers exist" nor "any basis for knowing what their character or contents immediately are." Similarly, the grand jury cannot be expected to anticipate the full range of criminal activity that might be connected with a possible criminal enterprise. Where the time period clearly is reasonable and the burden of production is limited, courts have accepted as sufficient showings of "some possible relationship, however indirect." This produces a relevancy standard very similar to the standard announced by the Supreme Court in applying Rule 17(c)'s reasonableness requirement. See § 7.6(b).

Objections to a subpoena duces tecum based solely upon the burden and expense of assembling a large quantity of records are almost always doomed to failure. With the advent of photocopying and the easy reproduction of computerized records, the possibility that the subpoenaed party will be unable to carry on its business without the relinquished records—a major concern in *Hale*—is largely mooted. Courts commonly have viewed the expense of assembling and duplicating the materials as simply another cost of doing business, particularly where the subpoenaed party is a large corporation. Moreover, in cases where that expense imposes a true financial hardship, the government may respond by offering reimbursement of all costs. The end result is that the burden of production is given weight primarily where the court has substantial doubts as to the relevancy of the documents or the reasonableness of the time span. Without such concerns, subpoenas have been upheld which required production of as much as fifty tons of documents.

(c) **Application of the Fourth Amendment to Other Subpoenas: *Dionisio* and *Mara*.** In *U. S. v. Dionisio* (1973) and *U.S. v. Mara* (1973), the Court left no doubt that the Fourth Amendment ordinarily does not apply to subpoenas apart from the "too sweeping" limitation upon subpoenas for documents. *Dionisio* and *Mara* were companion cases arising from separate grand jury investigations. In *Dionisio,* the grand jury had subpoenaed approximately 20 persons, including Dionisio, to give voice exemplars for comparison with recorded conversations that were material to the grand jury's investigation. In *Mara*, the witness was directed to produce handwriting exemplars for the purpose of determining whether he was the author of certain writings considered by the grand jury. Both witnesses claimed that the subpoenas constituted unreasonable searches and seizures because there was no showing of a reasonable basis for requiring their exemplars. The Court of Appeals agreed. It compared the dragnet effect of the subpoena in *Dionisio* to the mass police roundup of possible suspects for fingerprinting that was condemned in *Davis v. Miss* (§ 2.8(g)). The *Davis* opinion had suggested that a court order detaining a suspect for the purpose of obtaining identification evidence might be possible on a showing of less than probable cause (i.e., a reasonable suspicion), but the subpoena here had not been supported by anything other than a prosecutor's claim that the exemplars were "essential and necessary." The lower court reasoned that "interposition of the grand jury between the witnesses and the government" should not "eliminate the Fourth Amendment protection that would [otherwise] bar the government's obtaining the evidence."

The *Dionisio* majority concluded that the lower court's analogy to police detention was flawed because "a subpoena to appear before a grand jury is not a 'seizure' in the Fourth Amendment sense." There was a dramatic difference in the "compulsion exerted" by a subpoena as opposed to an "arrest or even an investigative stop". The "latter is abrupt, is effected with force or the threat of it and often in demeaning circumstances, and, in the case of arrest, results in a record involving social stigma." A grand jury subpoena, on the other hand, "is served in the same manner as other legal process; it involves no stigma whatever; if the time for appearance is inconvenient, this can generally be altered; and it remains at all times under the control and supervision of a court."

The *Dionisio* majority acknowledged that a grand jury subpoena, though differing from the arrest or investigative stop, could be both "inconvenient" and "burdensome." Any "personal sacrifices" required, however, were merely incidental to the "historically grounded obligation of every person to appear and give his evidence before the grand jury." The addition here of directives to give identification evidence did not alter the nature of the burden imposed. Neither the voice exemplar nor the handwriting sample invaded a privacy interest protected under the Fourth Amendment. Both related to physical characteristics "constantly exposed to the public" and were to be distinguished, for example, from the taking of a blood sample.

Having found that the Fourth Amendment had no application to either the summons to appear nor the directive to provide identification exemplars, the Court concluded that there was "no justification for requiring the grand jury to satisfy even the minimal requirement of 'reasonableness' imposed by the Court of Appeals." The grand jury "could exercise its 'broad investigative powers' on the basis of 'tips, rumors, evidence offered by the prosecutor, or [the jurors] own personal knowledge,'" and it should not be required to explain the basis for each of its subpoenas. To "saddle a grand jury with minitrials and preliminary showings would assuredly impede its investigation and frustrate the public's interest in the fair and expeditious administration of the criminal laws."

The *Dionisio* opinion clearly did not go so far as to hold the Fourth Amendment inapplicable to subpoenas compelling the production of any and all types of identification evidence. Indeed, in noting that a subpoena directive to produce a voice sample was "immeasurably further removed" from Fourth Amendment protection than the taking of a blood sample, the Court intimated that a grand jury subpoena requiring a witness to furnish such a sample might well be subject to Fourth Amendment limitations. Not surprisingly, several lower court cases subsequently held that the Fourth Amendment does apply to a blood-sample subpoena. Whereas *Dionisio* and *Mara* involved the production of physical characteristics exposed to the public, which had previously been held in other contexts not to invade a reasonable expectation of privacy, the taking of blood constitutes a penetration of the skin and production of internal fluid, which had long been held to constitute a search when performed under the direction of the police. Courts have noted the possibility that the taking of other identification evidence (the hair root, though not a hair clipping, and saliva) also may be subject to Fourth Amendment limitations.

The issue that has troubled the courts where the Fourth Amendment applies to the taking of identification evidence is whether the presence of a grand jury subpoena makes the search reasonable on less than the probable cause that presumably would be necessary for the taking of that evidence at the direction of the police. Some courts have concluded that the grand jury subpoena makes no difference, and probable cause is required. Other courts reject that conclusion. They note that there is no arrest involved, that the grand jury cannot be expected to show probable cause that the blood will constitute evidence of a crime where its very purpose is to determine whether there is probable cause to charge a person with a crime, and that the subpoena affords the opportunity for challenge prior to the taking of the blood. One court has viewed the lesser Fourth Amendment standard of "reasonable suspicion" to be appropriate, while another has described the appropriate standard as a "reasonable basis for believing * * * that a blood sample will provide test results that will significantly aid * * * the grand jury in their investigation of circumstances in which there is good reason to believe a crime ha[s] been committed."

§ 7.6　Challenges to Misuse of the Subpoena Authority

(a) **Improper Subject of Investigation.** It generally is conceded that "a subpoenaed [grand jury] witness has no right to know the subject matter of the inquiry or the person[s] against whom the investigation is directed." Ordinarily, however, the witness will become aware of at least the general area of inquiry through a designation of the subject matter in the subpoena, the questions asked, or the documents requested. In rare instances, this information may suggest that the grand jury is investigating an activity for which it cannot indict. Although such an investigation would ordinarily be beyond the grand jury's investigative authority, a witness' objection on that ground generally will be unavailing. *Blair v. U.S.* (1919), though it involved a rather convoluted subject matter objection, is generally viewed as barring all witness challenges to the grand jury's "jurisdiction" to investigate.

In *Blair,* the witness claimed that the transaction under investigation was beyond the grand jury's investigative authority because the applicable federal criminal statute was unconstitutional. The Supreme Court initially noted that consideration of the constitutionality of the statute at this point, prior to any indictment, would be contrary to the long-established practice of "refrain[ing] from passing upon the constitutionality of an act of Congress unless obliged to do so." It then proceeded, however, to speak in quite general terms of a witness' lack of capacity to challenge the "authority * * * of the grand jury," provided the jury had "de facto existence and organization." The Court treated the position of the grand jury witness as analogous to that of the trial witness. Neither could raise objections of "incompetency or irrelevancy," for those matters were of "no concern" to a witness, as opposed to a party. For the same reasons, witnesses also should not be allowed "to take exception to the jurisdiction of the grand jury or the court over the particular subject matter that is under investigation." The grand jury operates as a "grand inquest," which requires broad investigative powers. It must have authority, in particular, "to investigate the facts in order to determine the question of whether the facts show a case within [its] jurisdiction."

(b) Relevancy Objections. In commenting upon the objections of a witness, either at trial or before the grand jury, *Blair* noted that "[h]e is not entitled to urge objections of incompetency or irrelevancy, such as a party might raise, for this is no concern of his." This statement was commonly viewed by federal courts as barring all witness objections to the relevancy of information sought by a grand jury. Although relevancy was properly considered in making the Fourth Amendment determination as to whether a subpoena duces tecum was "too sweeping to be reasonable," a subpoena duces tecum limited in scope could not be challenged solely on the ground that it was seeking information not material to the inquiry. Thus, *U.S. v. Mara* (see § 7.5(c)) overturned a lower court ruling that had required, as a Fourth Amendment prerequisite, a preliminary government showing of relevancy as to a grand jury subpoena duces tecum that clearly was not overbroad, as it simply mandated production of a handwriting exemplar. Similarly, a witness could not object to questions put to him on the ground that they had no bearing upon the subject of the inquiry.

Federal Rule 17(c), which provides the grounding for the issuance of a subpoena duces tecum on behalf of the grand jury, authorizes the quashing of such a subpoena where "compliance would be unreasonable or oppressive." *In U.S. v. R. Enterprises*, (1974), the Court held that requiring compliance with a subpoena duces tecum would be "unreasonable" if the subpoena failed to meet a minimum standard of relevance. The lower court there had applied to a grand jury subpoena for business records the three prerequisites established in *U.S. v. Nixon* (1974) for a trial subpoena—that the documents sought be relevant, admissible in evidence, and adequately specified. The element of specificity was not disputed, but with *Nixon* applicable, the government had to make a preliminary showing as to admissibility and relevancy. Justice O'Connor's opinion for Court cited several reasons for refusing to extend the *Nixon* standard to grand jury proceedings. Insofar as that standard looked to the evidentiary admissibility of the items subpoenaed, it contradicted a line of earlier Supreme Court rulings holding that the grand jury could consider, and issue an indictment based upon, evidence that would be inadmissible at trial. Applying the *Nixon* standard to grand juries also would present unacceptable administrative difficulties. It "would invite procedural delays and detours while courts evaluate the relevancy and admissibility of documents sought by a particular subpoena." In *Dionisio*, the Court had "expressly stated that grand jury proceedings should be free of such delays." So too, in requiring a preliminary showing of relevancy, the *Nixon* standard would be inconsistent with the "strict secrecy requirements" of grand jury proceedings. "Requiring the Government to explain in too much detail the particular reasons underlying a subpoena" would "compromise 'the indispensable secrecy of grand jury proceedings,'" and it would "afford the targets of the investigation far more information about the grand jury's internal workings * * * than the Federal Rules of Criminal Procedure appear to contemplate."

Having rejected the application of the *Nixon* standard, Justice O'Connor then turned to the more difficult task of "fashion[ing] an appropriate standard of reasonableness" in the application of Rule 17(c). It was well established that "the investigatory powers of the grand jury are * * * not unlimited." The grand jury could not, for example, "engage in arbitrary fishing expeditions" or "select targets of investigation out of malice or an intent to harass." Applying such limits, however, required consideration of conflicting elements in the grand jury process. On the one hand, the decision as to the appropriate charge "is routinely not made until after the grand jury has concluded its investigation," and "one simply cannot know in advance whether information sought during the investigation will be relevant and admissible in the prosecution for a particular offense." On the other hand, the subpoenaed party "faces a difficult situation" in challenging the improper use of a subpoena. Grand juries ordinarily "do not announce publicly the subjects of their investigations," and the subpoenaed party therefore "may have no conception of the Government's purpose in seeking production of the requested information." Thus, what was needed was a standard of reasonableness that "gives due weight to the difficult position of subpoena recipients but does not impair the strong governmental interests in affording grand juries wide latitude, avoiding minitrials on peripheral matters, and preserving a necessary level of secrecy."

Turning to the specific guidelines that would give substance to such a standard, Justice O'Connor noted initially that "the law presumes, absent a strong showing to the contrary, that a grand jury acts within the legitimate scope of its authority." Consequently, "a grand jury subpoena issued through normal channels is presumed to be reasonable, and the burden of showing unreasonableness must be on the recipient who seeks to avoid compliance." Reasonableness requires relevancy, but in light of the presumption, a relevancy challenge "must be denied unless the district court determines that there is no reasonable possibility that the category of materials the Government seeks will produce information relevant to the general subject of the grand jury's investigation."

Recognizing that the above standard imposed an "unenviable task" upon the party raising a relevancy challenge, Justice O'Connor suggested that the district court had authority to ease that task through appropriate procedures. The subpoenaed party in this instance was aware of the "nature of the investigation," but where that was not the case, the District Court could take steps to offset that disadvantage consistent with the "strong governmental interests in maintaining secrecy, preserving investigating flexibility, and avoiding procedural delays." Thus, "to ensure that subpoenas are not routinely challenged as a form of discovery, a district court may require that the Government reveal the subject of the investigation to the trial court *in camera*, so that the court may determine whether the motion to quash has a reasonable prospect for success before it discloses the subject matter to the challenging party."

Although the Court in *R. Enterprises* was unanimous in rejecting application of the *Nixon* standard, there was division as to the specific guidelines advanced in Justice O'Connor's opinion. Justice Scalia did not join the paragraph discussing the district court's possible authority to require the prosecution to set forth the general subject of the investigation. Three justices, in a separate opinion by Justice Stevens, argued that the burden imposed upon the challenging party will vary with the nature of the subpoena. They noted, in particular, that a less rigorous showing of lack of relevancy should be sufficient where other significant interests are involved (e.g., where the subpoena "would intrude significantly on * * * privacy interests or call for disclosure of trade secrets or other confidential material"). Admittedly, Justice O'Connor's opinion did not propose a standard for such special circumstances, but Justice Stevens expressed concern that the Court's opinion "not be read to suggest that the deferential relevance standard the Court has formulated will govern decision in every case, no matter how intrusive or burdensome the request."

(c) Oppressiveness Objections. Federal Rule 17(c) and similar state provisions authorize quashing subpoenas where compliance would be "unreasonable or oppressive." In setting forth oppressiveness as an alternative ground, Rule 17(c) implicitly recognizes that a demand may be reasonable as measured by the *R. Enterprises* standard of relevancy, yet nonetheless be oppressive. Typically claims of oppressiveness rest on the costs and disruption associated with collecting and relinquishing large quantities of documents, with the subpoenaed party arguing that the prosecution should be required to narrow the subpoena by reference to time or category of documents. These claims are analyzed in much the same fashion as the largely identical claims brought under the Fourth Amendment overbreadth doctrine, discussed in § 7.5(b). Another fairly common type of oppressiveness claim rests on the alleged chilling impact of compliance on the exercise of some right. These claims are discussed in subsection (d) below.

(d) "Chilling Effect" Objections. Grand jury witnesses in several contexts have argued that even where the testimony or documents demanded of them clearly would be relevant, the grand jury should be required to show a "compelling need" for that information where the impact of its inquiry would be to chill the exercise of a constitutionally protected right. Those challenges commonly are grounded on the court's authority to protect the constitutional right said to be chilled. They also may be framed as Rule 17(c) challenges to the oppressiveness of the subpoena. The two claims of this character receiving the most attention involve the alleged chilling impact of grand jury subpoenas upon the exercise of First Amendment rights and upon the lawyer-client relationship.

First Amendment claims. "Chilling impact" claims based upon the First Amendment stand apart from any testimonial privileges that may bear upon the exercise of rights of free speech, freedom of association, and the free exercise of religion. Where the information sought falls within a statutory or common law privilege recognized in the particular jurisdiction (e.g., a clergy or journalist privilege), that privilege will afford protection. First Amendment claims look to the First Amendment itself to restrict grand jury access to information on the theory that its disclosure will chill the exercise of a First Amendment right. Such claims have been raised by a variety of persons with respect to a variety of activities, including: reporters contending that being forced to reveal their sources, to produce their notes, or simply to be required to appear before the grand jury would chill their capacity to gather and report news; reporters contending that being forced to furnish information about the internal operations of a newspaper would chill the newspaper's capacity to print controversial articles; sellers of sexually explicit materials contending that their First Amendment right to convey non-pornographic materials would be chilled by subpoenas that require them to disclose copies of the materials distributed or business records that reveal the identity of their customers; a religious organization contending that a grand jury demand for its financial records would injure its standing in the community and chill its capacity to attract new members; organizations engaged largely or partly in political advocacy contending that being required to furnish documents that identify their members would chill the participation of those members and restrict their capacity to attract new members; a private association of a controversial character (Hells Angels Motorcycle Club) contending that a grand jury demand for information relating to its membership, funding, and organizational structure would chill the members' freedom of association; a public official contending that his right of association was chilled by a grand jury demand that he produce his calendar and schedule for past years; and the author of a book who contended that a subpoena requiring him to produce records of alleged interviews cited in the book would chill future publications. With few exceptions, such challenges have not succeeded in obtaining the quashing of the grand jury directive. However, the courts have been far less consistent in their analysis of the legal standards applicable to these "chilling-impact" claims than in their disposition of the claims.

The one Supreme Court decision directly addressing such a challenge is *Branzburg v. Hayes* (1972). A closely divided Court there rejected the contention of newspaper reporters that they could not be compelled to reveal to state grand juries their confidential sources (who were apparent participants in drug offenses) unless the prosecution first established a compelling need for obtaining that information. Justice White's majority opinion acknowledged that requiring the reporters to testify might deter future confidential sources, but noted that the extent of that deterrence was "unclear." Moreover, even if there would be some negative impact upon news gathering, that impact did not outweigh the interest of the public in the grand jury's investigation of crime. This result was not leaving "newsgathering" without any "First Amendment protections." Judicial control of the grand jury process always was available to provide an appropriate remedy if the grand jury process was misused to harass the press. Justice Powell (who provided the majority's fifth vote and joined Justice White's opinion) offered an illustration of what might be deemed harassment in his separate concurring opinion: He noted: "If the newsman is called upon to give information bearing only a remote and tenuous relationship to the subject of the investigation, or if he has some other reason to believe that his testimony implicates confidential source relationships without a legitimate need of law enforcement, he will have access to the court on a motion to quash and an appropriate protective order may be entered."

Reading *Branzburg* narrowly (as a case dealing with something less than an established chilling impact on a First Amendment right), some lower courts view *Branzburg* as not inconsistent with their requiring the government to bear a special burden of justification for a subpoena clearly having a chilling impact on the exercise of a basic First Amendment right. These courts insist initially that the objecting witness make a prima facie showing that compliance with the subpoena will chill the future exercise of First Amendment protected activity, notwithstanding the secrecy that attaches to grand jury testimony. Once this prima facie case is established, the government is required to justify that impact by showing that the information sought by the subpoena is "substantially related" to a "compelling government interest." *Branzburg*, however, is viewed as having established that a government interest in investigating crime is per se a "compelling interest." Thus, absent a showing by the objecting witness strongly suggesting that the grand jury investigation was initiated in bad faith, the critical issue is whether the information sought is "substantially related" to the investigation of crime. This government burden typically requires no more than an explanation as to why the information sought clearly is relevant to the grand jury's investigation.

Still other courts, relying on *Branzburg*, have rejected entirely the contention that the government must make a special showing to sustain a subpoena that may chill the exercise of First Amendment rights. They reason that adoption of a substantial relationship prerequisite would be contrary to the reasoning of *Branzburg*. In particular, Justice Powell, in explaining the Court's decision, had noted that the district court's capacity to respond to a "bad faith exercise of grand jury powers" would allow for "striking * * * a proper balance between freedom of the press and the obligation of all citizens to give relevant testimony with respect to criminal conduct," but that balance would be struck on a case-by-case analysis of the facts, not through a threshold imposition of "constitutional preconditions." The lesson of *Branzburg*, under this view, is that, to protect adequately First Amendment interests, it is sufficient that the district court simply apply, "with special sensitivity where values of expression are potentially implicated," the general standards of *R. Enterprises*. *R. Enterprises*, it is noted, also recognized that " 'grand juries are not licensed to engage in arbitrary fishing expeditions, nor may they select targets out of malice or an intent to harass.' "

Attorney-client relationships. Chilling impact objections have also been raised in connection with grand jury subpoenas requiring attorneys to testify in connection with the investigation of past or current clients. Of course, insofar as questions posed to the attorney/witness seek information protected by the attorney-client privilege, that privilege can be relied upon to refuse to furnish that information. However, certain essential facts that are likely to be sought by the grand jury (e.g., client identity and fee information) commonly are not protected by the privilege. Here, attorneys have argued that, because of the chilling impact that such disclosure would have upon the attorney-client relationship, the grand jury should not be allowed to force disclosure from the attorney in the absence of an initial showing of special need and relevance. This position has been consistently rejected, however, by both federal and state appellate courts.

In refusing to require that the government make a special showing of need, the courts have noted that: (1) the attorney-client privilege and work product doctrine provide adequate protection of the attorney-client relationship; (2) even where the subpoenaed attorney currently is representing the client, it typically is at a point where the client is simply a target of the investigation and therefore has no Sixth Amendment right to that representation; (3) neither is the subpoena likely to interfere with the target/client's future Sixth Amendment right to counsel (assuming a subsequent indictment) because the possibility that the attorney's grand jury testimony will lead to the attorney's disqualification at trial tends to be no more than an "abstract possibility," hinging upon the happenstance of a variety of speculative occurrences; and (4) the attorney/witness is asking for exactly the kind of preliminary showing that the Supreme Court warned against in *Dionisio* and *Branzburg* as causing indeterminate delays in grand jury investigations. The appellate courts further note, however, that the supervisory court has sufficient discretionary authority under provisions like Rule 17(c) (prohibiting "oppressive" subpoenas) to quash or delay enforcement of a subpoena to an attorney where requiring immediate compliance would interfere with counsel's representation of the defendant in a currently pending trial. In such situations, the supervisory court may insist that the government make some showing of a need to obtain the information sought prior to that trial, at least where counsel shows that compliance with the subpoena will disrupt preparation for the trial.

Several states have adopted standards of professional responsibility directing prosecutors not to subpoena lawyers in grand jury or other criminal proceedings for the purpose of obtaining information "about a past or present client" unless (1) the evidence sought is "essential," and not otherwise available, and (2) the subpoena is authorized by a court after providing an opportunity for an adversarial hearing. When Congress in 1998 adopted the Citizen's Protection Act (CPA), which subjects attorneys for the federal government to state professional responsibility standards, it was argued that the traditional position of federal courts, as described above, would have to be altered for federal courts sitting in such states. Lower courts have held, however, that (1) a requirement of pre-issuance judicial approval of a subpoena, which is contrary to Rule 17, goes beyond an "ethical standard" and therefore is not made applicable by the CPA, and (2) the remedy for violating a standard of professional responsibility cannot be extended beyond a disciplinary sanction, to also exclude evidence obtained through such a violation, as that would contradict the Federal Rules of Evidence.

(e) **Use for Civil Discovery.** In *U.S. v. Procter & Gamble* (1958), the lower court granted broad disclosure of grand jury testimony to defendants in a civil antitrust action, with its ruling apparently influenced by the belief that the government had used the grand jury process "to elicit evidence" that it could later introduce in its civil action. The Supreme Court rejected the disclosure order as not supported by a showing of particularized need, but it also acknowledged that the alleged government subversion of the criminal process could constitute "good cause" warranting such extensive disclosure to the opposing party in the civil suit. There had been no finding, however, that the grand jury proceeding had in fact "been used as a short cut to [civil discovery] goals otherwise barred or more difficult to reach." If the grand jury had been employed in that fashion, the Court noted, the government clearly would have been guilty of "flouting the policy of the law," both as to the grand jury's proper function and the prescribed procedures for civil discovery.

Lower courts applying the civil misuse standard of *Procter & Gamble* agree that whether or not an abuse exists depends upon the government's purpose in using the grand jury process, rather than the relevancy of the requested information to possible civil litigation. They recognize that a proper criminal investigation may readily encompass elements that also relate to civil cases, and that in some areas of the law (e.g., antitrust), the overlap between the criminal and civil investigation will be substantial. Some disagreement appears to exist, however, as to exactly how "pure" the government's purpose must be. Several courts have suggested that the *Procter & Gamble* standard is violated only when the investigation was aimed "primarily" at civil discovery. The issue, as they see it, is whether the grand jury proceedings were a "cover" or "subterfuge" for a civil investigation. Other courts suggest that the grand jury can be used only to conduct investigations that are in their inception "exclusively criminal." This standard arguably would bar an investigation that is initiated with "a completely open mind as to what the appropriate remedy should be, criminal, civil, or both." If so, it probably goes beyond what the Supreme Court had in mind in *Procter & Gamble*.

To establish an improper purpose, the party claiming misuse must overcome the traditional "presumption of regularity," in the grand jury process. That burden clearly is the heaviest when the objection is made during an ongoing investigation by a motion to quash a subpoena or terminate the investigation. Courts hesitate to project the purpose of an investigation while it is still ongoing. Even where the surrounding circumstances strongly suggest misuse (e.g., where the grand jury investigation was instituted shortly after the target's legal challenges stymied a civil investigation), courts have been willing on a motion to quash or terminate to accept a prosecution affidavit of good faith as a sufficient response. A more appropriate assessment, it is argued, can be made after the investigation is ended, with adequate relief still available to the target. If the grand jury should return an indictment, that act will constitute strong evidence "that there has been no perversion of grand jury processes." If an indictment has not been returned, the target retains the opportunity to challenge the proceeding when and if a civil agency requests court-ordered disclosure for use in connection with a civil suit. At that point, a more detailed government affidavit may be required, or the court may hold an evidentiary hearing. Exactly how much explanation will be demanded from the government will vary with the strength of the suggestion of possible misuse in the surrounding circumstances. As one court noted, in the end, the judge's ruling on a misuse objection must seek to strike an equitable balance between "(1) the need of the [prospective civil] defendants to ascertain whether there has been an abuse of the grand jury process, and (2) the policies of grand jury secrecy and freedom in government decisionmaking."

(f) Use for Post–Indictment Criminal Discovery. The grand jury is given its broad investigative powers to determine whether a crime has been committed and an indictment should issue, not to gather evidence for use in cases in which indictments have already issued. Accordingly, both state and federal courts hold that it is an abuse of the grand jury process to use grand jury subpoenas "for the sole or dominating purpose of preparing an already pending indictment for trial." Those courts also hold, however, that where the primary purpose of the investigation is to determine whether others not indicted were involved in the same criminal activity, or whether the indicted party committed still other crimes, the government may go forward with the inquiry even though one result may be the production of evidence that could then be used at the trial of the pending indictment. They note also that, prior to indictment, nothing prevents the prosecution from bringing before the grand jury evidence that will fully explore the case, beyond what is needed for probable cause, although one consequence is to better prepare the prosecution for trial on the indictment it hopes the grand jury will issue.

In ruling on a motion to quash alleging a dominant purpose of post-indictment discovery, courts adopt an approach very much like that applied to a motion to quash alleging misuse to obtain civil discovery. Here too, courts start with the principle that a "presumption of regularity" attaches to the grand jury proceeding and that the objecting party bears the burden of overcoming that presumption. Courts also have noted their reluctance to interfere with an ongoing investigation, suggesting that the true purpose of the investigation can best be assessed after it is completed. Where the objecting party can point to surrounding circumstances highly suggestive of improper use, the court may require a governmental affidavit explaining the purpose of the post-indictment investigation or it may examine the grand jury transcript in camera to determine that purpose.

(g) Prosecution or Police Usurpation of the Subpoena Power. The subpoena power of the grand jury is designed for its own use, not to further independent investigations of the prosecutor or police. In most jurisdictions, the prosecutor may have subpoenas issued without advance authorization of the grand jury, but the purpose of the subpoena must be to produce evidence for use by the grand jury. This does not bar the prosecutor from screening the requested information before it is formally presented to the grand jury. Documents produced pursuant to a grand jury subpoena duces tecum commonly are first viewed and summarized by the prosecution staff, and in some instances, only the summaries are actually presented to the jurors. Similarly, it is not uncommon for prosecutors to use the occasion of the witness' grand jury appearance to conduct a preliminary interview. The prosecutor may not, however, have the grand jury subpoena issued "as a ploy to secure the attendance of a witness at the prosecutor's office." Nor may the prosecutor use the subpoena authority to force a witness to submit to an office interview. Similarly, while the prosecutor may utilize the grand jury subpoena to compel testimony from a witness after he has first refused to provide information to the police, this may be done only if the information sought truly is needed for the grand jury inquiry. Thus, when a person refuses to give the police information that may assist in locating a fugitive, the prosecutor may not then seek to compel that testimony through a grand jury subpoena, absent a situation in which the grand jury has a legitimate interest in obtaining the testimony of the fugitive or in determining whether the fugitive has been assisted in his flight.

Courts have divided as to whether special safeguards are needed to ensure that subpoenas for identification exemplars are really directed at a grand jury inquiry rather than at assisting an independent police investigation. Some courts have treated such subpoenas no differently than any other subpoena duces tecum. Other courts have concluded, however, that the potential for misuse requires special prerequisites where a subpoena demands production of identification exemplars. They have held, for example, that such subpoenas should not issue unless first approved by the grand jurors, thereby ensuring that the grand jury has an interest in the evidence sought. One court, concerned that the grand jury not be used to bypass the showing required under local law for the police to place a non-arrestee in a lineup, imposed the requirement that "a prosecutor seeking judicial enforcement of a grand jury directive to appear in a lineup * * * make a minimal factual showing sufficient to permit the judge to conclude that there is a reason for the lineup which is consistent with the legitimate function of the grand jury."

(h) Harassment. In the course of upholding broad investigatory powers of the grand jury, courts frequently note that, of course, use of those powers for the purpose of "harassment" is always subject to judicial remedy. Precisely what a court has in mind by this reference to "harassment" is often left open, but it apparently refers to something more than simply using the grand jury process for some unauthorized purpose, such as civil discovery. Courts that have offered illustrations of harassment tend to stress a vindictive element in the use of the grand jury, usually a use designed to intimidate the witness. Thus, illustrations are offered of "bad faith harassment of a political dissident" by imposing the burdens (political and otherwise) of a grand jury appearance with "no expectation that any testimony concerning a crime would be forthcoming." Similarly, repeated subpoenas to appear before one grand jury after another may reflect harassment. So too, subpoenas utilized to provide leaks to the press would constitute harassment. It has also been argued that calling a witness before the grand jury solely to trap him into committing perjury constitutes a form of harassment.

(i) Target Standing. *U.S. v. Miller* (§ 8.1(c)) held that a customer lacks standing to object on Fourth Amendment grounds to a subpoena directing a third party service provider (e.g., a bank) to disclose its records of the customer's transactions. Although some of the records were originally created by the customer, in giving control over the records to the service provider, the customer assumed the risk of disclosure by the provider. In general, as in *Miller*, the target of the investigation has no standing to object to a subpoena directing a third party to produce information relating to the target. Certain misuses of grand jury authority, however, will directly impact the rights of the target, and here the target may challenge the subpoena even where directed at a third party. Thus, a target may challenge a grand jury's misuse of the subpoena to enhance the prosecutor's criminal discovery on an indictment pending against the target, or to gain discovery for a civil action to be brought against the target. So too, an employer/target had standing to object to subpoenas issued to its employees where it alleged that the government's design was to harass the employer by repeatedly calling its employees to testify.

§ 7.7 Grand Jury Inquiries Based on Illegally Obtained Evidence

(a) **The *Calandra* Rule.** In *U.S. v. Calandra* (1974), grand jury witness Calandra objected to questions about certain records that had been seized in violation of the Fourth Amendment in a previous search of his office. The lower court sustained the objection, relying on the exclusionary remedy of the Fourth Amendment. The questions were viewed as the fruits of the illegal search, and requiring the witness to respond was viewed as extending the original illegality. A divided Supreme Court reversed, holding that the exclusionary rule could not be invoked by a grand jury witness to bar questions based on unconstitutionally seized evidence.

Viewing the exclusionary rule as basically a prophylactic remedy, the *Calandra* majority concluded that its applicability in the grand jury setting should be determined by weighing "the potential injury [in the rule's application] to the historic role and functions of the grand jury" against the potential for increased deterrence of illegal searches. On the one side, "it [was] evident that this extension of the exclusionary rule would seriously impede the grand jury": "permitting witnesses to invoke the exclusionary rule would delay and disrupt grand jury proceedings," and the resulting "suppression hearings would halt the orderly progress of an investigation and necessitate extended litigation of issues only tangentially related to the grand jury's primary objective." On the other side, the incremental deterrent effect that might be achieved by applying the exclusionary rule in grand jury proceedings was "uncertain at best." Any "incentive to disregard the requirements of the Fourth Amendment" as to grand juries, the Court noted, "is substantially negated by the inadmissibility of the illegally-seized evidence in a subsequent criminal prosecution of the search victim." On balance, the Court would not "embrace a view that would achieve a speculative and undoubtedly minimal advance in the deterrence of police misconduct at the expense of substantially impeding the role of the grand jury." See also § 2.1(f).

Lower courts have viewed the balance struck in *Calandra* as going beyond Fourth Amendment violations. Accordingly, they have rejected witness objections to grand jury use of evidence obtained illegally through violations of other constitutional provisions and statutory prohibitions. Support for this position has been found in: (1) *Calandra's* concern that witnesses not be allowed to "delay and disrupt" the grand jury proceedings by raising challenges to the source that led to the grand jury's inquiry; and (2) *Calandra's* reliance upon Supreme Court precedent holding that an indictment cannot be a challenge based on a grand jury's reliance upon unconstitutionally obtained evidence—a precedent that has been applied to a variety of illegalities in the acquisition of evidence.

Courts have recognized, however, two exceptions to *Calandra*. The broader exception relating to illegal electronic surveillance, is discussed in subsection (b) below. The second and narrower exception relates to *Silverthorne Lumber Co. v. U.S.*(1920). *Calandra* distinguished in a footnote the *Silverthorne* case, which had upheld the right of indicted defendants to refuse to respond to a grand jury subpoena duces tecum which would have required them to produce the same documents that had been returned to them following their successful Fourth Amendment challenge to the police seizure of those documents. *Silverthorne* reasoned that the subpoena was the fruit of the poisonous tree, as knowledge of the documents came from the illegal search, and that knowledge was thereby rendered permanently inaccessible to the government. The *Calandra* footnote cited three distinguishing characteristics of *Silverthorne*: (1) "there, plaintiffs in error had previously been indicted * * * and thus could invoke the exclusionary rule on the basis of their status as criminal defendants"; (2) the "government's interest in recapturing the original documents was founded on a belief they might be useful in the criminal prosecution already authorized by the grand jury," rather than a "need to perform its investigatory or accusatorial functions"; and (3) "prior to the issuance of the grand jury subpoenas, there had been a judicial determination that the search and seizure were illegal" (in contrast to a claim of an illegal search "raised for the first time on a pre-indictment motion to suppress requiring interruption of grand jury proceedings"). Lower court opinions examining the *"Silverthorne* exception" suggest that all three distinguishing factors must be present to challenge a grand jury subpoena as derived from an illegal search.

(b) Illegal Electronic Surveillance. In *Gelbard v. U.S.* (1972), grand jury witnesses refused to answer questions put to them by the prosecutor, asserting that the questions were derived from electronic surveillance that violated Title III of the Omnibus Crime Control and Safe Streets Act (see § 3.6(b)). The issue before the Supreme Court was whether, assuming that the witnesses assertions were correct, such use of illegally intercepted communications constituted "just cause" for a refusal to answer (and therefore relieved the witnesses of contempt liability). The Court in a 5–4 decision held that: (1) § 2515 of Title III prohibited interrogation of grand jury witnesses based on illegally intercepted communications, and (2) the witness could advance this prohibition as "just cause" for refusing to testify. The Court had little difficulty on the first point since § 2515 specifically refers to grand jury proceedings as among those proceedings in which "no evidence derived [from an illegal interception] may be received." On the second point, some difficulty was presented by § 2518(10)'s failure to include grand jury proceedings among the specified proceedings in which a motion to suppress might be brought. This omission was viewed as not inconsistent with simply allowing a grand jury witness to refuse to respond to questions based on illegal interceptions. The Court noted, however, that it reserved the issue as to whether a witness could refuse to answer if the interceptions had been made pursuant to a court order issued under Title III. Speaking to that situation, Justice White, the crucial fifth vote for the *Gelbard* majority, noted that the presence of a court order for the interception required a "different accommodation between the dual functioning of the grand jury system and the federal wiretap statute." Allowance of a suppression hearing would result in "protracted interruption" of the grand jury proceedings. Moreover, the deterrent value of excluding the evidence where the prosecutor had relied in good faith on a court order would be "marginal at best."

Lower courts applying *Gelbard* have accepted Justice White's suggestion that a witness objecting to grand jury use of a court ordered interception should not be entitled to a full-blown suppression hearing, but have also sought to provide reasonable assurance that a witness is not required to respond to questions based upon an invalid court order. One line of cases has held that the proper accommodation requires no more than an in camera inspection of the surveillance documents to ensure that the court order is in compliance with the statute. Another line of decisions provides for witness access to the key documents unless the government can show that grand jury secrecy requires in camera review. The witness is still limited, however, to challenging defects found on the face of those documents.

Gelbard left to the lower courts the task of establishing procedures for determining whether grand jury questions were in fact based upon an electronic surveillance. Frequent *Gelbard* objections have produced a substantial number of lower courts opinions dealing in particular with two issues relating to those procedures: (1) the nature of the allegation that must be made by the witness to trigger a government obligation to make inquiry and respond as to the existence of wiretaps; and (2) the scope of the inquiry that must be made by the government before denying the existence of wiretaps. On the first issue, some courts accept a "mere assertion" of wiretapping as sufficient, but most require the witness to point to suspicious circumstance indicating the presence of a wiretap. As to the second, courts generally hold that the strength of the witness' showing as to a likely wiretap sets the needed scope of the prosecutor's investigation. Where the witness' showing is minimal, it is sufficient for the government to rely upon negative responses of the agents working directly on the case. Where the showing is stronger, the prosecutor's inquiry may have to include other agencies (perhaps more than once removed) that furnished information used by those agents.

§ 7.8   Grand   Jury   Testimony   and   the   Privilege   Against Self–Incrimination

(a) **The Availability of the Privilege.** *Counselman v. Hitchcock* (1892) put to rest any doubts as to whether the Fifth Amendment privilege against self-incrimination was available to a grand jury witness. The grand jury witness testifies pursuant to a subpoena so the requisite element of "compulsion" clearly is present. However, the Amendment states only that a person shall not be compelled to be a witness against himself "in a criminal case." The *Counselman* Court reasoned that the grand jury inquiry into criminal liability was itself a "criminal case," but that characterization was not, in any event, a prerequisite to the availability of the privilege. The Fifth Amendment's "criminal case" requirement, it noted, refers to the eventual use of the testimony, not the nature of the proceeding in which it is compelled. Accordingly, the Fifth Amendment applies to a witness "in any proceeding" who is being compelled to give testimony that might incriminate him in a subsequent criminal case.

Counselman's analysis of the function of the "criminal case" phrasing in the Fifth Amendment had significance far beyond the grand jury. It led to a long line of cases holding the self-incrimination privilege available to witnesses in various non-criminal proceedings, including civil cases and administrative agency hearings. These rulings traditionally were viewed, consistent with *Counselman's* analysis, as reflecting the command of the Fifth Amendment itself; but that position seemingly was rejected by a majority of the Court in *Chavez v. Martinez* (2003). Although *Chavez* did not involve the exercise of the privilege by a witness in a non-criminal proceeding, the Court considered the non-criminal cases relevant to the question before it: whether the Fifth Amendment was violated by coercive interrogation of a suspect that compelled a statement which was never used against the suspect in a criminal case (see § 5.2(b)). The non-criminal cases were deemed relevant because the privilege was being made available to witnesses in those proceedings notwithstanding that there was no assurance that the statement being compelled would later be used in a criminal case.

Six justices in *Chavez* discounted the non-criminal cases by explaining that the availability of the privilege there rested not on the language of the Amendment as read in *Counselman*, but on the authority of the Court to craft protective procedures to implement the basic constitutional right. Four justices described a witness' exercise of the privilege outside of a criminal case as the product of a prophylactic rule (see § 1.5(e)), designed to ensure that the Fifth Amendment was not later violated by the admission of that witness' compelled statement in a criminal trial. Two described that availability as resting in "law * * * outside the Fifth Amendment's core," which provided "complimentary protection" to the core's prohibition of "courtroom use of a criminal defendant's compelled self-incriminatory testimony." The impact of *Chavez's* characterization of the *Counselman* progeny is uncertain. It may well be limited to prohibiting a damage remedy for violations of the witness' right to exercise the privilege in non-criminal settings (the *Chavez* conclusion as to *Miranda* violations).

(b) The Standard of Potential Incrimination. Under the standard construction of the Fifth Amendment privilege, a broad range of information can be classified as potentially incriminating and therefore protected by the privilege. However, the concept of potential incrimination is not without limits. The threat posed by the information is limited only to possible criminal liability, and that liability must relate to the witness himself, not others. The threat must be "real and appreciable," not "imaginary and unsubstantial." Moreover, a witness' assertion of the privilege is not conclusive. "It is for the court to say whether his silence is justified, and to require him to answer 'if it clearly appears to the court that he is mistaken.'" The Supreme Court has indicated, however, that courts are to give the witness every benefit of the doubt in reviewing his assertion of the privilege. *Hoffman v. U.S.* (1951), sets forth the applicable standard:

> "The privilege afforded not only extends to answers that would in themselves support conviction * * * but likewise embraces those which would furnish a link in the chain of evidence needed to prosecute the claimant. * * * To sustain the privilege, it need only be evident from the implications of the question, in the setting in which it is asked, that a responsive answer to the question or an explanation of why it cannot be

answered might be dangerous because injurious disclosure could result."

Applying this standard, it will be a rare case in which a claim of the privilege, made in the grand jury context, will be rejected by a court.

(c) Incrimination Under the Laws of Another Sovereign. For many years, American courts took the position that the privilege protected only against incrimination under the laws of the sovereign which was attempting to compel the incriminating testimony. In applying this rule, which was said to be derived from the English common law, the individual states and the federal system were treated as separate sovereigns. Thus, if a witness appearing before a federal grand jury was granted immunity against federal prosecution, he could not refuse to testify on the ground that his answers might be incriminating under the laws of a state. In *Murphy v. Waterfront Commission* (1964), the Supreme Court rejected this "separate sovereign" doctrine as applied to state and federal prosecutions. Noting that a contrary position would allow a witness to be "whipsawed into incriminating himself under both state and federal law," the Court concluded that the "policies and purposes" of the Fifth Amendment required that the privilege protect "a state witness against incrimination under federal as well as state law and a federal witness against incrimination under state as well as federal law." This meant that thereafter the immunity granted in a state or federal grand jury proceeding to replace the witness' privilege had to extend to both state and federal prosecutions.

The *Murphy* opinion contained language suggesting that the separate sovereign limitation was flawed even in its refusal to consider other nations, and the privilege therefore should be available where the witness realistically feared that his responses could lead to prosecution in a foreign country. That position was rejected, however, in *U.S. v. Balsys* (1998), a case in which a resident alien, questioned as to possible participation in Nazi persecutions in World War II, claimed the privilege based on potential criminal liability in Lithuania and Israel. The Court explained that the *Murphy* reading was the product of the application of the self-incrimination clause to the states via the Fourteenth Amendment (see § 1.3(d)). Once the states become bound by the Fifth Amendment guarantee, the self-incrimination clause "could no longer be seen as framed for one jurisdiction (i.e., state or federal government) alone, each jurisdiction having instead become subject to the same claim of privilege flowing from the one limitation." This concept of applying a single guarantee also was consistent with "a feature unique to the [self-incrimination] guarantee," an "option to exchange the privilege for an immunity to prosecutorial use of any compelled testimony." That option remained available by viewing the state and federal governments as extending their immunity to prosecutions by the other (see § 7.9(b)). In contrast, as to foreign prosecutions, the Fifth Amendment guarantee was not part of the governing law, and neither state nor federal government could grant immunity.

(d) Compelling the Target to Appear. The self-incrimination privilege has long been held to prohibit the prosecution from forcing a defendant to appear as a witness at his own trial. Should the prosecutor similarly be prohibited from forcing the target of an investigation to appear before the grand jury, or is the Fifth Amendment satisfied by simply allowing the target-witness, like any other witness, to refuse to respond to individual questions where his answer might be incriminating? Several state courts have concluded that the target of an investigation is, in effect, a "putative" or "de facto" defendant, and he therefore should be allowed to exercise his privilege in much the same manner as a "de jure defendant" at trial. In some of these jurisdictions, the target/witness must initially claim the privilege before the grand jury, which then excuses him from further testifying. In others, the privilege is viewed as a bar to the subpoena itself, so the target/witness cannot be called to testify unless first formally waiving his right not to appear.

The federal courts and majority of state courts treat the target no differently than other witnesses as to being subpoenaed and exercising the privilege. As with grand jury witnesses generally, the self-incrimination privilege is said to present only "an option of refusal and not a prohibition of inquiry." The witness intending to exercise the privilege must appear in response to the subpoena and assert the privilege as to individual questions that would require an incriminating answer. In subjecting even target-witnesses to this requirement, courts stress that the grand jury is part of the investigatory stage of the process, which distinguishes the status of the target from that of the defendant at trial. The defendant's right of silence at trial grew out of the early common law rule on the incompetency of parties to testify, which had bearing only at trial. It also rested in part on the fear that a defendant "forced in open court to refuse to answer questions" might be viewed by the jury as having something to hide. This concern has less significance in the grand jury setting; since that body looks only to the issue of probable cause, its proceedings need not be conducted "with the assiduous regard for the preservation of procedural safeguards which normally attends the ultimate trial of the issues."

Courts have further argued that the right to subpoena targets is inherent in the grand jury's combined investigative and shielding roles. Having an obligation to "run down every available clue," the jury cannot ignore the possibility that any one participant in a criminal enterprise may be willing to identify others. Having an obligation to "shield against arbitrary accusations," it has a right to be certain that the target's own testimony might not explain away the evidence against him. Another concern is that the establishment of a right not to appear based upon whether the prosecutor knew or should have known someone was a "target" would create a new source of tangential disputation.

(e) Advice as to Rights. It generally is agreed that the Fifth Amendment does not demand that a non-target witness be advised of his privilege against self-incrimination. Courts are divided, however, as to whether such advice must be given to a target. In *U.S. v. Mandujano* (1976), the Supreme Court left that issue open for future consideration. *Mandujano* held that even if warnings were required, the failure to give the warnings could not constitute a defense to a perjury charge based on the witness' false grand jury testimony. Six justices, however, went on to speak to the need for warnings, with four suggesting that they were not required.

Although the witness in *Mandujano* had been informed of both his privilege against self-incrimination and his right to consult with counsel, the district court had held that warning insufficient. Since the witness was a "putative defendant," the district court reasoned, he should have been given full *Miranda* warnings, including notification of a right to appointed counsel. Chief Justice Burger's plurality opinion, speaking for four members of the Court, rejected the district court's reasoning. *Miranda,* he noted, applied only to "custodial interrogation," which clearly did not include questioning before the grand jury. The position of the subpoenaed witness could hardly be compared to that of the arrestee subjected to interrogation in the "hostile" and "isolated" setting of the police station. The appropriate analogy was to the questioning of a witness in an administrative or judicial hearing. As noted by Justice Frankfurter in *U.S. v. Monia* (1943), a witness in that setting, "if * * * he desires the protection of the privilege, * * * must claim it or he will not be considered to have been 'compelled' within the meaning of the Amendment." Justices Brennan and Marshall responded that the *Monia* principle had no bearing on the questioning of a target witness because here the prosecutor "is acutely aware of the potentially incriminating nature of the disclosures sought," and that knowledge carries with it an obligation to advise the witness of his rights so as to ensure that any waiver of the privilege is "intelligent and intentional."

Subsequently, in *Minn. v. Murphy* (1984), the Court again commented on the issue. In the course of holding that a probation officer need not provide *Miranda*-type warnings in questioning a probationer, the Court drew an analogy to the grand jury setting. The interview setting in *Murphy*, the Court noted, subjected the probationer to "less intimidating pressure than is imposed upon a grand jury witness," and the Court has "never held that [warnings] must be given to the grand jury witness." This "expansive dictum," along with the reasoning of the plurality opinion in *Mandujano*, has led the Seventh Circuit to conclude that "the Supreme Court would be reluctant to extend a warning requirement to grand jury proceedings."

Several state courts, on the other hand, have concluded that the special status of being viewed by the prosecutor as a target creates a constitutional obligation to inform the target/witness of his right to refuse to answer on self-incrimination grounds. Most jurisdictions have found it unnecessary to search the issue because prosecutorial practice renders it moot. In the federal system, departmental guidelines require that all "targets" and "subjects" be advised of their right to exercise the privilege "Target" is defined as a person against whom "substantial evidence" exists and who, in the judgment of the prosecutor is a "putative" defendant (a definition narrower than that suggested by Justice Brennan in *Mandujano*, as he would have looked only to the available evidence and not to the prosecutor's judgment as to likely prosecution). A "subject" is a person "whose conduct is within the scope of the grand jury inquiry." State prosecutors commonly follow the same practice, also as a matter of internal policy.

Justice Brennan's concurring opinion in *Mandujano* argued that target warnings had to go beyond simply explaining the availability of the self-incrimination privilege. In his view, the Fifth Amendment also required the prosecution to inform the target/witness that "he was currently subject to possible criminal prosecution for the commission of a stated crime." In *U.S. v. Washington* (1977), the Court rejected that position. The witness there had been given full *Miranda*-type warnings, but had not been told that he might be indicted in connection with his possession of a stolen motorcycle. The Court initially noted that previous discussions with the police and prosecutor had given the witness ample notice that he was a suspect in the motorcycle theft, but it then added that such awareness was, in any event, "largely irrelevant." A failure to give a potential defendant a target warning simply did not put the witness at a "constitutional disadvantage." His status as a target "neither enlarg[ed] nor diminish[ed]" the scope of his constitutional protection. He "knew better than anyone else" whether his answers would be incriminating, and he also knew that anything he did say, after failing to exercise the privilege, could be used against him. The "constitutional guarantee," the Court noted, ensures "only that the witness be not *compelled* to give self-incriminating testimony."

In the Federal system, internal Justice Department policy advises against calling a target as a witness absent exceptional circumstances. When the target is subpoenaed, that policy then directs the prosecutor to inform the target/witness that "[his] conduct is being investigated for possible violation of federal criminal law." Several states take the further step of imposing a statutory obligation upon prosecutors to inform targets of their target status prior to testifying.

(f) **Waiver.** Assuming the witness receives those warnings, if any, that are constitutionally required, the privilege may be relinquished by the witness without an express statement of waiver. When the witness answers the question, his waiver is automatically assumed as to the content of that answer. Moreover, by providing in that answer certain incriminating information, the witness may relinquish his right to raise the privilege with respect to further incriminating information. *Rogers v. U.S.* (1951) is the leading case on such "testimonial waiver." The witness there testified before a grand jury that, as treasurer of the Communist Party of Denver, she had been in possession of party records, but had subsequently delivered those records to another person. She refused, however, to identify the recipient of the records, asserting that would be incriminating. A divided Supreme Court affirmed her contempt conviction, holding the privilege inapplicable. The Court noted that Rogers had already incriminated herself by admitting her party membership and past possession of the records; disclosure of her "acquaintanceship with her successor present[ed] no more than a 'mere imaginary possibility' of increasing the danger of prosecution." A witness would not be allowed to disclose a basic incriminating fact and then claim the privilege as to "details." To uphold such a claim of the privilege would "open the way to distortion of facts by permitting a witness to select any stopping point in her testimony."

As with other constitutional rights, a waiver is acceptable only if voluntary. In the grand jury setting, as contrasted to in-custody police interrogation, the setting itself does not inherently exert pressures that might render the waiver involuntary. However, the waiver still may be rendered involuntary by unconstitutional burdens placed on the exercise of the privilege. Thus, in *Garrity v. N.J.* (1967), where police officers were warned that they would be removed from office if they did not waive their privilege and testify as to the fixing of traffic tickets, the Court held that their waivers were coerced and their testimony could not be used against them in subsequent criminal proceedings.

If the grand jury witness should voluntarily waive the privilege, the generally accepted rule is that he may still exercise the privilege as an accused in a subsequent criminal prosecution. Waiver of the privilege applies only to the particular proceeding, and the dominant view is that the grand jury investigation and the criminal prosecution are separate proceedings.

(g) Adverse Consequences. A witness who exercises the privilege before the grand jury is fully shielded against adverse legal consequences. The prohibition against drawing an adverse inference from a defendant's exercise of the privilege in a criminal trial has been held to apply as well to the grand jury's determination as to whether to indict a witness who exercised the privilege before the grand jury. The Supreme Court has held that a defendant who testifies at trial cannot be impeached by reference to his having asserted the privilege when questioned about the same events before the grand jury. The Court also has held that the state may not impose an administrative sanction (such as an employee discharge or a disqualification from government contracts) based upon an individual's exercise of the privilege before the grand jury.

§ 7.9   Immunity and Compelled Testimony

(a) Constitutionality. The use of immunity grants to preclude reliance upon the self-incrimination privilege predates the adoption of the Constitution. The English adopted an immunity procedure, known as providing "indemnity" against prosecution, "soon after the privilege against compulsory self-incrimination became firmly established," and a similar practice was followed first in the colonies and then in the states. Not surprisingly, *Brown v. Walker* (1896) concluded that the immunity procedure was consistent with the history and purpose of the Fifth Amendment privilege. The Court stressed that the Fifth Amendment could not be "construed literally as authorizing the witness to refuse to disclose any fact which might tend to incriminate, disgrace, or expose him to unfavorable comments." The history of the Amendment clearly indicated that its object was only to "secure the witness against criminal prosecution." Thus, the self-incrimination privilege had been held inapplicable where the witness' compelled testimony would relate only to an offense as to which he had been pardoned or as to which the statute of limitations had run. So too, the privilege had been held not to apply where the witness' response might tend to "disgrace him or bring him into disrepute" but would furnish no information relating to a criminal offense. Such rulings, the Court reasoned, implicitly sustained the constitutionality of the immunity procedure. Since the immunity grant removed the only danger against which the privilege protected the witness, the witness could no longer claim that he was being compelled to incriminate himself.

(b) The Required Scope of Immunity. In *Counselman v. Hitchcock* (1892), decided prior to *Brown,* the Court struck down a federal immunity statute that granted the witness protection only against the admission of his immunized testimony in evidence in a subsequent prosecution. The Court stressed that the statute failed to provide protection against derivative use of the witness' testimony, including "the use of his testimony to search out other testimony to be used in evidence against him." At the conclusion of its opinion, the Court spoke in terms of even broader protection, which would, "afford absolute immunity against future prosecution for the offense to which the question relates." This statement was taken as indicating that a valid immunity grant must absolutely bar prosecution for any transaction noted in the witness' testimony. Accordingly, Congress adopted a new immunity statute providing for such "transactional immunity." That statute provided that a witness directed to testify or produce documentary evidence pursuant to an immunity order could not be prosecuted "for or on account of any transaction, matter, or thing concerning which he may testify or produce evidence." The constitutionality of this provision was upheld in *Brown v. Walker,* and subsequent state and federal immunity statutes were largely patterned upon the *Brown* statute.

Later decisions—and the language of subsequent statutes—recognized two limitations in transactional immunity. The witness may still be prosecuted for perjury committed in his immunized testimony. Similarly, the immunity does not extend to a transaction noted in an answer totally unresponsive to the question asked. Thus, the witness cannot gain immunity from prosecution for all previous criminal acts by simply including a reference to those acts in his testimony without regard to the subject on which he was asked to testify.

In *Murphy v. Waterfront Commission* (1964), the Court first upheld immunity that was not as broad in scope as the traditional transactional immunity. *Murphy,* as discussed in § 7.8(c), held that the self-incrimination privilege extends to possible incrimination under both federal and state law. Accordingly, to be constitutionally acceptable, the immunity granted to a witness had to provide adequate protection against both federal and state prosecutions. If that protection had to encompass transactional immunity, the state immunity provisions would necessarily fail. Congress could use its legislative authority to preempt state prosecutions, but the states lacked authority to prohibit federal prosecutions. The Court held, however, that the immunity grant need not absolutely bar prosecution in the other jurisdiction. It was sufficient that the witness was guaranteed that neither his testimony nor any fruits derived from that testimony would be used against him in any criminal prosecution. The Court, to accommodate "the interests of State and Federal Governments in investigating and prosecuting crime," would exercise its supervisory power to prohibit the federal government from using in federal courts state immunized testimony or the fruits thereof.

Following *Murphy,* Congress adopted a new immunity provision for federal witnesses, replacing transactional immunity with a prohibition against use and derivative use as to both federal and state prosecutions. The statute provided that "no testimony or other information compelled under the [immunity] order (or any information directly or indirectly derived from such testimony or other information) may be used against the witness in any criminal case, except a prosecution for perjury, giving a false statement, or otherwise failing to comply with the order." In *Kastigar v. U.S.* (1972), a divided Court upheld the new federal provision. The "broad language in *Counselman,*" which suggested the need for transactional immunity, was discounted as inconsistent with the "conceptual basis" of the *Counselman* ruling. The crucial question, as *Counselman* noted, was whether the immunity granted was "coextensive with the scope of the privilege against self-incrimination." Both the immunity upheld in *Murphy* and the traditional Fifth Amendment remedy of excluding compelled statements and their fruits (as, for example, in the coerced confession cases) indicated that the privilege did not require an absolute bar against prosecution. A prohibition against use and derivative use satisfied the privilege by placing the witness "in substantially the same position as if * * * [he] had claimed his privilege."

The *Kastigar* majority rejected the argument, relied upon by the dissenters, that the bar against derivative use could not be enforced so effectively as to ensure that the witness really was placed in the same position as if he had not testified. The statute's "total prohibition on use," it noted, "provides a comprehensive safeguard, barring the use of compelled testimony as an 'investigatory lead,' and also barring the use of any evidence obtained by focusing investigation on a witness as a result of his compelled disclosures." Appropriate procedures for "taint hearings" could ensure that this prohibition was made effective. Those procedures, the Court noted, would be identical to the procedures prescribed in *Murphy.* Once the defendant demonstrates that he testified under a grant of immunity, the prosecution would "have the burden of showing that their evidence is not tainted by establishing that they had an independent, legitimate source for the disputed evidence."

This was deemed to constitute "very substantial protection, commensurate with that resulting from invoking the privilege itself."

In a companion case to *Kastigar,* the Supreme Court upheld a state immunity statute providing for use/derivative-use immunity. More than twenty states eventually moved from transactional to use/derivative-use immunity in their general immunity statutes. The remaining states, however, have retained transactional immunity either in their general statutes, or in special statutes dealing with particular types of inquiries. That position has been supported on the ground that the number of subsequent prosecutions lost by providing transactional rather than use/derivative-use immunity is small, and transactional immunity will better encourage full disclosure. Proponents of use/derivative-use immunity respond that persons testifying under such immunity are the more likely to provide complete testimony (recognizing that greater detail strengthens the evidentiary reach of the immunity) and are more likely to be accepted as credible by a jury. The proponents also contend that allowing subsequent prosecution has practical significance, especially where the government already has a complete case against a person, but cannot wait until it gets a final conviction on that case before compelling the person through immunity to testify against others.

(c) **Applying the Use/Derivative–Use Prohibition.** Where the government seeks to prosecute a previously immunized witness, *Kastigar* requires that prosecution establish that its evidence was derived from an independent source and not from the defendant's immunized testimony. Typically this burden must be carried at an evidentiary hearing (commonly described as a "taint hearing" or a "*Kastigar* hearing"), although in exceptional cases (e.g., where the government relies upon evidence produced in a prior trial), affidavits alone may be sufficient. Many courts insist that the hearing be held prior to trial, which incidentally gives the defense far broader pretrial discovery than it would ordinarily obtain, but others will allow the government to make its showing after the trial is completed and all of its evidence has been seen. As *Kastigar* noted, the government burden at the hearing is not limited to "negation of taint," but must include a showing that it has "an independent legitimate source for the disputed evidence." Typically, "to establish a 'wholly independent source', the government must demonstrate that each step of the investigative chain through which the evidence was obtained is untainted." The government's standard of proof, however, is the preponderance of evidence standard, rather than some higher standard.

Federal caselaw applying *Kastigar* suggests that the prosecution is most likely to meet its burden of showing an independent source when the investigation of the defendant was completed or substantially completed before the defendant was compelled to give immunized testimony. The preferred practice in such cases is for the prosecution to make a record of all of the evidence collected prior to the grant of immunity, to file that record with the court, and then at the taint hearing, note its intent to utilize only the previously acquired evidence and further evidence directly derived from that evidence. That procedure, however, is hardly foolproof. Thus, where trial witnesses gave grand jury testimony prior to the grant of immunity, but then became aware of the immunized testimony of others (usually because it was given in a public forum), their subsequent trial testimony is likely to be viewed as influenced by that immunized testimony (and therefore excludable) unless it provides a perfect match to their earlier grand jury testimony.

Although the *Kastigar* opinion spoke primarily of the protection afforded by barring introduction of the compelled testimony and evidence derived from that testimony, it also used language suggesting a more sweeping prohibition. The Court noted, for example, that the federal immunity statute (which refers to prohibiting use of "information" derived from immunized testimony) "prohibits the prosecutorial authorities from using the compelled testimony in *any* respect." Accordingly, several lower courts have held that the *Kastigar* prohibition extends to "tactical" or "nonevidentiary use" of the compelled testimony. Such strategic decisions include deciding to initiate prosecution, refusing to plea bargain, and a cross-examination strategy that stands apart from forcing disclosure of particular information. Other federal circuit courts have either rejected or seriously questioned the proposition that *Kastigar* bars all nonevidentiary uses of immunized testimony by the prosecution. They note that *Kastigar* described the requisite scope of the immunity as placing the individual in "substantially the same position" as if he had claimed the privilege, and that nonevidentiary uses are often so tangential to the presentation of the prosecution as to hardly alter the strength of a case against the defendant that is based exclusively upon independently derived evidence.

(d) Immunity Procedures. Several states authorize the prosecutor to grant immunity without a court order, and in a few, grand jury witnesses receive automatic immunity simply by testifying before the grand jury (absent their waiver of that immunity). In the vast majority, however, an immunity order issued by a court is required before a witness will be compelled to testify over an exercise of the privilege. However, the court has a quite limited role in issuing the order. Typically, the court is required to issue the immunity order upon a showing that the witness would not testify without immunity and that the prosecutor has concluded that granting immunity as to the specified inquiry is in the public interest. The court here may not refuse to grant the order on the ground that the prosecutor erred in arriving at that conclusion.

Once the immunity order is granted, the witness must either testify or face contempt sanctions, unless the witness has some legal justification (e.g., the attorney-client privilege) for refusing to respond. The witness may not refuse to testify because his answers will subject him to substantial civil liability. Neither may he refuse to testify because he is fearful of physical or economic retaliation by associates or others. Some courts have suggested a duress defense could be available where the witness reasonably feared a sufficiently immediate threat of death or serious bodily harm, but the government can then respond by making available its witness protection program.

(e) Informal Grants of Immunity. Where the witness is willing to testify under a grant of immunity, the prosecutor may prefer to provide immunity through an agreement whereby the witness agrees to testify in exchange for a promise of non-prosecution or non-use. For the prosecutor, non-statutory immunity offers primarily two advantages. First, it bypasses the statutory procedure for obtaining an immunity order, and that procedure may be viewed as cumbersome or likely to pose a risk to grand jury secrecy. Second, it permits the prosecutor to tailor the scope of the immunity to the needs of the case. Thus, a prosecutor in a jurisdiction with a use/derivative-use statute may believe that an informal grant of transactional immunity will be more effective in gaining witness cooperation. In other situations, the immunity provided by statute may be more than the witness requires or the prosecutor is willing to give; an informal grant may be limited to barring prosecution only as to certain aspects of the transaction, or it may provide only use and not derivative-use immunity. Finally, the prosecution can condition the immunity on full cooperation, allowing for use of information initially provided should the defendant fail to be fully forthcoming in subsequent testimony. For the witness, informal immunity has an advantage primarily where it will permit him to obtain broader protection than would otherwise be available.

§ 7.10 Self–Incrimination and the Compulsory Production of Documents

(a) The *Boyd* Precedent. Although a subpoena duces tecum may be used to compel production of various types of physical evidence, it is most frequently used, at least in the grand jury setting, to require the production of documents. *Boyd v. U.S.* (1886)

was the first Supreme Court case to consider the applicability of the self-incrimination privilege to court ordered production of documents. Under the analysis adopted in *Boyd*, a subpoena requiring the production of a document was subject to challenge under both the Fourth Amendment and self-incrimination clause of the Fifth Amendment. As noted in § 7.4(a), *Boyd's* Fourth Amendment analysis was soon thereafter modified so as to limit the Fourth Amendment challenge to subpoenas that were overly broad in the documents requested. *Boyd's* Fifth Amendment analysis survived for a considerably longer period and provided a far more significant barrier to the compelled production of documents.

Under current precedent, very little, if anything, remains of *Boyd's* Fifth Amendment analysis. Yet the *Boyd* analysis remains a universally accepted starting point for understanding the many strands of current Fifth Amendment doctrine applicable to the subpoena duces tecum. For much of the current doctrine was developed in the process of first limiting and then replacing the *Boyd* analysis. Moreover, there still remains a question, at least for some jurisdictions, as to whether some elements of the *Boyd* analysis might not have current vitality in limited situations.

Boyd reasoned that, just as the Fifth Amendment prohibited "compulsory discovery by extorting the party's oath," it also prohibited discovery by "compelling the production of his private books and papers." The documentary production order was simply another form of "forcible and compulsory extortion of a man's own testimony." In reaching this conclusion, the Court described the Fourth and Fifth Amendments as "run[ning] almost into each other" in prohibiting any "compulsory extortion of a man's own testimony or his private papers to be used as evidence against him." The compulsory disclosure of a document, by revealing its content, was viewed as equivalent to requiring a subpoenaed party to describe that content through his testimony. Although the Court spoke of "private books and papers," it obviously was not referring only to confidential documents relating to personal or private matters. The document at issue in *Boyd* was a business record that had not been prepared by the partners themselves but by the shipper of the item alleged to have been illegally imported.

Starting with *Hale v. Henkel* (1906), decided only two decades after *Boyd*, the Court gradually developed a series of doctrines that chipped away at the broad implications of *Boyd's* analysis of Fifth Amendment protection. Finally, in *Fisher v. U.S.* (1976), decided close to a century after *Boyd*, the Court majority was forced to conclude that all that remained of *Boyd* was a "prohibition against forcing the production of private papers" that had "long been a rule searching for a rationale." The subsections that follow discuss the most significant of the doctrinal developments that restricted the privacy analysis of *Boyd*, and the quite different act-of-production analysis that was adopted in *Fisher*. Taken together, the rulings in these cases provide the basic legal principles currently governing the application of the privilege against self-incrimination to a subpoena duces tecum (principles which clearly reject the *Boyd* ruling on its facts). The possibility that some remnant of the *Boyd* analysis remains is discussed in the last subsection. Because of its special significance and complexity, the act-of-production doctrine is given further attention in § 7.11, which discusses a variety of issues raised in applying that doctrine.

(b) The Entity Exception. *Hale v. Henkel* (1906) not only reconstructed *Boyd's* Fourth Amendment analysis (see § 7.4(a)), but also added a major exception to its Fifth Amendment rationale. *Hale* held that the self-incrimination privilege was not available to a corporation and therefore *Boyd* did not bar a grand jury subpoena duces tecum requiring production of corporate records. The Court's refusal to allow a corporation to utilize the privilege rested basically on two grounds. First, the self-incrimination privilege is designed in large part to protect interests unique to the individual. Thus, in a later case, the privilege was described as designed to prevent "inhumane" methods of compulsion, to ensure "respect for the inviolability of the human personality," and to maintain the "right of each individual to a private enclave where he may lead a private life." A corporation, as a fictional entity, needs no such protection. Second, *Hale* spoke of the state's greater regulatory power over corporations, which were merely "creature[s] of the state."

The Court in *Hale* took special note of the enforcement needs of the government in compelling the production of corporate records; if such production were precluded by a self-incrimination claim, "it would result in a failure of a large number of cases where the illegal combination was determinable only upon such papers." In light of this concern, it was not surprising that, in *Wilson v. U.S.* (1911), the Court subsequently rejected the claim of a corporate officer possessing subpoenaed corporate records that he could refuse to produce those records because they would personally incriminate him. The State's "reserved power of visitation," the Court noted, "would seriously be embarrassed, if not wholly defeated in its effective exercise, if guilty officers could refuse inspection of the records and papers of the corporation." As the records were those of the corporation, not personal records, and were held "subject to the corporate duty," the official could "assert no personal right * * * against any demand of the government which the corporation was bound to recognize."

In *U.S. v. White* (1944), the Court extended the *Hale* exception to other entities. *White* held that the president of an unincorporated labor union could not invoke his personal privilege against a subpoena demanding union records. Characterizing the Court's previous reliance on the State's visitorial power as "merely a convenient vehicle for justification of governmental investigation of corporate books and records," the *White* Court concluded that the exception recognized in *Hale* was derived from the inappropriateness of affording the privilege to an impersonal collective entity, whether or not that entity took the corporate form.

The *White* opinion characterized the labor union as an organization with "a character so impersonal in the scope of its membership and activities that it cannot be said to embody or represent the purely private or personal interests of its constituents, but rather to embody their common or group interests only." In *Bellis v. U.S.* (1974), however, the Court concluded that the entity exception remained applicable even though the entity embodied personal as well as group interests. The functional key was that the organization "be recognized as an independent entity apart from its individual members." Thus, a small law firm, organized as a partnership, was an entity for this purpose even though it "embodie[d] little more than the personal legal practice of the individual partners." The partnership was not an "informal association or a temporary arrangement for the undertaking of a few projects of short-lived duration," but a "formal institutional arrangement organized for the continuing conduct of the firm's legal practice." State law, through the Uniform Partnership Act, imposed a "certain organizational structure"; the firm maintained a bank account in the partnership name; it had employees who worked for the firm as such; and, the firm "held itself out to third parties as an entity with an independent institutional identity."

(c) The Required Records Exception. Building upon dictum in *Wilson* to the effect that the privilege did not extend to corporate records because they were required by law to be kept for the public benefit, *Shapiro v. U.S.* (1948) held that the same principle could apply to the records of individuals engaged in regulated businesses. *Shapiro* upheld against a self-incrimination objection a subpoena directing production of records of commodity sales that the petitioner, a wholesale fresh produce dealer, was required to keep, and to make available for inspection by federal regulators, under the wartime Emergency Price Control Act. The Court acknowledged that "there are limits which the Government cannot constitutionally exceed in requiring the keeping of records which may be inspected by an administrative agency and may be used in prosecuting statutory violations committed by the recordkeeper himself," but it concluded that there was no need in this case to define precisely where those limits might lie. For, the Court noted, "no serious misgivings that those bounds were overstepped would appear to be evoked where there is a sufficient relation between the activity sought to be regulated and the public concern so that the Government can constitutionally regulate or forbid the basic activity concerned." This broad description of the acceptable nexus between the records and regulating authority offered the possibility of a far reaching required records doctrine. However, in the companion cases of *Marchetti v. U.S.* (1968) and *Grosso v. U.S.* (1968), the Court later made clear that the required records doctrine could not be carried to that extreme.

Marchetti and *Grosso* presented self-incrimination challenges to federal wagering tax statutes that required gamblers to identify themselves by registering with the government and by paying an occupational tax. The government contended that the disclosure requirements, though raising a "real and appreciable" hazard of self-incrimination, were nonetheless constitutional because they fit within the rationale of the required records doctrine. In rejecting that contention, the Court identified "three principle elements" of the required records doctrine, as it was "described in *Shapiro*." Those three elements were: "[F]irst, the purpose of the United States' inquiry must be essentially regulatory; second, information is to be obtained by requiring the preservation of records of a kind which the regulated party has customarily kept; and third, the records themselves must have assumed 'public aspects' which render them at least analogous to public documents." These elements were not satisfied in the gambling registration requirement; it dealt with an actively largely illegal throughout the United States, required information not otherwise kept, and did not seek records that had a public aspect (a feature commonly associated with records of licensed activities).

(d) The *Schmerber* Rule. Though it did not restrict the *Boyd* ruling as such, the limitation of the Fifth Amendment to "testimonial" compulsion, as held in *Schmerber v. Cal.* (1966), did raise questions as to the scope of the *Boyd* analysis. As discussed in § 6.2(a), *Schmerber* held that the privilege did not prohibit the compelled extraction of a blood sample from an accused and the subsequent admission of that sample as incriminatory evidence at his trial. The Court reasoned that the history of the privilege limited its application to compelled production of an accused's "communications" or "testimony." While this protection extended beyond words compelled from "a person's own lips" and extended to "communications * * * in whatever form they may take," it did not encompass "compulsion which makes a suspect or accused the source of 'real or physical' evidence."

Applying *Schmerber's* testimonial prerequisite, *Doe v. U.S.* (1988) (*Doe II*) later held that a court order requiring an individual to sign a form directing any foreign bank to release the records of any account he might have at that bank did not compel "testimony." This was so since the government did not seek to use the consent form itself as a factual assertion of the individual, expressing the "contents of his mind." While the government did intend to use the contents of the documents, if any, released by the bank, those documents would constitute statements not of the defendant, but of a third party. The same analysis arguably could have been advanced in *Boyd* to reject the claim of the petitioners there that the contents of the invoice constituted their incriminating communications.

(e) Third–Party Production. *Couch v. U.S.* (1973) and *Fisher v. U.S.* (1976) both involved situations in which an individual had transferred records to an independent professional who was then served with an IRS summons requiring production of those records. In both cases, the taxpayers relied upon *Boyd,* arguing that the government was seeking to obtain disclosure of papers of an even more confidential nature than the invoice subpoenaed in *Boyd.* The taxpayers acknowledged that the IRS summonses required their agents rather than the taxpayers themselves to produce the documents, but contended that factor was irrelevant since they had maintained a reasonable expectation of privacy in the documents even after delivery to the agents. The Supreme Court rejected the taxpayers' position. The Fifth Amendment applied only to personal compulsion and there was none here. Unlike the importers in *Boyd,* the taxpayers here were not themselves required "to do anything." The Court was not persuaded by the contention that its focus on personal compulsion was too formalistic to serve adequately the goals of the privilege. Responding in *Fisher,* it noted: "We cannot cut the Fifth Amendment completely loose from the moorings of its language and make it serve as a general protector of privacy—a word not mentioned in its text and a concept directly addressed in the Fourth Amendment." The Fifth Amendment, it continued, "protects against 'compelling testimony, not the disclosure of private information.' "

Both *Fisher* and *Couch* acknowledged that "situations might exist where constructive possession is so clear or the relinquishment of possession is so temporary and insignificant as to leave the personal compulsions upon the accused substantially intact." Lower courts have suggested, however, that where documents have been delivered to an independent third party, this "constructive-possession exception" will be available only if the third party received the records strictly for custodial safekeeping and the owner retained ready access to the records. Constructive possession is more likely to be found where a sole proprietor seeks to raise the privilege in response to a subpoena directing an employee to produce company records kept by that employee. Even here, however, a constructive possession argument may be denied, and the employer barred from raising the privilege, where, for example, the employer was an absentee proprietor who had delegated exclusive responsibility for the records to the subpoenaed employee.

(f) Testimonial Aspects of Production. Because the documents in *Fisher* (an accountant's workpapers) had been transferred to a third party (an attorney), the taxpayer could not directly raise a self-incrimination claim. Under the attorney-client privilege, however, the attorney could refuse to produce documents that "would have been privileged in the hands of the client by reason of the Fifth Amendment." The taxpayer argued that the documents here would have been privileged against self-production under the *"Boyd* rule" that "a person may not be forced to produce his private papers." However, Justice White's opinion for the Court in *Fisher* took a quite different view of *Boyd*.

Justice White initially noted that *Boyd* had relied on a combined Fourth and Fifth Amendment theory that had "not stood the test of time." Much of *Boyd*'s Fourth Amendment analysis had been flatly rejected and the rulings in cases like *Schmerber* and *Bellis* had adopted a different view of the Fifth Amendment. What was left was a "prohibition against forcing the production of private papers [that] has long been a rule searching for a rationale consistent with the proscriptions of the Fifth Amendment against compelling a person to give 'testimony' that incriminates him." In light of *Schmerber*, that prohibition could not rest on the incriminating content of the subpoenaed records. The court order of production of preexisting records does not require the subpoenaed party to author those records. Where the preparation of subpoenaed records was voluntary, those records "cannot be said to contain compelled testimonial evidence." The records may contain incriminating writing, but whether the writing of the subpoenaed party or another, that writing was not a communication compelled by the subpoena. Accordingly, the prosecution's acquisition of that writing by subpoena is no more compelling testimony than its acquisition of physical evidence with similar incriminating content.

Having found that application of the privilege could not rest on the declarations contained in the writings, Justice White then turned to what the Court majority viewed as a more appropriate explanation of the *Boyd* rule. The act of producing subpoenaed documents, Justice White noted, "has communicative aspects of its own, wholly aside from the contents of the papers produced."

Compliance with a subpoena "tacitly concedes the existence of the papers demanded and their possession or control by the [subpoenaed party]." It also would indicate that party's "belief that the papers are those described in the subpoena," and in some instances this could constitute authentication of the papers. These three elements of production—acknowledgment of existence, acknowledgment of possession or control, and potential authentication by identification—are clearly compelled, but whether they also are "testimonial" and "incriminating" would depend upon the "facts and circumstances of particular cases or classes thereof." The resolution of that question, Justice White reasoned, should determine whether a particular documentary production is subject to a Fifth Amendment challenge.

Upon examining the implications of the act of production in the case before it, the *Fisher* Court, for reasons explored in § 7.11, concluded that the taxpayer did not have a valid self-incrimination claim. "In light of the records now before us," Justice White noted, "however incriminating the contents of the accountant's workpapers might be, the act of producing them—the only thing which the taxpayer is compelled to do—would not itself involve testimonial self-incrimination." Justice White also added, however, a comment that could be taken to significantly limit the Court's ruling. He noted: "Whether the Fifth Amendment would shield the taxpayer from producing his own tax records in his possession is a question not involved here; for the papers demanded here are not 'private papers,' see *Boyd v. United States*."

Following *Fisher*, some lower courts saw the act-of-production doctrine and *Boyd*'s content-based analysis as alternative grounds for sustaining a self-incrimination challenge to the compelled production of the business records of a sole proprietor. This position was taken notwithstanding that the *Fisher* majority had rejected the privacy-based analysis of *Boyd* that been offered in the *Fisher* concurring opinions by Justices Brennan and Marshall. In *U.S. v. Doe (Doe I)* (1984), the Court reaffirmed that the *Fisher* analysis had rejected the view that the self-incrimination privilege is available whenever a person is ordered to disclose the content of private papers.

Doe I involved a subpoena directing a sole proprietor to produce for grand jury use a broad range of records, including billings, ledgers, canceled checks, telephone records, contracts, and paid bills. The district court sustained the proprietor's claim of privilege under the act of production doctrine. It concluded that compliance with the subpoena would require the proprietor to "admit that the records exist, that they are in his possession, and that they are authentic" and that each of these testimonial elements of production was potentially incriminatory. The Third Circuit agreed with this reasoning, but also added that the privilege applied because the compelled disclosure of the contents of the documents violated the Fifth Amendment. Relying upon the privacy analysis of *Boyd*, it reasoned that the contents of personal records were privileged under the Fifth Amendment and that "business records of a sole proprietorship are no different from the individual's personal records." Justice Powell's opinion for the Court in *Doe I* affirmed the rulings below insofar as they relied on the act-of-production doctrine. It flatly rejected, however, the Third Circuit's conclusion that the contents of the subpoenaed documents were protected by the privilege.

Justice Powell initially acknowledged that the Court in *Fisher* had "declined to reach the question whether the Fifth Amendment privilege protects the contents of an individual's tax records in his possession." The "rationale" underlying *Fisher's* holding, however, was equally persuasive here. *Fisher* had emphasized that "the Fifth Amendment protects the person asserting the privilege only from *compelled* self-incrimination." That a record was prepared by a subpoenaed party and is in his possession is "irrelevant to the determination of whether its creation * * * was compelled." The business records here, like the accountant's workpapers in *Fisher*, had been prepared voluntarily, and therefore only their production, and not their creation, was compelled. The contention that the Fifth Amendment created a "zone of privacy" that protected the content of such papers had been rejected in *Fisher*. The subpoena recipient cannot avoid compliance "merely by asserting that the item of evidence which he is required to produce contains incriminating writing, whether his own or that of someone else."

(g) The Remnants of Boyd. Although *Doe I* flatly rejected the Third Circuit's "zone of privacy" analysis, the Court had before it only a subpoena to compel the production of business records. Arguably, the most private records of an individual could be treated differently. Justice White had noted at one point in *Fisher* that case did not raise "the special problems of privacy which might be presented by subpoena of a personal diary." However, the *Doe I* majority opinion did not suggest any opening for separate treatment of personal recollections in confidential documents. It emphasized that the key to the application of the self-incrimination clause was the testimonial and incriminating aspects of the act of production, not the content of the voluntarily prepared document. Based upon that analysis, if intimate personal papers were to receive greater production, it was only because the confidential nature of those papers made it more likely that their production would have those attributes that made the production of the document "testimonial." This reading of *Doe I* was made explicit in Justice O'Connor's concurring opinion in that case, which led to a responding concurring opinion by Justice Marshall, who had argued in his *Fisher* concurrence that the Fifth Amendment creates a "zone of privacy" that encompassed all "personal records" not widely shared with others.

Justice O'Connor, in her concurring opinion, suggested that the *Doe–Fisher* rationale rejected a content based analysis as to all types of documents. She noted that the Court's analysis in *Doe I* and *Fisher* made clear "that the Fifth Amendment provides absolutely no protection for the contents of private papers of any kind. The notion that the Fifth Amendment protects the privacy of papers originated in *Boyd v. United States,* but our decision in *Fisher v. United States* sounded the death-knell for *Boyd.*" Responding to Justice O'Connor, Justice Marshall noted that the case before the Court, "presented nothing remotely close to the question that Justice O'Connor eagerly poses and answers." The documents in question here were business records, "which implicate a lesser degree of concern for privacy interests than, for example, personal diaries." It accordingly could not be said that the Court had "reconsidered the question of whether the Fifth Amendment provides protection for the content of 'private papers of any kind.' "

In the years since *Doe I,* lower courts usually have found it unnecessary to decide whether anything remains of *Boyd.* "If the contents of papers are protected at all," they note, "it is only in rare situations, where compelled disclosure would break the heart of our sense of privacy." That might be the case as to subpoena compelling production of "intimate papers such as private diaries and drafts of letters or essays," but it certainly would not cover the business and other financial records that typically are in issue. A growing number of courts have considered the issue, however, and have concluded that the rationale of *Doe* and *Fisher* precludes self-incrimination protection of the contents of a voluntarily prepared document, no matter how personal the document. Thus, courts have held that the act-of-production doctrine provides the only protection for such personal records as diaries and pocket calendars.

In a concurring opinion in *U.S. v. Hubbell* (§ 7.11(a)), Justice Thomas, joined by Justice Scalia, held open the possibility of a complete resurrection of *Boyd.* Justice Thomas suggested the Court should reexamine *Fisher* and other rulings that assume that the self-incrimination privilege applies only when a subpoena compels a production with "testimonial content." Justice Thomas noted that "[a] substantial body of evidence suggests that the Fifth Amendment privilege [was intended to] protect against the compelled production not just of incriminating testimony, but of any incriminating evidence." The holding in *Boyd,* he added, was in accord with this broader reading of the privilege, though *Boyd* admittedly did not refer to the concept that a person is being a "witness" against himself when compelled to "furnish incriminating physical evidence." Restoring *Boyd* in this fashion would have the advantage, he noted, of rendering irrelevant "the difficult parsing of the act of responding to a subpoena duces tecum" as required by *Fisher*.

§ 7.11 Application of the Act-of-Production Doctrine

(a) **Testimonial Character and the Foregone Conclusion Standard.** As discussed in § 7.10(f), *Fisher v. U.S.* (1976) concluded that the act of producing subpoenaed documents could have "communicative aspects of its own, wholly aside from the contents of the papers produced." Three elements of production—acknowledgment of existence, acknowledgment of possession or control, and potential authentication by identification—are clearly compelled, and could also be "testimonial" and "incriminating," *Fisher* also concluded, however, that the act of production in the case before it was not testimonial as to any of these elements. As for authentication, since the taxpayer was not in a position to authenticate documents prepared by another, the act of production was seen as having no testimonial content. Existence and possession, however, presented greater difficulties.

In finding that the taxpayer's act of production would not have been testimonial in its acknowledgment of both the existence of the workpapers and possession by the taxpayer, the Court relied on what came to be known as the foregone conclusion analysis. The crux of that analysis was set forth in a single paragraph:

> It is doubtful that implicitly admitting the existence and possession of the papers rises to the level of testimony within the protection of the Fifth Amendment. The papers belong to the accountant, were prepared by him, and are the kind usually prepared by an accountant working on the tax returns of his client. Surely the Government is in no way relying on the "truthtelling" of the taxpayer to prove the existence of or his access to the documents. The existence and location of the papers are a foregone conclusion and the taxpayer adds little or nothing to the sum total of the Government's information by conceding that he in fact has the papers. Under these circumstances by enforcement of the summons "no constitutional rights are touched. The question is not of testimony but of surrender."

Justice Brennan, in his concurring opinion, criticized the Court's "foregone conclusion" rationale as relying upon "the untenable proposition" that an admission as to existence and possession is not testimonial "merely because the Government could otherwise have proved [those facts]." Undoubtedly, as Justice Brennan noted, in assessing whether compelled testimony falls within the privilege, courts have never deemed it significant that the government could otherwise establish the incriminating information that might be disclosed in the witness' testimony; the critical question is simply whether the witness' testimony would be usable against him. However, the *Fisher* Court was not dealing with a traditional form of testimony, but with what it viewed as a quite different issue—whether the incidental communicative aspects of a physical act (production) were "testimonial." The Court cited by analogy its rulings holding the Fifth Amendment inapplicable to a court order requiring an accused to submit a handwriting sample. Incidental to the performance of that act, the Court noted, the accused necessarily "admits his ability to write and impliedly asserts that the exemplar is his writing." But the government obviously is not seeking this information—the "first would be a near truism and the latter self-evident"—and therefore "nothing he has said or done is deemed to be sufficiently testimonial for purposes of the privilege." Where the existence and possession of the documents to be produced are a "foregone conclusion," the act of production similarly "adds little or nothing to the sum total of the government's information" and therefore is no more testimonial than other compelled physical acts. The government in such a case obviously is not seeking the assertions of the subpoenaed party as to the facts of existence and possession, and his incidental communication as to those facts, inherent in the physical act that the government had the authority to compel, therefore does not rise to the level of compelled "testimony."

The explanation in *Fisher* of the relationship of the foregone conclusion standard to the lack of "testimonial" compulsion was brief and perhaps somewhat obfuscated by a second analogy drawn by the Court—that of the required production of entity records through an entity. However, in a later case, *Doe v. U.S. (Doe II)* (1988), the Court made quite clear that the communicative element of an act, even the act of making a statement, rises to the level of testimony only where the government's objective is to seek to have the actor, through that act itself, "relate a factual assertion or disclose information." *Doe II* held that a court order requiring an individual to sign a form directing any foreign bank to release the records of any account he might have at that bank did not compel "testimony" for Fifth Amendment purposes. This was so since the government did not seek to use the signed form itself as a factual assertion of the individual (although it would use the documents that might be produced by the bank in response to the signed directive). Indeed, the form was carefully drafted so that the signing party noted that he was acting under court order and did not acknowledge the existence of any account in any particular bank. The form did not indicate whether the requested documents existed, and offered no assistance to the government in later establishing the authenticity of any records produced by the bank. Thus, while the signed form did constitute a communication, it did not constitute "testimony." The government was not relying on the "truth-telling" of the directive, but simply requiring the petitioner to engage in the act of producing that directive.

Similarly, where the communicative elements of the act of producing a preexisting document merely establishes what is already a foregone conclusion, that factor suggests that the government is compelling the act for what it will produce (the voluntarily prepared documents, with a content not itself compelled) rather than the communication inherent in the act. To allow the privilege to be claimed simply because the required act incidentally provided information, even though the government did not seek that information, would be to make every compelled act a testimonial communication, contrary to the *Schmerber* rule.

The *Fisher* Court concluded that the existence and location of the accountant's workpapers were a foregone conclusion, but the Court never explained why that was so—apart from noting that the papers were of the kind usually prepared by an accountant. In *United States v. Doe* (*Doe I*), in contrast to *Fisher*, the Court held the privilege applicable to an act of production, and noted that there the government had failed to "rebu[t] the respondent's claim" as it had not shown "that possession, existence, and authentication were a foregone conclusion." The Court explained that its holding in this regard was based on the factual determinations of the two courts below, which had agreed on this point. Thus, the significance of the *Doe* I precedent was unclear, although the case appeared to reject the contention that the foregone conclusion standard was automatically met where the records subpoenaed were commonplace business records (as they were in *Doe* I).

In *U.S. v. Hubbell* (2000), the Court again spoke only briefly about the foregone conclusion doctrine, but provided substantially more content than *Fisher or Doe I*. The subpoena in *Hubbell* called for 11 categories of documents, which were broadly stated (e.g., calling for "any and all materials * * * relating to any direct or indirect sources of money or other things of value" received over a three year period). The Court reasoned that, "given the breadth of the 11 categories, * * * the collection and production of the materials demanded was tantamount to answering a series of interrogatories asking a witness to disclose the existence and location of particular documents fitting broad descriptions." Thus, there obviously was a "communicative aspect" in the act-of-production, as "it was unquestionably necessary for respondent to make extensive use of the 'contents of his own mind' in identifying the hundreds of documents responsive to the subpoena." The government argued, however, that this "communicative aspect" of production was not sufficiently testimonial "because the existence and possession of such records by any businessman is a foregone conclusion." Rejecting that contention, the Court reasoned:

> Whatever the scope of this "foregone conclusion" rationale, the facts of this case plainly fall outside of it. While in *Fisher* the Government already knew that the documents were in the attorneys' possession and could independently confirm their existence and authenticity through the accountants who created them, here the Government has not shown that it had any prior knowledge of either the existence or the whereabouts of the 13,120 pages of documents ultimately produced by respondent. The Government cannot cure this deficiency through the overbroad argument that a businessman such as respondent will always possess general business and tax records that fall within the broad categories described in this subpoena. The *Doe [I]* subpoenas also sought several broad categories of general business records, yet we upheld the District Court's finding that the act of producing those records would involve testimonial self-incrimination.

Hubbell puts to rest the notion that the commonplace character of the document in itself establishes existence and possession as a foregone conclusion. It also precludes limiting *Doe I* to a situation in which the government could not tie the individual to the business activities reflected in the records; most of the records sought in the *Hubbell* subpoena were defined by reference to Hubbell's own activities. In describing why the foregone conclusion standard was met in *Fisher*, the Court noted the existence of an outside source (the accountants) who could "independently confirm * * * existence and authenticity," and while *Hubbell* did not declare that route to be exclusive, it is a common feature of many lower court rulings finding that the government had met the foregone conclusion standard. Still other rulings have relied on similar extrinsic evidence, such as the subpoenaed party have acknowledged existence and possession in another context, or similar documents in the government's possession indicating that the subpoenaed documents also exist and are in the subpoenaed person's possession. Similarly, as to authentication, courts have held that the foregone conclusion standard is met where the government can point to another person who can authenticate, or where authentication can be achieved by other means (e.g., comparison with other documents independently authenticated or matching the handwriting with that of the subpoenaed party).

(b) Potential Incrimination. To raise a successful self-incrimination claim based on the act of production doctrine, the subpoenaed party must establish not only that the communicative aspects of production rise to the level of testimony, but also that such testimony would meet the traditional standard of potential incrimination. Thus, in *Fisher*, after indicating that act of production there would not be testimonial, the Court went on to conclude that the Fifth Amendment claim failed in any event because there had been no showing that the communicative aspects of production posed a "realistic threat of incrimination to the taxpayer." "Surely," the Court noted, "it was not illegal to seek accounting help in connection with one's tax returns or for the accountant to prepare workpapers and deliver them to the taxpayer." Accordingly, "at this juncture," the Court was "quite unprepared to hold that either the fact of the existence of the papers or their possession by the taxpayer" posed a sufficient threat to raise a legitimate self-incrimination claim. The *Fisher* reference to the innocuous nature of accountant's workpapers on their face might be read to suggest that no weight should be given to the possibility that the documents have an incriminating content. Such a position would be contrary to the traditional application of the potential incrimination standard to testimony, but arguably supported by the *Fisher* conclusion that the contents of the documents are not protected by the privilege.

In *Doe I*, the Court returned to the issue of incrimination in a footnote that appeared to reject such a narrow view of potential incrimination. In that footnote, the *Doe I* Court responded to the government's contention that even if the act of production there were viewed as having sufficient "testimonial aspects," any incrimination would be "so trivial" that the Fifth Amendment would not be implicated. The Court agreed that the Fifth Amendment would only be implicated if the risk of incrimination were "substantial and real," not merely "trifling or imaginary." It rejected, however, the government's claim that the risk of incrimination here clearly did not meet that standard. Respondent Doe had never conceded that the records subpoenaed actually existed or were within his possession. As respondent also noted, "even if the government could obtain the documents from another source, by producing the documents, respondent would relieve the government of the need for authentication." These potential prosecution uses of respondent's production, the Court noted, "were sufficient to establish a valid claim of the privilege."

What apparently distinguished *Doe I* from *Fisher*, as to the potential for incrimination, were the circumstances in *Doe I* suggesting the possible incriminating content of the documents sought. The records described in the *Doe I* subpoena were as innocuous in their general character as the accountant's workpapers subpoenaed in *Fisher*. The potential for incrimination existed in tying the subpoenaed party to the contents of those records through his acknowledgment that he was aware of their existence and possessed them. The *Doe I* Court relied in this regard on the finding of the District Court, affirmed by Court of Appeals, that the potential for incrimination through the testimonial aspects of production was "substantial and real." The Court stated that this conclusion was based on a "determination of factual issues" which it would not revisit, but its descriptions of the lower court proceedings suggested at least a few of the factors that contributed to the lower court's determination. The subpoena was issued by a grand jury investigating corruption in the awarding of government contracts; the government had "conceded [before the District Court] that the materials sought in the subpoena were or might be incriminating"; and the government was seeking through the act of production to establish a connection between Doe and several businesses under investigation (a link it apparently otherwise could not establish).

In *Fisher,* in contrast to *Doe I,* the materials were subpoenaed in a standard IRS investigation, with no criminal overtones—a proceeding in which lower courts have commonly required the contesting party to make some showing of potential incrimination. The taxpayer had raised, however, no more than a blanket claim of the privilege as to the records as group. In stating that it was unprepared "at this juncture" to find a realistic threat of incrimination, the Court may have been leaving the door open for the taxpayer to make a more particularized showing of possible incrimination. Thus, a valid self-incrimination claim arguably could have been presented in *Fisher* if the taxpayer had pointed to particular records that posed a real and appreciable threat of containing incriminatory information and had indicated that the government was seeking to link the taxpayer to those potentially incriminatory records through his act of production.

Lower court cases, analyzing the self-incrimination issue in light of *Doe I* and *Fisher*, have rejected "blanket claims" of self-incrimination based on the testimonial aspects of the act of production. Where the documents to be produced are innocuous on their face, the witness has been asked to make a "contextual" showing indicating how the linkage to the documents established by the act of production (or further evidence derived from that linkage) "would, in any sense, create a hazard of prosecution against him or a link in a chain of evidence establishing guilt." The lower courts have allowed that showing to be made *in camera*, have permitted the showing to be made by reference to different categories of documents (rather than as to production of each individual document), and have been willing to take account of the possible contents of the document. The standard of potential incrimination is the same as that applied to testimony, but in requiring a contextual showing, even where the documents have been subpoenaed by a grand jury, these rulings demand more of the witness than would ordinarily be demanded as to testimony.

(c) **Act-of-Production Immunity.** *Doe I* also considered the possibility that the government could obtain and make use of documents, even where the self-incrimination protection applied to the act of production, by granting act-of-production immunity. The Court there rejected the contention that the courts could fashion an immunity procedure apart from the immunity statute. It recognized, however, that the government "could have compelled respondent to produce the documents" by utilizing the federal immunity statute providing for use/derivative-use immunity. Moreover, that immunity need not have covered the contents of the documents, but could have been limited to the act of production since "immunity need be only as broad as the privilege against self-incrimination."

Concurring in *Fisher*, Justice Marshall suggested that act-of-production immunity commonly would "effectively shield" the contents of the documents, as the contents would be a "direct fruit" of the "immunized testimony" contained in the act of production. Justice Marshall's assumption was that the testimonial component of the act of production would usually include an implicit admission of existence and possession, and the document itself would be the fruit of those admissions. Accordingly, if those implicit admissions were immunized, then the document itself would be immunized and the prosecution could not use either its contents or evidence derived from its contents. The situation would be different, however, where the act of production was testimonial only because of its implicit authentication of the document (i.e., where existence and possession were foregone conclusions, but authentication was not a foregone conclusion). Here, the immunity would not bar use of the document, as its existence would be independently established. The government would be precluded from using the act of production to authenticate, but if it found through the document's contents another means of authenticating (e.g., a reference to a third person who could authenticate or a handwritten entry that could be matched against the producer's handwriting sample), then it could use the document.

In contrast to Justice Marshall, the United States Department of Justice took the position that act-of-production immunity has no bearing on the use of the contents, irrespective of the range of the testimonial components in the particular act-of-production. It reasoned that, since the contents of the record are not privileged, the immunity is fully satisfied if the government is prohibited from in any way (investigative or evidentiary) looking to the act of production itself. Act-of-production immunity required only that the documents be viewed as if they "magically appear[ed] before the grand jury" from an unknown source.

In *U.S. v. Hubbell* (2000), the Supreme Court rejected the Department of Justice's position. The prosecution there argued that its grant of act-of-production immunity (resulting in the production of documents totaling 13,120 pages) did not impact the evidence to be used in its subsequent prosecution of the respondent. It was not using the documents produced by respondent under the immunity order, but other evidence discovered through an examination of the produced documents, and there was no need "to advert to respondent's act of production in order to prove the existence, authenticity or custody" of the documents that the government would introduce at trial. The Court rejected this explanation as inadequate since the government did not show (and could not show) that it had not made derivative use of the "testimonial aspects" of the respondent's act of production. The contention that the produced documents should be useable as if they "magically appeared in the prosecutor's office, like manna from heaven," was not persuasive; in fact those documents "arrived there only after respondent asserted his constitutional privilege, received a grant of immunity, and * * * took the mental and physical steps necessary to provide the prosecutor with an accurate inventory of the many sources of potentially incriminating evidence sought by the subpoena." "It was only through respondent's truthful reply to the subpoena that the Government received the incriminating documents of which it made 'substantial use ... in the investigation'."

The reasoning of *Hubbell* would appear to support Justice Marshall's position on the consequences of act-of-production immunity. The Court notes that without the witness' immunized truth-telling in producing the documents, the government would never have received them, as it could not establish existence and possession as a foregone conclusion. It would seem to follow that every bit of evidence derived from the receipt of the documents (which obviously includes evidence derived from the content of the documents) is immunized. However, the Court also took note of special circumstances in *Hubbell* that tied the government's evidence to the act of production apart from providing the documents themselves. In particular, in responding to the broadly stated subpoena, the witness made critical distinctions that provided the government with crucial information as to the use of particular documents and their relationship to particular transactions. Indeed, the act of production was compared in this regard to answering a series of interrogatories about the documents. This roadmap clearly had assisted the government in building its case. In sum, while language in *Hubbell* would appear to preclude use of the content of the document even when the government seeks pursuant to act-of-production immunity a specifically described document (e.g., a communication identified by date and source), that clearly was not the situation before the Court.

(d) Claims By Entity Agents. In many instances, the person subpoenaed to produce entity records may himself be incriminated by what is to be found in those records. However, as noted in § 7.10(b), the Supreme Court has held that the entity agent may not rely upon his personal privilege to refuse to produce the records. The individual who holds the entity records (whether or not a formally designated custodian) does so in a representative rather than individual capacity. By voluntarily accepting the custodianship of the records, he assumes the entity's responsibility for making the records available to a government agency (including a grand jury) entitled to see them. If the rule were otherwise, the Court has noted, the entity exception would be meaningless.

The Supreme Court rulings establishing these principles were decided prior to *Fisher's* adoption of the act-of-production rationale as the basic grounding for a self-incrimination objection to a subpoena requiring the production of documents. In *Braswell v. U.S.* (1988), the petitioner, a corporate president and sole shareholder who had been subpoenaed to produce various corporate records, argued that the act-of-production doctrine provided a new grounding for recognizing a corporate custodian's exercise of the privilege, which had been ignored in the Court's earlier entity rulings. Petitioner claimed that the Court's earlier rulings had assumed that the availability of the privilege flowed from the "privacy rationale" of *Boyd* and protected the contents of "personal books and records" (therefore excluding entity records), but had not considered the personal testimonial incrimination of the custodian that attends his act of producing those entity records. A closely divided Supreme Court rejected that contention and reaffirmed the unavailability of the privilege to a custodian of entity records.

The *Braswell* majority concluded that the earlier rulings had not ignored the testimonial aspects of the act of production, but rather had considered any testimonial elements of that act to be properly attributed to the entity rather than to the agent acting on its behalf. Even where the subpoena was directed to the custodian by name, rather than simply to the entity, the custodian was not performing "a personal act, but rather an act of the [entity]." *Fisher* itself had accepted this distinction in the course of analyzing the act-of-production rationale. Thus, the *Braswell* majority noted, "whether one concludes—as did the Court [in *Fisher*]—that a custodian's production of corporate records is deemed not to constitute testimonial self-incrimination or instead that a custodian waives the right to exercise the privilege, the lesson of *Fisher* is clear: A custodian may not resist a subpoena for corporate records on Fifth Amendment grounds."

Braswell, however, added an evidentiary limitation not mentioned in the earlier cases that had rejected self-incrimination claims by entity agents. Since the agent's act of production is an act of the entity and not the individual, the government "may make no evidentiary use of the 'individual act' against the individual." Illustrating this point, the Court noted that, "in a criminal prosecution against the custodian, the Government may not introduce into evidence before the jury the fact that the subpoena was served upon, and the corporation's documents were delivered by, one particular individual, the custodian." The government would be limited to showing that the entity had produced the document and to using that act of the entity in establishing that the records were authentic entity records that the entity had possessed and had produced. If the defendant's position in the entity were such that it could be assumed that he had possession or knowledge of the documents, the jury could make that assumption; it would not be doing so because of defendant's act of production but would be relying on reasonable inferences applicable without regard to who produced the documents.

In its discussion of the limited use the government might make of the act of production in a subsequent prosecution of the custodian, the Court, in a footnote, added what may be a very important caveat: it was "leav[ing] open the question [of] whether the agency rationale supports compelling a custodian to produce corporate records when the custodian is able to establish, by showing for example that he is the sole employee and officer of the corporation, that the jury would inevitably conclude that he produced the records." The petitioner in *Braswell* might himself have fit that description, but no showing directed at the inevitability of such a jury conclusion was made there. Where such a showing is made, one judicial response might be to require the custodian to produce the documents, but preclude the prosecution from making reference even to the corporation's act of production. This would put the burden on the government to authenticate and to establish entity possession through other means, but would still fall short of placing on the government the burden it would bear as to the lack of taint in other evidence if it had been required to grant act-of-production immunity (as the *Braswell* dissenters suggested). Still another possibility would be to direct the subpoena to the corporation itself, and require it to make production through some third-party custodian (e.g., counsel or an unaffiliated agent) who would not be incriminated by the act of production. This obligation presumably would require that the corporation, through the sole-participant/custodian, assist the third-party custodian in locating and identifying the subpoenaed records, but the government would then have to note that production was by the third-party agent, and refrain from referring to the assistance of the sole-participant/custodian in presenting the documents in evidence.

The responsibility of the custodian to produce the records ordinarily will encompass a duty to testify for the limited purpose of identifying the material produced. In *Curcio v. U.S.* (1957), the Supreme Court distinguished between such testimony and what was required there. In that case, defendant Curcio, a secretary-treasurer of a union, had informed the grand jury that he could not produce the subpoenaed records because they were not in his possession. Without challenging the truth of his statement, the prosecution sought to compel him to testify as to the whereabouts of the documents. Although Curcio exercised his privilege against self-incrimination at this point, the government argued that the custodial duty that required the production of the documents also carried with it a relinquishment of the privilege as to "auxiliary testimony" that would permit the government to locate the documents. The Supreme Court rejected that argument, noting that an entity agent did not "waive his constitutional privilege as to oral testimony by assuming the duties of his office."

Curcio did suggest, however, that where the documents are produced, the custodian has an obligation to provide basic authentication testimony—i.e., to testify as to "the location of the documents produced and that the produced records are those called for in the subpoena." In *Braswell*, the Court characterized *Curcio* as having drawn a line between the duty to produce the documents, and the giving of oral testimony. This characterization arguably suggests that *Curcio* assumed that a custodian's authenticating testimony could be demanded, not because the custodian had a duty to provide it as part of the act of production, but because authenticating testimony would not add to the incrimination already provided by the act of production. However, that may not always be the case, as the additional specifics provided by testimony as to matters such as the prior location of the documents may provide additional information incriminating to the custodian. *Braswell* also indicates that whatever authentication testimony may be compelled, that testimony may not be admitted against the custodian should he be prosecuted.

§ 7.12   The Witness' Right to Counsel

(a) **Constitutional Requirements.** Although the Supreme Court has not ruled directly on whether a grand jury witness has a constitutional right to the assistance of counsel, the justices have made major statements on that issue in two cases, *In re Groban* (1957) and *U.S. v. Mandujano* (1976). *Groban,* did not involve a grand jury proceeding, but rather a special investigative proceeding of a state fire marshall at which the witness was not allowed to be accompanied by counsel. In finding that the exclusion of counsel from that proceeding did not violate due process, the Court majority drew an analogy to the grand jury proceeding. There, it noted, the law was clear that "a witness cannot insist, as a matter of constitutional right, on being represented by counsel."

In *Mandujano,* a grand jury witness was told that "he could have a lawyer outside the room with whom he could consult," but he was not offered the assistance of an appointed attorney, although claiming to be indigent. The lower courts held that, as a "putative" or "virtual" defendant, he was in a position akin to an arrestee and should have been given complete *Miranda* warnings, including advice as to appointed counsel. As noted in § 7.8(e), the Court upheld Mandujano's perjury conviction without conclusively ruling on the lower court's analysis. Six members of the Court, however, did speak to that analysis, including the possible right to counsel.

Four justices, through Chief Justice Burger's plurality opinion, concluded that the advice given Mandujano as to the availability of counsel was fully consistent with any constitutional requirements. Since "no criminal proceedings had been instituted," the "Sixth Amendment right to counsel had not come into play." The prerequisite of an "initiation of adversary judicial proceedings," as set forth in *Kirby v. Ill.* (§ 6.3(b)), rendered the Sixth Amendment inapplicable. The *Miranda* right to counsel, "fashioned to secure the suspect's Fifth Amendment privilege," also did not apply. It was premised upon an "inherently coercive" interrogation setting, clearly distinguishable from grand jury questioning. Under "settled principles," as reflected in *Groban,* "the witness may not insist upon the presence of his attorney in the grand jury room." Justice Brennan, joined by Justice Marshall, responded that *Groban* should be reexamined in light of more recent decisions like *Miranda* and *Escobedo.*

In *Conn v. Gabbert* (1999), the Court noted: "A grand jury witness has no constitutional right to have counsel present during the grand jury proceeding, *United States v. Mandujano,* and no decision of this Court has held that a grand jury witness has a right to have her attorney present outside the courtroom. We need not decide today whether such a right exists, because Gabbert clearly had no standing * * *." A line of lower court rulings have reached that issue and have held that there is no right to counsel in any location, as a Sixth Amendment right simply has not "come into play" at the point of a grand jury inquiry. A few courts have suggested, however, that where a witness has retained counsel present in the anteroom, the privilege against self-incrimination carries with it a right to leave the grand jury room and consult with counsel should the witness be uncertain as to the availability of the privilege.

(b) Counsel Within the Grand Jury Room. In one of the major developments in grand jury reform, roughly twenty states today have statutes permitting at least certain witnesses to be assisted by counsel located within the grand jury room. About half of these provisions apply to all witnesses, but several are limited to either targets, witnesses who have not been granted immunity, or witnesses who have waived immunity. Some, but not all of these provisions, require the appointment of counsel when the qualified witness is indigent.

The statutes commonly contain provisions limiting the role of counsel while before the grand jury. Several state that the lawyer may "advise the witness," but "may not otherwise take any part in the proceeding." One jurisdiction also allows counsel to "interpose objections on behalf of the witness." Another provides for such participation upon agreement of the prosecutor and the foreperson. To ensure that the witness does not use the statutory right to delay his or her appearance, two provisions state that counsel's unavailability does not excuse the witness' failure to appear. Others impose time restraints on the witness' obtaining counsel of choice.

(c) Counsel in the Anteroom. Jurisdictions that prohibit counsel's presence in the grand jury room, such as the federal, typically will permit the witness, under at least some circumstances, to leave the grand jury room to consult with retained counsel located in the anteroom. Lawyers sometimes urge witnesses to consult after each question, which allows the lawyer to construct a complete record of the questions asked. Many federal courts permit such a practice, while others go almost that far, limiting witnesses to departures after every few questions. Other jurisdictions are more stringent. They note, for example, that the grand jury may properly refuse a witness' request to leave where the witness obviously is seeking "strategic advice" rather than counseling as to the exercise of any legal rights.

Chapter 8

SCOPE OF THE EXCLUSIONARY RULES

Table of Sections

§ 8.1 Standing: The "Personal Rights" Approach

(a) "Personal Rights" as to Searches, Confessions and Identifications. When a motion to suppress evidence is made in a criminal case on the ground that the evidence was obtained in violation of the Constitution, there may be put in issue the question of whether the movant is a proper party to assert the claim of illegality and seek the remedy of exclusion. This question is ordinarily characterized as one of whether the party has "standing" to raise the contention. One aspect of standing is that the party seeking relief must have an adversary interest in the outcome, as to which any defendant in a criminal case against whom evidence alleged to have been illegally seized is being offered surely qualifies. In most areas of constitutional law, however, it is also necessary that the adverse interest be based upon a violation of the rights of the individual raising the claim rather than the violation of the rights of some third party. This is generally true with respect to the various constitutional issues that might arise in the context of a suppression hearing.

For example, when a Fourth Amendment claim is involved it is not sufficient that the defendant claims prejudice only through the use of evidence gathered as a consequence of a search or seizure directed at someone else; rather, he must have been a victim of a search or seizure. "This standing rule," the Court explained in *United States v. Calandra* (1974), "is premised on a recognition that the need for deterrence and hence the rationale for excluding the evidence are strongest where the Government's unlawful conduct would result in imposition of a criminal sanction on the victim of the search." As for who should be deemed a "victim of the search" under this line of reasoning, the fundamental inquiry is whether the conduct that the defendant wants to put in issue involved an intrusion into *his* reasonable expectation of privacy. Because expectation-of-privacy analysis is also used in deciding whether any Fourth Amendment search has occurred, it has been concluded that there no longer exists a concept of standing "distinct from the merits" of a Fourth Amendment claim. But this notion that the search and standing "inquiries merge into one" is best avoided; the question traditionally labelled as standing (did the police intrude upon *this defendant's* justified expectation of privacy?) is not identical to the question of whether any Fourth Amendment search occurred (did the police intrude upon *anyone's* justified expectation of privacy?), and thus the former inquiry deserves separate attention no matter what label is put upon it.

Questions of standing seldom arise as to confessions because established evidentiary rules normally permit a confession to be admitted as substantive evidence only against the maker. But the issue comes to the fore when, for example, a confession obtained in violation of *Miranda* reveals the location of physical evidence then offered as evidence in the trial of another person. The physical evidence would be admissible under a "personal rights" analysis, for any constitutional violation that occurred intruded only upon the rights of the person who made the confession. Thus, even if the defendant was himself subjected to an arrest or search based upon a confession obtained from another in violation of *Miranda,* he would lack standing to claim that what was obtained by the arrest or search should be suppressed as the fruits of the *Miranda* violation.

If the confession had been obtained by coercive tactics, under the "personal rights" approach there would be no standing even as to such a confession. Thus, if the police beat *A* until he confesses his role as an accomplice in a murder and says that his gun (used by *B*) is in his house and the police then retrieve the gun from *A*'s house, defendant *B* is not entitled to have the gun suppressed as a fruit of *A*'s coerced confession. If *A* had said the gun was in *B*'s house and the police on that basis obtained a warrant to search *B*'s house and found the gun there, *B* would still lack standing to claim this was a fruit of the confession but would have standing to raise his own Fourth Amendment claim that the warrant was invalid because based upon information known to be unreliable. More problematical would be a case in which a coerced confession is itself offered, as might happen if *A* testifies at *B*'s trial on *B*'s behalf and the prosecution then wants to impeach that testimony with a confession coerced from *A*. Though *B* could not be impeached by a coerced or involuntary statement obtained from him, it is unclear whether it follows from this that he would have standing as to *A*'s confession. It may well be that *B* is entitled to an assurance that "the trustworthiness of the evidence satisfies legal standards," but this is a narrower proposition, for *A*'s confession could be coerced or involuntary in a due process sense but yet be trustworthy.

Standing issues also arise infrequently with respect to unconstitutional identification procedures. But they can occur, as where in an accomplice's trial identification evidence is offered to show that his principal committed the crime charged. Where the nature of the constitutional violation was denial of the right to counsel at a lineup provided under *United States v. Wade* (1967), it has been held by analogy to Fourth Amendment standing rules that the defendant lacks standing to raise the other person's Sixth Amendment rights. Doubtless the cases disallowing standing as to another's denial of counsel under *Miranda* might also be thought relevant here. But it may be seriously questioned whether either of these analogies is sound. *Wade,* after all, is grounded on the proposition that if a defendant's conviction rests on "a suspect pretrial identification which the accused is helpless to subject to effective scrutiny at trial, the accused is deprived of that right of cross-examination which is an essential safeguard to his right to confront the witnesses against him." In other words, the constitutional right at issue belongs to the person on trial rather than the person identified, and thus the defendant has standing, for otherwise there would be present a serious risk that the issue of his guilt or innocence might not be reliably determined. Whatever the result in such circumstances, surely a defendant has standing to object to an identification procedure conducted in violation of *Stovall v. Denno* (1967), for such a due process violation exists only when the procedure has been such as to create "a very substantial likelihood of irreparable misidentification." Such evidence is just as unreliable when it is directed toward the identity of a coparticipant in a crime as when it relates to the identity of the defendant on trial.

A final word of caution concerning the "personal rights" approach: in determining in any particular case whether a defendant has standing, it is critical that the police conduct being objected to be properly identified, for this may turn out to be determinative on the standing issue. A very useful illustration of this point is provided by *Wong Sun v. United States* (1963). Federal narcotics agents made an illegal entry into the premises of Toy and then illegally arrested him, after which Toy in response to questioning said he had no narcotics but that Yee did. The agents then went to and entered Yee's premises and obtained narcotics from him, which Yee said he had obtained from Toy and Wong Sun. The narcotics were later admitted against both Toy and Wong Sun. The Court concluded that Wong Sun had no standing to seek their suppression, for their seizure "invaded no right of privacy of person or premises which would entitle Wong Sun to object." This would mean that Toy would likewise lack standing if he were also objecting merely to the agents' conduct at the Yee premises. However, Toy was held to have standing because he was objecting to the actions of the agents at his own premises that led to Yee and thus made the narcotics obtained from Yee the "fruit of the poisonous tree" of the violation of his own Fourth Amendment rights.

(b) Residential Premises. It has long been true and is still so under the modern expectation-of-privacy test that an individual with a present possessory interest in the premises searched has standing to challenge that search even though he was not present when the search was made. This includes those who are tenants or other continuing lawful occupants of a house or apartment or who are renting a room in a hotel, motel or rooming house, and also includes an owner-occupant but of course not an owner who has by lease given the full possessory right to another. Family members regularly residing upon the premises, such as a spouse or offspring, have standing of essentially the same dimensions. In *Bumper v. North Carolina* (1968), for example, the Supreme Court summarily concluded that there could "be no question of the petitioner's standing" to challenge a search of his grandmother's home during his absence in light of the fact that he regularly resided there as well. (However, an absent occupant or owner would lack standing as violation of any Fourth Amendment requirement intended only for the benefit of those present—e.g., violation of the knock-and-announce rule without damage to the premises, violation of the rule on serving a copy of the warrant on a present party.)

Establishing such an interest in the premises searched itself suffices to establish standing, and thus the defendant need not also show an interest in the particular items seized by the police. As the Supreme Court explained in *Alderman v. United States* (1969): "If the police make an unwarranted search of a house and seize tangible property belonging to third parties * * * the home owner may object to its use against him, not because he had any interest in the seized items as 'effects' protected by the Fourth Amendment, but because they were the fruits of an unauthorized search of his house, which is itself expressly protected by the Fourth Amendment." The majority in *Alderman* thus concluded that a person should have standing to object to illegal electronic eavesdropping which "overheard conversations of * * * himself or conversations occurring on his premises, whether or not he was present or participated in those conversations." The *Alderman* approach was reaffirmed in *United States v. Karo* (1984), having to do with the monitoring of a "beeper" inside a container which revealed that this container was presently within a certain residence; the majority concluded that the tenants of this residence, who would have standing to object to a physical intrusion therein, also had standing regarding this nontrespassory search by beeper.

If a defendant claims standing derived from his interest in the premises searched, he will not prevail if it appears that he had abandoned the premises prior to the time the search being objected to occurred. But under the modern expectation-of-privacy approach the abandonment question must be examined in terms of reasonable expectations flowing from conduct rather than in a technical, property sense. In any event, abandonment must be distinguished from a mere disclaimer of a property interest made to the police prior to the search, which under the better view does not defeat standing.

It is sometimes important to ascertain the physical dimensions of defendant's property interest in the premises, as is reflected by the cases holding a lessee has no standing as to a portion of the premises not leased to him. But under the expectation-of-privacy approach it could be argued that at least sometimes one's justified expectations are somewhat broader than the area of exclusive possession. Consider *McDonald v. United States* (1948), where police illegally entered the house of defendant's landlady and then, by standing on a chair in a second-floor hallway, looked through the transom and saw illegal activity in defendant's room. One Justice helpfully commented that it seemed to him "that each tenant of a building, while he has no right to exclude from the common hallways those who enter lawfully, does have a personal and constitutionally protected interest in the integrity and security of the entire building against unlawful breaking and entry." This is a very sensible approach, but one cannot state with assurance it would be followed by the Supreme Court today, for the Court has sometimes (but not always) taken the unduly narrow position that one cannot have a legitimate expectation of privacy for standing purposes without having a "right to exclude other persons from access to" the place in question. But surely any family member residing there should be deemed to have standing to object to an illegal entry of the family residential unit, though if that entry is lawful it may well be that search into certain areas therein will only intrude on the privacy of a particular resident, in which case the other family members would lack standing as that search.

Yet another way by which one could acquire standing as to residential premises was recognized in *Jones v. United States* (1960), where defendant was present in the apartment of another at the time of the search and he testified that the apartment belonged to a friend who had given him the use of it and a key with which he had admitted himself. The Court held that "anyone legitimately on premises" at the time of the search had standing. But in *Rakas v. Illinois* (1978) the Court rejected this formulation on the view that "the holding in *Jones* can best be explained by the fact that Jones had a legitimate expectation of privacy in the premises he was using and therefore could claim the protection of the Fourth Amendment with respect to a governmental invasion of those premises, even though his 'interest' in those premises might not have been a recognized property interest at common law." *Rakas* did not question the *result* in *Jones*; the Court noted that Jones had been given a key and left alone in the apartment by the owner, so that, except with respect to the owner, "Jones had complete dominion and control over the apartment and could exclude others from it." But, the Court later held in *Minnesota v. Olson* (1990), this does not mark the outer limits of guest standing; "an overnight guest has a legitimate expectation of privacy in his host's home," even when the guest lacks such "complete dominion and control," as it is generally true "that hosts will more likely than not respect the privacy interests of their guests." Lower courts were split as to whether the logic of *Olson* extended as well to those visitors present for a shorter term, but in *Minnesota v. Carter* (1998) a majority of the Justices embraced the position that a *social* guest would not have to be an overnight guest in order to have standing in the premises of another. But the respondents in *Carter* were observed by an illegal search while they were in an apartment engaged with the tenant in bagging cocaine, and a different majority held that they lacked standing given "the purely commercial nature of the transaction engaged in here, the relatively short period of time on the premises, and the lack of any previous connection between respondents and the householder."

Assuming now a guest who *does* have standing, there remains the question of exactly what kinds of Fourth Amendment violations are encompassed within that guest's standing. It seems clear that such a guest has standing to object to an illegal warrantless entry that leads to his own arrest in the host's premises, for that was the situation in *Olson*. It would also seem that such a guest has standing with respect to an illegal search of the guest's effects there. *Olson* describes the guest's privacy expectation in terms of "a place where he and his possessions will not be disturbed by anyone but his host and those his host allows inside," and in *Rakas* the Court emphasized it was *not* suggesting "that such visitors could not contest the lawfulness of the seizure of evidence or the search if their own property were seized during the search." *Rakas* suggests a guest does not have standing in other circumstances. By way of supporting the holding there that passengers in cars do not have standing simply by virtue of their lawful presence, the Court indicated by analogy that it would not "permit a casual visitor who has never seen, or been permitted to visit the basement of another's house to object to a search of the basement if the visitor happened to be in the kitchen of the house at the time of the search." But such a result is not inevitable under *Rakas,* for the four dissenters and two concurring justices all noted that the Fourth Amendment also protects security of the person and that this aspect of the Amendment was not at issue because the defendants there had not challenged the constitutionality of the police action in stopping the vehicle initially. In a premises context, this means that if the police, without required notice or without probable cause or without a required search warrant, burst into *B*'s home and disrupt a dinner party at which *A* is present as a guest, then certainly *A* should be deemed to have standing to object; he has had *his* freedom, privacy and solitude intruded upon by the police, and thus he has standing to object to that encroachment upon *his* rights, even if it led to the discovery of evidence in *B*'s basement, a place *A* "has never seen, or been permitted to visit." On the other hand, it is fully consistent with the *Rakas* reasoning and result to say that if the intrusion itself was lawful, then *A*'s lawful presence would not alone give him standing as to any subsequent illegalities that did not increase appreciably the interference with *A*'s personal freedom. Unfortunately, lower courts frequently have not recognized this critical distinction.

Still another type of case is that in which the defendant claims standing with respect to search of *his* personal property at a place that is not his and at a time when he was not present there. Standing has frequently been recognized in such circumstances, often by reliance upon *United States v. Jeffers* (1951). There, police entered defendant's two aunts' hotel room, for which he had a key and their permission to enter at will, and found his stash of drugs; the Supreme Court concluded with little by way of explanation that the government was in error in claiming "the search did not invade respondent's privacy." The Court expressly rejected the contention that defendant's interest in the seized property must be disregarded because it was illegal to possess such property, but did not make it clear whether that interest alone conferred standing or whether his continuing access to the place was essential to the outcome. It has sometimes been held that absent such access there is not the expectation of privacy needed for standing, but it has been forcefully argued that a bailment arrangement without continued access confers standing because the bailor has sought to maintain the security and privacy of his possessions in a place he regarded as safe.

But that analysis and even the *Jeffers* result have been put into doubt as a result of *Rawlings v. Kentucky* (1980), where police searched the purse of defendant's female companion and found therein the drugs she was carrying for him. The Supreme Court ruled that defendant had no standing to object to that search because he had no reasonable expectation of privacy as to the purse, especially since he did not "have any right to exclude other persons from access to Cox's purse." But while a "right to exclude" may be an easy way to establish the requisite legitimate expectation of privacy, it hardly follows that it is the only way; as the *Rawlings* dissenters noted, "such a harsh threshold requirement was not imposed even in the heyday of a property rights oriented Fourth Amendment." A bailor's right to exclude others is important in Fourth Amendment law, but for another purpose: deciding the lawfulness of a search consented to by the bailee (see § 2.10(e)). To now utilize the same approach for standing would produce the incredible result that whenever the police could conduct a lawful search with the bailee's consent, they may instead proceed to make that search without the bailee's consent because the bailor will lack standing. This is not only wrong, but is inconsistent with the Court's prior and subsequent pronouncements on the law of standing.

As did *Rawlings* itself, lower courts applying *Rawlings* have looked to the totality of the circumstances in determining whether a person who stores property on the premises (or in the container) of another has sufficient indicia of security to establish the expectation of privacy needed for standing. Thus defendants have been held to have standing as to the search of their own closed containers stored on the premises of others with the permission of those persons. On the other hand, even before *Rawlings* several lower courts had held that storage of possessions on the person of another did not provide standing to object to the search of that person, and *Rawlings* has been viewed as reaffirming that position.

(c) Business Premises. Analysis similar to that in the preceding subsection is appropriate when the question concerns standing to challenge a search of business premises. In *Mancusi v. DeForte* (1968), for example, where state officials conducted a search and seized records belonging to a Teamsters Union local from an office defendant shared with several other union officials, the Court characterized the "crucial issue" as being "whether the area was one in which there was a reasonable expectation of freedom from governmental intrusion." The Court answered in the affirmative, reasoning that defendant would certainly have had standing if the search were of his private office and that the "situation was not fundamentally changed because DeForte shared an office with other union officers," for he "still could reasonably have expected that only those persons and their personal or business guests would enter the office, and that records would not be touched except with their permission or that of union higher-ups." Consistent with *Mancusi,* courts have held that a corporate or individual defendant in possession of the business premises searched has standing, and that an officer or employee of the business enterprise has standing if there was a demonstrated nexus between the area searched and the work space of the defendant. Exclusive use would seem clearly to establish standing, but (as *Mancusi* teaches) there can be a justified expectation of privacy even absent exclusivity. As noted earlier, the "legitimately on the premises" basis of standing has now been rejected by the Supreme Court; it was never a meaningful basis for analysis as to business premises of some size.

Sometimes the question is whether a person who was not present and who in addition was not related to the business premises, in the sense of being a participant in the business enterprise, might ever have standing as to those premises. If, as suggested above, standing may be based upon an expectation of privacy as to certain effects temporarily put into the custody of another (a matter put in doubt by *Rawlings v. Kentucky* (1980)), the answer would be yes. Thus, if *A* leaves his jacket at *B*'s dry cleaning establishment to be cleaned and the police thereafter enter that establishment and search or seize that jacket, *A* would by virtue of his privacy interest in that item have standing to bring that police action into question. But if the customer does not have effects of his own on the premises, he is apparently out of luck. This is the thrust of *United States v. Miller* (1976), holding that the customer of a bank lacks standing to challenge subpoenas directed at the bank for records of his transactions that were "the business records of the banks." As the Court put it, "[t]he depositor takes the risk, in revealing his affairs to another, that the information will be conveyed by that person to the government," and consequently has no standing to challenge the subpoenas (or, as the Court concluded in a later case, to challenge acquisition of such records by burglary!). The reasoning and result in *Miller* are open to serious question, as resolving the standing issue on the basis that the person had assumed the risk of disclosure by someone else makes no sense and cannot be squared with the Court's earlier standing decisions.

(d) Vehicles. In *Rakas v. Illinois* (1978), where police stopped what they believed to be a robbery getaway car, ordered the occupants out of the car, and then searched the vehicle and found a rifle under the seat and shells in the glove compartment, the Court concluded that the passengers, who claimed no ownership of the seized objects, lacked standing because "they made no showing that they had any legitimate expectation of privacy in the glove compartment or area under the seat of the car in which they were merely passengers. Like the trunk of an automobile, these are areas in which a passenger *qua* passenger simply would not normally have a legitimate expectation of privacy."

This should not be taken to mean that persons who are "merely passengers" will never have standing. As two concurring and four dissenting Justices agreed in *Rakas*, a passenger *does* have standing to object to police conduct which intrudes upon his Fourth Amendment protection against unreasonable seizure of his person. If either the stopping of the car or the passenger's removal from it are unreasonable in a Fourth Amendment sense, then surely the passenger has standing to object to those constitutional violations and to have suppressed any evidence found in the car that is their fruit. It is also significant that the passengers in *Rakas* disclaimed ownership of the gun and shells. Even when there has been nothing unlawful about either the stopping of the vehicle or removal of the passengers from it, certainly a passenger has standing as to any search into *his* effects in the car.

Rakas deals only with passengers and thus does not place into question the notion that some persons with a stronger interest in the vehicle will have standing even as to vehicle searches in their absence. This is unquestionably so as to the owner of the car if he has not abandoned it or made a substantial bailment of it, the bailee of the vehicle, family members who share in the use of the car, and others who share use of the vehicle with the owner on a regular and recurring basis. This is not to suggest that such persons will have standing as to every kind of Fourth Amendment violation occurring in the vehicle; consistent with the earlier analysis, the owner-driver could not object if following the lawful stopping of his car a passenger's purse was opened.

The "wrongful presence" exception to the standing rule of the *Jones* case has its counterpart in the vehicle search cases: most courts agree that an occupant of a vehicle cannot be said to have standing by virtue of his presence if he is in possession of a stolen or otherwise illegally possessed or controlled vehicle. It has been argued that this should be so only if the police know they are dealing with a stolen car, but this is unsound, for a person's reasonable expectation of privacy hardly depends upon what someone else knows. While a thief driving a stolen car thus cannot gain standing as to the car by his wrongful possession of it, that possession does not deprive him of standing he otherwise has. This means that a thief is still entitled to challenge unlawful interferences with his person, and consequently it would be open to him to question a search of the car that was a fruit of his illegal arrest.

§ 8.2   Standing: Other Possible Bases

(a) **"Automatic" Standing.** In *Jones v. United States* (1960), the defendant charged with narcotics offenses was found by the court below to lack standing to object to the search of the apartment where the narcotics were found and where he was present as an invitee at the time of the search. The Supreme Court concluded otherwise and held that the "same element in this prosecution which has caused a dilemma, i.e., that possession both convicted and confers standing, eliminates any necessity for a preliminary showing of an interest in the premises searched or the property seized, which ordinarily is required when standing is challenged." The Court in *Jones* indicated it would be improper "to permit the Government to have the advantage of contradictory positions as a basis for conviction." When later, in *Simmons v. United States* (1968), the Court took another look at the problem of a defendant who is confronted with the dilemma of having to give incriminating testimony to establish standing and came up with a different type of solution applicable to a broader range of cases: "when a defendant testifies in support of a motion to suppress evidence on Fourth Amendment grounds, his testimony may not thereafter be admitted against him at trial on the issue of guilt unless he makes no objection." *Simmons* gave rise to the question of whether the *Jones* automatic standing rule had lost its vitality, which the Court finally answered affirmatively in *United States v. Salvucci* (1980). *Simmons*, the Court declared, provides protection "broader than that of *Jones*" because it "not only extends protection against this risk of self-incrimination in all of the cases covered by *Jones,* but also grants a form of 'use immunity' to those defendants charged with nonpossessory crimes." As for the vice of prosecutorial contradiction, the Court stated it need not decide if that "could alone support a rule countenancing the exclusion of probative evidence on the grounds that someone other than the defendant was denied a Fourth Amendment right," for at least after *Rakas* it is clear "that a prosecutor may simultaneously maintain that a defendant criminally possessed the seized good, but was not subject to a Fourth Amendment deprivation, without legal contradiction," for a "person in legal possession of a good seized during an illegal search has not necessarily been subject to a Fourth Amendment deprivation."

(b) "Target" Standing. Assume that X is arrested for armed robbery and that some time thereafter, acting with the specific intention of finding additional evidence incriminating X with respect to that crime, the police conduct a fruitful illegal search of X's wife. Or, assume that the police are seeking robber Y, who was known to have taken refuge in a certain apartment building, and that they then conduct an apartment-by-apartment search until they find Y in the last apartment, as to which probable cause existed because of the other illegal searches. By virtue of their being the "target" of the searches, do X and Y have standing to object to those illegal searches? The Supreme Court finally confronted the issue directly in *Rakas v. Illinois* (1979) and concluded that "since the exclusionary rule is an attempt to effectuate the guaranties of the Fourth Amendment, * * * it is proper to permit only defendants whose Fourth Amendment rights have been violated to benefit from the rule's protections." "Conferring standing to raise vicarious Fourth Amendment claims," the Court noted, "would necessarily mean a more widespread invocation of the exclusionary rule," exacting "a substantial social cost."

A very forceful argument in favor of the concept of target standing can be put by merely reciting the facts of the remarkable case of *United States v. Payner* (1980). In 1965, the IRS launched an investigation into the financial activities of American citizens in the Bahamas. An IRS special agent, knowing that the vice president of a Bahamian bank would be in Miami, agreed to and participated in a scheme whereby that person's locked briefcase was stolen for a short period of time while the case was opened and 400 bank records photographed. This led to other information establishing that Payner had a bank account in that bank and that he had falsified his federal income tax return in that connection. This "briefcase caper," in fact a calculated and deliberate extreme violation of the banker's Fourth Amendment rights and also a criminal act, was undertaken with full understanding by the IRS agent that a person such as Payner—precisely the kind of violator they were seeking—would not have Fourth Amendment standing to object. It would seem that if ever a fact situation cried out for recognition of target standing, *Payner* was it. Nonetheless, the Supreme Court reaffirmed that there is no Fourth Amendment target standing, and even overturned the lower court's conferral of standing under the inherent supervisory power of the federal courts. As the *Payner* dissenters put it, that holding "effectively turns the standing rules created by this Court for assertion of Fourth Amendment violations into a sword to be used by the Government to permit it deliberately to invade one person's Fourth Amendment rights in order to obtain evidence against another person."

(c) **"Derivative" Standing.** In *McDonald v. United States* (1948), McDonald and Washington were together convicted of operating a lottery after McDonald's motion to suppress gambling paraphernalia was denied. The Supreme Court reversed and then, though assuming Washington was without personal standing, held he was also entitled to a new trial at which the seized items would not be admitted against him. The Court explained that denial of McDonald's motion "was error that was prejudicial to Washington as well" because if "the property had been returned to McDonald, it would not have been available for use at trial." But in *Wong Sun v. United States* (1963), the Court, without any mention of *McDonald,* held that defendant Wong Sun was not entitled to suppression of narcotics that were excluded as to codefendant Toy, as the "seizure of this heroin invaded no right of privacy of person or premises which would entitle Wong Sun to object to its use at his trial." And in *Alderman v. United States* (1969) the Court adhered to "the general rule that Fourth Amendment rights are personal rights" and thus concluded there was "no necessity to exclude evidence against one defendant in order to protect the rights of another."

Derivative standing must be distinguished from a line of Ninth Circuit cases adopting the so-called "coconspirator exception," under which a coconspirator was deemed to have obtained a legitimate expectation of privacy for Fourth Amendment purposes if he had either a supervisory role in the conspiracy or joint control over the place or property involved in the search or seizure. In *United States v. Padilla* (1993), a unanimous Supreme Court rejected that view. Noting that it is privacy expectations and property interests which govern as to standing issues, the Court declared: "Participants in a criminal conspiracy may have such expectations or interests, but the conspiracy itself neither adds nor detracts from them."

(d) Abolition of Standing. The California supreme court adopted its own search and seizure exclusionary rule early on, and shortly thereafter held that a defendant would be recognized as having standing in all circumstances in that jurisdiction. This conclusion, the court reasoned in *People v. Martin* (1955), was a logical result of the fact that the traditional standing requirement "virtually invites law enforcement officers to violate the rights of third parties and to trade the escape of a criminal whose rights are violated for the conviction of others by use of the evidence illegally obtained against them." But the Supreme Court in *Alderman v. United States* (1969) declined to adopt the *Martin* approach because it was "not convinced that the additional benefits of extending the exclusionary rule to other defendants would justify further encroachment upon the public interest in prosecuting those accused of crime and having them acquitted or convicted on the basis of all the evidence which exposes the truth."

§ 8.3 "Fruit of the Poisonous Tree" Theories

(a) Generally. In the simplest of exclusionary rule cases, the challenged evidence is quite clearly "direct" or "primary" in its relationship to the prior arrest, search, interrogation, lineup or other identification procedure. Such is the case when that evidence is an identification occurring at the confrontation between suspect and victim or witness, a confession or admission made in response to questioning, or physical evidence obtained by search or arrest. Not infrequently, however, challenged evidence is "secondary" or "derivative" in character. This occurs when, for example, a confession is obtained after an illegal arrest, physical evidence is located after an illegally obtained confession, or an in-court identification is made following an illegally conducted pretrial identification. In these situations, it is necessary to determine whether the derivative evidence is "tainted" by the prior constitutional or other violation. To use the phrase coined by Justice Frankfurter, it must be decided whether that evidence is the "fruit of the poisonous tree." As is apparent from the examples just given, the "poisonous tree" can be an illegal arrest or search, illegal interrogation procedures or illegal identification practices (the latter is discussed in ch. 7).

The genesis of the "taint" doctrine was in *Silverthorne Lumber Co. v. United States* (1920), where federal officers unlawfully seized certain documents from the Silverthornes, and after a district court ordered those documents returned the prosecutor caused the grand jury to issue subpoenas to the defendants to produce the very same documents. In holding that the subpoenas were invalid, the Court declared this did "not mean that the facts [illegally] obtained become sacred and inaccessible," for if "knowledge of them is gained from an independent source they may be proved like any others." *Nardone v. United States* (1939) established the doctrine of "attenuation" by authoritatively recognizing that the challenged evidence might sometimes be admissible even if it did not have an "independent source" because the "causal connection * * * may have become so attenuated as to dissipate the taint." Thus, in the later case of *Wong Sun v. United States* (1963), it was said that the question to be answered as to derivative evidence is "whether, granting establishment of the primary illegality, the evidence to which instant objection is made has been come at by exploitation of that illegality or instead by means sufficiently distinguishable to be purged of the primary taint."

(b) "But for" Rejected. In *Wong Sun,* the Court declined to "hold that all evidence is 'fruit of the poisonous tree' simply because it would not have come to light but for the illegal actions of the police." Thus the Court ruled that Wong Sun's confession was untainted by his illegal arrest because it was given after he had obtained his release and voluntarily returned to the station later, although there seemed to be no doubt that he would never have come in and confessed but for the prior arrest. But, it might quite appropriately be asked: Why not suppress the confession, for it was quite clearly caused by the arrest, and thus admission of the confession permits the government to profit from the Fourth Amendment violation? Complete exclusion of fruits would be excessive in light of the obvious competing considerations: that exclusion of evidence thwarts society's interest in convicting the guilty. The Court's rejection of the "but for" test, therefore, as one Justice later pointed out, "recognizes that in some circumstances strict adherence to the Fourth Amendment exclusionary rule imposes greater cost on the legitimate demands of law enforcement than can be justified by the rule's deterrent purposes."

(c) "Attenuated Connection". In neither *Nardone* nor *Wong Sun* did the Court elaborate upon the "attenuated connection" test, thus leaving it rather uncertain exactly what lower courts were expected to look for, to say nothing of what facts would be relevant to an "attenuation" determination. But here as well it is useful to view the question from the perspective of the exclusionary rule's deterrence function. The notion of the "dissipation of the taint" attempts to mark the point at which the detrimental consequences of illegal police action become so attenuated that the deterrent effect of the exclusionary rule no longer justifies its cost. In short, the underlying purpose of the "attenuated connection" test is to mark the point of diminishing returns of the deterrence principle. When courts lose sight of that point the results can be most unfortunate, as is illustrated by the not uncommon holding prior to *Brown v. Illinois* (1975) that the *Miranda* warnings alone supply the requisite attenuation between an illegal arrest and a confession. That is not attenuation in the deterrence function sense, for it is clear that "the effect of the exclusionary rule would be substantially diluted" under such an approach. Of course, an appellate court's judgment as to that point at which admission of the evidence will significantly dilute deterrence will be informed by the court's views on a variety of subsidiary questions, such as whether police are likely to view the court's ruling as providing a significant "incentive" to engage in illegal searches and whether judges ruling on suppression motions can and will readily identify those situations in which police act with the specific objective of exploiting the limitations of the fruits doctrine.

(d) "Independent Source". The Court in *Wong Sun* quoted from *Silverthorne* the proposition that "the exclusionary rule has no application" when "the Government learned of the evidence 'from an independent source.'" As ordinarily applied, this means that if not even the "but for" test can be met, then clearly the evidence is not a fruit of the prior violation. So stated, the "independent source" limitation upon the taint doctrine is unquestionably sound. It is one thing to say that officers shall gain no advantage from violating the individual's rights; it is quite another to declare that such a violation shall put him beyond the law's reach even if his guilt can be proved by evidence that has been obtained lawfully.

The problem, of course, is that there is no way to get the cat back into the bag, so that once illegally obtained evidence incriminating the defendant has been found it can always be asserted with some plausibility that any information acquired thereafter is attributable to the authorities being spurred on and their investigation focused by the earlier discovery. Thus the question is whether the "independent source" test sometimes can be met even though it may well be that "but for" the earlier violation the investigation which uncovered the tendered evidence would never have been commenced. Some courts take the view that where unconstitutional action only leads the police to "focus" their investigation on a particular individual, this should not, in effect, grant him immunity from prosecution. Others object to this view, reasoning that if the police know that their initial illegality can be covered up later by legal police work, then there is nothing to stop them from committing the initial illegality.

Another troublesome independent source problem is presented where the police (i) have probable cause to obtain a search warrant, (ii) subsequently enter the premises without a warrant and discover that the contraband is indeed there, and (iii) then leave the premises, obtain a warrant based on the previously obtained probable cause (without any reference to the information obtained during the unlawful entry), and return with the warrant and seize the contraband in the execution of the warrant. In *Murray v. United States* (1988), the Supreme Court concluded that the independent source doctrine would apply if the agents' decision to seek the warrant had not been "prompted" by what had been seen during the earlier unlawful entry (i.e., if the lower court found that the agents "would have sought a warrant [even] if they had not earlier entered the [premises]"). The dissenters argued that this ruling would encourage police officers to enter premises illegally for the purpose of making certain that the contraband is actually there before they undertake the "inconvenient and time-consuming task" of obtaining a warrant, but the majority responded it "would be foolish" for an officer to do so and "risk suppression of all evidence on the premises, both seen and unseen, since his action would add to the normal burden of convincing a magistrate that there is probable cause the much more onerous burden of convincing a trial court that no information gained from the illegal entry affected either the law enforcement officers' decision to seek a warrant or the magistrate's decision to grant it."

(e) **"Inevitable Discovery".** Yet another theory that has been utilized by many courts in dealing with "fruit of the poisonous tree" issues is the so-called "inevitable discovery" rule. This rule, which has now been accepted by the Supreme Court, is in a sense a variation upon the "independent source" theory. But it differs in that the question is not whether the police did in fact acquire certain evidence by reliance upon an untainted source but instead whether evidence found because of an earlier violation would inevitably have been discovered lawfully. Some have objected that the inevitable discovery rule is based on conjecture and can only encourage police shortcuts whenever evidence may be more readily obtained by illegal than by legal means. These concerns, though unquestionably legitimate, are directed not so much to the rule itself as to its application in a loose and unthinking fashion so as to encourage unconstitutional shortcuts. Because one purpose of the exclusionary rule is to deter such shortcuts, it has been suggested that the inevitable discovery exception should be applied only when it is clear that the police did not act in bad faith to accelerate the discovery of the evidence in question. But in *Nix v. Williams* (1984), the Supreme Court rejected a lower court holding to that effect, explaining that such a condition "would place courts in the position of withholding from juries relevant and undoubted truth that would have been available to police absent any unlawful police activity" and "would put the police in a *worse* position than they would have been in if no unlawful conduct had transpired."

Lower courts have had the least difficulty in applying the inevitable discovery doctrine where that discovery would have come about through a routine procedure invariably applied under the particular circumstances, as commonly is the case where the government argues that the evidence discovered through an illegal warrantless search would have been uncovered in an inventory search. But these courts often find more troubling a situation in which the government claims as its source of inevitable discovery an investigatory procedure that is not routine, but dependent upon a police determination that the procedure's potential value would outweigh its costs. Here, there is greater uncertainty as to whether the procedure would have been performed and often greater incentive for police to take shortcuts. However, the same type of argument could have been made in *Nix v. Williams*, where the discovery of the corpse through the *Massiah* violation allowed the police to cut short by several hours a systematic search of the highway that was utilizing the efforts of 200 volunteers. In light of the Court's willingness to apply the inevitable discovery doctrine in that situation, lower courts have applied the doctrine to various non-routine investigatory procedures where the government can establish that the investigative procedure, as in *Nix*, had already been initiated prior to the actual discovery through a constitutional violation.

More difficult proof problems are presented where the government can show only that, at the time of the actual discovery through an illegal procedure, the police had not yet started to pursue a non-routine procedure that would have uncovered the evidence. Illustrative is a situation in which the police claim that at the time of the illegal warrantless search, a separate evaluation of the case had been initiated and it would have led to obtaining and successfully executing a warrant, but that determination had not yet been made. If the inevitable discovery doctrine is to be treated as analytically similar to the independent source doctrine, then the government should not be precluded from establishing inevitable discovery in such a situation, but should be required to make a showing similar to that demanded in *Murray*, i.e., that the decision to obtain the warrant was not influenced by the illegal entry (which confirmed that the evidence was actually on the premises).

Of course, to gain application of the inevitable discovery doctrine, the government must establish not only that its employment of an independent, lawful investigative procedure was inevitable, but also that that procedure inevitably would have led to the discovery of the same evidence actually found through the Constitutional violation. "Inevitably," for this purpose means that the discovery definitely would have occurred, not that it "might" or "could" have occurred. However, *Nix* held that the Constitution is satisfied if the government establishes inevitability by a preponderance of the evidence; a higher burden of proof (e.g., clear and convincing evidence) is not constitutionally required. Typically, lower courts insist that the government introduce specific evidence (ordinarily, testimony by a police officer) establishing that another investigative procedure would have been employed and would have been successful. In some instances, however, the successful employment of that other procedure appears to the court to be so obvious that it will hold inevitably discovery applicable as a matter of judicial notice.

§ 8.4   Fruits of Illegal Arrests and Searches

(a) **Confessions.** The question of whether a confession, otherwise admissible, must be suppressed as the fruit of an antecedent illegal arrest was first dealt with by the Supreme Court in *Wong Sun v. United States* (1963). Federal agents broke into Toy's laundry and pursued him into his living quarters, where his wife and child were sleeping, and there held him at gunpoint and handcuffed him, after which Toy made incriminating statements also implicating Yee. The agents then recovered drugs from Yee, who said he had obtained them from Toy and Wong Sun, both of whom were thereafter arrested and then released on their own recognizance after being charged. Later Wong Sun, on being questioned by an agent who advised him of his right to withhold incriminating information and that he was entitled to advice of counsel, made a confession. The Court concluded that Toy's admissions were the fruits of his unlawful arrest in his premises; in response to the government's claim that the admissions resulted from "an intervening independent act of free will," the Court said that on the above facts "it is unreasonable to infer that Toy's response was sufficiently an act of free will to purge the primary taint of the unlawful invasion." By contrast, the connection between Wong Sun's confession and his earlier arrest had "become so attenuated as to dissipate the taint" because of his release from custody and voluntary return to make a statement days later.

The more typical case was assayed in *Brown v. Illinois* (1975), where following his illegal arrest defendant was taken to the station and given the *Miranda* warnings, after which he gave incriminating statements within two hours of the arrest. The Supreme Court first rejected the per se rule of the Illinois court whereunder the *Miranda* warnings were deemed to break the causal chain between the arrest and confession. The Court explained that the mere fact a statement was voluntary under *Miranda* did not make it untainted, for if "*Miranda* warnings, by themselves, were held to attenuate the taint of an unconstitutional arrest, regardless of how wanton and purposeful the Fourth Amendment violation, the effect of the exclusionary rule would be substantially diluted." The Court in *Brown* then declined to adopt a per se rule running the other direction, and instead concluded that such taint issues "must be answered on the facts of each case." It was explained that the "voluntariness of the statement is a threshold requirement"; this is obviously so, for absent voluntariness the statement could be suppressed without resort to any fruits analysis. Assuming voluntariness, various factors must be considered: (1) whether the *Miranda* warnings were given (though again, if they were not this would be a basis for suppression without reaching the fruits issue); (2) the "temporal proximity of the arrest and the confession"; (3) "the presence of intervening circumstances"; and (4) "the purpose and flagrancy of the official misconduct." This meant the confession in the instant case was poisoned fruit, for it was obtained just two hours after the arrest without any intervening event of significance, and the arrest was obviously illegal and was undertaken "in the hope that something might turn up."

The Court's assumption in *Brown* that the mere passage of time between the arrest and the confession increases the likelihood of the confession being untainted is not sound, for illegal custody becomes more oppressive as it continues uninterrupted, and thus it is fair to conclude, as the lower court cases indicate, that temporal proximity is the least important factor involved in the *Brown* formula. The "purpose and flagrancy" factor of *Brown* is certainly a legitimate consideration, for to maximize the policy of deterrence, the Fourth Amendment exclusionary rule should be most strictly applied in cases where flagrantly unlawful police activity has occurred. Lower courts have been especially willing to find taint if the arrest was made without any apparent justification, as part of a dragnet operation or upon a pretext, while suppression is less likely where the illegality is an arrest slightly short of probable cause after a lawful stopping for investigation or an arrest on evidence that would be sufficient but for its acquisition during a stopping for investigation on grounds barely insufficient.

As for intervening circumstances, this would include commitment by a magistrate, termination of the illegal custody, or consultation with counsel. Some courts have treated a volunteered statement, not made in response to police interrogation, as a significant intervening circumstance. That view is unobjectionable, but the same cannot be said for the conclusion that a statement given in response to interrogation following an illegal arrest is untainted because of the sense of remorse felt by the defendant or because the defendant was then confronted with his accomplice, who successfully urged him to confess. But such results may be more likely after *Rawlings v. Kentucky* (1980), where Rawlings and Ms. Cox were detained at a house while a search warrant was sought and when the warrant arrived Ms. Cox was compelled to empty her purse, after which she called upon Rawlings to claim what was his and he claimed the revealed controlled substances because he "wasn't going to try to pin that on her." The majority had "little doubt that this factor weighs heavily in favor of a finding that petitioner acted 'of free will unaffected by the initial illegality.'" The dissenters properly objected that Rawlings' statement was in response to Cox's demand, which was a product of the illegal search of her purse, which in turn was made possible by the illegal detention of the people at the house.

Given the nonutility of the "temporal proximity" factor, what ordinarily is required is a balancing of the last two *Brown* factors. The clearest indication of attenuation, such as release from custody, is called for where the official conduct was flagrantly abusive of Fourth Amendment rights. But when the police conduct is not flagrant, some lesser intervening circumstances (but more than mere *Miranda* warnings) will suffice.

The *Brown* approach, applied in that and other cases to situations in which the alleged poisonous tree was an arrest made without probable cause, was deemed inapplicable in *New York v. Harris* (1990), where the poisonous tree was an in-premises arrest on probable cause but without a required arrest warrant. The Court in *Harris* instead adopted a per se rule: "where the police have probable cause to arrest a suspect, the exclusionary rule does not bar the State's use of a statement made by the defendant outside of his home." The majority reasoned (i) that once Harris had been removed from his home his continued custody was lawful, so that his statement given at the police station was not the product of unlawful custody; and (ii) that the statement was likewise not a fruit of the arrest occurring in the home instead of somewhere else, as the *Payton* warrant requirement "is imposed to protect the home" and thus is vindicated by suppression of "anything incriminating the police gathered from arresting Harris in his home, rather than elsewhere."

Cases in which it is contended that a confession was the fruit of a prior illegal search are usually easier to resolve. In the typical case in which the defendant was present when incriminating evidence was found in an illegal search or in which the defendant was confronted by the police with evidence they had illegally seized, it is apparent that there has been an "exploitation of that illegality" when the police subsequently question the defendant about that evidence or the crime to which it relates. Because the realization that the cat is out of the bag plays a significant role in encouraging the suspect to speak, the more fine-tuned assessment used in *Brown* for determining when a confession is the fruit of an illegal *arrest* is ordinarily unnecessary when the "poisonous tree" is an illegal search. Giving the *Miranda* warnings in such a case clearly will not break the causal chain, for these warnings do not advise the defendant whether the evidence he is confronted with is unlawfully obtained or whether it will be admissible at trial. If a magistrate or counsel did unequivocally and clearly advise the defendant that the evidence had been illegally seized and neither it nor its fruits could be used against him, it would seem that this would dissipate the taint of the illegal search. Those cases which attribute defendant's confession to remorse or some similar feeling in holding that it is not a fruit of the earlier police illegality are unsound. More plausible, at least in some circumstances, is the claim that a confession was not the product of a prior illegal search because the defendant was equally influenced by other, lawfully obtained evidence already in the hands of the police.

(b) Searches. In the typical case in which an illegal arrest is followed by a search, no "fruits" problem of any magnitude is presented. Where the search of the person or the surrounding area has its only justification as being "incident to" the arrest, then unquestionably the evidence found in the search must be suppressed if the antecedent arrest was unlawful. This is direct rather than derivative evidence, and there is no occasion to be concerned about the limits of the fruit of the poisonous tree doctrine. But if the search is based upon a consent theory rather than a search-incident-to-arrest theory, the mere fact the consent was "voluntary" does not mean it is untainted. As noted earlier, in *Brown v. Illinois* (1975) the Court rejected the notion that a confession is untainted merely because it is voluntary, and thus it follows that the voluntariness of a consent does not alone remove the taint. Rather, the factors from *Brown* discussed earlier should be applied to this situation.

Yet another situation is that in which the search is undertaken pursuant to a search warrant based upon lawfully acquired probable cause, but the police attempted to ensure that the warrant could be successfully executed by illegally holding the defendant until the warrant was obtained and served. On such facts, some courts have held that the evidence obtained in execution of the warrant is a fruit of the illegal detention, reasoning that to hold otherwise would unquestionably run contrary to the deterrence objective of the exclusionary rule. Somewhat related to that situation, and perhaps dictating a different result even there, is *Segura v. United States* (1984), where police entered premises without a warrant and arrested the occupants and then remained on the scene several hours until a search warrant was obtained and executed there. The claimed "poisonous tree" was "the initial illegal entry and occupation of the premises," which the Court held did not require suppression of the evidence later obtained in execution of the search warrant. This was because the warrant affidavit was based only on information acquired prior to the illegal entry, and because the possibility that absent the illegal entry the evidence would have been removed or destroyed "was pure speculation." "Even more important," the *Segura* majority added, "we decline to extend the exclusionary rule, which already exacts an enormous price from society and our system of justice, to further 'protect' criminal activity, as the dissent would have us do." The four dissenters forcefully argued that such a conclusion "provides an affirmative incentive for warrantless and plainly unreasonable and unnecessary intrusions into the home" because police now know that if they illegally impound premises for the very purpose of facilitating a later successful warrant execution, that illegality will have no effect upon the evidence first discovered during the warrant execution. Whether this is so remains unclear, however, because of the limited scope of the *Segura* ruling, particularly the Court's rejection there of any link between the illegal entry/impoundment and the effectiveness of the later execution of the warrant.

Sometimes upon a motion to suppress evidence obtained in execution of a search warrant, a showing is made that some of the information in the affidavit presented to the magistrate was acquired in a prior illegal search. The question then becomes how this affects the status of the search warrant, which most courts have answered by saying that the warrant is nonetheless valid if it could have issued upon the untainted information in the affidavit. Some courts have been a bit more demanding, and rightly so. If illegally-obtained information is merely stricken and the balance of the affidavit assessed as if the tainted information had never been included, then police are tempted to make illegal searches to bolster what would otherwise be borderline affidavits. If the illegality is never uncovered, then they have a warrant solidly based on probable cause where otherwise their warrant application might have been rejected. If, on the other hand, the illegality comes to light, then the police are no worse off than if they had not made the illegal search. At a minimum, a warrant should be held invalid where the tainted information was used to bolster what would otherwise have been a doubtful showing of probable cause. This involves nothing more than depriving such warrants of the special treatment they would otherwise receive under *United States v. Ventresca* (1965), where the Court declared that "in a doubtful or marginal case a search under a warrant may be sustainable where without one it would fall."

(c) Arrests. If police by an illegal search discover evidence providing probable cause that a particular person has committed a crime, an arrest of that person based upon this information is unquestionably tainted, provided of course the arrestee had standing to object regarding the antecedent search. But the mere existence of such a prior illegal search does not inevitably taint a subsequent arrest, for it may be that the arrest will be found to have a sufficient factual basis apart from the illegal search. The reasoning of the cases in the preceding subsection is applicable here as well, and thus for example, an officer possessing legally obtained information constituting probable cause for arrest is not barred from making the arrest solely because he also has information that was unlawfully obtained. However if the lawfully acquired evidence established probable cause but illegally obtained information influenced the making of the arrest at a particular time or place, which had a bearing on what was uncovered in the search incident to arrest, this would be yet another basis for concluding that the arrest was the fruit of the prior illegality.

(d) Identification of Person. Yet another issue is whether identification evidence (e.g., fingerprints, photographs, face-to-face confrontation) acquired following an illegal arrest is a tainted fruit of the arrest. Assume, for example, that defendant is illegally arrested on suspicion of armed robbery, after which he is placed in a lineup and identified by a victim of the robbery as the perpetrator of the crime. If the victim is later called to testify at trial, may he give evidence of his stationhouse identification or now identify the defendant in court? As for the stationhouse identification, some decisions are to be found taking the position that this kind of evidence is not to be deemed the fruit of the prior illegal arrest, but the correct view under ordinary circumstances is that because a stationhouse lineup is the direct result of the illegal arrest, that identification is unlawful fruit of the poisonous tree. This is not inevitably the case, however, for what is required here is analysis essentially like that used in *Brown v. Illinois* (1975) in assaying the connection between the illegal arrest and the identification by considering the factors of "temporal proximity," "the presence of intervening circumstances," and "the purpose and flagrancy of the official misconduct."

Assuming now a case in which it may be concluded that the pretrial identification was a fruit of a prior illegal arrest and thus must be suppressed, what then of an at-trial identification by the same witness? The Supreme Court dealt with an analogous problem in *United States v. Wade* (1967), where the question was the admissibility of an in-court identification preceded by an at-the-station identification that was illegal for denial of counsel. *Wade* held the "taint" issue depended on "various factors," such as "prior opportunity to observe the alleged criminal act, the existence of any discrepancy between any pre-lineup description and the defendant's actual description, any identification prior to lineup of another person, the identification by picture of the defendant prior to the lineup, failure to identify the defendant on a prior occasion, and the lapse of time between the alleged act and the lineup identification," as well as "those facts which, despite the absence of counsel, are disclosed concerning the conduct of the lineup." Lower courts have used this same approach in determining whether an in-court identification is the fruit of a prior identification that was tainted because it occurred while defendant was being held in violation of the Fourth Amendment.

The correctness of this latter position was confirmed by the Supreme Court in *United States v. Crews* (1980), where the Court applied several of the factors in the *Wade* "independent origins" test: "the victim viewed her assailant at close range for a period of 5–10 minutes under excellent lighting conditions and with no distractions * * *; respondent closely matched the description given by the victim immediately after the robbery * * *; the victim failed to identify anyone other than respondent * * *, but twice selected respondent without hesitation in nonsuggestive pretrial identification procedures * * *; and only a week had passed between the victim's initial observation of respondent and her first identification of him * * *." It might well be argued, however, that facts which would suffice in a *Wade* context to show an in-court identification was reliable do not inevitably also show it was not obtained in exploitation of a prior Fourth Amendment violation, any more than showing a confession to be voluntary per se dissipates the taint. This reasoning appears to have been accepted by the Court in *Crews*. In a part of the opinion joined by all participating members of the Court, note was taken of defendant's contention that the *Wade* test "seeks only to determine whether the in-court identification is sufficiently reliable to satisfy due process, and is thus inapplicable in the context of this Fourth Amendment violation." The Court then agreed "that a satisfactory resolution of the reliability issue does not provide a complete answer to the considerations underlying *Wong Sun*," but concluded "that in the present case both concerns are met." It is far from clear exactly what the Court meant by this, and in particular whether a majority of the Court would agree with the conclusion of the court below, which was that the "extreme sanction" of suppressing the in-court identification would have been necessary had there been "egregious misconduct" (e.g., pretextual dragnet arrests made on information falling far short of probable cause for the precise purpose of identifying persons as perpetrators of recent criminality). But that conclusion is sound, for it is merely an application of the Supreme

Court's own teaching in *Brown v. Illinois* that sound fruit-of-the-poisonous-tree analysis necessitates very close attention to "the purpose and flagrancy of the official misconduct."

Turning now to the identification practice of viewing a photograph, one kind of case is that in which the illegal arrest and photographing was for the purpose of getting a picture that could be used in making such an identification, in which case the situation is indistinguishable from the face-to-face confrontation cases already discussed, and must be resolved in the same way. But, because photographs are typically taken as a matter of routine in the course of booking and then become a permanent part of the police files, it sometimes happens that a photograph routinely taken after an illegal arrest will on some future occasion serve to connect that person with some other crime totally unrelated to the reasons why the pre-photographing illegal arrest was made. In these circumstances, courts are understandably inclined to find attenuation, although a contrary result is called for if the original arrest was so far lacking probable cause as to justify the conclusion that it was made solely to acquire data regarding the defendant.

As for fingerprint identification, the Supreme Court dealt with it in *Davis v. Mississippi* (1969), where defendant's fingerprints, acquired when he was illegally arrested as part of a dragnet roundup conducted as part of a rape investigation, were matched with the prints at the crime scene. In holding the prints were the suppressible fruits of an illegal arrest, the Court rejected the state's claim that the taint concept should not be extended to fingerprints because of their inherent trustworthiness. (By like reasoning, it has been held that other trustworthy identification evidence, such as handwriting exemplars, may likewise be the fruit of an illegal arrest.) *Davis* must be distinguished from a case where the prints were taken as a matter of routine following an arrest that was illegal but not made for the express purpose of having the prints on file for later use, and then were used on a later occasion to connect the defendant with some crime totally unrelated to the reasons underlying the illegal arrest. On such facts, a finding of attenuation is likely.

(e) Testimony of Witness. In *United States v. Ceccollini* (1978), an officer in a flower shop on a social visit illegally picked up an envelope and found it to contain money and policy slips, and then learned from his friend, an employee there who did not notice his discovery, that the envelope belonged to defendant, who owned the shop. The information reached the FBI, and four months later an agent questioned the employee about defendant's activities without specific mention of the illegally discovered policy slips. She was most cooperative and later served as a witness against defendant at his trial for perjury based upon his grand jury testimony that he had not taken policy bets at the shop. The Court declined to accept the government's *"per se* rule that the testimony of a live witness should not be excluded at trial no matter how close and proximate the connection between it and a violation of the Fourth Amendment," but did renounce its earlier declaration in *Wong Sun v. United States* (1963) that "the policies underlying the exclusionary rule [do not] invite any logical distinction between physical and verbal evidence." The Court reasoned there should be greater reluctance to find testimony of a witness a suppressible fruit because (1) the "greater the willingness of the witness to freely testify, the greater the likelihood that he or she will be discovered by legal means and, concomitantly, the smaller the incentive to conduct an illegal search to discover the witness," and (2) exclusion "would perpetually disable a witness from testifying about relevant and material facts, regardless of how unrelated such testimony might be to the purpose of the originally illegal search or the evidence discovered thereby." The two dissenters in *Ceccollini* made two telling criticisms of the majority's logic: (1) the claim that the "greater the willingness of the witness to freely testify, * * * the smaller the incentive to conduct an illegal search to discover the witness" actually "reverses the normal sequence of events," for it is unlikely that "a witness' willingness to testify is known before he or she is discovered"; (2) the claim that exclusion would "perpetually disable" the witness ignores the fact that "at least as often the exclusion of physical evidence * * * will be as costly to the same societal interest."

The majority in *Ceccollini,* having concluded "that the exclusionary rule should be invoked with much greater reluctance where the claim is based on a causal relationship between a constitutional violation and the discovery of a live witness than when a similar claim is advanced to support suppression of an inanimate object," found that the taint had been dissipated in the instant case. The Court stressed the following factors, which have been utilized by lower courts in dealing with witness-as-a-fruit situations: (1) "the testimony given by the witness was an act of her own free will in no way coerced or even induced by official authority as a result of [the] discovery of the policy slips"; (2) the slips were not used in questioning the witness; (3) substantial time passed between the search and contact with the witness and between the contact and the testimony; (4) even before the search, "both the identity of [the witness] and her relationship with the respondent was well known to those investigating the case"; (5) there was "not the slightest evidence" that the officer made the search "with the intent of finding a willing and knowledgeable witness to testify against" defendant.

(f) New Crime. On occasion, when the police conduct an illegal arrest or an illegal search, this will prompt the person arrested or subjected to the search to react by committing some criminal offense. He might attack the officer, attempt to bribe him, or make some criminal misrepresentation in an effort to bring the incident to a close. In the bribery cases, the courts have consistently held that the evidence of the attempted bribe is admissible notwithstanding the prior illegal search of arrest. The most common explanation for this, that bribery attempts are sufficiently acts of free will to purge the taint, is not particularly satisfying, for it might be asked why the bribe offer is any more an act of free will than an incriminating admission or attempt to dispose of the evidence, neither of which is per se untainted. The answer may lie in the underlying deterrent purpose of the exclusionary rule, which is a prime consideration in marking the limits on fruit-of-the-poisonous-tree doctrine. Incriminating admissions and attempts to dispose of incriminating objects are common and predictable consequences of illegal arrests and searches, and thus to admit such evidence would encourage such Fourth Amendment violations in future cases. Bribery attempts, by comparison, are so infrequent and unpredictable that admission of evidence of such criminal activity in a particular case is not likely to encourage future illegal arrest and searches in order to accomplish the same result. In cases where the response has been a physical attack upon the officer making the illegal arrest or search, courts have again held that the evidence of this new crime is admissible; here as well the common explanation is that the attack was a free and independent action, but once more the better basis of distinction is that the rationale of the exclusionary rule does not justify its extension to this extreme.

§ 8.5 Fruits of Illegally Obtained Confessions

(a) The Confession as a "Poisonous Tree". Under the early common law, the inadmissibility of a confession obtained from the defendant had no effect upon the admissibility of other evidence that was acquired as a consequence of that confession. The rationale of this position was that the defendant's statement was suppressed solely because of its untrustworthiness, and thus there was no reason to extend the exclusion to other evidence that itself did not suffer from that defect. The early Supreme Court cases suppressing confessions on due process grounds also focused upon their purported unreliability, and thus the reliable fruits of such constitutional violations were deemed admissible no matter how close the connection. But as this due process theory expanded to encompass other concerns, that rule was put into question. Some courts nonetheless adhered to the old view, while other decisions reached a contrary conclusion on the ground that even indirect products of police misconduct violating our sense of fair play and decency must be suppressed.

As for a confession merely obtained in violation of *Miranda,* the Supreme Court did not speak fully to this issue until almost two decades after *Miranda* was decided. The *Miranda* case itself states that unless the prosecution shows at trial that defendant waived his rights, "no evidence obtained as a result of interrogation can be used against him." But this would seem to be obiter dictum, for none of the several cases considered in *Miranda* involved the admissibility of evidence other than the confessions themselves. Equally puzzling is the decision in *Michigan v. Tucker* (1974), dealing with the admissibility of the testimony of a witness whose identity had been learned by questioning a defendant who was not given the full *Miranda* warnings. Noting that the deviation from *Miranda* was slight because the police had merely failed to tell defendant that if he could not afford a lawyer one would be provided for him, the Court said this meant that "the police conduct here did not deprive respondent of his privilege against compulsory self-incrimination as such, but rather failed to make available to him the full measure of procedural safeguards associated with that right since *Miranda.*" Thus the *Wong Sun* fruits doctrine was dismissed, in effect, with the observation that there had been no constitutional violation, no "poisonous tree" for which the testimony of the witness could be a "fruit." Though *Tucker* thus might have been read as supporting the proposition that a confession obtained by violating *Miranda* cannot be a "poisonous tree," other aspects of the case (the interrogation occurred prior to *Miranda* and thus at a time when the police could not have been aware of a responsibility to give the omitted warning; the alleged fruit in *Tucker* was testimony of a witness, later treated in a special way favoring admissibility even in a Fourth Amendment context) made that a highly questionable interpretation.

Nonetheless, in *Oregon v. Elstad* (1985) the Court rejected such a narrow reading of *Tucker* and held that *Tucker*'s reasoning applied with "equal force when the alleged 'fruit' of a noncoercive *Miranda* violation is neither a witness nor an article of evidence but the accused's own voluntary testimony." In *Elstad,* two officers initially questioned defendant at his home without first giving him *Miranda* warnings. When they expressed their belief that he had been involved in a burglary, he responded, "Yes, I was there." That this statement was excludable under *Miranda* was not contested. However, the defendant was questioned again at the stationhouse; there, after being given the *Miranda* warnings, and after waiving his rights, he made an extensive statement explaining his exact involvement in the burglary. Defendant argued that this statement should be excluded as the fruit of the poisonous tree, but the *Elstad* majority held the fruits doctrine was inapplicable. The Court noted that the fruits doctrine had been developed in the context of the Fourth Amendment exclusionary rule, where the objective was to deter unreasonable searches no matter how probative their fruits, while the objective of the Fifth Amendment was to bar use of compelled statements. Moreover, the *Miranda* ruling, upon which petitioner relied, had adopted an exclusionary rule that "sweeps more broadly" than the Fifth itself by establishing an irrebuttable presumption that unwarned statements obtained through custodial interrogation are compelled, a prophylactic element of *Miranda* that should not be carried beyond prohibiting the state's use of the unwarned statement in its case in chief. Just as *Miranda* had been held not to bar use of an unwarned statement, if in fact voluntary, for impeachment use (see § 8.6(a)), so too it should not bar use of a subsequently obtained statement where there was compliance with *Miranda* in obtaining that statement and the earlier unwarned statement was voluntary. Violation of *Miranda*'s prophylactic safeguards does not in itself create a coercive atmosphere that renders involuntary any subsequent, properly warned, statement. The relevant inquiry should be "whether, in fact, the second statement was also voluntarily made," considering the "surrounding circumstances and the entire course of police conduct with respect to the suspect."

Because *Elstad* purported to be dealing only with a "simple failure to administer the warnings, unaccompanied by any actual coercion or other circumstances *calculated* to undermine the suspect's ability to exercise his free will," some courts have concluded that *Elstad* is inapplicable (even assuming voluntariness of the confession) if the police failed to honor the defendant's invocation of his right to silence or right to counsel. But because the *Elstad* majority's reasoning suggested a more sweeping rejection of the fruit of the poisonous tree doctrine as applied to *Miranda* violations, most lower court rulings have taken *Elstad* in that direction and thus advance the position that an admission or confession obtained in violation of *Miranda* should not be treated as a poisonous tree. This position, consistent with the results reached by the Supreme Court in more recent cases (*Patane* and *Seibert,* infra), distinguishes confessions obtained in violation of *Miranda* not only from confessions obtained in violation of due process (i.e., coerced confessions), but also from confessions held inadmissible under other doctrines similarly treated as creating a poisonous tree.

One such illegally obtained confession is one obtained in violation of the *Massiah* right to counsel. In that situation, it is clear that the constitutional violation occurs at the time of the deprivation of counsel, and thus it may be concluded that the confession can constitute a "poisonous tree" for purposes of fruits analysis.

The Supreme Court acknowledged as much when it indicated in *Brewer v. Williams* (1977) that on retrial it would be necessary to determine whether evidence of the body's location and condition was a fruit of defendant's confession, obtained in violation of his right to counsel, revealing where the body could be located.

(b) Searches. Where the confession was involuntary lower courts have held suppressible under the fruits doctrine physical evidence acquired through that illegally obtained confession, provided the connection between the confession and the acquisition of the physical evidence was rather close and direct. Such is the case when the confession supplies the probable cause for an evidence-producing arrest or search, when the defendant's statement indicates that the physical evidence is at a certain location and the police find it there as a consequence, or when the physical evidence was given to the police as part of the suspect's direct response to the illegal interrogation.

As for *Miranda* violations, both *Tucker* and *Elstad* could be distinguished from the "physical evidence" cases described above, for both involved situations in which the *Miranda* violation led to the claimed evidentiary fruit only through the decision of an individual to voluntarily provide the police with that evidence (the decision of the witness to testify in *Tucker,* and the decision of the defendant to make a second incriminating statement in *Elstad*). Nonetheless, there is much in the *Elstad* majority opinion suggesting that such distinctions would be irrelevant to the *Elstad* majority. Pointing in that direction are the *Elstad* opinion's broad reading of *Tucker*, its characterization of the fruits doctrine as standing apart from the basic objective of the Fifth Amendment (to bar use of compelled statements), its characterization of *Miranda* as imposing safeguards that extend beyond the compulsion that violates the self-incrimination clause, and its analysis of the appropriate limits of the prophylactic sanction of *Miranda*. Not surprisingly, most lower courts view *Elstad* as allowing admission of physical evidence discovered through a statement obtained in violation of *Miranda*, even where the link between the discovery and the statement is direct and immediate.

Some doubts were created by *Dickerson v. United States* (2000), holding *Miranda* announced a constitutional rule, but were tempered by the plurality's conclusion in *Chavez v. Martinez* (2003) that no self-incrimination violation occurs re a confession obtained in violation of *Miranda* unless and until it is admitted against the maker in a criminal trial. Then came *United States v. Patane* (2004), holding the physical evidence admissible. Three Justices reasoned failure to give the *Miranda* warnings is not itself a violation of a suspect's constitutional rights (or even of the *Mi-*

randa rule), which occurs only if the unwarned confession is admitted into evidence, meaning that exclusion of the confession is itself a sufficient remedy and that there is no need to apply the "fruits" doctrine to the mere failure to warn because there is nothing to deter. Two others deemed it unnecessary to decide such matters; given the important probative value of the physical evidence and the fact that admitting it does not risk admission of the unwarned statement as well, they rationalized such admission as an accommodation of *Miranda* with the other objectives of the criminal justice system. The main dissent stressed that the privilege against self incrimination "extends to the exclusion of derivative evidence" (certainly the case as to compelled testimony; see *United States v. Hubbell* (2000)), and that a *Miranda* violation "raises a presumption of coercion" properly applied in the instant context to serve its purpose of freeing courts from "the inherently difficult exercise of assessing the voluntariness of a confession" resulting from custodial interrogation.

In *Nix v. Williams* (1984), the Supreme Court applied the inevitable discovery doctrine in the context of a Sixth Amendment violation that produced a statement which led police to physical evidence. The logical implication of *Nix* is that the fruits doctrine does apply to physical evidence discovered through a statement inadmissible under the Sixth Amendment, unless that discovery falls within one of those limitations (e.g., inevitable discovery) that makes that doctrine inapplicable.

(c) Confessions. As for the admissibility of a confession obtained subsequent to an earlier one illegally obtained from the same party, one approach is reflected in *Lyons v. Oklahoma* (1944). There a confession was coerced from defendant, but 12 hours later in the presence of different persons and after having been transferred from a jail to a prison, defendant gave a second confession. The Court in *Lyons* first declared that the "admissibility of the later confession depends upon the same test—is it voluntary," and then ruled that while sometimes the "effect of earlier abuse may be so clear as to forbid any other inference than that it dominated the mind of the accused to such an extent that the later confession is involuntary," this was not such a case. The fruit-of-the-poisonous-tree doctrine was never mentioned and quite obviously was not being applied. The issue, as the Court saw it, was whether the events at the time of the first confession—not the confession itself—brought about the second confession, and the focus was not on the impact of the first confession on the second but on the continuing effect of *prior coercive practices*. On other facts, the Court has held a second confession involuntary because the coercive circumstances of the first carried over to the second.

In *United States v. Bayer* (1947), the lower court applied the fruit-of-the-poisonous-tree doctrine to exclude a second confession that, while preceded by a warning that it might be used against the defendant, was made after defendant had reread the first confession without being told it could not be used against him. But the Supreme Court reversed. The majority in *Bayer* first noted that though "after an accused has once let the cat out of the bag by confessing * * * [h]e can never get the cat back in the bag," this does not mean "that making a confession under circumstances which preclude its use, perpetually disables the confessor from making a usable one after those conditions have been removed." That conclusion is unobjectionable, but some questioned whether the same could be said for the Court's next statement that the lower court improperly used a fruits theory here because the Supreme Court's earlier cases in that line "did not deal with confessions but with evidence of a quite different category and do not control this question."

Although some lower courts read *Bayer* narrowly and continued to apply the fruits doctrine to successive confessions, that interpretation was open to serious question even before *Elstad*. In a series of post-*Bayer* decisions involving an initial confession that had been involuntary, the Court had asked the question posed in *Lyons*—whether the second confession was itself involuntary— rather than whether the second confession was a fruit of the first. The critical issue was whether there was a "break in the stream of events" sufficient to "insulate" the later confession from the coercive practices that had rendered the first involuntary. Although this approach looked to many of the same factors as a fruits analysis, such as temporal attenuation, intervening circumstances, and the "flagrancy" of the coercive practices that rendered the initial confession involuntary, it apparently placed less emphasis on the impact of the initial confession on the willingness of the individual to make a second statement.

The difference between the two approaches was brought home in *Elstad,* where the Court explicitly rejected application of the fruits doctrine to determine the admissibility of a second confession that followed a first obtained in violation of *Miranda.* The crucial issue, the Court noted, was whether the second confession was voluntary, not whether it could be tied to the first under a fruits doctrine developed for determining the Fourth Amendment's exclusionary rule. The Court noted in this regard that it previously had refused to automatically exclude all second confessions under a "cat-out-of-the-bag" theory, and it was certainly not about to do so when the original confession was excludable only because of a *Miranda* violation. Any psychological compulsion that flowed from an unwarned but entirely voluntary statement was too speculative and attenuated, as it relates to official coercion, to justify exclusion of a second statement itself obtained after the administration of *Miranda* warnings. While it was true that the defendant had not been told prior to his second statement that the first statement was excludable, the Court "has never embraced the theory that the defendant's ignorance of the full consequences of his decisions vitiates their voluntariness." The officers here had not attempted to "exploit the [earlier] unwarned admission to pressure [the suspect] into waiving his right to remain silent," and they should not be expected to give the suspect legal advice as to the inadmissibility of his earlier statement. As noted in *Fellers v. United States* (2004), the Supreme Court has not yet decided whether the rationale of *Elstad* applies when the first confession was obtained in violation of the defendant's Sixth Amendment right to counsel.

When the Court later, in *Missouri v. Seibert* (2004), limited the impact of *Elstad*, it did so in a manner that did not require the first confession to be treated as a poisonous tree. *Seibert* involved an increasingly popular "police protocol for custodial interrogation that calls for giving no warnings of the rights to silence and counsel until interrogation has produced a confession," utilized "to get a confession the suspect would not make if he understood his rights at the outset," a likely consequence because giving the warnings *after* the defendant has already confessed "could lead to an entirely reasonable inference that what he had just said will be used, with subsequent silence being of no avail." The Court held Seibert's second confession must be suppressed, *not* because it was the fruit of the first confession, but simply because the circumstances in which the *Miranda* warnings were given meant they could not "function 'effectively' as *Miranda* requires."

(d) Testimony of Witness. *Harrison v. United States* (1968) involved these facts: after three confessions allegedly made by defendant were introduced at his trial, he took the stand and testified to his own version of the events, making damaging admissions in the process; his conviction was later reversed on the ground that the confessions had been obtained in violation of the *McNabb–Mallory* rule; upon retrial the prosecution introduced defendant's testimony at the first trial, and he was convicted once again. The Supreme Court reversed. Noting that but for the erroneous admission of defendant's confessions he "might not have testified at all" and certainly would not "have admitted being at the scene of the crime and holding the gun when the fatal shot was fired." the Court concluded it "has not been demonstrated, therefore, that the petitioner's testimony was obtained 'by means sufficiently distinguishable' from the underlying illegality 'to be purged of the primary taint.'"

The Court in *Harrison* cautioned that it was reserving for future decision the question of whether testimony by some other person could be a fruit. This question was later raised in *Michigan v. Tucker* (1974), where after incomplete *Miranda* warnings defendant gave a statement which identified a person the prosecution used as a witness at trial. The Court declined to treat that testimony as a suppressible fruit, but, for the reasons stated earlier, it is impossible to draw any general conclusions from *Tucker*. However, some courts have concluded that the testimony of persons discovered thereby is not a fruit of a confession obtained in violation of *Miranda,* but that a fruits inquiry is appropriate if the confession is either involuntary or obtained in violation of the Sixth Amendment right to counsel. Even as to the latter situations, however, it is well to remember the Supreme Court's "special" approach to claims that testimony is an inadmissible fruit, designed to limit the circumstances in which such evidence would be suppressed, for doubtless it is applicable in this context as well. And in any event, the testimony of the discovered witness will be held admissible under the "inevitable discovery" rule if it appears to the court that sooner or later his identity would have been independently revealed by standard investigation procedures.

§ 8.6 Permissible Use of Illegally Obtained Evidence at Trial

(a) **Impeachment.** Under the various exclusionary rules, if a constitutional violation has occurred then upon a timely objection by a defendant with standing the fruits of that illegality must be suppressed and consequently may not be introduced into evidence at the criminal trial of that defendant. There exist, however, a few exceptions to that statement, one of which concerns the use of that evidence for impeachment purposes. The dimensions of that particular exception have broadened over the years, which can best be seen by a brief chronological look at the Supreme Court's leading decisions in this area, starting with *Agnello v. United States* (1925). Defendant, charged with conspiracy to sell cocaine, testified on direct examination that he received certain packages without knowing they contained cocaine, and on cross-examination said he had never seen narcotics, at which point the government was permitted to introduce in rebuttal a can of cocaine that had been illegally seized from his room and suppressed from the government's case in chief. A unanimous Court reversed, relying upon its earlier statement that the "essence of a provision forbidding the acquisition of evidence in a certain way is not merely that evidence so acquired shall not be used before the court but that it shall not be used at all."

A somewhat similar case, *Walder v. United States* (1954), later reached the Court; there, defendant testified on direct and cross-examination that he had never purchased, sold or possessed any narcotics, which the government was allowed to impeach by questioning defendant concerning heroin illegally seized from his home two years earlier. The Court upheld this procedure, reasoning that the defendant could not use the exclusionary rule to "provide himself with a shield against contradiction of his untruths" where he had been "free to deny all the elements of the case against him" without the impeached "sweeping claim that he had never dealt in or possessed any narcotics." *Walder* thus appeared to say that where a defendant (i) on direct examination (ii) did not merely deny the elements of the case against him but instead made sweeping claims putting his character in issue, then the government could introduce illegally obtained evidence (iii) for the limited purpose of impeachment (iv) if the evidence was obtained as a consequence of police misconduct unrelated to the instant case. So viewed, *Walder* seemed to strike a reasonable balance between the competing interests involved.

In the third case, *Harris v. New York* (1971), after the defendant upon direct examination denied having made the charged sale of narcotics, the prosecutor was allowed to impeach the defendant's credibility by resort to a statement made by him to the police under circumstances that concededly made that statement inadmissible under *Miranda*. The Supreme Court affirmed, reasoning that though in *Walder* defendant "was impeached as to collateral matters" while here he "was impeached as to testimony bearing more directly on the crimes charged," this did not amount to a "difference in principle" between the two cases:

> The impeachment process here undoubtedly provided valuable aid to the jury in assessing petitioner's credibility, and the benefits of this process should not be lost, in our view, because of the speculative possibility that impermissible police conduct will be encouraged thereby. Assuming that the exclusionary rule has a deterrent effect on proscribed police conduct, sufficient deterrence flows when the evidence in question is made unavailable to the prosecution in its case in chief.
>
> Every criminal defendant is privileged to testify in his own defense, or to refuse to do so. But that privilege cannot be construed to include the right to commit perjury. * * * Having voluntarily taken the stand, petitioner was under an obligation to speak truthfully and accurately, and the prosecution here did no more than utilize the traditional truth-testing devices of the adversary process.

Harris was rightly criticized because it selectively quoted from *Walder*, carefully excising any reference to the broader principle that the defendant "must be free to deny all the elements of the case against him without thereby giving leave to the Government to introduce by way of rebuttal evidence illegally secured by it," and also because it claimed to be extending a general rule laid down in *Walder* when in truth *Walder* was a limited exception to the general rule established in *Agnello,* which thus was overruled without even being cited.

Next came *United States v. Havens* (1980), where on direct examination defendant denied being involved with his codefendant in the transportation of cocaine, and on cross-examination denied being involved in sewing a pocket (in which drugs were found) into his codefendant's clothing or having in his own suitcase cloth from which the swatch was cut to make the pocket. That testimony was impeached by admitting the illegally seized cloth, but the appellate court reversed because the impeached testimony was not given on direct examination. But the Supreme Court, again in a 5–4 decision, ruled otherwise: "In terms of impeaching a defendant's seemingly false statements with his prior inconsistent utterances or with other reliable evidence available to the government, we see no difference of constitutional magnitude between the defendant's statements on direct examination and his answers to questions put to him on cross-examination that are plainly within the scope of the defendant's direct examination."

What started out in *Walder* as a narrow and reasonable exception has thus taken on awesome proportions. Under *Havens,* statements elicited on cross-examination now may be impeached. This violates the waiver doctrine of *Walder,* and actually encourages constitutional violations for purposes of "boxing in" the defendant, for now, the *Havens* dissenters noted, "even the moderately talented prosecutor [can] 'work in * * * evidence on cross-examination * * * [as it would] in its case in chief * * *,' " and "a defendant will be compelled to forego testifying on his own behalf" to avoid this consequence. Secondly, *Harris* (as the Court later put it in *Havens*) "made clear that the permitted impeachment by otherwise inadmissible evidence is not limited to collateral matters," but may relate directly to commission of the offense itself. Of course, the defendant's testimony must open the door to such impeachment, but neither *Harris* nor *Havens* indicated precisely how far the defendant had to go in his testimony relating to an element of the offense to permit impeachment as to that element. As a consequence, some courts allow impeachment when the defendant does no more than deny the elements of the crime, though many courts refuse to read *Harris* as bringing about such an unfair result. Thirdly, as *Havens* makes plain, a defendant may now be impeached by evidence bearing directly upon the crime charged. This departure from *Walder* is also most unfortunate, for the discarded limitation minimized the danger that a jury might view unconstitutionally obtained impeaching evidence as establishing guilt, even if instructed to consider it only for credibility purposes.

Yet another question that must be asked about the impeachment exception concerns what kinds of constitutional or other violations are encompassed within the exception. *Walder* and *Havens* make it clear that Fourth Amendment violations qualify. What then if instead the evidence was obtained in violation of Title III of the Omnibus Crime Control Act of 1968, which imposes limitations upon resort to eavesdropping and wiretapping? Though this legislation expressly provides that "no part" of the contents of an invalid interception and "no evidence derived therefrom may be received in evidence in any trial," the legislative history indicates that this and related provisions were not intended to press the scope of the suppression rule beyond present search and seizure law, and thus the result in such cases is no different.

The reasons justifying some sort of impeachment exception as to Fourth Amendment violations might well be thought not to carry over to violations of the Fifth Amendment privilege against self-incrimination. For one thing, illegally seized tangible evidence is inherently reliable, but the same cannot necessarily be said where there has been a *Miranda* violation. Moreover, the Fourth Amendment exclusionary rule is a court-created device intended to deter the police, and thus arguably ought not be applied when the objective of deterrence is outweighed by other considerations, while by contrast the Fifth Amendment on its face prohibits the government from using "compelled" statements "against" a defendant. But in *Harris,* where the defendant was not given the complete *Miranda* warnings and it was asserted he made "no claim that the statements made to the police were coerced or involuntary," the Court unhesitantly extended the impeachment exception to *Miranda* violations. The same result was reached in *Oregon v. Hass* (1975), although there the suspect was advised of his rights and then asked for counsel but was questioned without his request being honored. The majority saw the case as indistinguishable from *Harris* because "inadmissibility would pervert the constitutional right into a right to falsify," while the two dissenters argued that *Hass* was far worse because it provided police with an incentive for dishonoring such requests—they had nothing to lose and something significant to gain, "a statement which can be used for impeachment if the accused has the temerity to testify in his own defense."

In *New Jersey v. Portash* (1979), the Court emphasized that "central to the decisions" in *Harris* and *Hass* was the fact that the defendant made no claim the statements were coerced or involuntary. That served to distinguish the statements obtained in the instant case, defendant's testimony before a grand jury given in response to a grant of use immunity, which was "the essence of coerced testimony." Confronted with "the constitutional privilege against compulsory self-incrimination in its most pristine form," the Court concluded that the balancing of interests undertaken in *Harris* and *Hass* was "impermissible" in the present context. And in *Mincey v. Arizona* (1978) the Court again distinguished *Harris* and *Hass* and declared that use of an "involuntary statement" even for impeachment purposes would constitute "a denial of due process of law." The Court did not comment on the fact that in a particular case a statement could be involuntary but yet very truthworthy.

In *Michigan v. Harvey* (1990), the Supreme Court overturned a state court ruling that because defendant's statement after arraignment and appointment of counsel was taken "in violation of defendant's Sixth Amendment right to counsel" it could not be used for impeachment purposes. The majority focused upon the state court's reliance upon *Michigan v. Jackson* (1986), which held that after a defendant requests assistance of counsel, any waiver of Sixth Amendment rights given in a discussion initiated by police is presumed invalid. Because it "simply superimposed the Fifth Amendment analysis" of *Edwards v. Arizona* (1981) onto the Sixth Amendment right, the majority reasoned, *Jackson* did not mark the exact boundary of the Sixth Amendment right itself but rather constituted a "prophylactic rule * * * designed to ensure voluntary, knowing, and intelligent waivers of the Sixth Amendment right to counsel." From this, it was deemed to follow that the reasoning of such cases as *Hass* and *Havens* carried over to the instant case: once again, "the 'search for truth in a criminal case' outweighs the 'speculative possibility' that exclusion of evidence might deter future violations of rules not compelled directly by the Constitution in the first place."

It is important to note that the *Harvey* majority did *not* hold that the fruits of a violation of the Sixth Amendment right to counsel may be used for purposes of impeachment. Having characterized the case as it did, the Court did not have to "consider the admissibility for impeachment purposes of a voluntary statement obtained in the absence of a knowing and voluntary waiver of the right to counsel," that is, in a situation in which the prosecution even apart from the *Jackson* presumption could not carry its burden of proving such a waiver. (The four dissenters cogently argued (1) that the Sixth Amendment right, unlike *Miranda,* extends "to all efforts to elicit information from the defendant whether for use as impeachment or rebuttal at trial or simply to formulate trial strategy"; (2) that "exclusion of statements made by a represented and indicted defendant outside the presence of counsel follows not as a remedy for a violation that has preceded trial but as a necessary incident of the constitutional right itself"; and (3) that under the majority's rule the police after formal charge "have everything to gain and nothing to lose by repeatedly visiting with defendant and seeking to elicit as many comments as possible about the pending trial.")

Sometimes the question is whether defendant's silence may be utilized for impeachment purposes. In *Doyle v. Ohio* (1976), the Court held that impeachment by defendant's post-arrest silence after he had received the *Miranda* warnings was impermissible. Not only is "every post-arrest silence * * * insolubly ambiguous" because it "may be nothing more than the arrestee's exercise of [his] *Miranda* rights," but use of the silence to impeach "would be fundamentally unfair" given the fact that the warnings carry the implicit "assurance that silence will carry no penalty." *Doyle* has been distinguished in three later cases. In *Anderson v. Charles* (1980), impeachment by prior inconsistent statements given after *Miranda* warnings was permitted because "a defendant who voluntarily speaks after receiving *Miranda* warnings has not been induced to remain silent." In *Jenkins v. Anderson* (1980), where at his murder trial defendant claimed self defense, the Court ruled it was permissible to impeach that story by defendant's prearrest silence in not reporting the stabbing to the authorities for at least two weeks. This was not compelled self-incrimination, for, as the Court had concluded many years earlier, the possibility of impeachment by prior silence is not an impermissible burden upon the exercise of Fifth Amendment rights. Nor was it a denial of fundamental fairness, for unlike *Doyle* "no government action induced petitioner to remain silent before arrest." The claim has been made that the silence in *Jenkins* was just as equivocal as that in *Doyle,* for an individual's reluctance to hand himself over to the police and admit a stabbing, in self-defense or otherwise, is not probative of guilt. But in *Fletcher v. Weir* (1982) the Court followed *Jenkins* and distinguished *Doyle* in allowing impeachment by post-arrest silence not preceded by *Miranda* warnings, explaining that this was not "a case where the government had induced silence by implicitly assuring the defendant that his silence would not be used against him." So too, *Brecht v. Abrahamson* (1993) held that where defendant did not receive *Miranda* warnings until his arraignment, the prosecution did not violate due process insofar as it impeached him by reference to his post-arrest silence up to that point. The Supreme Court has not passed on use of such silence as substantive evidence of guilt in the prosecution's case-in-chief, a matter on which lower courts are divided.

An effort to extend the impeachment exception from the defendant's own testimony to the testimony of all defense witnesses was rejected in *James v. Illinois* (1990). The Court concluded that such an expansion of *Walder* "would not promote the truth-seeking function to the same extent as did creation of the original exception, and yet it would significantly undermine the deterrent effect of the general exclusionary rule," thus serving to "frustrate rather than further the purposes underlying the exclusionary rule." The same beneficial effects would not be present, the Court reasoned, because (1) the threat of subsequent criminal prosecution is alone more likely to deter a defense witness than a defendant, already facing conviction for the underlying offense; and (2) such expansion "likely would chill some defendants from presenting their best defense—and sometimes any defense at all—through the testimony of others," as a variety of factors make it problematical whether a defense witness will testify as expected and thus avoid such impeachment. Moreover, there would be present under such expansion greater threat to "the exclusionary rule's deterrent effect on police misconduct"; the expansion would "vastly increase the number of occasions on which such evidence could be used" and would serve to deter not only perjury but also the calling of defense witnesses in the first place, from which "police officers and their superiors would recognize that obtaining evidence through illegal means stacks the deck heavily in the prosecutions's favor." In an earlier, more limited ruling, relying upon *Doyle,* the Supreme Court held in *Wainwright v. Greenfield* (1986) that the prosecution's use of defendant's post-arrest, post-*Miranda*-warnings silence as evidence of his sanity violates due process.

(b) Defense Tactics That "Open the Door". In the impeachment case of *Walder v. United States* (1954), the Court emphasized that it was the defendant who "opened the door" to the admissibility of the illegally seized evidence by his sweeping assertions upon direct examination. On rare occasion, defense tactics that likewise seek to gain extraordinary advantage from the fact of suppression of certain evidence may also be deemed to have "opened the door" to at least limited receipt of that evidence. Defense tactics are more likely to be found to have opened the door if they involved a calculated effort to create a high degree of confusion based upon knowledge that any adequate explanation would require some reference to evidence previously suppressed. But this does not mean, however, that merely because the defendant intrudes an issue into the trial as to which illegally obtained evidence would be relevant, the door has thereby been opened to receipt of that evidence on the issue. Thus, the mere fact that insanity is an affirmative defense, so that proof of sanity is not part of the prosecution's case-in-chief, does not mean that evidence obtained in violation of *Miranda* and the Fourth Amendment can be used generally to rebut an insanity defense.

(c) Prosecution for Perjury or Other "New" Offense. In *Walder v. United States* (1954), the Court saw no "justification for letting the defendant affirmatively resort to perjurious testimony in reliance on the Government's disability to challenge his credibility," and, as we have seen, this same view has been taken in the later impeachment cases. From this, it might be argued that illegally obtained evidence should be admissible in the prosecution's case in chief on a charge of perjury. While this argument has been accepted in several lower court cases, such a result should be reached only when it is clear that no significant additional deterrent effect could be realized by suppression and that the benefits to be derived from admission are substantial. In a case where the evidence was obtained in an illegal search, this means (1) that the search must have preceded the perjured testimony, for otherwise there would be incentive to conduct such searches against individuals suspected of perjury; and (2) actual awareness of the search by the defendant at the time his testimony was given is essential, as if that were not so there would be incentive to make undisclosed illegal searches and then subpoena the search victim. As for whether this exception to the exclusionary rules needs to be limited to perjury prosecutions, one court suggested the answer is no because "no significant additional deterrent effect could be realized by suppressing the evidence at a trial of the search victim for a crime committed after the illegal search and with the knowledge that the illegal search occurred," and suppression in such circumstances "would in effect give the victim of an illegal search a license to commit any new crimes he cares to, free from the concern that the illegally seized evidence might be used against him in prosecution for these subsequent crimes." Some courts have so held.

Chapter 9

ADMINISTRATION OF THE EXCLUSIONARY RULES

Table of Sections

§ 9.1   The Pretrial Motion to Suppress

(a) **Contemporaneous Objection or Pretrial Motion.**
Some states continue to follow the "contemporaneous objection rule," which only requires that an objection be made at trial at the time the prosecution seeks to introduce the illegally obtained evidence. However, the great majority of jurisdictions have abandoned the contemporaneous objection rule in favor of a requirement that objections be raised before trial by way of a pretrial motion to suppress. This requirement usually applies to exclusion based on all grounds relating to the illegal acquisition of the evidence.

The minority of jurisdictions following the contemporaneous objection rule view it as a more efficient procedure. However, there are many valid reasons underlying the prevailing practice of requiring pretrial motions. The pretrial motion requirement eliminates from the trial disputes over police conduct not immediately relevant to the question of guilt, and avoids interruptions of a trial in progress with such auxiliary inquiries. It also prevents having to declare a mistrial because the jury has been exposed to unconstitutional evidence. Moreover, it is to the advantage of both the prosecution and defense to know in advance of the time set for trial whether certain items will or will not be admitted into evidence. If the pretrial motion is granted, this could result in abandonment of the prosecution, thus avoiding the waste of prosecutorial and judicial resources occasioned by preparation of a trial, or in the prosecution changing the theory of its case or developing untainted evidence. If the pretrial motion is denied, then the defendant is in a position at that time either to plead guilty and gain whatever concessions might be obtained by so pleading without causing the commencement of a trial, or to go to trial with a somewhat different defense strategy. Finally, in those jurisdictions where interlocutory appeal by the prosecution is permitted, the requirement of a pretrial motion to suppress protects that right of immediate appeal.

(b) **Form of the Motion.** The pretrial motion to suppress, which in many jurisdictions must be in writing, must identify the evidence the defendant seeks to suppress and specify with particularity the grounds upon which the motion is based. This requirement is one of specificity in the statement of defendant's legal theory, which may be met, for example, by alleging that the evidence in question was obtained from the defendant incident to an arrest that was not made upon probable cause. Many jurisdictions require a defendant making a pretrial suppression motion also to set out facts in support of the motion, and it may even be necessary that defendant's motion be accompanied by an affidavit or affidavits on behalf of the defendant setting forth all facts within his knowledge upon which he intends to rely in support of the motion. This requirement has been held constitutional, which perhaps it is so long as the holding in *Simmons v. United States* (1968)—that testimony given by the defendant at the hearing on his motion is not admissible against him at trial on the question of guilt or innocence—is extended to such affidavits.

(c) Pre-charge Motions Distinguished. The pretrial motion to suppress, made in the context of criminal proceedings, must be distinguished from the action that may be taken in many jurisdictions prior to the filing of criminal charges, in order to challenge continued government possession of objects acquired in an earlier search. Though this precharge motion is sometimes referred to as a motion to suppress, it is more correct to call it a motion for return of property or a motion to quash a search warrant, for even if the movant is successful it does not necessarily follow that this evidence will be suppressed if a criminal prosecution is later undertaken.

Such anomalous jurisdiction in the federal system is exercised with caution and restraint and subject to equitable principles. A foremost consideration is whether there is a clear and definite showing that constitutional rights have been violated. A second consideration is whether the plaintiff has an individual interest in and need for the material whose return he seeks, as where those goods are necessary to conduct a legitimate business. Yet a third consideration is whether the plaintiff would be irreparably injured by denial of the return of the property or instead has an adequate remedy at law. But courts are disinclined to grant relief when a criminal prosecution is anticipated, for they usually take the view that in such circumstances intervention would impede prosecuting officers and interfere with the grand jury.

Pre-charge proceedings to quash search warrants or for the return of items seized in searches are also available in many states. They are commonly authorized by statutes governing the issuance of warrants, but in some jurisdictions are permitted by courts of equity without express statutory authority. Where such proceedings rest exclusively upon statute, they may be limited to searches made pursuant to a warrant or even to warrants for certain types of property (e.g., obscene materials).

§ 9.2   Waiver or Forfeiture of Objection

(a) Failure to Make Timely Objection. In those jurisdictions requiring a contemporaneous objection to the introduction of illegally obtained evidence, failure to make such an objection ordinarily bars consideration of any subsequent objection at trial or on appeal. Similarly, in states requiring that a pretrial motion to suppress be made by a specified time, a motion that is not made until trial or even until some later pretrial stage is not timely and thus ordinarily will not receive consideration. Noncompliance with these requirements is commonly characterized as a "waiver" of the constitutional objection, but because such a failure does not ordinarily involve an intentional relinquishment of a constitutional right it is better to view it as a "forfeiture."

In many jurisdictions a court may in its discretion entertain a suppression motion even when the motion could be barred as untimely. If the court entertains the motion and receives evidence going to the merits, under the prevailing view it may still decline to suppress on the ground that the motion was not timely. The minority position is that once the hearing has been held the timeliness of the motion becomes moot and can no longer be a proper ground for denial. In any event, if an untimely motion is denied on the merits, this denial may be appealed after conviction.

All jurisdictions grant relief from pretrial motion requirements when it is shown that the defendant lacked a reasonable opportunity to raise the objection by the required time. Statutes and court rules articulating this exception vary somewhat in their phrasing, and this may influence to some degree how courts construe its breadth. It is fair to say, however, that there is a general disinclination to find such lack of opportunity except under the most compelling circumstances. Ignorance of the legal grounds for having the evidence suppressed will not suffice, but ignorance by the defendant that the item in question had been seized will. If the defendant was personally aware of the police action that led to their acquisition of the evidence, he is responsible for informing counsel of those facts.

In *Henry v. Mississippi* (1965), the Supreme Court, applying the "proposition that a litigant's procedural defaults in state proceedings do not prevent vindication of his federal rights unless the State's insistence on compliance with its procedural rule serves a legitimate state interest," concluded that the less demanding contemporaneous objection rule did serve such an interest. But the Court went on to say that the purpose of this rule was substantially served by the motion defendant had made at the close of the state's evidence, and thus suggested that noncompliance with the rule could not be deemed an independent state ground supporting defendant's conviction. A few states have read *Henry* as placing constitutional limits upon their power to treat failure to comply with a timely objection rule as a waiver of the constitutional objection. In the main, however, the courts have not read *Henry* as barring enforcement of either the contemporary objection rule or the pretrial motion rule, though *Henry* may have influenced some jurisdictions to be somewhat more ready to find the existence of good cause for failure to comply.

The Court in *Henry* found it unnecessary to resolve the independent state ground issue because the record suggested defendant's counsel had deliberately bypassed the opportunity to make a timely objection, which the Court concluded would constitute a forfeiture of the constitutional claim even "without prior consultation with an accused" by counsel. This branch of *Henry* has been relied upon by courts in holding that noncompliance with a timely objection rule, prompted by counsel's deliberate and strategic choice not to attempt to have the evidence in question suppressed, is binding upon the defendant even if that choice was made without the defendant's knowledge or participation.

(b) Failure to Renew Objection. In most jurisdictions a defendant will have preserved the suppression issue for appeal simply by having made the requisite pretrial motion that was denied. But some states require that the defendant renew his objection at the time the evidence is offered at trial. In support, it is argued that such a requirement ensures that the trial judge (as opposed to some lesser judicial officer) will have passed on the issue, serves to bar appeal where defendant later concludes as a matter of trial strategy that he would prefer to have the evidence admitted, also bars appeal where defense counsel later concludes the motion was without merit, and ensures reconsideration upon the added facts developed at trial. But requiring renewal robs the pretrial motion of its greatest benefit: the saving of much time during and immediately prior to trial.

Even where renewal of the motion is not generally required, special circumstances may make renewal essential. Such is the case where it appears at the pretrial hearing that the facts cannot be fully developed at that point, so that the judge defers ruling on the motion until trial or denies the motion "without prejudice" to renewal at trial. Even absent such circumstances, renewal is the safer course in a jurisdiction in which the pretrial order is not binding on the trial judge. If the motion is renewed and reconsidered by the trial court, then it is customary for the appellate court on review to consider all the evidence available to the trial judge up to that point.

Defense counsel must be alert to other traps for the unwary. For example, in some jurisdictions it is the law that even if the defendant made a timely pretrial motion to suppress and (if required) a contemporaneous objection at the time the evidence was offered against him, the issue is *still* not preserved for appellate review unless the objection is made yet another time in a motion for a new trial.

(c) Testimony by Defendant. A small number of jurisdictions adhere to the position that a defendant may not complain on appeal about the admission of illegally obtained evidence, notwithstanding timely objection at or before trial, if the defendant gave testimony at trial admitting possession of that evidence. A variety of reasons have been given for this result: that defendant's admission is a "waiver" of the constitutional objection; that it amounts to a judicial confession; and that it makes admission of the evidence harmless error. The rule has been applied when defendant's testimony was equivocal, remote in its relationship to the evidence, or given to explain away the evidence and make possession of it appear innocent. The rule serves no legitimate state interest, and places the defendant in the dilemma where he must either ignore the damaging evidence introduced against him or waive his right to appeal its erroneous introduction, and thus it is encouraging that some states have abandoned the rule. Some courts have concluded that the rule is unconstitutional in light of *Harrison v. United States* (1968), where the Supreme Court held defendant's trial testimony was a "fruit" of his illegally obtained confessions earlier admitted into evidence. But, as a dissent in *Harrison* objected, the majority, contrary to earlier "fruits" decisions, had used a "broad 'but for' sense of causality," and hence it is by no means clear that the minority rule under discussion here is unconstitutional, for the Supreme Court's more recent "fruits" cases have instead focused upon the issue of "exploitation" and upon the notion of deterrence.

(d) Plea of Guilty or Nolo Contendere. A plea of guilty is an admission of guilt and a waiver of all non-jurisdictional defects. It "represents a break in the chain of events which has preceded it in the criminal process," and thus once a valid plea is received defendant may not appeal on the ground that his earlier suppression motion was erroneously denied. The same is true of a valid nolo contendere plea. As for a *Harrison*-type argument that the plea was a fruit of the prior illegality, this is "at most a claim that the admissibility of his confession was mistakenly assessed and that since he was erroneously advised * * his plea was an unintelligent and voidable act." And, the Supreme Court added in *McMann v. Richardson* (1970), this is not a claim that will prevail if the attorney's advice "was within the range of competence demanded of attorneys in criminal cases." Some jurisdictions have by statute or court rule created an exception to the general rule, so that a "conditional" plea may be made reserving the right to appeal an earlier denial of the suppression motion.

§ 9.3　Burden of Proof

(a) **Generally.** The term "burden of proof" actually encompasses two separate burdens. One burden is that of producing evidence, sometimes called the "burden of evidence" or the "burden of going forward." If the party who has the burden of producing evidence does not meet that burden, the consequence is an adverse ruling on the matter at issue. The other burden is the burden of persuasion, which becomes crucial only if the parties have sustained their respective burdens of producing evidence and only when all the evidence has been introduced. It becomes significant if the trier of fact is in doubt; if he is, then the matter must be resolved against the party with the burden of persuasion. It is not inevitably true that the burden of production and the burden of persuasion must both fall upon the same party, but the prevailing practice is to allocate the two burdens jointly to one party or another. Sometimes courts expressly state that this is what they are about, but more commonly it results as a consequence of a general ruling that the "burden of proof" on the motion to suppress rests upon either the defendant or the state.

Various principles are often advanced in the course of discussions of where, as a matter of sound policy, the burden of proof should lie in various circumstances. In summary, they are: (1) that the burdens should be placed on the party who has the best access to the relevant facts; (2) that the burdens should be placed on the party desiring change; (3) that the burdens should be allocated so as to avoid providing an incentive for use of the objection primarily to gain general discovery of the other side's case, particularly where discovery is otherwise quite limited; (4) that the burdens should be allocated so as to have one party proving a limited ground rather than the other party disproving many grounds; (5) that the burdens should be allocated in accordance with the best judicial estimate of the probabilities of the particular event having occurred; and (6) that the burdens should be used to "handicap" disfavored contentions. These principles will sometimes be helpful in working out burden of proof issues, but they do not inevitably all point in the same direction and thus will not always show where as a matter of policy the burden would best be placed.

(b) **Search and Seizure.** With respect to the issue that is usually central in a Fourth Amendment suppression hearing—the reasonableness of the challenged search or seizure—most states follow the rule utilized in the federal courts: if the search or seizure was pursuant to a warrant, the defendant has the burden of proof; but if the police acted without a warrant the burden of proof is on the prosecution. The warrant-no warrant dichotomy is typically explained on the ground that when the police have acted with a warrant an independent determination on the issue of probable cause has already been made by a magistrate, thereby giving rise to a presumption of legality, while when they have acted without a warrant the evidence comprising probable cause is particularly within the knowledge and control of the arresting agencies.

Some jurisdictions, however, do not draw a distinction between warrant and no-warrant cases in allocating the burden of proof. A few uniformly place the burden of proof upon the prosecution on the ground that the state is the party seeking to use the evidence and thus ought to bear the burden of establishing that it was lawfully come by. Some states place the burden of proof uniformly upon the defendant. By way of explanation, it is commonly stated that the burden is so placed because (a) the burden should be upon the moving party, (b) there is a presumption of regularity attending the actions of law enforcement officials, (c) relevant evidence is generally admissible and thus exceptions must be justified by those claiming the exception, and (d) it will deter spurious allegations wasteful of court time. Placing the burden upon the defendant even in the no warrant situation would seem to place him in a most disadvantageous position. It would be impossible, for example, for a defendant to prove a lack of probable cause in the abstract, as he cannot be expected to prove such a lack until he knows on what the government bases its claim of its existence. However, the situation is not necessarily this bad in jurisdictions purporting to place the burden of proof upon the defendant, for they may in fact permit the defendant to shift the burden to the prosecution with a minimum of effort.

There are certain types of Fourth Amendment issues that customarily receive special treatment with respect to burden of proof. One of these is that of whether a so-called consent search occurred. In *Bumper v. North Carolina* (1968), the Supreme Court held: "When a prosecutor seeks to rely upon consent to justify the lawfulness of a search, he has the burden of proving that the consent was, in fact, freely and voluntarily given. This burden cannot be discharged by showing no more than acquiescence to a claim of lawful authority." *Bumper* so places the burden as a matter of constitutional law, meaning states may not adopt a contrary rule. Another issue ordinarily singled out for special treatment is that of whether the defendant has standing. In *Jones v. United States* (1960), the Court emphasized that the Fourth Amendment exclusionary rule keeps out evidence "otherwise competent" as "a means for making effective the protection of privacy," and thus concluded that it was "entirely proper to require of one who seeks to challenge the legality of a search as the basis for suppressing relevant evidence that he alleged, and if the allegation be disputed that he establish, that he himself was the victim of an invasion of privacy." Most lower courts follow *Jones* and place the burden on the defendant to establish standing, though a few have gone the other way.

Yet another issue usually receiving special burden-of-proof treatment is that of whether any "search" in the Fourth Amendment sense has actually occurred. Thus, in *Nardone v. United States* (1939), where the defendant contended that the case against him was based upon evidence acquired as a consequence of an illegal wiretap, the Court ruled that the burden was on him to show that such a wiretap had occurred. The Court in *Nardone* expressed concern that if the rule were otherwise the defendant would obtain full pretrial discovery of the prosecution's case, but doubtless was influenced by the fact that unless the burden were on the defendant there would likely be a flood of frivolous claims of wiretapping. The lower courts have generally placed the burden on the defendant to prove the existence of a wiretap. Some courts also apply the *Nardone* rule to other occurrence-of-search issues, such as whether or not the object seized was in plain view, though some place the burden on the prosecution in such circumstances on the ground that plain view is a justification for not having a warrant and as such ought to be established by the party claiming the exception. (The Supreme Court is divided on the question of whether the was-there-a-search burden should always fall on the defendant.) The defendant also has the burden of proof as to whether there was sufficient government involvement in seemingly private conduct and whether a seizure occurred.

Nardone is also relevant with respect to yet another special situation, namely, that in which the issue is whether certain evidence is the fruit of some prior Fourth Amendment violation. The Court said that once wiretapping was established the defendant would have an opportunity "to prove that a substantial portion of the case against him was a fruit of the poisonous tree," after which the government would have an opportunity "to convince the trial court that its proof had an independent origin." This language was cited with approval in *Alderman v. United States* (1969), holding that in such a situation the defendant "must go forward with specific evidence demonstrating taint," upon which the government "has the ultimate burden of persuasion to show that its evidence is untainted." This would mean, for example, that the government could prevail by showing an independent source for its evidence or that the evidence would inevitably have been discovered by lawful means. In the main, the lower courts have followed the *Nardone–Alderman* allocation of burdens in fruit-of-the-poisonous-tree situations.

The extent to which the states remain free to allocate the burden of proof in Fourth Amendment cases is a matter of considerable uncertainty. It appears clear the Court has held, albeit without any extended discussion of the issue, that the burden of proof *must* be on the prosecution when it is claimed the evidence was obtained in a search by consent. However, the Court has not spoken in such direct terms about the allocation of the burden in other situations. True, the Court has frequently spoken of the burden being on those who claim an exemption from the Fourth Amendment warrant requirement, but these assertions are subject to varying interpretations. They may be read as referring only to the state's burden in appellate argument of justifying any request that the Court recognize any new or expanded exception to the warrant requirement. Or, as some courts have concluded, they may be interpreted as signaling a requirement that the burden of proof be placed upon the state whenever the police have acted without a warrant. The latter interpretation seems closer to the mark. At least, it is most unlikely the Court would find it constitutionally permissible for a state to impose burdens of proof upon defendants to such a degree and extent as to foreclose "a reliable and clearcut determination" of Fourth Amendment claims, as would be the case, for example, if a defendant had to bear the burden of production and persuasion on the issue of whether the police lacked probable cause for a warrantless arrest.

(c) **Confessions.** When the issue at a suppression hearing is whether a confession obtained from the defendant was voluntary, most jurisdictions place the burdens of production and persuasion upon the prosecution. A few states, however place the burden of proving involuntariness on the defendant. The Supreme Court's decision in *Lego v. Twomey* (1972) raises serious doubts as to the constitutionality of the latter position. Though the Court was concerned primarily with the applicable standard of proof, *Lego* indicated that it was the constitutional obligation of the prosecution to meet that standard of proof. The Court declared that "the prosecution must prove at least by a preponderance of the evidence that the confession was voluntary." As for compliance with the requirements of the *Miranda* case, it is clear that as a constitutional matter the burden is on the prosecution. The Court in that case declared that "a heavy burden rests on the Government to demonstrate that the defendant knowingly and intelligently waived his privilege against self-incrimination and his right to retained or appointed counsel," explaining: "Since the State is responsible for establishing the isolated circumstances under which the interrogation takes place and has the only means of making available corroborated evidence of warnings given during incommunicado interrogation, the burden is rightly on its shoulders."

When a "fruits" issue arises with respect to a confession, either that the confession is the fruit of some earlier illegality or that some later-acquired evidence is the fruit of an illegal confession, it is customary to use the *Nardone* approach. This means that once the defendant has established a relationship between the unlawful police activity and the evidence to which objection is made, the burden is on the prosecution to show that the unlawful taint has been dissipated. So too, where the defendant gave immunized testimony, the prosecution bears the burden in any subsequent prosecution of establishing that its evidence is not tainted.

(d) **Identification.** If a lineup or other identification procedure is conducted at a time and in a manner so that it is a "critical stage" for right to counsel purposes, then resort to such procedure without counsel imposes upon the prosecution the burden of establishing that defendant intelligently waived his right to counsel. If such a showing is not made, a per se rule of exclusion applies as to testimony about that identification, while an at-trial identification by the witness who made the earlier identification is barred only if it is the fruit of the previous constitutional violation. In *United States v. Wade* (1967), the Court held as a constitutional matter that the burden must be on the government to show "that the in-court identifications were based upon observations of the suspect other than the lineup identification."

An identification procedure may also be challenged on the ground that it was so unnecessarily suggestive as to violate due process. In such circumstances many courts have assumed, typically without extensive discussion, that the defendant has the burden of proving the due process violation because he is the moving party. But the prosecution should bear the burdens of production and persuasion whenever the identification procedure was conducted out of the presence of defendant's attorney, for in such a situation the defendant may not even be aware that witnesses were seeking to identify him (e.g., where a "showup" was conducted through a one-way mirror), and even if aware, he still may be unable to know what facts existed that might make the procedure unnecessarily suggestive. Some jurisdictions have divided the burden of proof between the defense and the prosecution; the defense carries the burden of showing that the identification procedure was unnecessarily suggestive, and the burden then shifts to the prosecution to show that the identification nevertheless was sufficiently reliable to be accepted under due process.

Under the due process approach, a later, at-trial identification must be excluded if there was an earlier identification "unnecessarily suggestive" to the degree that there was "a very substantial likelihood of irreparable misidentification." In making the latter calculation, the factors to be considered are essentially the same as those utilized in determining whether an at-trial identification is the fruit of a lineup held in violation of defendant's right to counsel. This being the case, it is not surprising that some courts have concluded that here as well the burden must be on the government to show that the in-court identification is not so tainted. However, in the due process cases the question whether the at-trial identification is unreliable in light of what occurred earlier is not a "fruits" issue at all, but is part and parcel of the basic question of whether any violation of the constitution has occurred. Because this is so (and assuming that establishment of the due process violation is otherwise a burden that may be placed on the defendant), it may well be permissible to put on the defendant the burden of showing the unreliability of the at-trial identification.

§ 9.4   Standard of Proof

(a) **Generally.** Various standards of proof are used in the law. In the trial of criminal cases, as the Supreme Court held in *In re Winship* (1970), it is a requirement of due process that the defendant be proved guilty beyond a reasonable doubt. In civil cases, by contrast, the standard usually is a preponderance of evidence, commonly defined as proof that leads the jury to find that the existence of the contested fact is more probable than its nonexistence. But in certain circumstances a standard somewhere between these two is utilized; it is usually called the clear and convincing evidence standard, and means that the factfinder must be persuaded that the truth of the contention is highly probable. Depending upon the jurisdiction and the matter at issue, any one of these three standards of proof may be used in the context of a suppression hearing. In large measure, the choice of the standard is a matter of local law, but at least in some circumstances the Constitution may compel use of something beyond the preponderance standard.

(b) **Confessions.** In *Lego v. Twomey* (1972), the Court rejected the contention that the voluntariness of a confession must be established beyond a reasonable doubt. The Court first concluded that *Winship* was not controlling:

> Since the purpose that a voluntariness hearing is designed to serve has nothing whatever to do with improving the reliability of jury verdicts, we cannot accept the charge that judging the admissibility of a confession by a preponderance of the evidence undermines the mandate of *In re Winship*. * * * A high standard of proof is necessary, we said, to ensure against unjust convictions by giving substance to the presumption of innocence. A guilty verdict is not rendered any less reliable or

less consonant with *Winship* simply because the admissibility of a confession is determined by a less stringent standard.

Lego also rejected the contention that application of a reasonable doubt standard was necessary "to give adequate protection to those values that the exclusionary rules are designed to serve." The Court responded that it was "unconvinced that merely emphasizing the importance of the values served by exclusionary rules is itself sufficient demonstration that the Constitution also requires admissibility to be proved beyond a reasonable doubt." Taking into account the long experience with exclusion of illegally obtained confessions and physical evidence, the Court declared that "our experience over this period of time no substantial evidence has accumulated that federal rights have suffered from determining admissibility by a preponderance of the evidence." The Court could see no good reason "for moving further in this direction," "particularly * * * since the exclusionary rules are very much aimed at deterring lawless conduct by police and prosecution and it is very doubtful that escalating the prosecution's burden of proof in Fourth and Fifth Amendment suppression hearings would be sufficiently productive in this respect to outweigh the public interest in placing probative evidence before juries for the purpose of arriving at truthful decisions about guilt or innocence." Though the Supreme Court in *Lego* concluded that due process was satisfied by application of the preponderance standard and was not even persuaded "to impose the stricter standard of proof as an exercise of supervisory power" over federal courts, note was taken that the states were always "free, pursuant to their own law, to adopt a higher standard." Some states have adopted the reasonable doubt test, but a substantial majority now follow the preponderance standard.

As for confessions challenged on *Miranda* grounds, the Supreme Court in that case declared that "a heavy burden rests on the Government to demonstrate that the defendant knowingly and intelligently waived his privilege against self-incrimination and his right to retained or appointed counsel." But in *Colorado v. Connelly* (1987), the Court reaffirmed *Lego* and applied it in this context as well: "If, as we held in *Lego v. Twomey*, the voluntariness of a confession need be established only by a preponderance of the evidence, then a waiver of the auxiliary protections established in *Miranda* should require no higher burden of proof." Although the federal courts and many states utilize the preponderance standard, other states continue to apply, as a matter of state law, either the reasonable doubt or the clear and convincing standard.

(c) Search and Seizure. That part of *Lego* rejecting the claim that *Winship* governs at the suppression stage of a criminal case is equally applicable or perhaps even more applicable to Fourth

Amendment suppression hearings. And the other branch of *Lego,* focusing upon the purpose of exclusionary rules, expressly encompasses Fourth Amendment suppression cases as well. Thus it is as a general matter constitutional to conclude, as the Supreme Court later put it in *United States v. Matlock* (1974), that "the controlling burden of proof at suppression hearings should impose no greater burden than proof by a preponderance of the evidence." Again, states are free to impose a higher standard, but state courts have generally held that the preponderance standard applies at a hearing where a search or seizure is challenged. Significantly, this position has been taken even in jurisdictions that apply a reasonable doubt standard when the voluntariness of a confession is at issue. This can be explained by the fact that an involuntary confession may be unreliable while illegally seized evidence is always reliable, and by the added fact that the police have a greater capacity to keep records and otherwise to prepare to meet a higher standard of proof in establishing the events surrounding a custodial interrogation as opposed to a typical warrantless search.

Some authority is to be found seeming to require more than a preponderance of evidence under certain circumstances. In particular, at least some courts have found the higher clear and convincing evidence standard appropriate when the prosecution's claim is that the search was consented to or that the evidence was obtained after a voluntary abandonment of it by the defendant, or that the illegally obtained evidence would inevitably have been lawfully discovered. The policy judgment underlying these cases—that a higher standard is called for in situations where it would be particularly easy for the police to manipulate events or fabricate an interpretation of events that could not be effectively challenged by the defendant—does not conflict with the reasons given above as to why the preponderance standard should ordinarily suffice.

This is not to suggest that the states are constitutionally required to use this higher standard in those circumstances. True, the Supreme Court instructed in *Schneckloth v. Bustamonte* (1973) that "[t]o approach [consent] searches without the most careful scrutiny would sanction the possibility of official coercion." But *Schneckloth* also teaches that the test to be applied in determining the validity of a consent is "voluntariness," the meaning of which "has been developed in those cases in which the Court has had to determine the 'voluntariness' of a defendant's confession." Because the Court in *Lego* was not prepared to require more than the preponderance standard where the question to be resolved was the voluntariness of a confession, there is no reason to believe that a higher standard will be imposed when the question is the voluntariness of a consent to a search.

(d) Identification. In *United States v. Wade* (1967), establishing a right to counsel at certain pretrial identification proceedings, the Court expressly stated that the burden was on the government "to establish by clear and convincing evidence that the in-court identifications were based upon observations of the suspect other than the lineup identification." It is thus clear that the states are constitutionally compelled to utilize a standard at least this demanding. Some states have carried this concept over to in-court identifications allegedly tainted by an out-of-court identification procedure that violated due process. Once the court concludes that the initial, out-of-court identification procedure violated due process, the state assumes the burden of establishing by clear and convincing evidence the independent reliability of the in-court identification. As to the due process violation in the original identification procedure, here the burden is usually placed on the defendant (at least in part), and the defendant's burden typically is limited to a preponderance of the evidence standard.

§ 9.5   The Suppression Hearing

(a) The Trier of Fact. Prior to the Supreme Court's decision in *Jackson v. Denno* (1964), at least three different factfinding allocations were used in determining whether a confession was voluntary. In states following the "orthodox rule," voluntariness was determined solely and finally by the judge. If the judge found the confession voluntary, it was admissible without any separate determination by the jury. Evidence relating to police methods in obtaining the confession might well be admitted to assist the jury in its assessment of the credibility of the confession, but the jury was not called upon to consider the voluntariness of the confession. By comparison, under the "Massachusetts rule" a determination that a confession was voluntary had to be made twice. Once again the trial court initially ruled on the admissibility of the confession, and if the judge concluded the confession was involuntary his ruling excluding it was final. But if the judge found the confession voluntary, it was then admitted at trial subject to the jury's independent determination of voluntariness. The jury received evidence of the circumstances surrounding the confession, was charged as to the voluntariness standard, and was instructed that it could not consider the confession unless it first found it to be voluntary. Under the third alternative, the so-called "New York rule," the determination of voluntariness was left primarily to the jury. The judge would make an initial determination as to whether reasonable persons could differ on the issue of voluntariness, as where testimony was in conflict or different inferences could be drawn from undisputed facts. Unless there were "no circumstances" under which the confession could be voluntary, the voluntariness issue was passed along to the jury. The jury was instructed on the voluntariness standard and told to consider the confession only if it found it to be voluntary.

In the *Jackson* case, the Court held the New York procedure unconstitutional. The crux of the majority's reasoning in *Jackson*, as later summarized in *Lego v. Twomey* (1972), was

> that the New York procedure was constitutionally defective because at no point along the way did a criminal defendant receive a clear-cut determination that the confession used against him was in fact voluntary. The trial judge was not entitled to exclude a confession merely because he himself would have found it involuntary, and, while we recognized that the jury was empowered to perform that function, we doubted it could do so reliably. Precisely because confessions of guilt, whether coerced or freely given, may be truthful and potent evidence, we did not believe a jury could be called upon to ignore the probative value of a truthful but coerced confession; it was also likely, we thought, that in judging voluntariness itself the jury would be influenced by the reliability of a confession it considered an accurate account of the facts.

As also noted in *Lego,* the Court in *Jackson* "cast no doubt upon the orthodox and Massachusetts procedures." As for the latter, the *Jackson* majority found it to be significantly different from the New York procedure because the judge "himself resolves evidentiary conflicts and gives his own answer to the coercion issue," so that the jury only considers those confessions the judge believes to be voluntary. The dozen or so states that had theretofore used the New York procedure were thus free to adopt either of the others. The orthodox rule is now followed in the federal courts and in most states, while a substantial minority use the Massachusetts rule. The better view, however, is that the latter rule is inappropriate when the confession has been challenged on *Miranda* grounds, as then the determination that must be made is more complex than a question of voluntariness. But even where the orthodox rule obtains, the defendant must be allowed to put before the jury testimony about the environment in which the police secured his confession so that he may thereby put its credibility into issue. Denial of that opportunity infringes upon the constitutional right to "a meaningful opportunity to present a complete defense," derived from the Fourteenth Amendment due process clause and the Sixth Amendment confrontation and compulsory process clauses.

Only the orthodox rule is generally utilized outside the confession cases. The legality of a search is a matter of law to be determined by the court and not the jury, and this is so even when resolution of the matter depends upon a determination of the credibility of various witnesses and even when the motion was properly made during the course of the trial. Likewise, the admissibility of testimony claimed to be the fruit of unconstitutional identification procedures is a matter to be decided by the court; thereafter, the jury will determine the credibility of the identification by considering the conditions under which the observation was made, the physical ability of the witness to observe the defendant, and any possible problems that could distort the witness' observation powers and judgment.

(b) **Presence of Jury.** Ordinarily, if the motion to suppress is made before trial, the admissibility issue will be decided before the jury is selected. But if defendant's objection is made initially at trial or the court has delayed a hearing on a pretrial motion to avoid inconvenience to witnesses, it would be possible for the hearing to be conducted in the presence of the jury. Courts have rather consistently ruled this should not be done as to search and seizure claims, reasoning that if suppression was ordered an admonition to the jury to disregard the evidence would hardly suffice. Such reasoning would seem to extend to other suppression hearings as well, and explains why the prevailing practice squares with the Supreme Court's teaching that the most prudent course of action is to hold hearings on the admissibility of confessions and eyewitness identifications out of the presence of the jury. In some jurisdictions, however, it is at least sometimes the practice to hold such hearings while the jury is present, apparently for the reason that this will avoid the necessity of "a replay" of the same testimony later so that the jury can determine the weight to be given the evidence if it is admitted by the judge.

The Supreme Court, dealing only with instances in which the suppression hearing before a jury did *not* result in exclusion of evidence, has declined to hold that there is a per se rule requiring all such hearings be held outside the jury's presence. In *Pinto v. Pierce* (1967), concerning a hearing on whether a confession should be suppressed as involuntary, the Court ruled the trial judge had not acted contrary to *Jackson v. Denno* (1964) in holding the hearing in the jury's presence. But the Court placed considerable emphasis upon the fact that defendant through his counsel consented to that procedure. More recently, in *Watkins v. Sowders* (1981), the Court held there was no per se rule requiring all hearings into the constitutionality of witness identification procedures to be held outside the presence of the jury. Over a vigorous dissent, the majority reasoned that the notion a jury would not follow instructions to disregard certain evidence, perhaps acceptable in confession cases where a very reliable but coerced confession would be suppressed, had no application in the instant case because if identification evidence were suppressed it would be because of its unreliability. (Such reasoning suggests that in eyewitness identification cases the Court would reach the same result if, as was not the case in *Watkins,* the judge had suppressed the evidence.) As for the claim that the presence of the jury deterred defense counsel from vigorously and fully cross-examining the witnesses, the majority in *Watkins* found no specific instances in which counsel were so deterred and opined that defense counsel in this context runs only the usual risks in cross-examining an adverse witness.

(c) Testimony by Defendant. Often it will be necessary for the defendant to be a witness at a suppression hearing. The defendant may testify in a suppression hearing without waiving his right to decline to take the stand in his own defense at trial or any other rights stemming from his choice not to testify. If he testifies, he may be subjected to cross-examination, but he does not, by testifying upon a preliminary matter, subject himself to cross-examination as to other issues in the case. Nonetheless, the cross-examination may enable the prosecutor to elicit incriminating information beyond that offered on direct examination, and this might be helpful to the prosecution in developing its case or deciding its trial strategy.

In *Simmons v. United States* (1968), the Court held that testimony given at the hearing by a defendant in order to establish his standing to object to illegally seized evidence may not be used against him at his trial on the question of guilt or innocence. The logic of *Simmons,* namely, that a defendant should not be "obliged either to give up what he believed, with advice of counsel, to be a valid Fourth Amendment claim or, in legal effect, to waive his Fifth Amendment privilege against self-incrimination," indicates that the same protection must be given to any testimony by the defendant at the suppression hearing. Some courts have read *Simmons* with *Harris v. New York* (1971), holding that a confession obtained in violation of *Miranda* may be introduced at trial for impeachment purposes, so as to permit use of defendant's suppression hearing testimony for impeachment purposes at trial. It may be objected that this conclusion is incorrect in light of *New Jersey v. Portash* (1979), holding that testimony given after a grant of use immunity cannot be admitted even for impeachment purposes because such testimony "is the essence of coerced testimony" in that it was compelled under threat of contempt. So the argument goes, testimony by the defendant at a suppression hearing is likewise "compelled" in light of the Hobson's choice described in *Simmons.* But more recently in *United States v. Salvucci* (1980), a majority of the Supreme Court, while claiming the issue remained open, asserted that "the protective shield of *Simmons* is not to be converted into a license for false representations."

(d) **Evidentiary Rules.** As noted in *United States v. Matlock* (1974), the "rules of evidence normally applicable in criminal trials do not operate with full force at a hearing before the judge to determine the admissibility of evidence." Though it has long been clear that hearsay could be received on the issue of probable cause to search, *Matlock* held that hearsay statements could also be admitted on other issues as well. There, in an effort to show the search was consented to by defendant's roommate, the prosecution sought to put in evidence the roommate's out-of-court statements regarding her joint occupancy of the premises and representation that she was defendant's wife. The Supreme Court held that the trial judge erred in excluding those statements as hearsay, noting that a provision in the proposed (and since adopted) federal evidence rules specifically provided that on a preliminary question, such as the "admissibility of evidence," the trial court "is not bound by the rules of evidence except those with respect to privileges." The Court added that there was "much to be said for the proposition that in proceedings where the judge himself is considering the admissibility of evidence, the exclusionary rules [such as the hearsay prohibition] should not be applicable, and the judge should receive the evidence and give it such weight as his judgment and experience counsel." Even if a trial court could not go that far, the Court declared, it certainly should not exclude hearsay statements where, as here, "the court was quite satisfied that the statement had in fact been made" and "there is nothing in the record to raise serious doubts about the truthfulness of the statements themselves."

(e) **Right of Confrontation.** As indicated in *McCray v. Illinois* (1967), defendant's right of cross-examination at the suppression hearing may be substantially narrower than that available at trial. *McCray* held that neither due process nor the confrontation clause was violated when the suppression hearing judge refused to allow defense counsel to force the arresting officer, on cross-examination, to reveal the name and address of the informant alleged to have provided probable cause for defendant's arrest. Lower courts similarly have held that the combination of the limited function of the suppression hearing and valid security interests justify receiving certain prosecution evidence in camera (i.e., with the defendant excluded). Courts have stressed, however, that limitations on the opportunity for confrontation must be carefully circumscribed to fit the state's justification for restricted disclosure. And while the court may restrict cross-examination by defense counsel to avoid manipulation of the suppression hearing for discovery purposes, it may not cut off questioning that clearly is relevant to the defense challenge.

(f) Right of Compulsory Process. The constitutional right of compulsory process is essentially a trial right; when the defendant's guilt or innocence is at issue, due process requires that the accused be able to present witnesses in his own defense to the jury so it may decide where the truth lies. But this right, albeit a fundamental one, is not absolute, and thus it may yield to policy considerations such as the interest in the orderly conduct of trials. Whatever lesser right of compulsory process exists at suppression hearings is likewise not absolute, and thus may be outweighed by various policy concerns. Thus, where there is other evidence of probable cause to arrest, the defendant may not call the undercover officer to testify about defendant's drug sale in his presence when such testimony might compromise the undercover officer's safety or the integrity of pending investigations. And similarly, at a suppression hearing which has not otherwise produced evidence raising substantial issues as to the credibility of the lineup, the interest in protecting complainants against harassment has been deemed sufficient to bar the defendant from calling the complainant to inquire about any suggestive actions by the police.

Of course, the right to compulsory process is contingent upon a defense right to present evidence, and a court may conclude under some circumstances that the receipt of defense evidence is not necessary. That is most likely to occur where the court concludes that even if one accepts the facts alleged in the defense motion and accompanying affidavits, the facts alleged provide no basis for relief. At times, a court also will hold that an evidentiary hearing is not required in light of counter-affidavits filed by the prosecution. This is acceptable where the court concludes that there is no significant dispute between the parties as to the relevant facts, but not where its decision rests on a resolution of disputed fact by reference to the conflicting affidavits.

§ 9.6   The Ruling and Its Effect

(a) Findings. In some jurisdictions the judge ruling on a motion to suppress is required to make specific findings of fact and law, while elsewhere formal findings are not required and it will suffice that a record is made supporting the ruling. In *Sims v. Georgia* (1967), the Supreme Court noted that the due process requirements of *Jackson v. Denno* (1964) did not mandate that the judge "make formal findings of fact or write an opinion," though "his conclusion that the confession is voluntary must appear from the record with unmistakable clarity." Appellate courts, however, have urged trial judges to make findings because in their absence appellate review is often more difficult. Indeed, it has been said that findings are all but essential in multi-issue cases where the basis of the trial judge's decision would otherwise be in doubt.

If a defendant puts forward several alternative grounds for suppression, may a judge ruling in his favor on one of them not inquire into the others? There are competing considerations. On the one hand, it would seem superfluous to inquire into the other grounds after a basis for suppression has already been found; on the other, failure to consider the remaining grounds is at odds with the goal of pretrial determination of all such issues. The judge is thus left with considerable discretion in deciding whether judicial economy would best be served by conducting a full hearing on all the grounds urged or by bifurcating the issues. The desirable course of action will depend on a variety of factors, including the number of grounds for the motion to suppress, the number of witnesses expected to be called in support of each ground, and the extent to which the evidence on the first ground pertains to the other grounds.

(b) Recommendations. It is sometimes provided by law that a motion to suppress may be heard by a lesser judicial officer than the judge who has the ultimate responsibility for deciding the matter. Such is the case in the federal system, and in *United States v. Raddatz* (1980) the Supreme Court had occasion to assess the respective responsibilities of the hearing magistrate and the district judge. Prior to trial, Raddatz moved to suppress his incriminating statements, and the judge referred the matter to a magistrate for an evidentiary hearing. This was done pursuant to the Federal Magistrates Act, which authorizes a district court to refer such a motion to a magistrate and thereafter to decide the motion based on the record developed before the magistrate, including the magistrate's proposed findings of fact and recommendations, and which also provides that the judge shall make a "de novo determination" of those portions of the magistrate's report, findings or recommendations to which objection is made, and that the judge may accept, reject or modify, in whole or in part, the magistrate's findings or recommendations and that alternatively the judge may receive further evidence or recommit the matter to the magistrate with instructions. Based on his view of the credibility of the testimony, the magistrate found the statements voluntary and thus recommended the motion be denied. The district court accepted that recommendation over defendant's objection, but the court of appeals reversed on the ground Raddatz had been deprived of due process by the district court's failure personally to hear the controverted testimony.

After finding that the statute, by calling for a "de novo determination" rather than a de novo hearing, did not require the district court to rehear the testimony, the Court concluded "that the statute strikes the proper balance between the demands of due process and the constraints of Art. III." As for the Article III question, the *Raddatz* Court concluded that because "the entire process takes place under the district court's total control and jurisdiction," the "delegation does not violate Art. III so long as the ultimate decision is made by the district court." On the due process issue, the Court, after noting that "the guarantees of due process call for a 'hearing appropriate to the nature of the case,' " concluded that "the nature of the issues presented and the interests implicated in a motion to suppress evidence" do not "require that the district court judge must actually hear the challenged testimony." This is because the interests underlying such a hearing "do not coincide with the criminal law objective of determining guilt or innocence." But there are limits on what the district judge may do with respect to the magistrate's findings and recommendations. It would be a rare case in which a district judge could resolve credibility choices contrary to the recommendations of the magistrate without himself having had an opportunity to see and hear the witnesses testify. And even if matters of credibility are not central to decision of the suppression motion, the district judge may not reject the recommendation of the magistrate without *at least* consulting the transcript of the hearing before the magistrate.

(c) Reconsideration at Trial. Except in those jurisdictions that actually require renewal of a suppression motion at trial, reconsideration at trial of a motion previously denied is a disfavored procedure. Such reconsideration, it is said, defeats the benefits of pretrial motion practice and unfairly imposes upon the prosecution the obligation of proving legality twice. Thus, the trial judge will usually rely upon the prior ruling as the law of the case. However, the law of the case doctrine operates only as a discretionary rule of practice, for to view the pretrial ruling as binding would be to proscribe correction of its own error by the trial court.

A defendant is not likely to obtain reconsideration unless at trial new or additional evidence is produced bearing on the issue or substantially affecting the credibility of the evidence adduced at the pretrial hearing of the motion. The state cases in the main treat such a situation as one in which the court *may* reconsider, while federal cases commonly speak of a *duty* to reconsider where matters appearing at trial cast reasonable doubt on the pretrial ruling. But in light of the fact that a constitutional objection is deemed forfeited absent a showing of good cause for not complying with a pretrial motion rule, it would seem that a defendant is entitled to a redetermination of his claim at trial only if new evidence comes to light that was unavailable at the time of the original hearing on the motion through no fault of the movant.

There is some authority that if defendant's pretrial suppression motion was granted, the prosecution may obtain a reconsideration of that ruling at trial under essentially the same circumstances in which reconsideration would be permitted in the defendant's behalf: where there is new relevant evidence available and good cause is shown as to why that evidence was not introduced at the pretrial hearing. But, while the doctrines of res judicata and collateral estoppel do not bar such reconsideration, the prosecution will not often be able to show cause for reconsideration because it is more able than the defendant to insure a full and fair resolution of any issue at a pretrial proceeding. In jurisdictions where the prosecutor may take an interlocutory appeal from the pretrial granting of a suppression motion, reconsideration at trial may well be barred as to matters that could have been raised by appeal. But there are differences between appellate review and reappraisal of a pretrial ruling at trial, and thus it cannot be said that the availability of interlocutory appeal bars any reconsideration.

(d) Effect of Ruling in Other Cases. If defendant's motion to suppress was granted but the prosecution later seeks to have the same evidence admitted against the defendant at a trial on a different charge, is relitigation of the admissibility issue barred? As a constitutional matter, an argument that the collateral estoppel doctrine of the double jeopardy clause bars relitigation cannot prevail if the charges were dropped in the first case, as then defendant was never placed in jeopardy. But it has been argued that in such circumstances the defendant might prevail because of collateral estoppel protections flowing from the due process clause. Whether the collateral estoppel doctrine has any application here remains in doubt, but if it does apply surely it is necessary that in the first case the state has had an opportunity for a full hearing on suppression and at least one appeal as of right.

Even if the Constitution, either as a general matter or in particular circumstances, does not require that the prosecution be bound by the granting of a suppression motion in another case, it is possible that the law of the jurisdiction will have this effect. This may occur, for example, where a statute declares that if a suppression motion is granted the evidence shall not be admissible "at any trial." In the absence of such law, the judge in the second case might nonetheless not reconsider the matter if he is convinced it was fully explored in the earlier case.

Assume now the reverse situation in which the motion was denied in an earlier case. Though the constitutional doctrine of collateral estoppel regarding a prior verdict in a criminal case does not run both ways, that does not prevent a state from adopting the position that collateral estoppel principles preclude a defendant from obtaining suppression of evidence he unsuccessfully tried to suppress in an earlier case. But even when the earlier denial of the defendants suppression motion does not have such preclusive effect, the judge in the second case may nonetheless accept the admissibility ruling in the earlier case, absent a showing of new evidence or some other basis for reconsideration, provided that the defendant was convicted at the first trial and thus had an opportunity to obtain appellate review of the ruling.

For a ruling on a motion to suppress in a prior case to have either conclusive or presumptive effect in a later case, there must be an identity of parties. Thus, notwithstanding prior suppression by a state court, a federal court may make an independent determination as to admissibility. And if the same evidence is offered in the separate trials of two defendants in the same jurisdiction, the ruling in the first of these cases is not binding in the second.

Chapter 10

THE RIGHT TO COUNSEL

Table of Sections

The constitutional right to counsel has been described as the "most pervasive" of all criminal process rights, in part because it extends to many different stages of the process, but also because it provides the vehicle through which all other criminal process rights are presented in a judicial setting. We have discussed in previous chapters the constitutional right to counsel as it bears directly on a particular investigative practice (e.g., custodial interrogation). This chapter considers basic elements of the right to counsel, as they relate to the availability and performance of counsel, and thereby impact the presentation of legal challenges to investigative practices at the various judicial proceedings that are a part of the criminal justice process. An understanding of these basic elements also helps to place in their doctrinal context the various aspects of the right to counsel during the investigative process that have been discussed in previous chapters.

§ 10.1 Diverse Constitutional Groundings

Although courts commonly speak of a single constitutional right to counsel. There are in fact several different groundings for a constitutional right to counsel, and in that sense, several different constitutional rights to counsel. These rights apply at different stages of the criminal justice process. But once a particular grounding establishes a constitutional right to counsel, the requirements flowing from the right (e.g., effective assistance by counsel) commonly are the same without regard to the particular grounding.

(a) **Sixth Amendment Rights.** The Sixth Amendment provides that "in all criminal prosecutions, the accused shall enjoy the right * * * to have the assistance of counsel for his defense." That this provision guaranteed a right to representation by privately retained counsel was obvious from the outset; that it also included an obligation of the state to provide at public expense defense counsel for the indigent defendant (i.e., the defendant financially unable to retain a lawyer) was far less certain. Unlike the right to retained counsel, a right to appointed counsel lacked any substantial historical grounding. Nonetheless, the Court eventually came to interpret the Sixth Amendment as granting a right to representation by counsel to all defendants, with the state required to provide counsel where the defendant was indigent. Moreover, that Supreme Court precedent also indicates that the proceedings encompassed by the Sixth Amendment right to counsel are precisely the same whether the issue is allowing representation by retained counsel or requiring the state to appoint counsel for the indigent.

The first major Supreme Court discussion of the constitutional right to counsel came in *Powell v. Ala.* (1932), which considered the rights of defendants both to utilize retained counsel and to be provided with court appointed counsel. *Powell* was not itself a Sixth Amendment case. It involved a state prosecution and was decided under the then prevailing "fundamental fairness" interpretation of Fourteenth Amendment due process (see § 1.3(b)). Nonetheless, it has had continuing significance through subsequent interpretations of the Sixth Amendment right to counsel. When the Court later discarded the fundamental fairness interpretation in favor of a selective incorporation analysis that made the Sixth Amendment directly applicable to the states (through the Fourteenth Amendment), its interpretation of the Sixth Amendment rested heavily upon *Powell*'s analysis of the need for counsel.

The Supreme Court had before it in *Powell* a prosecution that was to become a cause célébre in the fight against racial injustice. Nine black youths had been charged with the rape of two white girls in the vicinity of Scottsboro, Alabama. Eight of the youths had been convicted, with the jury imposing the death sentence. On appeal, the defendants raised two claims relating to the right to counsel. First, they claimed that they had a constitutional right to retain counsel to represent them at trial and that the trial court had violated this right by failing to give them sufficient opportunity to seek retained counsel. Second, they claimed that, assuming arguendo that they would have been unable to employ counsel even if they had been given that opportunity, the trial court would then have had an obligation to make an effective appointment of counsel. The trial judge at their arraignment had announced that he was appointing "all of the members of the bar" to represent them, but defendants argued that this had been an empty gesture, made in such a haphazard way that the local bar member who eventually stepped forward to represent them at trial (in consultation with an outside attorney) was largely unprepared. The Supreme Court sustained both of defendants' claims, finding that each separately established a denial of due process.

The *Powell* opinion initially considered the trial court's failure to give defendants an adequate opportunity to retain counsel. The opinion concluded that the due process clause of the Fourteenth Amendment guaranteed to defendants a right to be represented by retained counsel, and to implement that right, a trial court must give the defendant reasonable time and opportunity to secure counsel. The Court here relied heavily upon the historical developments that had led to the adoption of the Sixth Amendment and similarly worded state provisions. The practice in England had been to allow the complete assistance of retained counsel in misdemeanor trials, but to deny defendants the right to utilize their counsel at felony trials, except for arguments on legal questions. This limitation had not been accepted in the American colonies, where defendants were allowed the full assistance of retained counsel in felony as well as misdemeanor trials. At the time of the adoption of the Constitution, twelve of the thirteen states had rejected the English rule on felony cases, and the Sixth Amendment, not surprisingly, did the same. The *Powell* opinion concluded that the right to utilize retained counsel, as reflected in these state and federal provisions, readily fit within the concept of due process. For due process guaranteed a right to a fair hearing, and such a hearing, "[h]istorically and in practice, in our country at least, has always included the right to the aid of counsel when desired and provided by the party asserting the right."

When the *Powell* opinion turned to the defendants' second claim, asserting an indigent defendant's right to appointed counsel, it did not look to the history underlying the Sixth Amendment or to the early state provisions. This was understandable since the right of the indigent defendant to counsel provided by the state had a much narrower historical base. Where the original states provided for the appointment of counsel, they usually did so only in capital cases. Similarly, Congress, shortly before the ratification of the Sixth Amendment, had adopted a statutory provision requiring an appointment of counsel that was limited to capital crimes. Indeed, at the time of the *Powell* decision, almost half of the states apparently did not provide appointed counsel in most felony cases.

A constitutional right to appointed counsel could be derived, however, if not from historical traditions, from the due process right to a fair hearing. In concluding that the right to retained counsel was an essential element of due process, the first portion of the *Powell* opinion had stressed that the "right to be heard would be, in many cases, of little avail if it did not comprehend the right to be heard by counsel." The indigent defendant, the Court reasoned, was as much entitled to a fair hearing as the more affluent defendant who could afford to retain a lawyer. The state accordingly had a due process obligation to provide the indigent defendant with a lawyer where counsel's assistance would be necessary to achieve a fair hearing. Language in the first portion of the opinion arguably also suggested that a lawyer would almost always be needed to provide a fair hearing. Even the "intelligent and educated layman," the opinion had noted, needs the "guiding hand of counsel" to cope with the intricacies of the law. The *Powell* Court's holding on appointed counsel, however, was carefully limited to the type of situation presented in the case before the Court—"a capital case, where the defendant is unable to employ counsel, and is incapable adequately of making his own defense because of ignorance, feeble-mindedness, illiteracy, or the like."

The *Powell* reasoning suggested that there were two distinct and separately grounded constitutional rights to counsel. First, as a result of the rejection of the English common law rule, the defendant had gained a right to be represented by counsel provided at his own expense. Whether or not a lawyer was needed in the particular case did not matter; that was for the defendant to decide, and the state had to respect his decision, as only his resources were involved. Second, a constitutional right to appointed counsel arose out of the state's obligation to provide a fair hearing. That obligation carried with it an affirmative duty to provide counsel for the indigent defendant where a lawyer's assistance was needed to ensure a fair and accurate guilt-determining process. This right arguably was narrower in scope than the right to retained counsel. Since public funds were being expended, the provision of counsel could be tied to cases where it was actually needed. Thus, the *Powell* ruling on appointed counsel had been restricted to the special circumstances of that case, while its ruling on the right to use retained counsel had spoken of a general right applicable in all felony cases.

Six years after *Powell,* in *Johnson v. Zerbst* (1938), the Court drew no distinction between the right to retained counsel and the right to appointed in its interpretation of the Sixth Amendment. *Johnson* involved a federal prosecution in which two apparently indigent defendants, charged with the felony of counterfeiting, had been refused appointed counsel because theirs was not a capital case. The Court held that their trial without counsel violated the Sixth Amendment, which applies by its terms to "all criminal prosecutions." The *Johnson* opinion reasoned that the Sixth Amendment "embodies a realistic recognition of the obvious truth that the average defendant does not have the professional legal skill to protect himself" in a criminal trial. It therefore "withholds from the federal courts, in all criminal proceedings, the power and authority to deprive an accused of his life or liberty unless he has or waives the assistance of counsel." This constitutional prerequisite for a valid conviction applied to all defendants, including those unable to afford counsel.

The *Johnson* opinion did not refer to the historical developments that had been cited in *Powell*. It focused instead upon the language in *Powell* noting that the right to be heard often would be of little value without the assistance of counsel. That language was seen as supporting a reading of the Sixth Amendment that treated representation by counsel as a prescribed prerequisite for the criminal trial, no different than the elements of jury trial, notice, confrontation, and compulsory process. It was the trial court's obligation to ensure that these rights were available to defendant (although, as to the right to counsel, that did not preclude making the defendant bear the financial cost if he was able to do so). If the assistance of counsel otherwise would be unavailable because the defendant lacked funds to retain counsel, then the court had to make that assistance available by appointing counsel.

For a twenty-five year period following *Johnson,* the Supreme Court refused to extend that ruling to state cases. Although *Johnson* had held that the Sixth Amendment required appointed counsel in all cases encompassed by that Amendment, state cases were governed by the "less rigid and more fluid" requirement of the Fourteenth Amendment's due process clause. Relying upon a fundamental fairness analysis, the Court held in *Betts v. Brady* (1942) that due process required the appointment of counsel only where the special circumstances of the particular case indicated that the indigent defendant needed a lawyer to obtain a fair trial. *Powell* and other capital cases presented one illustration of such special circumstances. The need for appointed counsel could also be established by the complicated nature of the offense or possible defenses thereto, events during trial that raised difficult legal questions, and personal characteristics of the defendant, such as youthfulness or mental incapacity. The special circumstances test of *Betts v. Brady* was sharply criticized by commentators, who argued that it was virtually impossible to render a retrospective judgment that a defendant forced to proceed pro se had not been prejudiced by the lack of counsel.

In *Gideon v. Wainwright* (1963), the Court rejected the special circumstances rule of *Betts* and extended the right to appointed counsel in state cases to all indigent felony defendants. Unlike *Betts, Gideon* appeared to proceed from the premise, consistent with the selective incorporation doctrine (see § 1.3(d)), that the Fourteenth Amendment rendered the Sixth Amendment right to counsel directly applicable to the states as a fundamental right. However, rather than simply relying on *Johnson v. Zerbst's* holding under the Sixth Amendment, *Gideon* returned to *Powell's* discussion of the need for counsel. It concluded that "reason and reflection require us to recognize that in our adversary system of criminal justice, any person hauled into court, who is too poor to hire a lawyer cannot be assured a fair trial unless counsel is provided for him."

Gideon, like *Johnson v. Zerbst*, viewed the Sixth Amendment as prescribing the invariable prerequisites of a fair trial and including the assistance of counsel among those prerequisites. It follows from this premise that no Sixth Amendment distinction should exist between the affluent defendant's right to retained counsel and the indigent defendant's right to appointed counsel. Where a particular proceeding is deemed to be a stage in the "criminal prosecution" for Sixth Amendment purposes, both should have an automatic right to representation by counsel (in the case of the indigent, at state expense). On the other hand, where the proceeding is not within the span covered by the Sixth Amendment's reference to the "criminal prosecution," neither should have a Sixth Amendment right to counsel. Whether a Sixth Amendment right to counsel exists should depend on the nature of the proceeding and not on whether the claim relates to retained or appointed counsel.

This conception of the Sixth Amendment as a single right found further support in later cases determining the stages of the criminal justice process to which the Sixth Amendment applies (see § 10.2(b)) and determining when counsel performance was so deficient as not to constitute the requisite assistance of counsel (see § 10.4(a)). Its end consequence is that the state has no Sixth Amendment obligation to allow representation by retained counsel in a proceeding as to which it has no Sixth Amendment obligation to appoint counsel for the indigent. It does not necessarily follow, however, that the state has absolute freedom constitutionally to bar representation by retained counsel. As will be seen in the next subsection, due process can provide a constitutional grounding for assistance of counsel where the Sixth Amendment does not apply, and that right may preclude an unreasonable state interference with representation by retained counsel even where there is no constitutional right to appointed counsel.

(b) Due Process Rights. While *Powell v. Ala.* (1932) recognized due process rights to the assistance of appointed and retained counsel in the context of a proceeding that today would be subject to the Sixth Amendment, *Powell*'s due process analysis did not disappear with the selective incorporation of the Sixth Amendment. Rather, it had continuing significance for other proceedings not encompassed by the Sixth Amendment. In the post-incorporation ruling of *Gagnon v. Scarpelli* (1973), a due process right to appointed counsel in parole and probation revocation hearings was thought to flow logically from hearing rights previously mandated under the due process clause. Past precedent had established that the parolee or probationer was entitled to substantial procedural safeguards in a revocation hearing, including the rights to present evidence and confront opposing witnesses. *Gagnon* concluded that due process also requires the state to provide appointed counsel where, under the facts of the particular case, counsel is needed to ensure the "effectiveness of the [hearing] rights guaranteed by [due process]." The *Gagnon* Court refused to formulate "a precise and detailed set of guidelines" for determining when counsel was needed to ensure the effective operation of the hearing rights demanded by due process. It did note that counsel ordinarily should be provided where there is a significant factual dispute or the individual relies upon contentions that a layman would have difficulty presenting. At the same time, it cited other situations in which appointment of counsel ordinarily would not be necessary.

Speaking to the possibility of imposing a flat requirement of counsel in all revocation cases, the *Gagnon* Court acknowledged that such a requirement "had the appeal of simplicity." However, "it would impose direct costs and serious collateral disadvantages without regard to the need or the likelihood in a particular case for a constructive contribution by counsel." In most revocation cases, the issue presented simply did not require that expertise of a lawyer. Quite often, "the probationer or parolee has been convicted of committing another crime [which automatically establishes grounds for revocation] or has admitted the charges against him." Although he may still contend that revocation would be too harsh in light of the nature of his violation, "mitigating evidence of this kind is often not susceptible of proof or is so simple as not to require either investigation or exposition by counsel." On the other side, "the introduction of counsel" would "alter significantly the nature of the [revocation] proceeding." The state would respond by retaining its own counsel and the role of the hearing body would become "more akin to that of a judge at trial, and less attuned to the rehabilitative needs of the individual probationer." In addition, the revocation proceedings would be prolonged, and "the financial cost to the State—for appointed counsel, counsel for the State, a longer record and the possibility of judicial review—[would] not be insubstantial."

In contrast to *Gagnon*, which adopted a case-by-case approach similar to that of *Betts* (§ 10.1(a)), the Court adopted a flat "in-or-out" approach in assessing due process claims to other proceedings that occur after the criminal prosecution is ended (and the Sixth Amendment therefore ceases to apply). In *Ross v. Moffitt* (1974), the Court rejected the contention that due process required appointment of counsel to assist indigent defendants in preparing their applications for second-tier, discretionary appellate review. *Pa. v. Finley* (1987) and *Murray v. Giarratano* (1989) similarly held that due process did not require appointment of counsel for collateral challenges to a conviction (e.g., habeas corpus). *Evitts v. Lucey* (1985), on the other hand, held that due process establishes a right to retained and appointed counsel on a first appeal granted by state law as a matter of right.

Ross, the first of these due process rulings, stressed the difference position of the defendant who seeks to challenge a conviction in a postconviction proceeding, as opposed to the defendant who seeks to avoid a conviction at trial. The defendant at trial has need for an attorney "as a shield to protect him against being 'haled into court' by the State and stripped of his presumption of innocence." On appeal, in contrast, the attorney is to be utilized "as a sword to upset [a] prior determination of guilt." The defendant here is "seeking not to fend off the efforts of the State's prosecutor but rather to overturn a finding of guilt made by a judge or jury below." As one of the factors to be considered under a due process analysis is the "risk of an erroneous deprivation" of the protected liberty interest without the claimed procedural safeguard, a defendant stands in a lesser position when he claims a right to appointed counsel following a conviction.

Despite this "lesser position" of a person challenging a conviction, *Evitts* recognized a due process to counsel for a first appeal as a matter of right. Moreover, it did so as flat rule, rather than looking to the circumstances of the case, as in *Gagnon*. This was so even though, in contrast to *Gagnon*, the Court was not building upon other due process prerequisites for the proceeding involved. Indeed, the Court had held that the Constitution imposes no obligation upon a state to grant appeals of right in criminal cases— a factor noted by *Ross* in explaining why the defendant on appeal occupies a lesser position than the defendant at trial (who, of course, has a constitutional right to a fair trial).

At issue in *Evitts* was a due process right to representation by a retained counsel (such a right being a prerequisite for defendant's claim of ineffective assistance by his retained appellate counsel, see § 10.4(a)). Prior to *Evitts*, in *Douglas v. Cal.* (1963), the Court had recognized an equal protection right of an indigent defendant to the assistance of appointed counsel on a first appeal granted by state law as a matter of right. *Evitts* held the *Douglas* ruling also had a constitutional grounding in due process and that grounding necessarily established as well a right to be represented by retained counsel. *Douglas* had reasoned that, while the state had no constitutional obligation to establish an appellate process, once it had established such appellate review as " 'an integral part of [its] system for finally adjudicating the guilt or innocence of a defendant,' " it could not, first structure the appeal so that it was basically a "meaningless ritual" for a defendant lacking the assistance of counsel, and then fail to include a right to utilize counsel's assistance. Drawing an analogy to *Gideon,* the Court noted that under the state's appellate procedure, as under its trial procedure, "the services of a lawyer will for virtually every layman be necessary" to effectively present his case. Here too, the defendant faced an "adversarial system of justice" in which "lawyers are 'necessities,' not luxuries." Accordingly, due process, as to the first appeal of right, mandated a right to counsel parallel to the trial-level right established in *Gideon* under the Sixth Amendment. The *Gideon* argument, as *Evitts* noted, lent itself to a due process grounding, as it looked to the fairness of the adjudication process.

The imposition of a flat requirement in *Evitts* can be explained on several grounds. The Court indicated that the appellate process was so complicated that here a lawyer always was needed to ensure the appeal was not simply a "meaningless ritual." In this respect the setting was similar to the trial setting presented in *Gideon* where the Court also had rejected applying a case-by-case analysis to determine when counsel was needed. Also, the costs of a flat rule here, in contrast to *Gagnon,* were insubstantial. With *Douglas* already requiring appointed counsel in all first appeals as a matter of right, recognizing a due process right to retained counsel imposed no additional financial burden on the state. As for administrative burdens, recognizing a constitutional right to utilize retained counsel certainly did not alter the character of the proceeding except to allow incompetency challenges by defendants, and as the *Evitts* Court noted, both state courts and lower federal courts had long recognized and adjudicated such claims without "dire consequences."

In contrast to *Douglas* and *Evitts*, *Ross* found that, where the lesser position of the person challenging a conviction was combined with the quite different function of a second appeal that was discretionary, adjudication fairness did not mandate the assistance of appointed counsel. The Court stressed that the defendants in this setting have already received a full appellate review, assisted by counsel, on their first appeal as of right. Accordingly, further assistance of counsel is not necessary to provide "meaningful access" to the higher appellate courts. In considering a defendant's petition for review, those higher courts will have before them the trial transcript, the intermediate court brief prepared by counsel, and in most instances, the opinion of the state's intermediate appellate court. Those materials, supplemented by any personal statement of the defendant, provide an "adequate basis" for determining whether to grant review. This is especially so because of the discretionary nature of the second-tier appellate review. The traditional standard utilized in determining whether to grant such discretionary review is whether the appeal presents issues worthy of high court consideration because of their general legal significance, rather than whether there has been a "correct adjudication of guilt" in the individual case.

In *Pa. v. Finley* (1987), the majority characterized the issue before it as whether due process required the state to appoint counsel to assist the respondent in preparing a collateral attack upon her conviction under a state postconviction relief procedure. The state there had appointed counsel, but counsel had then been allowed to withdraw after concluding that the collateral attack lacked arguable merit. The Court majority reasoned that the withdrawal procedure would present a constitutional issue only if respondent had an underlying constitutional right to the appointment of counsel. Turning to that question, the Court did not focus on the possible need for counsel. Arguably, a stronger case could be made here than in *Ross,* as collateral challenges in state proceedings commonly present issues that were not raised at trial or on appeal. The *Finley* Court stressed, instead, the place of the collateral attack within the totality of the proceedings for determining guilt. The majority noted that "postconviction relief is even further removed from the criminal trial than is discretionary direct review," is not "part of the criminal proceedings itself," and "normally occurs only after the defendant has failed to secure relief through direct review of his conviction." In such a setting, the Court concluded, "the fundamental fairness mandated by the Due Process Clause does not require that the State supply a lawyer as well."

In *Murray v. Giarratano* (1989), a sharply divided Court refused to create an exception to *Pa. v. Finley* based on the special character of the particular postconviction proceeding in that case.

At issue in *Murray* was the claim of Virginia's death row inmates that they were entitled to appointed counsel to assist them in preparing collateral attack challenges to their convictions and sentences. In upholding that claim, the Fourth Circuit had viewed the inmates' situation as presenting special circumstances that distinguished *Finley*. First, here, unlike *Finley,* the inmates had been sentenced to the death penalty. Second, the district court here had made special factual findings as to the inmates' need for counsel. That court had concluded "that death row inmates had a limited amount of time to prepare their petitions, that their cases were unusually complex, and that the shadow of impending execution would interfere with their ability to do legal work." While the state did assign "unit attorneys" to each penal institution, the district court had also found that those attorneys could not adequately assist the death row inmates because their role was limited to that of "legal advisor" rather than counsel for the inmate. Those district court findings were seen as providing a case-specific showing of the essentiality of counsel that had not been present in *Finley*.

Speaking for four justices, Chief Justice Rehnquist authored a plurality opinion that flatly rejected both of the distinctions cited by the lower court. The plurality emphasized the *Finley* precedent and the fact that the Court's post-*Gideon* rulings on the right to counsel "ha[d] been categorical holdings as to what the Constitution requires with respect to a particular stage of a criminal proceeding in general." This "tack" had been adopted in light of "the Court's dissatisfaction with the case-by-case approach in *Betts v. Brady* that led to the adoption of the categorical ruling * * * in *Gideon.*" There was nothing in the nature of the collateral proceeding that justified departure from the continued use of categorical holdings. In response, Justice Stevens' dissenting opinion, also speaking for four justices, argued that "particular circumstances" necessarily shape the scope of the due process right to counsel. Here the circumstances cited by the lower court, as well as additional circumstances, clearly distinguished *Finley*.

With eight justices evenly divided as to the significance of the special circumstances presented by the Virginia inmates, the deciding vote in *Murray* was cast by Justice Kennedy. His very brief opinion appeared to give some weight to special circumstances, although Justice O'Connor found no inconsistency in the Kennedy and Rehnquist opinions and joined both. Justice Kennedy initially accepted Justice Stevens' analysis insofar as it established (1) that "collateral proceedings are a central part of the review process for prisoners condemned to death" and (2) that the "complexity of our jurisprudence in this area * * * makes it unlikely that capital defendants will be able to file successful petitions for collateral relief without the assistance of persons learned in the law." He noted, however, that the necessary assistance can be provided in "various ways" and there was no showing that Virginia's approach had been unsatisfactory. For "no prisoner on death row in Virginia ha[d] been unable to obtain counsel to represent him in postconviction proceedings, and Virginia's prison system is staffed with institutional lawyers to assist in preparing petitions for postconviction relief." Accordingly, Justice Kennedy concurred in the reversal of the lower court ruling based "on the facts and record of this case."

The division of the Court in *Murray* leaves open the extent to which the Court majority will give weight to the special elements of a procedural setting, as it relates to a particular type of litigant, in assessing a due process claim to appointed counsel. Arguably, the division among the justices was limited to the capital case. There was no suggestion that special circumstances could play a role on a discretionary appeal (*Ross*) or a collateral proceeding (*Finley*) in a non-capital case. Yet, there remains *Gagnon v. Scarpelli,* a case utilizing a special-circumstances approach outside of the capital offense context, which was not discussed in any of the *Murray* opinions. Certainly the thrust of the Court's rulings is not so firmly settled as to impose a significant barrier to the adoption in future cases, especially by a Court of changed composition, of an approach that more strongly favors either categorical rulings (e.g., *Evitts, Finley,* and *Ross*) or special-circumstances rulings (e.g., *Gagnon*).

The Court's rulings also leave open the possibility of a due process right to counsel in other proceedings that are not within the coverage of the Sixth Amendment, yet may affect the loss of liberty flowing from a criminal conviction. The Court has not, for example, directly considered whether due process requires appointed counsel where a discretionary appeal is the only appeal available to the defendant (unlike *Ross,* where the discretionary appeal followed a first appeal granted as a matter of right). So too, in *Coleman v. Thompson* (1991), the Court specifically left open the question of whether there exists an exception to *Finley* where state law provides that a claim of ineffective assistance of trial counsel cannot be raised on appeal but must be presented in a state collateral proceeding.

Still another issue left in limbo is whether the due process right to utilize retained counsel may have a broader scope than the due process right to appointed counsel. Pre-*Gideon* rulings had indicated that the right to representation by retained counsel had a broader due process grounding than the right to appointed counsel. Thus, during the same period in which the accused's right to appointed counsel in a noncapital felony case was controlled by the special circumstances rule of *Betts,* the right of such a defendant to representation by retained counsel was characterized as "unqualified." Indeed, *Powell v. Ala.* (§ 10.1(a)) had suggested in dicta that due process would be denied if a court, even in a civil case, "were arbitrarily to refuse to hear a party by counsel, employed by and appearing for him." On the other hand, as previously noted, the later Sixth Amendment rulings have indicated that the rights to appointed and retained counsel are equivalent under that Amendment. The same could be true of due process. While due process analysis might be distinguishable as allowing for consideration of the burden placed upon the state in providing counsel at its expense, the Court's due process rulings rejecting claims to appointed counsel have tended to emphasize other factors, such as the limited role of collateral challenges in ensuring the reliability of verdicts. Those other factors could be deemed equally controlling in rejecting claims as to retained counsel—unless the Court recognizes an independent due process interest of the litigant not to be prevented from utilizing his own resources to present his case through counsel if he so chooses. Support for recognizing such an interest may be found in historical practice. As to almost all proceedings relating to criminal liability that are not themselves part of the criminal prosecution (e.g., appeals and collateral challenges), there is a longstanding history of allowing representation by retained counsel.

The possibility that a state could refuse to permit retained counsel where it need not appoint counsel was raised in *Gagnon*. After holding that due process required appointment of counsel in probation and parole revocation cases where the circumstances made counsel necessary to ensure the "effectiveness" of due process guaranteed hearing rights, the *Gagnon* Court cited several concerns in refusing to impose a flat requirement of appointed counsel in all revocation cases. Among those concerns was the potentially adverse impact of automatic representation by counsel upon the special nature of the revocation proceeding (where the state typically did not use counsel and the focus often was upon a "predictive and discretionary" determination as to rehabilitative potential). That impact, of course, would flow from frequent representation by retained counsel as well as by appointed counsel. The Court added a warning, however, should a state decide to restrict the use of retained counsel. It stated in a footnote: "We have no occasion to decide in this case whether a probationer or parolee has a right to be represented at a revocation hearing by retained counsel in situations other than those where the State would be obliged to furnish counsel for an indigent." In other contexts, lower courts have noted that should a state seek to bar the assistance of retained counsel in a proceeding that relates to the criminal justice process, it must at least be able to point to the pernicious impact of counsel on the special character of the proceeding. This view finds support in *Wolff v. McDonnell* (1974), where the Court held that prisoners did not have a right to "either retained or appointed counsel" in prison disciplinary proceedings as a result of various difficulties that would arise from the "insertion of counsel" into such proceedings.

(c) Derivative Rights to Counsel. A constitutional right to the assistance of counsel also can be derived from other constitutional guarantees besides the due process right to a fair hearing. Thus, *Miranda v. Ariz.* (1966) held that the right to consult with counsel was indispensable to the protection of the self-incrimination privilege of a person subjected to custodial interrogation. The Court there required that the police inform such a person that "he has a right to consult with a lawyer and to have the lawyer with him during interrogation," and that "if he is indigent, a lawyer will be appointed to represent him." This requirement extends beyond the Sixth Amendment right to counsel since custodial interrogation often occurs before the individual is an "accused" in a "criminal prosecution." The *Miranda* right, however, rests on a condition that, as a practical matter, typically will be eliminated if the individual exercises that right. The *Miranda* right exists only if the arrestee is subjected to custodial interrogation, and if the arrestee refuses to waive the right to counsel, the police have the option of not pursuing the interrogation, which relieves them of the obligation to obtain counsel.

The *Miranda* approach, requiring an opportunity to consult with counsel as a means of safeguarding another constitutional guarantee, has also been advanced in other situations not encompassed by the Sixth Amendment. In *Kirby v. Ill.* (1972), this approach was urged by the dissenters in arguing that a suspect placed in a lineup should have a right to the presence of retained or appointed counsel, but it was rejected by the majority (see§ 6.3(b)). In *U.S. v. Mandujano* (1976), two justices argued that the self-incrimination privilege of a target-witness before a grand jury carried with it a right to consult with retained or appointed counsel prior to questioning. While the Court did not find it necessary to rule on that contention, the *Mandujano* plurality opinion argued against a right to counsel, and later cases have approvingly cited that discussion (see § 7.12(a)). Thus, the prospects for recognition of further derivative rights to counsel, beyond that established in *Miranda,* currently appear dim.

(d) Equal Protection and Appointed Counsel. Assume that a state allows a person to be represented by retained counsel in a proceeding as to which neither due process nor the Sixth Amendment requires the appointment of counsel. Does the equal protection guarantee then require the state to provide appointed counsel for indigent persons so as to ensure equal treatment?

Supreme Court precedent indicates that the equal protection guarantee may impose an independent obligation upon the state to provide appointed counsel, but also indicates that this obligation is limited largely to situations in which due process would also require appointment of counsel. The key cases in assessing the scope of the state's obligation under the equal protection clause are *Douglas v. Cal.* (1963) and *Ross v. Moffitt* (1974). An analysis of those rulings, however, must begin with an examination of the earlier case of *Griffin v. Ill.* (1963). While *Griffin* did not involve the appointment of counsel, it is the seminal ruling on the state's general obligation to provide "equal justice" in the criminal justice process.

Griffin dealt with a state law that gave every defendant the right to appeal, but then conditioned appellate review on defendant's presentation of a trial record that often could not be prepared without a stenographic trial transcript. Defendant, who was indigent, asked the state to provide him with a free transcript so that he could prepare his appeal, but the state refused to do so. The Supreme Court held that this refusal resulted in a denial of due process and equal protection. Both Justice Black's plurality opinion and Justice Frankfurter's separate concurring opinion acknowledged that the state had no constitutional obligation to provide appellate review of criminal convictions. However, once the state had granted defendants a right to appeal, it could not condition the exercise of that right upon a prerequisite that discriminated against those defendants who were indigent. "In criminal trials," Justice Black noted, "a State can no more discriminate on account of poverty than on account of religion, race, or color" since "the ability to pay costs in advance bears no relationship to defendant's guilt or innocence." Commenting generally upon this country's dedication "to affording equal justice to all," Justice Black added, in an oft-quoted statement: "There can be no equal justice where the kind of trial a man gets depends on the amount of money he has."

Notwithstanding the sweeping language in Justice Black's opinion, it was far from certain that the *Griffin* ruling would be extended to the appointment of counsel for the indigent. By requiring a transcript to perfect an appeal, the state had denied the indigent defendant access to an integral part of its process for ensuring against unjust convictions. In contrast, the indigent defendant denied appointed counsel on appeal still had his right to appellate review. However, in *Douglas v. Cal.* (1963), the Court extended *Griffin* to the right to counsel.

Douglas held invalid on equal protection grounds an intermediate appellate court's practice of refusing to appoint counsel on appeal when the court, after reviewing the trial record, concluded that "such appointment would be of no value to either the defen-

dant or the court." The majority opinion found this practice inconsistent with the *"Griffin* principle." Here too, there was "discrimination against the indigent," with "the kind of appeal a man enjoys
depend[ing] on the amount of money he has." Unlike the indigent,
the more affluent defendant was not required to "run [the] gaunt-
let of a preliminary showing of merit" to have his case presented by
counsel. As the Court saw the state's procedure, "the indigent,
where the record was unclear or errors were hidden, had only the
right to a meaningless ritual, while the rich man had a meaningful
appeal." The *Douglas* opinion stressed, however, that it was not
requiring "absolute equality" throughout the criminal justice process. What was at stake here was the first level of appeal, the "one
and only appeal an indigent has as of right." The Court was not
here concerned with review "beyond the stage in the appellate
process at which the claims have once been presented by a lawyer
and passed upon by an appellate court."

In stressing the importance of the first appeal, and in characterizing a defendant's presentation of his appeal without counsel as
a "meaningless ritual," the *Douglas* opinion cited factors that
arguably would have supported a due process right to appointed
counsel in that case. Indeed, in *Evitts v. Lucey* (§ 10.1(b)), the
Court looked to the reasoning of *Douglas* in finding a due process
right to retained counsel on a first appeal as a matter of right.
When *Ross v. Moffitt* (1974) refused to extend *Douglas* to indigent
defendants seeking appointed counsel to prepare petitions for a
discretionary second appeal, it looked to both due process and equal
protection. The Court did note that each clause "depend[s] on a
different inquiry which emphasizes different factors." For due
process the emphasis is on "fairness between the State and the
individual dealing with the State, regardless of how other individuals in the same situation may be treated." "Equal protection, on
the other hand, emphasizes disparity in treatment by a State
between classes of individuals."

In refusing to extend *Douglas* to the petition for second-level
discretionary review, the *Ross* majority examined separately the
impact of the two clauses, and found that neither lent support to
the defendant's claim. In discussing the due process element, the
Court stressed the quite different relationship of the defendant and
the state on an appeal as opposed to a trial. As discussed in
subsection (b), the defendant's role as the person pressing the
appeal and challenging a determination of guilt reduced the
strength of his claim for procedural safeguards. Accordingly, the
state does not "automatically * * * act unfairly" in leaving indigent defendants to pursue on their own a discretionary determination as to second tier review. "Unfairness results only if indigents
are singled out * * * and denied meaningful access to the appellate

system because of their poverty, [and] that question is more profitably considered under an equal protection analysis."

Analyzing the question under equal protection, the *Ross* majority found that there was no denial of meaningful access based on poverty. It stressed the ease with which an appellate court could determine whether to grant discretionary review even where the application had not been prepared by counsel. It acknowledged that "a skilled lawyer, particularly one trained in the somewhat arcane art of preparing petitions for discretionary review," could prove helpful to his client. However, the state had no "duty to duplicate the legal arsenal that may be privately retained by a criminal defendant in a continuing effort to reverse his conviction, but only to assure the indigent defendant an adequate opportunity to present his claims fairly in the context of the state appellate process." Here, unlike *Douglas,* that opportunity was available without counsel.

The combination of *Ross* and *Evitts* appears to establish that, as to the right to counsel, equal protection is unlikely to add anything to the assistance due the indigent defendant. Where due process fails to require the appointment of counsel, equal protection will not do so simply because the jurisdiction allows retained counsel to participate in the proceeding. On the other hand, where equal protection requires appointed counsel, defendant's need for counsel will be such that due process will similarly require appointed counsel. Notwithstanding the impression arguably conveyed by *Douglas,* a distinction does exist between the scope of the equal protection right to assistance of the type presented in *Griffin,* and the equal protection right to counsel. Thus, *Mayer v. Chicago* (1971) held that an indigent defendant convicted of an ordinance violation punishable only by fine was entitled under *Griffin* to a free transcript that would permit him to challenge on appeal the sufficiency of the evidence supporting his conviction. Since the defendant was not threatened with the loss of liberty, the interest he advanced was less than what due process and Sixth Amendment cases require for establishing a right to appointed counsel (see § 10.2(a)). *Mayer* nonetheless deemed that interest sufficient to justify an equal protection right to a transcript that was, in effect, a prerequisite for obtaining appellate review.

§ 10.2   Scope of the Indigent's Right to Counsel

(a) Right to Appointed Counsel: Misdemeanor Prosecutions. Prior to *Argersinger v. Hamlin* (1972), all of the appointed counsel cases decided by the Supreme Court had involved felony prosecutions. Though the Sixth Amendment refers to "all criminal prosecutions," several lower courts had ruled that the Sixth

Amendment right to appointed counsel, like the Sixth Amendment right to jury trial, did not apply to prosecutions for "petty offenses" (basically misdemeanors punishable by no more than six months imprisonment). That position was presented to the Court in *Argersinger,* where it was unanimously rejected. The Court could find no substantial reason for extending the petty offense exception to the counsel clause. While there was "historical support" for the jury trial exception, "nothing in the history of the right to counsel" suggested "a retraction of the right in petty offenses, wherein the common law previously did require that counsel be provided." There also was no functional basis for drawing the line at petty offenses. The "problems associated with * * * petty offenses," the Court noted, "often require the presence of counsel to insure the accused a fair trial." It could not be said that the legal questions involved in a misdemeanor trial were likely to be less complex because the jail sentence did not exceed six months. Neither is there less need for advice of counsel prior to entering a plea of guilty to a petty offense. Indeed, petty misdemeanors may create a special need for counsel because their great volume "may create an obsession for speedy dispositions, regardless of the fairness of the result."

Since the defendant in *Argersinger* had been sentenced to jail, the Court found it unnecessary to rule on the defendant's right to appointed counsel where "a loss of liberty was not involved." The opinion laid the foundation, however, for distinguishing between cases involving sentences of imprisonment and those in which only fines are imposed. Both *Johnson v. Zerbst* (§ 10.1(a)) and *Gideon v. Wainwright* (§ 10.1(a)) had referred to counsel's assistance as necessary to ensure "the fundamental human rights of life and liberty." The special significance of the loss of liberty to both the accused and society could not be denied. As the *Argersinger* opinion noted: "[T]he prospect of imprisonment for however short a time will seldom be viewed by the accused as a trivial or petty matter and may well result in quite serious repercussions affecting his career and his reputation."

The *Argersinger* opinion also cited to the practicability of applying an "actual imprisonment" standard. Responding to the contention that appointment of counsel for minor offenses was beyond the capacity of "the Nation's legal resources," it noted that an actual imprisonment standard would limit significantly the burden imposed upon the states. Although many jurisdictions classified traffic offenses as criminal, only a minute portion of all such offenses were likely to be "brought into the class where imprisonment actually occurs." Indeed, the opinion stated, "the run of misdemeanors will not be affected by today's ruling."

A major objection advanced against an actual imprisonment standard was that it would require the magistrate (who often would also be the misdemeanor trial judge) to "prejudge" the case in determining whether appointed counsel is necessary. The magistrate would have to determine prior to trial whether imprisonment might be imposed if the defendant were convicted. The Court, however, did not see any insurmountable difficulties in requiring the magistrate to make this "predictive evaluation of each case." It apparently assumed that the magistrate's determination would be based in large part upon the general character of the offense charged. The *Argersinger* opinion quoted at length from an ABA report noting that there were many offenses theoretically punishable by imprisonment but so "rarely if ever" resulting in incarceration that "for all intents and purposes the punishment they carry is at most a fine." If the judge had doubts as to whether a particular offense might merit imprisonment, he could always appoint counsel. However, if he failed to do so, that would preclude the imposition of imprisonment no matter what new information came to his attention during the course of the trial.

In *Scott v. Illinois* (1979), the Court refused to carry the Sixth Amendment right to appointed counsel in misdemeanor cases beyond the actual imprisonment standard suggested in *Argersinger*. The petitioner there was an indigent defendant who had been convicted of shoplifting. Although that misdemeanor offense was punishable by a maximum sentence of one year in jail and a $500 fine, petitioner had been sentenced to only a fine of $50.00. Referring to both the Sixth Amendment and the Fourteenth Amendment's due process clause, the Supreme Court concluded that the "federal constitution does not require a state trial court to appoint counsel for a criminal defendant such as petitioner." *Argersinger*, the Court stated, had rested on the "conclusion that incarceration was so severe a sanction that it should not be imposed * * * unless an indigent has been offered appointed counsel." It had thereby "delimit[ed] the constitutional right to appointed counsel in state criminal proceedings." The "central premise of *Argersinger*—that actual imprisonment is a penalty different in kind from fines or the mere threat of imprisonment"—was not altered by the fact that the misdemeanor involved here carried a potential punishment that took it beyond the petty offense category. The key for all misdemeanors is whether the judge imposes a sentence of imprisonment on conviction of the misdemeanor offense. The Court also noted that the actual imprisonment standard "had proved reasonably workable, whereas any extension would create confusion and impose unpredictable, but necessarily substantial, costs in 50 quite diverse states."

Scott was a 5–4 decision, with Justice Powell noting that he had joined the majority opinion only to provide "clear guidance" to the lower courts. However, in light of subsequent cases building upon *Argersinger* and *Scott,* the Court appears firmly committed to utilizing the actual imprisonment standard as the sole Sixth Amendment dividing line for requiring appointed counsel in misdemeanor cases. It has shown no inclination to build upon Justice Powell's reluctant concurrence, and require appointment of counsel, under a due process analysis, in a particularly compelling nonimprisonment misdemeanor case. Indeed, it has even suggested that the actual imprisonment standard might be incorporated into the right to consult with a lawyer established under *Miranda.* In *Berkemer v. McCarthy* (1984), in holding that *Miranda* warnings were not required prior to roadside questioning of a person stopped for a traffic misdemeanor (see § 5.6(e)), the Court left open for future decision the question of "whether an indigent suspect has a right, under the Fifth Amendment, to have an attorney appointed to advise him regarding his responses to custodial interrogation when the alleged offense about which he is being questioned is sufficiently minor that he would not have a right, under the Sixth Amendment, to the assistance of appointed counsel at trial."

In *Ala. v. Shelton* (2002), the Court made clear that the no imprisonment standard applied not simply to the immediate sentence, but also to subsequent imprisonment based on the sentence. Thus, a state could not sentence a person on an uncounseled conviction to a sentence of probation that could result in incarceration upon a subsequent revocation of probation. The Court distinguished *Nichols v. U.S.* (1994), which held that an uncounseled misdemeanor conviction valid under *Scott* (no term of incarceration having been imposed) could be used to enhance the imprisonment sentence for a subsequent conviction. In *Shelton*, although the imprisonment would be triggered by a probation violation, the sentence was for the underlying conviction (not the probation violation). In *Nichols*, in contrast, the sentence was for the subsequent conviction on which the defendant had counsel. There the earlier conviction was simply being considered as an element of the defendant's criminal background, in much the same way as other past behavior.

Of course, the states remain free to provide counsel in situations where the Constitution does not compel appointment. A large group of states require appointment for all offenses that carry an authorized punishment of incarceration. Many others, however, utilize a standard that is tied in some way to actual imprisonment. Some of these states have a statutory standard requiring that counsel be appointed for all misdemeanors carrying an authorized punishment of incarceration unless the judge declares on the record prior to trial that a sentence of incarceration will not be imposed. Other employ a general directive to appoint counsel if the judge concludes that incarceration is a "practical possibility."

(b) Right to Appointed Counsel: Stages of the Proceeding. The Sixth Amendment right to appointed counsel applies only to "critical stages" in the criminal prosecution. There is no need for the assistance of appointed counsel unless the "substantial rights of the accused may be affected" at the particular proceeding. Since the trial clearly is a critical stage in the criminal prosecution, most of the cases applying the critical stage test have concerned pretrial proceedings. Applying that test, the Supreme Court has held that an "accused" has the right to the assistance of counsel at a preliminary hearing, *Coleman v. Ala.* (1970), at some pretrial identification procedures (but not others) (see § 6.3(a)), and when subjected to police or prosecutor efforts to elicit inculpatory statements (see § 5.4(a)). The first appearance before a magistrate and the arraignment before the trial judge may or may not be a critical stage depending upon the state's treatment of the defendant's actions at that proceeding. Thus, *Hamilton v. Ala.* (1961) held that an indigent defendant was entitled to appointed counsel at an arraignment where state law viewed defenses not raised at that point as abandoned. Similarly, *White v. Md.* (1963) found that the first appearance was a critical stage where defendant was asked there to enter only a non-binding plea, but a non-binding plea of guilty, though later withdrawn, could still be used against him at trial.

Of course, no matter how significant the particular proceeding, the Sixth Amendment right does not apply if the proceeding is not part of the "criminal prosecution." The starting point for the criminal prosecution is the initiation of "adversary judicial proceedings." It is at that point that the individual becomes an "accused" person entitled to the application of the Sixth Amendment guarantee. Precisely what constitutes the initiation of adversary judicial proceedings is an issue most commonly raised in connection with police investigative procedures, and it has been discussed previously in §§ 5.4(d) and 6.3(b). As those discussions indicate, the initiation of adversary judicial proceedings ordinarily requires a formal commitment of the government to prosecute, as evidenced by the filing of charges. This may occur even prior to the issuance of an indictment or information, as where the arrestee is brought before the magistrate for a "first appearance" on charges filed in the form of a complaint.

In *U.S. v. Gouveia* (1984), the Court reaffirmed, however, that a person has not become an accused for Sixth Amendment purposes simply because he has been detained by the government with the intention of filing charges against him. There, prison inmates had been assigned to a special Administrative Detention Unit (ADU) on suspicion that they were responsible for the murder of an inmate. After prison officials concluded they had participated (following a disciplinary hearing), the inmates were kept in the ADU for substantial periods (19 months in one case) until finally indicted. The Supreme Court rejected their claim that they had a right to appointed counsel over this period. The Court acknowledged the concern of the lower courts that, in prison cases, the government might delay initiation of charges, and that could result in the loss of evidence that might have been preserved through the preindictment investigation of appointed counsel. It concluded, however, that such concerns were appropriately addressed under other procedural protections (e.g., the due process protection against prejudicial delay in bringing charges), rather than the Sixth Amendment right to counsel. The Court noted that it had "never held that the right to counsel attaches at the time of arrest," and had "never suggested that the purpose of the right * * * is to provide a defendant with a preindictment private investigator." On the contrary, the right was limited by its objective "of protecting the unaided layman at critical confrontations with his adversary," and it therefore demanded the initiation of adversary judicial proceedings, which marked the point at which "the adverse positions of government and defendant have solidified."

Once started, the Sixth Amendment's "criminal prosecution" continues through to the end of the basic trial stage, including sentencing. In the course of ruling upon due process and equal protection claims, a series of cases, as discussed in § 10.1(b), have clearly indicated that the "criminal prosecution" has ended where the defendant is pursuing an appeal from his conviction. Less clear is the status of post-sentencing proceedings before the trial judge that similarly present challenges to the conviction. The answer may depend, in part, upon the nature of issues presented. If the proceeding involves no more than an extension of a trial ruling, and occurs shortly after trial, as in a post-verdict motion for judgment of acquittal, it should be treated as subject to the Sixth Amendment. On the other hand, a motion for a new trial based on new evidence, which can occur months after the conviction, might be treated as closer to a collateral attack, which clearly is outside the criminal prosecution.

While timing is a significant factor in assessing post-trial proceedings in the trial court, it is not necessarily conclusive. Thus, a probation revocation proceeding that occurred months after defendant's conviction was held to be a part of the criminal prosecution where that proceeding also involved the setting of the defendant's basic prison term for the crime. In that case, *Mempa v. Rhay*

(1967), the trial judge placed the defendant on probation without fixing the term of imprisonment that would be imposed if probation were later revoked. The Supreme Court concluded that the subsequent determination and imposition of a prison sentence at the probation revocation proceeding was as much a part of the criminal prosecution as the sentencing of a defendant immediately after trial. In contrast to *Mempa, Gagnon v. Scarpelli* (1973) held that a probation revocation hearing is not part of the criminal prosecution when a prison sentence had previously been imposed but then suspended in favor of probation. The only issue presented in such a hearing is whether to revoke probation, and that determination is based on defendant's subsequent conduct rather than the commission of the original offense.

Of course, even though a proceeding is not part of the criminal prosecution, there may still be a right to appointed counsel drawn from a constitutional provision other than the Sixth Amendment. Thus, *Douglas* (§ 10.1(d)) and *Evitts* (§ 10.1(b)) established an equal protection and due process right to appointed counsel on a first appeal provided as a matter of right, and *Gagnon* (§ 10.1(b)) established a due process right to appointed counsel under special circumstances in a probation or parole revocation proceeding. On the other hand, *Ross v. Moffitt* held that neither equal protection nor due process required appointment of counsel to assist an indigent convicted defendant in preparing an application for second-level discretionary review of a conviction, and *Pa. v. Finley* and *Murray v. Giarratano* found no constitutional basis for requiring appointment of counsel to assist an indigent prisoner in filing a habeas petition or other collateral attack upon his conviction. See § 10.1(b).

In many states, appointed counsel is provided in various settings where the indigent clearly does not have a constitutional right to appointed counsel. Very often this is a product of judicial practice rather than a legal right under state law. A very common practice of this type is the appellate court practice of directing counsel appointed for the first appeal to assist their clients in preparing timely applications for subsequent discretionary appellate review within the state judicial system. While states less often establish a legal right to the assistance of appointed counsel where not constitutionally mandated, such state-created rights are fairly common at certain stages of the criminal justice process. In the federal system and numerous states, indigents are entitled to appointed counsel in all probation revocation hearings, without regard to the special circumstances test of *Gagnon v. Scarpelli*. Discretionary authority to provide counsel in a collateral proceeding challenging a conviction is fairly widely recognized, but a statutory right to such assistance—apart from capital cases—is granted only by a much smaller group of states.

§ 10.3   Waiver of the Right to Counsel

(a) General Requirements. Just as the right to counsel extends through various stages in the criminal justice process, waiver of that right can occur at each of those stages. In some respects, what is required for a valid waiver will vary with the particular stage. Thus, the standards for a waiver of counsel in the course of a police investigation differ in certain respects from the standards governing a waiver in a judicial proceeding. A judge accepting a waiver at trial, for example, may be required to conduct a type of inquiry as to the defendant's state of mind that simply would not be feasible for a police officer accepting a waiver prior to custodial interrogation. The requisites for a valid waiver in the course of investigatory procedures have been discussed in previous chapters. Our focus in this section is upon waivers in judicial proceedings, particularly at trial.

While the standards governing waiver vary with the nature of the proceeding, there are several general principles that apply to all waivers of the right to counsel. To be valid, a waiver of counsel must be made "knowingly, intelligently, and voluntarily." There must be "an intentional relinquishment or abandonment of a known right or privilege," and it may not be the product of governmental tactics that amount to "coercion."

The Supreme Court repeatedly has warned the lower courts against simply assuming that the defendant has the necessary knowledge and understanding to make a constitutionally acceptable waiver. It has in fact directed those courts to "indulge in every reasonable presumption against waiver." Consistent with this approach, a waiver may not be presumed from a "silent record"; the record must show that the defendant was informed specifically of his right to the assistance of appointed or retained counsel and that he clearly rejected such assistance. "No amount of circumstantial evidence that the person may have been aware of his right will suffice to stand" in place of a specific notification of rights. Having been informed of his right, the defendant's relinquishment of that right must be clear and unequivocal.

(b) Waiver at Trial: The Necessary Inquiry. Assume that a defendant, having been informed of his right to counsel (including appointed counsel, if indigent), states unequivocally that he wishes to proceed without counsel. Is that enough to establish that his waiver was made "intelligently" as well as "knowingly"? While it may be enough for a waiver in the course of a police investigatory practice, establishing an acceptable waiver before the trial court typically requires much more. On direct appeal from a conviction, the prosecution ordinarily must be able to point to a trial court inquiry establishing the necessary level of understanding by the defendant. When a waiver is challenged on collateral attack (e.g., habeas corpus), "it is the defendant's burden to prove that he did not competently and intelligently waive his right to the assistance of counsel." *Iowa v. Tovar* (2004). Here, the lack of an adequate inquiry will not be sufficient in itself to invalidate the waiver, as the defendant must show that he actually lacked the needed understanding (which could have been obtained apart from the judicial inquiry).

The Supreme Court has refused to "prescrib[e] any formula or script to read to a defendant," or questions to be directed to a defendant, to ensure that the waiver of counsel is intelligent. It has noted that "the information a defendant must possess in order to make an intelligent election * * * will depend on a range of case-specific factors, including the defendant's education or sophistication, the complex or easily grasped nature of the charge, and the stage of the proceeding." *Tovar*. Speaking to the importance of the stage of the proceeding, the Court has stressed the need for "a 'pragmatic approach to the waiver question,' one that asks 'what purposes a lawyer can serve at the particular stage of the proceedings in question, and what assistance he could provide to an accused at that stage,' in order 'to determine the * * * type of warnings and procedures that should be required before a waiver of that right will be recognized.'" *Tovar* [quoting *Patterson v. Ill.* (§ 5.4(e))]. Thus, the Court has required the most extensive inquiry where the defendant desires to waive counsel and proceed to trial representing himself. There, it has held that the trial court must warn the defendant of the specific "dangers and disadvantages" of self-representation, so that the record establishes his awareness of the general skills that counsel could have brought to the litigation process. *Faretta v. Cal.* (1975).

Tovar refused to require similar warnings where the defendant sought to waive counsel and enter a guilty plea. The state court here had concluded that the waiver of counsel was inadequate under the Sixth Amendment because the trial court had: "(1) [failed to] advise the defendant that 'waiving the assistance of counsel in deciding whether to plead guilty entails the risk that a viable defense will be overlooked'; and (2) [failed to] 'admonish' the defendant that by waiving his right to an attorney he will lose the opportunity to obtain an independent opinion on whether, under the facts and applicable law, it is wise to plead guilty'." A unanimous Supreme Court responded:

"[N]either warning is mandated by the Sixth Amendment. The constitutional requirement is satisfied when the trial court informs the accused of the nature of the charges against him, of his right to be counseled regarding his plea, and of the range of allowable punishments attendant upon the entry of a guilty plea."

In the guilty plea context, the "purposes a lawyer can serve" were likely to be "more obvious, requiring less rigorous warnings" to ensure that the defendant understands how the waived right "would apply in *general* in the circumstances" of his waiver.

The *Tovar* Court also noted, however, that it need not decide whether the simple guilty plea colloquy in the case before it was sufficient in itself to establish the understanding needed for a constitutionally acceptable waiver of counsel. That colloquy, in its discussion of counsel's assistance, consisted of the trial court noting its understanding that defendant desired to waive application for court appointed counsel and represent himself, the defendant stating that the court's understanding was correct, and the court then explaining the trial rights (including counsel's assistance at trial) relinquished by pleading guilty. The Court noted that defendant also waived counsel at his first appearance and at a subsequent sentencing hearing ("where he could have withdrawn the guilty plea"), and "the State does not contest that a defendant must be alerted to his right to the assistance of counsel in entering a plea" (assistance the state described as involving "working on issues of guilt and sentencing"). The Court further noted that the states remain free to adopt under state law required inquiries that go beyond the constitutional minimum (as many states have done).

(c) Forfeiture of the Right. A long line of state and federal cases have sustained trial court rulings that forced defendants to proceed pro se because they failed to obtain counsel prior to the trial date. In these cases, defendants were advised of their right to retain counsel, given ample time to obtain counsel prior to the scheduled trial date, and nevertheless appeared in court on that date without counsel and without a reasonable excuse for having failed to obtain counsel. The courts typically have characterized such conduct by defendant as a "waiver" or "waiver by conduct" of the right to counsel. However, the circumstances in many of these cases clearly did not fit the traditional definition of a defense waiver in the right to counsel context—that is, a defendant's "intentional relinquishment or abandonment of a known right." Initially, the facts strongly suggested that the defendant had not intended to relinquish his right to counsel. Secondly, the trial court in some instances dispensed with even the barest inquiry that would have been needed for a true waiver. Finally, even if such an inquiry may be unnecessary where defendant's conduct unequivocally shows an intentional abandonment of his right, that characterization would appear to depend upon a prior warning as to the consequences of that conduct (i.e., failing to have counsel at the time scheduled for trial), and the cases do not always refer to such a warning having been given.

Most often, the analysis offered by the courts fits the category of "forfeiture" rather than "waiver." As the Supreme Court explained in *U.S. v. Olano* (1993), a forfeiture rests on the failure to make "a timely assertion of a right" rather than an intentional abandonment of the right. What these courts have held, in effect, is that the state's interest in maintaining an orderly trial schedule and the defendant's negligence, indifference, or possibly purposeful delaying tactic, combined to justify a forfeiture of defendant's right to counsel in much the same way that the defendant's assault upon his counsel can result in his loss of representation by counsel. Some courts, however, have refused to adopt such an analysis, insisting that there be at least some evidence of a intentional relinquishment in the defendant's failure to retain counsel prior to the scheduled trial date.

§ 10.4   The Right to Effective Assistance of Counsel: Guiding Principles

(a) The Prerequisite of a Constitutional Right to Counsel. The Supreme Court first recognized a constitutional right to the effective assistance of counsel in *Powell v. Ala.* (1932). *Powell* noted that where due process requires the state to provide counsel for an indigent defendant, "that duty is not discharged by an assignment at such a time or under such circumstances as to preclude the giving of effective aid in the preparation and trial of the case." Subsequent cases, involving Sixth Amendment and equal protection rights to counsel, similarly held that the right to counsel encompassed a right to effective assistance by that counsel. For "a party whose counsel is unable to provide effective representation is in no better position that one who has no counsel at all."

Taken together, the various rulings establish that a constitutional requirement of effective assistance extends to counsel's performance in any proceeding as to which there would be a constitutional right both to appointed counsel for the indigent and to retained counsel for the non-indigent. Where there is no such constitutional right to counsel's assistance, however, even the most negligent performance of counsel will not give rise to an ineffective assistance claim.

Thus, in *Wainwright v. Torna* (1982), the Court rejected defendants claim that he had been denied the effective assistance of counsel when his retained attorney failed to file a timely application for discretionary review at the state's second-level of appeal. Noting that "*Ross v. Moffitt* [had] held that a criminal defendant does not have a constitutional right to counsel to pursue [such] discretionary state appeals [see § 10.1(b)]," the per curiam majority opinion concluded that the lawyer's negligence therefore did not violate any constitutional right of the defendant. The Court reasoned: "Since respondent had no constitutional right to counsel, he could not be deprived of the effective assistance of counsel by his retained counsel's failure to file the application timely." While *Torna* involved retained counsel, subsequent cases adopted the same analysis as to the performance of appointed counsel in a postconviction proceeding, as the state had no constitutional obligation to appoint counsel in that proceeding. So too, lower courts have rejected constitutional claims based on the allegedly incompetent performance of retained counsel in advising a suspect during conversations with police that took place before the Sixth Amendment right to counsel took hold.

As discussed in § 10.1(b), in proceedings in which there is no right to appointed counsel (such as that involved in *Torna*), there may be a due process right to proceed through retained counsel absent a compelling state interest for excluding counsel. Since the right to use retained counsel here would not be based on a constitutional need for counsel to ensure a fair hearing, but simply on a "state's duty to refrain from unreasonable interference with the individual's desire to defend himself in whatever manner he deems best," the right would not carry with it a state obligation to ensure that retained counsel provided effective assistance. The defendant alone would bear the consequences of his unwise choice of counsel, notwithstanding constitutional protection of his right to proceed by counsel rather than pro se.

In some instances, unlike *Torna*, the proceeding in which the state had no obligation to provide counsel may nonetheless be a proceeding that it has a constitutional obligation to provide. Here, the completely deficient performance of counsel, whether retained or appointed, might be utilized by defendant to challenge the adequacy of the proceeding itself. Such a possibility would be presented, for example, by the ineffective assistance of retained counsel at a misdemeanor trial which resulted in the imposition only of a fine (and therefore was not a proceeding at which the Sixth Amendment would guarantee a right to appointed counsel). The defendant could argue here that the ineffectiveness of counsel resulted in a proceeding in which defendant was so deprived of his ability to make use of the procedural rights constitutionally guaranteed to him in such a trial that the proceeding itself did not comport with due process. The state might respond that its due process obligation was only to make those hearing rights available to the defendant, and the failure of the defendant to take advantage of those rights due to counsel's incompetency is not the state's responsibility, just as the loss of the appeal was not the state's responsibility in *Torna*. Here, however, what is at stake is the state's basic authority to impose a sanction, which is conditioned constitutionally on a fair determination of liability. In light of that constitutional prerequisite, the state might not so readily be allowed to ignore the actions of counsel, though it had no duty to provide or allow for counsel, where counsel's actions rendered meaningless the rights afforded the defendant to ensure that fair determination of liability.

(b) Retained vs. Appointed Counsel. Prior to *Cuyler v. Sullivan* (1980), many lower courts utilized different standards for reviewing ineffective assistance claims depending upon whether counsel was appointed or privately retained. Some of the earlier cases had refused on an agency rationale to even recognize ineffectiveness claims involving retained counsel. Other courts recognized that the law of agency was misplaced as applied to criminal cases, but found a basis in the state-action requirement of the Fourteenth Amendment for applying a less stringent standard of review to the alleged incompetency of retained counsel.

Cuyler put to rest this division among the lower courts. The ineffective assistance claim in *Cuyler* was based upon a retained attorney's multiple representation of codefendants with possibly conflicting interests. Although arguing that counsel was not ineffective, the prosecution also claimed that, in any event, "the alleged failings of * * * retained counsel cannot provide a basis for a * * * [constitutional violation] because the conduct of retained counsel does not involve state action." Rejecting that contention, the Supreme Court reasoned that "a proper respect for the Sixth Amendment disarms [the prosecution's] contention that defendants who retain their own counsel are entitled to less protection than defendants for whom the State appoints counsel. * * * Since the State's conduct of a criminal trial itself implicates the State in the defendant's conviction, we see no basis for drawing a distinction between retained and appointed counsel that would deny equal justice to defendants who must choose their own lawyers." Adhering to the obvious thrust of this reasoning, lower courts have refused to limit the Court's analysis to the multiple representation situation presented in *Cuyler*. Since *Cuyler,* they have uniformly held that the standard of review applied to all types of ineffectiveness claims will not vary with the status of counsel as retained or court-appointed.

(c) The Adversary System Touchstone. The companion cases of *U.S. v. Cronic* (1984) and *Strickland v. Washington* (1984) provide the general framework for the analysis of ineffective assistance claims. The critical element, both opinions noted, is to evaluate the performance of counsel in light of the underlying purpose of the constitutional right to counsel. Since both cases involved challenges to the performance of counsel at the trial level, the opinions focused on the purpose of the Sixth Amendment right to counsel. However, since the Court indicated that the role of counsel under that Amendment flowed from the adversary nature of the trial process, and that the same principles would apply to other stages of the criminal justice process that are "sufficiently like a trial in its adversarial format and in the existence of standards for decision," the analysis of *Cronic* and *Strickland* also has been applied to the various stages of the process at which due process or equal protection establish a constitutional right to counsel.

The Sixth Amendment right to counsel, the Court noted in *Strickland,* is aimed, like other Sixth Amendment rights, at providing the "basic elements of a fair trial." A key component of that fair trial is the adversarial system of litigation. The Sixth Amendment included a guarantee of assistance of counsel because "it envisions counsel playing a role that is critical to the ability of the adversarial system to produce just results." The " 'very premise of our adversary system * * * is that partisan advocacy on both sides of a case will best promote the ultimate objective that the guilty be convicted and the innocent go free,' " and it is this " 'very premise' that underlies and gives meaning to the Sixth Amendment." Effective assistance therefore must be measured by reference to the functioning of the adversary process in the particular case. "The right to effective assistance," the *Cronic* opinion noted, is "the right of the accused to require the prosecution's case to survive the crucible of meaningful adversary testing. When a true adversarial criminal trial has been conducted—even if defense counsel may have made demonstrable errors—the kind of testing envisioned by the Sixth Amendment has occurred." The critical question therefore is whether counsel's performance was so deficient that the process "lost its character as a confrontation between adversaries," producing an "actual breakdown of the adversary process."

In tying the concept of effective assistance to the functioning of the adversary process, the Court clearly rejected a measurement based solely on a comparison of counsel with his or her peers. The key is not how close counsel came to gaining for defendant the best possible result that an attorney might have realistically achieved. Neither is it the grade counsel might receive as measured against some model for attorney performance, whether theoretical or reflective of empirical data. Rather the focus is on the presence of the requisite adversarial testing. The most obvious case of ineffectiveness would be that in which counsel simply did not act as an advocate, either because he was prevented from doing so or simply did not make the effort. Where counsel sought to perform as an advocate, the question will then be whether his effort provided a "meaningful adversary testing." What is "meaningful" for this purpose will be measured by reference to the operation of the adversary process to achieve its basic objective, ensuring the reliability of the adjudication. Thus, as the *Cronic* opinion noted, a failing to provide adversarial testing as to a single issue, when that issue is critical to a finding of guilt, may in itself produce a breakdown in the adversarial process. On the other hand, as *Strickland* further noted, meaningful adversarial testing hardly requires that challenges be made and investigations be directed at each and every point without regard to its likely insignificance in testing the strength of the prosecution's case.

(d) **Per Se vs. Actual Ineffectiveness.** The adversary system touchstone advanced in *Cronic* and *Strickland* appeared to call for a determination of "actual ineffectiveness" under the facts of the particular case. A constitutional challenge could be found only upon a determination both that counsel had actually failed in some respect to discharge the duties of an advocate in an adversarial system and that counsel's failure so affected the adversary process as to undermine confidence in the result it produced. These determinations suggest a fact-sensitized judgment that evaluates the nature and impact of counsel's representation under the circumstances of the individual case. Not all of the Court's previous rulings, however, had adopted such a "judgmental" approach. Some had seemingly relied upon per se standards of ineffective assistance. In cases in which trial courts had prevented counsel from utilizing certain adversarial procedures (e.g., a closing argument), the Supreme Court had found ineffective assistance without looking to other aspects of counsel's performance. In cases in which counsel had acted upon a conflict of interest, the Court had also found ineffective assistance without examining all aspects of counsel's performance.

In *Cronic*, the Court was presented with a case in which the lower court had extended the per se approach of the earlier cases to conclude that counsel was inherently incapable of providing effective assistance. The lower court in *Cronic* had sustained defendant's ineffectiveness claim without referring to any specific error or inadequacy in counsel's performance. Instead, it had inferred that "counsel was unable to discharge his duties" based upon five aspects of the circumstances surrounding counsel's appointment (including the lateness of the appointment, the complexity of the case, and counsel's lack of experience). Justice Stevens' opinion for the *Cronic* Court rejected this "inferential approach." It concluded that a determination of actual effectiveness is the standard prerequisite for sustaining an ineffective assistance claim, and the use of a presumption of inherent ineffectiveness therefore must be limited to unique circumstances presented in extreme cases.

Justice Stevens' opinion initially stressed that a judicial evaluation of an ineffectiveness claim must "begin by recognizing that the right to the effective assistance of counsel is recognized not for its own sake, but because of the effect it has on the ability of the accused to receive a fair trial." Accordingly, establishment of an ineffectiveness claim ordinarily requires some showing of an adverse effect on the reliability of the trial process. Moreover, because "we presume that the lawyer is competent," the burden ordinarily rests on the accused to make that showing. "There are, however, circumstances that are so likely to prejudice the accused that the cost of litigating their effect in a particular case is unjustified." In such situations, constitutional ineffectiveness, amounting to a "breakdown of the adversarial process," could be presumed. However, upon turning to the Court's past decisions, Justice Stevens found only three settings in which such a presumptive approach was justified.

First, there was the situation in which "counsel was either totally absent or prevented from assisting the accused during a critical stage of the proceeding." Falling in this category were cases in which the trial court had unconstitutionally refused to appoint counsel or had restricted counsel's assistance. The second situation was that in which counsel was physically present, but completely absent in effort. As the Court put it, "if counsel entirely fails to subject the prosecution's case to meaningful adversarial testing, then there has been a denial of Sixth Amendment rights that makes the adversary process itself presumptively unreliable." Finally, there were "occasions when, although counsel is available to assist the accused during trial, the likelihood that any lawyer, even a fully competent one, could provide effective assistance is so small that a presumption of prejudice is appropriate without inquiry into the actual conduct of the trial." *Powell v. Ala.* was such a case. The trial court there had utilized such a haphazard process of appointment—ordering admittedly unprepared outstate counsel to proceed with whatever help the local bar, appointed en masse, might provide—that ineffective assistance was properly presumed without further inquiry. Apart from these three situations, the focus must be on the actual performance of counsel and its impact on the case (although where counsel operated under a conflict of interest and took a position adverse to his client, a prejudicial impact upon the outcome ordinarily will be presumed).

(e) **The *Strickland* Standards.** The governing standard for assessing counsel's actual performance was set forth in *Strickland*. The Court there announced a two pronged test for determining whether counsel's performance was so defective as to deny defendant his constitutional right to counsel; to establish constitutionally ineffective representation, the defendant must prove both incompetence and prejudice. Incompetency is judged by an "objective standard of reasonableness": "Whether in light of all the circumstances, the identified acts or omissions [of counsel] were outside the range of professionally competent assistance." The standard for the element of prejudice is whether "there is a reasonable probability that, but for counsel's unprofessional errors, the result of the proceeding would have been different." A "reasonable probability" in this regard is "a probability sufficient to undermine confidence in the outcome."

Performance. Prior to *Strickland*, several lower courts had relied heavily upon generally accepted guidelines for counsel's performance, such as the A.B.A. Standards, in judging competency. Indeed, some had suggested that any substantial deviation from those guidelines automatically established incompetency. The *Strickland* majority flatly rejected this approach in explaining its standard of reasonableness. The "performance inquiry" the Court noted, "must be whether counsel's assistance was reasonable under all the circumstances" and "more specific guidelines are not appropriate." Utilizing specific guidelines as per se test for competent performance was inappropriate because (i) "no particular set of detailed rules for counsel's conduct can satisfactorily take account of the variety of circumstances faced by defense counsel or the range of legitimate decisions regarding how best to represent a criminal defendant," and (ii) "reliance on such guidelines * * * could distract counsel from the overriding mission of vigorous advocacy of the defendant's cause." Of course, prevailing norms of practice help to define reasonableness, but the ultimate point of reference is whether counsel's performance met a level consistent with "the proper functioning of the adversarial process"—for that is what sets "the range of competence demanded of attorneys in criminal cases."

Consistent with its emphasis upon a fact-sensitized judgment respecting "the wide latitude counsel must have in making tactical decisions," the *Strickland* majority also warned lower courts against "second-guess[ing]" counsel's performance: "Judicial scrutiny * * * must be highly deferential. * * * A fair assessment of attorney performance requires that every effort be made to eliminate the distorting effects of hindsight, to reconstruct the circumstances of counsel's challenged conduct, and to evaluate the conduct from counsel's perspective at the time. Because of the difficulties inherent in making the evaluation, a court must indulge a strong presumption that counsel's conduct falls within the wide range of reasonable professional assistance; that is, the defendant must overcome the presumption that, under the circumstances, the challenged action 'might be considered sound trial strategy.' "

Prejudice. Prior to *Strickland*, lower courts had taken a wide variety of positions on the element of prejudice in an ineffective assistance claim, ranging from presuming prejudice upon a finding of incompetency to placing a heavy burden on defendant to show prejudice. *Strickland* sought to resolve those differences in its explanation of its prejudice prong. The Court initially noted that, since the underlying function of the constitutional right to counsel is to "ensure * * * the assistance necessary to justify reliance on the outcome of the proceeding," any deficiency in counsel's performance "must be prejudicial to the defense in order to constitute ineffective assistance."

Moreover, here, unlike the situation in the state interference cases, or conflict of interest cases, such prejudice could not be presumed: "Attorney errors come in an infinite variety and are as likely to be utterly harmless in a particular case as they are to be prejudicial." As for the requisite likelihood of prejudice, the Court described its "reasonable probability" standard as falling between the overly lenient "some conceivable effect" standard (which would invariably lead to a finding of prejudice) and the overly rigorous "more likely than not" test (which would ignore the constitutional grounding of defendant's claim by placing upon defendant the same burden applied to newly discovered evidence).

In light of the function of the prejudice requirement, the Court has warned against "an analysis focusing solely on mere outcome determination, without attention to whether the result of the proceeding was fundamentally unfair or unreliable." *Lockhart v. Fretwell* (1993). Prejudice does not automatically follow from a reasonable probability of a different result had counsel acted otherwise. Thus, *Nix v. Whiteside* (1986) held that defendant, "as a matter of law," could not establish prejudice where he claimed that his counsel had improperly prevented him from presenting perjured testimony which could have swayed the jury. So too, in *Lockhart*, the Court held that there was "no 'prejudice' within the meaning of *Strickland*" where counsel's incompetence consisted of failing to present an objection that was supported by precedent at the time of trial, but later was rejected with the overturning of that precedent.

In *Kimmelman v. Morrison* (1986), counsel's incompetence was in failing to present a Fourth Amendment exclusionary rule claim, and the Court remanded for consideration of the prejudice issue.

Arguably implicit in the remand was the assumption that prejudice would be established if there was a reasonable likelihood that the exclusion of the illegally seized evidence would have altered the outcome. However, three concurring justices argued that the failure to gain exclusion of evidence that clearly was reliable, though illegally seized, did not lead to "an unjust or fundamentally unfair result" and therefore could not constitute prejudice.

(f) **State Interference.** The "right to the assistance of counsel," the Supreme Court noted in *Herring v. N.Y.*(1975), "has been understood to mean that there can be no restrictions upon the function of counsel in defending a criminal prosecution in accord with the traditions of the adversary factfinding process." Accordingly, state action, whether by statute or trial court ruling, that prohibits counsel from making full use of traditional trial procedures may be viewed as denying defendant the effective assistance of counsel. In considering the constitutionality of such "state interference," courts are directed to look to whether the interference denied counsel "the opportunity to participate fully and fairly in the adversary factfinding process." If the interference had that effect, then both the overall performance of counsel apart from the interference and the lack of any showing of actual outcome prejudice become irrelevant. The interference in itself establishes ineffective assistance and requires automatic reversal of the defendant's conviction. The leading cases finding such interference include *Geders v. U.S.* (1976) (trial court prevented counsel from consulting with the accused during an overnight recess that separated the direct examination of the accused from his forthcoming cross-examination) and *Herring v. N.Y.* (1972) (trial counsel prevented counsel from delivering a closing argument in a bench trial).

Also sometimes categorized as state interference cases are situations in which state agents invade the lawyer-client relationship. However, such invasions differ from the direct impediments involved in cases like *Geders* and *Herring* in that they do not necessarily restrict the lawyer's performance. Indeed, the circumstances surrounding the invasion may often negate any realistic likelihood that the invasion had any adverse impact upon counsel's performance. In *Weatherford v. Bursey* (1977), the Supreme Court held that, at least in some such cases, it will not find a Sixth Amendment violation. In that case, Weatherford, in order to maintain his undercover status, attended, at defendant Bursey's request, two pretrial meetings between Bursey and his lawyer. Weatherford did not disclose to his superiors any information derived from those discussions that related to defense plans for the trial. Similarly, when Weatherford was unexpectedly called as a prosecution witness at that trial, he carefully limited his testimony so as not to touch upon anything he might have learned through the lawyer-client meetings.

The basic issue presented in *Weatherford v. Bursey* was whether the Supreme Court would adopt what it described as a "per se" or "prophylactic rule." The lower court had adopted such a rule. Relying on Supreme Court precedent, it had held that "whenever the prosecution knowingly arranges or permits intrusions into the attorney-client relationship the right to counsel is sufficiently endangered to required reversal and a new trial." A divided Supreme Court held that the lower court had misread the relevant precedent and had adopted a rule that failed to give sufficient weight to the "necessity of undercover work and the value it often is to effective law enforcement." In *Hoffa v. U.S.* (1966), another case in which an undercover agent had been present during attorney-client conversations, the Court had assumed, without deciding, that a conviction would be overturned if the informer had reported the substance of those conversations to the authorities. Here, however, as in *Hoffa,* the undercover agent had not reported the substance of the lawyer-client conversations and his trial testimony had not related to those conversations. The Court noted that "Bursey would have a much stronger case" if either (1) Weatherford had testified at trial as to those conversations, (2) the "State's evidence [had] originated from those conversations," (3) the "overheard conversations had been used in any other way to the substantial detriment of Bursey," or (4) "even had the prosecution learned from Weatherford * * * the details of the * * * conversations about trial preparations." But with "none of these elements * * * present here," there was no basis for finding a Sixth Amendment violation.

Weatherford presented an invasion of the lawyer-client relationship that had a significant investigative justification. That was not the case in *U.S. v. Morrison* (1981). In that case, D.E.A. agents, although aware that the defendant had been indicted and had retained counsel, met with defendant without defense counsel's knowledge or permission, and while seeking her cooperation, disparaged her retained attorney. The lower court held that defendant's right to counsel was violated irrespective of the lack of proof of prejudice to her case, and that the only appropriate remedy was a dismissal of the prosecution with prejudice. The Supreme Court unanimously reversed. The Court found it unnecessary to rule on the government's contention that a Sixth Amendment violation could not be established here without "some [defense] showing of prejudice." Even if it were assumed that there had been a Sixth Amendment violation, the remedy imposed by the lower court was incorrect because it was not "tailored to the injury suffered." Since "[r]espondent has demonstrated no prejudice of any kind, either transitory or permanent to the ability of her counsel to provide adequate representation in these criminal proceedings," there was "no justification" for such "drastic relief" as a dismissal with prejudice.

In declining to reach the government's contention that a showing of prejudice would be needed to establish a Sixth Amendment violation, the *Morrison* opinion left open the possibility that the Court might adopt a standard of automatic conviction reversal where there has been a state invasion of the lawyer-client relationship that was not supported by any legitimate state motivation. The federal lower courts have divided on this issue on postconviction review of cases in which the prosecution had intentionally obtained, without any legitimate justification, information passed between the defendant and his lawyer. Some have concluded that the intentional invasion of the lawyer-client relationship producing such disclosure constitutes a per se Sixth Amendment violation, with no need to show that the defendant was prejudiced at trial as a result of the disclosure. Others have held that the defendant must show prejudice (e.g., the government's use of the information gained to its advantage), and the First Circuit has taken a "middle position," with the government bearing the "high burden" of showing that it did not use the information against the defendant.

*

Table of Cases

A

Abel v. United States, 362 U.S. 217, 80 S.Ct. 683, 4 L.Ed.2d 668 (1960)— **§ 2.1(d).**

Adams v. New York, 192 U.S. 585, 24 S.Ct. 372, 48 L.Ed. 575 (1904)— **§ 2.1(a).**

Adams v. Williams, 407 U.S. 143, 92 S.Ct. 1921, 32 L.Ed.2d 612 (1972)— **§ 2.8(d), (e).**

Adamson v. California, 332 U.S. 46, 67 S.Ct. 1672, 91 L.Ed. 1903 (1947)— **§ 1.3(c).**

Agnello v. United States, 269 U.S. 20, 46 S.Ct. 4, 70 L.Ed. 145 (1925)— **§ 8.6(a).**

Aguilar v. Texas, 378 U.S. 108, 84 S.Ct. 1509, 12 L.Ed.2d 723 (1964)— **§ 2.3(c); § 2.8(d).**

Alabama v. Shelton, 535 U.S. 654, 122 S.Ct. 1764, 152 L.Ed.2d 888 (2002)— **§ 10.2(a), (b).**

Alabama v. White, 496 U.S. 325, 110 S.Ct. 2412, 110 L.Ed.2d 301 (1990)— **§ 2.8(d).**

Albright v. Oliver, 510 U.S. 266, 114 S.Ct. 807, 127 L.Ed.2d 114 (1994)— **§ 1.4(c).**

Alderman v. United States, 394 U.S. 165, 89 S.Ct. 961, 22 L.Ed.2d 176 (1969)—**§ 3.6(b), (d); § 8.1(b); § 8.2(c), (d); § 9.3(b).**

Alexander v. United States, 390 F.2d 101 (5th Cir.1968)—**§ 2.10(c).**

Allen v. Illinois, 478 U.S. 364, 106 S.Ct. 2988, 92 L.Ed.2d 296 (1986)— **§ 5.10(e).**

Almeida–Sanchez v. United States, 413 U.S. 266, 93 S.Ct. 2535, 37 L.Ed.2d 596 (1973)—**§ 2.9(f).**

Alvarez–Sanchez, United States v., 511 U.S. 350, 114 S.Ct. 1599, 128 L.Ed.2d 319 (1994)—**§ 5.3(b).**

Andresen v. Maryland, 427 U.S. 463, 96 S.Ct. 2737, 49 L.Ed.2d 627 (1976)— **§ 2.2(i).**

Argersinger v. Hamlin, 407 U.S. 25, 92 S.Ct. 2006, 32 L.Ed.2d 530 (1972)— **§ 10.2(a).**

Arizona v. Evans, 514 U.S. 1, 115 S.Ct. 1185, 131 L.Ed.2d 34 (1995)— **§ 2.1(h).**

Arizona v. Fulminante, 499 U.S. 279, 111 S.Ct. 1246, 113 L.Ed.2d 302 (1991)—**§ 5.2(c).**

Arizona v. Hicks, 480 U.S. 321, 107 S.Ct. 1149, 94 L.Ed.2d 347 (1987)— **§ 2.4(k); § 2.6(g).**

Arizona v. Mauro, 481 U.S. 520, 107 S.Ct. 1931, 95 L.Ed.2d 458 (1987)— **§ 5.7(a), (c).**

Arizona v. Roberson, 486 U.S. 675, 108 S.Ct. 2093, 100 L.Ed.2d 704 (1988)— **§ 5.9(f).**

Arizona v. Youngblood, 488 U.S. 51, 109 S.Ct. 333, 102 L.Ed.2d 281 (1988)— **§ 1.4(a).**

Arkansas v. Sanders, 442 U.S. 753, 99 S.Ct. 2586, 61 L.Ed.2d 235 (1979)— **§ 2.5(e); § 2.7(c).**

Arkansas v. Sullivan, 532 U.S. 769, 121 S.Ct. 1876, 149 L.Ed.2d 994 (2001)— **§ 2.1(d).**

Ash, United States v., 413 U.S. 300, 93 S.Ct. 2568, 37 L.Ed.2d 619 (1973)— **§ 6.3(c).**

Atwater v. City of Lago Vista, 532 U.S. 318, 121 S.Ct. 1536, 149 L.Ed.2d 549 (2001)—**§ 2.5(a); § 2.8(b).**

B

Baggot, United States v., 463 U.S. 476, 103 S.Ct. 3164, 77 L.Ed.2d 785 (1983)—**§ 7.3(f).**

Balsys, United States v., 524 U.S. 666, 118 S.Ct. 2218, 141 L.Ed.2d 575 (1998)—**§ 7.8(c).**

Bank of Nova Scotia v. United States, 487 U.S. 250, 108 S.Ct. 2369, 101 L.Ed.2d 228 (1988)—**§ 1.2(h).**

Banks, United States v., ___ U.S. ___, 124 S.Ct. 521, 157 L.Ed.2d 343 (2003)—**§ 2.4(h); § 2.6(b).**

Baxter v. Palmigiano, 425 U.S. 308, 96 S.Ct. 1551, 47 L.Ed.2d 810 (1976)— **§ 5.10(e).**

D

E

F

N

O

*

INDEX

571

†